New Developments
in Productivity
Measurement and Analysis

Studies in Income and Wealth
Volume 44

National Bureau of Economic Research
Conference on Research in Income and Wealth

New Developments in Productivity Measurement and Analysis

Edited by John W. Kendrick
and Beatrice N. Vaccara

The University of Chicago Press

Chicago and London

JOHN W. KENDRICK is professor of economics at George Washington University.

BEATRICE N. VACCARA is deputy assistant secretary for domestic economic policy in the U.S. Department of the Treasury.

The University of Chicago Press, Chicago 60637
The University of Chicago Press, Ltd., London

Library of Congress Cataloging in Publication Data

Conference on New Developments in Productivity
    Measurement and Analysis, Williamsburg, Va., 1975.
    New developments in productivity measurement and
analysis.

    (Studies in income and wealth ; v. 44)
    Bibliography: p.
    Includes index.
    1.   Industrial productivity—United States—
Congresses.   2.   Industrial productivity—Congresses.
3.   Productivity accounting—Congresses.   I.   Kendrick,
John W.   II.   Vaccara, Beatrice N.   III.   Title.
IV.   Series: Conference on Research in Income and
Wealth.   Studies in income and wealth ; v. 44.
HC106.3.C714   vol. 44   [HC110.I52]   330′.08s   79–20399
ISBN 0–226–43080–4   [338′.06]

Since this volume is a record of conference proceedings, it has been exempted from the rules governing critical review of manuscripts by the Board of Directors of the National Bureau (resolution adopted 6 July 1948, as revised 21 November 1949 and 20 April 1968).

Contents

Prefatory Note

This volume contains the papers presented at the Conference on New Developments in Productivity Measurement and Analysis held at Williamsburg, Virginia, on 13–14 November 1975. We are indebted to the National Science Foundation and to the National Center for Productivity and Quality of Working Life for their support, and to Beatrice N. Vaccara and John W. Kendrick, who served as cochairmen.

Introduction

John W. Kendrick and Beatrice N. Vaccara

Seventeen years elapsed between the previous Income and Wealth conference on productivity held in 1958, which eventuated in the volume *Output, Input and Productivity Measurement* (1961), and the 1975 conference, of which the proceedings are contained in the present volume. During the intervening years, interest in productivity measurement and analysis grew perceptibly. The chief impetus for the first conference was concern with the role of productivity in economic growth and development. Since that time, the course of the U.S. and world economies has focused attention on other aspects of productivity. In particular, the apparent slowdown after the mid-1960s in the U.S. average rate of productivity growth has been associated with an acceleration of general price inflation, a sluggish growth in real wage rates and income per capita, and problems of the international competitiveness of American goods. In addition to the observed decline in the longer term growth rates for productivity there was increased cyclical variability of production and an absolute decline in productivity during the contraction of 1973–75. One of the papers in this volume suggests that, as far as major manufacturing industries are concerned, the increased variability of changes in output completely explains the retardation in growth rates. Be that as it may, the economic developments of the decade prior to the 1975 conference definitely enhanced interest in concepts, measurement, and analysis of productivity—with respect not only to causal factors, but also to the interrelationships of productivity, costs, and prices (both cyclically and secularly) in the U.S. and other major economies.

John W. Kendrick is at George Washington University; Beatrice N. Vaccara is at the U.S. Department of the Treasury.

1

One visible evidence of increased federal government concern over productivity was the creation in June 1970 of a National Commission on Productivity, and the continuance of its objectives via the National Center for Productivity and Quality of Working Life (1975–78), and the present National Productivity Council. A number of states have also established productivity centers or their equivalents. In early 1977, C. Jackson Grayson, former chairman of the Price Commission (1971–73), founded the private-sector American Productivity Center to help promote productivity growth. As an objective measure of increasing work on productivity matters, the successive annotated bibliographies on productivity compiled by the Bureau of Labor Statistics have become progressively thicker.[1]

The purpose of the 1958 conference was to "bring theoretician and statistician together to try to sharpen our concepts of output, input, and productivity, and to suggest needed improvements in methods of estimation and basic data."[2] The 1975 conference provides a sampling of the subsequent work designed to sharpen concepts and improve measures of productivity and to analyze relationships of productivity changes or differences to selected associated variables. In this Introduction, we present an overview of the contents of the volume but not full summaries of the papers, which are included in the reviews of the discussants. We also provide background and perspective on developments relating to the concept and measurement of productivity, which is a major focus of four of the papers. This orientation may also help in interpreting the primarily analytical papers.

Conceptual and Methodological Developments

Prior to World War II, all productivity estimates were of the simple output-per-worker or per-hour variety. This was true of the first estimates prepared in the Bureau of Labor by Carrol Wright in the nineteenth century, the work of the National Research Project of the Works Progress Administration in the 1930s, the subsequent program of the Bureau of Labor Statistics, and the various industry studies of the National Bureau of Economic Research—to mention only the major productivity measurement initiatives. The concept of a production function involving capital as well as labor inputs had been developed in the

1. See Bureau of Labor Statistics, U.S. Department of Labor, *Productivity: A Selected Annotated Bibliography, 1971–75*, Bull. 1933 (1977) and Bull. 1914 (1966). The earlier volume contained an average of 60 items per year; the latest an average of 216 items per year.

2. *Output, Input and Productivity Measurement*, Studies in Income and Wealth, vol. 25 (Princeton: Princeton University Press for the National Bureau of Economic Research, 1961), p. 3.

1920s by Paul Douglas and Charles Cobb in a simple form amenable to statistical estimation of parameters. But their results using available figures for U.S. manufacturing did not indicate any upward trend in the "technological scalar," and this evoked skeptical comments by Sumner Slichter and J. M. Clark on the Cobb-Douglas paper at the American Economic Association meeting in 1927. Little further empirical work by others trying to measure productivity change within the framework of a complete production function was undertaken for a couple of decades.[3]

At the first meeting of the Conference on Research in Income and Wealth in 1936, Morris Copeland did suggest that the relationship of real product to real factor costs (input), using the framework of the national income and product accounts (which, of course, are grounded in the theory of production), yields an efficiency measure.[4] But, as pointed out in the paper by Christensen, Cummings, and Jorgenson (CCJ), the first empirical attempt to measure total factor productivity was made by Jan Tinbergen in 1942 in a remarkable but neglected article in which estimates were presented for four countries, including the United States, over a forty-four-year period. The first estimates of total factor productivity we know of prepared in the United States were those of George Stigler for manufacturing presented in a 1947 volume of the National Bureau of Economic Research.[5]

The concept of total factor productivity (TFP) was further elaborated by John Kendrick at a 1951 Income and Wealth conference, and he used it as the framework for his subsequent NBER study of total and partial productivity trends in the United States private domestic economy.[6] Work by several others during the 1950s (as noted by CCJ),[7] including Robert Solow who explicitly used a production function framework, helped to establish TFP as an operational concept.

In 1962, the conceptual and analytical frontiers of the field were expanded further by the imaginative work of Edward F. Denison in his

3. See Solomon Fabricant, "Perspective on Productivity Research," *Conference on an Agenda for Economic Research on Productivity* (Washington: National Commission on Productivity, April 1973).

4. Morris A. Copeland, "Concepts of National Income," Studies in Income and Wealth, vol. 25 (New York: National Bureau of Economic Research, 1937), p. 31.

5. George J. Stigler, *Trends in Output and Employment* (New York: NBER, 1947).

6. John W. Kendrick, *National Productivity and Its Long-Term Projection*, Studies in Income and Wealth, vol. 16 (New York: NBER, 1954); *Productivity Trends: Capital and Labor*, Occasional Paper 53 (New York: NBER, 1956); and *Productivity Trends in the United States* (Princeton: Princeton University Press for NBER, 1961).

7. They might also have included the comprehensive Columbia University dissertation by Irving Siegel, "Concepts and Measurement of Production and Productivity," unpublished.

Sources of United States Economic Growth and the Alternatives before Us. In his 1957 article, Solow had already noted the substantial magnitude of the residual difference between rates of growth of real product and weighted rates of growth of labor and capital inputs as conventionally measured. This residual was challengingly called by Abramovitz a "measure of our ignorance,"[8] and the search was on for the factors that would explain changes in TFP, narrow the residual, and thus reduce our ignorance concerning sources of economic growth. In his initial work (1962), later updated and refined (1974),[9] Denison sought to narrow the residual in two ways: One was by including in his labor input measure estimates of the effect of increased education, shortened hours of work, the changing age-sex composition of the labor force, and other factors that changed the quality of labor over time. The second way was to attempt to quantify the contributions to growth of all major factors other than advances of knowledge, so that his final residual would primarily reflect the impact of that basic dynamic element.

Following Denison, Dale Jorgenson and several collaborators—Griliches (1966, 1967, 1972), Christensen (1969), and Gollop in the present volume—extended to capital the principle of weighting input components by marginal products, and they used a more elaborate system than Denison in adjusting labor inputs for quality shifts. After correction of the early Jorgenson-Griliches estimates for errors pointed out by Denison in their famous exchange (1972),[10] the estimates by Jorgenson and Christensen, and by Gollop and Jorgenson (GJ) in this volume show a substantially larger increase in real factor inputs and a correspondingly smaller increase in the residual than Denison's. Most of the difference is due to the different methodologies used in measuring capital.

As described in their paper, for each of the 51 industries examined, GJ differentiated four types of real capital, which are weighted by the rates of return in four economic sectors. These rates of return are adjusted for the effects of taxation of property income, and for the impact of differences in service lives and rates of change in prices of different types of capital assets.

With respect to labor input, GJ decomposed hours worked by eight age groups, ten occupational categories, five educational attainment

8. See Moses Abramovitz, *Resource and Output Trends in the United States since 1870*, Occasional Paper 52 (New York: NBER, 1956).

9. Edward F. Denison, *The Sources of Economic Growth in the United States and the Alternatives before Us* (New York: Committee for Economic Development, 1962); and *Accounting for United States Economic Growth, 1948–1969* (Washington: the Brookings Institution, 1974).

10. See *Survey of Current Business*, Part 2, May 1972.

levels, two employment classes, and both sexes. They then weighted hours worked by average hourly labor compensation in each of the 1600 cells. This is the most elaborate measure of labor input yet prepared. By dividing indexes of labor and capital inputs adjusted for quality by the corresponding indexes of unadjusted input, GJ obtained measures of the increase in efficiency of labor and capital inputs stemming from relative shifts in the composition of the inputs.

In his more recent work on productivity,[11] Kendrick continued to compute factor inputs unadjusted for quality change, preferring to view the increases in quality as part of the explanation of the broader residual. In a still more recent volume, Kendrick has tried to measure the impact of improving quality of the factors by an approach which differs from those of both Denison and Jorgenson et al.[12] He estimates the real capital stocks resulting from intangible investments designed to improve the efficiency of the factors—R and D, education and training, health and safety, and mobility. He then estimates the contribution of the growth in these intangible capital stocks to economic growth generally, and to the productivity residual in particular. His final residual, while of the same order of magnitude as Denison's, has a somewhat different meaning, of course.

In the last analysis, it is perhaps not so important whether input quality changes are counted as part of changes in the quantity of inputs or as part of the explanation of productivity change, so long as the variables are identified and their separate contributions to growth are quantified. The differences in accounting schemes can then be reconciled.

The separate presentation of quality improvement indexes by GJ also makes possible comparisons with other estimates of the same variable. Although CCJ in principle use the same theoretical framework as GJ, the necessity of preparing consistent total factor productivity estimates for all nine countries necessitated some differences from GJ in the factor input measures for the United States. Thus, CCJ adjusted labor inputs based only on educational attainment data. Surprisingly, for the United States the results are very similar to those obtained by the much more elaborate GJ procedure. The basic capital adjustment procedure was similar in both studies, except that disaggregation and weighting by industry was not done by CCJ, with the result that the indicated increase in capital quality is less in that study than in GJ's.

A valuable contribution to the range of productivity estimates was also made by GJ through relating gross output to total input including

11. John W. Kendrick, *Postwar Productivity Trends in the United States, 1948–1969* (New York: NBER, 1973).
12. John W. Kendrick, *The Formation and Stocks of Total Capital* (New York: NBER, 1976).

intermediate products consumed as well as factor services. For consistency with the nonduplicative national income accounts framework, most previous studies have related real product to factor inputs. But GJ persuasively argue that for purposes of analyzing industry productivity movements, gross output measurement is a preferable approach since substitutions occur among all inputs in response to relative price changes, and innovations affect requirements for intermediate inputs as well as for primary factors.

Perhaps the most important contribution of the GJ and CCJ papers, as stressed by discussant Berndt, is that they incorporated significant recent developments in production and cost theory and in index number theory and practice. Specifically, they used translog production functions, suitable for their multiple-output, multiple-input models; and they consistently employed Törnquist's discrete version of the Divisia form of index numbers for the major components and aggregates of output and input. CCJ also develop the dual of their production function, demonstrating that changes in total factor productivity are equal to changes in the ratio of input price to output price composites. Although Berndt notes several problems with the GJ and CCJ methodology, he considers it a major advance over earlier work employing more restrictive production functions and inflexible Laspeyres or Paasche quantity and price indexes, which are still standard in federal government statistical time series.

A contribution of the GJ and CCJ papers is that they provide future researchers a body of total productivity estimates with factor quality components for the U.S. business economy by industry group, and for nine countries on a consistent basis. CCJ note that, after Tinbergen's pioneering work in 1942, five other economists between 1964 and 1974 prepared total factor productivity estimates for five to nine countries. But the CCJ estimates are the most comprehensive. Their discussant, Don Daly, offers a number of criticisms, some of which the authors used to improve their estimates as described, others of which they reject in a reply to Daly.

Two of the other papers make considerable contributions to matters of methodology, particularly with regard to problems of defining and measuring outputs and inputs in selected service sectors—transportation and government. In the first of these, Meyer and Gómez-Ibáñez (MGI) investigate in some depth the special characteristics of three major transportation modes, with particular reference to the specification and weighting of outputs and of inputs. The measures they produce show significant differences in movement from earlier estimates, although the authors have admittedly not solved all of the puzzles they pose. The inference is inescapable that studies which use standard conventions for measuring outputs and inputs for many industries may, though consistent in a narrow sense, lead to distortions in productivity measures for industries that are regulated or have other special characteristics. Certainly, more careful monographic industry studies of productivity such as GMI's should result in noticeable improvements in the measures available for interindustry comparisons, as well as for analysis of the specific industries. Actually, a considerable monographic literature on productivity in individual industries and sectors has accumulated,[13] but much more remains to be done.

The paper by Searle and Waite (SW) assesses current efforts to measure productivity in the public sector from the viewpoint of adequacy for developing true real product estimates for general government. At present, real government product is measured in terms of real labor compensation, without allowance for productivity change. Granted the input approach as a proxy for measuring real product of nonbusiness sectors, real property compensation should also be included. SW note that BEA is developing estimates of real capital stocks owned by general governments which could serve as a basis for estimating real capital inputs into the public sector.

After reviewing earlier private and governmental efforts to measure outputs, inputs, and productivity in the public sector, SW concentrate most of their attention on the federal program, begun in 1971, which eventuated in productivity estimates prepared annually by BLS covering outputs produced by 65% of federal civilian government employees in 245 organizational elements in 48 agencies. When government enterprises are excluded, coverage drops to approximately 50% of civilian employment. SW observe that the output indicators do not represent ultimate public goods, but rather the flow of work units defined in an instrumental sense. Even if this narrower concept were accepted, they point out various problems such as uneven coverage of functions and the mixing of intermediate with final outputs, particularly from a consolidated, government-wide viewpoint. Whereas the measures are undoubtedly valuable for their primary use as a management tool, SW review the kinds of improvements in the measures needed to warrant their use for adjusting federal civilian labor inputs for productivity change as a means of producing more adequate measures of real product. The discussant, Jerry Mark, is optimistic that continued gradual improvements in coverage and measurement of outputs will eventually justify their use for national-income accounting purposes. This is encouraging, since Mark, as head of the BLS Office which prepares the estimates, is in a position to promote their improvement.

Productivity measurement at the state and local government levels lags far behind the federal government work. But, as SW point out, the

13. See Bureau of Labor Statistics, *Bulletin 1933*, pp. 15–21.

BLS achievements point the way to progress at that level, which now employs over twice as many civilian workers as the federal government. Continued encouragement from the National Productivity Council will help, but it would appear that it will be many years before coverage of state and local government outputs and inputs, even in noneducational functions, is adequate to permit true real product and productivity estimates for the sector.

The Analytical Papers

The remaining seven papers presented at the conference are concerned primarily with analyzing the effects of selected variables on productivity change. None of the papers essays the heroic task Denison set for himself of quantifying the effects on economic growth and productivity of all the major causal factors. Rather, most of the authors attempt to study in depth the productivity effects of one, or a few, variables. This is, of course, the kind of specialized research that will eventually make possible increasingly satisfactory comprehensive explanations of productivity changes and differences.

The broadest in scope of the primarily analytical papers is one by Yamada and Ruttan (YR) on international comparisons of productivity in agriculture. They assemble estimates of agricultural output per worker for six countries for the period 1880–1970, building on an earlier work by Hayami and Ruttan (1971) which contained data only for the United States and Japan. Although they note that total productivity estimates are available for the agricultural sector of at least nine countries, they choose to work with labor productivity estimates which they are also able to assemble for a cross-sectional analysis of forty-one countries for 1970, supplementing the analysis for 1960 conducted in the earlier study. They find it analytically useful to view output per worker as the product of output per hectare of land and the number of hectares per worker, for which they also provide data, as well as for a number of interrelated variables. They then proceed to analyze and interpret both bodies of data within the framework of the induced innovation hypothesis. Their results, summarized succinctly by discussant Schuh and shown graphically in the YR paper, add significantly to our understanding of the interrelationships between differences and changes in relative factor endowments, relative factor prices, types of technological innovation (biological and mechanical), patterns of input use, partial productivity ratios, and several associated variables. Schuh does question YR's use of a Cobb-Douglas production function and the significance of a number of coefficients. For example, he believes the high degree of importance their regression analysis accords to human capital in the form of general and technical education may be picking up the effect of interrelated variables of scale and specialization not included in the analysis. We agree with Schuh's assessment that the YR paper is, nevertheless, a particularly rich bag, and the data are there for those who may prefer to try different types of statistical analysis.

In view of the importance of R and D as a fountainhead of technological progress, three of the conference papers were devoted to empirical studies of the productivity effects and returns to R and D in the private sector. Terleckyj attempts to estimate both the direct and indirect effects of industrial R and D on the productivity growth of twenty manufacturing and thirteen nonmanufacturing industry groups, using Kendrick's estimates of total factor productivity. Employing a Cobb-Douglas production function and standardizing for a number of other related variables, he confirms the findings of his earlier study (1974), that returns to private R and D financed within the various manufacturing industries is high; and that returns to indirect R and D embodied in capital goods and intermediate products purchased from other industries is much higher. For the nonmanufacturing industries, he finds no return to direct R and D (which is small in most of them), but a very high return to indirect R and D. No productivity effects of government-financed R and D are discovered.

Interesting aspects of Terleckyj's paper are his use of the GJ factor quality indexes as standardizing variables, and his later substitution of the GJ total factor productivity indexes for Kendrick's in the twenty manufacturing industries. As might be expected, introduction of the quality indexes results in a significant decrease in the privately financed direct R and D coefficient. Use of the GJ productivity measures not only decreases the R^2s, but both the direct and indirect privately financed R and D coefficients become statistically insignificant. These findings suggest that there may be a high degree of correlation between the education level of the employees and the degree to which a firm invests in R and D, a good portion of which could be "in-house." Indeed, discussant Globerman suggests that possible collinearity between the factor quality indexes and other variables included in the productivity equation may explain the disappearance of productivity effects of R and D with use of the GJ productivity measures. Globerman also comments on various issues relating to model specifications, measurement problems, and the single-equation estimation procedure, although he judges Terleckyj's findings to be generally plausible. He notes that publication of the author's data series will facilitate further testing and extension of his work by others.

Griliches based his analysis of returns to R and D in six industry groups on time series data (1957–65) for 883 large U.S. manufacturing companies. These companies accounted for about 90% of sales and a bit more of R and D. Information from the annual NSF Census R and

D surveys was supplemented by data on value added, assets, and depreciation based on a match with the 1958 and 1963 Census of Manufactures and Enterprise Statistics. Although constrained by confidentiality restrictions, inability at the time to include still other bodies of data, and various simplifying assumptions, Griliches was able to develop some interesting findings and suggest directions for future research.

Specifically, fitting Cobb-Douglas type production functions with data for levels in 1963 and rates of growth for the period 1957–65, Griliches obtained an elasticity of output with respect to R and D investments of around .07, which is consistent with findings of others. The elasticities were higher for the research-intensive groups, and lower for the less intensive groups. For most of his groups, total private rates of return were in the 30 to 40% range, about double that earned by physical capital during the same period, but lower than the Terleckyj estimates which Globerman suspects are too high. But supporting the direction of Terleckyj's results, Griliches found that the two industries with the largest proportion of federal R and D financing showed the lowest rates of return on R and D. Finally, he finds no support for the notion that larger firms (among those with over 1,000 employees) "have either a higher propensity to invest in R and D or are more effective in deriving benefits from it." This also accords with findings of prior studies.

In his comments, Mansfield notes the lag between R and D investments and derived commercial innovations, and presents some relevant data. He also offers results of a case study of private rates of return from investments in R and D and related innovative activity, which are not inconsistent with the findings of Griliches. He suggests that the social rates of return are higher than the private, but that both have probably fallen since the period studied by Griliches. Griliches agrees that a study of the post-1965 period would be useful, particularly since it is a period when real R and D growth ended for many firms.

Nadiri and Bitros (NB) approach the analysis of R and D and productivity growth at the level of the firm. The discussant, Richard Levin, notes that the novelty of their paper lies in its focus on the short-run disequilibrium dynamics of R and D outlays, within a general dynamic model of input demands and factor substitutions. Using data for sixty-two firms for the period 1965–72, NB find that the firm's decisions regarding employment, capital accumulation, and R and D are closely related in a dynamic interaction process. All of the decisions, including R and D activities as well as demands for labor and tangible capital, are influenced significantly by both sales and relative input prices. The output elasticities of the inputs over the long run are quite similar, suggesting constant returns to scale. Demand for the inputs, including R and D, appears quite stable when firms are stratified by asset-size classes. The most important conclusion from the viewpoint of the conference topic is that both labor productivity and tangible investment demand of firms are significantly affected by their R and D outlays, particularly over the long run.

Levin notes various data problems, and expresses serious reservations concerning NB's basic model. Nevertheless, he considers the paper an important step forward and hopes the authors will pursue their line of inquiry further using richer bodies of data and appropriate joint estimation information techniques.

Klotz, Madoo, and Hansen (KMH) address themselves to a study of high and low value added per production worker-hour (VA/H) establishments in U.S. manufacturing. Because of confidentiality restrictions, KMH deal with quartiles of establishments (discussant Siegel recommends deciles) in a maximum set of 195 four-digit industries for which data were deemed satisfactory, and a subset of 102 industries. Although KMH had initially referred to VA/H as "labor productivity" in their title, in the floor discussion Lipsey pointed out that VA/H is not really an efficiency measure but is more like a proxy for factor proportions, reflecting differences in capital and nonproduction workers per production worker, plus differences in factor prices (including profits) and indirect business taxes among establishments.

Since Lipsey's comment was well taken, it is not surprising that KMH's multiple regressions indicate that differences in factor proportions and in monopoly power contribute to an explanation of high VA/H. But even these factors explain a relatively small portion of interquartile differences, particularly in the low VA/H plants, and experiments with other presumably explanatory variables do not help. This leads KMH to conclude that the strength of transitory, disequilibrium elements casts doubt on any static explanation of productivity differences. In one of the more humorous comments at the conference, Siegel stated: "Any reader of the paper who stays the course not only feels sadder and wiser at the end but is also inclined to congratulate the data for withstanding the torments of advanced technique without confessing what they did not really know and, therefore, could not tell." Siegel concurs with the authors that longitudinal studies, relating differential rates of change in real value added per unit of input to associated variables among groups of establishments, would yield more useful results.

Certainly, firm and establishment level productivity studies are of great potential importance, since that is where the action is with respect to innovational decisions, large and small, and relative efficiency of operations under given technologies. The promising BLS program of plant level productivity measurement and analysis, started after World War II, was terminated after several years because of high cost. But the OECD and some other countries have continued to stress interfirm and interplant comparisons. In recent years, the National Center for Productivity, the Department of Commerce, the Conference Board, and most recently the American Productivity Center have promoted company productivity measurement. The expansion of company information systems to include productivity data is not only helping internal management programs to increase efficiency, but, as Siegel points out, the increased quantity and quality of "atomic" information will contribute to improved productivity measurement, analysis, and policy formulation at the macro as well as the micro levels.

Myers and Nakamura (MN) contribute a paper on the timely topic of the effects on investment and productivity of antipollution and occupational safety and health requirements, and of large unexpected increases in the price of energy. MN develop a putty-clay model with the usual assumptions, including one of steady cost-reducing technological progress over successive vintages of capital—and two outputs, a good and a bad (with a negative price). They conclude that the accelerated obsolescence and induced investment effects of environmental and health-safety standards and energy price hikes will provide significant productivity offsets to the trade-off of fewer goods with given inputs, which reduces productivity as usually measured.

Their discussant, Cremeans, argues that MN have not realistically assessed the management decision to invest in new and presumably better facilities, in light of actual regulatory practices and uncertainties regarding future standards. He also notes that they fail to take account of effects on the cost of capital of increased capital demand stemming from accelerated obsolescence. Cremeans advises MN to examine empirically their assumption that new vintages of facilities incorporating antipollution and energy-conserving features have significant cost advantages over older vintages. For these and other reasons, he recommends that the authors revise their model and research plan. Despite the criticisms, MN are congratulated on pioneering and imaginative work on assessing the productivity effects of contemporary developments that are widely believed to have contributed to the productivity slowdown of recent years.

To test the proposition that the productivity slowdown after 1966 was due to greater cyclical output instability than in the 1956–66 period, Michael Mohr uses a translog model of interrelated (stock-adjustment) factor demand with quarterly data on six inputs for ten two-digit SIC manufacturing industries. Without our trying to describe his complicated model (which discussant Humphrey does admirably), suffice it to say that Mohr maintains that, when demand exhibits increasing variation, firms adjust by altering labor hours and capacity utilization rates in preference to adding to fixed capital stocks. Consequently, output per hour is lower when demand is more erratic because more of the adjustable short-run labor input is used to produce a given output than during periods of steadier growth in demand and production. His estimate of labor and other factor demands that are independent of changes in the adjustment sequence due to increased variability of output indicates that labor productivity would have grown as fast in the 1966–72 period as in the prior decade if output growth had been as steady.

This is an important conclusion, if valid. Humphrey points out that the results are affected by exclusion from the model of variables such as changes in age-sex mix, to which the slowdown has also been attributed. But if Mohr is right, it means that the retardation in productivity growth is reversible. If his results can be generalized from manufacturing to the business economy as a whole, it means that we may return to the pre-1966 trend rate of productivity advance in coming years if macroeconomic policies result in at least as stable a rate of growth as was experienced in the 1946–56 decades.

Despite the findings of Mohr, it is most likely that a combination of factors, only one of which was increased cyclical instability, was responsible for the 1966–76 slowdown in productivity growth. Certainly, the significant changes in age-sex mix of the work force, the changing industrial distribution of employment, the decline in R and D outlays relative to GNP, accelerating inflation, the decline in the rate of growth of physical capital per worker, environmental, health, and safety regulations, and the 1971–74 wage-price control episode, as well as other socioeconomic trends, have all contributed to the retardation. Consequently, policies to accelerate productivity growth will require more than just the resumption of steadier economic growth, although that is an important economic objective for reasons transcending its favorable impact on productivity.

In any case, the important progress that has been made in the past couple of decades, as evidenced in this volume, puts us in a far better position to track and analyze productivity developments. This in turn improves our ability to prescribe policy measures that can promote productivity advance and thereby the attainment of the important economic goals that are associated with it.

I.   Labor and Multifactor Productivity by Industry

1   U.S. Productivity Growth by Industry, 1947–73

Frank M. Gollop and Dale W. Jorgenson

The objective of this paper is to describe and analyze postwar patterns of productivity growth by industry for the U.S. economy. In section 1.1 we present a model of production and technical change that permits an analysis of sources of growth in output for individual industrial sectors. The model includes a production function for each sector, giving output as a function of intermediate input, capital input, labor input, and time. The model also includes conditions for producer equilibrium. Given the production function and the conditions for producer equilibrium, we can generate index numbers for sectoral output, sectoral capital, labor, and intermediate input, the corresponding prices, and sectoral productivity.

We present disaggregated measures of labor input in section 1.2. These measures are index numbers constructed from detailed data on labor input for each year, cross-classified by age, sex, education, occupation, and class of worker for each sector. We present disaggregated measures of capital input in section 1.3. These measures are index numbers constructed from detailed data on capital input for each year, cross-classified by type of asset and legal form of organization for each

Frank M. Gollop is at the University of Wisconsin; Dale W. Jorgenson is at Harvard University.

The development of the data base described in this report has left us with a series of obligations that we can acknowledge, but never adequately repay. Our colleagues William Barger, Peter Chinloy, and Charles Hulten contributed to the development of both methods and data. The results of their own work are reported in their doctoral dissertations, included in our list of references. However, we would like to express our appreciation to them for their contributions to our work. We have also much appreciated the valuable advice and assistance of Barbara Fraumeni in the construction of our capital data and of Peter Derksen and Mieko Nishimizu in the generation of our labor data. Without their help the industrial sector. In section 1.4 we present annual measures of output and intermediate input for each industrial sector. Finally, we combine sectoral intermediate input, capital input, labor input, and output into an index of productivity for each sector for the period 1947–73.

1.1   Sectoral Production and Technical Change

1.1.1   Technical Change

Our methodology for productivity measurement is based on a model of production and technical change. The point of departure for this model is a production function for each industrial sector, giving output as a function of intermediate input, capital input, labor input, and time. To analyze substitution among primary factors of production and intermediate goods, we combine the production function for each sector with necessary conditions for producer equilibrium for that sector. These conditions take the form of equalities between the shares of each input in the value of output of each sector and the elasticity of sectoral output with respect to the corresponding input. The elasticities depend on inputs and time, the variables that enter the production function for each sector. To analyze changes in substitution possibilities over time, we consider the rate of technical change for each sector, defined as the rate of growth of the output of that sector, holding all inputs into the sector constant. The rate of technical change, like the elasticities of sectoral output with respect to sectoral inputs, depends on inputs and time.

---

development of these data would have been impossible. Finally, we wish to acknowledge the able research assistance of David Carvalho, Blake Evernden, and David Robinson.

Our capital and output data owe much to the efforts of Jack Faucett, President of Jack Faucett Associates, and his staff. We are very grateful to them and to Ron Kutscher, Ken Rogers, and John Tschetter of the Bureau of Labor Statistics for assisting us in the effective use of the results. Thomas Vasquez of the Office of Tax Analysis kindly made available his unpublished study of depreciation practices. Finally, the staff of the Bureau of Economic Analysis has been extremely helpful in all phases of our work. We wish to mention, especially, the assistance of Robert Clucas, Tony Eckman, Jack Gottsegan, William Gullickson, John Hinrichs, Mimi Hook, Shirley Loftus, James Milton, John Musgrave, Robert Parker, Eugene Roberts, Colleen Scanlon, Arlene Shapiro, Al Walderhaug, and Paula Young.

Comments on the original draft of our manuscript by Ernst Berndt, Geoffrey Moore, and Beatrice Vaccara were very useful to us in preparing the final manuscript. Financial support of our work by the Federal Preparedness Agency and the National Science Foundation is gratefully acknowledged. None of the individuals or institutions listed above shares our responsibility for any remaining deficiencies in this study.

We consider production under constant returns to scale for each sector, so that a proportional increase in all inputs results in a proportional change in sectoral output. Under constant returns to scale the sum of elasticities of each sector's output with respect to all inputs is equal to unity, so that the value shares of all inputs sum to unity for each sector. The necessary conditions for producer equilibrium for each sector can be combined with growth rates of intermediate input, capital input, labor input, and output to produce an index number for the sectoral rate of technical change that depends on the prices and quantities of inputs and outputs for the sector.

Our sectoral models of production and technical change are based on production functions $\{F^i\}$ for each of the n sectors, characterized by constant returns to scale:

$$Z_i = F^i\,(X_i, K_i, L_i, T), \qquad (i = 1, 2, \ldots, n),$$

where $\{Z_i\}$ is the set of outputs, $\{X_i\}$ is the set of intermediate inputs, $\{K_i\}$ is the set of capital inputs, and $\{L_i\}$ is the set of labor inputs for all n sectors, and T is time. Denoting the prices of outputs by $\{q_i\}$, the prices of intermediate inputs by $\{p^i_X\}$, the prices of capital inputs by $\{p^i_K\}$, and the prices of labor inputs by $\{p^i_L\}$, we can define the shares of intermediate input, say $\{v^i_X\}$, capital input, say $\{v^i_K\}$, and labor input, say $\{v^i_L\}$, in the value of output for each of the sectors by

$$v^i_X = \frac{p^i_X X_i}{q_i Z_i},$$

$$v^i_K = \frac{p^i_K K_i}{q_i Z_i},$$

$$v^i_L = \frac{p^i_L L_i}{q_i Z_i}, \qquad (i = 1, 2, \ldots, n).$$

Necessary conditions for producer equilibrium for each sector are given by equalities between the value shares of each input into the sector and the elasticity of output with respect to that input:

$$v^i_X = \frac{\partial \ln Z_i}{\partial \ln X_i}\,(X_i, K_i, L_i, T),$$

$$v^i_K = \frac{\partial \ln Z_i}{\partial \ln K_i}\,(X_i, K_i, L_i, T),$$

$$v^i_L = \frac{\partial \ln Z_i}{\partial \ln L_i}\,(X_i, K_i, L_i, T), \qquad (i = 1, 2, \ldots, n).$$

The production function for each industrial sector is defined in terms of sectoral output, intermediate input, capital input, and labor input. Under constant returns to scale for each sector, the elasticities and the value shares for all three inputs sum to unity. Each of the inputs is an aggregate that depends on the quantities of individual intermediate inputs, capital inputs, and labor inputs to the sector. Constant returns to scale imply that the aggregates for each sector are characterized by constant returns to scale; proportional changes in all the inputs that comprise each aggregate input result in proportional changes in the aggregate:

$$X_i = X_i (X_{1i}, X_{2i}, \ldots, X_{ni}),$$

$$K_i = K_i (K_{1i}, K_{2i}, \ldots, K_{pi}),$$

$$L_i = L_i (L_{1i}, L_{2i}, \ldots, L_{qi}), \qquad (i = 1, 2, \ldots, n),$$

where $\{X_{ji}\}$ is the set of n intermediate inputs from the jth sector ($j = 1, 2, \ldots, n$), $\{K_{ki}\}$ the set of p capital inputs, and $\{L_{li}\}$ the set of q labor inputs, all into the ith sector ($i = 1, 2, \ldots, n$).

Denoting the prices of capital inputs by $\{p^i{}_{Kk}\}$ and the prices of labor inputs by $\{p^i{}_{Ll}\}$, we can define the shares of the n intermediate inputs, say $\{v^i{}_{Xj}\}$, in the value of intermediate input, the shares of the p capital inputs, say $\{v^i{}_{Kk}\}$, in the value of capital input, and the shares of the q labor inputs, say $\{v^i{}_{Ll}\}$, in the value of labor input in the ith sector ($i = 1, 2, \ldots, n$) by

$$v^i{}_{Xj} = \frac{q_j X_{ji}}{p^i{}_X X_i}, \qquad (i, j = 1, 2, \ldots, n),$$

$$v^i{}_{Kk} = \frac{p^i{}_{Kk} K_{ki}}{p^i{}_K K_i}, \qquad (i = 1, 2, \ldots, n; k = 1, 2, \ldots, p),$$

$$v^i{}_{Ll} = \frac{p^i{}_{Ll} L_{li}}{p^i{}_L L_i}, \qquad (i = 1, 2, \ldots, n; l = 1, 2, \ldots, q).$$

Necessary conditions for producer equilibrium for each sector are given by equalities between the shares of each individual input in the value of the corresponding aggregate and the elasticities of the aggregate with respect to the individual inputs:

$$v^i{}_{Xj} = \frac{\partial \ln X_i}{\partial \ln X_{ji}} (X_{1i}, X_{2i}, \ldots X_{ni}),$$

$$v^i{}_{Kk} = \frac{\partial \ln K_i}{\partial \ln K_{ki}} (K_{1i}, K_{2i}, \ldots, K_{pi}),$$

$$v^i{}_{Ll} = \frac{\partial \ln L_i}{\partial \ln L_{li}} (L_{1i}, L_{2i}, \ldots, L_{qi}), \quad (i = 1, 2, \ldots, n).$$

Under constant returns to scale, the elasticities and the value shares sum to unity for each of the three aggregates for each sector.

Finally, we can define rates of technical change, say $\{v^i{}_T\}$, for all n sectors, as rates of growth of output with respect to time, holding intermediate input, capital input, and labor input constant:

$$v^i{}_T = \frac{\partial \ln Z_i}{\partial T}(X_i, K_i, L_i, T), \qquad (i = 1, 2, \ldots, n).$$

Under constant returns to scale the rate of technical change for each sector can be expressed as the rate of growth of the corresponding sectoral output less a weighted average of the rates of growth of intermediate input, capital input, and labor input into the sector, where the weights are given by the corresponding value shares:

$$\frac{d \ln Z_i}{d T} = \frac{\partial \ln Z_i}{\partial \ln X_i}\frac{d \ln X_i}{d T} + \frac{\partial \ln Z_i}{\partial \ln K_i}\frac{d \ln K_i}{d T}$$

$$+ \frac{\partial \ln Z_i}{\partial \ln L_i}\frac{d \ln L_i}{d T} + \frac{\partial \ln Z_i}{\partial T},$$

$$= v^i{}_X\frac{d \ln X_i}{d T} + v^i{}_K\frac{d \ln K_i}{d T} + v^i{}_L\frac{d \ln L_i}{d T}$$

$$+ v_{iT}, \qquad (i = 1, 2, \ldots, n).$$

We refer to the expressions $\{v^i{}_T\}$ as the *Divisia quantity indexes of sectoral rates of technical change*.

The Divisia quantity indexes of sectoral technical change are defined in terms of sectoral aggregates for intermediate input, capital input, and labor input. Under constant returns to scale the rate of growth of each sectoral aggregate can be expressed as a weighted average of rates of growth of its components, where weights are given by the corresponding value shares:

$$\frac{d \ln X_i}{dT} = \Sigma v^i{}_{Xj}\frac{d \ln X_{ji}}{dT},$$

$$\frac{d \ln K_i}{dT} = \Sigma v^i{}_{Kk}\frac{d \ln K_{ki}}{dT},$$

$$\frac{d \ln L_i}{dT} = \Sigma v^i{}_{Ll}\frac{d \ln L_{li}}{dT}, \qquad (i = 1, 2, \ldots, n).$$

We refer to these expressions $\{X_i, K_i, L_i\}$ as *Divisia indexes of sectoral intermediate input, capital input, and labor input*.[1]

If the production function for each individual sector gives output Z_i

---

1. These quantity indexes and the analogous price indexes discussed below were introduced by Divisia (1925, 1928, 1952). The Divisia index of technical change was introduced by Solow (1957) and has been discussed by Hulten (1973a), Jorgenson and Griliches (1967, 1971), Merrilees (1971), Nelson (1973), Richter (1966), and Usher (1974).

as a function of a sectoral aggregate for input, say W_i, we can write this function in the form

$$Z_i = G^i [W_i(X_i, K_i, L_i), T], \qquad (i = 1, 2, \ldots, n),$$

where input is homogeneous of degree one in intermediate input X_i, capital input K_i, and labor input L_i for the sector. The production function G^i is homogeneous of degree one in input W_i, so that sectoral technical change is *Hicks-neutral* and we can rewrite the function in the form

$$Z_i = A_i(T) \cdot W_i(X_i, K_i, L_i), \qquad (i = 1, 2, \ldots, n).$$

The sectoral rate of technical change is independent of intermediate, capital, and labor input and depends only on time:

$$v^i_T = \frac{d \ln A_i(T)}{dT}, \qquad (i = 1, 2, \ldots, n);$$

similarly, sectoral input is independent of time and depends only on intermediate, capital, and labor input. The rate of growth of sectoral input can be expressed as a weighted average of rates of growth of these inputs:

$$\frac{d \ln W_i}{dT} = v^i_x \frac{d \ln X_i}{dT} + v^i_K \frac{d \ln K_i}{dT}$$

$$+ v^i_L \frac{d \ln L_i}{dT}, \qquad (i = 1, 2, \ldots, n).$$

We refer to this expression $\{W_i\}$ as the *Divisia index of sectoral input.*[2]

Under constant returns to scale the existence of a sectoral aggregate for input is equivalent to Hicks neutrality of sectoral technical change. We do not require the existence of such an aggregate in constructing an index of sectoral technical change; equivalently, we do not require that sectoral technical change be Hicks-neutral. Our disaggregated production account includes data on output, intermediate input, capital input, and labor input in current and constant prices and data on sectoral productivity for each sector. We do not present data on aggregate input for each sector, and the assumption of Hicks neutrality is not employed in the construction of our indexes of sectoral technical change.

1.1.2 Duality

Under constant returns to scale the necessary conditions for producer equilibrium imply that the value of output is equal to the sum of the values of intermediate, capital, and labor input into each sector:

2. The definition of technical change that is neutral in the sense that the ratio of marginal products of capital and labor for any ratio of capital and labor input is independent of time is due to Hicks (1932). This definition is generalized to more than two inputs by Burmeister and Dobell (1969).

$$q_i Z_i = p^i{}_X X_i + p^i{}_K K_i + p^i{}_L L_i, \qquad (i = 1, 2, \ldots, n).$$

Our data on output, intermediate input, capital input, and labor input in current prices for each sector satisfy this equality as an accounting identity. Given this equality for each sector, equalities between the value shares of each input into the sector and the elasticity of sectoral output with respect to that input, we can express the price of sectoral output as a function, say P^i, of the prices of intermediate input, capital input, labor input, and time:

$$q_i = P^i(p^i{}_X, p^i{}_K, p^i{}_L, T), \qquad (i = 1, 2, \ldots, n).$$

We refer to these functions as the *sectoral price functions*.[3]

Under constant returns to scale the values of intermediate, capital, and labor input are equal to the sum of the values of their components:

$$p^i{}_X X_i = \Sigma q_j X_{ji},$$

$$p^i{}_K K_i = \Sigma p^i{}_{Kk} K_{ki},$$

$$p^i{}_L L_i = \Sigma p^i{}_{Ll} L_{li}, \qquad (i = 1, 2, \ldots, n).$$

Our data on the components of intermediate, capital, and labor input for each sector satisfy these equalities as accounting identities. The prices of intermediate, capital, and labor input are functions of the prices of their components:

$$p^i{}_X = p^i{}_X(q_1, q_2, \ldots, q_n),$$

$$p^i{}_K = p^i{}_K(p^i{}_{K1}, p^i{}_{K2}, \ldots, p^i{}_{Kp}),$$

$$p^i{}_L = p^i{}_L(p^i{}_{L1}, p^i{}_{L2}, \ldots, p^i{}_{Lq}), \qquad (i = 1, 2, \ldots, n).$$

We can express the rate of growth of the price index for each sectoral aggregate as a weighted average of the rates of growth of its components:

$$\frac{d \ln p^i{}_X}{dT} = \Sigma v^i{}_{Xj} \frac{d \ln q_j}{dT},$$

$$\frac{d \ln p^i{}_K}{dT} = \Sigma v^i{}_{Kk} \frac{d \ln p^i{}_{Kk}}{dT},$$

$$\frac{d \ln p^i{}_L}{dT} = \Sigma v^i{}_{Ll} \frac{d \ln p^i{}_{Ll}}{dT}, \qquad (i = 1, 2, \ldots, n).$$

We refer to these expressions $\{p^i{}_X, p^i{}_K, p^i{}_L\}$ as the *Divisia price indexes of sectoral intermediate input, capital input, and labor input.*

We can define rates of technical change for all n sectors as the negative of rates of growth of the prices of sectoral output with respect to

---

3. The price function was introduced by Samuelson (1953).

time, holding the prices of intermediate input, capital input, and labor input constant:

$$v^i_T = -\frac{\partial \ln P^i}{\partial T}(p^i_X, p^i_K, p^i_L, T), \quad (i = 1, 2, \ldots, n).$$

We can express the rate of technical change for each sector as a weighted average of rates of growth of prices of input into the sector, less the rate of growth of the price of sectoral output, where the weights are given by the corresponding value shares:

$$\frac{d \ln q_i}{dT} = v^i_X \frac{d \ln p^i_X}{dT} + v^i_K \frac{d \ln p^i_K}{dT} + v^i_L \frac{d \ln p^i_L}{dT}$$

$$- v^i_T, \quad (i = 1, 2, \ldots, n).$$

We refer to these expressions $\{v^i_T\}$ as the *Divisia price indexes of sectoral technical change.*

If sectoral output is a function of an aggregate for sectoral input, the price of sectoral output can be expressed as a function of the price of input, say p^i_W:

$$q_i = \frac{p^i_W(p^i_X, p^i_K, p^i_L)}{A_i(T)}, \quad (i = 1, 2, \ldots, n).$$

The rate of sectoral technical change depends only on time and the price of sectoral input depends only on the prices of intermediate, capital, and labor input. The existence of a quantity aggregate for sectoral input is equivalent to the existence of a price aggregate for sectoral input, and either is equivalent to Hicks neutrality of technical change. It is important to emphasize that we do not employ the assumption of Hicks neutrality, since we do not require the existence of quantity or price indexes for sectoral input in constructing our indexes of sectoral productivity.

The product of Divisia price and quantity indexes for an aggregate is equal to the sum of the values of its components. For example, the product of the price and quantity indexes for intermediate input into a sector is equal to the sum of the values of intermediate inputs that make up the aggregate. Second, Divisia indexes have the *reproductive property* that a Divisia index of Divisia indexes is also a Divisia index of the components of each index. For example, if sectoral input is composed of three subaggregates—intermediate input, capital input, and labor input—the Divisia index of sectoral input can be defined in two equivalent ways. First, sectoral input is a Divisia index of Divisia indexes of sectoral intermediate, capital, and labor input. Alternatively, sectoral input is a Divisia index of the individual intermediate, capital, and labor inputs into the sector. Divisia price indexes also have the reproductive property.

1.1.3 Index Numbers

While Divisia price and quantity indexes are useful in defining sectoral output, sectoral intermediate, capital, and labor input, and sectoral productivity in terms of data on quantities and prices, we find it essential to extend our methodology to incorporate price and quantity data at discrete points of time.[4] For this purpose we consider specific forms of the sectoral production functions $\{F^i\}$:

$$Z_i = \exp\left[\alpha^i_0 + \alpha^i_X \ln X_i + \alpha^i_K \ln K_i + \alpha^i_L \ln L_i\right.$$

$$+ \alpha^i_T \cdot T + \frac{1}{2}\beta^i_{XX}(\ln X_i)^2$$

$$+ \beta^i_{XK}\ln X_i \ln K_i + \beta^i_{XL}\ln X_i \ln L_i$$

$$+ \beta^i_{XT}\ln X_i \cdot T + \frac{1}{2}\beta^i_{KK}(\ln K_i)^2$$

$$+ \beta^i_{KL}\ln K_i \ln L_i + \beta^i_{KT}\ln K_i \cdot T$$

$$+ \frac{1}{2}\beta^i_{LL}(\ln L_i)^2 + \beta^i_{LT}\ln L_i \cdot T$$

$$\left. + \frac{1}{2}\beta^i_{TT}\cdot T^2\right], \qquad (i = 1, 2, \ldots, n).$$

For these production functions, sectoral outputs are transcendental or, more specifically, exponential functions of the logarithms of inputs. We refer to these forms as *transcendental logarithmic production functions* or, more simply, translog production functions.[5]

The translog production function for an industrial sector is characterized by constant returns to scale if and only if the parameters for that sector satisfy the conditions

$$\alpha^i_X + \alpha^i_K + \alpha^i_L = 1,$$

$$\beta^i_{XX} + \beta^i_{XK} + \beta^i_{XL} = 0,$$

$$\beta^i_{XK} + \beta^i_{KK} + \beta^i_{KL} = 0,$$

$$\beta^i_{XL} + \beta^i_{KL} + \beta^i_{LL} = 0,$$

$$\beta^i_{XT} + \beta^i_{KT} + \beta^i_{LT} = 0, \qquad (i = 1, 2, \ldots, n).$$

For each sector the value shares of intermediate, capital, and labor input can be expressed as

---

4. Nelson (1973) and Usher (1974) have pointed out the need to define indexes appropriate for discrete points of time.

5. The translog production function was introduced by Christensen, Jorgenson, and Lau (1971, 1973). The treatment of technical change outlined below is due to Diewert (1977) and to Jorgenson and Lau (1977).

$$v^i_X = \alpha^i_X + \beta^i_{XX} \ln X_i + \beta^i_{XK} \ln K_i + \beta^i_{XL} \ln L_i$$
$$\quad + \beta^i_{XT} \cdot T,$$

$$v^i_K = \alpha^i_K + \beta^i_{XK} \ln X_i + \beta^i_{KK} \ln K_i + \beta^i_{KL} \ln L_i$$
$$\quad + \beta^i_{KT} \cdot T,$$

$$v^i_L = \alpha^i_L + \beta^i_{XL} \ln X_i + \beta^i_{KL} \ln K_i + \beta^i_{LL} \ln L_i$$
$$\quad + \beta^i_{LT} \cdot T, \qquad (i = 1, 2, \ldots, n).$$

The rate of sectoral technical change can be expressed as

$$v^i_T = \alpha^i_T + \beta^i_{XT} \ln X_i + \beta^i_{KT} \ln K_i$$
$$\quad + \beta^i_{LT} \ln L_i + \beta^i_{TT} \cdot T, \qquad (i = 1, 2, \ldots, n).$$

If we consider data for an industrial sector at any two discrete points of time, say T and $T - 1$, the average rate of sectoral technical change can be expressed as the difference between successive logarithms of sectoral output less a weighted average of the differences between successive logarithms of sectoral intermediate, capital, and labor input with weights given by average value shares:

$$\ln Z_i(T) - \ln Z_i(T-1) = \bar{v}^i_X[\ln X_i(T)$$
$$\quad - \ln X_i(T-1)] + \bar{v}^i_K[\ln K_i(T) - \ln K_i(T-1)]$$
$$\quad + \bar{v}^i_L[\ln L_i(T) - \ln L_i(T-1)]$$
$$\quad + \bar{v}^i_T, \qquad (i = 1, 2, \ldots, n),$$

where

$$\bar{v}^i_X = \frac{1}{2}[v^i_X(T) + v^i_X(T-1)],$$

$$\bar{v}^i_K = \frac{1}{2}[v^i_K(T) + v^i_K(T-1)],$$

$$\bar{v}^i_L = \frac{1}{2}[v^i_L(T) + v^i_L(T-1)],$$

$$\bar{v}^i_T = \frac{1}{2}[v^i_T(T) + v^i_T(T-1)], \qquad (i = 1, 2, \ldots, n).$$

We refer to these expressions for the average rate of sectoral technical change $\{\bar{v}^i_T\}$ as the *translog indexes of the sectoral rates of technical change*.

Similarly, we can consider specific forms for sectoral intermediate, capital, and labor input as functions of individual intermediate, capital, and labor inputs into each industrial sector. For example, sectoral intermediate input can be expressed as a translog function of individual intermediate inputs:

$$X_i = \exp \left[\alpha^i_1 \ln X_{1i} + \alpha^i_2 \ln X_{2i} + \ldots + \alpha^i_n \ln X_{ni} \right.$$

$$+ \frac{1}{2} \beta^i_{11} (\ln X_{1i})^2$$

$$+ \beta^i_{12} \ln X_{1i} \ln X_{2i} + \ldots$$

$$\left. + \frac{1}{2} \beta^i_{nn} (\ln X_{ni})^2 \right], \qquad (i = 1, 2, \ldots, n).$$

Intermediate input for an industrial sector is characterized by constant returns to scale if and only if the parameters for that sector satisfy the conditions

$$\alpha^i_1 + \alpha^i_2 + \ldots + \alpha^i_n = 1,$$
$$\beta^i_{11} + \beta^i_{12} + \ldots + \beta^i_{1n} = 0,$$

$$\cdot \quad \cdot \quad \cdot \quad \cdot \quad \cdot \quad \cdot \quad \cdot \quad \cdot$$

$$\beta^i_{1n} + \beta^i_{2n} + \ldots + \beta^i_{nn} = 0, \qquad (i = 1, 2, \ldots, n).$$

For each sector the value shares of individual intermediate inputs $\{X_{ji}\}$ can be expressed as

$$v^i_{Xj} = \alpha^i_j + \beta^i_{1j} \ln X_{1i} + \ldots$$

$$+ \beta^i_{jn} \ln X_{ni}, \qquad (i = 1, 2, \ldots, n).$$

Considering data on intermediate inputs into an industrial sector at any two discrete points of time, we can express the difference between successive logarithms of sectoral intermediate input as a weighted average of differences between successive logarithms of individual intermediate inputs into the sector with weights given by average value shares:

$$\ln X_i (T) - \ln X_i (T-1) = \Sigma \bar{v}^i_{Xj} [\ln X_{ji} (T)$$

$$- \ln X_{ji} (T-1)], \qquad (i = 1, 2, \ldots, n),$$

where

$$\bar{v}^i_{Xj} = \frac{1}{2} [v^i_{Xj} (T) + v^i_{Xj} (T-1)], \quad (i = 1, 2, \ldots, n).$$

Similarly, if capital and labor input into each industrial sector are translog functions of their components, we can express the difference between successive logarithms of sectoral capital and labor input in the form

$$\ln K_i (T) - \ln K_i (T-1) = \Sigma \bar{v}^i_{Kk} [\ln K_{ki} (T)$$

$$- \ln K_{ki} (T-1)],$$

$$\ln L_i\,(T) - \ln L_i\,(T-1) = \Sigma \bar{v}^i_{Ll}\,[\ln L_{li}\,(T)$$
$$- \ln L_{li}\,(T-1)], \qquad (i=1,2,\ldots,n),$$

where

$$\bar{v}^i_{Kk} = \frac{1}{2}\,[v^i_{Kk}\,(T) + v^i_{Kk}\,(T-1)],$$
$$(i=1,2,\ldots,n; k=1,2,\ldots,p),$$

$$\bar{v}^i_{Ll} = \frac{1}{2}\,[v^i_{Ll}\,(T) + v^i_{Ll}\,(T-1)],$$
$$(i=1,2,\ldots,n; l=1,2,\ldots,q).$$

We refer to these expressions for sectoral intermediate, capital, and labor input $\{X_i, K_i, L_i\}$ as *translog indexes of sectoral intermediate, capital, and labor input.*[6]

The product of price and quantity indexes of sectoral intermediate, capital, and labor input must be equal to the sum of the values of the individual intermediate, capital, and labor inputs into each sector. For example, we can define the price index corresponding to the translog quantity index of sectoral intermediate input as the ratio of the value of intermediate input into the sector to the translog quantity index. Price indexes corresponding to the translog quantity indexes of sectoral capital and labor input can be defined in the same way. The resulting price indexes of sectoral intermediate, capital, and labor input do not have the form of translog price indexes, but they can be determined from data on prices and quantities at any two discrete points of time. Translog quantity indexes do not have the reproductive property we have described above for Divisia indexes; the translog index for an aggregate depends on the structure of the subaggregates on which it is defined.[7]

1.2   Labor Input

1.2.1   Introduction

In describing and analyzing postwar patterns of productivity growth in the U.S. economy, our initial objective is to construct measures of

6. The quantity indexes were introduced by Fisher (1922) and have been discussed by Tornqvist (1936), Theil (1965), and Kloek (1966). These indexes were first derived from the translog production function by Diewert (1976). The corresponding index of technical change was introduced by Christensen and Jorgenson (1970). The translog index of technical change was first derived from the translog production function by Diewert (1977) and Jorgenson and Lau (1977). Earlier, Diewert (1976) had interpreted the ratio of translog indexes of output and input as an index of technical change under the assumption of Hicks neutrality.

7. This corrects an error in Christensen and Jorgenson (1973a), p. 261.

labor input in current and constant prices for each industrial sector.[8] Measures of labor input in constant prices are index numbers constructed from data on hours worked and compensation per hour for each sector. Our data on hours worked and labor compensation for each industry are cross-classified by sex, age, education, employment status, and occupation of workers. To construct measures of labor input that are consistent with the U.S. national income and product accounts we have controlled these data to industry totals based on establishment surveys. To disaggregate labor input by industrial and demographic characteristics of the work force we have exploited the detail on employment, hours worked, and compensation available from household surveys. To achieve consistency between establishment and household survey data we have used the household survey results to distribute industry totals based on establishment surveys.

We have disaggregated the labor input of all employed persons into cells cross-classified by the two sexes, eight age groups, five education groups, two employment classes, ten occupational groups, and fifty-one industries listed in table 1.1. This breakdown of labor input characteristics is based on the groupings employed by the Bureau of Census in reporting data from household surveys. The census data provide the only source of consistent time series on the work force cross-classified by industrial and demographic characteristics. With few exceptions, data on labor input for the fifty-one industry groups listed in table 1.1 are also available from establishment surveys employed in construction of the U.S. national income and product accounts. Neither household nor establishment surveys provide data on hours worked and labor compensation for the 81,600 cells of a matrix cross-classified by the characteristics given in table 1.1.[9] Moreover, we require four such matrices, one for each of four components of labor input: employment, hours, weeks, and labor compensation. While the complete cross-classifications are not available directly, marginal totals cross-classified by two, three, and sometimes four characteristics of labor input are available for each year from 1947 to 1973.

8. The initial design of our approach to the measurement of labor input, the collection of data, and much of the required estimation were carried out in collaboration with Peter Chinloy. The results of his measurement and analysis of labor input for the U.S. economy at the aggregate level are reported in his doctoral dissertation. See Chinloy (1974).

9. The 81,600 cell total is the product of the number of characteristic divisions within each industrial and demographic dimension: $(51) \cdot (2) \cdot (2) \cdot (8) \cdot (5) \cdot (10)$. A substantial number of these cells will have zero entries; an example is the number of "fourteen- or fifteen-year old" laborers with "four or more years of college" in each of the 2040 cells cross-classified by industry, occupation, sex, and employment class. In implementing the multiproportional matrix model discussed below we need not identify the empty cells prior to estimation; these cells are treated symmetrically with those for which entries are different from zero.

Table 1.1   **Characteristics of Labor Input**

Sex
- (1) Male
- (2) Female

Age
- (1) 14–15 years
- (2) 16–17 years
- (3) 18–24 years
- (4) 25–34 years
- (5) 35–44 years
- (6) 45–54 years
- (7) 55–64 years
- (8) 65 years and over

Education
- (1) 1–8 years grade school
- (2) 1–3 years high school
- (3) 4 years high school
- (4) 1–3 years college
- (5) 4 or more years college

Employment Class:
- (1) Wage and salary worker
- (2) Self-employed/unpaid family worker

Occupation:
- (1) Professional, technical, and kindred workers
- (2) Farmers and farm managers
- (3) Managers and administrators, except farm
- (4) Clerical workers
- (5) Sales workers
- (6) Craftsmen and kindred workers
- (7) Operatives
- (8) Service workers, including private household
- (9) Farm laborers
- (10) Laborers, except farm

Industry:
- (1) Agricultural production
- (2) Agricultural services, horticultural services, forestry, and fisheries
- (3) Metal mining
- (4) Coal mining
- (5) Crude petroleum and natural gas extractions
- (6) Nonmetallic mining and quarrying, except fuel
- (7) Construction
- (8) Food and kindred products
- (9) Tobacco manufactures
- (10) Textile mill products
- (11) Apparel and other fabricated textile products
- (12) Paper and allied products
- (13) Printing, publishing, and allied industries
- (14) Chemicals and allied products

Table 1.1 (continued)

(15) Petroleum and coal products
(16) Rubber and miscellaneous plastic products
(17) Leather and leather products
(18) Lumber and wood products, except furniture
(19) Furniture and fixtures
(20) Stone, clay, and glass products
(21) Primary metal industries
(22) Fabricated metal industries
(23) Machinery, except electrical
(24) Electrical machinery, equipment, and supplies
(25) Transportation equipment, except motor vehicles, and ordnance
(26) Motor vehicles and motor vehicle equipment
(27) Professional photographic equipment, and watches
(28) Miscellaneous manufacturing industries
(29) Railroads and railway express service
(30) Street railway and bus lines and taxicab service
(31) Trucking service and warehousing and storage
(32) Water transportation
(33) Air transportation
(34) Pipelines, except natural gas
(35) Services incidental to transportation
(36) Telephone, telegraph, and miscellaneous communication services
(37) Radio broadcasting and television
(38) Electric utilities
(39) Gas utilities
(40) Water supply, sanitary services, and other utilities
(41) Wholesale trade
(42) Retail trade
(43) Finance, insurance, and real estate
(44) Services
(45) Private households
(46) Nonprofit institutions
(47) Federal public administration
(48) Federal government enterprises
(49) Educational services, government (state and local)
(50) State and local public administration
(51) State and local government enterprises

Our first task is to construct matrices cross-classified by the industrial and demographic characteristics listed in table 1.1 for all four components of labor input for each year of the period 1947–73. To accomplish this goal we introduce a multiproportional matrix model, generalizing the RAS method introduced by Stone (1962). The statistical principles underlying this model are a straightforward extension of those that underlie the biproportional matrix model of Bacharach (1965). We present the multiproportional matrix model in section 1.2.2. We have employed all the available published information on marginal totals for each component of labor input available from the Census of Population and the Current Population Survey. The sources for the data on employment, hours, weeks, and labor compensation and the procedures we have adopted in constructing the matrices that underlie our index numbers for labor input are outlined in the following sections. In section 1.2.3 we describe our estimates of hours worked per year; our estimates of labor compensation per hour worked are described in section 1.2.4.

The desirability of disaggregating labor input by industrial and demographic characteristics of the work force has been widely recognized, for example by Denison (1962), Griliches (1960), Jorgenson and Griliches (1967), Kendrick (1961), and others. Kendrick has developed measures of labor input disaggregated by industry for much of the postwar period, but his measures do not incorporate a cross-classification of labor input by age, sex, education, or other demographic characteristics of the work force. Denison has developed measures of labor input for the U.S. economy as a whole based on data disaggregated by sex, age, education, and employment status, but not by occupation or industry.[10]

Data on labor input cross-classified by characteristics such as employment class, occupation, and industry are required in studies of labor demand; data cross-classified by characteristics such as sex, age, and education are required in studies of labor supply. In the absence of data disaggregated by both industrial and demographic characteristics, measures of labor input that fail to reflect differences in productivity among workers remain in common use. A recent illustration is provided by a study of the growth of labor input during the postwar period by the Bureau of Labor Statistics (1973b). The study provides data on hours worked for broadly defined age-sex groups and five major industrial groups. No attempt is made to construct measures of labor input that reflect differences in productivity among workers:

> All manhours published in this bulletin are treated as homogeneous units. In other words, changes in the quality of labor, as reflected in shifts toward high skilled workers and increased wage rates, are not reflected in the estimates.[11]

10. Kendrick purposely avoids disaggregating the employed population by demographic characteristics. Any difference in the productivity of an hour's work by laborers of differing personal characteristics should, in Kendrick's view, be captured not in a measure of factor input but in an index of productivity change. By contrast, Denison posits that disaggregation by personal characteristics is essential in measuring labor input. In his view, shifting composition by industrial and occupational characteristics does not reflect changes in the level of labor input but should be included in the measure of productivity change.

11. U.S. Bureau of Labor Statistics (1973b), p. 32.

We present indexes of labor input for the fifty-one industry groups included in our study in section 1.2.5. Our data base can be used to generate indexes of labor input cross-classified by each of the characteristics we have employed in compiling data on hours worked and compensation per hour.

1.2.2 Multiproportional Matrix Model

For each year in the period 1947–73 we require matrices of data on hours worked and labor compensation per hour, cross-classified by the demographic and industrial characteristics of labor input listed in table 1.1. This cross-classification involves a total of 81,600 entries for each matrix for each year. Data on the components of labor input—employment, hours per week, weeks per year, and labor compensation—are not available in published form for such a detailed cross-classification. However, considerable detail is available for individual years on the basis of two-way, three-way, and even four-way cross-classifications. Data from the decennial Census of Population is more detailed than data from the annual Current Population Survey. Our objective is to exhaust the detail available from both sources in constructing matrices for each component of labor input for each year.

In constructing matrices for employment, hours per week, weeks per year, and labor compensation we employ the published cross-classifications as control totals. The problem that remains is to generate estimates of each component of labor input for all 81,600 cells of the cross-classification presented in table 1.1 for each year. For this purpose we have developed a multiproportional matrix model, generalizing the RAS method introduced by Stone (1962) and formalized by Bacharach (1965) as the biproportional matrix model. To illustrate the multiproportional matrix model we find it useful to consider the biproportional matrix model as an example. Consider two nonnegative matrices, say A and B. The elements of the first matrix, say $\{a_{ij}\}$, are known. The problem is to estimate the unknown elements, say $\{b_{ij}\}$ of the second matrix, where only the row and column sums $\{u_i\}$ and $\{v_j\}$,

$$\sum_{j=1}^{n} b_{ij} = u_i, \qquad (i = 1, 2, \ldots, m),$$

$$\sum_{i=1}^{m} b_{ij} = v_j, \qquad (j = 1, 2, \ldots, n),$$

are known.

To specify the problem of estimating the unknown elements $\{b_{ij}\}$ more precisely, we introduce the assumption that the matrix B is *biproportional* to the matrix A, that is,

$$b_{ij} = r_i s_j a_{ij}, \qquad (i = 1, 2, \ldots, m; j = 1, 2, \ldots, n),$$

where r_i is a factor associated with the ith row of A and s_j is a factor associated with the jth column of A. The problem of estimating the unknown elements of the matrix B reduces to the problem of choosing row and column factors $\{r_i, s_j\}$ so that the row and column sums are equal to the known row and column sums $\{u_i, v_j\}$ and the elements of B are nonnegative. To state the problem more formally we can introduce the diagonal matrix $\hat{r}$ with diagonal elements $\{r_i\}$ and the diagonal matrix $\hat{s}$ with diagonal elements $\{s_j\}$. We can represent sequences of such matrices by $\{\hat{r}^t, \hat{s}^t\}$. The set of matrices B that are biproportional to the matrix A is defined by the conditions

$$B = \lim_{t \to \infty} \hat{r}^t A \, \hat{s}^t,$$

$$B \geq 0,$$

$$B\iota = \boldsymbol{u},$$

$$\iota' B = \boldsymbol{v},$$

where ι is a vector of ones, $\boldsymbol{u}$ is a vector with elements $\{u_i\}$, and $\boldsymbol{v}$ is a vector with elements $\{v_j\}$.

The matrices B that are biproportional to a given matrix A can be written in the "RAS" form

$$B = \hat{r} A \, \hat{s},$$

or as the limit of such matrices. Bacharach shows that for any matrix A such that every row and every column has at least one positive element, and for any vectors $\boldsymbol{u}$ and $\boldsymbol{v}$ with all elements positive and

$$\Sigma u_i = \Sigma v_j,$$

there exists a unique nonnegative matrix B that is biproportional to nonnegative matrix A.[12] The method for constructing the matrix B proposed by Stone (1962) and others involves an iterative process. The first iteration requires two steps:

1. Multiply the ith row by a scalar, say $r^1{}_i$, such that the row sum is equal to the given total u_i.

2. Multiply the jth column by a scalar, say $s^1{}_j$, such that the column sum is equal to the given total v_j.

The result of this process is a new, nonnegative matrix, say A^1, that serves as the starting point of the next iteration. Successive iterations of the process define a sequence of matrices $\{A^t\}$ defined by

12. Bacharach (1965), pp. 302–8.

$$A^t = \hat{r}^t A^{t-1} \hat{s}^t, \qquad (t = 1, 2, \ldots),$$

where

$$A^0 = A.$$

Bacharach shows that the process converges to the unique biproportional matrix B.[13]

We next consider the multiproportional matrix model. In defining this model we find it useful to rewrite the nonnegative matrix A, where

$$A = [a_1, a_2 \ldots a_n],$$

and a_j is the jth column of A, as a column vector, say a, where

$$a = \begin{bmatrix} a_1 \\ a_2 \\ \cdot \\ \cdot \\ \cdot \\ a_n \end{bmatrix}.$$

Next, we consider any partition of the elements of a, that is, any set of subsets of the elements of a such that each element is assigned to one and only one subset. We restrict consideration to partitions of the elements of a such that each subset contains at least one positive element. As before, the elements of the matrix A or the column vector a are known. The problem is to estimate the unknown elements of a matrix B, where

$$B = [b_1, b_2 \ldots b_n],$$

and b_j is the jth column of B, or the column vector b:

$$b = \begin{bmatrix} b_1 \\ b_2 \\ \cdot \\ \cdot \\ \cdot \\ b_n \end{bmatrix}.$$

We consider a partition of the vector b corresponding to any given partition of the vector a, denoting the sum of all elements in the ith subset of the jth partition of b by $u^j{}_i$, where all such sums are positive and the sum over all subsets is the same for all partitions. We say that the vector b is *multiproportional* to the vector a if the following conditions are satisfied:

13. Ibid., p. 304.

1. There are factors $\{r^j{}_i\}$ such that each element of b can be represented either as the product of such factors, one for each partition, and the corresponding element of a or as the limit of a sequence of products of this type.
2. The vector b is nonnegative.
3. The sum of elements of b in the ith subset of the jth partition is equal to $u^j{}_i$.

There exists a unique nonnegative vector b that is multiproportional to a nonnegative vector a.

To construct the vector b that is multiproportional to a vector a, we employ an iterative process. The first iteration requires as many steps as there are partitions of the vector a. At the jth step we multiply the elements in the ith subset of the jth partition by a scalar, say $r^{j1}{}_i$, such that the sum of elements in the subset is equal to the given total $u^j{}_i$. The result of this process is a new, nonnegative vector, say a^1, that serves as the starting point of the next iteration. Successive iterations of the process define a sequence of vectors $\{a^t\}$ such that each element is the product of the scalars $\{r^{jt}{}_i\}$ and the corresponding element from the preceding iteration, where

$$a^0 = a.$$

This process converges to the unique multiproportional vector b.

As an illustration of the multiproportional matrix model, consider the case where one has available information separately classified by each of two characteristics and wishes to construct a matrix cross-classified by these characteristics. Both marginal distributions can be used as input into the multiproportional matrix model, following the iterative procedure outlined above. If a three-way cross-classification is the objective and the data set includes all three possible two-way cross-classifications, the multiproportional matrix model can be applied in four ways. Any pair of two-way cross-classifications can be employed or all three can be used simultaneously. Fortunately, the appropriate choice can be made on elementary grounds. In estimating the elements of the multiproportional matrix, the number of degrees of freedom can be reduced to a minimum by using as much overlapping marginal information as is available. In this example, all three two-way cross-classifications would be employed in the model as marginal distributions.

1.2.3 Annual Hours Worked

Introduction

The task of developing measures of labor input cross-classified by sex, age, education, employment status, and occupation for each industry can be divided between compiling data on annual hours worked and compiling data on labor compensation. In this section we present our methodology and data sources for constructing annual data on hours worked; we discuss the development of data on labor compensation in the following section. Our first step in measuring annual hours worked is to construct employment matrices for the civilian work force for each postwar year, cross-classified by sex, age, education, employment class, occupation, and industry of employment. Marginal totals for employment are based on the last three decennial Censuses of Population and the postwar Current Population Survey. We combine data from these sources by means of the multiproportional matrix model presented in the preceding section. The resulting employment matrices are adjusted to employment totals by industry from the U.S. national income and product accounts.

The second step in measuring annual hours worked is to incorporate differences in hours worked by different groups of workers. Since establishment-based surveys provide data on hours paid rather than hours worked, hours paid have often been substituted for hours worked in measuring labor input. The latter is clearly more appropriate as a measure of labor input. The growing importance of hours that are paid but not worked due to vacations, illness, personal leaves, and holidays leads to an upward bias in the growth of hours worked if data on hours paid are substituted for data on hours worked. To avoid the deficiencies of establishment-based data on hours paid we employ data on hours worked from household surveys reported in the decennial census and the Current Population Survey. We employ the multiproportional matrix model in constructing matrices of hours worked per week, cross-classified by sex, age, employment class, occupation, and industry for each year. The resulting hours-worked matrices are adjusted to industry totals from the national accounts. We define annual hours worked for each category of labor input as the product of employment, hours worked per week, and the number of weeks in the calendar year, fifty-two.

Employment

Our first step in constructing employment matrices for the civilian work force for each postwar year is to assign each worker to one of 81,600 cells, cross-classified by sex, age, education, employment class, occupation, and industry of employment. Information for the years of the decennial Census of Population—1950, 1960, and 1970—is considerably more detailed than information available for other years from the Current Population Survey. We employed two-way, three-way, and four-way cross-classifications of employment from the census in generating the full six-way cross-classification for each census year. The value of employment for each cell in the detailed cross-classification was initialized at unity; all available marginal totals from each Census of

Population were used in the multiproportional matrix model to control the distribution of employment among cells for the corresponding year. We then ranked intermediate years by the detail available for marginal totals in each year. We initialized the employment matrix for each intermediate year by a weighted average of employment matrices from the nearest years for which an employment matrix was already available, beginning with a weighted average of matrices based on the decennial censuses. All available marginal totals available for each year were incorporated by means of the multiproportional matrix model. For the years 1947, 1948, 1949, 1971, 1972, and 1973 this process was initialized with the nearest year for which an employment matrix was available.

The incorporation of Alaska and Hawaii into U.S. census data in 1960 and the redefinition of census labor force concepts[14] beginning with the 1967 household survey necessitated special approaches to the labor input data for these years. The resolution of the discontinuity between 1959 and 1960 is straightforward. We have constructed two employment matrices for 1960—one defined on a basis comparable with earlier years, the other to later years. Since the 1960 census was the first survey to incorporate data for Alaska and Hawaii, we create a separate employment matrix for the forty-ninth and fiftieth states by means of the multiproportional matrix model. The matrix for the two states is then subtracted from the matrix for all fifty states to create a second 1960 matrix that is comparable with 1959 and earlier years.

Fortunately, most of the definitional changes introduced by the Bureau of the Census in January 1967 affect the distinction between the unemployed and those who are not in the labor force and did not affect data on the employed labor force. Three changes did affect the employment data. First, employed persons who are not at work during the survey week and are looking for another job had their classification changed from unemployed to employed:

Up to now (January 1967) the small group of persons absent from their jobs the entire survey week because of vacations, illness, strikes,

---

14. Most of the definitional changes introduced by the Census Bureau in January 1967 affect the distinction between the unemployed and those who are not in the labor force. See Stein (1967). These changes do not influence this study. However, changes in the interviewers' questioning policy and the bureau's classificatory criteria do have an impact. Beginning in January 1967, (i) those persons, previously classified as unemployed, who were absent from their jobs during the entire survey week because of vacations, strikes, etc., but were looking for other jobs were now classified as employed; (ii) former proprietors who later incorporated their businesses were now assigned to the wage and salary class rather than the self-employed category; and (iii) all fourteen- and fifteen-year-old laborers were no longer considered part of the labor force.

bad weather, etc., who were looking for other jobs was classified as unemployed. Starting in January 1967, such persons are classified as employed—that is, among others "with a job but not at work."[15]

This definitional change shifted approximately 80,000 persons[16] from the unemployed to the employed category.

We ultimately control our employment data to totals based on establishment surveys. Since these totals include all workers who received pay during the survey period, whether or not they actually worked during the period, the establishment survey classifies workers receiving pay from one job, though physically absent and looking for another job, as employed. The control totals for our employment data are unaffected by the first census redefinition. Since there is no evidence to suggest that the industrial and demographic characteristics of the 80,000 persons reclassified from unemployed to employed are different from the characteristics of the employed population, we made no adjustments in the distribution of workers in our employment matrices based on household surveys.

The second census redefinition involved a more accurate classification of employed persons between wage and salary workers and self-employed and unpaid family workers. Prior to January 1967 a person was simply asked in which of the two classes he or she belonged. By the early sixties it had become clear that some proprietors who had incorporated their businesses were still defining themselves as part of the self-employed when, in actuality, they should be classified as employees of a corporate business. After January 1967, whenever a census-taker received a "self-employed" response, an additional question was asked to determine whether the "proprietor's" business was incorporated. The respondent was then properly classified into one of the two employment classes. The Census Bureau estimated that this question accounted for a shift of approximately 750,000 workers[17] from the self-employed to the wage and salary class.

To provide a basis for constructing continuous time series, the Census Bureau conducted a separate survey of 17,500 households, the Monthly Labor Survey, during 1966. This survey was based on the new questionnaire which was to become effective in January 1967. Paralleling this was the traditional Current Population Survey of 35,000 households. We could have treated this shift of 750,000 laborers in the same manner as the introduction of Alaska and Hawaii. We could have constructed a second 1966 matrix based on the Monthly Labor Survey. This matrix would be defined in terms consistent with 1967 and all later years.

15. Stein (1967), p. 7.
16. Ibid., p. 10.
17. Ibid.

However, unlike the addition of new states at a point in time, which leaves all labor matrices preceding the date of statehood unaffected, the reallocation of the corporate self-employed affects labor matrices in all years prior to 1967. Consequently, we find it essential to adjust all pre-1967 household matrices for the corporate self-employed.

The Bureau of Economic Analysis used the two 1966 census surveys to estimate the number of workers misclassified as self-employed in each industry in 1966. The Bureau then linearly extrapolated each industry's corporate self-employed back to 1948, assuming that the corporate self-employed were one-third the 1966 total in 1958 and zero in 1948. All the post-1947 employment totals reported in the national accounts were adjusted to reflect this reclassification. Although our employment matrices are controlled to totals from the Bureau of Economic Analysis, we require estimates of the demographic characteristics of the corporate self-employed. These workers are more likely to share the demographic characteristics of the self-employed than those of wage and salary workers.

For each industry and each year from 1948 to 1966 we distributed the corporate self-employed by sex, age, education, and occupation characteristics by allocating totals from the Bureau of Economic Analysis in proportion to the distribution of self-employed and unpaid family workers from the household survey.[18] We then subtracted this matrix for each industry and each year from the corresponding household employment matrix for self-employed workers and added it to the employment matrix for wage and salary workers. This procedure not only accounts for the definitional shifts occurring in 1967 but also corrects misallocations affecting the measure of labor input in each year from 1948 to 1966.

The final and most perplexing change introduced in 1967 involved the decision to drop all employed fourteen- and fifteen-year-olds from the census's definition of the labor force. While the Department of Commerce no longer provides data on these young workers cross-classified by the demographic characteristics previously reported, limited demographic data on employed fourteen- and fifteen-year-olds is still collected by the census bureau and reported separately from the usual labor force data. This information was used together with employment matrices representing those sixteen years old or over to construct a complete 1947–73 series for all employed persons fourteen years of age and older.

While census data based on household surveys provide the best source of data on labor input cross-classified by industrial and demographic

---

18. Results based on the Current Population Survey were used to initialize the multiproportional matrix model for 1966 and earlier years.

characteristics, industry totals must be reconciled with data based on establishment surveys. First, census reports suffer from a slight undercount. Part of the undercount can be attributed to the bureau's decision to classify a multiple job holder only in the industry where he works the most hours. A valid measure of annual hours worked requires a count of jobs held in the economy rather than a count of employed persons. This necessitates counting each laborer holding multiple jobs as employed in each industry in which he works no matter how insignificant the number of hours in his secondary jobs. Establishment-based surveys meet this requirement. Second, industry totals from establishment surveys include those employed workers who are less than fourteen years old. Since their contribution to output is captured in production measures, their labor input must be incorporated into a measure of total labor input.

Establishment surveys provide an enumeration of jobs rather than persons at work. The resulting employment data are based on annual average job counts from surveys of establishments. These data include workers who received pay but were not at work during the survey week, while household surveys count only those who were actually at work during the survey week. A worker who is absent from his job but paid during the survey week or employed at other times during the year is not absent for all fifty-two weeks of the calendar year. Exclusion of these workers would lead to a downward bias in annual labor input for the corresponding category of labor input. Using an establishment count of employees paid and later assigning to absent workers the average annual hours worked by workers with comparable demographic characteristics who received pay during the survey period provides a more attractive approach to measuring annual hours worked.

Both the Bureau of Economic Analysis and the Bureau of Labor Statistics publish annual establishment-based estimates of the number of employed persons by industry. Integration of our measure of labor input with the U.S. national income and product accounts requires that we use the Bureau of Economic Analysis estimates. These estimates are largely based on annual averages of the employment returns by individual establishments to state unemployment insurance bureaus. The payroll data account for nearly 80% of wages and salaries and almost 95% of wages and salaries in private industry. While the Bureau of Labor Statistics also bases its employment series to state unemployment insurance data, it controls its industry totals to the March returns rather than to annual averages. In addition, the Bureau of Labor Statistics data do not include agricultural and private household sectors, while data from the national income and product accounts include these sectors. After each year's census matrices had served as marginal inputs into the multiproportional matrix model, the resulting household matrices of employment were then adjusted to totals by industry from the national accounts. The result is a complete time series of matrices cross-classifying all employed persons by industrial and demographic characteristics for the period 1947–73.

Hours

Measures of labor input must incorporate differences in hours worked by different groups of workers. The Bureau of Labor Statistics publishes data on hours paid based on establishment surveys. Hours data are compiled only for production labor in manufacturing and nonsupervisory workers in nonmanufacturing, so that hours worked for supervisory, self-employed, and unpaid family workers are unavailable. A more important limitation in the series published by the Bureau of Labor Statistics is that hours data by industry are not cross-classified by demographic characteristics. To avoid the deficiencies of establishment-based hours data we use the hours data collected and published by the Bureau of the Census. The census reports only those hours that were actually *worked* during the survey week and thus automatically excludes vacations, holidays, illness, personal leave, and all other circumstances during which an employed person may be paid for hours he did not work.

The Census provides data on hours worked cross-classified by the demographic and industrial characteristics listed in table 1.1. An analysis of the hours-worked data published by the Bureau of the Census reveals that the total hours worked per week associated with individuals in each cell has a distribution that can be accurately represented by the lognormal distribution. We therefore assume that the hours worked by the individuals in each cell have a lognormal distribution with unknown location and dispersion parameters. Assigning each employed person to the appropriate cell cross-classified by sex, age, employment status, occupation, and industry[19] and imposing this lognormality assumption on the distribution of hours worked, we can estimate the two unknown parameters by the method of maximum likelihood.

The method of maximum likelihood cannot be applied directly to census data on hours worked, since the data are not presented as individual observations, but rather as empirical frequency distributions. For example, for a given set of labor input characteristics, the census presents the number of laborers who fall within each of the following discrete hour classes: 0 hours worked, 1–14, 15–26, 27–34, 35–40, 40, and 41 or more. Gjeddebaek (1949) has provided an adaptation of the method of maximum likelihood which is directly applicable to

19. Unfortunately, there are no available data covering the postwar period which classify hours worked by education.

data in frequency form.[20] The raw frequency data are interpreted as drawings from a multinomial model where the units within any given cell are divided into mutually exclusive groups corresponding to the census intervals. Using the lognormal distribution to describe the probabilities of observing individuals in each interval, the likelihood of observing any given empirical distribution of hours worked can be maximized.

While the multinomial model enables us to obtain estimates of mean hours worked for each demographic cell in each marginal distribution provided by the census, these averages will be biased upward unless they are adjusted for holders of multiple jobs. This bias arises because the census classifies a person holding more than one job as employed only in that industry in which he works the most hours. Furthermore, the census allocates to that industry the multiple job holder's total hours worked at all jobs regardless of the industry in which the hours were actually worked. This accounting framework incorrectly assigns the total number of hours to the primary job, while neglecting to assign the appropriate number of hours worked by multiple job holders to their secondary jobs.

The separate effects of the census's procedure of assigning employed persons and their hours worked solely to primary industries reinforce each other, leading to mean estimates that are biased upward. Consider two industries A and B which together employ three workers. The first works 5 hours in A, the second works 20 hours in A and 15 in industry B, and the third works 10 hours in B and 5 hours in A. The true mean hours worked in each industry are as follows:

Industry A: $\dfrac{(5 + 20 + 5)}{3} = 10,$

Industry B: $\dfrac{(15 + 10)}{2} = 12.5.$

Calculating these averages on the basis of raw data reported by the census would lead to the following estimates:

Industry A: $\dfrac{(L_1 + L_2)}{2} = \dfrac{(5 + 35)}{2} = 20,$

Industry B: $\dfrac{(L_3)}{1} = 15.$

Thus, failure to adjust for multiple job holders clearly leads to an upward bias in all industries where multiple job holders play a role.

---

20. Barger (1971) has applied Gjeddebaek's method to the estimation of mean earnings from data available in frequency form.

Using data on hours published in the *Special Labor Force Reports*, we subtract from each cell created directly from the census reports those hours that were worked in other industries and add these hours to the appropriate secondary industries. The multiproportional matrix model is then used to construct a matrix of average weekly hours worked by persons cross-classified by sex, age, employment class, occupation, and industry. We first construct matrices of hours worked for the years of the decennial Census of Population, initializing the matrix for each year with the corresponding employment matrix and incorporating all available marginal totals. For intermediate years the matrix is initialized by a matrix with entries equal to the product of the entries from the corresponding employment matrix and a weighted average of the entries from matrices of average hours worked from the nearest years for which an hours matrix was available.

The household survey data on employment and hours worked for the 1948–66 period are based on a set of definitions allocating the corporate self-employed to the class of self-employed and unpaid family workers. Applying the multinomial model to the frequency distributions of hours worked by the self-employed as reported in both the Current Population Survey and the Monthly Labor Survey for 1966, we determined that weekly hours worked in 1966 by the corporate self-employed are not statistically different from the weekly hours worked by all self-employed workers, but are different from the weekly hours worked by wage and salary workers. In most cases, the corporate self-employed worked more hours per week than their wage and salary counterparts. Using the demographic and industrial distribution of the corporate self-employed, as described above, and estimating average weekly hours worked by these workers from data on average weekly hours worked by self-employed workers with comparable demographic and industrial characteristics, we adjust each entry in our matrices of weekly hours for wage and salary workers for the years 1948 to 1966 to reflect the weekly hours worked by the corporate self-employed. No adjustment of the matrices on average weekly hours worked by self-employed workers is required.

Using data on annual totals of hours worked by industry, recently compiled and published by the Bureau of Economic Analysis, we control our estimates of annual hours worked within each industry to totals for the industry. Our first step is to convert BEA estimates of annual hours worked for each industry to weekly hours worked by dividing by the number of weeks in a calendar year, fifty-two. Controlling our weekly hours matrices to these totals and dividing by our employment matrices enumerating jobs, we obtain estimates of average weekly hours per job. It is important to emphasize that the corresponding frequency distributions of hours worked from the census household surveys include workers "with a job but not at work" as reporting zero hours worked in the survey week. These workers are included in our estimates of average hours worked, so that we obtain weekly hours worked per job for each category of worker. Consequently, we control our estimates of weekly hours worked per job for each industry to estimates of weekly hours worked per job from the Bureau of Economic Analysis data on hours worked and employment. The result is an annual series of matrices of average weekly hours *worked* per job, cross-classified by the demographic and industrial characteristics presented in table 1.1.

1.2.4 Labor Compensation

Introduction

The choice of an appropriate accounting framework for measuring the compensation of labor input is important for at least two reasons. First, labor compensation is required in order to weight hours worked in forming an index of labor input for each industry. Second, the total wage bill must reflect labor's share in total cost in the measurement of productivity. Our approach to the measurement of labor compensation is based on data for average compensation for the civilian work force from the last three decennial Censuses of Population. These data provide estimates of average compensation per person; our employment data provide estimates of the number of jobs. Our first step in measuring labor compensation is to provide a basis for converting average compensation per person to average compensation per job. For this purpose we construct matrices of weeks paid per year, cross-classified by sex, age, employment class, occupation, and industry for each year, using the multiproportional matrix model. The average number of weeks paid per year for each category of workers, divided by fifty-two, provides an estimate of the number of jobs per person in each category.

The second step in our measurement of labor compensation is to construct matrices giving average compensation per person for the civilian labor force for each postwar year, cross-classified by sex, age, education, employment class, occupation, and industry of employment. Marginal totals for average compensation are based on data on wage and salary income from the three last decennial Censuses of Population. These data are interpolated and extrapolated from the benchmark years to obtain estimates of wage and salary income for each year from 1947 to 1973. The wage and salary data for each year are adjusted to incorporate employers' contributions to social security and unemployment compensation and other supplements to wages and salaries. We divide average compensation per person by the ratio of the average number of weeks paid per year to fifty-two to obtain average compensation per job for each category of workers. The resulting compensation matrices are adjusted to control totals for labor compensation by industry from the U.S. national income and product accounts.

Weeks

In estimating labor compensation from census data it is essential to recall that the census provides an enumeration of persons on the basis of household surveys, while data on employment from establishment surveys provide an enumeration of jobs rather than persons. If a job is filled by two workers during a given year, each paid for twenty-six weeks, employment data from establishment surveys will report one person employed while compensation data from household surveys will report the compensation received by both workers. Multiplying average compensation per person in a given category by the number of jobs in that category would produce a downward bias in the resulting estimate of labor compensation. To eliminate this source of bias we divide average compensation per person by the number of jobs per person, estimated as the ratio of the number of weeks paid for each person to fifty-two. In our example, we would divide average compensation for each of our two workers by the ratio of twenty-six weeks paid for each worker to fifty-two to produce an average compensation per job equal to twice the average compensation per person.

The Bureau of the Census provides the only source of data on weeks cross-classified by demographic and industrial characteristics of the work force. As indicated in the following census definition, these data are compiled on a weeks-paid basis rather than on a weeks-worked basis.

> The data on weeks worked pertain to the number of different weeks in which a person did any work for pay or profit (including paid vacation and sick leave) or worked without pay on a family farm or in a family business.[21]

Census data on weeks paid from household surveys are compiled on the same basis as data on employment from establishment surveys, which include all jobs for which payment is made rather than the number of workers actually at work during the survey period. At this point we find it useful to emphasize that the employment matrices we have generated from household surveys are controlled to industry totals from establishment surveys.

A problem in the use of the weeks data arises from the census's policy of assigning all weeks for which a worker was paid during the past year to the cell representing that worker's present demographic and industrial characteristics. This may introduce a bias if the worker has crossed

21. U.S. Department of Commerce, Bureau of the Census, *U.S. Census of Population—1960. Industrial Characteristics*, PC(2)–7F, p. xvi.

occupation, class, or industry boundaries during the past year. The data constrain our options and allow us to do little more than acknowledge this limitation. However, two qualifying notes may be appended. First, according to Bancroft (1963), fewer than 6% of all employed persons actually crossed such boundaries in 1961.[22] While this percentage may shift over time, a second and more important finding of this same study of job mobility reveals that 96.7% of the job changes were self-canceling[23]—that is, except for 3.3% of the sample, job shifts away from each class-occupation-industry category were fully offset by employment shifts into the same category. Consequently, unless the cumulative weeks paid of workers leaving a particular job differ substantially from the weeks paid of incoming laborers, little bias is introduced by the census procedure.

Since the census reports weeks paid in the form of empirical frequency distributions, the steps used to construct weeks matrices are very similar to those used in deriving the hours-worked matrices. First, we assign each person to the appropriate cell. Assuming that weeks paid for the individuals in each cell have a lognormal distribution, we estimate the unknown parameters of this distribution from the empirical frequency distributions reported by the Bureau of the Census. No data are available on the weeks paid for multiple job holders for principal and secondary jobs; however, Perrella (1970) reports that almost half of all multiple job holders worked at both principal and secondary jobs in all twelve months preceding a survey taken in May 1969.[24] Accordingly, we assume that the average of weeks paid for multiple job holders is equal to the average number of weeks paid in each industry of employment.

The multiproportional matrix model is used in constructing a matrix of weeks paid for employed persons, cross-classified by sex, age, employment class, occupation, and industry. The matrix for each decennial census year is initialized by means of the corresponding employment matrix; all available marginal totals of weeks paid for each year are then incorporated. Matrices for intermediate years are initialized by a matrix with entries equal to the product of the entries from the corresponding employment matrix and a weighted average of entries from matrices of average weeks paid from the nearest years for which weeks matrices were available. No marginal totals were available for 1947 and 1948, so that we employ the matrix for average weeks paid for 1949 to represent the corresponding matrices for 1947 and 1948. Similarly, no marginal totals are available for 1971, so that we use an average of the matrices for average weeks paid for 1970 and 1972 to represent the

22. Bancroft (1963), tables F and G.
23. Ibid.
24. Perrella (1970), p. 3.

matrix for 1971. A procedure identical to that applied to hours worked was used to adjust the 1948–66 data on weeks worked for reallocation of the corporate self-employed to the wage and salary class.

Labor Compensation

The first problem in measuring labor compensation is the selection of a concept that reflects differences among the marginal products of individual workers. The available census compensation data include total income, earnings, and wage and salary earnings. Earnings include the return to capital invested by self-employed workers in their private businesses, as the following definition indicates:

> Earnings are the sum of wages and salary income and self-employment income. Self-employment income is defined as net money income (gross receipts minus operating expenses) from a business, farm, or professional enterprise in which the person was engaged on his own account.[25]

Earnings reflect differences in marginal products of workers, but also incorporate differences in income from the use of capital. The wage and salary income of wage and salary workers is a more appropriate starting point for the measurement of labor compensation.

A second problem in measuring labor compensation is that the cost of labor input from the point of view of the firm is the sum of both direct payments to labor in the form of wages and salaries and indirect payments that take the form of supplements. The Bureau of the Census reports compensation from the point of view of the household, so that the incomes reported are measures of wage and salary income rather than the total of wages, salaries, and supplements. Household surveys exclude employers' contributions to social security, pension plans, unemployment insurance, and all the other programs that are combined under the heading of supplements. Differentials in the proportion of supplements in labor compensation are sufficient to make suspect any assumption of proportionality of direct labor payments to total labor cost. For example, employers' contributions to social security and unemployment insurance are calculated by applying a percentage to each worker's annual earnings, but only up to a fixed maximum.

A third problem in measuring labor compensation concerns the appropriate time period for comparisons of the marginal productivities among distinct labor groups. A worker's average compensation per hour provides a good approximation to the worker's marginal productivity. Annual compensation, even based on labor earnings for each worker, is hardly an adequate proxy for compensation per hour, since

25. U.S. Department of Commerce, Bureau of the Census, *U.S. Census of Population—1960. Industrial Characteristics*, PC(2)–7F, p. xvi.

annual labor compensation is the product of annual hours and hourly compensation. Annual hours may differ widely among groups and over time. If annual hours worked vary over demographic and industrial groups, then differences in labor compensation based on variations in annual earnings do not parallel differences in marginal productivity. An appropriate measure of labor compensation requires estimates of average compensation per hour for each of the categories of labor to be aggregated.

The fourth problem in measuring labor compensation is whether weights based on compensation per hour worked should be fixed over the whole time period or should vary from year to year. To account for shifting demand conditions, changing production techniques, or the impact of constraints on labor supply, the best approach is to construct a set of weights based on compensation per hour worked for each year. We have undertaken the construction of measures of hourly compensation for each of the postwar years 1947 through 1973. Just as for data on hours and weeks, annual compensation data are presented in the form of empirical frequency distributions for the three benchmark years 1949, 1959, and 1969. Since economists investigating the distribution of labor income in the United States have long observed that the distributions can be approximated by a lognormal probability distribution, we have employed Gjeddebaek's adaptation of the method of maximum likelihood to estimate the parameters of this distribution. We have employed this method to estimate average wage and salary income for each category of labor input. It is important to note that this estimate refers to the wage and salary income of persons and not to the sum of wage payments to all workers occupying a given job.

Estimates based on Bureau of the Census data identify the amount of income workers receive and not the total labor cost incurred by the firm. To estimate labor cost we have distributed employers' contributions to social security among employees by adding to wage and salary income the appropriate dollar amount as determined by the workers' annual wages or salaries and the year's social security tax laws as described by Pechman (1971). Similarly, we added unemployment compensation contributions by employers to the wage and salary income matrices. These two adjustments account for nearly 70% of all earnings supplements.

Up to this point we have defined average labor compensation per person rather than average compensation per job. Two persons reporting $10,000 each for twenty-six weeks' work earn a different sum of supplements than a single laborer reporting $20,000 income for a full year's work. To convert the census data on average compensation per person to data on average compensation per job we divide average compensation for each category of worker by the ratio of the number of weeks paid to the number of weeks in a calendar year, fifty-two. The resulting matrices of annual labor compensation of wage and salary workers are inputs into the multiproportional matrix model.

Control totals for annual labor compensation by industry are taken directly from table 6.1 in the national income issue of the *Survey of Current Business.* These labor compensation data include all employer supplements. In addition to guaranteeing correct industry totals, these data provide the basis for the distribution of the 30% of labor supplements not accounted for directly. In addition, establishment-based control totals assure that the compensation of multiple job holders is appropriately distributed among each worker's industries of employment. Finally, the national income and product accounts provide a continuous time series of labor compensation for the period 1947 through 1973. The labor compensation matrix for each intermediate year is initialized by a matrix with entries equal to the product of annual hours worked for the corresponding cell and a weighted average of wages and salaries per hour worked for the nearest census years with weights given by log-linear interpolation.

The hourly wage estimates for the benchmark years include employers' contributions to social security and unemployment insurance as well as all payments to employee pension funds and similar programs. These payments vary from year to year depending on the current tax laws, union contracts, and so on. Failure to account for these changes would introduce a bias when using data reported for census years to estimate wage rates for intermediate years. To adjust wage data so that wage rates do not reflect employers' tax contributions and other indirect payments, a matrix of annual labor compensation is generated with all nontax supplements excluded. Second, a matrix of benchmark wage rates exclusive of each year's social security and unemployment insurance taxes paid by employers is generated. We initialize each intermediate year's compensation model with an initial estimate of annual wages excluding supplements.

We next estimate wage rates for each intermediate year. We first adjust the earnings estimates to reflect wage and salary totals, exclusive of employer supplements, published by the Bureau of Economic Analysis. Next we estimate the appropriate level of employer contributions to social security and unemployment insurance for each cell; to account for the remaining supplements we adjust data from all cells to control totals from the national income and product accounts. To obtain wages earned per hour worked, where wages represent the sum of the employers' direct and indirect payments to labor, we divide labor compensation by hours worked, defined by the product of employment, weekly hours worked, and the number of weeks per calendar year, fifty-two. Together with the decennial census matrices described above, these estimates for intermediate years form a complete time series of employers' direct plus indirect hourly payments to labor for the period 1947–73.

Since earnings reported to the census by self-employed laborers are a combination of labor income and the return to noncorporate capital, the procedure we have described for estimating labor compensation can be applied only to wage and salary workers. An index of labor input requires an estimate of the labor compensation of self-employed and unpaid family workers. Given the compensation of employees and noncorporate income by industry from the national income and product accounts, two options present themselves. Holding sex, age, education, occupation, and industry constant, we could assume that both classes of workers earn identical hourly wages. Using the employment, hours, and weeks matrices generated above, an estimated wage bill for the self-employed could be calculated for each industry. Subtracting this total from noncorporate income, we would obtain property compensation. Alternatively, we could assume that both corporate and noncorporate capital earn the same after-tax return. Noncorporate property income for each industry could then be subtracted from total noncorporate income to obtain labor compensation. The residual would represent the labor return to that industry's self-employed and unpaid family workers. This wage bill could be distributed among the self-employed so as to preserve the wage differentials observed among that industry's classified wage and salary workers.

We have chosen to assume that after-tax rates of return are the same for corporate and noncorporate business. Differences in individual preferences and barriers to entry of some wage and salary workers into the self-employed category are sufficient to make suspect any claim that wages are equal, even controlling for labor characteristics. By contrast, there is less reason to expect that immobility of capital results in differential after-tax rates of return in the corporate and noncorporate sectors. The cost of incorporating a noncorporate business is relatively modest, and small corporations can be treated in the same manner as noncorporate businesses from the point of view of the corporate income tax. The legal form of organization, corporate or noncorporate, can be altered with little impact on the use of capital, so that capital is freely mobile between sectors.

1.2.5   Indexes of Labor Input

We have outlined the development of data on annual hours worked and labor compensation per hour for each industrial sector, cross-classified by sex, age, education, employment class, and occupation of workers. To construct an index of labor input for each industrial sector we assume that sectoral labor input, say $\{L_i\}$, can be expressed as a translog function of its individual components, say $\{L_{li}\}$. The corresponding index of sectoral labor input is a translog quantity index of individual labor inputs:

$$\ln L_i(T) - \ln L_i(T-1) = \sum \bar{v}^i_{Ll}\,[\ln L_{li}(T)$$
$$- \ln L_{li}(T-1)], \qquad (i = 1, 2, \ldots, n),$$

where weights are given by average shares of each component in the value of sectoral labor compensation:

$$\bar{v}^i_{Ll} = \frac{1}{2}\,[v^i_{Ll}(T) + v^i_{Ll}(T-1)],$$
$$(i = 1, 2, \ldots, n; l = 1, 2, \ldots, q),$$

and

$$v^i_{Ll} = \frac{p^i_{Ll}\,L_{li}}{\sum p^i_{Ll}\,L_{li}},$$
$$(i = 1, 2, \ldots, n; l = 1, 2, \ldots, q).$$

The value shares are computed from data on hours worked $\{L_{li}\}$ and compensation per hour $\{p^i_{Ll}\}$ for each component of sectoral labor input, cross-classified by sex, age, education, employment class, and occupation of workers. Labor compensation for the sector as a whole $\sum p^i_{Ll}\,L_{li}$ is controlled to labor compensation by industry from the U.S. national income accounts.

For each of the components of labor input into an industrial sector $\{L_{li}(T)\}$, the flow of labor services is proportional to hours worked, say $\{H_{li}(T)\}$:

$$L_{li}(T) = Q^i_{Ll}\,H_{li}(T),$$
$$(i = 1, 2, \ldots, n; l = 1, 2, \ldots, q),$$

where the constants of proportionality $\{Q^i_{Ll}\}$ transform hours worked into a flow of labor services. The translog quantity indexes of sectoral labor input $\{L_i\}$ can be expressed in terms of their components $\{L_{li}\}$ or in terms of the components of sectoral hours worked $\{H_{li}\}$:

$$\ln L_i(T) - \ln L_i(T-1) = \sum \bar{v}^i_{Ll}\,[\ln L_{li}(T)$$
$$- \ln L_{li}(T-1)]$$
$$= \sum \bar{v}^i_{Ll}\,[\ln H_{li}(T) - \ln H_{li}(T-1)],$$
$$(i = 1, 2, \ldots, n).$$

We form sectoral indexes of labor input from data on hours worked by industry, cross-classified by sex, age, education, employment class, and occupation. Changes in the logarithms of hours worked for each component are weighted by average shares in sectoral labor compensation.

We can define *sectoral hours worked*, say $\{H_i(T)\}$, as the unweighted sum of its components,

$$H_i(T) = \Sigma H_{li}(T), \qquad (i = 1, 2, \ldots, n).$$

Similarly, we can define *sectoral indexes of the quality of hours worked*, say $\{Q^i{}_L(T)\}$, that transform sectoral measures of hours worked into the translog indexes of labor input:

$$L_i(T) = Q^i{}_L(T)H_i(T), \qquad (i = 1, 2, \ldots, n).$$

The sectoral indexes of the quality of hours worked can be expressed in the form

$$\ln Q^i{}_L(T) - \ln Q^i{}_L(T-1)$$

$$= \Sigma \bar{v}^i{}_{Ll} [\ln H_{li}(T) - \ln H_{li}(T-1)]$$

$$- [\ln H_i(T) - \ln H_i(T-1)],$$

$$(i = 1, 2, \ldots, n),$$

so that these indexes reflect changes in the composition of hours worked within each sector.[26] Sectoral labor quality remains unchanged if all components of hours worked within a sector are growing at the same rate. Sectoral quality rises if components with higher flows of labor input per hour worked are growing more rapidly and falls if components with lower flows per hour worked are growing more rapidly.

We have generated translog indexes of labor input for each industrial sector listed in table 1.1. There are 1600 categories of labor input for each industry and 51 industries. Based on the employment, hours, weeks, and labor compensation data described above, translog indexes of labor input for the private domestic economy and for a number of sectoral divisions are presented in column (4) of tables 1.2 through 1.13. Unweighted indexes of hours worked based on the same data are given in column (2). The ratio between these two series, presented in column (3), measures the change in labor quality. To facilitate comparisons with unweighted and industry-weighted hours indexes, industry series employed by the Bureau of Labor Statistics and by Kendrick are presented in columns (1) and (5). Kendrick's labor indexes have been taken directly from his *Postwar Productivity Trends in the United States: 1948–1969.*[27]

26. Detailed discussions of quality indexes and applications to disaggregated labor data can be found in doctoral dissertations by Barger (1971) and Chinloy (1974).

27. See Kendrick (1973), pp. 240–359. For a complete discussion of his methods, see pages 154–58 of the same book.

The primary source of hours and employment estimates for the BLS productivity studies is the Department of Labor's Current Employment Statistics Program. Establishment data on employment and average paid weekly hours of production workers in manufacturing and nonsupervisory workers in nonmanufacturing are developed from this program and published in BLS (1973a) Bulletin no. 1312, "Employment and Earnings Statistics of the United States." The methods currently adopted by BLS in constructing its hours series have evolved considerably from the original procedures outlined in BLS (1960) Bulletin no. 1249. A working paper describing these methods is available on request from the Productivity and Technology Division of the Bureau of Labor Statistics. The following passage has been extracted from this working paper and, along with published and unpublished man-hours data made available by BLS, forms the basis for the indexes found in column (1):

> In the manufacturing sector, separate estimates for production and nonproduction worker manhours are derived and then aggregated to the manufacturing total. Production workers and nonproduction worker employment and production worker average weekly hours are taken directly from published sources (BLS Bulletin 1312). Average weekly hours for nonproduction workers are developed from BLS studies of wages and supplements in the manufacturing sector which provide data on the regularly scheduled workweek of white collar employees. It is assumed that scheduled hours are equivalent to paid hours for nonproduction workers in manufacturing. . . .
>
> For nonmanufacturing sectors, employment and weekly hours paid are taken from published sources (BLS Bulletin 1312) . . . . Although average weekly hours data refer only to nonsupervisory workers (who comprise about 85 percent of total employment), it is assumed that the length of the workweek for nonsupervisory workers in each nonmanufacturing industry is the same for all wage and salary workers.
>
> Manhours are computed by multiplying employment by average weekly hours in each sector and inflated to annual levels using a constant factor of 52. Each manhour is treated as a homogeneous unit; no distortion is made between workers with different skill levels or rates of pay.[28]

28. U.S. Bureau of Labor Statistics (1973b), p. 3. The scheduled weekly hours for nonproduction workers are calculated from data collected by BLS for the study, *Employer Expenditures for Selected Supplementary Remuneration Practices for Production Workers in Manufacturing Industries, 1962*, BLS Bulletin 1428 (1965).

While not mentioned in this excerpt, estimated annual man-hours for proprietors and unpaid family workers are derived by BLS from the National Income Accounts and the Current Population Survey and are added to industry employee totals. The BLS indexes presented in column (1) of tables 1.2 through 1.16 similarly include these estimates.

Table 1.2   **Private Domestic Economy (1972=1.000)**

Year	Hours Worked		Labor Quality (3)	Labor Input	
	BLS (1)	MPM Model (2)		Translog (4)	Kendrick (5)
1947	.821	.855	.846	.723	.771
1948	.823	.859	.851	.730	.781
1949	.794	.823	.850	.700	.746
1950	.806	.845	.861	.728	.766
1951	.836	.877	.871	.763	.806
1952	.844	.880	.886	.780	.817
1953	.855	.889	.893	.794	.825
1954	.822	.856	.895	.766	.784
1955	.855	.880	.897	.790	.814
1956	.866	.893	.902	.806	.829
1957	.855	.880	.911	.802	.824
1958	.818	.847	.912	.773	.784
1959	.848	.872	.920	.802	.813
1960	.854	.871	.947	.825	.822
1961	.841	.865	.934	.809	.811
1962	.858	.881	.951	.838	.830
1963	.863	.887	.953	.846	.841
1964	.877	.899	.963	.866	.860
1965	.907	.927	.967	.896	.890
1966	.929	.952	.981	.934	.927
1967	.935	.957	.987	.944	.932
1968	.954	.970	.993	.964	.951
1969	.978	.994	.995	.989	.978
1970	.966	.975	1.007	.983	
1971	.966	.972	1.006	.978	
1972	1.000	1.000	1.000	1.000	
1973	1.033	1.040	1.006	1.046	

Table 1.3   **Agriculture (1972=1.000)**

Year	Hours Worked		Labor Quality (3)	Labor Input	
	BLS (1)	MPM Model (2)		Translog (4)	Kendrick (5)
1947	2.491	2.542	.921	2.341	2.736
1948	2.387	2.456	.904	2.221	2.662
1949	2.361	2.349	.912	2.142	2.671
1950	2.176	2.289	.934	2.137	2.462
1951	2.068	2.190	.916	2.007	2.329
1952	1.972	2.111	.932	1.968	2.211
1953	1.926	2.064	.929	1.916	2.057
1954	1.874	2.013	.933	1.877	1.993
1955	1.918	1.952	.931	1.817	2.026
1956	1.814	1.825	.933	1.703	1.934
1957	1.691	1.692	.933	1.579	1.771
1958	1.575	1.619	.939	1.520	1.641
1959	1.573	1.592	.939	1.495	1.638
1960	1.553	1.506	.974	1.467	1.609
1961	1.460	1.472	.944	1.390	1.505
1962	1.405	1.437	.958	1.376	1.469
1963	1.328	1.381	.945	1.304	1.389
1964	1.280	1.293	.955	1.235	1.334
1965	1.249	1.258	.965	1.213	1.300
1966	1.139	1.139	.988	1.125	1.182
1967	1.131	1.091	.998	1.088	1.142
1968	1.115	1.081	1.000	1.080	1.116
1969	1.047	1.048	.999	1.047	1.047
1970	.995	1.015	1.026	1.042	
1971	.983	.997	.999	.997	
1972	1.000	1.000	1.000	1.000	
1973	.987	1.004	1.007	1.011	

Table 1.4 **Mining (1972=1.000)**

Year	Hours Worked		Labor Quality (3)	Labor Input	
	BLS (1)	MPM Model (2)		Translog (4)	Kendrick (5)
1947	1.447	1.439	.868	1.249	
1948	1.453	1.520	.871	1.323	1.542
1949	1.258	1.316	.872	1.148	1.314
1950	1.274	1.372	.878	1.205	1.373
1951	1.332	1.416	.882	1.249	1.404
1952	1.297	1.379	.893	1.232	1.363
1953	1.259	1.333	.899	1.199	1.301
1954	1.154	1.206	.903	1.089	1.168
1955	1.214	1.267	.905	1.148	1.236
1956	1.259	1.332	.910	1.213	1.297
1957	1.246	1.305	.917	1.197	1.269
1958	1.099	1.138	.929	1.057	1.098
1959	1.114	1.123	.935	1.051	1.088
1960	1.082	1.089	.939	1.023	1.059
1961	1.027	1.044	.947	.988	1.009
1962	1.004	1.026	.958	.982	.996
1963	.997	1.007	.956	.963	.985
1964	1.002	1.006	.964	.970	.985
1965	1.007	1.019	.964	.983	1.000
1966	1.008	1.021	.971	.991	1.000
1967	.985	.992	.974	.966	.975
1968	.974	.986	.980	.966	.969
1969	1.001	1.014	.987	1.000	1.001
1970	1.004	1.013	.991	1.004	
1971	.969	.982	1.004	.985	
1972	1.000	1.000	1.000	1.000	
1973	1.026	1.023	1.000	1.023	

Table 1.5 **Contract Construction (1972=1.000)**

Year	Hours Worked		Labor Quality (3)	Labor Input	
	BLS (1)	MPM Model (2)		Translog (4)	Kendrick (5)
1947	.692	.682	.895	.611	
1948	.738	.728	.907	.661	.732
1949	.722	.693	.908	.629	.697
1950	.765	.748	.909	.679	.749
1951	.824	.810	.917	.743	.810
1952	.834	.822	.927	.762	.826
1953	.806	.796	.929	.740	.792
1954	.760	.760	.934	.709	.749
1955	.789	.777	.937	.728	.767
1956	.837	.817	.935	.764	.806
1957	.811	.790	.935	.739	.782
1958	.767	.760	.939	.713	.752
1959	.810	.790	.941	.744	.781
1960	.790	.775	.943	.731	.767
1961	.779	.777	.947	.736	.766
1962	.801	.797	.961	.766	.783
1963	.819	.819	.963	.788	.805
1964	.837	.843	.973	.820	.828
1965	.872	.879	.973	.856	.866
1966	.890	.901	.983	.886	.891
1967	.872	.897	.988	.886	.879
1968	.880	.920	.995	.915	.891
1969	.950	.969	.997	.966	.950
1970	.929	.941	.987	.928	
1971	.961	.961	1.011	.971	
1972	1.000	1.000	1.000	1.000	
1973	1.051	1.072	1.004	1.076	

Table 1.6   **Manufacturing (1972=1.000)**

Year	Hours Worked		Labor Quality	Labor Input	
	BLS (1)	MPM Model (2)	(3)	Translog (4)	Kendrick (5)
1947	.814	.821	.873	.716	
1948	.825	.840	.874	.734	.819
1949	.750	.767	.876	.671	.745
1950	.812	.829	.880	.729	.800
1951	.875	.896	.888	.795	.872
1952	.890	.913	.903	.824	.891
1953	.932	.951	.911	.867	.930
1954	.852	.872	.918	.800	.849
1955	.898	.919	.917	.843	.893
1956	.912	.932	.921	.858	.906
1957	.897	.916	.928	.850	.897
1958	.824	.836	.936	.782	.813
1959	.879	.892	.938	.836	.871
1960	.874	.886	.956	.847	.873
1961	.850	.865	.951	.823	.848
1962	.885	.903	.964	.870	.888
1963	.894	.911	.961	.875	.898
1964	.913	.929	.966	.897	.927
1965	.960	.978	.963	.942	.969
1966	1.021	1.043	.972	1.014	1.039
1967	1.018	1.041	.981	1.022	1.015
1968	1.040	1.053	.985	1.038	1.037
1969	1.055	1.070	.986	1.055	1.055
1970	1.000	1.002	.994	.996	
1971	.961	.960	1.007	.967	
1972	1.000	1.000	1.000	1.000	
1973	1.053	1.057	1.000	1.057	

Table 1.7　　　　　**Transportation (1972＝1.000)**

Year	Hours Worked		Labor Quality (3)	Labor Input	
	BLS (1)	MPM Model (2)		Translog (4)	Kendrick (5)
1947	1.126	1.138	.943	1.072	
1948	1.128	1.156	.950	1.098	1.255
1949	1.025	1.054	.947	.998	1.130
1950	.992	1.041	.938	.976	1.105
1951	1.049	1.099	.944	1.038	1.169
1952	1.043	1.088	.952	1.035	1.157
1953	1.054	1.088	.953	1.037	1.141
1954	.986	1.014	.952	.965	1.044
1955	1.013	1.035	.953	.986	1.068
1956	1.035	1.049	.953	1.000	1.080
1957	1.030	1.034	.955	.988	1.062
1958	.946	.951	.956	.909	.959
1959	.974	.966	.960	.927	.969
1960	.961	.954	.963	.919	.959
1961	.932	.931	.964	.898	.926
1962	.939	.935	.974	.911	.925
1963	.936	.937	.972	.911	.928
1964	.951	.949	.980	.930	.944
1965	.970	.968	.977	.945	.961
1966	.988	.996	.988	.984	.990
1967	.991	1.002	.994	.996	.985
1968	1.004	1.016	1.001	1.017	1.006
1969	1.015	1.026	1.002	1.029	1.015
1970	1.010	1.006	.999	1.005	
1971	.986	.994	1.013	1.006	
1972	1.000	1.000	1.000	1.000	
1973	1.030	1.027	1.008	1.035	

Table 1.8   **Communications and Public Utilities (1972=1.000)**

Year	Hours Worked		Labor Quality	Labor Input	
	BLS (1)	MPM Model (2)	(3)	Translog (4)	Kendrick (5)
1947	.770	.642	.854	.548	
1948	.783	.693	.859	.596	.681
1949	.760	.688	.861	.593	.680
1950	.777	.687	.864	.593	.679
1951	.806	.714	.870	.622	.706
1952	.814	.724	.884	.640	.714
1953	.819	.746	.885	.660	.738
1954	.788	.754	.899	.678	.743
1955	.808	.770	.902	.695	.759
1956	.818	.802	.903	.724	.790
1957	.813	.808	.907	.733	.795
1958	.778	.780	.919	.717	.773
1959	.775	.773	.931	.719	.768
1960	.781	.779	.954	.743	.779
1961	.772	.774	.948	.733	.769
1962	.774	.774	.961	.744	.772
1963	.776	.779	.964	.751	.777
1964	.794	.795	.975	.775	.793
1965	.821	.821	.976	.801	.819
1966	.851	.851	.979	.833	.851
1967	.863	.868	.989	.858	
1968	.879	.882	.992	.875	
1969	.932	.939	.995	.934	
1970	.968	.988	.994	.982	
1971	.957	.980	1.010	.990	
1972	1.000	1.000	1.000	1.000	
1973	1.031	1.031	1.003	1.034	

Table 1.9   **Trade (1972=1.000)**

Year	Hours Worked		Labor Quality (3)	Labor Input	
	BLS (1)	MPM Model (2)		Translog (4)	Kendrick (5)
1947	.715	.795	.936	.744	
1948	.726	.776	.944	.733	.725
1949	.727	.774	.945	.732	.720
1950	.734	.779	.948	.738	.730
1951	.759	.815	.946	.770	.762
1952	.770	.819	.953	.780	.770
1953	.773	.819	.955	.782	.768
1954	.767	.811	.954	.773	.759
1955	.791	.831	.947	.786	.782
1956	.807	.852	.936	.798	.799
1957	.803	.849	.939	.797	.801
1958	.793	.841	.939	.789	.795
1959	.815	.855	.943	.807	.813
1960	.828	.862	.978	.842	.828
1961	.815	.855	.955	.817	.820
1962	.822	.859	.972	.835	.825
1963	.824	.860	.975	.838	.832
1964	.843	.878	.978	.859	.851
1965	.872	.901	.976	.880	.875
1966	.887	.915	.991	.907	.895
1967	.894	.914	.994	.909	.899
1968	.914	.926	1.001	.927	.914
1969	.937	.954	.995	.949	.937
1970	.948	.963	1.018	.980	
1971	.966	.981	1.011	.992	
1972	1.000	1.000	1.000	1.000	
1973	1.024	1.026	1.007	1.033	

Table 1.10   Finance, Insurance, and Real Estate (1972=1.000)

Year	Hours Worked		Labor Quality (3)	Labor Input	
	BLS (1)	MPM Model (2)		Translog (4)	Kendrick (5)
1947	.476	.480	.873	.419	
1948	.492	.500	.877	.439	.486
1949	.493	.501	.878	.440	.490
1950	.506	.519	.870	.452	.507
1951	.530	.543	.885	.481	.532
1952	.557	.565	.901	.509	.558
1953	.580	.590	.913	.539	.583
1954	.606	.614	.922	.566	.606
1955	.627	.635	.922	.586	.624
1956	.635	.655	.919	.602	.635
1957	.643	.664	.923	.613	.645
1958	.657	.673	.928	.625	.663
1959	.675	.689	.942	.649	.679
1960	.693	.703	.981	.690	.694
1961	.704	.722	.962	.694	.707
1962	.729	.736	.976	.718	.727
1963	.751	.755	.976	.737	.750
1964	.767	.774	.986	.763	.763
1965	.782	.799	.987	.789	.785
1966	.804	.823	.997	.820	.810
1967	.822	.846	.991	.838	.828
1968	.857	.884	.994	.878	.856
1969	.902	.923	.990	.914	.902
1970	.922	.941	.999	.940	
1971	.957	.971	1.009	.980	
1972	1.000	1.000	1.000	1.000	
1973	1.028	1.053	1.011	1.064	

Table 1.11   Services, Excluding Private Households and Nonprofit Institutions and Including Government Enterprises (1972=1.000)

Year	Hours Worked		Labor Quality (3)	Labor Input	
	BLS (1)	MPM Model (2)		Translog (4)	Kendrick (5)
1947	.457	.504	.977	.492	
1948	.456	.512	.981	.502	.525
1949	.458	.513	.985	.505	.523
1950	.455	.519	1.004	.521	.524
1951	.472	.537	.988	.530	.529
1952	.498	.555	.997	.553	.559
1953	.505	.565	.998	.563	.567
1954	.516	.569	1.003	.571	.565
1955	.520	.585	.993	.581	.578
1956	.529	.611	.988	.604	.595
1957	.546	.629	.991	.623	.610
1958	.546	.638	.993	.634	.612
1959	.569	.660	.994	.655	.630
1960	.602	.680	1.025	.697	.660
1961	.625	.702	.998	.700	.672
1962	.653	.725	1.010	.732	.687
1963	.685	.749	1.004	.752	.708
1964	.711	.779	1.006	.784	.726
1965	.751	.808	1.004	.811	.759
1966	.786	.847	1.003	.849	.786
1967	.813	.873	1.006	.878	
1968	.854	.897	1.007	.903	
1969	.903	.935	1.007	.941	
1970	.937	.944	1.027	.969	
1971	.958	.960	1.009	.968	
1972	1.000	1.000	1.000	1.000	
1973	1.038	1.047	1.003	1.050	

Table 1.12   **Private Households and Nonprofit Institutions (1972=1.000)**

Year	Hours Worked BLS (1)	Hours Worked MPM Model (2)	Labor Quality (3)	Labor Input Translog (4)	Labor Input Kendrick (5)
1947	.820	.842	.815	.687	
1948	.816	.853	.824	.703	.668
1949	.818	.854	.831	.710	.675
1950	.876	.905	.835	.756	.716
1951	.901	.889	.841	.748	.720
1952	.887	.833	.857	.714	.713
1953	.895	.823	.863	.710	.733
1954	.865	.778	.877	.682	.699
1955	.970	.869	.856	.744	.756
1956	1.023	.909	.849	.771	.781
1957	1.027	.906	.857	.776	.794
1958	1.048	.931	.855	.797	.820
1959	1.056	.947	.870	.824	.840
1960	1.077	.980	.902	.884	.885
1961	1.075	.986	.899	.886	.895
1962	1.084	1.002	.916	.918	.914
1963	1.080	1.000	.922	.922	.941
1964	1.074	1.000	.931	.931	.955
1965	1.056	.994	.942	.936	.991
1966	1.031	.994	.957	.952	1.031
1967	1.057	1.058	.953	1.009	
1968	1.051	1.040	.971	1.010	
1969	1.034	1.047	.986	1.033	
1970	1.008	1.004	.999	1.003	
1971	.997	1.003	1.005	1.008	
1972	1.000	1.000	1.000	1.000	
1973	.984	.982	1.016	.997	

Table 1.13   **General Government, Private Households, and Nonprofit Institutions (1972=1.000)**

Year	Hours Worked		Labor Quality	Labor Input	
	BLS (1)	MPM Model (2)	(3)	Translog (4)	Kendrick (5)
1947	.483	.521	.847	.441	.443
1948	.491	.535	.851	.455	.449
1949	.500	.554	.856	.474	.470
1950	.523	.576	.853	.491	.489
1951	.555	.603	.882	.531	.585
1952	.561	.604	.913	.551	.622
1953	.566	.604	.914	.552	.623
1954	.568	.597	.932	.556	.615
1955	.602	.629	.917	.577	.624
1956	.638	.656	.913	.599	.637
1957	.658	.670	.926	.620	.649
1958	.675	.689	.927	.639	.658
1959	.694	.704	.934	.657	.666
1960	.711	.726	.948	.688	.683
1961	.727	.750	.950	.712	.699
1962	.743	.767	.965	.740	.730
1963	.764	.785	.967	.759	.746
1964	.780	.806	.973	.784	.766
1965	.816	.829	.979	.812	.791
1966	.847	.864	.984	.850	.845
1967	.893	.905	.985	.891	.892
1968	.912	.924	.998	.922	.925
1969	.927	.945	.998	.942	.942
1970	.935	.951	.995	.946	
1971	.965	.974	1.005	.979	
1972	1.000	1.000	1.000	1.000	
1973	1.018	1.018	1.010	1.028	

A comparison of rates of growth in BLS, Kendrick, and translog indexes of labor input over the 1948–66 period is presented for all fifty-one industries in table 1.14. In addition, rates of growth of the translog indexes of sectoral labor input are presented for five subperiods of the period 1947–73. Rates of growth of labor input for the period as a whole are also reported in table 1.14.

1.3 Capital Input

1.3.1 Introduction

Our next objective is to construct measures of capital input by industrial sector for the U.S. economy in current and constant prices. Our measures of capital input in constant prices are index numbers constructed from data on the services of capital stocks and rental prices for capital services. At a conceptual level these indexes are strictly analogous to the measures of labor input in constant prices presented in the preceding section. Capital input takes the form of services of capital stock just as labor input involves the services of the work force. Capital services are compensated at rental prices just as labor services are compensated at wage rates. Pursuing this analogy, a possible approach to construction of measures of capital input would be to compile data on rental transactions in capital services. This method provides the basis for measuring capital services associated with the use of dwellings in the U.S. national income and product accounts. Data on rental prices for tenant-occupied dwellings are used to measure rental prices for owner-occupied dwellings. Data on the stock of both tenant-occupied and owner-occupied dwellings are used in constructing estimates of the rental value of housing.

A substantial portion of the assets employed in the U.S. economy involves capital goods with active rental markets. Most types of land and structures can be rented, and a rental market exists for many types of equipment—transportation equipment, construction equipment, electronic computers, office equipment and furniture, and so on. Unfortunately, very little effort has been devoted to compiling data from rental transactions, so that the construction of measures of capital input based on sources analogous to those we have employed for labor input is not feasible. An alternative approach is to infer the level of capital stocks at each point of time from data on flows of investment up to that point. Rental prices required for indexes of capital input in constant prices can be inferred from data on prices of investment goods and on property compensation. To construct measures of capital input that are consistent with the U.S. national income and product accounts, we have controlled our data on investment by industrial sector to totals for all

Table 1.14 Labor Input: Rates of Growth

Industry	1948–1966 (average annual rates of growth)			Translog Index of Labor Input (average annual rates of growth)					
	BLS	Kendrick	Translog	1947–1973	1947–1953	1953–1957	1957–1960	1960–1966	1966–1973
Agricultural production			−.0408	−.0352	−.0357	−.0505	−.0251	−.0495	−.0183
Agricultural services			.0133	.0202	.0158	−.0098	−.0353	.0492	.0402
Metal mining	−.0107	−.0096	−.0031	−.0025	.0204	.0035	−.0457	−.0070	−.0031
Coal mining	−.0696	−.0689	−.0683	−.0391	−.0789	−.0569	−.1227	−.0189	.0236
Crude petroleum and natural gas	.0053	.0065	.0141	.0155	.0602	.0332	−.0322	−.0046	.0046
Nonmetallic mining and quarrying	.0126	.0134	.0160	.0101	.0304	.0159	−.0138	.0178	−.0070
Contract construction	.0104	.0109	.0163	.0218	.0320	−.0003	−.0033	.0319	.0277
Food and kindred products	−.0028		−.0005	.0044	.0272	−.0081	−.0016	.0025	−.0039
Tobacco manufacturers	−.0157	−.0082	−.0015	−.0028	.0098	−.0166	.0078	−.0083	−.0054
Textile mill products	−.0147	−.0148	−.0121	−.0061	−.0210	−.0392	−.0087	.0158	.0079
Apparel and other fabr. textile prod.	.0099	.0081	.0085	.0081	.0148	−.0120	.0101	.0227	.0005
Paper and allied products	.0193	.0185	.0256	.0206	.0301	.0174	.0230	.0264	.0084
Printing and publishing	.0157	.0135	.0196	.0174	.0220	.0137	.0360	.0137	.0107
Chemicals and allied products	.0212	.0206	.0312	.0206	.0206	.0240	.0214	.0284	.0117
Petroleum and coal products	−.0107	−.0133	−.0024	.0001	.0160	.0045	−.0306	−.0159	.0107
Rubber and misc. plastic products	.0300	.0301	.0343	.0396	.0557	.0130	.0114	.0555	.0395

Table 1.14 (continued)

Industry	1948–1966 (average annual rates of growth)			Translog Index of Labor Input (average annual rates of growth)					
	BLS	Kendrick	Translog	1947–1973	1947–1953	1953–1957	1957–1960	1960–1966	1966–1973
Leather and leather products	−.0053	−.0048	−.0043	−.0110	−.0052	−.0109	−.0098	.0046	−.0300
Lumber and wood prod. excluding furniture	−.0151	−.0160	−.0147	.0042	.0373	−.0474	−.0077	.0068	.0081
Furniture and fixtures	.0164	.0132	.0165	−.0015	−.0589	−.0031	.0005	.0358	.0157
Stone, clay and glass products	.0101	.0073	.0143	.0169	.0287	.0055	.0192	.0176	.0119
Primary metal industries	.0045	.0033	.0096	.0053	.0178	−.0088	−.0295	.0283	−.0022
Fabricated metal industries	.0195	.0168	.0217	.0177	.0309	.0017	−.0081	.0341	.0126
Machinery excluding electrical	.0200	.0196	.0240	.0155	.0116	−.0045	−.0184	.0547	.0112
Electrical machinery, eqpt., and supplies	.0370	.0366	.0436	.0350	.0717	.0062	.0391	.0474	.0077
Trans. eqpt. and ord. ex. motor vehicles	.0539		.0616	.0349	.1635	.0022	−.0517	.0454	−.0284
Motor vehicles and equipment	.0091		.0165	.0161	.0472	−.0420	−.0148	.0393	.0159
Prof. photographic eqpt. and watches	.0289	.0308	.0384	.0400	.0984	.0144	.0100	.0380	.0190
Misc. manufacturing industries	.0007	.0005	.0057	.0129	.0420	−.0212	.0029	.0232	.0030
Railroads and rail express service		−.0504	−.0385	−.0345	−.0385	−.0408	−.0714	−.0174	−.0263

Table 1.14 (continued)

Industry	1948–1966 (average annual rates of growth)			Translog Index of Labor Input (average annual rates of growth)					
	BLS	Kendrick	Translog	1947–1973	1947–1953	1953–1957	1957–1960	1960–1966	1966–1973
Street rail, bus lines, and taxicabs			−.0200	−.0183	−.0241	−.0325	−.0186	−.0119	−.0106
Trucking services and warehousing			.0316	.0299	.0456	.0184	.0192	.0335	.0245
Water transportation		−.0052	−.0047	.0078	.0673	.0070	−.0355	.0096	−.0256
Air transportation		.0574	.0587	.0563	.0638	.0851	.0439	.0461	.0475
Pipelines ex. natural gas		−.0281	−.0185	−.0131	.0102	−.0074	−.0303	−.0334	−.0115
Transportation services			.0188	.0215	.0117	−.0149	.0139	.0468	.0321
Telephone, telegraph, misc. comm. services		.0105	.0187	.0251	.0314	.0288	−.0085	.0226	.0341
Radio broadcasting and television			.0451	.0472	.0801	.0410	.0305	.0341	.0410
Electric utilities			.0092	.0169	.0128	.0318	.0006	.0085	.0263
Gas utilities			.0252	.0259	.0491	.0009	.0462	.0153	.0206
Water supply and sanitary services			0.133	.0157	.0271	.0048	−.0019	.0203	.0157
Wholesale trade	.0175	.0161	.0202	.0207	.0161	.0136	.0278	.0245	.0223
Retail trade	.0142	.0095	.0086	.0094	.0056	.0012	.0145	.0077	.0167
Finance, insurance, and real estate		.0270	.0347	.0358	.0418	.0323	.0395	.0288	.0372
Services, excl. priv. households and institutions			.0295	.0294	.0190	.0279	.0364	.0346	.0319
Private households			−.0152	−.0168	−.0218	.0067	−.0003	−.0285	−.0230

Table 1.14 (continued)

Industry	1948–1966 (average annual rates of growth)			Translog Index of Labor Input (average annual rates of growth)					
	BLS	Kendrick	Translog	1947–1973	1947–1953	1953–1957	1957–1960	1960–1966	1966–1973
Institutions			.0476	.0416	.0436	.0385	.0852	.0419	.0227
Federal public administration			.0239	.0172	.0443	−.0060	.0055	.0280	.0029
Federal government enterprises			.0222	.0198	.0336	.0091	.0286	.0227	.0079
State and local educ. services			.0562	.0518	.0522	.0586	.0628	.0535	.0413
State and local public administration			.0392	.0403	.0472	.0430	.0270	.0394	.0204
State and local govt. enterprises			.0360	.0404	.0783	.0022	.0647	.0204	.0364

sectors from the national product accounts. Similarly, we have controlled our data on property compensation by industry to totals from the national income accounts.

We have disaggregated the capital input of each industrial sector into cells cross-classified by six types of assets and three legal forms of organization listed in table 1.15. The classification by asset class corresponds to the breakdown of investment flows from the U.S. national product accounts. The classification by legal form of organization corresponds to the breakdown of property compensation from the U.S. national income accounts. Data on property compensation are available for forty-six of the fifty-one industry groups included in the list of industries presented in table 1.1 above. Data on property compensation for the five sectors corresponding to federal and state and local governments are not available. We have constructed indexes of capital input for the forty-six sectors of private industry for which data on property compensation are available. For two of these sectors—private households and nonprofit institutions—the legal form of organization is limited to households and institutions. The remaining forty-four sectors are divided between corporate and noncorporate business.

Our first task is to construct estimates of capital stock for each type of asset and each legal form of organization for forty-six sectors of private industry for each year for the period 1947–73. Consumers' durable equipment is used only by private households, while producers' durable equipment is used in every sector except private households. Residential structures are allocated between owner-occupied dwellings, assigned to the private household sector, and tenant-occupied dwellings, assigned to finance, insurance, and real estate. Nonresidential structures are assigned to every sector except private households. Inventories are employed in every sector except private households and nonprofit institutions. Land is employed in all forty-six sectors. For depreciable assets

Table 1.15   Characteristics of Capital Input

Asset Class
(1) Producers' durable equipment
(2) Consumers' durable equipment
(3) Residential structures
(4) Nonresidential structures
(5) Inventories
(6) Land

Legal Form
(1) Corporate business
(2) Noncorporate business
(3) Households and institutions

—equipment and structures—we employ the perpetual inventory method to estimate capital stocks from data on investment. For inventories and land our estimates are based on balance-sheet data. We describe our data sources and the resulting estimates of capital stock in section 1.3.2.

Our second task is to construct estimates of rental prices by industrial sector for each type of asset and each legal form of organization for the period 1947–73. Our approach is based on the dual to the perpetual inventory method proposed and implemented by Christensen and Jorgenson (1969, 1973). The perpetual inventory method is based on the relationship between capital stock at a point of time and investment up to that point. The dual to the perpetual inventory method is based on the relationship between the price of an investment good at a point of time and rental prices of capital services from that point forward. Each rental price of capital services involves the nominal rate of return for the industrial sector, rates of depreciation and capital loss or gain for the type of asset, and variables incorporating the tax structure for the legal form of organization. We assume that the nominal rate of return after taxes is the same for all assets within a given sector and that the sum of rental payments for all assets is equal to total property compensation. On the basis of these assumptions we can allocate property compensation for each industry sector among types of assets and legal forms of organization. We describe our data sources and the resulting estimates of rental prices for capital services in section 1.3.3.

The desirability of disaggregating capital input by industrial sector, class of asset, and legal form of organization has been recognized by Christensen and Jorgenson (1969), Denison (1972), Griliches and Jorgenson (1966), Jorgenson and Griliches (1967, 1972), Kendrick (1973), and others. Kendrick has developed measures of capital input disaggregated by industry for much of the postwar period, but his measures do not incorporate a cross-classification by class of asset or legal form of organization. Denison has developed measures of capital input for the U.S. economy as a whole disaggregated by class of asset and by legal form of organization, but not by industry.

Data on capital input cross-classified by characteristics such as legal form of organization and industry are required for studies of capital demand and investment behavior; data cross-classified by asset class are required for studies of investment goods supply. Measures of capital input that fail to reflect differences in productivity among capital assets remain in common use. Kendrick's recent study of postwar productivity trends provides data on capital stock by industry; no attempt is made to construct measures of capital input that reflect differences in productivity among capital assets. We present indexes of capital input for the forty-six industry groups included in our study in section 1.3.4. Our data base can be used to generate indexes of capital input cross-classified by class of asset or legal form of organization for industrial sectors.

1.3.2   Capital Stock

We next describe the methodology and data sources employed in constructing estimates of capital stock by industry for each year for the period 1947–73. We construct estimates for each of the six asset classes and each of the three legal forms of organization listed in table 1.15. For equipment and structures we employ the perpetual inventory method,[29] assuming that replacement requirements follow a declining balance pattern for each asset, so that the relationship between investment and capital stock takes the form

$$A(T) = I(T) + (1-\delta)A(T-1),$$

where δ is the rate of replacement.

Jack Faucett Associates (1973a) has compiled annual time series data on investment by industrial sector for equipment and structures. These data are available for manufacturing industries through 1971 and for nonmanufacturing industries through 1970. The time series for equipment for each industry except nonprofit institutions begins in 1920 and covers investment in producers' durable equipment. We have employed estimates of investment in producers' durable equipment by nonprofit institutions from the Bureau of Economic Analysis *Capital Stock Study* (1976a).[30] Faucett's time series for structures for each industry except nonprofit institutions begins in 1890 and covers investment in nonresidential structures. The series for finance, insurance, and real estate also includes tenant-occupied residential structures. We have employed estimates of investment in nonresidential structures by nonprofit institutions and investment in owner-occupied residential structures by private households from the Bureau of Economic Analysis *Capital Stock Study*.

We have updated Faucett's investment series through 1972 for both manufacturing and nonmanufacturing industries. We have controlled the sum of investment for all sectors, including nonprofit institutions, for producers' durable equipment to total investment in producers' durables from the U.S. national product accounts for the period 1929–72 and to data from the *Capital Stock Study* for the period before 1929. Similarly, we have controlled the sum of investment in nonresidential structures for all sectors, including nonprofit institutions, to total investment in nonresidential structures from the U.S. national product accounts and the *Capital Stock Study*. Finally, we have controlled the sum

29. This account of the perpetual inventory method is based on that of Christensen and Jorgenson (1973), pp. 265–83; see also Jorgenson (1973).
30. See also Musgrave (1976).

of investment in residential structures for finance, insurance, and real estate and for private households to total investment in residential structures from the U.S. national product accounts and the *Capital Stock Study*.

The investment data compiled by Jack Faucett Associates are distributed among industrial sectors on an establishment basis. We have reallocated the investment data for nonmanufacturing industries so that the ratio of historical cost capital consumption allowances for the period 1947–73 to capital consumption allowances from the Bureau of Economic Analysis study of gross product originating is the same for all sectors. Finally, we have deflated the investment data from Jack Faucett Associates and the *Capital Stock Study* to obtain investment in constant prices; the deflators are based on investment goods prices from the U.S. national product accounts for the period 1929–72 and from the *Capital Stock Study* for the period before 1929.

Given time series data on investment in equipment and structures by industry, we have compiled estimates of capital stock by industry and by type of asset annually for the period 1947–73, expressing capital stock for each year as a weighted sum of past investments. We assume that the rate of replacement is twice the reciprocal of the lifetime of the corresponding asset for each industry from Jack Faucett Associates or the *Capital Stock Study*. This assumption results in double declining balance replacement patterns for all assets. Since the time series for investment in equipment begin in 1920 and our estimates of capital stock begin in 1947, we have set the level of investment for periods before 1920 equal to zero. Similarly, the time series for structures begin in 1890 and we have set the level of investment equal to zero before 1890. The final step in construction of our estimates of capital stock is to allocate stocks for each sector, except for private households and nonprofit institutions, between corporate and noncorporate business. We allocate stocks for each year in proportion to capital consumption allowances for corporate and for noncorporate business from the Bureau of Economic Analysis study of gross product originating.

Our construction of estimates of stocks of land begins with estimates of the value of land for the economy as a whole generated by Christensen and Jorgenson (1969, 1973). Christensen and Jorgenson based their estimates on the earlier studies of Goldsmith (1962) and Manvel (1968).

To establish a benchmark for land we assume that land is 39 percent of the value of all private real estate in 1956. This is based on a study of the value of real estate and land by Manvel. Taking the value of residential and nonresidential structures in 1956 to be 61 percent of the value of all private real estate, we obtain a benchmark for the value of land in 1956. . . . We take the price index of land to be the same as Goldsmith's through 1958. We estimate the rate of growth of land prices between 1956 and 1966 to be 6.9 percent; we use this rate of growth to extrapolate Goldsmith's price index from 1958 to 1967 (in our case 1973).[31]

Using this price index, we estimated the market value of all private land annually for the period 1947–73. Following the procedure of Christensen and Jorgenson,[32] this current dollar aggregate was first allocated among sectors[33] using 1956 proportions from Manvel (1968). The land assigned to each sector was then allocated among legal forms of organization (corporate, noncorporate, and household) in proportion to data reported for 1956 by Goldsmith (1962). These data provided control totals for our estimates of land by industrial sector.

We employ balance sheet data from the IRS *Statistics of Income* (1974) to distribute the market value of land for the economy as a whole among industrial sectors. Fortunately, balance sheet data on book value of land by industrial sector are available for corporations for all years for the period 1947–73; however, the data are classified by industries defined on a company rather than establishment basis. The transformation of the balance sheet data to an establishment basis was accomplished by using the 1958 establishment-company ratios available in the Bureau of the Census *Enterprise Statistics* (1958). In addition, the *Statistics of Income* detail for nonmanufacturing industries is less than the industrial detail used throughout this study; the book value of land was distributed among subindustries using current dollar shares in total plant. Finally, the book values for each industry were adjusted proportionately so that their sum equaled the controlling market value total for corporate land. We assume that the ratio of market value to book value is constant across industries but not over time. Goldsmith's economy-wide index, extrapolated to the present by Christensen and Jorgenson, is employed as a land deflator for all industries. Dividing each industry's current dollar value of corporate land by this deflator, we obtain the quantity of land held by the corporate sector of each industry.

Noncorporate land data for partnerships and proprietorships are separately available from the *Statistics of Income* for only a limited number of years: four for partnerships and two for proprietorships. We began by generating a consistent set of industry data for each of the benchmark years (1953, 1959, 1963, and 1965) according to a method first suggested by Hulten (1973*b*):

---

31. Christensen and Jorgenson (1969), p. 296.
32. Ibid., p. 301.
33. The land aggregate for each year was distributed among farm, residential, and nonfarm nonresidential uses.

(1) The *Statistics of Income* estimates are inflated from "partnership with balance sheets" to the level of "all partnerships" using the ratio of total receipts for the latter to total receipts for the former. (2) The resulting estimates are then adjusted to include sole proprietorships (to bring the estimates up to the noncorporate level). This is accomplished by calculating the ratio of total receipts of proprietorships and partnerships to total receipts of partnerships and using the result to inflate the partnership land estimates. (3) Data for missing industries are then estimated by allocating the total unaccounted-for land in the same proportion as the corresponding corporate book values. The result is a consistent set of benchmarks for the book values of noncorporate land.[34]

We then interpolated between and extrapolated beyond each industry's benchmark values using the book-value growth rates for the corporate land held by that sector. Dividing each current dollar industry series by our land deflator resulted in the desired series of quantities of land held by the noncorporate sector of each industry.

Sales and purchases of commodities held as inventories are frequently occurring events. This makes the estimation of current market values for inventory conceptually straightforward. The Bureau of Economic Analysis has constructed annual data on current and constant dollar inventory stocks by industry. Loftus and Hinrichs of the National Income and Wealth division kindly made available postwar time series of corporate and noncorporate inventory stocks and corresponding reflators[35] for twenty-one two-digit manufacturing sectors and nine nonmanufacturing aggregates. These estimates are consistent with establishment-basis industry definitions used throughout this research and, like all our other data series, are controlled to U.S. national income and product account totals. For the six nonmanufacturing sectors that require disaggregation,[36] we employ the stock distributions available from constant-dollar inventory stocks from *Measures of Working Capital* prepared by Jack Faucett Associates (1973b) and constant-dollar value added available for each industry from the Bureau of Economic Analysis (1974a).[37] We employ the inventory reflators for both corpo-

34. See Hulten (1973b), p. 67.
35. The reflators are the same for corporate and noncorporate stocks. For a discussion of the methodology underlying the construction of stocks of business inventories, see Loftus (1972).
36. These industries are agriculture, mining, transportation, communications and public utilities, finance and real estate, and services. The remaining three, construction and wholesale and retail trade, already had a one-to-one correspondence with our fifty-one-order list.
37. We assume that sectors within each industry aggregate, sharing similar technologies and product demand characteristics, have a common relation between inventories and value added.

rate and noncorporate stocks for all sectors included in each nonmanufacturing sector of the Bureau of Economic Analysis study.

1.3.3   Property Compensation

The dual to the perpetual inventory method originated by Christensen and Jorgenson (1969, 1973) provides the theoretical framework for our measures of the rental prices of capital services. For an asset with a declining pattern of replacement requirements, the rental price of capital services takes the form

$$p_K(T) = p_I(T-1)r(T) + \delta p_I(T) - [p_I(T)$$
$$- p_I(T-1)].$$

The rental price is the sum of the nominal return to capital $p_I(T-1)$ $r(T)$ and depreciation $\delta p_I(T)$, less revaluation $p_I(T) - p_I(T-1)$. We can also express the rental price of capital services in terms of the price of investment goods, the own rate of return on capital in period T,

$$r(T) - \frac{p_I(T) - p_I(T-1)}{p_I(T-1)},$$

and depreciation:

$$p_K(T) = p_I(T-1) \left[r(T) - \frac{p_I(T) - p_I(T-1)}{p_I(T-1)} \right]$$
$$+ \delta p_I(T).$$

In the absence of taxation the value of capital services is the product of the rental price and the level of capital stock at the end of the preceding period:

$$p_K(T) \cdot A(T-1) = \{p_I(T-1)r(T)$$
$$+ \delta p_I(T) - [p_I(T) - p_I(T-1)]\}$$
$$\times A(T-1).$$

Given the level of capital stock, the price of investment goods, and the rate of replacement, the rate of return on capital is the only variable that remains to be determined in the rental price of capital services.

For a sector not subject to direct or indirect taxes on property income, the value of property compensation is equal to the value of capital services. We can solve for the rate of return, given data on property compensation for the sector:

$$r(T) =$$

$$\frac{\text{property compensation} - \{\delta p_I(T) - [p_I(T) - p_I(T-1)]\}A(T-1)}{p_I(T-1)A(T-1)}.$$

The rate of return is the ratio of property compensation less depreciation and plus capital gains to the value of assets at the beginning of the period. For a sector with more than one type of asset the value of property compensation is equal to the sum of the values of capital services over all assets. We assume that the rate of return is the same for all assets, so that we can solve for the rate of return as the ratio of property compensation for the sector less depreciation and plus capital gains for all assets to the value of all assets at the beginning of the period.

We have constructed estimates of capital stock by industry, cross-classified by the three legal forms of organization and six types of assets listed in table 1.15. Private households and nonprofit institutions are treated as separate sectors; capital stocks for the remaining forty-four industrial sectors are divided between noncorporate and corporate business. In measuring rates of return employed in our estimates of rental prices of capital services we must take into account differences in the tax treatment of property compensation among legal forms of organization. Households and institutions are not subject to direct taxes, but they are subject to property taxes. Noncorporate business is subject to direct taxation through the personal income tax. Corporate business is subject to both personal and corporate income taxes. Both noncorporate and corporate businesses are also subject to property taxes.

We can modify our expression for the rental price of capital services to incorporate property taxes by adding the rate of taxation, say $\tau(T)$, multiplied by the price of investment goods, to the rental price:

$$p_K(T) = p_I(T-1)r(T) + \delta p_I(T) - [p_I(T)$$
$$- p_I(T-1)] + p_I(T)\tau(T).$$

To estimate the rate of return we set property compensation equal to the value of capital services, as before. The rate of return is the ratio of property compensation less depreciation, plus capital gains, and less property taxes, to the value of assets at the beginning of the period. Depreciation, capital gains, property taxes, and the value of assets are sums over all assets for a sector with more than one type of asset.

In measuring the value of capital services for private households and nonprofit institutions we first derive the value of services of owner-occupied residential real estate, including both land and residential structures, from data on the value of the use of dwellings in the U.S. national income and product accounts. To obtain the rate of return on capital we take the ratio of the value of the services of owner-occupied residential real estate less depreciation, plus capital gains, and less property taxes to the value of land and residential structures at the beginning of the period. We assume that the rate of return for consumers' durable equipment in private households and for all assets in nonprofit institutions—producers' durable equipment, nonresidential structures, and land—is the same as for owner-occupied residential real estate. Given the prices of each of these investment goods, rates of replacement for equipment and structures, and tax rates, we can determine the rental price of each type of asset utilized by private households and nonprofit institutions. Rates of replacement and the prices of investment goods are taken from those employed in construction of our estimates of capital stock, as described above. Effective rates of tax are equal to property taxes on each type of asset given in the U.S. national income and product accounts.

For each of the industrial sectors listed in table 1.1, excluding the five government sectors, private households, and nonprofit institutions, property compensation is defined on the basis of data included in the Bureau of Economic Analysis study of gross product originating. Property compensation for corporate business is defined as follows:

Corporate property compensation
  = corporate capital consumption allowances
    + corporate business transfer payments
    + corporate business property and other taxes
    + corporate profits before tax
    + corporate inventory valuation adjustment
    + corporate net interest paid.

Property compensation for noncorporate business is defined as follows:

Noncorporate property compensation
  = noncorporate capital consumption allowances
    + noncorporate business transfer payments
    + noncorporate business property and other taxes
    + income of unincorporated enterprises
    − labor compensation of self-employed and unpaid family workers
    + rental income of persons
    + noncorporate inventory valuation adjustment
    + noncorporate net interest paid.

To estimate rental prices for the corporate sector of each industry we must take the taxation of corporate income into account. For producers' durable equipment the rental price of capital services, modified to take the corporate income tax and indirect business taxes into account, takes the form

$$p_K(T) = \left[\frac{1 - u(T)z(T) - k(T) + y(T)}{1 - u(T)} \right]$$
$$\times \{ p_I(T-1)r(T) + \delta p_I(T)$$
$$- [p_I(T) - p_I(T-1)] \} + p_I(T)\tau(T),$$

where $u(T)$ is the corporate income tax rate, $z(T)$ is the present value of capital consumption allowances on one dollar's worth of investment, $k(T)$ is the rate of the investment tax credit, and $y(T)$ is a variable used in accounting for the fact that the investment credit was deducted from the value of an asset in calculating depreciation for tax purposes in 1962 and 1963:

$$y(T) = k(T)u(T)z(T), \qquad (T = 1962, 1963),$$
$$= 0, \qquad (T \neq 1962, 1963).$$

For residential and nonresidential structures the rental price of capital services is the same as for producers' durable equipment, except that the rate of the investment tax credit $k(T)$ is equal to zero. For inventories and land the rate of replacement δ, the present value of capital consumption allowances $z(T)$, and the rate of investment tax credit $k(T)$ are all equal to zero.

We estimate the effective rate of indirect taxation $\tau(T)$ for the corporate sector of each industry as the ratio of corporate business property and other taxes to the value of all corporate assets at the beginning of the period. We measure the effective rate of the corporate income tax $u(T)$ for each industry as the ratio of corporate tax liabilities plus the investment tax credit to corporate property compensation less corporate business property and other taxes and less the imputed value of capital consumption allowances for tax purposes. Imputed capital consumption differs from capital consumption allowances actually claimed for tax purposes in reflecting the present value of future capital consumption allowances; the present value depends on the depreciation formulas and lifetimes of assets allowed for tax purposes and the rate of return. We assume that the rate of return used in discounting future capital consumption allowances in the corporate sector is constant at 10%

In January 1973, the Treasury Department initiated a survey to determine the use and effectiveness of its then recently introduced Accelerated Depreciation Range system.

The Asset Depreciation Range (ADR) initiated on March 12, 1971, provides a range of asset lives for various classes of assets placed in service after December 31, 1971. A taxpayer may elect to base the tax depreciation of an asset on any number of years within the designated range of years allowable for the particular guideline class of the asset . . . . The designated range for each class allows a minimum asset life 20% below and a maximum life 20% above the "Guideline" lives previously in effect.[38]

38. See Vasquez (1974), p. 2.

As useful by-products of this Treasury study, the Office of Tax Analysis compiled a detailed table of the 1970 (pre–ADR) and 1971 (ADR) equipment tax lives reported by both ADR electors and nonelectors within each of thirty-six industries. A similar table reporting separate percentage distributions over the various depreciation methods used by electors and nonelectors in 1971 was also produced. The four major depreciation formulas covered in the survey were straight-line, 1.5 declining balance, 2.0 declining balance, and sum-of-years digits. In addition, the Treasury report by Vasquez (1974) compares the depreciation methods and asset lives used by corporate taxpayers during 1954, 1954–59, 1970 (pre–ADR), and 1971 (ADR).[39] Given these Treasury data, we have constructed an annual time series of depreciation methods and tax lives for each of our forty-six industrial sectors.

Before 1954, taxpayers were limited to the straight-line method. We therefore imposed this depreciation pattern on each of our sectors. In 1954 depreciation allowances were liberalized to allow accelerated depreciation. Declining balance methods at twice the straight-line rate as well as the sum-of-years digits method were introduced. The Treasury report presents the average percentage use of these principal methods for the period immediately following the 1954 tax law change (1954–59) for eight industry aggregates. We moved these average distributions over the six-year period using annual manufacturing and nonmanufacturing data compiled and published by Young (1968).[40] Given the absence of industry detail in the Vasquez report, we assumed that the distribution of depreciation methods was identical for each industry within each of Vasquez's eight aggregates. A similar procedure was employed to interpolate the distributions of depreciation methods between the 1959 breakdowns and those presented by the Office of Tax Analysis (1973) for 1971. The 1971 data were then extrapolated to yield 1972 and 1973 distributions. The estimation of tax lives for equipment followed similar lines. Young (1968) prepared a set of economy-wide equipment tax life changes over the years prior to 1954.[41] We were able to use these to move the 1954 lives for ten industries reported by Vasquez[42] back to 1947. Once again, tax lives for all industries within each aggregate were assumed to move in the same proportion. Vasquez's 1954–59 averages were again moved in proportion to Young's estimates to levels given by the Treasury for thirty-six industries for 1970. Data for 1971 were also available from the Treasury and were extrapolated to produce 1972 and 1973 estimates.

39. See Vasquez (1974), pp. 34–37.
40. See Young (1968), p. 19.
41. See Young (1968), p. 20. We used his recommended "approximation I."
42. See Vasquez (1974), p. 37.

Since the ADR system applies only to investment in producers' durables, the Treasury study did not include an analysis of depreciation practices for structures. As a result, the only source of information on tax lives and methods of depreciation now available is based on the work of Young (1968). Young presents the distribution of depreciation methods for total manufacturing and nonmanufacturing for each year from 1954 to 1959 and an average for the period 1960–66.[43] We applied these estimates to each industry. The 1960–66 average was extrapolated through 1973. For tax service lives in 1945, 1950, 1952, 1955, 1957, 1960, 1961, and the 1962–66 period, Young presents economy-wide estimates of each year's percentage relationship to the average service life for structures purchased in 1940. Combining this time series with the Christensen-Jorgenson (1969) estimate of the lifetime for structures in 1953 (35.3 years),[44] we were able to convert Young's index to lifetimes. We then interpolated and extrapolated this series to generate estimates for the full 1947–73 period, applying the series to data on corporate structures in each industry.

Given data on depreciation methods and tax lives for structures and equipment, we estimated the present value of capital consumption allowances $z(T)$ for each asset as a weighted average of the present values for each depreciation method. The weights are the corporate investment shares in total corporate investment for the industry by firms using straight-line, 1.5 declining balance, 2.0 declining balance, and sum-of-years digits methods. The formulas for calculating that year's discounted present value of depreciation expenses according to the relevant depreciation methods are given by Hall and Jorgenson (1967, 1971); we adjusted these formulas to take into account the "half-year convention," permitting six months' depreciation to be taken for tax purposes during the year of acquisition.

Since Young (1968) distinguishes between straight-line and all accelerated methods for corporate structures, we used the double declining balance formula for all accelerated methods applied to corporate structures; second, since the Treasury report distinguishes between the depreciation practices of ADR electors and nonelectors in 1970 and 1971, each of the components of present value was divided between these two categories of taxpayers for 1970–73. Assuming that the after-tax rates of return are the same for all assets within each industry, corporate property compensation was set equal to the sum of rental payments for all types of capital services—equipment, structures, land, and inventories—in order to determine the rate of return after corporate income

43. See Young (1968), pp. 19–21. Prior to 1954 only the straight-line method was allowed.
44. See Christensen and Jorgenson (1969), p. 311.

taxes. Given the rate of return for each industry, the prices of capital goods, rates of replacement for equipment and structures for each industry, variables describing the corporate tax structure—$u(T)$, $z(T)$, $k(T)$—and the rate of property taxes, $\tau(T)$, for each industry, we can determine the rental price of each type of asset utilized by the corporate sector of each industry.

Our approach to the estimation of rental prices for each type of asset utilized by the noncorporate sector of each industry is similar to that for the corporate sector. We set all variables describing the corporate tax structure equal to zero. We estimate the effective rate of indirect taxation $\tau(T)$ for the noncorporate sector of each industry as the ratio of noncorporate business property and other taxes to the value of all noncorporate assets at the beginning of the period. We assume that the noncorporate rate of return is equal to the corporate rate of return after corporate taxes. Given the noncorporate rate of return for each industry, prices of investment goods, rates of replacement for each industry, and the noncorporate rate of property taxes for each industry, we can determine the rental price of each type of asset by industry. Noncorporate property compensation is equal to the sum of rental payments for all types of capital services—equipment, structures, land, and inventories. Labor compensation of self-employed and unpaid family workers is equal to the difference between all the components of noncorporate property compensation listed above, including income of unincorporated enterprises, and the sum of rental payments.

1.3.4   Indexes of Capital Input

We have outlined the development of data on capital stock and the rental price of capital services for each industrial sector, cross-classified by asset class and legal form of organization. To construct an index of capital input for each industrial sector we assume that sectoral capital input, say $\{K_i\}$, can be expressed as a translog function of its individual components, say $\{K_{ki}\}$. The corresponding index of sectoral capital input is a translog quantity index of individual capital inputs:

$$\ln K_i(T) - \ln K_i(T-1) = \sum \bar{v}^i_{Kk}[\ln K_{ki}(T)$$
$$- \ln K_{ki}(T-1)], \qquad (i = 1, 2, \ldots, n),$$

where weights are given by average shares of each component in the value of sectoral property compensation:

$$\bar{v}^i_{Kk} = \frac{1}{2}[v^i_{Kk}(T) + v^i_{Kk}(T-1)],$$

$$(i = 1, 2, \ldots, n; k = 1, 2, \ldots, p),$$

and

$$v^i_{Kk} = \frac{p^i_{Kk} K_{ki}}{\sum p^i_{Kk} K_{ki}},$$

$$(i = 1, 2, \ldots, n; k = 1, 2, \ldots, p).$$

The value shares are computed from data on capital services $\{K_{ki}\}$ and the rental price of capital services $\{p^i_{Kk}\}$ for each component of sectoral capital input, cross-classified by asset class and legal form of organization. Property compensation for the sector as a whole $\sum p^i_{Kk} K_{ki}$ is controlled to property compensation by industry from the U.S. national income accounts.

For each of the components of capital input into an industrial sector $\{K_{ki}(T)\}$ the flow of capital services is proportional to capital stock, say $\{A_{ki}(T-1)\}$:

$$K_{ki}(T) = Q^i_{Kk} A_{ki}(T-1),$$

$$(i = 1, 2, \ldots, n; k = 1, 2, \ldots, p),$$

where the constants of proportionality $\{Q^i_{Kk}\}$ transform capital stock into a flow of capital services. The translog quantity indexes of sectoral capital input $\{K_i\}$ can be expressed in terms of their components $\{K_{ki}\}$ or in terms of the components of sectoral capital stock $\{A_{ki}\}$:

$$\ln K_i(T) - \ln K_i(T-1) = \sum \bar{v}^i_{Kk}[\ln K_{ki}(T)$$
$$- \ln K_{ki}(T-1)]$$
$$= \sum \bar{v}^i_{Kk}[\ln A_{ki}(T-1) - \ln A_{ki}(T-2)],$$

$$(i = 1, 2, \ldots, n).$$

We form sectoral indexes of capital input from data on capital stock by industry, cross-classified by asset class and legal form of organization. Changes in the logarithms of capital stock for each component are weighted by average shares in sectoral property compensation.

We can define sectoral capital stock, say $\{A_i(T-1)\}$, as the unweighted sum of its components:

$$A_i(T-1) = \sum A_{ki}(T-1), \qquad (i = 1, 2, \ldots, n).$$

Similarly, we can define *sectoral indexes of the quality of capital stock*, say $Q^i_K(T)$, that transform sectoral measures of capital stock into the translog indexes of capital input:

$$K_i(T) = Q^i_K(T) \cdot A_i(T-1), \qquad (i = 1, 2, \ldots n).$$

The sectoral indexes of the quality of capital stock can be expressed in the form

$$\ln Q^i{}_K(T) - \ln Q^i{}_K(T-1)$$
$$= \sum \bar{v}^i{}_K[\ln A_{ki}(T-1) - \ln A_{ki}(T-2)]$$
$$- [\ln A_i(T-1) - \ln A_i(T-2],$$
$$(i = 1, 2, \ldots, n),$$

so that these indexes reflect changes in the composition of capital stock within each sector. Sectoral capital quality remains unchanged if all components of capital stock within a sector are growing at the same rate. Sectoral quality rises if components with higher flows of capital input per unit of capital stock are growing more rapidly and falls if components with lower flows are growing more rapidly.

We have generated translog indexes of capital input for the forty-six industries in the private domestic sector of the U.S. economy listed in table 1.1. Based on the capital stock and property compensation data described above, translog indexes of capital input for the private domestic economy and for a number of sectoral divisions are presented in column (4) of tables 1.16 through 1.26. Unweighted indexes of capital stock based on the same data are given in column (2). The ratio between these series, presented in column (3), measures the change in capital quality. To facilitate comparisons with unweighted and industry-weighted capital stock indexes, industry series employed by Kendrick are presented in columns (1) and (5). These capital indexes have been taken directly from his *Postwar Productivity Trends in the United States: 1948–1969* (1973). A comparison of rates of growth in Kendrick with translog indexes of capital input over the 1948–66 period is presented for all forty-six industries in table 1.27. In addition, rates of growth of the translog indexes of sectoral capital input are presented for five subperiods of the period 1947–73. Rates of growth of capital input for the period as a whole are also reported in table 1.27.

1.4 Output, Intermediate Input, and Productivity

1.4.1 Introduction

One of the principal features that distinguishes our approach to productivity from its predecessors is the definition of output at the sectoral level. At the economy-wide level the appropriate definition of output is based on deliveries to final demand—consumption, investment, government, and net exports. The corresponding definition of input is based on value added by primary factors of production—capital and labor input. The value of output is equal to the value of capital and labor input. At the sectoral level capital and labor input are combined with inputs of intermediate goods to produce output, so that the value of

Table 1.16 **Private Domestic Economy (1972=1.000)**

Year	Capital Stock		Capital Quality (3)	Capital Input	
	Kendrick (1)	Translog (2)		Translog (4)	Kendrick (5)
1947	.435	.446	.715	.319	.392
1948	.451	.470	.742	.349	.407
1949	.470	.485	.774	.375	.423
1950	.489	.513	.764	.392	.437
1951	.514	.536	.787	.422	.461
1952	.535	.552	.814	.450	.485
1953	.554	.569	.819	.466	.503
1954	.572	.584	.831	.485	.519
1955	.594	.609	.822	.501	.536
1956	.618	.631	.842	.531	.560
1957	.639	.647	.858	.556	.581
1958	.653	.657	.877	.576	.592
1959	.671	.675	.869	.587	.606
1960	.691	.692	.877	.607	.624
1961	.707	.706	.889	.627	.638
1962	.724	.725	.886	.642	.653
1963	.744	.747	.892	.666	.671
1964	.766	.771	.897	.691	.694
1965	.796	.801	.898	.720	.722
1966	.835	.835	.913	.762	.762
1967		.862	.939	.809	
1968		.891	.950	.847	
1969		.921	.965	.888	
1970		.942	.991	.933	
1971		.967	.996	.963	
1972		1.000	1.000	1.000	
1973		1.037	1.015	1.053	

Table 1.17   **Agriculture (1972=1.000)**

Year	Capital Stock		Capital Quality (3)	Capital Input	
	Kendrick (1)	Translog (2)		Translog (4)	Kendrick (5)
1947		.628	.775	.487	.706
1948		.675	.759	.512	.719
1949		.685	.810	.555	.736
1950		.712	.795	.566	.751
1951		.740	.820	.607	.769
1952		.767	.828	.635	.782
1953		.773	.862	.666	.789
1954		.785	.866	.680	.794
1955		.800	.864	.691	.798
1956		.781	.907	.708	.796
1957		.794	.874	.694	.794
1958		.812	.853	.693	.794
1959		.811	.874	.709	.796
1960		.818	.877	.718	.798
1961		.817	.880	.718	.798
1962		.834	.867	.723	.802
1963		.860	.856	.736	.807
1964		.862	.884	.762	.809
1965		.879	.886	.779	.810
1966		.928	.876	.813	.813
1967		.932	.915	.853	
1968		.964	.920	.887	
1969		1.024	.893	.915	
1970		1.035	.915	.947	
1971		1.054	.922	.971	
1972		1.000	1.000	1.000	
1973		1.038	.944	.980	

Table 1.18   **Mining (1972=1.000)**

Year	Capital Stock		Capital Quality (3)	Capital Input	
	Kendrick (1)	Translog (2)		Translog (4)	Kendrick (5)
1947		.626	.850	.532	
1948		.643	.906	.583	1.080
1949		.640	.949	.607	
1950		.644	.946	.609	
1951		.650	.949	.617	
1952		.668	.937	.627	
1953		.676	.965	.652	1.060
1954		.684	.968	.662	
1955		.725	.922	.669	
1956		.743	.969	.720	
1957		.765	.959	.734	1.081
1958		.776	.969	.752	
1959		.798	.966	.771	
1960		.820	.973	.798	1.113
1961		.854	.963	.822	
1962		.866	.984	.852	
1963		.869	.999	.869	
1964		.901	.973	.877	
1965		.918	.994	.913	
1966		.933	1.000	.933	.933
1967		.939	1.023	.961	
1968		.939	1.028	.965	
1969		.951	1.022	.972	
1970		.956	1.028	.982	
1971		.964	1.026	.989	
1972		1.000	1.000	1.000	
1973		1.014	1.024	1.038	

Table 1.19   **Contract Construction (1972=1.000)**

Year	Capital Stock Kendrick (1)	Capital Stock Translog (2)	Capital Quality (3)	Capital Input Translog (4)	Capital Input Kendrick (5)
1947		.158	.925	.146	
1948		.173	1.032	.178	.223
1949		.184	1.064	.196	.259
1950		.222	.940	.209	.270
1951		.254	.982	.250	.315
1952		.286	.989	.283	.346
1953		.282	1.127	.318	.352
1954		.314	1.003	.315	.353
1955		.341	1.018	.347	.359
1956		.371	1.028	.381	.390
1957		.405	1.014	.411	.434
1958		.429	1.051	.451	.462
1959		.472	1.002	.473	.480
1960		.494	1.055	.521	.507
1961		.541	1.002	.542	.535
1962		.574	1.003	.576	.568
1963		.614	1.001	.614	.612
1964		.661	1.003	.663	.661
1965		.718	.991	.712	.714
1966		.758	1.019	.772	.772
1967		.820	1.004	.823	
1968		.826	1.062	.877	
1969		.852	1.052	.896	
1970		.890	1.048	.932	
1971		.915	1.062	.971	
1972		1.000	1.000	1.000	
1973		1.037	1.039	1.077	

Table 1.20   **Manufacturing (1972=1.000)**

Year	Capital Stock		Capital Quality (3)	Capital Input	
	Kendrick (1)	Translog (2)		Translog (4)	Kendrick (5)
1947	.429	.475	.811	.385	
1948	.452	.493	.856	.422	.404
1949	.469	.491	.902	.442	.415
1950	.480	.506	.867	.438	.417
1951	.515	.552	.818	.451	.443
1952	.554	.570	.877	.500	.484
1953	.579	.588	.885	.521	.502
1954	.591	.590	.914	.539	.505
1955	.602	.610	.893	.545	.508
1956	.631	.644	.889	.573	.538
1957	.658	.658	.926	.609	.558
1958	.665	.654	.960	.628	.566
1959	.671	.657	.955	.627	.575
1960	.685	.669	.950	.635	.587
1961	.694	.678	.953	.646	.593
1962	.707	.694	.947	.657	.603
1963	.722	.706	.958	.676	.628
1964	.742	.731	.947	.693	.654
1965	.776	.770	.941	.724	.698
1966	.833	.833	.926	.771	.771
1967		.890	.942	.838	
1968		.926	.961	.889	
1969		.957	.969	.928	
1970		.981	.988	.969	
1971		.985	1.008	.993	
1972		1.000	1.000	1.000	
1973		1.028	.996	1.024	

Table 1.21　　　Transportation (1972=1.000)

Year	Capital Stock		Capital Quality (3)	Capital Input	
	Kendrick (1)	Translog (2)		Translog (4)	Kendrick (5)
1947		.664	.723	.480	
1948		.650	.808	.525	.564
1949		.634	.829	.525	.580
1950		.628	.825	.519	.593
1951		.621	.847	.527	.609
1952		.625	.840	.524	.626
1953		.634	.842	.533	.640
1954		.621	.879	.546	.651
1955		.625	.870	.544	.660
1956		.622	.893	.556	.669
1957		.629	.883	.555	.679
1958		.625	.913	.570	.686
1959		.653	.873	.570	.690
1960		.665	.922	.613	.697
1961		.669	.941	.629	.701
1962		.691	.919	.635	.706
1963		.701	.955	.669	.712
1964		.722	.942	.680	.720
1965		.760	.928	.706	.735
1966		.806	.940	.758	.758
1967		.842	.969	.816	
1968		.888	.967	.858	
1969		.936	.969	.907	
1970		.969	.990	.959	
1971		.985	1.000	.985	
1972		1.000	1.000	1.000	
1973		1.019	.998	1.017	

Table 1.22   **Communications and Public Utilities (1972 = 1.000)**

Year	Capital Stock		Capital Quality (3)	Capital Input	
	Kendrick (1)	Translog (2)		Translog (4)	Kendrick (5)
1947		.334	.880	.294	
1948		.345	.895	.308	.244
1949		.353	.921	.325	.268
1950		.359	.945	.339	.289
1951		.363	.962	.349	.310
1952		.388	.914	.355	.332
1953		.399	.960	.383	.356
1954		.401	.996	.400	.379
1955		.408	.996	.407	.401
1956		.420	.994	.417	.422
1957		.442	.971	.429	.450
1958		.461	.989	.456	.484
1959		.475	1.008	.479	.504
1960		.495	1.001	.495	.530
1961		.511	1.021	.522	.550
1962		.529	1.020	.539	.567
1963		.557	1.008	.561	.586
1964		.586	1.017	.596	.609
1965		.619	1.019	.630	.634
1966		.653	1.024	.669	.669
1967		.691	1.026	.709	
1968		.732	1.025	.750	
1969		.789	1.009	.797	
1970		.843	1.020	.860	
1971		.915	1.007	.922	
1972		1.000	1.000	1.000	
1973		1.104	.990	1.092	

Table 1.23   **Trade (1972=1.000)**

Year	Capital Stock		Capital Quality (3)	Capital Input	
	Kendrick (1)	Translog (2)		Translog (4)	Kendrick (5)
1947		.320	.812	.260	
1948		.363	.855	.310	.348
1949		.381	.919	.350	.380
1950		.431	.858	.369	.402
1951		.449	.924	.415	.439
1952		.456	.945	.431	.447
1953		.464	.938	.436	.450
1954		.472	.934	.441	.453
1955		.509	.883	.450	.467
1956		.524	.930	.488	.497
1957		.529	.950	.502	.518
1958		.532	.958	.510	.525
1959		.556	.926	.515	.535
1960		.579	.938	.543	.552
1961		.583	.974	.568	.570
1962		.608	.954	.580	.586
1963		.638	.952	.607	.615
1964		.669	.959	.641	.646
1965		.709	.954	.676	.681
1966		.762	.947	.722	.722
1967		.789	.998	.787	
1968		.827	.995	.823	
1969		.863	1.007	.870	
1970		.895	1.022	.915	
1971		.943	1.006	.948	
1972		1.000	1.000	1.000	
1973		1.040	1.024	1.064	

Table 1.24   **Finance, Insurance, and Real Estate (1972=1.000)**

Year	Capital Stock		Capital Quality (3)	Capital Input	
	Kendrick (1)	Translog (2)		Translog (4)	Kendrick (5)
1947		.689	.566	.390	
1948		.707	.550	.389	
1949		.716	.582	.417	
1950		.733	.599	.439	
1951		.751	.629	.473	
1952		.751	.675	.507	
1953		.766	.660	.506	
1954		.783	.679	.531	
1955		.794	.709	.563	
1956		.818	.712	.583	
1957		.833	.748	.623	
1958		.837	.782	.655	
1959		.846	.782	.661	
1960		.855	.782	.668	
1961		.867	.800	.693	
1962		.879	.815	.717	
1963		.891	.836	.745	
1964		.903	.834	.752	
1965		.920	.807	.743	
1966		.925	.847	.783	
1967		.938	.860	.807	
1968		.949	.887	.842	
1969		.958	.915	.877	
1970		.966	.962	.929	
1971		.980	.980	.960	
1972		1.000	1.000	1.000	
1973		1.020	1.056	1.077	

Table 1.25   **Services, Excluding Private Households and Nonprofit Institutions and Including Government Enterprises (1972=1.000)**

Year	Capital Stock		Capital Quality (3)	Capital Input	
	Kendrick (1)	Translog (2)		Translog (4)	Kendrick (5)
1947		.499	.907	.452	
1948		.490	.929	.455	
1949		.481	.933	.448	
1950		.475	.928	.441	
1951		.466	.929	.433	
1952		.458	.925	.424	
1953		.453	.914	.414	
1954		.444	.925	.411	
1955		.455	.880	.401	
1956		.469	.891	.418	
1957		.483	.901	.435	
1958		.492	.918	.452	
1959		.523	.889	.466	
1960		.540	.917	.495	
1961		.568	.921	.523	
1962		.598	.922	.552	
1963		.639	.917	.586	
1964		.674	.939	.632	
1965		.715	.941	.673	
1966		.762	.953	.727	
1967		.783	.999	.782	
1968		.839	.960	.806	
1969		.899	.975	.877	
1970		.933	1.015	.948	
1971		.958	1.017	.975	
1972		1.000	1.000	1.000	
1973		1.055	.989	1.044	

Table 1.26   **Private Householders and Nonprofit Institutions (1972=1.000)**

Year	Capital Stock		Capital Quality (3)	Capital Input	
	Kendrick (1)	Translog (2)		Translog (4)	Kendrick (5)
1947		.341	.754	.257	
1948		.368	.774	.285	.372
1949		.394	.796	.314	.380
1950		.431	.796	.343	.392
1951		.457	.847	.387	.405
1952		.478	.866	.414	.417
1953		.501	.865	.434	.429
1954		.525	.874	.459	.443
1955		.558	.864	.482	.460
1956		.583	.891	.520	.477
1957		.604	.905	.546	.498
1958		.619	.917	.568	.521
1959		.644	.903	.582	.545
1960		.665	.913	.607	.571
1961		.680	.923	.628	.597
1962		.701	.916	.643	.625
1963		.727	.916	.666	.653
1964		.755	.921	.695	.685
1965		.787	.927	.729	.726
1966		.817	.943	.770	.770
1967		.843	.963	.812	
1968		.875	.967	.846	
1969		.904	.984	.889	
1970		.925	1.006	.930	
1971		.956	1.002	.959	
1972		1.000	1.000	1.000	
1973		1.043	1.013	1.057	

Table 1.27   Capital Input: Rates of Growth

Industry	1948–1966 (average annual rates of growth)		Translog Index of Capital Input (average annual rates of growth)					
	Kendrick	Translog	1947–1973	1947–1953	1953–1957	1957–1960	1960–1966	1966–1973
Agricultural production		.0238	.0248	.0511	.0088	.0097	.0180	.0238
Agricultural services		.0685	.0651	.1077	.0490	.0444	.0568	.0540
Metal mining	.0234	.0878	.0604	.0743	.0785	.2175	.0421	−.0135
Coal mining	−.0164	.0281	.0480	.1378	−.0653	.0482	.0453	.0380
Crude petroleum and natural gas	−.0237	.0122	.0102	−.0042	.0264	.0057	.0169	.0095
Nonmetallic mining and quarrying	.0472	.1051	.0979	.1864	.1030	.0989	.0745	.0387
Contract construction	.0691	.0814	.0768	.1294	.0643	.0792	.0655	.0475
Food and kindred products		.0203	.0237	.0408	.0138	.0155	.0208	.0209
Tobacco manufacturers	.0193	.0156	.0138	.0297	.0074	.0120	.0151	.0034
Textile mill products	.0007	.0233	.0320	.0701	.0064	−.0355	.0302	.0446
Apparel and other fabr. textile prod.	.0393	.0279	.0355	.0383	.0141	.0044	.0444	.0510
Paper and allied products	.0388	.0499	.0513	.0767	.0647	.0376	.0371	.0398
Printing and publishing	.0227	−.0022	.0078	−.0155	−.0125	.0014	.0168	.0346
Chemicals and allied products	.0514	.0419	.0453	.0637	.0384	.0235	.0441	.0439
Petroleum and coal products	.0302	.0133	.0179	.0135	.0421	−.0026	−.0018	.0334
Rubber and misc. plastic products	.0371	.0046	.0262	−.0792	.0548	.0319	.0585	.0702
Leather and leather products	.0028	.0127	.0155	.0494	.0077	−.0243	.0028	.0190
Lumber and wood prod. excluding furniture	.0192	.0250	.0319	.0693	.0320	−.0113	.0120	.0354
Furniture and fixtures	.0152	.0248	.0313	.0299	.0234	.0174	.0327	.0416
Stone, clay, and glass products	.0408	.0439	.0431	.0705	.0666	.0409	.0235	.0238
Primary metal industries	.0319	.0242	.0244	.0341	.0294	.0197	.0141	.0239
Fabricated metal industries	.0406	.0367	.0400	.0562	.0435	.0182	.0349	.0380
Machinery excluding electrical	.0278	.0454	.0505	.0691	.0462	.0281	.0431	.0529

Table 1.27 (continued)

Industry	1948–1966 (average annual rates of growth)		Translog Index of Capital Input (average annual rates of growth)					
	Kendrick	Translog	1947–1973	1947–1953	1953–1957	1957–1960	1960–1966	1966–1973
Elec. machinery, eqpt., and supplies	.0626	.0545	.0575	.0874	.0553	.0071	.0555	.0565
Trans. eqpt. and ord. ex. motor vehicles		−.0054	.0160	−.0349	.0278	−.0066	.0160	.0627
Motor vehicles and equipment		.0357	.0355	.0513	.0638	−.0222	.0363	.0300
Prof. photographic eqpt. and watches	.0506	.0714	.0705	.1144	.0820	.0336	.0433	.0654
Misc. manufacturing industries	.0740	.0215	.0334	.0140	.0382	.0076	.0349	.0569
Railroads and rail express service	.0330	−.0100	−.0087	−.0144	−.0085	−.0180	−.0038	−.0041
Street rail, bus lines, and taxicabs		−.0211	−.0032	−.0037	−.0405	−.0255	.0011	.0244
Trucking services and warehousing		.0696	.0805	.1343	.0530	.0816	.0662	.0620
Water transportation	.0002	−.0353	−.0241	−.0724	−.0493	−.0057	−.0112	.0127
Air transportation	.0230	.0992	.0994	.0435	.0926	.2034	.1121	.0956
Pipelines ex. natural gas	.0772	−.0109	−.0055	−.0036	−.0203	−.0412	.0047	−.0079
Transportation services		.0205	.0105	−.0663	.0204	.0686	.0642	−.0001
Telephone, telegraph, and misc. comm. services	.0598	.0550	.0678	.0520	.0331	.0521	.0872	.0913
Radio broadcasting and television		.1194	.1012	.0886	.2077	.1039	.1066	.0455
Electric utilities		.0334	.0411	.0310	.0355	.0314	.0294	.0671
Gas utilities		.0276	.0306	.0678	−.0218	.0626	.0112	.0316
Water supply and sanitary services		.0486	.0506	.0266	.0416	.0689	.0489	.0700
Wholesale trade	.0502	.0527	.0587	.0928	.0412	.0274	.0481	.0619
Retail trade	.0361	.0433	.0512	.0815	.0318	.0253	.0470	.0510
Finance, insurance, and real estate		.0389	.0391	.0432	.0520	.0236	.0264	.0456
Services, excl. priv. households and institutions		.0260	.0322	−.0149	.0128	.0428	.0639	.0518
Private households		.0557	.0552	.0891	.0585	.0348	.0391	.0466
Institutions		.0426	.0363	.0356	.0352	.0414	.0513	.0224

output includes the value of intermediate input as well as the value of capital and labor input.

We define the value of output and input for each sector from the point of view of the producer. For each sector of the economy we measure revenue as proceeds to the sector and outlay as expenditures of the sector. The value of output includes the value of primary factor inputs, capital and labor, and the value of intermediate input. The value of output is net of indirect business taxes on output, sales and excise taxes, as well as all trade and transportation margins associated with deliveries of output to consuming sectors; the value of input includes all taxes on intermediate, capital, and labor input and all trade and transport costs incurred in taking delivery of intermediate input. In the preceding sections we have described our approach to the measurement of price and quantities of capital and labor input. In this section we turn our attention to the measurement of prices and quantities of output and intermediate input.

Consistent time series data on output in current and constant prices for the manufacturing industries listed in table 1.1 above are available from the Interindustry Economics Division of the Bureau of Economic Analysis (1974b). These data incorporate the value of shipments and the cost of goods sold from the *Annual Survey of Manufactures*. The data are based on industry definitions from the U.S. national income and product accounts. Jack Faucett Associates (1975) has developed data on output in current and constant prices for nonmanufacturing industries for two classifications of these industries—the 160-order Economic Growth Sectoring Plan of the Bureau of Labor Statistics and the 80-order sectoring of interindustry transactions by the Bureau of Economic Analysis. These classifications are far more detailed than the breakdown of nonmanufacturing industries given in table 1.1 above. However, the data are based on industry definitions employed in interindustry accounts rather than those used in the national income and product accounts.

For the twenty-one manufacturing industries listed in table 1.1, we have used the BEA data on output in current and constant prices. For twenty nonmanufacturing sectors, we have employed data on output in current and constant prices developed by Faucett, adjusted so as to conform with industry definitions used in the national income and product accounts. For the remaining ten nonmanufacturing sectors, our estimates of output in current and constant prices are derived from data provided by the Bureau of Economic Analysis (BEA). By comparing nonmanufacturing industry definitions used by Faucett, BEA, and BLS, we were able to identify the standard industrial classification (SIC) appropriate for each nonmanufacturing industry. To make our estimates conform with national accounting concepts, a number of adjustments are required. Principal among these are a reallocation of each sector's output of secondary products and a reconciliation of interindustry and national accounts industry definitions.

Activity redefinitions and SIC reclassifications account for the major differences between the interindustry and the national income and product accounts industry definitions. While the national accounts adhere strictly to SIC conventions, input-output sectors are defined so as to achieve more homogeneous product groupings. An example of an SIC reclassification initiated for interindustry accounts is the reallocation of veterinary services from the agricultural sector to the services sector; an example of interindustry activity redefinitions is the reallocation from the railroad to the construction sector of all construction and installation work performed by railroad employees in the railroad sector. With the aid of unpublished 80-order data on sectoral input provided by the Bureau of Economic Analysis,[45] we were able to reallocate the output associated with each interindustry activity redefinition and industry reclassification in Faucett's data to the appropriate national accounts sectors. This reconciled our industry definitions with those that underlie the national accounts.

A second adjustment required to make our estimates conform to national accounting conventions involves the reallocation of each sector's production of secondary products. In the national accounts all primary and secondary products are allocated to the sector in which they are produced. There are no transfers in or out. By contrast, the interindustry data follow the convention of transferring into each sector the goods that are secondary to other industries but primary to the receiving sector. "The secondary output is treated as if sold by the producing industry to the industry to which it is primary, and is added to the output of the primary industry for distribution to users."[46] Fortunately, the data required to eliminate transfers of output are available from the current dollar transactions tables in each of the six postwar interindustry studies used in this research. Faucett's output data for nonmanufacturing, adjusted for transfers and redefinitions, together with manufacturing data from the BEA, form a consistent set of time series for sectoral output for the period 1947–73, conforming to national income and product accounts industry definitions.

The need to include intermediate goods and services in a study of sectoral productivity is easily demonstrated. The supermarket manager

45. See Walderhaug (1973) for a full discussion of the redefinition and reclassification adjustments necessary to bridge national accounts and input-output definitions.

46. U.S. Department of Commerce, Bureau of Economic Analysis, "The Input-Output Structure of the U.S. Economy: 1967," *Survey of Current Business* 54 (February 1974); 56.

may choose to have his own employee display the frozen ice cream products in the frozen foods cabinet or he may contract with the raw materials supplier to have its deliveryman display the product. The former is a direct labor cost to the supermarket; the latter is an expense related to intermediate inputs. Presumably the store manager makes this choice such that the ratio of marginal products equals the corresponding ratio of factor prices. Should the marginal product of intermediate inputs increase, the manager may be capable of producing the same level of output with reduced labor and intermediate input requirements. Productivity change will be measured accurately only if all inputs are treated symmetrically.

The Bureau of Economic Analysis (1974b) makes available a complete set of data on intermediate input in current and constant prices for each of the manufacturing sectors (table 1.1). These data are constructed from disaggregated industry data according to industry definitions used in the national income and product accounts. We derive an estimate of intermediate input in current prices for nonmanufacturing industries by subtracting estimates of value added in current prices from the corresponding estimates of output in current prices described above. In converting these current price estimates into constant prices we take account of the composition of the intermediate inputs in each industry. Interindustry transactions in current prices published by the BEA are used to allocate intermediate input among the industries supplying each sector. Sectoral output deflators inclusive of indirect business taxes to the supplying sectors are used to convert the purchasing industry's intermediate input to constant prices.

1.4.2   Output and Intermediate Input

A measure of output in current and constant prices is essential to productivity measurement. The value of output is also indispensable in generating a measure of intermediate input. Data on output in current and constant prices for manufacturing sectors are available from the Interindustry Economics Division of the Bureau of Economic Analysis (1974b). Jack Faucett Associates (1975) has assisted the Bureau of Labor Statistics in developing data on output in current and constant prices for nonmanufacturing sectors classified according to the BLS Economic Growth Sectoring Plan, a 160-order classification of industries, and the BEA 80-order interindustry classification of industries. We have employed data from the BEA study of manufacturing industries directly. We have adjusted data from the Faucett study of nonmanufacturing industries to conform with industry definitions used in the national income and product accounts.

In table 1.28 we present a detailed cross-classification of industry definitions employed in the national income and product accounts, the

Table 1.28   Industrial Classifications[a]

National Income (1)	Interindustry (2)	BLS (3)	SIC[b] (4)
1	*1,2	1–5	01[c]
2	*3,4	6,7	07,(−0713),08,09[d]
3	*5,6	8–10	10
4	*7	11	11,12
5	*8	12	13[e]
6	*9,10	13,14	14
7	11,12	15–20	15,16,17[f]
8	14	23–32	20,0713[g]
9	15	33	21
10	16,17,18.01–18.03	34–37	22
11	18.04,19	38–39	23[h]
12	24,25	45–46	26
13	26	47–49	27
14	27–30	50–57	28[i]
15	31	58	29
16	32	59–61	30
17	33,34	62	31
18	20,21	40–42	24
19	22,23	43–44	25
20	35,36	63–67	32
21	37,38	68–72	33[j]
22	39–42	73–79	34
23	43–52	80–90	35
24	53–58	91–99	36
25	13,60,61	21,22,101–105	19,37(−371)
26	59	100	371
27	62,63	106–110	38
28	64	111–113	39[k]
29	65.01	*114	40[l]
30	65.02	*115	41
31	65.03	*116	42[m]
32	65.04	*117	44
33	65.05	*118	45
34	65.06	*119	46
35	65.07	*120	47[n]
36	66	121	48(−483)
37	67	122	483
38	68.01	*123	491,pt. 493
39	68.02,68.03	*124	492,496,pt. 493[o]
40	68.03	*125	494,495,497[o]
41	69.01	*126	50
42	69.02	*127	52–59,pt. 8099[p]
43	*70,71	128–132	60,61,63–67[q]
44	*72,73,75–77	133–146	70,72,73[n],75,76,78,79,80[s], 81,82,84,89[t]
45	86	159	88

Table 1.28 (continued)

National Income (1)	Interindustry (2)	BLS (3)	SIC[b] (4)
46	77.05	146	86[t]
47	pt. 84	pt. 157	9190
48	78	147–149	9101–9189
49	pt. 84	pt. 157	9282,9382
50	pt. 84	pt. 157	9290,9390
51	79	150–151	9201–9289(–9282)
			9301–9389(–9382)

*Indicates whether Faucett's BLS or interindustry accounts data set was used for the nonmanufacturing national accounts sector identified in column (1). The absence of an asterisk in any line indicates either that we did not use the Faucett data for reasons described in the text or that Faucett reported no output estimates for that sector.

[a]Industry titles corresponding to each of the numerical references to national accounts sectors are listed separately in table 1.1. The digits used to identify the interindustry, BLS, and SIC industry boundaries are the conventional numerical codes respectively described in the *Survey of Current Business*, Faucett (1975), and Executive Office of the President (1967).

[b]The SIC codes correspond to national accounts definitions. Superscripted characters reference footnotes describing how interindustry accounts boundaries definitionally differ from the national accounts codes. Unless noted otherwise, all references to interindustry reclassifications apply also to the corresponding BLS sectors.

[c]Interindustry (I/O) sector 1.03 includes pt. 0729.
[d]I/O 4 includes 0713 and excludes 0722 and pt. 0729.
[e]I/O 8 excludes 138; BLS 12 includes 138.
[f]I/O 11.01 includes pt. 6561 and I/O 11.05 includes pt. 138. I/O 12.02 includes pt. 138; BLS 15–20 excludes 138.
[g]I/O 14 excludes 0713.
[h]I/O 18.04 includes 39996.
[i]I/O 27.01 excludes 28195.
[j]I/O 38.04 includes 28195.
[k]I/O 64.12 excludes 39996.
[l]I/O 65.01 includes 474.
[m]I/O 65.03 includes 473.
[n]I/O 65.07 excludes 473 and 474.
[o]I/O 68.03 includes 496 and pt. 493.
[p]I/O 69.02 includes 7396.
[q]I/O 71 excludes pt. 6561.
[r]I/O 73.01–.02 excludes 7396.
[s]I/O 77.03 includes 0722.
[t]I/O 77.05 includes 84, 86, 8921.

interindustry accounts, and the BLS Economic Growth Sectoring Plan.[47] Standard industrial classification (SIC) codes corresponding to each of

47. We include manufacturing industries in table 1.29 for completeness.

the three industrial classifications are given together with details on industrial classifications where exact correspondence with the SIC codes is lacking.[48] The first step in our procedure is to identify the BLS and interindustry classifications corresponding most closely to each nonmanufacturing industry from the national income and product accounts. Specifically, if a particular national accounts sector (for example, industry 4) maps exactly into one or more of Faucett's 80-order interindustry sectors (in this case, industry 7), we then chose the output series from that interindustry sector as a first approximation to the desired national accounts series. If, however, a national accounts sector (for example, industry 34) maps into only some disaggregated part of an interindustry sector's boundaries (in this example, industry 65.06) but into one or more BLS sectors (BLS industry 119), we then used Faucett's data for the BLS sectors as the initial estimate for the national accounts sector. In table 1.28, an asterisk identifies which of the two Faucett series was chosen as the initial estimate of output for each industry in the national accounts.

After initial estimates for each nonmanufacturing sector had been identified from the interindustry and BLS classifications, we adjusted data on the value of output in current prices to eliminate transfers among disaggregated BLS sectors within a single industry in the interindustry accounts. Eight of the sectors included in the interindustry accounts are the same as the corresponding sectors in the more detailed BLS accounts. For all but six sectors in the interindustry accounts the value of output is the sum of the values of outputs of the component sectors in the BLS accounts. However, for six sectors in the interindustry accounts,[49] the value of output is not equal to the sum of component sectors due to transfers within an industry. We adjusted data on the value of output for components of these six sectors to eliminate transfers, so that the value of output for each interindustry accounts sector is equal to the sum of the values of output of its components.

Finally, for a number of nonmanufacturing sectors (those lines in table 1.28 without an asterisk), we had to construct estimates of output from sources other than the Faucett report. First, the Faucett report publishes no results for the following nonmanufacturing sectors from the interindustry accounts:

---

48. Industry boundaries in the Economic Growth Sectoring Plan and the interindustry accounts are identical. Discrepancies listed in the notes to table 1.29 apply to the relationship between national income and product accounts definitions and the interindustry and equivalent BLS conventions.

49. The six interindustry sectors are numbered 6, 65, 68, 70, 73, and 77.

Interindustry Accounts Sector	Name
11	New construction
12	Maintenance and repair construction
66	Communications, except radio and TV
67	Radio and TV broadcasting
84	Government industry
86	Household industry

We obtained unpublished data on output in current and constant prices for contract construction from the Interindustry Economics Division of the BEA. These data are constructed according to conventions of the national income and product accounts, so that no further adjustments are required.

For the two communication sectors we constructed estimates of output in current and constant prices by moving the six current and constant price benchmarks from BEA studies of interindustry transactions[50] by the gross product originating series published annually in the July *Survey of Current Business* (1976*b*). By interpolating the ratios of gross product originating to output between benchmark years and using the intermediate-year figures we obtained output for the communication sectors.

Faucett found it unnecessary to construct estimates of output for government and household sectors, since value of production in these sectors is equivalent to value added. The Bureau of Economic Analysis prepares annual value-added estimates for the household and government sectors according to industry definitions from the national income and product accounts (1974*a*, 1977). Our annual value-added estimates for the household sector represent the sum of labor compensation, an estimate of the rental value of owner-occupied dwellings, and an estimate of the service flow of consumer durables. In the three government sectors (federal public administration, state and local educational services, and state and local public administration), the value-added totals equal labor compensation. Though the BEA is currently engaged in estimating capital stocks for each government sector, the data are not presently available. Since the value of output is wholly defined in terms of the value of inputs in the government and household

50. We employed BEA interindustry transaction data for 1947, 1958, 1961, 1963, 1966, and 1967. Data for 1958, 1963, and 1967 are published in the *Survey of Current Business* (1965, 1969, 1974*c*). Data for 1947, 1961, 1966 were obtained from unpublished studies by BEA (1968, 1970, 1972). The 1968, 1969, 1970, and 1971 transaction tables became available too late to be incorporated in this study.

sectors, no analysis of productivity change can be undertaken for national accounts sectors 45, 47, 49, and 50.

Second, although Faucett reports current and constant-dollar output series for nonprofit institutions and both federal and state and local enterprises, we chose not to adopt his estimates. For the two government enterprise sectors no estimates are available for capital services. An analysis of productivity change must await the completion of the Bureau of Economic Analysis study of capital stocks in all government sectors. Faucett's output estimates for nonprofit institutions are equivalent to value added. In place of the Faucett series, we applied a procedure like that used for the communications sectors to derive annual current and constant-dollar estimates of output in nonprofit institutions.

The output estimates for the manufacturing and contract construction sectors are used directly since they are constructed by conventions and industry definitions consistent with those used throughout the national income and product accounts. The value of output in these sectors includes all primary and secondary products originating in each producing sector. By contrast, our estimates of output for the communication sectors and nonprofit institutions and Faucett's output estimates for the remaining nonmanufacturing industries are derived according to the interindustry accounts convention of transferring into each sector the goods that are secondary to other industries but primary to the receiving sector. This results in the double counting of transferred output and would result in upward-biased estimates of intermediate inputs into each sector. Current dollar transactions tables available for each of the six interindustry accounts benchmark years make it possible to correct the Faucett series for transfers.

All output data presented by Faucett are set equal to output from the benchmark tables. In particular, Faucett's output in current prices equals the output reported in the transactions table minus imports that are allocated to that industry as substitute goods and import margins. To eliminate the secondary product transfers we employ the ratio of transfers to sector output reported in the 80-order or 367-order input-output tables.[51] Defining this ratio in terms consistent with Faucett's definition of output, a time series of output for each sector adjusted for transfers is formed by eliminating transfers from Faucett's unadjusted output series. We interpolated and extrapolated these ratios for the six benchmark years to obtain ratios for nonbenchmark years.[52]

51. Data for the more detailed tables are required for industries obtained from Faucett's BLS industry classification. The less detailed tables are required for industries from Faucett's interindustry classification.

52. The more detailed tables are available on a consistent basis only for 1963 and 1967.

In addition to secondary output transfers, activity redefinitions and SIC reclassifications account for important differences between the interindustry or BLS accounts and the national income and product accounts industry definitions, as indicated by Walderhaug:

> The GPO [NIPA gross product originating] estimates adhere strictly to the Standard Industrial Classification (SIC). In the I-O system, however, some industries are reclassified in order to achieve industry groups that are more homogeneous and that thus have a more stable input structure. [A sample of] these reclassifications consists of shifting veterinary services from the agricultural sector to the services sector, oil and gas field drilling services from mining to construction, and trading stamp companies from services to wholesale and retail trade. . . . [There are also] differences between the GPO and I-O value-added estimates that are due to the "redefinition" of certain activities [rather than whole SIC industries] from one industry to another. [Most] differences are due to the fact that in the I-O system all construction and installation work performed by employees in establishments not in the construction industry [i.e., force account construction] is redefined to be in the construction industry. [Other redefinitions include:] manufacturing and service activities that occur in the trade and transportation industries are shifted to the appropriate manufacturing and service industries; trade activities occurring in other industries are shifted to wholesale and retail trade; and manufacturer's sales offices are shifted from wholesale trade to manufacturing.[53]

Walderhaug kindly prepared and made available a full 80-order interindustry–national accounts reconciliation of 1963 industry value added that is similar to the more aggregated appendix table that appears in his contribution to the April 1973 issue of the *Survey of Current Business*. With this table we can calculate the fraction of net output (measured in current dollars) of each interindustry sector that had to be added to or subtracted from the Faucett interindustry or BLS sectors. If we had had data on redefined and reclassified output rather than value added, we would have required only the net addition to or subtraction from the output of each sector caused by redefinitions and reclassifications. However, given data on value added and the fact that the ratio of output to value added varies considerably across industries, we first identify the value added that was redefined or reclassified from each industrial sector and adjust it to reflect shifts in output. The adjustment for redefined and reclassified output is based on the ratio of value added redefined and reclassified for 1963 to total value added for that year. Since the Walderhaug table applies only to 1963, we were compelled to assume that the fractional addition or deduction reported by Walderhaug

53. Walderhaug (1973), pp. 42–43.

for each industry's value added remains constant for all years.[54] After adjusting the Faucett data series for transfers, redefinitions, and reclassifications, we obtained output series in current prices on the basis of industry definitions from the national income and product accounts.

The derivation of the output in constant prices from the BLS and interindustry series reported by Faucett was straightforward. In fact, we needed to make no adjustment to the Faucett series except for the redefinitions and reclassifications described above. Our elimination of secondary product transfers from data on output in current prices left each sector's output deflator unaffected. Transfers are treated as comparable to the primary output of the receiving rather than producing sectors. Consequently, in assigning deflators to secondary product flows, Faucett chose price indexes calculated from output in current and constant prices for goods actually produced in the receiving sector. These deflators required no alterations for our estimates of output in current prices for industrial sectors from the national income and product accounts. The same conclusion applies to the shifts of redefined and reclassified industry output away from a given sector. The products within each sector have a common deflator. Reclassifying some of the sector's output elsewhere leaves the supplying sector's deflator unaffected. Transfers of redefined or reclassified output into a given sector, however, would affect the output deflator for the receiving sector. We adjusted Faucett's price index for output to reflect the price movements in the industries in which the redefined or reclassified goods originate.

We have described the construction of output in accord with industry definitions from the national income and product accounts. One final adjustment to output in current prices is required; output must be valued in producers' prices—that is, exclusive of trade and transportation margins and all indirect business taxes. The current dollar series for manufacturing and construction taken directly from the national accounts and estimated for nonmanufacturing sectors from Faucett's data are net of trade and transportation margins but gross of sales and excise taxes. We thus subtracted from each industry's current dollar value of output the dollar value of sales and excise taxes reported in the national income and product accounts by the Bureau of Economic Analysis. This implies a symmetrical adjustment to each sector's output deflator since, while taxes do not affect the measure of constant dollar output, the elimination of indirect business taxes alters the series of producers' prices for output. The adjusted deflator is calculated by dividing the original deflator gross of sales and excise taxes by $(1+t)$, where t is the indirect tax rate.

---

54. This assumption was also made by Faucett (1975), so that our adjustments are consistent with those made by Faucett.

Data on intermediate input in current and constant prices are available for the manufacturing industries listed in table 1.1 above from the Bureau of Economic Analysis. These data are classified on the basis of the industry definitions employed in the national income and product accounts and can be employed directly in our study. For the nonmanufacturing industries we have constructed estimates of output in current and constant prices as described in the preceding section. Data on value added in these industries are available in current prices from the Bureau of Economic Analysis. We constructed estimates of intermediate input in current prices by subtracting value added from output, both in current prices. The problem that remains is to construct estimates of intermediate input in constant prices.

Our first step in constructing estimates of intermediate input in constant prices was to determine the ratio of intermediate input in current prices to output in current prices for each of the sectors from the interindustry accounts and BLS accounts employed in our construction of estimates of output in current prices. These ratios were obtained from tables of interindustry transactions constructed by the Bureau of Economic Analysis; for years that interindustry transaction tables were unavailable, we obtained these ratios by interpolation and extrapolation. Our second step was to obtain estimates of the current dollar value of intermediate input for each industry in the interindustry and BLS accounts by multiplying that industry's ratio of the value of intermediate input to the value of output by the value of its redefinition, reclassification, and transfer adjusted output. We adjusted these estimates so that the current dollar value of intermediate input for each industry in the national income and product accounts is equal to the sum of its interindustry or BLS accounts components. The interindustry and BLS accounts sectors corresponding to each industry from the national income and product accounts are indicated in table 1.28. We assumed that the ratio of the value of intermediate input to the value of output was the same for industries classified according to interindustry accounting definitions as for industries classified according to national income and product accounting conventions.

Third, after allocating intermediate input in current prices among the appropriate interindustry and BLS accounts sectors, we identified the source industries producing those goods as final products and used output deflators in purchasers' prices for each industry to convert deliveries of intermediate input into constant prices. The exact procedure adopted to accomplish this result can be described as follows. Using the input-output coefficients in current prices published in the six benchmark input-output studies, we allocated intermediate input by sector of origin for each industry. These coefficients are interpolated and extrapolated to obtain shares of intermediate input by sector of origin for each industry for all years. Finally, the output deflators for each sector of origin are weighted by the corresponding shares to obtain a deflator for intermediate input for each industry. Finally, having deflated the current dollar value of intermediate input into each interindustry and BLS accounts sector, we summed the resulting constant dollar quantities of intermediate input for all sectors included in an industry from the national income and products accounts to obtain intermediate input in that national accounts sector.

It is important to note that the output deflator used in measuring the current dollar value of a sector's output is not equivalent to the deflator used in evaluating the current dollar value of that sector's output as intermediate input into a purchasing sector's production process. The former is measured in producers' prices; the latter is measured in consumers' prices. The former is net of all sales and excise taxes and trade and transportation margins; the latter is gross of sales and excise taxes attributed to the output of the sector supplying the intermediate input. The trade and transportation margins paid by the consuming sector are captured in the intermediate input flows from the trade and transport sectors.

A final issue in measuring output and intermediate input involves the use of energy consumption to adjust potential capital services for the actual level of services utilized. This approach, originally introduced by Griliches and Jorgenson (1966), was subsequently withdrawn by Christensen and Jorgenson (1973). Kendrick has argued that capital stock should not be adjusted for utilization:

> In contrast to the human population, the entire living population of capital goods is available for productive use at all times, and involves a per annum cost, regardless of degree of use. The purpose of capital assets is for use in production of current output and income. The degree of capital utilization reflects the degree of efficiency of enterprises and the social economy generally. Hence, in converting capital stocks into inputs, we do not adjust capital for changes in rates of capacity utilization, and thus these are reflected in changes in the productivity ratios.[55]

Denison also argues against adjustment for utilization:

> In the short run, the intensity of capital utilization fluctuates with variations in the pressure of demand, but in this respect capital input is not different from land input or labor input. . . . The hours that capital is used may also change in the longer run but such changes,

55. Kendrick (1973), p. 26.

if they occur, are merely manifestations of changes in other output determinants that are separately measured so need not be given separate consideration.[56]

The use of energy per unit of capital input employed as a relative utilization adjustment by Griliches and Jorgenson (1966) and Jorgenson and Griliches (1967, 1972) involves the substitution of energy, a component of intermediate input, for capital. This substitution is fully accounted for in our measures of intermediate input, since these measures are based on a model of production and technical change that incorporates substitution among intermediate, capital, and labor inputs as well as the rate of technical change. No further adjustment of capital input or intermediate input is required.

1.4.3   Indexes of Productivity

We have described the development of data on prices and quantities of output and intermediate input for each industrial sector. We have generated prices and quantities of output for all fifty-one industrial sectors of the private domestic sector of the U.S. economy listed in table 1.1. For six of these sectors—private households and the five government sectors—output is equal to value added and intermediate input is zero. We have generated prices and quantities of intermediate input for the remaining forty-five industrial sectors. Rates of growth of output for all fifty-one sectors and rates of growth of intermediate input for forty-five sectors are presented in table 1.29.

To construct an index of productivity for each industrial sector we assume that sectoral output $\{Z_i\}$ can be expressed as a translog function of sectoral intermediate input $\{X_i\}$, capital input $\{K_i\}$, and labor input $\{L_i\}$. The corresponding index of productivity is the translog index of sectoral technical change $\{\bar{v}^i_T\}$:

$$\bar{v}^i_T = [\ln Z_i(T) - \ln Z_i(T-1)]$$
$$- \bar{v}^i_X [\ln X_i(T) - \ln X_i(T-1)]$$
$$- \bar{v}^i_K [\ln K_i(T) - \ln K_i(T-1)]$$
$$- \bar{v}^i_L [\ln L_i(T) - \ln L_i(T-1)],$$
$$(i = 1, 2, \ldots, n),$$

where weights are given by average shares of sectoral intermediate input, capital input, and labor input in the value of sectoral output:

56. Denison (1974), p. 56.

$$\bar{v}^i{}_T = 1/2 \; [v^i{}_T(T) + v^i{}_T(T-1)],$$

$$\bar{v}^i{}_X = 1/2 \; [v^i{}_X(T) + v^i{}_X(T-1)],$$

$$\bar{v}^i{}_K = 1/2 \; [v^i{}_K(T) + v^i{}_K(T-1)],$$

$$\bar{v}^i{}_L = 1/2 \; [v^i{}_L(T) + v^i{}_L(T-1)], \quad (i = 1, 2, \ldots, n),$$

and

$$v^i{}_X = \frac{p^i{}_X X_i}{q_i Z_i},$$

$$v^i{}_K = \frac{p^i{}_K K_i}{q_i Z_i},$$

$$v^i{}_L = \frac{p^i{}_L L_i}{q_i Z_i}, \qquad (i = 1, 2, \ldots, n).$$

The value shares are computed from data on output and its price $\{q_i\}$, intermediate input and its price $\{p^i{}_X\}$, capital input and its price $\{p^i{}_K\}$, and labor input and its price $\{p^i{}_L\}$. The value of output is equal to the sum of the values of intermediate, capital, and labor input.

We have generated translog indexes of productivity for each industrial sector listed in table 1.1. For the five government sectors output is equal to labor input, so that productivity change is zero. For private households output is equal to an index of capital and labor input; again, productivity change is zero. For the remaining forty-five sectors we present indexes of productivity in table 1.30. To facilitate comparisons with indexes of productivity for value added developed by Kendrick, we have generated translog indexes of productivity for value added $\{\bar{v}_{VT}\}$ for each industrial sector for the period 1948–66, the period covered by Kendrick's study. These indexes are generated from the translog indexes for output as follows:

$$\bar{v}^i{}_{VT} = \bar{v}^i{}_V \; \bar{v}^i{}_T, \qquad (i = 1, 2, \ldots, n),$$

where the weights $\{\bar{v}^i{}_V\}$ are given by the average shares of value added in the value of sectoral output. Value added is equal to the sum of the values of capital and labor input. For comparison, indexes employed by Kendrick are presented for each industry included in his study. These indexes have been taken directly from his *Postwar Productivity Trends in the United States: 1948–1969* (1973).

Table 1.29 Output and Intermediate Input: Rates of Growth

Industry	Output (average annual rates of growth)						Intermediate Input (average annual rates of growth)					
	1947–1973	1947–1953	1953–1957	1957–1960	1960–1966	1966–1973	1947–1973	1947–1953	1953–1957	1957–1960	1960–1966	1966–1973
Agricultural production	.0179	.0114	.0223	.0184	.0162	.0222	.0144	−.0011	.0238	.0066	.0210	.0201
Agricultural services	.0306	.0517	.0110	.0418	.0107	.0359	.0484	.0692	.0349	.0780	−.0168	.0815
Metal mining	.0178	.0317	.0194	−.0053	.0075	.0237	.0474	.1012	.0054	.0169	−.0181	.0946
Coal mining	−.0086	−.0592	.0122	−.0604	.0306	.0115	.0017	−.0548	−.0043	−.0635	.0199	.0658
Crude petroleum and natural gas	.0304	.0537	.0350	.0094	.0235	.0225	.0323	.0283	.0223	.0058	.0555	.0330
Nonmetallic mining and quarrying	.0479	.0553	.0720	.0395	.0466	.0325	.0447	.0403	.0993	.0473	.0490	.0126
Contract construction	.0379	.0674	.0411	.0403	.0348	.0125	.0429	.0832	.0484	.0244	.0363	.0187
Food and kindred products	.0292	.0192	.0294	.0514	.0232	.0331	.0282	.0160	.0277	.0663	.0241	.0262
Tobacco manufacturers	.0125	.0066	−.0017	.0639	.0030	.0118	.0040	.0096	−.0326	.0618	−.0091	.0065
Textile mill products	.0442	.0329	.0061	.0336	.0635	.0637	.0446	.0408	.0000	.0398	.0679	.0555
Apparel and other fabr. textile prod.	.0345	.0308	.0293	.0227	.0406	.0406	.0344	.0218	.0483	.0188	.0469	.0331
Paper and allied products	.0434	.0436	.0285	.0366	.0551	.0447	.0462	.0510	.0371	.0358	.0517	.0469
Printing and publishing	.0332	.0201	.0432	.0447	.0436	.0250	.0363	.0288	.0414	.0681	.0396	.0233

Table 1.29 (continued)

Industry	Output (average annual rates of growth)						Intermediate Input (average annual rates of growth)					
	1947–1973	1947–1953	1953–1957	1957–1960	1960–1966	1966–1973	1947–1973	1947–1953	1953–1957	1957–1960	1960–1966	1966–1973
Chemicals and allied products	.0681	.0722	.0610	.0632	.0769	.0632	.0584	.0627	.0492	.0612	.0723	.0467
Petroleum and coal products	.0408	.0566	.0311	.0310	.0336	.0431	.0379	.0602	.0334	.0307	.0238	.0366
Rubber and misc. plastic products	.0578	.0397	.0113	.0768	.0789	.0736	.0599	.0433	.0327	.0775	.0818	.0632
Leather and leather products	.0028	−.0052	.0038	−.0038	.0107	.0050	.0030	.0109	.0194	−.0096	.0000	−.0052
Lumber and wood prod. excluding furniture	.0240	.0136	.0046	.0372	.0357	.0283	.0277	.0352	.0133	.0548	.0259	.0194
Furniture and fixtures	.0390	.0370	.0245	.0256	.0535	.0425	.0411	.0411	.0293	.0422	.0570	.0337
Stone, clay, and glass products	.0407	.0553	.0340	.0441	.0455	.0265	.0480	.0746	.0427	.0640	.0440	.0247
Primary metal industries	.0227	.0503	−.0310	−.0188	.0615	.0143	.0287	.0533	−.0245	−.0055	.0591	.0265
Fabricated metal industries	.0357	.0457	.0085	.0196	.0548	.0332	.0349	.0463	.0052	.0242	.0547	.0297
Machinery excluding electrical	.0412	.0413	−.0062	.0101	.0916	.0384	.0415	.0446	−.0091	.0201	.0908	.0346
Elec. machinery, eqpt, and supplies	.0612	.0834	−.0048	.0645	.1065	.0397	.0505	.0769	−.0241	.0635	.0904	.0306

Table 1.29 (continued)

Industry	Output (average annual rates of growth)						Intermediate Input (average annual rates of growth)					
	1947–1973	1947–1953	1953–1957	1957–1960	1960–1966	1966–1973	1947–1973	1947–1953	1953–1957	1957–1960	1960–1966	1966–1973
Trans. eqpt. and ex. motor vehicles	.0550	.2191	−.0249	−.0411	.0625	−.0054	.0543	.2368	−.0368	−.0475	.0515	−.0042
Motor vehicles and equipment	.0483	.0753	−.0021	.0224	.0676	.0487	.0460	.0775	−.0091	.0096	.0688	.0464
Prof. photographic eqpt. and watches	.0559	.0685	.0138	.0831	.0590	.0549	.0479	.0628	.0164	.0845	.0600	.0272
Misc. manufacturing industries	.0386	.0323	.0052	.0676	.0509	.0402	.0375	.0247	.0020	.0904	.0533	.0326
Railroads and rail express service	−.0052	−.0174	−.0021	−.0197	−.0062	.0106	−.0259	−.0150	−.0305	−.0078	−.0882	.0130
Street rail., bus lines, and taxicabs	−.0459	−.0583	−.0360	−.0357	−.0784	−.0175	−.0647	−.0272	−.0333	−.0346	−.1758	−.0323
Trucking services and warehousing	.0457	.1241	.0393	.0308	−.0107	.0367	.0324	.1215	.0219	.0283	−.0647	.0471
Water transportation	.0083	−.0464	.0511	−.0582	.0080	.0596	−.0030	−.0318	.0209	−.0441	−.0179	.0386
Air transportation	.1068	.1459	.1204	.0958	.0868	.0874	.0687	.1115	.0827	.1249	.0187	.0430
Pipelines ex. natural gas	.0474	.0795	.0654	.0180	.0088	.0554	−.0152	.0518	.0599	.0330	−.1217	−.0449
Transportation services	−.0079	−.0072	.0319	−.0676	−.0739	.0510	−.0017	.0046	.0994	−.0735	−.1366	.0814
Telephone, telegraph, misc. comm. services	.0712	.0763	.0564	.0536	.0804	.0749	.0582	.0656	.0294	.0381	.0689	.0676

Table 1.29 (continued)

Industry	Output (average annual rates of growth)						Intermediate Input (average annual rates of growth)					
	1947–1973	1947–1953	1953–1957	1957–1960	1960–1966	1966–1973	1947–1973	1947–1953	1953–1957	1957–1960	1960–1966	1966–1973
Radio broadcasting and television	.0668	.1182	.0658	.0357	.0515	.0498	.0672	.1123	.0316	.0566	.0864	.0371
Electric utilities	.0665	.0803	.0673	.0620	.0644	.0580	.0541	.0247	.0323	.0273	.0866	.0753
Gas utilities	.0702	.1224	.0745	.0666	.0504	.0415	.0777	.1396	.0867	.0943	.0420	.0430
Water supply and sanitary services	.0392	.0649	.0062	.0545	.0468	.0231	.0448	−.0058	−.0089	.0972	.1055	.0444
Wholesale trade	.0465	.0327	.0442	.0561	.0610	.0430	.0445	.0258	.0316	.0890	.0693	.0278
Retail trade	.0306	.0267	.0294	.0134	.0371	.0364	.0164	−.0045	.0157	−.0074	.0155	.0456
Finance, insurance, and real estate	.0493	.0402	.0613	.0374	.0489	.0559	.0663	.0251	.1276	.0193	.0432	.1067
Services, excl. priv. households and institutions	.0384	.0224	.0368	.0322	.0506	.0450	.0538	.0367	.0443	.0252	.0633	.0779
Private households	.0512	.0801	.0552	.0342	.0359	.0444						
Institutions	.0355	.0352	.0308	.0550	.0462	.0208	.0224	.0211	.0149	.0217	.0428	.0106
Federal public administration	.0175	.0449	−.0099	.0029	.0322	.0032						
Federal government enterprises	.0199	.0358	.0063	.0281	.0237	.0073						
State and local: Educ. services	.0526	.0535	.0568	.0591	.0571	.0429						
Public administration	.0400	.0484	.0385	.0238	.0421	.0387						
Gov't enterprises	.0409	.0802	−.0011	.0634	.0233	.0366						

Table 1.30   Productivity: Rates of Growth

Industry	Total Factor Productivity 1948–1966 (average annual rates of growth)		Translog Index of Productivity (average annual rates of growth)					
	Kendrick	Translog	1947–1973	1947–1953	1953–1957	1957–1960	1960–1966	1966–1973
Agricultural production		.0379	.0168	.0194	.0221	.0202	.0147	.0120
Agricultural services		−.0038	−.0085	.0033	−.0062	.0100	−.0113	−.0254
Metal mining	.0239	−.0335	−.0155	−.0363	.0065	−.0353	.0120	−.0253
Coal mining	.0508	.0356	−.0002	−.0222	.0501	.0128	.0223	−.0349
Crude petroleum and natural gas	.0319	.0171	.0098	.0360	.0096	.0098	−.0071	.0020
Nonmetallic mining and quarrying	.0260	−.0094	−.0000	−.0243	.0000	.0011	.0007	.0197
Contract construction	.0146	.0137	.0007	.0009	.0089	.0223	−.0016	−.0116
Food and kindred products	.0108	−.0097	.0001	.0005	.0090	−.0466	.0030	.0123
Tobacco manufacturers	.0395	.0079	.0028	−.0048	.0238	−.0335	.0080	.0085
Textile mill products	.0188	.0374	.0154	.0062	.0173	.0190	.0131	.0225
Apparel and other fabr. textile prod.	.0249	.0077	.0067	.0110	.0027	−.0144	.0020	.0183
Paper and allied products	.0262	.0046	.0001	−.0064	−.0077	−.0224	.0124	.0094
Printing and publishing	.0475	.0143	.0057	−.0000	.0211	−.0306	.0187	.0061
Chemicals and allied products	.0296	.0468	.0233	.0206	.0208	.0269	.0218	.0267
Petroleum and coal products	.0386	−.0208	.0069	.0095	.0002	−.0134	.0162	.0094
Rubber and misc. plastic products	.0165	.0269	.0099	.0025	−.0174	.0433	.0084	.0187
Leather and leather products	.0341	−.0379	−.0068	−.0132	−.0038	−.0871	.0088	.0179
Lumber and wood prod. excluding furniture	.0290	−.0063	−.0061	−.0285	.0107	−.0691	.0177	.0102
Furniture and fixtures	.0240	.0049	.0121	.0401	.0086	−.0352	.0068	.0148
Stone, clay, and glass products	.0157	.0132	.0023	.0004	.0010	−.0269	.0143	.0070
Primary metal industries	.0184	−.0079	−.0049	.0094	−.0174	−.0594	.0160	−.0046
Fabricated metal industries	.0256	.0045	.0019	.0039	.0012	−.0329	.0096	.0090
Machinery excluding electrical	.0364	.0102	.0055	.0080	−.0064	−.0272	.0218	.0105
Elec. machinery, eqpt., and supplies		.0367	.0148	.0081	−.0013	.0006	.0380	.0160

Table 1.30 (continued)

Industry	Total Factor Productivity 1948–1966 (average annual rates of growth)		Translog Index of Productivity (average annual rates of growth)					
	Kendrick	Translog	1947–1973	1947–1953	1953–1957	1957–1960	1960–1966	1966–1973
Trans. eqpt. and ord. ex. motor vehicles		.0207	.0074	.0297	−.0065	−.0324	.0161	.0059
Motor vehicles and equipment		.0171	.0054	.0075	.0057	−.0183	.0092	.0104
Prof. photographic eqpt. and watches	.0310	.0154	.0066	−.0153	−.0101	.0219	.0115	.0243
Misc. manufacturing industries	.0288	.0221	.0085	.0014	.0097	−.0020	.0107	.0166
Railroads and rail express service	.0340	.0513	.0220	.0060	.0294	.0121	.0436	.0171
Street rail, bus lines, and taxicabs		−.0266	−.0099	−.0335	−.0022	−.0064	.0057	−.0087
Trucking services and warehousing		.0355	.0067	.0217	.0153	−.0009	.0013	−.0033
Water transportation	.0506	.0281	.0122	−.0341	.0374	−.0176	.0191	.0443
Air transportation	.0053	.0970	.0382	.0588	.0355	−.0114	.0485	.0345
Pipelines ex. natural gas	.0769	.0814	.0542	.0568	.0437	.0196	.0635	.0647
Transportation services		−.0733	−.0165	−.0058	−.0363	−.0255	−.0279	−.0007
Telephone, telegraph, and misc. comm. services	.0400	.0339	.0233	.0325	.0261	.0308	.0217	.0121
Radio broadcasting and television		.0018	.0010	.0230	.0000	−.0195	−.0205	.0097
Electric utilities		.0561	.0266	.0565	.0339	.0396	.0207	−.0035
Gas utilities		.0319	.0114	.0171	.0259	−.0146	.0182	.0037
Water supply and sanitary services		.0069	−.0001	.0482	−.0128	−.0010	−.0092	−.0259
Wholesale trade	.0245	.0185	.0121	−.0023	.0214	.0128	.0196	.0122
Retail trade	.0238	.0265	.0132	.0138	.0190	.0053	.0215	.0055
Finance, insurance, and real estate		.0080	.0021	.0021	−.0065	.0109	.0167	−.0093
Services, excl. priv. households and institutions		.0015	.0004	.0006	.0049	−.0013	.0038	−.0045
Institutions		−.0006	−.0003	−.0006	−.0017	−.0012	.0005	.0007

References

Bacharach, Michael. 1965. Estimating non-negative matrices from marginal data. *International Economic Review* 6: 294–310.

Bancroft, Gertrude, and Garfinkle, Stuart. 1963. Job mobility in 1961. *Special Labor Force Report*, no. 35, August, tables F and G.

Barger, William J. 1971. The measurement of labor input: U.S. manufacturing industries, 1948–1966. Ph.D. dissertation, Harvard University.

Bureau of the Census. 1958. *Enterprise statistics: 1958, part 3 link of census establishment and IRS corporation data*, ser. ES3, no. 3. Washington: U.S. Department of Commerce.

———. 1963. *U.S. census of population—1960, industrial characteristics*, PC(2)–7F. Washington: U.S. Department of Commerce, p. xvi.

Bureau of Economic Analysis. 1965. Transactions table of 1958 input-output study and revised direct and total requirement data. *Survey of Current Business*, vol. 45, no. 9 (September). Washington: Government Printing Office.

———. 1968. Input-output transactions: 1961. Staff paper in economics and statistics, no. 16. Washington: U.S. Department of Commerce.

———. 1969. Input-output structure of the U.S. economy: 1963. *Survey of Current Business*, vol. 49, no. 11 (November). Washington: Government Printing Office.

———. 1970. The input-output structure of the United States economy: 1947, March. Washington: U.S. Department of Commerce.

———. 1972. Input-output transactions: 1966, February. Staff paper in economics and statistics, no. 19. Washington: U.S. Department of Commerce.

———. 1974*a*. Gross national product by industry, work file 1205–01–01. Washington: U.S. Department of Commerce.

———. 1974*b*. Gross national product by industry, work file 1205–04–06. Washington: U.S. Department of Commerce.

———. 1974*c*. The input-output structure of the U.S. economy: 1967. *Survey of Current Business*, vol. 54, no. 2 (February). Washington: U.S. Department of Commerce.

———. 1976*a*. *Fixed nonresidential business and residential capital in the United States, 1925–1975*, PB–253 725. Washington: U.S. Department of Commerce, National Technical Information Service.

———. 1976*b*. U.S. national income and product accounts, 1973 to Second Quarter 1976. *Survey of Current Business*, vol. 56, no. 7 (July). Washington: Government Printing Office.

————. 1977. *The national income and product accounts of the United States, 1929–1974: Statistical tables.* Washington: Government Printing Office.

Bureau of Labor Statistics. 1960. *Trends in output per man-hour in the private economy, 1909–1958,* Bulletin no. 1249. Washington: U.S. Department of Labor.

————. 1965. *Employer expenditures for selected supplementary remuneration practices for production workers in manufacturing industries, 1962,* Bulletin no. 1428. Washington: U.S. Department of Labor.

————. 1973*a. Employment and earnings statistics of the United States,* Bulletin no. 1312. Washington: U.S. Department of Labor.

————. 1973*b.* Historical productivity measures. Unpublished working paper prepared by the Productivity and Technology Division of the Bureau of Labor Statistics, Department of Labor.

Burmeister, Edwin, and Dobell, Rodney. 1969. Disembodied technological change with several factors. *Journal of Economic Theory* 1 (June): 1–8.

Chinloy, Peter T. 1974. Issues in the measurement of labor input. Ph.D. dissertation, Harvard University.

Christensen, Laurits R., and Jorgenson, Dale W. 1969. The measurement of U.S. real capital input, 1929–1967. *Review of Income and Wealth,* ser. 15, no. 4 (December), pp. 293–320.

————. 1970. U.S. real product and real factor input, 1929–1967. *Review of Income and Wealth,* ser. 16, no. 1 (March), pp. 19–50.

————. 1973. Measuring the performance of the private sector of the U.S. economy, 1929–1969. In M. Moss, ed., *Measuring economic and social performance* (New York: National Bureau of Economic Research), pp. 233–338.

Christensen, Laurits R.; Jorgenson, Dale W.; and Lau, Lawrence J. 1971. Conjugate duality and the transcendental logarithmic production function. *Econometrica* 39: 255–56.

————. 1973. Transcendental logarithmic production frontiers. *Review of Economics and Statistics* 55 (February): 28–45.

Denison, Edward F. 1962. *Sources of economic growth in the United States and the alternatives before us.* New York: The Committee for Economic Development.

————. 1972. Final comments. *Survey of Current Business* 52 (May): 95–110.

————. 1974. *Accounting for United States economic growth, 1929 to 1969.* Washington: The Brookings Institution.

Diewert, W. Erwin. 1976. Exact and superlative index numbers. *Journal of Econometrics* 4 (May): 115–46.

————. 1977. Aggregation problems in the measurement of capital. Discussion paper 77–09, Department of Economics, University of British Columbia.

Divisia, F. 1925. L'indice monétaire et la théorie de la monnaie. *Revue d'Économie Politique* 39: 842–61, 980–1008, 1121–51.

————. 1928. *Économique rationnelle.* Paris: Gaston Doin.

————. 1952. *Exposés d'économique,* vol. 1. Paris: Dunod.

Executive Office of the President. 1967. *Standard industrial classification manual.* Washington: Bureau of the Budget.

Fisher, I. 1922. *The making of index numbers.* Boston: Houghton Mifflin.

Gjeddebaek, N. F. 1949. Contribution to the study of grouped observations: Application of the method of maximum likelihood in case of normally distributed observations. *Skand. Aktuar. Tidskr.* 32: 135.

Goldsmith, R. W. 1962. *The national wealth of the United States in the postwar period.* New York: National Bureau of Economic Research.

Griliches, Zvi. 1960. Measuring inputs in agriculture: A critical survey. *Journal of Farm Economics* 42: 1411–27.

Griliches, Zvi, and Jorgenson, Dale W. 1966. Sources of measured productivity change: Capital input. *American Economic Review* 56: 50–61.

Hall, R. E., and Jorgenson, D. W. 1967. Tax policy and investment behavior. *American Economic Review* 57: 391–414.

————. 1971. Application of the theory of optimum capital accumulation. In G. Fromm, ed., *Tax incentives and capital spending.* Amsterdam: North-Holland, pp. 9–60.

Hicks, J. R. (1932). *The theory of wages.* London: Macmillan (2nd ed., 1963).

Hulten, Charles. 1973a. Divisia index numbers. *Econometrica* 41: 1017–26.

————. 1973b. *The measurement of total factor productivity in U.S. manufacturing, 1948–1966.* Ph.D. dissertation, University of California.

Internal Revenue Service. 1974. *Source book, statistics of income: Active corporation income tax returns.* Washington: Government Printing Office.

Jack Faucett Associates, Inc. 1973a. *Development of capital stock series by industry sector.* Washington: Office of Emergency Preparedness.

————. 1973b. *Measures of working capital.* Washington: U.S. Department of the Treasury.

————. 1975. *Output and employment for input-output sectors.* Washington: U.S. Bureau of Labor Statistics.

Jorgenson, Dale W. 1973. The economic theory of replacement and depreciation. In W. Sellekaerts, ed., *Econometrics and Economic Theory*. New York: Macmillan, pp. 189–221.

Jorgenson, Dale W., and Griliches, Zvi. 1967. The explanation of productivity change. *The Review of Economic Studies* 34: 249–83.

———. 1971. Divisia index numbers and productivity measurement. *Review of Income and Wealth*, ser. 17, no. 2, pp. 53–55.

———. 1972. Issues in growth accounting: A reply to Edward F. Denison. *Survey of Current Business* 52: 65–94.

Jorgenson, D. W., and Lau, L. J. 1977. *Duality and Technology*. Amsterdam: North-Holland.

Kendrick, John W. 1961. *Productivity trends in the United States*. Princeton: Princeton University Press for the National Bureau of Economic Research.

———. 1973. *Postwar productivity trends in the United States, 1948–1969*. New York: National Bureau of Economic Research.

Kloek, T. 1966. *Indexcijfers: enige methodologisch aspecten*. The Hague: Pasmans.

Loftus, Shirley F. 1972. Stocks of business inventories in the United States, 1928–1971. *Survey of Current Business* 52: 29–32.

Manvel, A. D. 1968. Trends in the value of real estate and land, 1956–1966. *Three Land Research Studies*. Washington: The National Commission on Urban Problems.

Merrilees, W. J. 1971. The case against Divisia index numbers as a basis in a social accounting system. *Review of Income and Wealth*, ser. 17, no. 1, pp. 81–86.

Musgrave, John. 1976. Fixed nonresidential business and residential capital in the United States, 1925–1975. *Survey of Current Business* 56: 46–52.

Nelson, Richard R. 1973. Recent exercises in growth accounting: new understanding or dead end. *American Economic Review* 63: 462–68.

Office of Tax Analysis. 1973. Unpublished tables: Investment and asset life by industry and type of equipment; use of depreciation methods by industry and equipment type; and investment by industry. Washington: U.S. Department of the Treasury (typewritten).

Pechman, Joseph A. 1971. *Federal tax policy*, rev. ed. Washington: The Brookings Institution.

Perrella, Vera C. 1970. Multiple job holders in May, 1969. *Special Labor Force Report*, no. 123, p. 3.

Richter, M. K. 1966. Invariance axioms and economic indexes. *Econometrica* 34: 239–55.

Samuelson, P. A. 1953. Prices of factors and goods in general equilibrium. *Review of Economic Studies* 21: 1–20.

Solow, Robert M. 1957. Technical change and the aggregate production function. *Review of Economics and Statistics* 39: 312–20.

Stein, Robert L. 1967. New definitions for employment and unemployment. *Employment and Earnings and Monthly Report on the Labor Force* 13, no. 8: 3–27.

Stone, R., and Brown, J. A. C. 1962. *A computable model of economic growth (A programme for growth 1)*. London: Chapman and Hall.

Theil, H. 1965. The information approach to demand analysis. *Econometrica* 33: 67–87.

Tornqvist, Leo. 1936. The Bank of Finland's consumption price index. *Bank of Finland Monthly Bulletin*, no. 10, pp. 1–8.

Usher, Dan. 1974. The suitability of the Divisia index for the Measurement of economic aggregates. *Review of Income and Wealth*, ser. 20, no. 3, pp. 273–88.

Vasquez, Thomas. 1974. ADR Paper. Washington: U.S. Department of the Treasury, Office of Tax Analysis (typewritten).

Walderhaug, Albert J. 1973. The composition of value added in the 1963 input-output study. *Survey of Current Business* 53 (April): 34–44.

Young, Allan. 1968. Alternative estimates of corporate depreciation and profits: part I. *Survey of Current Business* 48: 17–28.

Comment   Ernst R. Berndt

The Gollop-Jorgenson (hereafter GJ) paper represents the culmination of a mammoth project involving an enormous amount of data gathering, consultation with government statistical officials, and data manipulation. Even without adjusting for the obvious quality of the labor input, one cannot help but be overwhelmed with the massive real factor input embodied in this paper. Annual productivity measures are obtained for each of 51 industries over the 1947–73 period;[1] labor data are broken down into classifications of sex (two groups), age (eight), occupation (ten), education (five), and type of employment (two). Capital data

Ernst R. Berndt is at the University of British Columbia.

The original versions of the paper and comments were prepared for presentation at the NBER Conference on New Developments in Productivity Measurement, Williamsburg, Virginia, 1975 November 13–14. The comments below are on the revised version of the Gollop-Jorgenson paper, dated September 1977. I have benefited from discussions with Dale W. Jorgenson, who clarified a number of issues regarding data procedure.

1. In the original version of the paper, data were prepared for 67 industries. The finance, insurance, and real estate sectors, among others, have been aggregated in the revised version.

are disaggregated into three types of organization (corporate business, noncorporate business, households and institutions), and six asset classes (producers' durable equipment, consumers' durable equipment, residential structures, nonresidential structures, inventories, and land). Finally, intermediate goods are introduced into the growth accounting framework. Thus this paper represents an enormous effort in applied economic research.

In addition to the presentation of indices of total factor productivity for each of 51 industries, the GJ study offers three substantial discussions: (i) theoretical underpinnings for the indexing of total factor productivity, (ii) the derivation, calculation, and interpretation of labor and capital quality indices, and (iii) the introduction of intermediate goods into growth accounting.

In these comments I will focus most of my attention on theoretical underpinnings, crucial assumptions, and method of approach.[2] I begin with a discussion of theoretical underpinnings.

If we wish to obtain indices of total factor productivity, it is imperative that we first develop a clear notion of what it is that we are trying to measure. Historically, the theory and practice of indexing was closely associated with the theory of production. In recent years substantial developments in the theory of production, cost, and duality have taken place; a number of these developments are explicitly incorporated into the GJ paper.

Suppose there exists a transformation function relating inputs (denoted $X_1, X_2, \ldots, X_n$) and outputs (denoted $Y_1, Y_2, \ldots, Y_m$) at different points in time (denoted by t). More formally, let us specify a general transformation function of the form

(1) $$H(Y_{1t}, Y_{2t}, \ldots, Y_{mt}; X_{1t}, X_{2t}, \ldots, X_{nt}; t) = 0,$$

where H satisfies the appropriate differentiability and curvature properties. Let us denote a scalar index of the m outputs at time t as Y_t, a scalar index of the m inputs as X_t, and the time derivaties as $\dot{Y}/Y$ and $\dot{X}/X$. The index of total factor productivity (hereafter TFP) is typically computed as

(2) $$\text{TFP} = \frac{\dot{Y}}{Y} - \frac{\dot{X}}{X}.$$

This suggests that one might want to ask what conditions must be placed on (1) in order to measure TFP in the above manner. A set of sufficient conditions is that a consistent index of aggregate output and a

---

2. These revised comments are considerably shorter than in the original version, since a number of suggestions have been incorporated by GJ in their revised paper.

consistent index of aggregate input exists; thus it is assumed that (1) can be written in the homothetic weakly separable form

(3)
$$H\,(Y_{1t},Y_{2t},\ldots Y_{mt};\,X_{1t},\,X_{2t},\ldots,\,X_{nt};\,t)$$
$$= H^*\,[G^*\,(Y_{1t},\,Y_{2t},\ldots,\,Y_{mt}),F^*\,(X_{1t},\,X_{2t},\ldots X_{nt})]$$
$$= H^{**}[G^{**}(Y_t),\,F^{**}(X_t,t)],$$

where Y_t and X_t are "composite goods" or "consistent aggregates." If in addition it is assumed that the homothetic separability is of the additive type, we can specify the familiar production function

(4)
$$G\,(Y_t)\,-\,F\,(X_t,t)\,=\,0,\text{ or } G\,(Y_t)\,=\,F\,(X_t,t).$$

Gollop and Jorgenson also assume that G and F are characterized by constant returns to scale. While this assumption is not necessary, it traditionally has been convenient for purposes of data construction and accounting. Under these assumptions, the notion of total factor productivity is simply the partial derivative

(5)
$$\epsilon_{Ft} = \frac{\partial \ln F\,(X_t,t)}{\partial t}\text{, input quantities fixed,}$$

which is approximated empirically by (2).

An alternative notion of TFP can be derived using the theory of duality. If H, G, and F have the appropriate curvature properties and input markets are competitive, then corresponding with the production function (4) there exists a dual cost function of the form

(6)
$$C_t = C^*\,(Y_t,\,P_{1t},P_{2t},\ldots,\,P_{nt},\,t),$$

where C is the minimum total cost of producing output Y, and $P_1,P_2,\ldots,P_n$ is the vector of input prices. The elasticity of costs with respect to output is defined as

(7)
$$\epsilon_{CY} = \frac{\partial \ln C}{\partial \ln Y}\text{, input prices fixed}$$

and the associated dual rate of returns to scale is of course

(8)
$$\epsilon^{-1}{}_{CY} \equiv \frac{1}{\epsilon_{CY}} = 1/(\partial \ln C/\partial \ln Y).$$

Finally, one can define the dual rate of total cost diminution as

(9)
$$\epsilon_{Ct} = \frac{-\partial \ln C}{\partial t}\text{, input prices and output quantity fixed.}$$

Naturally the question arises as to the relationship between total factor productivity (5) viewed from the primal and total cost diminution (9) viewed from the dual. Makoto Ohta (1974) has shown that, in general,

(10) $\qquad \epsilon_{Ft} = \epsilon^{-1}{}_{CY} \, \epsilon_{Ct},$

i.e., total factor productivity viewed from the primal side is equal to dual returns to scale times the rate of total cost diminution. If returns to scale are greater than unity, then of course $\epsilon_{Ft} > \epsilon_{Ct}$. In the GJ framework where constant returns to scale are imposed, $\epsilon_{Ft} = \epsilon_{Ct}$, i.e.,

(11) $\qquad \dfrac{\partial \ln F(X_t, t)}{\partial t} = \dfrac{-\partial \ln C(P_t, Y_t, t)}{\partial t},$

where P_t is a vector of the n input prices. Hence in the present context the primal and dual notions of productivity are equal.

It should be noted that this notion of total factor productivity as presented by GJ does not require neutrality of technical change. TFP is simply a time derivative—which can be the outcome of nonneutral technical change. Indeed, TFP can be viewed as a weighted sum of input-specific technological change biases. Suppose, for example, that technical change is of the constant exponential factor augmenting form

(12) $\qquad X^*{}_{it} = X_{it} \, exp \, (\lambda_i T), \quad i = 1, \dots, n,$

or, equivalently, of the input price diminishing form

(13) $\qquad P^*{}_{it} = P_{it} \, exp \, (-\lambda_i T),$

where $X^*{}_{it}$ and X_{it} are input quantities measured in efficiency and "natural" units, respectively, $P^*{}_{it}$ and P_{it} are input prices measured in efficiency and "natural" units, $T = t - t_o$, where t_o is an initial point in time, and λ is the constant exponential rate of factor quantity augmentation (price diminution). It can be shown that total factor productivity is the weighted sum of input augmentation rates

(14) $\qquad \text{TFP} = \dfrac{\partial \ln G}{\partial t} = -\dfrac{\partial \ln C}{\partial t} = \sum_{i=l}^{m} M_i \, \lambda_i,$

where M_i is the cost or value share of the ith input in total cost or total value. Thus TFP does not require neutrality of technical change.[3] Incidentally, in the above example, the rate of total factor productivity is endogenous; exogenous rates of augmentation for each input are weighted by endogenous cost-minimizing factor shares.

The above represents theoretical underpinnings of TFP measurement. It might be noted that TFP in the Gollop-Jorgenson framework is clearly restricted to the production sector; in particular, TFP has no

---

3. A clear statement of nonneutral technical change and TFP in the context of a CES production function is offered by Paul A. David and Th. van de Klundert, "Biased Efficiency Growth and Capital-Labor Substitution in the U.S., 1899–1969," *American Economic Review* 55 (1965): 357–94. An analogous presentation for translog cost functions is found in Berndt and Jorgenson (1975).

clear relationship to "welfare" or "social well-being," even when prices accurately reflect social costs.

In the revised version of their paper, Gollop and Jorgenson specify the vital link between the production or cost function and the precise index-number formulas. The issue here is how one empirically approximates the derivatives $\partial \ln G/\partial\, t$ or $\partial \ln C/\partial\, t$ in (11).

Let us denote the output of a specific production-functional form F at times t and $t-1$ as Y_t and Y_{t-1}, and particular index-number measures of output as I_t and I_{t-1}. The particular index number is said to be *exact* for the functional form F if[4]

$$(15) \qquad \frac{Y_t}{Y_{t-1}} = \frac{I_t}{I_{t-1}}.$$

Gollop and Jorgenson employ a discrete version of the Divisia index developed by Törnqvist. Thus it is of interest to ask what the functional form is for which the Törnqvist index is exact. Diewert has shown that if the production function is homogeneous translog, then the Törnqvist quantity index will be exact; similarly, if the cost function is homogeneous translog, then the Törnqvist price index will be exact. This then provides a theoretical foundation for using the Törnqvist index in productivity analyses and explains why GJ call their index a "translog" index. Other index number formulas (such as Fisher's ideal index) are exact for alternative functional forms. Various index numbers could therefore be employed. Diewert has defined an index number as *superlative* if it is exact for an F which can provide a second-order approximation to an arbitrary linear homogeneous function. He introduces an entire family of superlative index numbers, and shows that the Törnqvist index belongs to this family; the Paasche and Laspeyres indices do not, however, belong. The implication of Diewert's results is that productivity researchers may be well advised not to use the restrictive Paasche or Laspeyres indices, and instead employ one of the superlative index numbers such as the Törnqvist (translog) or Fisher ideal index.

Although the translog index used by GJ has attractive properties for indexing TFP, it also suffers slightly from several drawbacks. First, in their computations, GJ use translog quantity indices; implicit price indices are computed by dividing value by the translog quantity index. All the GJ results would be altered slightly if they initially computed a translog price index and then computed the quantity index implicitly by dividing value by translog price index. This occurs because the translog index satisfies the factor reversal test only approximately. The implication is that if GJ had done all the necessary computations, they would have observed that $\partial \ln G/\partial\, t \simeq -\partial \ln C/\partial\, t$—the equality would not have held exactly, but only approximately.

4. This discussion is largely based on Diewert (1976).

Secondly, although the continuous Divisia index is reproducible (i.e., a Divisia index of Divisia indices is itself a Divisia index), the translog approximation does not in general possess this property.[5] Thus, if GJ first compute a capital index as a translog index of diverse capital inputs, then compute a labor index as a translog index of diverse labor input characteristics, and then finally compute total primary inputs as a translog index of the translog capital and translog labor inputs, they would obtain a different number than if in a single step they had computed total primary input as a translog index of all the diverse capital and labor inputs. The difference, I suspect, is in most cases likely to be very small if not negligible.

In summary, a significant contribution of the GJ paper is that it provides an explicit, rigorous theoretical foundation for the measurement of TFP. Several issues remain, however. First, since TFP is indexed essentially as a residual ($\dot{Y}/Y - \dot{X}/X$), anything not explained by changes in real factor input is attributed to technical change. Producer errors in optimizing behavior, departures from constant returns to scale, and errors in data measurement all become components of TFP. It would be useful to have a discussion on some of these issues. In particular, it should be possible to derive analytically the effect of TFP on errors in optimizing behavior and departures from constant returns to scale.

Secondly, the GJ theoretical discussion suggests that an interesting empirical extension would be to use econometric techniques and to test whether in fact TFP is an empirically meaningful notion. To do that, one would want to estimate the parameters of a flexible multiple input, multiple output transformation function and then use statistical inference to test for the validity of hypotheses relating to (i) homothetic or homogeneous additive separability of inputs from outputs, (ii) constant returns to scale, (iii) the existence of "labor," "capital," or "primary factor" composite indices,[6] and (iv) various forms of technical change (e.g., factor augmenting, Hicks-neutral, Harrod-neutral, Solow-neutral,

5. Diewert has shown that the Törnqvist (translog) index is reproducible if and only if the "true" subfunctions and the "true master" functions are linear homogeneous translog.

6. A procedure for testing separability restrictions using the translog production or cost functions has been developed by Berndt and Christensen (1974). There are, however, two problems with this approach. First, if one interprets the translog functions as a function in its own right, one can only impose separability conditions on the translog by simultaneously imposing additional restrictions on the separable subfunction; thus, if this separability restriction is rejected, one cannot at present determine whether the separability or the unavoidable additional restrictions "caused" the rejection. For further discussion, see Blackorby, Primont, and Russell (1977). An alternative procedure is to treat the translog as an approximation to the "true" function, and then test for separability at the

or Leontief-neutral). If (iii) were followed, evidence would be available on whether the notion of labor productivity, capital productivity, or primary factor productivity could be justified on the basis of appropriate separability restrictions. Incidentally, it would be particularly interesting to test whether the value-added notion of productivity is justified; recent evidence accumulated in my research suggests that the data in U.S. manufacturing may not be consistent with value-added restrictions (Berndt and Wood 1975).

Let me now turn to a second major contribution of the GJ paper—the discussion on labor *quality*. GJ devote a major portion of their paper to the construction of labor indices. Since labor is heterogeneous, and since numerous compositional and work-related changes have taken place over time, it is important that the composite index reflect the net effects of these changes. For each of the fifty-one industries, GJ decompose labor input into 1600 cells—eight age groups, ten occupational categories, five educational attainment levels, two sexes, and two employment categories. Since this is done for twenty-seven years in each of fifty-one industries, the total number of labor cells is 2,203,200—although many cells are empty. To do this, data from a number of sources—primarily the decennial census and the annual current population survey—are utilized. Since household and establishment totals frequently do not agree, extensive use is made of the suitably generalized RAS method. This raises the issue of how much error is introduced into the labor quantity and quality figures through the widespread use of the generalized RAS multiproportional adjustment method. Although GJ have gone to extraordinary lengths to employ all possible reliable data, one cannot help but question the reliability of the resulting labor quality and TFP measures. In an earlier paper (Jorgenson 1966), Professor Jorgenson has expended some effort discussing the sensitivity of measured TFP to errors in the construction of capital price data. At this point, some Monte Carlo–type research on the effects of measurement errors on computed TFP appears to be a useful direction for further research.

GJ attempt in their analysis to measure hours worked rather than hours paid for; the reason is that hours worked rather than hours paid for enters as an input into the production function. Hours paid for enters indirectly through the price of labor viewed from the vantage of

point of approximation (expansion). This procedure has been advocated by Christensen, Jorgenson, and Lau (1975). The problem with this approach is that the test results will vary with the data point chosen as the point of approximation (expansion), and thus this procedure could lead to inference which lacked robustness.

the producer, for price per unit of labor worked is computed as wage bill plus supplementary benefits (including paid holidays and employers' contributions to social insurance—an increasing portion of wages and salaries) divided by actual hours worked. GJ introduce and implement procedures on the measurement of hours worked which reflect an unusually thorough and detailed effort in measuring labor input. I suspect, however, that a number of errors still remain; in particular, the accuracy of census data on number of hours worked by "white-collar" workers, and the representativeness of the survey week in the context of the entire year are potential sources of considerable error.

The GJ indexing procedure for measuring labor input is valid of course only if the weights (cost or value shares) accurately reflect logarithmic marginal revenue products. Departures from this will introduce errors into the calculations. If, for example, employers invest firm-specific training in their workers, then marginal revenue product may be greater than wage paid, because the firm will want to recoup a share of its investment. In the present context, this may introduce considerable error into the time series data for certain white-collar occupational groups. Although a bit out of context, it is of interest to speculate on the effects of wage discrimination against women on measured productivity. If women have been paid wage rates less than their marginal revenue product, then postwar increases in the labor force activity of women have been weighted by downward-biased shares; measured total factor input then understates true total factor input, and measured TFP is biased upward. Alternatively, other things being equal, if discrimination against women declines, *measured* (but not necessarily actual) TFP will likely fall.

Let me now move on to capital input. GJ devote considerable care to the development of capital data, along with their extensive discussion on labor data. Remarks made above concerning labor quality indices carry over of course for capital quality. GJ are forced for data reasons to make several important assumptions. First, the assumption of *exogenous geometric decay* is made for all equipment and structures. There is some evidence to suggest that this assumption may not be unrealistic for certain types of equipment; on the other hand, the assumption appears less justifiable for other assets such as nonresidential structures. Further, recent events with respect to energy prices suggest that we may want to develop theoretical frameworks which make rates of decay, scrapping, and obsolescence endogenous and variable, rather than exogenous and constant. Second, GJ assume that in any given year the nominal rate of return is the same across assets in each industry, but that this common rate of return varies across industries. There may in fact be data reasons for doing this, but these are not discussed by GJ.

Third, GJ compute real capital input as a translog index of producers' durable equipment, nonresidential structures, land, and inventories. Working capital is not included; indeed, the issue of whether money ought to enter the production function and therefore enter the accounts of TFP is not discussed. Further consideration of this issue would be useful.

The final substantial contribution of this study is the introduction of intermediate goods into the detailed productivity calculations. Although the inclusion of intermediate goods might appear novel, in fact Vernon W. Ruttan already concerned himself with such issues in the early 1950s.[7]

Appropriately, GJ first address themselves to the issue of why intermediate materials ought to be included in the calculation of TFP. Their answer is straightforward and convincing: the measurement of TFP is based on the theory of production behavior; to a producer, intermediate inputs are treated symmetrically with all other inputs. The cost-minimizing firms will choose that set of capital, labor, and intermediate inputs which minimizes total cost given output. Therefore intermediate inputs, along with capital and labor, should enter in the calculation of TFP.

One of the reasons researchers have ignored intermediate inputs in many previous empirical studies is that a large portion of American studies have been done at the national level, and at the national level almost all intermediate transactions except imports and exports "cancel out"; thus, failing to include intermediate inputs in the aggregate American studies involved neglecting a relatively small amount (imports minus exports accounted for about 5% of U.S. gross national product) of transactions. At the industry level, however, intermediate inputs are quite important.

Apparently it still is not widely known that for a single industry TFP measured using value-added techniques will generally be greater than or equal to TFP measured using gross output. This significant inequality relationship seems to have been discovered several times. In his 1954 U.S. Department of Agriculture Marketing Research Report,[8] Vernon W. Ruttan discusses the value added–gross output relationship at some length, and attributes the TFP inequality discovery to an un-

---

7. See Vernon W. Ruttan, "Technological Progress in the Meat Packing Industry, 1919–1947," Ph.D. dissertation, Department of Economics, University of Chicago, 1952; this thesis was published in abridged form under the same title as United States Department of Agriculture Marketing Research Report No. 59, January 1954. Also see the article by Ruttan, "The Contribution of Technological Progress in Farm Output," *Review of Economics and Statistics* 38 (February 1956).

8. See previous note.

published (and apparently undated) paper by Herbert A. Simon.[9] The same inequality was derived independently in 1961 by Evsey Domar, was discovered once more by Spencer Star in 1974, and then was generalized by Charles Hulten in 1974. Hence discussion of the implications of using intermediate inputs in growth accounting has a rather extensive lineage.

There is one issue regarding intermediate inputs, however, which remains troublesome. In his 1961 paper Domar noted that the measure of TFP depends critically on what one means by an intermediate input. Suppose one computes TFP and includes in a sector's outputs and inputs sales of one firm in the sector to another firm in the same sector; call this "double counting" version TFP_1. Suppose that another researcher computes TFP_2 excluding these intrasectoral transfers but including all intersectoral sales. Domar showed that $TFP_1 < TFP_2$. A further contribution of the Domar paper was the development of a measure of TFP with intermediate inputs that was invariant to how one defined intermediate inputs, i.e., how one disaggregated a sector. Unfortunately, this aspect of TFP measurement has not been discussed by GJ, nor have alternative TFP measures been presented. As a result, comparison among sectors is very difficult. I submit that the issue of invariant measures of TFP in the Domar sense ought to be high on the list of future research priorities.[10]

Finally, on page 111 GJ address themselves to the important issue of how capital data might be adjusted to reflect more accurately the amount of capital services actually utilized. The interested reader will remember that this issue of "adjusting for utilized capital" over the years has been a contentious one in the productivity measurement debates between Jorgenson and Griliches and Denison. In the present context, GJ measure total factor input in such a way that variations in energy consumption are included in the productivity calculation. This leads GJ to conclude that "no further adjustment of capital input or intermediate input is required" (p. 112). The principal feature of the GJ procedure here is that for given real capital, labor, and nonenergy intermediate material input, measured total factor input will vary with energy usage, and thus measured total factor productivity will be affected by variations in energy demand. Note, however, that measured

9. Ruttan's citation is as follows: Herbert A. Simon, "Some Models for the Study of the Economic Effects of Technological Change," Cowles Commission Discussion Paper 213 (unpublished).

10. It follows, of course, that at the aggregate national level international comparisons of TFP are practically meaningless unless exports and imports are fully incorporated; if these intermediate inputs are neglected, other things being equal, countries with relatively larger foreign sectors can be expected to show greater TFP growth.

real capital input is completely independent of energy usage; variations in energy expenditures in no way alter measured real capital input.

In my judgment, the GJ procedure of this paper is clearly preferable to the practice whereby capital is adjusted using some type of relative electricity capacity index, e.g., actual electricity consumption divided by nameplate capacity. The latter procedure not only is confined solely to electricity and raises measurement issues in how one defines "capacity," but also assumes that the relationship between capital and energy is one of strict proportionality. In contrast, the GJ technique treats energy just like any other input, and does not make any assumption on whether the relationship between energy and capital is one of substitutability, strict proportionality, or complementarity.[11]

Let me now conclude my comments with some suggestions for further research and with a few remarks on the productivity measurement debates. The recent developments in productivity measurement have occurred simultaneously with a very substantial set of developments in the theory of production. In particular, we now have moved far beyond the restrictive two-input, single-output Cobb-Douglas, and CES production models and instead deal with multiple-input, multiple-output "flexible" or generalized functional forms. We have also recently witnessed the revival of index number theory which relates closely to the "flexible" production models. These index theory results suggest that we no longer should use fixed-weight Paasche or Laspeyres indices, but should rather use the chained ideal Fisher or chained translog indices. In both cases, we have made substantial progress by generalization. I personally would like very much to see the theoretical underpinnings of TFP measurement generalized from zero profits, perfect competition, constant returns to scale to zero profit, monopolistic competition, and possibly increasing returns to scale. There appears to be some evidence that at the establishment or two-digit level, slightly increasing returns to scale occur—although it should be pointed out that all the studies have, I believe, been based on value added rather than gross output functions. The reason we have so frequently assumed constant returns to scale and perfect competition is for convenience in data construction and in the establishment of national real and financial accounting frameworks. It appears to this reader that the zero-profits assumption is rather crucial, but that data construction and consistent accounting frameworks could be derived under monopolistic competition with zero profits and increasing returns to scale. One other additional area for further research is the incorporation of dynamic ("disequilibrium" or

11. For a development of the energy-capital and "utilized capital" discussion, see Berndt and Wood (1977).

"temporary equilibrium") considerations into the theory of production, cost, and the measurement of TFP.

In summary, this paper embodies many of the recent developments in the theory and measurement of productivity; a number of issues, however, still remain. Let us suppose that these remaining issues were resolved; that would, of course, constitute a noteworthy accomplishment. Where would we then stand? I am reminded of the statement, "Understanding the atom is child's play compared with understanding child's play." In the present context, where we still need an enormous amount of research effort is in the area of why and how productivity gains are realized; how can we adequately model the costly process of innovation, implementation, and technical change? How are these processes affected by market structure? How is the rate and bias of technical change affected by changes in relative prices? How is technical change transferred among countries through international trade? Cynics might argue that it is possible that economists will agree on how to measure productivity long before we will understand why and how it takes place.

One final comment. You probably have noticed that in these comments I have not mentioned ways in which the GJ approach differs from the procedures adopted by Edward Denison and John Kendrick. I believe the present paper offers a clue as to why these researchers differ. As I read the lengthy debate carried on by Griliches, Jorgenson, Christensen, Gollop, Denison, and Kendrick, I am struck by the following: Although there are substantial differences in details, Griliches, Jorgenson, Christensen, Gollop, and frequently Denison essentially agree on what they want to measure—namely, real output and real factor input, including all quality changes. From the vantage of this reader, however, Kendrick has something different in mind than the task of accounting for real outputs and real inputs. The reason Kendrick does not adjust labor and capital for quality changes may well be that Kendrick has a more profound notion in mind—that of measuring changes in "welfare" over time; for example, Kendrick appears to be interested in how "well off" the worker is, how much output on average the worker will obtain for a measured man-hour of input. Such a welfare notion is of course extremely difficult to measure, and could provide material for endless debates and conferences. But then the argument of which approach is "right"—Griliches, Jorgenson, Denison, or Kendrick —may well be misplaced. When researchers are attempting to quantify different notions, it is not surprising that they fail to agree on methods of measurement. Perhaps the most important contribution of the present GJ paper is that it clearly and rigorously defines the concept of TFP and then proceeds with a detailed and careful implementation.

References

Berndt, E. R., and Christensen, L. R. 1974. Testing for the existence of a consistent aggregate index of labour inputs. *American Economic Review* 64: 391–404.

Berndt, E. R., and Jorgenson, D. W. 1975. Energy, intermediate goods, and production in an inter-industry econometric model of the U.S., 1947–71. Paper presented at the World Congress of the Econometric Society, Toronto.

Berndt, E. R., and Wood, D. O. 1975. Technology, prices, and the derived demand for energy. *Review of Economics and Statistics* 57: 259–68.

————. 1977. Engineering and econometric approaches to energy conservation and capital formation: A reconciliation. MIT Energy Laboratory Working Paper.

Blackorby, C.; Primont, D.; and Russell, R. 1977. On testing separability restrictions with flexible functional forms. *Journal of Econometrics* 5: 195–209.

Christensen, L. R.; Jorgenson, D. W.; and Lau, L. J. 1975. Transcendental logarithmic utility functions. *American Economic Review* 65: 367–83.

Diewert, W. E. 1976. Exact and superlative index numbers. *Journal of Econometrics* 4: 115–45.

Domar, Evsey. 1961. On the measurement of technological change. *Economic Journal* 71: 709–29.

Hulten, Charles R. 1974. Growth accounting with intermediate inputs. Working paper in Economics no. 9, Department of Political Economy, Johns Hopkins University.

Jorgenson, D. W. 1966. The embodiment hypothesis. *Journal of Political Economy* 74: 1–17.

Ohta, M. 1974. A note on the duality between production and cost functions: Rate of returns to scale and rate of technical progress. *Economic Studies Quarterly* 25: 63–65.

Star, S. 1974. Accounting for the growth of output. *American Economic Review* 64: 123–35.

2

The Long-Term Structure of Production, Factor Demand, and Factor Productivity in U.S. Manufacturing Industries

Michael F. Mohr

2.1 Introduction

The rate of future productivity growth has been a primary concern of policy makers and economic analysts in recent years. The reason for this concern lies largely in the fact that a least-squares time trend of private-sector labor productivity shows an annual rate of growth of 3.2% from 1947 to 1966 but only 2.4% from 1966 to 1973; the overall trend was 3.1% for the 1947–73 interval.

Opinion has varied widely concerning the sources of this productivity slowdown. For instance, Eckstein and Shields (1974), in a study for the National Commission on Productivity and Work Quality, conclude that cyclical factors[1] and energy constraints are behind the measured decrease in productivity growth. Alternatively, Jerome Mark (1975), assistant commissioner of BLS' Office of Productivity and Technology,

Michael F. Mohr was formerly with the Bureau of Labor Statistics, Division of Productivity Research, and is currently with the office of the Chief Economist, U.S. Department of Commerce.

The author is indebted to J. Randolph Norsworthy, chief of the Division of Productivity Research, David B. Humphrey, Beatrice N. Vaccara, John W. Kendrick, and Leo Sveikauskas for their comments on earlier drafts of this paper.

The opinions and conclusions expressed are those of the author and do not necessarily represent those of the Bureau of Labor Statistics.

1. Cyclical factors include (1) changes in the composition of demand of the economic aggregate under study because of sectoral differences in the short-run income and price (both measured and expected income and price) elasticities of demand, e.g., between durable and nondurable goods; and (2) changes in the utilization of labor and capital because of raw materials bottlenecks, tight money, or a general decline in aggregate demand. For more information see Fair (1969, 1971), Clark (1973), Jorgenson and Griliches (1967), Hirsch (1968), Friedman (1957), Hayek (1951), Hawtrey (1913), and Hicks (1950).

has suggested that secular forces[2] account for the post-1966 decline in productivity. Nordhaus (1972) takes a similar position. In a study covering the period 1948–71, Nordhaus asserted that cyclical factors played a small part in the reduced rate of productivity since 1965, and that most of the deceleration can be explained by changes in the composition of demand—specifically, by shifts to low-productivity from high-productivity industries rather than shifts between industries with high and low rates of productivity growth.

Most attempts to isolate and remove the cyclical influences in observed series on labor productivity consist of either mechanical least-squares trend fits or ad hoc single-equation multiple regression procedures employing a "cyclical" variable such as the unemployment rate (see, e.g., Nordhaus 1972). Such procedures give no insight into the determinants of factor productivity in general or labor productivity in particular. They tell us little as to why productivity moved the way it did or where it was going because they are not based on any meaningful representation of the decision-making behavior of the economic agents under consideration.

The purpose of this paper is to set forth a procedure which is firmly grounded in production and cost theory, and which can be used to partition the observed productivity series in individual industries into cyclical and secular components. This study predates the energy problem by analyzing data only through the fourth quarter of 1972, and it avoids the shifting-mix problem to a large extent by analyzing two-digit manufacturing sectors. This disaggregation seems appropriate in view of the evidence[3] that the productivity slowdown cannot be laid solely to changes in the composition of output among broadly defined aggregates,[4] as in the Nordhaus study, but rather is indigenous to the components of these aggregates. To eliminate seasonal changes in productivity,

2. Some of the secular forces most frequently discussed in the literature include the following: (1) secular changes in the composition of output and labor attributed to the individual industries of the economic aggregate being studied (Denison 1973; Nordhaus 1972); (2) changing age-sex composition of the labor force (Perry 1971; Denison 1974); and (3) a slowdown in the growth of the capital-labor ratio (Christensen, Cummings, and Jorgenson 1980).

3. The evidence indicates that the productivity slowdown is not confined to a few sectors but is pervasive at a detailed industry level. According to the BLS, more than two-thirds of the industries the bureau studied had lower rates of productivity gain during the 1966–73 period than in the 1948–66 period (see Mark 1975, p. 21).

4. In fact, the research of the BEA indicates that studying productivity at too high a level of aggregation can even conceal the extensiveness of the slowdown. Thus, the BEA study shows that while the productivity of aggregate nondurable manufacturing slowed very little among the individual nondurable sectors, only 20% of the output in 1970 was accounted for by industries that did not experience a slowdown (see comments by Vaccara in Nordhaus 1972, p. 541).

this study uses seasonally adjusted quarterly data for ten two-digit manufacturing studies.[5]

Basically, the model posits that cyclical and secular influences can be individually captured by a partial adjustment model. The goal of this adjustment process is the long-run or least-cost combination of inputs $X^*_i(Y;P)$ $(i = 1, \ldots, n)$ appropriate for gross output level Y, and the vector of factor prices levels, P.[6] Thus, the functions X^*_i describe the classical instantaneous adjustment expansion path which is defined in this study to be the long-run objective of entrepreneurs. When the X^*_i are imbedded in an interrelated dynamic adjustment model, a system of equations results which describes both the short-run and long-run technology of the industry in question.

Such a model provides a general equilibrium framework for analyzing both the long-run and actual expansion paths of the studied industries. The parameters for the complete system are simultaneously estimated by a generalized least-squares method. Having estimated and isolated the parameters describing the long-term of least-cost expansion path[7] we are then in a position to simulate this path and compare it to the actual expansion path. The simulations produced by this study will show a sharp contrast in overall efficiency of resource use in most of the ten industries between the relatively stable growth period between 1961 and 1966 and the unstable period between 1966 and 1972. In short, this study will show that the prolonged period of economic instability between 1966 and 1972 resulted in a general decline in the productive efficiency of the input mix in general and of production workers in particular. This condition arose because the unstable post-1966 eco-

---

5. The following industries are included:

SIC 20 Food and beverages	SIC 330 = (331 + 332) Primary ferrous metals
SIC 22 Textile mill products	
SIC 26 Paper and allied products	SIC 333 = (33 − 330) Primary non-ferrous metals
SIC 28 Chemical and allied products	
SIC 30 Rubber and plastic products	SIC 35 Nonelectrical machinery
SIC 32 Stone, clay, and glass products	SIC 371 Motor vehicles and equipment

In 1971, BEA's gross product originating (GPO) data show that these industries comprised 74% of gross output in nondurable goods manufacturing, 51% in durable goods manufacturing, and 62% in total manufacturing.

6. Since the work of Parks (1971) and Berndt and Wood (1975) suggests that a value-added approach may bias the substitution relationship between inputs, a total factor approach is taken in this study.

7. It should be understood at the outset that the end product of this study is not a smooth secular productivity path. On the contrary, the long-run path will be heavily impacted by the effects of changes in output and factor prices. In summary, the long-run expansion path indicates what factor demand and factor productivity would be if entrepreneurs could instantaneously adjust from one least-cost input combination to another as suggested by the traditional comparative static model of production.

nomic climate, in contrast to the 1961–66 period, did not allow for stable output projections and consequently provided no prolonged period of stable growth in which to bring the actual input mix into line with the least-cost mix. This kind of analysis cannot be provided by crude approaches to isolating the impact of the business cycle.

The model developed in this study is similar in some respects to the Nadiri and Rosen model but, as will be discussed, there are important differences in specification, method of estimation, and internal consistency between the two models. It will also be seen that our dynamic specification renders a significant improvement in statistical results over the Berndt and Christensen comparative static approach to modeling the structure of production and factor demand. These models, while employing a rich flexible functional form, are contaminated with serially correlated residuals—a problem which our partial adjustment approach shows considerable improvement on. Moreover, in contrast to the Berndt and Christensen and Berndt and Wood studies, we find no evidence of complementarity between inputs on the long-run expansion path, even though such relationships are found to exist in the short run. We suspect that specification and/or aggregation bias may be responsible for the complementarity findings of the above-mentioned authors.

The remainder of this paper is organized as follows: section 2.2 provides a detailed description of the model to be used in this study; section 2.3 describes the method used to transform our measures of least-cost input shares into least-cost or long-run measures of factor demand and factor productivity; section 2.4 provides a detailed discussion of the empirical results for the ten industrial sectors examined and contains the results of tests which examine the structure of production for each industry; and section 2.5 summarizes our findings and conclusions. The data, their sources, and the methodological considerations pertinent in their construction are described in a brief appendix.

2.2 Model Structure and Theory

2.2.1 Introduction

The theoretical model used in this study hypothesizes that cost minimization is the modus operandi of entrepreneurs. The structure of the model results from a melding of the duality theorem of Shepherd (1953, 1970), the translog production function of Christensen, Jorgenson, and Lau (1971, 1973) and the dynamic interrelated factor demand model of Nadiri and Rosen (1969, 1973). The model views the entrepreneurs as attempting to satisfy expected gross output (measured as shipments plus inventory change) at the lowest cost—the locus of such points describing a firm's long-run expansion path. Much of the literature on the derived demand for factors of production attempts to model this least-cost expansion path directly, i.e., by a comparative statics model employing constant returns to scale and perfect competition assumptions. This approach not only ignores adjustment costs[8] but also may be the cause of the autocorrelated disturbances usually found in such models (e.g., Berndt and Christensen 1974; Berndt and Wood 1975).[9] Thus, it may be possible for a firm or industry to accommodate output variations by adjusting the flow of services from its inputs, but it may not be possible to adjust the stock variables which embody these service flows.[10] For instance, the hours worked per employee can be adjusted more rapidly than the level of employment; the utilization rates of plant and equipment can be adjusted more rapidly than the stocks of either capital input. Apart from purely logistical reasons, some of the sluggishness in the adjustment rates of the stock variables is no doubt due to reluctance on the part of entrepreneurs to respond to economic stimuli they suspect are short-run; that is, they take a wait-and-see attitude. However, for both reasons the actual input adjustment path is going to heavily reflect the effect of short-term or interim input adjustments which differ from the optimal ones which would be made in a world where perfect certainty and perfect adjustment capabilities prevailed. Finally, when it is recognized that input adjustments are interrelated (e.g., a decision to increase the utilization rates of the capital stocks in

8. In addition, such a comparative statics model has a number of other deficiencies including the following: (1) Returns to scale may be other than linear homogeneous in particular and homothetic in general. (2) Perfect competition may not exist in the product or factor markets. (3) The form of the production function regularly used in such models (Cobb-Douglas or CES) assumes separability of inputs, and strong separability at that, since the elasticity of substitution $\sigma_{ij} = k$ for all i and j. Note that Berndt and Christensen (1974) and Berndt and Wood (1975) treat separability as a testable, not a maintained, hypothesis.

9. In their note 8, Berndt and Wood indicate that they could not reject the null hypothesis of no autocorrelation against the alternative of a nonzero diagonal autocovariance matrix. In the view of this author, the Berndt and Wood alternative hypothesis is biased toward rejection. This is not only because the R matrix of Berndt and Wood in the context of a system of share equations must be diagonal, but also all elements on the diagonal must be equal. The individual equation Durbin-Watson statistics reported by Berndt and Wood suggest that this is probably not the case, with the K and E equations manifesting positive autocorrelation and the L and M equations zero autocorrelation.

10. Flow variables in this study are loosely defined as that dimension of an input which moves most closely in tandem with the short-run variation in output. For example, the composite measure of production labor input in this study is defined as $E_t (HS + HO_t)$, where E_t, HS_t, HO_t stand for employment, straight-time hours, and overtime hours, respectively. Of these three components, HO_t has the most pronounced cyclical movement, and so only HO_t is described as a flow variable. Capacity utilization is also a flow variable, while intermediate materials inputs share elements of both flow and stock variables.

excess of their desired levels may also necessitate increasing the average number of hours worked by the labor stocks) the following stock-adjustment model can be used to decompose the short-run and long-run movements in factor demand:

(1) $$\Delta X_t = B[X^*_t(Y;P) - X_{t-1}] + U_t \qquad (t = 1, \ldots, n)$$

where

$\Delta X_t =$ a $(k \times 1)$ vector of first differences in the k observed input levels where the components of ΔX_t are $X_{it} - X_{it-1}$ $(i = 1, \ldots, k)$.

$X^*(Y;P) =$ a $(k \times 1)$ vector of functions which describes the least-cost expansion path of the inputs X^*_i. The arguments of X^*, i.e., Y and P, are measures of output and input prices, respectively.

$B =$ a $(k \times k)$ matrix of partial adjustment coefficients which include both own and cross effects.

$U_t =$ a $(k \times 1)$ vector of random disturbances assumed to be distributed normally with $E(u_{it}) = 0$ for all i, and where across the whole set of observations, n, the variance-covariance matrix for U is assumed to have the following form:

$$\Sigma = E(UU) = \begin{bmatrix} \kappa_{11} & \kappa_{12} \cdots & \kappa_{1k} \\ \kappa_{21} & \kappa_{22} & \kappa_{2k} \\ \cdot & \cdot & \cdot \\ \cdot & \cdot & \cdot \\ \cdot & \cdot & \cdot \\ \kappa_{k1} & \kappa_{k2} & \kappa_{kk} \end{bmatrix} \times I,$$

where I is a unit matrix of order $n \times n$.

The form assumed for Σ states that the disturbance in any single equation is homoscedastic and nonautocorrelated, and that there is non-zero correlation between contemporaneous disturbances across equations. In short, equation (1) suggests that movements in observed input levels are composed of an interrelated partial adjustment factor, where the goal of the adjustment mechanism is $X^*(Y;P)$ which describes the long-run input expansion path. In what follows we will formulate and assemble the pieces of the theoretical puzzle presented as equation (1).

2.2.2 Optimization in Production

We begin our discussion with the following assumptions: (1) entrepreneurs are cost-minimizers; (2) the long-run input expansion path can be closely approximated by a translog cost function,

$$\ln C^*(Y;P) = \min_x \Sigma P_i x_i;$$

(3) technology is Hicks-neutral.

Assumption (1) is a weaker assumption than profit-maximization since it does not require that entrepreneurs know their demand curve and thus conforms more closely with the accuracy of the information actually available to decision makers.[11] An advantage of a cost-minimization model is that optimization is invariant to the degree of competition in the product market.

Assumption (2) is an improvement over much of the earlier literature in that it includes other model formulations (notably Cobb-Douglas and CES) as special cases and enables the researcher to easily test for input separability and the nonhomotheticity of production rather than imposing these conditions on an estimating form.

Given the output level, Y, and input prices, P, our model's comparative static expansion path can be described by a six-input translog cost function:

$$(2) \qquad \ln C^*_t(Y_t;P_t) = \alpha_y \ln Y + \alpha_t T + \sum_{i=1}^{6} \ln P_i$$

$$+ \frac{1}{2} \sum_{i=1}^{6} \sum_{j=1}^{6} \delta_{ij} \ln P_i \ln P_j + \sum_{i=1}^{6} \beta_i \ln Y \ln P_i,$$

where Y_t and P_t are observed gross output and prices,[12] respectively and T is time. For (2) to be considered a "well-behaved" cost function, it must satisfy the following conditions:

i) Symmetric Hessian (Young's theorem)

In this study we treat the translog cost function as a second-order approximation to any continuous, twice differentiable cost function. As a result, the matrix of δ_{ij}'s in (2) is equivalent to the Hessian of the Taylor series expansion of the true cost function. Thus by Young's theorem this matrix must be symmetric or

---

11. Profit-maximization implies that firms are capable of adjusting output levels so as to satisfy the necessary condition for profit-maximization, namely, the equality between marginal revenue and marginal cost. This requires that firms have a knowledge of both their demand and cost curves. The author's position is that (1) knowledge of the cost curve is more likely to be part of the information set available to the firm; (2) output price is more likely to be administered; (3) production goals to satisfy expected current demand at that price and inventory investment (to satisfy unexpected current demand) are determined at the start of the production period from information exogenous to the cost function (e.g., the previous period's level of demand, the level of beginning inventories, and the size of the backlog of new orders).

12. The vectors of inputs are indexed as follows: $X_1 =$ hours of production workers; $X_2 =$ nonproduction worker employment; $X_3 =$ equipment stock; $X_4 =$ plant stock; $X_5 =$ capacity utilization; $X_6 =$ materials including energy. The prices of these inputs are indexed analogously. The construction of gross output Y, inputs $(X_i \mid i = 1, \ldots, 6)$ and input prices $(P_i \mid i = 1, \ldots, 6)$ is discussed in the Data Appendix.

$$\delta_{ij} = \delta_{ji} \qquad (i, j = 1, \ldots, 6; i \neq j).$$

ii) Linear homogenity in prices: a doubling of prices doubles cost. This implies that

$$\sum \alpha_i = 1, \quad \sum_i \delta_{ij} = 0, \quad \sum_j \delta_{ij} = 0, \quad \sum \beta_i = 0.$$

This condition follows from the logic that a proportional increase in the price of all inputs will not change the input mix for a given level of output.

iii) Monotonicity: The cost function must be an increasing function of prices such that

$$\frac{\partial \ln C^*}{\partial \ln P_i} = \alpha_i + \Sigma \delta_{ij} \ln P_j + \beta_i \ln Y > 0.$$

Since $\partial \ln C^* / \partial \ln P_i$ is the cost share of input X^*_i, (iii) will be satisfied as long as the input shares are positive.

iv) Concavity of input prices: the Hessian of second partials, H, of equation (2) must be negative semidefinite within the range of observed input prices.

Since equation (2) is linear homogenous in factor prices, the Hessian will be singular but concavity is assured if the principal minors of H alternate in sign starting with negative.

The vector of coefficients, $\boldsymbol{\beta}$, in equation (2) represents nonhomothetic output effects on factor demand. Statistical tests of their significance from zero provides a test of the homotheticity of production.[13]

According to the approach used in this study, (2) is not expected to hold instantaneously; rather, it represents the objective to which the decision maker aspires in acquiring and assembling his inputs since it represents the least-cost input combination given an output level, Y, and a vector of input prices, $\boldsymbol{P}$.

2.2.3 Derived Demand Equations

By Shephard's lemma (1953, 1970) it is known that the partial derivative of the cost function, $C^*(Y;P)$, with respect to input price P_i gives the derived demand equation for input X_i, i.e.,

$$\frac{\partial C^*}{\partial P_i} = X_i(Y;P) \qquad (i = 1, \ldots, 6).$$

13. If the cost function, $C = F(Y;P)$, can be written as separable functions in output and factor prices $C = H(Y)G(P)$, the structure of production is homothetic. Further, if $\partial \ln C / \partial \ln Y = k$, a constant, then the structure of production is homogeneous. For further discussion of the concepts of homotheticity and homogeneity in production see Clemhout (1968), Zellner and Revankar (1969), Wolkowitz (1971), Parks (1971), and Diewert (1974).

The analogue of this for the translog function (2) gives a set of cost share equations:

(4) $$\frac{\partial \ln C^*}{\partial \ln P_i} = S_i(Y;P) = \alpha_i + \sum_{j=1}^{6} \delta_{ij}\ln P_j + \beta_i \ln Y$$

$$(i = 1, \ldots, 6).$$

There are two subtle points affecting the system described by equations (2) and (4). The first point deals with the correct measure of cost for which equation (2) determines the minimum level. The second point refers to the fact that the system of cost-share equations in (4) is singular.

1) Real versus measured total factor cost (RTFC vs. MTFC). The objective of the firm is to minimize the cost of producing a given level of output subject to a production function constraint. Mathematically, the problem can be stated as

(5) $$\min \text{MTFC} = X_1 P_1 + X_2 P_2$$
$$+ X_3\{[q_{e,\,t-1}\, r_t - (q_{et}$$
$$- q_{et-1}) + q_{et}\delta_e\,(1 + X_5 - \overline{X}_5)^2]\,\tau_e\}$$
$$+ X_4\{[q_{s,\,t-1}\, r_t - (q_{st}$$
$$- q_{st-1}) + q_{st}\delta_s\,(1 + X_5 - \overline{X}_5)^2]\,\tau_s\}$$
$$+ X_6 P_6,$$

subject to $\hat{Y} - f(X_1, \ldots, X_6) = 0$

where the terms within braces are shown in the data appendix to be equal to P_3 and P_4, respectively. These are modifications to Hall and Jorgenson (1967) rental prices. The first relationship in equation (5) is measured total factor cost (MTFC) and is a simple accounting relationship. However, note that MTFC is nonlinear in X_3, X_5, and X_4, X_5. Using the method of the Lagrangean multiplier, we can rewrite equation (5) as

(6) $$\min L = \text{MFTC} + \lambda[\hat{Y} - f(X_1, \ldots, X_6)].$$

The well-known first-order conditions for equation (6) are $P_i = \lambda MP_i$, $i = 1, \ldots, 6$, where P_1 through P_6 are defined in the data appendix. The set of relationships derived from equation (6) dictate that in order to minimize cost subject to the production function constraint it is necessary for the firm to use each input to the point where the marginal factor cost or shadow price of that input is equal to the product of marginal cost, λ, and the marginal product of the input, MP_i.[14] These

14. See Samuelson (1963), pp. 57–89.

first-order conditions are important to the derivation of the Allen partial elasticities of substitution (AES) since it can be shown that the AES_{ij} $(i, j, = 1, \ldots, 6)$ are contingent on the following definition of cost:[15,16]

$$(7) \qquad RTFC = \sum_{i=1}^{6} P_i X_i,$$

that is, a definition based on the shadow prices of the inputs.[17] We will hereafter refer to (7) as the definition of real total factor cost (RTFC). It differs from MTFC by the term $P_5 X_5$ which is the marginal factor cost of increasing the rate of capital use. Note that throughout this study we assume that the rates of utilization of plant and equipment are the same since this is the best that available data will allow.

2) The singularity of the system of cost share equations. The set of

---

15. Note, in contrast to the typical textbook example, the nonlinearity of MTFC in X_3, X_5 and X_4, X_5 destroys the usual equality between MTFC and $\sum P_i X_i$. Thus, the transformation of (9a) into (9b) requires the use of RTFC in place of MTFC.

16. To see this consider that the Allen partials ($AES_{ij} = \sigma_{ij}$) can be defined equivalently as

$$(8a) \qquad \sigma_{ij} = \frac{\sum_{h=1}^{6} MP_H \cdot X^*_H}{X^*_i X^*_j} \frac{|F_{ij}|}{|F|},$$

where $|F|$ is the determinant of the bordered Hessian matrix and $|F_{ij}|$ is the cofactor of the ijth element of F, or equivalently as either

$$(8b) \qquad \frac{\sum_{h=1}^{6} P_H X^*_H}{X^*_i X^*_j} \frac{\partial^* X_i}{\partial P_j}$$

or

$$(8c) \qquad \frac{C^* C^*_{ij}}{C^*_i C^*_j},$$

where C^* is defined by equation (2). Equation (8c) follows from equations (8a) and (8b) by Shephard's lemma,

$$(9a) \qquad \frac{\partial C(Y,P)}{\partial P_i} = C^*_i = X^*_i,$$

from which it follows that

$$(9b) \qquad \frac{\partial^2 C^*(Y,P)}{\partial P_i \partial P_j} = C^*_{ij} = \frac{\partial X_i}{\partial P_j},$$

and by the set of relationships derived from (6) which are instrumental in transforming (8a) into (8b), from which the equality $C^* = \sum P_H X^*_H$ follows immediately.

17. Becker and Lewis (1973) make a similar point in the context of utility theory.

cost share equations defined by (4) constitutes a singular system. To see this, note that

$$(10) \qquad \sum_{i=1}^{6} S^*{}_i = \frac{\sum_{i=1}^{6} P_i X^*{}_i}{C^*} = 1.$$

From equation (10) it follows that, given any five of the six equilibrium shares, say the first five, the sixth share is definitionally equal to

$$(11) \qquad S^*{}_6 = 1 - \sum_{i=1}^{5} S^*{}_i.$$

In this study we arbitrarily drop the long-term share equation for materials, choosing the remaining five equations to form a nonsingular system.[18]

In conclusion, letting $\ln P_i = R$, the comparative static model, with symmetry, linear homogenety in prices, and (10) imposed contains the following independent equations:[19]

$$(12) \qquad S^*{}_{1t} = \frac{P_{1t} X^*{}_{1t}}{C^*} \sum_{j=2}^{6} = \alpha_1 + \delta_{1j}[R_j - R_1] + \beta_1 \ln Y,$$

$$S^*{}_{2t} = \frac{P_{2t} X^*{}_{2t}}{C^*} \sum_{\substack{j=1\\j \neq 2}}^{6} = \alpha_2 + \delta_{2j}[R_j - R_2] + \beta_2 \ln Y,$$

$$S^*{}_{3t} = \frac{P_{3t} X^*{}_{3t}}{C^*} \sum_{\substack{j=1\\j \neq 3}}^{6} = \alpha_3 + \delta_{3j}[R_j - R_3] + \beta_3 \ln Y,$$

$$S^*{}_{4t} = \frac{P_{4t} X^*{}_{4t}}{C^*} \sum_{\substack{j=1\\j \neq 4}}^{6} = \alpha_4 + \delta_{4j}[R_j - R_4] + \beta_4 \ln Y,$$

$$S^*{}_{5t} = \frac{P_{5t} X^*{}_{5t}}{C^*} \sum_{\substack{j=1\\j \neq 5}}^{6} = \alpha_5 + \delta_{5j}[R_j - R_5] + \beta_5 \ln Y,$$

where, recall, symmetry determines that $\delta_{ij} = \delta_{ji}$

2.2.4   Disequilibrium—The Dynamics of Adjustment

Up to this point, the discussion has been presented primarily in the context of a comparative statics model. The system of equations in (2)

18. As will be discussed below, the method of estimating the parameters assures that these estimates are invariant to the equation deleted.

19. The coefficients for the sixth share equation are determined as follows:

$$\alpha_6 = 1 - (\alpha_1 + \alpha_2 + \alpha_3 + \alpha_4 + \alpha_5); \; \delta_{i6} = -(\delta_{i1} + \delta_{i2}$$
$$+ \delta_{i3} + \delta_{i4} + \delta_{i5}) \; i = 1, \ldots, 5;$$
$$\delta_{66} = -(\delta_{16} + \delta_{26} + \delta_{36} + \delta_{46} + \delta_{56}); \; \beta_6 = -(\beta_1$$
$$+ \beta_2 + \beta_3 + \beta_4 + \beta_5).$$

and (4) describes the objective of the firm, and it contains the information necessary to chart the least-cost input expansion path. With this type of behavior as a maintained hypothesis, we can now address more clearly the dynamic manner in which the firm achieves long-run cost minimization. The point to be made here is that even when the firm can perfectly discriminate between cyclical and secular components in input prices and output, it still cannot move instantaneously from one long-run equilibrium point to another; rather, it follows a disequilibrium path along which all inputs are dynamically and interrelatedly adjusted to compensate for deficiencies between the desired and actual levels of the respective inputs. This is essentially the model formulated by Nadiri and Rosen (1973). Eisner and Strotz (1963) have provided a rationale for modeling adjustment costs in the context of a geometrically declining lag structure. The model estimated by Nadiri and Rosen is the analogue to (1) in log form,

$$(13) \qquad \ln X_t - \ln X_{t-1} = \beta[\ln X^*_t(Y;P) - \ln X_{t-1}] + e_t,$$

with the following important exceptions: first, Nadiri and Rosen (1973) assume first-order serial correlation in the individual equation disturbance term but do not allow for cross equation correlation of disturbances; this is directly opposite to the hypothesis maintained in (1);[20] second, $X^*(Y;P)$ is based on a very restrictive Cobb-Douglas formulation of productive technology where it is assumed that inputs are strongly separable;[21] third, Nadiri and Rosen take as a maintained hypothesis that technology is Hicks-neutral but estimate a model which does not support this hypothesis.

The estimation model used in this study is the direct analogue to (1) in share form,

$$(14) \qquad \Delta S_t = \theta[S^*_t(Y;P) - S_{t-1}] + \epsilon_t,$$

20. This difference in stochastic specification is especially important when there are cross equation parameter restrictions. This is the case in system (13) and as well as in (14) below. Nadiri and Rosen neglect to impose any cross equation equality restrictions on their parameters and then proceed to estimate the parameters for the system using a Cochrane-Orcutt single equation estimation technique, thereby causing overidentification of the parameters determining X^*_{it} in (13). To eliminate this problem (13) should have been estimated by a simultaneous estimation procedure, such as was used to estimate (15) (see section 2.4.2 below), in which the covariance matrix was taken into account. Nadiri and Rosen (1973, pp. 56–58) decide against this procedure and as a result destroy much of the meaning and consistency in their theoretical model.

21. Nadiri and Rosen's empirical results do not support a Cobb-Douglas specification since their derived estimates of both long and short-run elasticities of substitution differ measurably from one and in fact are close to zero. Nadiri and Rosen suggest that this is due to the fact that they do not constrain their model to the production frontier (Nadiri and Rosen 1973, p. 56).

where ΔS_t is a (6×1) vector of quarterly first differences in the six cost shares; $S^*_t(Y;P) - S_{t-1}$ is a (6×1) vector of first differences between the six minimum cost shares and lagged actual cost shares where the components of $S^*(Y;P)$ are as in (12) above; θ is a (6×6) matrix of own and cross partial adjustment coefficients; and ϵ_t is a (6×6) vector of disturbances assumed to have the same stochastic properties as U_t in (1) except that $\Sigma \epsilon_{it} = 0$ $(t = 1, \ldots, n)$ because of the adding-up condition discussed below.[22]

The system in (14) contains only five independent equations for reasons analogous to those for the system in (4), i.e., the adding-up condition holds for actual shares as well as for long-run or cost-minimizing shares. Thus, analogous to (10), we have

22. The system of equations set out in (14) can be written

(i) $$S_t = \theta S^*_t + \phi S_{t-1} + \epsilon_t,$$

where

$$\phi = I - \theta.$$

By process of repeated substitution into (i), it can be shown that (i) can be written

(ii) $$S_t = \phi^{K+1} S_{t-K-1} + \sum_{\lambda=0}^{K} M_\lambda S^*_{t-\lambda} + \sum_{\lambda=0}^{K} \phi^\lambda \epsilon_{t-\lambda},$$

where $M_\lambda = \phi^\lambda \theta$. Now, as K goes to infinity, (ii) reduces to

(iii) $$S_t = \sum_{\lambda=0}^{\infty} M_\lambda S^*_{t-\lambda} + \phi^\lambda \epsilon_{t-\lambda},$$

provided

$$\lim_{\lambda \to \infty} \phi^\lambda = 0.$$

Specification (iii) is known as the final form of (ii). It can be shown that (iii) is stable provided the eigenvalues of the ϕ matrix are all less than one in absolute value (Theil 1971, p. 464). If this condition is met, the following results hold for a constant level of Y_t, and P_t:

(iv) $$\sum_{\lambda=0}^{\infty} M_\lambda S^*_t = \theta[I + \phi + \phi^2 + \ldots + \phi^n] S^*_t,$$

and since $\phi = I - \theta$, we have

$$\sum_{\lambda=0}^{\infty} M_\lambda S^*_t = S^*_t,$$

and

(v) $$E(\Sigma \phi^\lambda \epsilon_{t-\lambda}) = E(\epsilon_t) + \phi E(\epsilon_{t-1})$$
$$+ \phi^2 E(\epsilon_{t-2}) + \ldots + \phi^n E(\epsilon_{t-n}) = 0,$$

since we have assumed $E(\epsilon_{t-\lambda}) = 0$ for all λ. Therefore, the expected value of the set of factor cost shares in the long run is

(vi) $$E(S_t) = S^*_t.$$

(15) $$\sum_{i=1}^{6} S_{it} = \frac{\Sigma P_i X_i}{C} = 1,$$

where C_t is the cost identity computed as in (7). This implies that

$$\sum_{i=1}^{6} \epsilon_{it} = 0 \ (t = 1, \ldots, n)$$

and that $E(\epsilon_t \epsilon'_t)$ is singular for all t. However, as shown by Berndt and Savin (1975), invariant maximum-likelihood estimates of the parameters in (14) can be obtained by arbitrarily deleting any one of the six equations. As before, the materials cost share equation is arbitrarily dropped since its coefficients are contained either implicitly or explicitly in the remaining five equations.[23]

Combining equation (15) with (10), we obtain in matrix form the following system of five independent equations:

(16) $$\Delta S'_t = T[S^{*'}_t \ (Y;P) - S'_{t-1}]$$

$$+ \ \epsilon'_t \qquad (t = 1, \ldots, n),$$

where $\Delta S'_t$, S'_t, S'_{t-1}, and ϵ'_t are defined as in equation (15) after netting out the sixth equation, and the elements of T, namely, T_{ij} $(i, j = 1, \ldots, 5)$ are defined as the composite coefficients $\theta_{ik} - \theta_{ij}$ $(i, k = 1, \ldots, 5)$.

System (16) makes explicit the following points: first, the system of equations involving S_1, S_2, S_3, S_4, S_5, and S_6 constitutes a singular system by virtue of equation (15); second, adjustment to long-run equilibrium is interrelated[24] in all inputs X_1 through X_6, and third, the system of equations involving the long-run equilibrium paths of S^*_1, S^*_2, S^*_3, S^*_4, S^*_5, and S^*_6 also constitutes a singular system by virtue of (10).

Finally, the reader should be aware that individual own and cross adjustment coefficients, θ_{ii} and θ_{ij}, cannot be obtained from a knowledge

23. The long-run equilibrium coefficients can be separately identified by the relationships set out under equations (2) and (12) above. However, the individual adjustment coefficients can be obtained for (14) only under certain conditions, as will be explained below.

24. The reader should be aware of the importance of the cross adjustment coefficients in model (14). Disregarding the cross effects would imply, for example, that a disequilibrium in equipment stock did not involve compensating adjustments in other inputs. Brainard and Tobin (1968) have described the type of system in (17) as a "general disequilibrium" framework for the dynamics of adjustment to a "general equilibrium system." Moreover, for production theory Nadiri and Rosen (1973) observed that a system of unrelated adjustment paths implies that the firm is off its production function, i.e., is using inputs inefficiently. While from a theoretical point of view, we see no reason to constrain output to the production frontier during the adjustment process, we also do not see any virtue in ignoring the obvious interrelationships that exist between inputs in disequilibrium as well as equilibrium.

of the composite coefficients, $\theta_{ij} - \theta_{i6}$. The only constraints put on the adjustment coefficients in a singular system involving cost shares is[25]

$$(17) \qquad \sum_{i=1}^{n} \theta_{ij} = R \qquad (j = 1, \ldots, n).$$

However, due to (15) we can only identify the composite effects $\theta_{ij} - \theta_{i6}$ $(i, j = 1, \ldots, 5$, and (17) assures that

$$\sum_{i=1}^{6} \theta_{ij} - \sum_{i=1}^{6} \theta_{i6} = 0 \qquad (j = 1, \ldots, 5).$$

Therefore, we can identify $\theta_{6i} - \theta_{66}$ $(j = 1, \ldots, 5)$ but we have no information to identify any of the individual elements θ_{ij}.[26] This, however, does not prevent us from reaching our goal, which is to estimate adjustment-free parameters for S^*_i $(i = 1, \ldots, 6)$.

2.2.5 An Alternative View of the Adjustment Process

It may be argued that the variables in (2) are observed prices and output, and that the firm is not likely to undertake major decisions on the makeup of its capital, materials, and employment stock inputs on the basis of current levels of these variables.[27] Rather, since the firm operates in an atmosphere of uncertainty, it views the array of observed input prices and output demand as consisting of a permanent and a

25. To see this, observe that (15) and (16) give

$$\sum_{i=1}^{6} S_{it} = \sum_{i=1}^{6} \sum_{j=1}^{6} \theta_{ij}[S_{jt} - S_{jt} - 1] - \sum_{i=1}^{6} S_{it} - 1.$$

Therefore, since

$$\sum_{i=1}^{6} S_{it} = 1$$

and

$$\sum_{i=1}^{6} S_{it} = 1,$$

it is necessary that $\Sigma\theta_{i1} = R$; $\Sigma\theta_{i2} = R$; $\Sigma\theta_{i3} = R$; $\Sigma\theta_{i4} = R$; $\Sigma\theta_{i5} = R$; $\Sigma\theta_{i6} = R$.

26. A sufficient condition for identifying the θ_{ij} $(i,j, = 1, \ldots, 6)$ when

$$\sum_{i=1}^{6} \theta_{ij} = R \qquad (j = 1, \ldots, 6)$$

is that

$$\sum_{j=1}^{6} \theta_{ji} = R_i \qquad (i = 1, \ldots, 6).$$

For a general discussion of identification of parameters in singular systems, see Berndt and Savin (1975).

27. This position has been taken by Birch and Siebert (1975).

transitory[28] component, that is, $Y_t = Y^P{}_t + Y^T{}_t$, and $P_t = P^P{}_t + P^T{}_t$. In this scenario, the entrepreneur is likely to be very reluctant to undertake input stock investments, disinvestments, or reorganizations based on the levels of variables until he feels certain that there has been a permanent change in the levels of these variables.

The firm is also likely to make short-term adjustments in its flow variables (hours and utilization) to accommodate cyclical shocks in demand but less likely to do so in the case of cyclical shocks in prices. This suggests that the long-run expansion path would be composed primarily of stock variable adjustments and the short-run expansion path primarily of flow variable adjustments. This process can be illustrated with the aid of figure 2.1. Suppose at initial time $t = 0$ the firm is in equilibrium, producing output level Y_0 at the minimum cost input combination specified by point $A(L^P{}_0, K^P{}_0)$. Now, if output demand increases in period $t = 1$ to Y_1, the firm might satisfy this demand with alternative input combinations depending on (1) its ability to adjust inputs rapidly, (2) its perception of the permanency of Y_1, and (3) the cost of making adjustments which might be wrong. Thus, if Y_1 is viewed as a permanent increase in output, the firm will aspire to move along its long-run (minimum-cost) expansion path to point $B(L^P{}_1, K^P{}_1)$. On the labor side, this expansion will largely involve increasing employment, E_t, with little change in average straight-time hours, HRS_t, and possibly a decrease or total elimination in overtime hours, HRO_t, per employee.

However, if the firm views Y_1 as only a transitory or cyclical change, then it might satisfy this demand in a short-run cost minimization sense by moving to point $C(L^P{}_1, K^P{}_0)$. That is, the firm will attempt to satisfy Y_1 by using an efficient combination of inputs, defined as any input combination on Y_1 to the left of B, but, recognizing that mistakes might be costly, it chooses not to use the long-run combination which would require an expansion of capital stock. If Y_1 turned out to be transitory and the firm increased capital to $K^P{}_1$, it would be forced to disinvest $(K^P{}_1 - K^P{}_0)$ in order to return to its long-run expansion path. In contrast to the situation where Y_1 is considered a permanent level of demand, the increase in labor input will come primarily from increasing overtime hours, with smaller increases likely in the employment and straight-time hours.[29]

28. The term *transitory* here is meant to include cyclical as well as purely random movements in P_t and Y_t.

29. The logic is symmetric with respect to a decline in aggregate demand. Thus, suppose the firm is initially in equilibrium at point B for output level Y_1, but output demand decreases to Y_0. If the firm views this decrease in output as a transitory or cyclical change in output, it will likely move from point B on Y_1 to point D on Y_0 primarily by reducing overtime hours.

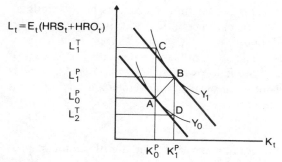

$L_t = E_t(HRS_t + HRO_t)$

L_1^T

L_1^P

L_0^P

L_2^T

K_0^P K_1^P

K_t

Fig. 2.1   Short- and Long-Run Expansion Paths

This expectational variable approach has an important conceptual[30] difference from the interrelated dynamic adjustment model of Nadiri and Rosen. This is because the Nadiri and Rosen model implies that the firm has static expectations concerning output and relative factor prices and thus expects the current level of output and price to continue. Accordingly, there is no need for the firm to discriminate between transitory and permanent components in the observed variables so that the movement from point A to point C in figure 2.1 represents a partial adjustment of all inputs (both stock and flow) toward a new equilibrium at point B, although the initial adjustment to point C is likely to impact most strongly on the flow variables.

30. The conceptual difference notwithstanding, mathematically there are strong similarities in form between the two approaches. It is shown in footnote 22 that equation (14) can be rewritten as an infinite distributed lag of current and past desired share levels:

(14a)
$$S_t = \sum_{\lambda=0}^{K} \theta[I - \theta]^\lambda S^*_{t-\lambda} + [I - \theta]^{K+1} S_{t-K} +$$
$$\sum_{\lambda=0}^{K} [I - \theta]^\lambda \epsilon_{t-\lambda}.$$

Utilizing equations (4) and (14), this can be written equivalently as

(14b)
$$S_t = \sum_{\lambda=0}^{K} \theta[I - \theta]^\lambda \begin{bmatrix} \alpha_1 & \delta_{11} & \delta_{12} \cdots \delta_{16} & \beta_1 \\ \alpha_2 & \delta_{21} & \delta_{22} \cdots \delta_{26} & \beta_2 \\ \cdots\cdots\cdots\cdots\cdots\cdots\cdots \\ \alpha_6 & \delta_{61} & \delta_{62} \cdots \delta_{66} & \beta_6 \end{bmatrix}$$
$$\begin{bmatrix} 1 \\ LnP_{1t-\lambda} \\ LnP_{2t-\lambda} \\ LnP_{6t-\lambda} \\ \cdots\cdots\cdots \\ LnY_{t-\lambda} \end{bmatrix}$$

2.3 Decomposition of Factor Demand and Labor Productivity

In section 2.2 we set forth a model that allowed us to discriminate between long-run and short-run parameters. Up to this point the analysis was developed in the context of relative cost shares; now we proceed to measure the long-run (cost-minimizing) demand for factors of production and output per production worker hour and develop a relationship between the short-term (or cyclical) movements in the observed data and these long-run measures.

2.3.1 Long-Run Demand for Factors of Production

From equation (15), the equilibrium share for the ith factor of production is

$$+[I - \theta]^{K-1}S_{t-K-1} + \sum_{\lambda=0}^{K} [I - \theta]^{\lambda}\epsilon_{t-\lambda}.$$

In vector notation (14b) becomes

(14c)
$$S_t = \sum_{\lambda=0}^{K} \theta[I - \theta]^{\lambda}\delta V_{t-\lambda} + [I - \theta]^{K+1} S_{t-K-1}$$

$$+ \sum_{\lambda=0}^{K} [I - \theta]^{\lambda}\epsilon_{t-\lambda} = \delta \sum_{\lambda=0}^{K} \theta[I - \theta]^{\lambda}V_{t-\lambda}$$

$$+ [I - \theta]^{K+1}S_{t-K-1} + \sum_{\lambda=0}^{K} [I - \theta]^{\lambda}\epsilon_{t-\lambda}.$$

The term

$$\sum_{\lambda=0}^{K} \theta[I - \theta]^{\lambda}V_{t-\lambda}$$

represents a distributed lag of current and past output prices. This leads naturally to an expectational variable interpretation such that the expectation of V_t, say $\hat{V}_t$, is

$$\hat{V}_t = \sum_{\lambda=0}^{K} \theta[I - \theta]^{\lambda}V_{t-\lambda}.$$

From this we can write (14c) as

(14d)
$$S_t = \delta\hat{V}_t + [I - \theta]^{K+1}S_{t-K-1} + \sum_{\lambda=0}^{K} [I - \theta]^{\lambda}\epsilon_{t-\lambda}.$$

Thus, while the direct estimation of (14d) would require a more elaborate generalized least-squares approach than (14), since the residuals in (14d) would definitely be autocorrelated despite the fact that individual elements in $\sum[I-\theta]^{\lambda}\epsilon_{t-\lambda}$ were assumed independent within each equation in (14), the model to be estimated in this study does implicitly contain a special case of an expectational-variable model. Preliminary attempts by the author to replace observed output and prices in (14) with permanent output and price components based on a rational expectations approach have not proved fruitful. This may suggest that the observed variables in the context of the lagged adjustment model (14) adequately represent the proper set of decision-making arguments.

$$S^*_i = \frac{P_i X^*_i}{C^*} = \alpha_i + \sum_{j=1}^{6} \delta_{ij} R_j + \beta_i \ln Y$$

$$(i = 1, \ldots, 6),$$

where C^* is defined by equation (2). It follows that the minimum-cost input of X_i is determined as

(18) $$X^*_{it} = S^*_{it} \frac{C^*_t}{P_{it}}.$$

The problem is that C^*_t is unobservable and some estimate of it must be made in order to determine X^*_{1t}.

The method used, while not perfect, is an attempt to derive an input series which eliminates most of the cyclical adjustment impact in the raw data and is therefore closer to the input set on the long-run expansion path.[31] The process consists of the following steps:

1. For each year in the sample, compute an average of quarterly inputs, factor prices, and output designated as X^A_i, P^A_i $(i = 1, \ldots, 6)$, and Y^A, respectively.

2. Use the input and price series from point (1) to construct a proxy measure for C^*_t, namely

$$\text{RTFC}^A = C^{\hat{*}A}_t = \sum_{i=1}^{6} P^A_i X^A_i.$$

3. Use the parameters estimates from (14), Y^A, P^A_i, and $C^{\hat{*}A}_i$, to form the relationship

(19) $$Z^{\hat{*}} = \alpha_{At} T + \alpha_Y \ln Y^A_t + v_t,$$

where

$$Z_t = \ln C^{\hat{*}A}_t - \sum_{i=1}^{6} \hat{\alpha}_i R^A_{it} - \frac{1}{2} \sum_{i=1}^{6} \sum_{i=1}^{6} \hat{\delta}_{ij} R^A_{it} R^A_{jt}$$

$$= \Sigma \hat{\beta}_i R^A_{it} \ln Y^A_t$$

and $R^A_i = \ln P^A_i$. Now, (19) is an approximation to (2) and α_{At}, α_Y are measures of Hicks-neutral technical progress and homothetic returns to scale, respectively. There are two obvious reasons why $Z^{\hat{*}}_t$ is likely to contain measurement error: first, because $C^{\hat{*}A}_t \neq C^{*A}_t$, and second, because estimated values of the parameters in (14) are used in place of the actual parameters. Suppose, then, that the true value, Z^*_t, is related to the measured value as

---

31. One approach we rule out directly is an estimate of C^*_t based on (7) using the actual quarterly date for P_i and X_i. We exclude this method because (1) it is a maintained hypothesis of this study that these quarterly input observations are the result of an adjustment process; and (2) the model contains no constraints to keep the firm on its production function.

(20) $Z^{\hat{*}}{}_t = Z^*{}_t + d_t,$

where d_t is the measurement error in $Z^{\hat{*}}{}_t$. Further, suppose that the true relationship which we are attempting to capture by (19) is

(21) $Z^*{}_t = \alpha_{At} T + \alpha_Y \ln Y^A{}_t + e_t,$

where e_t is the stochastic element in $Z^*{}_t$. By substituting equation (21) into (20) we see that $v_t = d_t + e_t$ in equation (19).

As long as d_t is uncorrelated with the independent variable in (19), it can be shown that the parameter estimates for α_{At} and α_Y from equations (19) and (21) have the same expected value.[32] With the estimates of α_t and α_Y from equation (19) we are now in a position to derive quarterly estimates of $C^*{}_t$ as

(22) $C^{\hat{*}}{}_t = [\,\dfrac{1}{4}\,\hat{\alpha}_{At} T + \hat{\alpha}_Y \ln Y_t + \Sigma\hat{\alpha}_i R_{it}$

$$+ \frac{1}{2} \Sigma\Sigma \hat{\delta}_{ij} R_{it} R_{jt} + \Sigma\beta_i R_i \ln Y_t].$$

The results of (22) are used in (18) to obtain $X^*{}_i$ $(i = 1, \ldots, 6)$.

2.3.2   Cyclical Effects on Factor Demand

The difference between the observed and the least-cost inputs of the ith factor of production,

(23) $DX_{it} = X_{it} - X^*{}_{it}$ $(i = 1, \ldots, n)$

constitutes a measure of the impact of short-run adjustments to changes in relative factor prices, and output. For each industry study we measure (23) at each quarter between three sets of peaks in the respective industry's output data.[33] The first interval is from the mid-1950s peak to the quarter with the highest output level in 1972. The second interval is between the mid-1950s peak and the mid-1960s peak. The third interval is from the mid-1960s peak to the 1972 peak. For each quarter in the sample, (23) is expressed as a percentage of the long-run factor input level for the quarter or

(24) $\%DX_{it} = \dfrac{X_{it} - X^*{}_{it}}{X^*} \times 100.$

32. See Rao and Miller (1971), pp. 179–84.

33. The peak quarters chosen to delineate the three intervals do not necessarily correspond to the peaks in the constant-dollar output series for each of the three periods. This is because the peak quarters chosen were made to reconcile with peaks in the utilization series. This approach to choosing the peaks was adopted because of possible errors in the construction of the gross output series.

We then sum (24) over the quarters in each of the intervals and divide by the number of quarters in each interval to obtain a measure of the average percentage deviation of short-term or cyclical adjustments from the long-run expansion path for production worker hours $(A\%DX^{p}{}_{1}{}^{-p}{}_{2})$, that is,

$$(25) \qquad A\%DX_i{}^{p}{}_1{}^{-p}{}_2 = \frac{\displaystyle\sum_{t=p_1}^{p_2} \%DX_{it}}{q_{p_1-p_2}},$$

where p_1 is the beginning peak in the interval; p_2 is the ending peak in the interval (so p_1-p_2 defines the interval); and $q_{p_1-p_2}$ is the number of quarters in the interval from p_1 to p_2.

The differential measured by equation (23) is not a measure of cyclical influence in the sense that the deviation between the actual input level and a peak-to-peak trend level of input might be considered a measure of business cycle influence. Rather, since $X^*{}_{it}$ represents the input demand resulting from an instantaneous adjustment to changes in output and price levels, its path in a period of economic instability will manifest a very cyclical character. In fact, for inputs such as plant and equipment, which have a long adjustment lag, the least-cost path is likely to show much more cyclical movement than the actual path. Nevertheless, DX_{it} does provide a measure of the extent to which changes in the economic climate affect the operating efficiency of an industry at a point in time.[34]

At any point in time, the value of DX_{it} may be the result of several influences which affect the relative speed at which a certain input can be adjusted to its least-cost level. Thus, one or more of the following factors may affect DX_{it}: (1) the underlying short-term technology in the industry;[35] (2) a change in economic conditions affecting an industry, as when a secular decline in either the growth rate or level of demand in an industry generates excess capacity which requires time to reduce; (3) the presence of institutional restraints such as labor union

34. This fact shows up very well in figs. 2.2–2.11, especially in the growth recession and absolute recession period between 1969 and 1972.

35. For example, we might expect production worker-hours and employment to adjust fairly rapidly to economic conditions. However, a basic tenet of the model described by (14) is that hours are not adjusted independently of other inputs—hours may be a short-term substitute for one input and short-term complement to another input—and the net effect of disequilibrium in the components of the input set which co-operate with production workers may in some industries substantially slow the adjustment process toward the least-cost expansion.

contracts which may prevent or at least substantially lengthen the adjustment process of actual input levels to least-cost levels; (4) the extent to which competitive pressures are strong enough to force an industry's management to adopt minimum-cost production procedures; and (5) the degree to which an industry's managers possess the skills necessary to define and organize a least-cost technology.[36]

A more long-term perspective on not only the relative ability of an industry to adjust quickly to business cycle conditions but also on the adequacy of the cost-minimization hypothesis as a characterization of the long-run behavior of an industry is provided by (25). Thus, while we would expect to see fluctuations—both positive and negative—in the value of DX_{it}, we would also expect an industry which follows a conscious policy of cost minimization to be fairly close, on the average, to the long-run expansion path. Moreover, in a sustained growth period, such as that characterized by the interval between 1961 and 1966, we would expect to find a high degree of correspondence between the actual and long-term paths with a low value for (25) relative to an unstable period such as between 1966 and 1972.

2.3.3 Labor Productivity

The long-term path of labor productivity is defined as the level of output per production worker hour on the long-run expansion path:

$$(26) \qquad P^*r_1 = Y/X^*_{1t},$$

while actual labor productivity is defined as the level of output per production worker hour on the actual expansion path:

$$(27) \qquad Pr_1 = Y/X_{1t}.$$

As before, the deviation between the observed and long-run levels ($DPr_1 = Pr_1 - P^*r_1$) is a measure of the short-term adjustment component in the observed series, and

---

36. Industry 22 offers a case where the actual and least-cost expansion paths for hours, equipment, and plant showed substantial divergence between the midfifties and mid-sixties peaks. A BLS profile of the industry published in 1966 bears heavily on points (2), (4), and (5) and states that

> interest in plant modernization is stronger now than at any time in the last 50 years. . . . The push for technological improvements is being stimulated by intensified efforts to meet foreign and interfiber competition, an improved financial position, and the emergence of larger companies with more professional experience.

See *Technological Trends in Major American Industries*, Bulletin no. 1474, Feb. 1966, p. 148.

$$(28) \qquad A\%DPr_1{}^{P_1-P_2} = \frac{\displaystyle\sum_{t=P_1}^{P_2} \%DPr_1}{q_{P_1-P_2}}$$

where $\%\ DPr_1$, defined analogously to (24), is a measure of the average percentage deviation of the cyclical adjustments from the long-run productivity expansion path. In other words, (28) is a long-term measure of the difference in the levels of output per man-hour on the actual and least-cost expansion path.

Finally, we are in a position to address the basic question of this study: What is the underlying rate of productivity growth? The hypothesis maintained is that this path is described by (26) and so the question is, What does relationship (26) for each of the ten industry sectors suggest about the growth rates of productivity from the mid fifties to the mid sixties, and from the mid sixties to the 1972 output peak? Further, how does this picture compare with the picture derived from (27)? To answer this question we divide the results from (26) and (27) for each industry into intervals determined by output peaks discussed under equation (23). For each equation we then fit a least-squares trend to each of the three intervals, taking specific note of the two shorter intervals contained within the long interval. Two points of comparison result from this process: first, we are able to contrast the levels of the rates of growth between the actual and long-run series; second, we are able to contrast changes in the rates of growth between the two short intervals for each series. Of course, the basic question is, Does the long-run path indicate a productivity slowdown?

2.3.4   Real Total Factor Cost—Actual versus Long-Run

As mentioned several times throughout this study, a primary consideration of this paper is to determine the underlying or long-term path of productivity for the purpose of discovering whether the observed slowdown in labor productivity is of cyclical or secular origin. Measuring the growth rate of labor productivity is important primarily because productivity helps to control the rise in prices. However, labor is only one of several inputs in the production process, and the rise in production costs and therefore in output prices depends on the productivity of the other co-operating inputs as well. Therefore, we calculate what may be the most important measure produced by this study, namely, the levels and rates of growth of actual and long-term real total factor cost. Actual real total factor cost, defined by (7) and repeated here, is

$$\text{RTFC} = \sum_{i=1}^{6} P_i X_i.$$

The long-run measure of RTFC is

(29) $$\text{RTFC}^* = \sum_{i=1}^{6} P_i X^*_i.$$

To compare the levels of RTFC and RTFC* we compute a measure analogous to (25) and (28), namely,

(30) $$A\%\text{RTFC}^{p_1-p_2} = \frac{\displaystyle\sum_{t=p_1}^{p_2} \%\,DRTFC_t}{q_{\overline{p}_1-p_2}},$$

where

$$\%\,DRTFC_t = \frac{\text{RTFC}_t - RTFC^*_t}{\text{RTFC}^*_t} \times 100.$$

The value of $A\%DRTFC^{\,p_1-p_2}$ indicates for the interval p_1-p_2 the average percentage amount by which RTFC exceeded RTFC*. Especially in industries where unit cost pricing prevails, this measure would be highly suggestive of how much lower the level of prices could have been if the industry could have followed its least-cost expansion path.

From the point of view of inflation, however, the critical question is how fast RTFC grows in comparison to RTFC*. To answer this question, we compute least-squares rates of growth for each of these cost measures for the three peak-to-peak intervals described previously.

2.4   Empirical Results

2.4.1   Introduction

In order to simplify the orderly presentation of the mass of statistical results generated by our research, the contents of this section are presented and generally discussed according to the broad categories of nondurable and durable goods manufacturing rather than for each of the ten sectors individually.[37] The reader is reminded at the outset that there are three main objectives in this research effort: first, to determine the "best" representation of the structure of production for each industry; second, to use this structure to estimate the long-term path of demand for factors of production and production worker productivity; third, to contrast these long-term paths with the paths of the measured or observed variables. The reader is provided with tables and charts to assist in evaluating the discussion on each of these aforementioned ob-

---

37. See note 5.

jective.[38] These tables include the following: Table 2.2 gives the F-test results for three alternative specifications of the long-term structure of production and two alternative specifications of the dynamics of adjustment. Table 2.3 gives the matrix of "best" model mean Allen partial elasticity of substitution coefficients for the years between 1957 and 1972. Table 2.4 provides the values of the "best" model Allen partials by industry for 1957, 1965, and 1972. Table 2.5 provides estimates of the "best" model Hicks-neutral technical progress and the homothetic returns to scale coefficients for each sector.[39]

Tables 2.6A–2.15A provide the contrasting measures of the least-squares rates of growth for the actual versus the long-run measures of production worker input, relative cost share, productivity, and real total factor cost. For these variables these tables also provide a measure of the average cycle effect computed according to formulas (25), (28), and (30) in each of the peak-to-peak intervals.[40] Finally, these tables also provide a measure of the average cycle effect on output for each of the peak-to-peak intervals. This effect is defined as

$$\left[\left(\sum_{t=P_1}^{P_2} \text{abs } \frac{Y_t - YTR_t}{YTR_t}\right) \Bigg/ q_{P_1 - P_2}\right] \times 100,$$

where YTR is equal to the mid-fifties peak-to-peak trend level of output, q, P_1, and P_2 are as defined in section 2.3.2, and "abs" stands for absolute value. Tables 2.6B–2.15B provide the contrasting measures of the least-squares rates of growth for the actual versus the long-run measures of nonproduction worker employment, equipment, plant, capacity utilization, and materials. For these five nonproduction worker inputs, these tables also provide a measure of the average cycle effect computed according to formula (25) for the three peak-to-peak intervals.[41]

---

38. A complete set of tables and graphs for each industry is provided in Mohr (1978). Included are the estimation results for (16) under both homothetic and nonhomothetic specifications; estimates of the Allen partial elasticities of substitution for the homothetic and nonhomothetic versions of (12); tables and graphs profiling each of the variables used in estimating (16); and a set of graphs profiling and contrasting the paths of the actual and long-run values for each of the six factors of production.

39. See discussion in section 2.3.1.

40. See discussion in section 2.3.2.

41. The method used to construct the investment price of plant helped to safeguard against unreasonable first- to fourth-quarter jumps in the level of the constructed quarterly plant investment prices. (See Data Appendix in Mohr 1978). However, it is not designed to prevent such jumps in the first difference of the constructed plant investment prices, and the first difference as well as the levels of these prices is part of the constructed rental prices of plant for each industry.

In addition to these twenty summary tables (2.6A–2.15A and 2.6B–2.15B), there are also provided for each industry four charts (parts A through D of figs. 2.2–2.11) which profile and contrast the paths of actual and long-run values for plant and equipment as well as for production worker productivity and real total factor cost.

2.4.2   Method of Estimation

The system in (16) and all variants of it discussed below were estimated on a 1956.2 to 1972.4 quarterly data set. Since we chose to interpret the translog cost function in (2) as a second-order approximation to an arbitrary twice-differential cost function, all the arguments in (16) and its variants were indexed to $1 = 1963$.

Since the system of cost share equations (14) is assumed to have not only contemporaneous cross equation correlation in the vector of error terms $(e_{1t}, e_{2t}, \ldots, e_{6t})$ for all t, but also symmetry, adding-up, and homogenity restrictions,[42] all factor share models in this study were estimated using a generalized least-squares (GLS) technique known as iterative Zellner-efficient estimation (IZEF). If the regressors are independent of the disturbances in each equation and if IZEF converges, it converges to maximum-likelihood estimation (Kmenta and Gilbert 1968). Further, Pollak and Wales (1969) have shown that maximum-likelihood estimation of *any* subset of $n-1$ independent equations in a set of n equations provides maximum-likelihood estimates of the parameters of the entire set. In particular, Berndt and Savin (1975, pp. 974–50) show that all the parameters of the established nonlinear model (16) are invariant to the equation deleted.

It may be argued that the correct estimation technique for (14) is IZEF combined with two-stage least-squares (2SLS) to form iterative three-stage least squares (I3SLS). However, in view of the massive amount of data constructed here, I3SLS seemed to be an unnecessary refinement.[43]

An inspection of the quarterly constructed plant rental price series showed a large outlier in 1956.1 which was not obvious in the constructed plant investment price data. Our original simulation with the outlier in it seriously distorted the relationship between the long-run and actual paths of plant demand. As a consequence, for all industries the mid-fifties to mid-sixties average cycle effect on plant was estimated with 1956.2 as the beginning year. Also, the plot of the actual and long-run plant demand in figs. 2.2A–2.11A always begins with 1956.2.

42. See conditions (i) and (ii) under equation (2) and equations (10) and (15).

43. Berndt and Christensen (1973b) reported that, based on a model estimated on aggregate manufacturing data, their results from IZEF and I3SLS were very similar.

2.4.3 Testing the Structure of Production

Two sets of criteria were used in deciding upon the "best" model to represent the structure of production in each industry. The first criterion is statistical and the second is theoretical. To understand how the statistical tests were constructed, consider that the model of production (14) is composed of two structures: first, the long-term or comparative static structure (12), and second, the short-term or partial adjustment structure. Each of these structures represents areas where tests of alternative theories can be conducted. The series of tests described below amounts to the imposition of parameter restrictions on the basic model (14), and as such the validity of these restrictions can be ascertained by an F-test.[44]

The maintained long-term hypothesis embodied in (14) is (12), i.e., the long-term structure of production conforms to a nonhomothetic translog cost function. Therefore, the first series of tests we wish to construct is aimed at testing widely used alternatives to (12), namely, homothetic translog and Cobb-Douglas specifications. Note that the validity of the adjustment process is being maintained in this first series of tests. Now, when the null hypothesis to (12) is homothetic translog, this amounts to constraining the five β_i parameters in (12) and (14) to zero. Further, when the null hypothesis is not only homothetic but also Cobb-Douglas, an additional fifteen zero-parameter restrictions are being imposed on δ_{ij}'s in (12) and (14). Thus, we can construct a series of nested F-tests where each successive stage in the series is conditioned on the acceptance of the null hypothesis in the preceeding stage.[45] At each stage in the series the change in the weighted sum of squared residuals from restrictions imposed at this stage is calculated, and then divided by the sum of squared residuals at the previous stage. Of course, both the numerator and denominator of this ratio are adjusted by the appropriate degrees of freedom. Accordingly, the first F-test on the long-term structure is computed as

$$F_1 = \frac{[RSS_H - RSS_{NH}]/(50-5)}{RSS_{NH}/(335-50)},$$

where the subscripts H and NH stand for homothetic and nonhomothetic, respectively; 50 is the number of free parameters in the maintained hypothesis embodied by (12) and (14); 5 is the number of zero restrictions imposed by the null hypothesis of homothetic translog; and 335 is the number of observations in the stacked regressions for all the

---

44. See Theil (1971), pp. 402–3.
45. See Christensen, Jorgenson, and Lau (1973), pp. 38–45.

models estimated in each industry. Conditional on the acceptance of homothetic translog in F_1, we then test the validity of a Cobb-Douglas specification of (12) and (14) as

$$F_2 = \frac{[RSS_{CD} - RSS_H]/(45–15)}{RSS_H/(335–45)},$$

where the subscripts CD and H refer to Cobb-Douglas and homothetic translog, respectively; 45 is the number of free parameters in the homothetic translog version of (12) and (14); and 15 is the number of additional zero restrictions which are imposed on the homothetic versions of (12) and (14) when the null hypothesis is that long-term structure of production is Cobb-Douglas. F_2 is both a test of the Nadiri-Rosen model and also a test of complete global functional separability of the factors of production.[46] The overall level of significance for this first series of tests is set at .02 and is allocated among the two stages equally, i.e., at the .01 level.

The second series of tests to be constructed bears on the short-term or partial adjustment structure of (14). In effect, the null hypothesis to be tested here is that adjustment is rapid enough to be adequately captured by a direct comparative static model. In particular, we test the null hypothesis that the model is homothetic and translog without any adjustment parameters. Except for the fact that a production function instead of a cost function is embodied in (14), the null hypothesis to be tested here is a test of the Jorgenson, Christensen, and Berndt approach to modeling the structure of production.[47] As with the first series of tests, the second can be tested in two stages. The first stage is a test of the homotheticity of the long-run structure which has already been described in F_1. Conditional on the acceptance of homotheticity, the second stage amounts to testing the validity of imposing additional zero-parameter restrictions on all twenty-five of the composite adjustment parameters, $T_{ij} = \theta_{ij} - \theta_{i6}$ ($ij = 1, \ldots, 5$), in (16). Therefore, we construct a second series of nested F-tests where the first stage has already been computed by F_1 above, and the second stage is computed as

$$F_3 = \frac{[RSS_H - RSS_{DTL}]/(45–25)}{RSS_H/(335–45)},$$

where the subscript DTL stands for direct translog and twenty-five is the number of zero restrictions which would be imposed on a homothetic translog version of (16) when the null hypothesis is that adjustment is instantaneous. As before, we set an overall level of significance at .02 and distribute it evenly between F_1 and F_3. Critical values em-

46. See Berndt and Christensen (1973*a*, *b*).
47. See Christensen, Jorgenson, and Lau (1973) and Berndt and Christensen (1973*b*, *c*). See also Berndt and Wood (1975) where a cost function is used.

ployed in our tests are given in table 2.1. The results of the F-tests for each industry are reported in table 2.2. By comparing the values of F_1, F_2, and F_3 with their respective critical values in table 2.1 we reach the following conclusions: (1) the null hypothesis of homethetic translog is accepted by F_1 at both the 1% and 2.5% significance levels in all sectors but 330 and 371; (2) the additional parameter restrictions required for the Cobb-Douglas and direct translog null hypothesis are rejected at the 1% and 2.5% levels for all sectors by F_2 and F_3, respectively.

In addition to these purely statistical criteria, two theoretical considerations were instrumental in determining the "best" structure of production for each industry. These considerations are the monotonicity and

Table 2.1   Critical Values of F (v_1, v_2)

Degrees of Freedom		Level of Significance		
			.01	.025
$V_1 = 45$ $V_2 = 285$	$F_1 \ (45,285)$	$F(40, 120)$ $F(40, \infty)$	1.76 1.59	.161 .148
$V_1 = 30$ $V_2 = 290$	$F_2 \ (30,290)$	$F(30, 120)$ $F(30, \infty)$	1.86 1.70	1.69 1.57
$V_1 = 20$ $V_2 = 290$	$F_3 \ (20,290)$	$F(20, 120)$ $F(20, \infty)$	2.03 1.88	1.82 1.71

Table 2.2   Computed F-Values by Industry Category

Industry	$F_1(45, 285)$	$F_2(30, 290)$	$F_3(20, 290)$
Nondurable Goods			
SIC 20	0.5300	24.7602	40.7589
SIC 22	0.7380	5.7674	19,1618
SIC 26	0.1488	15.8936	21.4285
SIC 28	0.5948	15.4192	63.4757
SIC 30	1.1098	7.9747	24.0836
Durable Goods			
SIC 32	0.1601	8.4502	26.8025
SIC 330	2.9790	17.9297	17.2086
SIC 333	1.2932	6.1363	58.3244
SIC 35	1.1501	9.6322	58.2023
SIC 371	3.6695	9.2421	29.5406

SOURCE: *Biometrika Tables for Statisticians,* vol. 1, ed. by E.S. Pearson and H.O. Hartley (Cambridge: Cambridge University Press, 1954), pp. 160–61.

concavity conditions described in section 2.2.2. The monotonicity condition was tested for both the homothetic and nonhomothetic versions of (14) for all industries. Only the homothetic version of SIC 22 failed to satisfy this condition.

As pointed out in section 2.2.2, concavity requires that H be negative semidefinite. However, it can be shown that an equivalent condition is that σ be negative semidefinite, where σ is the symmetric matrix of Allen partial elasticities of substitution (AES). When all $\sigma_{ij} < 0$ ($i \neq j$), a necessary condition for σ to be negative semidefinite is that all of the own AES (σ_{ii}) < 0.[48]

This necessary condition for concavity was most closely met in the data for industries 330 and 371 in homothetic form. It will also be noted by studying tables 2.3 and 2.4 that the durable goods industries come much closer to satisfying this condition than the nondurable sectors. Also, the more variation existing in the output data, the more closely this condition is satisfied; SIC 20 with the least amount of output variation constitutes the major exception. (Compare the results of tables 2.3 and 2.4 with the measure of output variation in tables 2.6A–2.15A.)

While the inequality condition on σ_{ii} is not explicitly met for most of the industries, it is still possible that this condition is satisfied provided that the own substitution parameters, δ_{ii}, in (4) are not statistically different from zero since the own AES's are defined as

$$\sigma_{ii} = \frac{1}{S^{*2}_i} (\delta_{ii} + S^{*2}_i - S^*_i) \qquad (i = 1, \ldots, 6),$$

where S^*_i are the long-run cost shares defined by (4). Therefore, if $\delta_{ii} = 0$, $\sigma_{ii} = 1 - (S_i/S^{*2}_i)$, where $S^*_i/S^{*2}_i > 1$, so that $\sigma_{ii} < 0$. Now, the δ_{ii} are not computed directly, but residually, as

$$\delta_{ii} = \sum_{\substack{j=1 \\ i \neq j}}^{n} \delta_{ij} \qquad (i = 1, \ldots, 6),$$

so that δ_{ii} is a linear combination of the δ_{ij} ($i \neq j$). Therefore, the variance of δ_{ii} can be expressed as

$$V(\delta_{ii}) = b'V (\delta_{ij})\, b \qquad (i = j; i = 1, \ldots, 6),$$

where b is a (5×1) unit vector and $V (\delta_{ij})$ is the (5×5) variance-covariance matrix for the five δ_{ij} used to compute δ_{ii}. Unfortunately, the software necessary to compute $V(\delta_{ij})$ was not available so no test of significance on the δ_{ii} could be calculated. However, an inspection of

---

48. If this condition is satisfied, it follows from (8b) that the derived demand curve for the inputs is downward-sloping since by (8b) $\sigma_{ii} > 0$ if and only if $\partial X_i/\partial P_i > 0$, i.e., if and only if the demand curve is upward-sloping.

the t-statistics indicated that, based just on the variance components of $V(\delta_{ij})$, we could often conclude that the δ_{ii} are not significant.[49]

The theoretical considerations formed the overriding criteria in deciding on the "best" long-term structure, so that, for instance, in SIC 26 where the results of F_1 supported the null hypothesis of homotheticity, the null hypothesis was rejected by the theoretical criteria.

In summary, the results of the F-test and theoretical criteria combined led to the following conclusions: first, in all cases the Cobb-Douglas and instantaneous adjustment hypotheses were overwhelmingly rejected by the results of F_2 and F_3; second, homothetic translog was accepted in all industries except 330 and 371 by the results of F_1; third, when the theoretical criteria are considered, homotheticity is accepted for all industries but 22 and 26. Finally, the reader will notice from tables 2.3 and 2.4 that all inputs are substitutes in the long-run even though the signs on the adjustment parameters (not shown here) indicated that some inputs are short-term complements.[50]

2.4.4 Estimating Hicks-Neutral and Homothetic Scale Parameters

Estimates of Hicks-neutral technical progress[51] (total factor productivity) and homothetic returns to scale[52] are OLS estimates based on a

---

49. Simulation analysis conducted by Wales (1976) brings out a very important point: even though the data are the result of an optimization process—utility-maximization or cost-minimization—the translog model parameters may fail to satisfy the required regularity conditions and thus fail to verify that the underlying model, which assumes such behavior, is an accurate description of the economic conduct of the agents in question (in this study, the firms in the ten selected industries). However, Wales's results show that the translog share equation generally fitted the data very well, as measured by the R^2 or by the divergence between the true and estimated price elasticity, even when the curvature conditions were violated. These two facts imply that the parameters of the estimated function are probably not far from their true values. Furthermore, since our cross Allen partial estimates were much closer to 1 than zero, Wales's results point toward improvement in raw source data and/or methods of data construction as a possible key to satisfying the curvature condition for cost-minimization, i.e., negatively signed σ_{ii}. Some candidates for data improvement are discussed in section 2.5.

50. The reader will recall from the discussion in section 2.2.4 that the adjustment parameters estimated here are composite parameters. Therefore, we are not capable of identifying with certainty either the magnitude or sign of the individual adjustment coefficients, although reasonable conjectures about the signs can be made more easily than about magnitude. A negative sign on a θ_{ij} indicates that input i is a short-term complement to input j, while a positive sign indicates i is a short-term substitute for j.

51. When interpreting the Hicks-neutral coefficient in tables 2B and 3B, the reader should bear in mind that a cost function and not a production function was used to obtain these estimates. Therefore, a negative sign on the coefficient

1956–72 annual sample (see table 2.5). The results of these latter estimations must be viewed with some caution since (19) is estimated with prior parameter restrictions, for example, those from the share equations in (14); also, the constant term is maintained to be zero in (19), and Z^* is assumed to be an adequate proxy for Z^* in (19). In the case of industry 22 one or more of these prior constraints seems to be overly restrictive as is evidenced by the fact that $R^2 = -7.36$ for the specification represented by (19). The inclusion of a constant term for this industry noticeably improved the fit but rendered the Hicks-neutral term positive and insignificant and the homothetic scale term negative and insignificant. The former result is inconsistent with the extraordinarily high rate of labor productivity growth in sector 22 (4.44% between 1956.1 and 1972.3). The latter result implied that marginal cost in SIC 22 was negative.[53]

---

indicates positive technical progress, the reverse being true for a positive-signed coefficient.

52. Long-run returns to scale in an industry can be defined by the shape of the long-run average cost curve, C^*/Y. Returns to scale are increasing, constant, or decreasing, according to $\partial(C^*/Y)/ \leq 0$. An equivalent result is obtained when $(1 - \partial \ln C^*/\partial \ln Y) \leq 0$, where $\ln C^*$ is defined by (2). In general, the long-run cost function can be written as $C^* = H(Y)G(P;Y)$ or $\ln C^* = \ln H(Y) + \ln G(P;Y)$, where $\ln H(Y)$ describes the homothetic returns-to-scale relationship. However, in this study we use the term homothetic in a restricted sense, i.e., we have restricted $\ln H(Y)$ in (2) in such a way that $\partial \ln C^*/\partial \ln Y = \partial \ln H(Y)/\partial \ln Y = \alpha_Y$, a constant. Thus, $\ln H(Y)$ has been restricted to the class of homogeneous functions in this study, but has not been restricted to being linear homogeneous where $\alpha_Y = 1$.

53. A well-behaved cost function must exhibit positive marginal cost in the relevant range. Long-run marginal cost is defined as dC^*/dY, and from (2) it follows that

$$\frac{dC^*}{dY} \frac{C^*}{Y} = \frac{d\ln C^*}{d\ln Y} = \alpha_Y + \Sigma \beta_i \ln P_i,$$

or that

$$\frac{dC^*}{dY} = [\alpha_Y + \Sigma \beta_i \ln P_i] \, Y/C^*.$$

Therefore, for the nonhomotheic case,
$$dC/dY > 0$$

implies

$$\alpha_Y + \Sigma \beta \ln P_i > 0,$$

since Y/C^* is by definition positive for positive values of Y. Since $\Sigma \beta_i \ln P_i < 0$ in SIC 22, a negative sign on α_Y assures violation of the positivity condition. Again, if (2) is homothetic, then

$$\frac{dC^*}{dY} = \alpha_Y \, Y/C^*$$

and $dC^*/dY > 0$ if and only if $\alpha_Y > 0$.

For the remaining industries, the Durbin-Watson (DW) statistic is low, but DW is not a valid indicator of serial correlation when the constant term is excluded from the regression. When (19) was estimated using iterative Cochran-Orcutt, the parameter values were not noticeably affected, but their significance was greatly reduced. In addition, when (19) was estimated with a constant term, the uniform result was that the technical progress parameter became negative, and quite often insignificant, while all improvement over time in unit cost became the result of positive economies of scale. By contrast, the use of (19) directly gives a much more plausible result: only sectors 330, 35, and 371 show increasing returns to scale. Since these three industries experienced much lower operating rates than the other seven sectors during the 1956–72 period (see note 62), it is reasonable to suspect that the observed data pertain to operations in the increasing returns-to-scale range of the long-run average cost curve. In summary, the estimates of the homothetic scale parameters from specification (19) suggest that industries SIC 22, SIC 26, SIC 28, SIC 30, SIC 32, and SIC 333 are characterized by decreasing returns to scale, industries SIC 35, SIC 330, and SIC 371 are characterized by increasing returns to scale, while industry SIC 20 exhibits constant returns to scale. The technical progress parameters in table 2.5 also form a reasonable pattern. The industries rank in the following order: SIC 28, SIC 22, SIC 26, SIC 30, SIC 32, SIC 371, SIC 333, SIC 20, SIC 330, SIC 35. This ranking is roughly equivalent to that based on the rate of actual labor productivity growth in tables 2.6A–2.15A;[54] the major exceptions are SIC 20 and 35, which rank fourth and fifth, respectively, among the ten industries in the rate of growth of labor productivity.

On balance, in spite of the cautions, the consistent use of specification (19) to estimate the Hicks-neutral and returns-to-scale parameters for each industry not only has resulted in reasonable estimates for the sectors individually but also has facilitated comparisons of these parameters among the sectors. In this respect, table 2.5 brings to light an interesting dichotomy in the long-term structure of production between the nondurable and durable goods–producing industries. The former are characterized by high rates of growth in technical progress (except for SIC 20) and decreasing returns to scale (except for SIC 20). By contrast, three out of the five durable goods industries (SIC 35, 330, and 371) showed increasing returns to scale, and only SIC 32 showed

54. The industry ranking of the growth rates in actual output per actual production hour between the mid-fifties and 1972 peaks is as fcllows: SIC 28, SIC 22, SIC 26, SIC 20, SIC 35, SIC 371, SIC 30, SIC 32, SIC 333, SIC 330. The rank correlation coefficient between the Hicks-neutral and labor productivity rates is .61. Excluding sectors 20 and 35 from the list of sectors results in a rank correlation coefficient of .93.

decreasing returns to scale comparable to that found in the nondurable sectors. Only two durable goods–producing industries (SIC 32 and 371) showed significant rates of increase in total factor productivity growth, but in each case the growth was substantially smaller than that of any nondurable goods sectors except SIC 20.

2.4.5   Patterns in the Long-Run Structure of Production, Output, and Productivity

In this section we use the information in tables 2.3, 2.4 and 2.5 to examine patterns in the "best" model long-term structure of production.[55] Also, as a prelude to examining the contribution of the business cycle to the slowdown in productivity growth after the mid sixties, we discuss the major patterns found in the measured data on output and productivity in tables 2.6A–2.15A. Because of space limitations, the discussion will generally be in terms of the two broad classes of manufacturing—nondurable and durable goods manufacturing.[56]

Patterns in the Structure of Production

First, in the recent production-theory literature, several authors have raised questions concerning the validity of the standard value-added approach to estimating the structure of production.[57] In the light of this controversy, all models estimated in this study are based on a gross-output concept of production. This approach is superior to a value-added approach for analyzing the determinant of factor demand and factor productivity over time unless at least one of the following conditions is satisfied:[58] (1) the ratio of materials to gross output (X_6/Y) is always constant over time; (2) the ratio of the price of materials to the price of output (P_6/P_Y) is always constant over time; (3) the in-

55. As pointed out in section 2.2.4, model (14) lacks sufficient restrictions to identify the individual short-term adjustment parameters. A heuristic approach to identifying the sign and magnitude of the θ_{ij}'s in (14) from a knowledge of the T_{ij}'s in (16) is given in Mohr (1978), but no discussion of the short-term structure of production is attempted here.

56. A detailed discussion of each of the ten industries is given in Mohr (1978).

57. See, for instance, Parks (1971), Diewert (1973), and Berndt and Woods (1975).

58. Berndt and Wood (1975) employ a four-factor, gross output, translog cost function to analyze factor demand in U.S. manufacturing for the period 1947–71. The four factors include the following: labor, capital, materials, and energy. Under the assumption that the production function is linear homogenous, Berndt and Wood test to see if any of the three sufficient conditions for validating a value-added approach to production theory and factor demand are met. They state not only that none of these conditions are met by the annual data for U.S. manufacturing in the 1947–71 period, but also that "we must call into question the reliability of investment and factor demand studies for United States manufacturing based on the value added specification."

puts X_1, X_2, X_3, X_4, and X_5 are weakly separable from X_6, implying that $\sigma_{16} = \sigma_{26} = \sigma_{36} = \sigma_{46} = \sigma_{56}$; also, if condition (1) stems from the technological nonsubstitutability of X_6, then, $\sigma_{16} = \sigma_{26} = \sigma_{36} = \sigma_{46} = \sigma_{56} = \sigma_{66} = 0$. While no formal tests of the presence of any of these three conditions were undertaken, there is evidence that none of them is met in any sector for the sample period 1956.2–1972.4. First, in the process of constructing the materials measure described in the appendix, it became apparent that the ratio X_6/Y was not constant; second, the process of constructing the output and materials price deflators indicated that the ratio P_6/P_Y also was not constant; third, an inspection of "best" model Allen partials for each industry (see tables 2.3 and 2.4) suggests that the equalities set out under condition (3) are not satisfied between 1957 and 1972. Thus, exclusion of materials from the mix of simultaneously determined inputs is likely to eliminate an important source of factor substitution. For example, process-saving advances in the quality and in the degree of fabrication of the materials supplied by the chemical and plastic industries to the auto industry have enabled the latter to substitute the capital, labor, and technology of the former for their counterparts in the auto industry.

Second, an inspection of tables 2.3 and 2.4 shows that, for all ten industries, our "best" model results suggest that all inputs are long-term substitutes regardless of their short-term relationships. The sixth and twelfth columns of table 2.3 give the unweighted averages of the elasticity of substitution coefficients for the five nondurable goods sectors and for the five durable goods sectors for the period 1957 to 1972. Comparing these numbers with a 1959–71 average of the substitution coefficients in Berndt and Wood (1975, table 4, p. 264) for all manufacturing, we discover that our numbers compare very well for the capital-labor coefficients. Berndt and Wood estimate a 1959–71 average σ_{KL} of 1.01, while we estimate a 1957–72 average $\sigma^{ND}_{13} = 1.06$, $\sigma^{ND}_{14} = .98$, $\sigma^{ND}_{23} = 1.01$, $\sigma^{ND}_{24} = .98$, $\sigma^D_{13} = .99$, $\sigma^D_{14} = .95$, $\sigma^D_{23} = .89$, $\sigma^D_{24} = .96$.[59] For the elasticity of substitution between labor and materials, we estimate a $\sigma^{ND}_{16} = .78$, $\sigma^{ND}_{26} = .83$, $\sigma^D_{16} = .91$, $\sigma^D_{26} = 1.04$. Thus, Berndt and Wood's estimate of $\sigma_{LM} = .60$ corresponds much more closely to what we find on the average in nondurable manufacturing and in particular to the σ_{16} for production workers and mate-

---

59. $\sigma_{ij} = \mathrm{AES}_{ij}$ in tables 2.3 and 2.4 and $\sigma^{ND}_{ij} =$ the unweighted average of the AES_{ij} for the five nondurable sectors shown in table 2.3, while σ^D_{ij} is the counterpart for the five durable sectors. Also, while Berndt and Wood's model uses an aggregate capital input K (plant plus equipment) and an aggregate labor input L (production plus nonproduction worker-hours), the present study uses plant and equipment and production and nonproduction worker inputs as separate factors. Thus, the σ_{KL} of Berndt and Wood must be compared with our σ_{13}, σ_{23}, σ_{14}, and σ_{24} in both durable and nondurable emanufacturing (see note 12).

Table 2.3   Mean Values of "Best" Model Long-Run Allen Partials for 1957 to 1972

Own-and Cross-Allen Partials	Nondurable Goods Industries						Durable Goods Industries					
	SIC 20 (1)	SIC 22 (2)	SIC 26 (3)	SIC 28 (4)	SIC 30 (5)	Unweighted Avg. of 5 Ind. (6)	SIC 32 (7)	SIC 330 (8)	SIC 333 (9)	SIC 35 (10)	SIC 371 (11)	Unweighted Avg. of 5 Ind. (12)
AES11	−19.267	11.822	−.442	11.240	16.777	4.026	1.504	−5.272	.827	3.948	−4.922	−.783
AES12	1.010	.993	.945	1.002	.973	.985	1.003	.998	.998	1.000	.939	.987
AES13	1.142	.993	.997	1.129	1.037	1.060	1.012	1.020	.917	1.036	.973	.992
AES14	.996	.954	.992	.956	.988	.977	.940	.895	.991	.995	.950	.954
AES15	.814	.682	.844	.780	.815	.787	.753	.881	.939	.864	.929	.873
AES16	1.019	.613	.931	.817	.507	.777	.932	.977	.999	.742	.910	.912
AES22	29.018	4.566	−7.333	−.430	8.406	6.846	.044	.773	−9.046	−5.027	1.417	−2.367
AES23	.962	.963	1.000	1.119	.989	1.007	1.032	.899	.842	.834	.856	.893
AES24	.974	.984	.973	.977	.994	.980	.987	.843	.987	.973	.993	.957
AES25	.862	1.019	.890	.847	.955	.915	.817	1.055	.958	1.039	.984	.971
AES26	.490	.986	.843	.855	.995	.834	.891	.987	1.121	1.240	.965	1.041
AES33	−8.647	−1.097	.417	1.116	.217	−1.599	.646	−3.311	−1.920	−10.288	−5.526	−4.080
AES34	.975	.968	.976	1.023	.914	.971	1.009	.843	.969	.744	.823	.878
AES35	1.060	.960	.926	.903	.959	.962	.944	1.094	.993	1.163	1.005	1.040
AES36	.973	.916	.849	.740	.889	.873	.762	.890	.972	1.092	.950	.933
AES44	.857	5.892	.790	2.166	6.781	3.297	.147	.863	5.470	4.871	−3.042	.632
AES45	.995	.990	.993	.985	1.001	.993	.988	.965	.996	1.009	.939	.979
AES46	.997	.987	.995	.990	1.000	.994	.982	1.044	.998	1.012	.999	1.007
AES55	−2.801	−1.182	−1.026	−.304	−1.131	−1.289	−.847	−2.368	−3.006	−3.771	−4.250	−2.849
AES56	.891	1.031	1.008	1.043	1.094	1.014	1.061	.894	.847	.768	.828	.880
AES66	−.173	.389	−.209	1.612	.651	.454	.846	−1.493	.624	2.593	.810	.934

Table 2.4A **"Best" Model Long-Run Allen Partials for 1957, 1965, and 1972**

A. Nondurable Goods Industries

Own-and Cross-Allen Partials	SIC 20			SIC 22			SIC 26			SIC 28			SIC 30		
	1957	1965	1972	1957	1965	1972	1957	1965	1972	1957	1965	1972	1957	1965	1972
AES11	−15.812	−19.204	−27.412	19.270	9.233	−1.812	−1.543	−1.218	0.732	7.571	6.399	20.302	16.157	12.350	17.941
AES12	1.006	1.011	1.013	0.992	0.992	0.993	1.007	1.008	1.008	1.002	1.002	1.002	0.973	0.974	0.975
AES13	1.090	1.135	1.223	1.058	1.047	1.060	0.998	0.998	0.997	1.119	1.102	1.162	1.032	1.030	1.043
AES14	0.997	0.997	0.994	1.016	1.014	1.020	0.994	0.993	0.990	0.957	0.966	0.942	0.990	0.991	0.985
AES15	0.841	0.829	0.754	0.638	0.727	0.665	0.890	0.861	0.796	0.828	0.812	0.696	0.841	0.845	0.776
AES16	1.017	1.019	1.023	0.457	0.644	0.676	0.931	0.934	0.930	0.821	0.820	0.806	0.425	0.543	0.586
AES22	61.086	16.024	20.663	5.845	4.638	3.256	−8.148	−8.091	−6.078	−1.498	−1.661	1.826	7.205	5.921	11.741
AES23	0.961	0.968	0.956	0.966	0.965	0.960	1.050	1.055	1.075	1.113	1.101	1.140	0.990	0.990	0.986
AES24	0.968	0.980	0.972	0.987	0.985	0.980	0.977	0.978	0.966	0.977	0.981	0.972	0.995	0.995	0.992
AES25	0.817	0.893	0.873	1.080	1.079	1.085	0.916	0.900	0.859	0.877	0.862	0.803	0.962	0.960	0.942
AES26	0.277	0.554	0.560	0.983	0.985	0.988	0.833	0.850	0.848	0.857	0.852	0.859	0.994	0.995	0.995
AES33	−11.808	8.567	6.338	−0.953	−1.072	−1.163	0.746	0.500	0.203	0.991	1.457	0.952	0.517	0.349	−0.113
AES34	0.979	0.974	0.974	0.965	0.968	0.972	1.036	1.040	1.036	1.021	1.023	1.022	0.913	0.905	0.921
AES35	1.046	1.064	1.073	1.021	1.022	1.023	0.922	0.930	0.931	0.886	0.910	0.912	0.958	0.960	0.960
AES36	0.981	0.975	0.966	0.939	0.925	0.894	0.888	0.864	0.815	0.753	0.789	0.685	0.918	0.903	0.847
AES44	2.001	1.857	1.011	13.184	7.233	1.607	1.718	2.307	−0.863	1.113	3.541	1.029	10.818	12.294	0.525
AES45	0.996	0.995	0.995	0.991	0.990	0.988	0.992	0.994	0.993	0.981	0.986	0.986	1.000	1.000	1.000
AES46	0.997	0.997	0.996	0.991	0.989	0.982	0.996	0.996	0.994	0.990	0.992	0.988	1.000	1.000	1.001
AES55	−2.806	−2.955	−2.778	−1.171	−1.176	−1.208	−0.895	−1.059	−1.073	−0.087	−0.319	−0.451	−1.026	−1.147	−1.224
AES56	0.884	0.878	0.899	1.114	1.099	1.074	1.095	1.071	1.051	1.051	1.047	1.031	1.122	1.099	1.062
AES66	−0.141	−0.157	−0.197	0.194	0.311	0.632	−0.307	−0.271	−0.092	1.232	1.059	2.466	0.320	0.498	1.257

Table 2.4B   "Best" Model Long-Run Allen Partials for 1957, 1965, and 1972

B. Durable Goods Industries

Own-and Cross-Allen Partials	SIC 32			SIC 330			SIC 333			SIC 35			SIC 371		
	1957	1965	1972	1957	1965	1972	1957	1965	1972	1957	1965	1972	1957	1965	1972
AES11	0.640	1.024	1.613	−5.370	−5.317	−5.172	−0.029	−0.312	2.040	3.059	2.541	6.382	−4.906	−4.922	−4.874
AES12	1.002	1.002	1.003	0.998	0.998	0.998	0.998	0.998	0.998	1.000	1.000	0.999	1.001	1.001	1.001
AES13	1.012	1.011	1.013	1.075	1.076	1.097	0.928	0.930	0.900	1.028	1.030	1.051	0.967	0.975	0.976
AES14	1.002	1.002	1.002	0.893	0.898	0.883	0.993	0.993	0.988	0.996	0.996	0.993	1.012	1.012	1.014
AES15	0.788	0.764	0.749	0.888	0.886	0.866	0.948	0.949	0.924	0.878	0.886	0.829	0.922	0.929	0.933
AES16	0.940	0.931	0.935	1.039	1.039	1.045	0.999	0.999	0.999	0.730	0.767	0.732	0.899	0.912	0.919
AES22	−1.448	−0.657	−0.494	1.530	1.067	9.808	−9.442	−9.692	−9.391	−5.122	−5.005	−5.047	11.715	0.934	1.640
AES23	1.031	1.029	1.031	0.903	0.902	0.874	0.856	0.861	0.833	0.856	0.850	0.801	0.801	0.864	0.861
AES24	0.987	0.988	0.985	0.828	0.838	0.812	0.989	0.989	0.985	0.975	0.977	0.968	0.992	0.993	0.991
AES25	0.838	0.822	0.820	1.118	1.119	1.140	1.018	1.018	1.023	1.038	1.035	1.041	0.980	0.984	0.984
AES26	0.901	0.888	0.900	1.053	1.052	1.059	1.190	1.179	1.163	1.274	1.229	1.207	1.036	1.028	1.027
AES33	0.515	0.789	0.614	−3.523	−3.452	−3.068	−1.979	−1.977	−1.837	−13.395	−10.831	−7.231	−4.930	−5.834	−5.870
AES34	1.010	1.009	1.008	0.862	0.851	0.835	0.967	0.968	0.972	0.763	0.730	0.744	0.782	0.828	0.868
AES35	0.938	0.947	0.943	1.150	1.149	1.164	1.057	1.055	1.054	1.140	1.161	1.184	1.074	1.063	1.063
AES36	0.745	0.788	0.743	0.900	0.898	0.885	0.975	0.974	0.966	1.069	1.086	1.128	1.014	1.012	1.013
AES44	−0.114	0.558	−0.869	−0.985	−0.905	−0.890	9.418	7.932	1.133	−4.290	−4.380	−5.570	−1.002	−3.020	−5.421
AES45	0.987	0.988	0.986	0.963	0.966	0.966	0.996	0.996	0.996	1.008	1.008	1.010	1.001	1.001	1.002
AES46	0.981	0.984	0.978	1.110	1.104	1.107	0.998	0.998	0.997	1.010	1.011	1.017	0.999	0.999	0.999
AES55	−0.849	−0.848	−0.847	−2.395	−2.329	−2.317	−3.186	−3.130	−2.702	−3.823	−3.892	−3.431	−4.263	−4.132	−4.154
AES56	1.062	1.065	1.057	0.891	0.893	0.897	0.828	0.835	0.879	0.742	0.761	0.817	0.826	0.832	0.837
AES66	0.965	0.580	1.145	−1.500	−1.499	−1.511	−0.565	−0.587	−0.718	−2.171	−2.534	−3.210	−0.788	−0.802	−0.854

Table 2.5   **Estimates of Hicks–Neutral and Homothetic Scale Parameters by Industry Category***

Industry	Total Factor Productivity	Homothetic Returns to Scale
	Nondurable Goods	
SIC 20	− 0.0023	0.9890
	(− 2.1746)	(910.3445)
SIC 22	− 0.0623	1.3006
	(−20.8986)	(355.2507)
SIC 26	− 0.0424	1.4835
	(−19.4785)	(559.6018)
SIC 28	− 0.0746	1.7448
	(−30.5885)	(633.2446)
SIC 30	− 0.0290	1.2490
	(−10.3674)	(342.6716)
	Durable Goods	
SIC 32	− 0.0232	1.4314
	(− 9.3291)	(454.5437)
SIC 330	0.0025	0.7501
	(1.3791)	(351.1755)
SIC 333	− 0.0033	1.0718
	(− 0.9962)	(261.5576)
SIC 35	0.0039	0.7505
	(4.0806)	(709.7000)
SIC 371	− 0.0161	0.9112
	(−10.3424)	(522.9985)

*Numbers in parentheses are T-statistics.

rials. However, with respect to the relationship between capital and materials, Berndt and Wood's estimates are substantially lower than ours, and the fact that Berndt and Wood separate energy from materials and find that energy and capital are complements does not help to explain this difference. In any event, both studies find materials and capital to be substitutes with Berndt and Wood's results giving a 1959–71 average $\sigma_{KM} = .54$ while we estimate a 1957–72 average $\sigma^{ND}_{36} = .87$, $\sigma^{ND}_{46} = .99$, $\sigma^{D}_{36} = .93$, $\sigma^{D}_{46} = 1.01$. Berndt and Wood's finding of 1959–71 average $\sigma_{KE} = -3.3$ suggests that our estimates of the relationships between capital and materials should be lower than theirs, not higher. In another context Berndt and Christensen (1974) find that nonproduction workers and capital are complements, while our results do not. We question, then, whether the complementarity found by Berndt and Wood between capital and energy and the complementarity found by Berndt and Christensen between capital and nonproduction workers is the result of misspecification bias, i.e., results from using a model which applies that adjustment is instantaneous. We earlier overwhelmingly rejected such a model in each of the ten sectors.[60]

Third, a closer look at the patterns in the elasticity of substitution coefficients in table 2.3 shows that, in both nondurable and durable goods manufacturing, equipment is more substitutable for the services of production workers than any other input. We also discover that, while they are substitutes for both labor inputs, materials and capacity utilization in both manufacturing aggregates are more complementary with the input of production workers than with the input of nonproduction workers. Also, in both manufacturing sectors, the use rate of capital is strongly substitutable for increases in the stocks of both types of capital, and materials are more substitutable for plant than for equipment.

Comparing patterns between the two aggregate manufacturing sectors, we see the following differences (see sixth and twelfth columns of table 2.3): $\sigma^{ND}_{13} > \sigma^{D}_{13}$ by 6.9%, $\sigma^{ND}_{23} > \sigma^{D}_{23}$ by 12.7%, $\sigma^{ND}_{34} > \sigma^{D}_{34}$ by 10.7%, $\sigma^{ND}_{56} > \sigma^{D}_{56}$ by 15.2%; while $\sigma^{D}_{15} > \sigma^{ND}_{15}$ by 10.9%, $\sigma^{D}_{25} > \sigma^{ND}_{25}$ by 6.1%, $\sigma^{D}_{26} > \sigma^{ND}_{26}$ by 24.8%, $\sigma^{D}_{35} > \sigma^{ND}_{35}$ by 8.1%, and $\sigma^{D}_{36} > \sigma^{ND}_{36}$ by 6.8%. In short, durable goods manufacturing shows significantly greater opportunities than nondurable goods manufacturing to substitute materials and increases in the use rate of capital for inputs of production workers and equipment, while nondurable goods manufacturing shows substantially greater ability to replace the services of both types of labor as well as plant with the services of equipment.

Fourth, tables 2.4A and 2.4B show that all inputs are not only long-run substitutes in each sector but are also relatively stable ones. On an industry-by-industry basis the following 1957–72 trends emerge from tables 2.4A and 2.4B (more detailed tables support these results):[61]

SIC 20—Nonproduction workers, equipment, and materials show an increasing degree of substitutability for production worker hours, while capacity utilization shows a decreasing ability to be substituted for hours of production workers. Utilization has become more substitutable for nonproduction workers and equipment, while materials have become more (less) substitutable for nonproduction workers (equipment).

SIC 22—Materials have become increasingly substitutable for both labor inputs and less substitutable for plant, equipment, and capacity

---

60. These complementarities may also be the result of aggregation bias since, in both the Berndt and Wood and Berndt and Christensen studies, aggregate manufacturing data are used, while this study uses disaggregate manufacturing data.

61. For a discussion of the forces behind these trends in each of the ten sectors, see Mohr (1978, pp. 76–299).

utilization, with the latter relationships possibly reflecting an increasing degree of complementarity between the energy component of materials and capital goods.

SIC 26—Utilization has become decreasingly substitutable for production worker hours, nonproduction workers, and materials, while nonproduction workers have become less (more) substitutable for equipment (materials).

SIC 28—Equipment has become more substitutable for production worker hours and nonproduction worker employment and less substitutable for materials; capacity utilization has become a decreasing substitute for production worker hours, nonproduction worker employment, and materials; materials have become less substitutable for production worker hours.

SIC 30—Materials are a relatively weak but increasing substitute for production workers and a relatively strong but decreasing substitute for equipment and utilization; capacity utilization is a strong but decreasing substitute for the services of production and nonproduction workers.

SIC 32—Capacity utilization has become a decreasing substitute for the services of production and nonproduction workers.

SIC 330—Equipment has become an increasing (decreasing) substitute for production worker hours (nonproduction workers); plant and equipment have become decreasing substitutes. The ability to substitute materials for plant decreased between 1957 and 1964–65 but rose from 1964 to 1972.

SIC 333—The coefficients AES13, AES15, AES23, AES24, AES25, AES36, and AES56 were all fairly constant between 1957 and 1964–65, but AES13, AES15, AES23, AES24, and AES36 decreased between 1964–65 and 1972, while AES25 and AES56 increased.

SIC 35—Equipment has become more (less) substitutable for production workers hours (nonproduction workers); materials have become more substitutable for equipment, plant, and capacity utilization; capacity utilization has become less substitutable for the hours of production workers.

SIC 371—The ability to substitute equipment plant and materials for production worker services has increased; capital use rates and equipment have become less substitutable. The level of substitutability between capital use rates and materials has increased.

The most obvious general characteristic in terms of trend for both durable and nondurable manufacturing sectors is the decreasing ability to substitute capacity utilization for production worker hour. However, upon closer inspection, a more meaningful pattern emerges: the ability to substitute increases in the use rate of capital for both types of labor inputs shows an abrupt decrease in the 1965–72 period relative to the

1957–65 period—only the textile and auto industries (SIC 22 and 371) deviate from this pattern. This result is consistent with the fact that the average operating rates in each of the ten sectors is substantially higher in the post-1965 period than in the pre-1965 period.[62] The general state of capital underutilization during the pre-1965 period relative to the post-1965 period is reflected in figures 2.2A–2.11A and 2.2B–2.11B, where it is seen that the least-cost expansion paths for the stocks of plant and equipment in most industries are often below their corresponding actual paths in the pre-1965 period. The post-1965 period shows a very different pattern. In particular, the period between 1965.1 and 1969.3, which is the last half of the long economic expansion that began in 1961, shows strong evidence of a capital shortage developing in pulp and paper, chemicals, rubber and plastics, iron and steel, and nonferrous metals—all basic materials–producing industries. In short, after 1965 the ability of the manufacturing sector as a whole to utilize more efficiently the inputs of production workers through higher operating rates rather than increases in the co-operating stocks of capital has diminished relative to the pre-1965 period.

By way of contrast, table 2.4A shows that between 1957 and 1972 the ability to substitute materials for capacity utilization has been declining in the nondurable goods sectors (SIC 20 is the only exception), while table 2.4B shows that in durable goods manufacturing this ability has been increasing since 1957 (SIC 32 is the only exception).

Finally, as mentioned in section 2.4.4, four out of the five nondurable goods industries show decreasing returns to scale coupled with high rates of technical progress, while the five durable goods sectors show much lower rates of technical progress, with three of the five sectors showing increasing returns to scale (see table 2.5).

It is evident, then, that continued productivity growth in nondurable goods sectors depends greatly on developing and implementing cost-saving innovations; otherwise, sustained output growth will lead to reduced productivity growth. In durable goods manufacturing, on the other hand, the outlook for future improvement in the rate of labor productivity growth depends more on economies of scale than on technological progress—a prolonged period of sustained output growth should increase the rate of productivity growth.

Patterns in the Growth of Output and Production Worker Productivity

An inspection of the peak-to-peak output growth rates in tables 2.6A–2.15A shows that on average the nondurable goods sectors en-

---

62. The 1955–56 (1966–72) average operating rates by industry are as follows: SIC 20—.903 (.954); SIC 22—.853 (.942); SIC 26—.846 (.952); SIC 28—.837 (.944); SIC 30—.816 (.923); SIC 32—.925 (.921); SIC 330—.820 (.879); SIC 333—.834 (.911); SIC 35—.770 (.870); SIC 371—.800 (.849).

joyed substantially higher rates of growth than did the durable goods sectors. The unweighted average of the mid-fifties to mid-sixties growth rates of the five nondurable sectors was 4.93% versus 3.90% for the five durable goods sectors. In the mid-sixties to 1972 interval the corresponding numbers were 3.63% for nondurables and 0.40% for durables. Thus, the average rate of output growth fell by 26% in nondurables but more than triple that—89%—in durables. Much of this discrepancy in output growth rates can be explained by the greater sensitivity of the durable goods industries to business cycle conditions. As shown in tables 2.6A–2.15A, with the exception of stone, clay, and glass (SIC 32), the average absolute percentage deviation of output from its mid-fifties to 1972 peak-to-peak trend level in durable goods manufacturing is about twice that in nondurable goods manufacturing in both peak-to-peak subintervals. Finally, while each of the ten industries studied experienced a slowdown in output growth after the mid-sixties, the industries most affected were iron and steel (a 282% drop in growth rate); nonferrous metals (a 113% drop in growth rate); nonelectrical machinery (an 80% drop in growth rate); autos (a 46% drop in growth rate). Since these are all capital goods–related industries, a clear picture emerges of the extent to which business cycle conditions in the era after the mid sixties eroded incentives in the business community to expand stocks of plant and equipment.

Tables 2.6A–2.15A also show that the growth rates of production worker productivity were also generally higher in nondurable than durable goods manufacturing in each of the peak-to-peak intervals. The unweighted average of the productivity growth rates in the five nondurable goods industries was 4.26 and 3.23% in the respective peak-to-peak intervals versus 3.05 and 1.87% in the five durable goods industries. Thus, the rate of productivity growth fell by 24% in nondurables and 39% in durables. This large discrepancy in the rate of decline of productivity growth between the two broad classes of manufacturing is consistent with our earlier finding on technical progress and returns-to-scale patterns within the two manufacturing sectors. Thus, productivity in nondurable goods, with its high rates of technical progress and decreasing returns to scale, would be less affected by cyclical slowdowns than durable goods where technical progress has been occurring at a much lower rate and where returns to scale are increasing in three out of the five industries. Finally, as opposed to the pattern in output growth, where all ten industries experienced a decline after the mid-sixties output peak, only eight of the ten industries experienced a decline in the rate of growth in output per production worker hour (see tables 2.6A–2.15A). SIC 26 and 35 managed to maintain their pre–mid-sixties rate of growth. The slowdown in the productivity growth rate was most pronounced in SIC 330 (a drop of 75%) and SIC 333 (a drop of 74%).

Before proceeding to analyze the contribution of business cycle conditions on the slowdown in production worker productivity, it is important to note that a close inspection of the output paths in each of the ten sectors studied shows that the interval between the mid-fifties and mid-sixties peaks contained a long period of sustained output growth, usually between 1961 and 1966.[63] In contrast, the period following the mid-sixties peak is marked by a very depressed and erratic output pattern. In fact, the overall economy experienced a growth recession in 1967 and 1969, and an absolute recession in 1970. As will be discussed, the effects of this concentrated instability played a major role in the productivity slowdown after the mid sixties.

2.4.6 Factor Demand, Factor Productivity, and the Business Cycle

Having described the broad outlines in the productivity of the actual (measured) input of production workers, we now investigate in detail the impact of the business cycle on the efficiency of resource use in general and production worker productivity in particular. To do this we use the estimated parameters for (14) and (19) which, according to the hypothesis maintained in this study, describe the long-run structure of production. The object of our endeavors is to use this information to simulate the least-cost path of the six inputs, production worker productivity, and long-run real total factor costs. These simulations show what the factor use levels, productivity, and total factor cost would have been net of the short-term or lagged adjustment process. By comparing these simulated paths to the actual paths of the respective variables, we obtain a clearer picture of the impact of business cycle conditions, as they are manifested through the lagged adjustment process, on the efficiency of resource use. Our analysis here is based on the discussion in section 2.3 with specific reference to formulas (18), (26), and (29), which are used to simulate the long-run or least-cost path of the variables indicated above, and formulas (25), (28), and (30), which are used to compute the average cycle effects on each of these least-cost measures between the mid-fifties to mid-sixties, and the mid-sixties to 1972 output peaks. The results of our analysis for each industry are summarized in tables 2.6A–2.15A and 2.6B–2.15B.

Actual versus Long-Run Factor Demand and Factor Efficiency

An inspection of the average cycle effects on inputs in tables 2.6A–2.15A and 2.6B–2.15B provides the first bit of evidence that the productivity slowdown is due to cyclical rather than secular causes. These tables clearly show a general pattern of decline in the efficiency of resource use in the post–mid-sixties period relative to the pre–mid-

63. See Mohr (1978); especially Chart 6 for each industry.

sixties period. For example, the average percentage by which the actual
levels of inputs exceed their least-cost levels shows a consistent tendency
to be larger in the period following the mid-sixties output peak. The
only exceptions to this pattern are in SIC 20, SIC 22, and SIC 330.[64]
The explanation of the contrast in efficiency of resource use between

64. The failure of the three industries (SIC 20, 22, and 330) to follow the
general pattern is due to special circumstances which affected these industries in
the pre–mid-sixties period. For two of the sectors—SIC 20 and 22—these circumstances are very similar—namely, both sectors were involved in major programs
to modernize, close, and replace outmoded plants and equipment during the
period between the mid-fifties and mid-sixties output peaks. (See *Technological
Trends in Major American Industries*, BLS Bulletin 1974, Feb. 1966, pp. 114–140,
148–154.) The obsolete state of capital in the food and textile industries is manifested by the following: in 1957 SIC 20 ranked fourth and SIC 22 ranked third
among the ten sectors studied in the proportion of their plant stock which was
over ten years old in 1957, while ranking second and first, respectively, in the
proportion of their equipment stock more than five years old in 1957. The average
cycle effects in tables 2.6 and 2.7 for SIC 20 and 22 indicate substantial discrepancies between the least-cost and actual input expansion paths during the pre–mid-
sixties adjustment process. Tables 2.6 and 2.7 also indicate that in the post–mid-
sixties period, with the long period of adjustment behind, the correspondence
between the least-cost and actual input expansion paths has improved markedly.
In short, the mid-fifties to mid-sixties average cycle effects on inputs in SIC 20
and 22 are not measures of the impact of short-term output fluctuations on the
efficiency of resource use but rather are measures of the degree to which the input
mixes of these industries have historically been in disequilibrium vis-à-vis a least-
cost mix during this period. Since the magnitude of this disequilibrium and the
period of adjustment were so extensive, they dwarf the truer measures of business
cycle effects on the efficiency of resource use captured in the interval between the
mid-sixties and 1972 output peaks. As a final point, SIC 20 differs from SIC 22
in the fact that, even though it shows substantial divergence on the average between the least-cost and actual levels of the individual inputs in the pre–mid-
sixties period, it nevertheless was able to achieve a level of real total factor cost
which was on the average close to the least-cost level (see average cycle effect on
real total factor cost in tables 2.6 and 2.7). The industry was able to achieve this
result because the isoquants for several pairs of inputs on the industry's long-run
production surface are flat relative to those of other industries, thereby allowing
for a wider range of near least-cost input combinations. For example, a comparison of the "best" model Allen partials for production workers in each industry
(see tables 2.3 and 2.4) indicates that the food industry shows a higher ability
to substitute nonproduction workers and equipment for production workers than
any other industry. Also, it can substitute materials for production workers to a
greater extent than any other sector but steel. Finally, it ranks fourth among the
ten sectors in its ability to substitute plant for production workers, and ranks first
among the nondurable industries in its ability to substitute equipment stocks for
increases in the use rate of capital inputs. The evidence from table 2.6 is that the
industry took advantage of this flexibility and heavily substituted the other inputs
for production workers, with the plant-to-hours ratio showing the least rate of
growth between 1956.1 and 1964.2. This flexibility also explains the food industry's ability to operate with an actual input of production-worker hours that

the two subperiods is directly linked to the 1961–66 period of stable output growth referred to in the previous section. That is, it was this prolonged period of stable growth which allowed the respective industries time to adjust their input mixes to the least-cost input combination. By inspecting figures 2.2D–2.11D, one can see that most industries experienced a considerable amount of cyclical influences in 1956, 1958, 1960, 1967, and in the period between 1969.3 and 1972.4. Thus, the decade of the 1960s is bracketed at both ends by periods of considerable instability. Figures 2.2D–2.11D show that in every industry, real total factor cost exceeded long-run real factor cost for the most of the interval spanned by each of these strong business cycle periods. In addition, figures 2.2D–2.11D also show a clear pattern of convergence between the long-run and actual cost paths beginning after the 1960 recession and continuing through 1969.3, with a major interruption being induced by the growth recession period of 1967. The impressions provided by figures 2.2D–2.11D are also supported by an inspection of the average cycle effects on real total factor cost in tables 2.6A–2.15A. In every sector but SIC 22, 26, and 330 the average percentage by which actual cost exceeded long-run cost was larger in the period after the mid-sixties output peak. In summary, the time profiles of the actual and long-run real total factor cost paths give strong evidence that not only was the overall efficiency of resource use (productivity) substantially improved by the stability of output growth between 1961 and

---

averaged 12.13% less than the corresponding least-cost levels during the interval between 1956.1 and 1964.2. While the pattern of the average cycle effects in the steel industry (SIC 330) is similar to that found in SIC 20 and SIC 22, there are two very important differences: first, the size of these effects is of a much smaller order of magnitude. In fact, the steel industry operates very close on the average to a least-cost expansion path in both peak-to-peak subintervals as indicated by the size of the average cycle effects of real total factor cost in table 2.12B; secondly, the reason that the pre–mid-sixties average cycle effects on inputs exceed the post–mid-sixties effects is of a quite different origin. The primary reason is that the magnitude and frequency of output fluctuations induced by the business cycles spanning 1956.4–1959.2 and 1960.1–1961.3 as well as the strike activity of 1956 and 1959.3 and .4 were very severe relative to anything experienced by the industry in the interval between 1961.3 and 1972.4 (see fig. 2.8D). Accordingly, figs. 2.8C and D show that, in the relatively stable growth period between 1961.3 and 1965.4, the correspondence between the least-cost and measured variables is much closer on the average than correspondence which exists in the more unstable periods before and after the interval between 1961.3 and 1965.4. Thus, in contrast to sectors 20 and 22, it was business cycle–type conditions which were responsible for the pre–mid-sixties average cycle effect on inputs being larger than the post–mid-sixties average cycle effects. Furthermore, had the output fluctuations between 1956.2 and 1961.3 been less severe, the pattern of average cycle effects on input usage in SIC 330 would have followed the pattern exhibited by the other seven industrial sectors.

1969.3, but also that the period experiencing the major benefit of this stable growth was the period before the mid-sixties output peaks. By way of contrast between the efficiency of resource use in durable and nondurables, tables 2.6A–2.15A show that, except for SIC 20, the industries showing the greatest correspondence between their least-cost and actual expansion paths are all durable goods industries. Except for the interval between 1966.3 and 1972.4 in SIC 333, the average percentage deviation between actual and long-run total factor cost never exceeds 2% in any durable goods industry or in SIC 20, and only occasionally exceeds 1%. On the other hand, the average percentage deviation between the actual and long-run total factor costs in non-durables (excluding SIC 20) exceeds 2% in all but two instances— the 1966.3–1972.4 interval in SIC 26 and the 1955.4–1966.1 interval in SIC 30. Finally, in the context of a unit cost pricing policy, a direct assessment of the inflationary impact of being off the long-run or least-cost expansion path can be gained by comparing the rates at which cost increased on the long-run path to the corresponding rates on the actual path (see tables 2.6A–2.15A). The results of such an analysis indicate that in all ten sectors prices and costs on the least-cost expansion path would have risen at a slower rate than on the actual expansion path in the interval from the mid sixties to 1972. Furthermore, in sectors 22, 26, 28, 30, 330, and 333, the difference is substantial—greater than one percentage point. Conversely, during the mid-fifties to mid-sixties interval, the rate of increase of total factor cost on the long-run expansion path exceeded the rate on the actual expansion path in every industry but SIC 22 and 26. However, only in sectors 30 and 333 was the difference in rates more than one percentage point. We conclude, for the manufacturing sector as a whole, that the concentration of business cycle forces in the post–mid-sixties era caused (1) a reduction in the efficiency of resource use; (2) a higher level of prices and costs; (3) a higher rate of increase in prices and costs.

Actual versus Long-Run Production Worker Productivity

Having concluded that the productivity of the mix of co-operating inputs declined after the mid sixties because of business cycle effects, we now investigate the contribution of the business cycle to the post–mid-sixties decline in the rate of production worker productivity. As indicated earlier, this decline is observed in all sectors but SIC 26 and 35. By contrast, tables 2.6A–2.15A show that on the long-run expansion path, the rate of productivity growth declines in only two sectors —SIC 32 and SIC 371—but in both cases the decline is very small, especially in relation to the decline manifested on the actual expansion path. A more detailed chronology of the movements in production worker productivity is provided by figures 2.2C–2.11C. By comparing the movements in the actual and long-run paths in these figures, we see that, consistent with our earlier findings on the productivity of the overall mix of resources, the level of productivity per production worker hour is higher on the long-run path in both the highly cyclical periods bracketing the period between 1961 and 1969.3. SIC 20, for reasons explained earlier, is the only industry which deviates from this general pattern. Figures 2.2C–2.11C and tables 2.6A–2.15A also show that in general the correspondence between the actual and long-run levels of productivity is much greater in the period before the mid-sixties peak than in the period after, which again highlights the contribution of the 1961–66 stable growth period to least-cost production. As expected from our earlier discussion, SIC 20 and 22 do not follow this pattern. Another pattern made apparent by figures 2.2C–2.11C and generally comfirmed by tables 2.6A–2.15A is that the rate of growth of production worker productivity was generally faster on the long-run than on the actual expansion path throughout the post–mid-sixties period. The only exceptions to this pattern from tables 2.6A–2.15A are SIC 30, 35, and 371. However, figures 2.6C, 2.10C, and 2.11C for these three sectors clearly show that the long-term rate of growth exceeded the actual rate of growth for most of this period. Conversely, tables 2.6A–2.15A show that the rate of growth of productivity was higher in every industry on the actual expansion path in the period between the mid-fifties and mid-sixties output peaks. However, this phenomenon is easily explained by the fact that the level of productivity falls noticeably during a business downturn on the actual expansion path but not on the least-cost path. In fact, for those industries experiencing decreasing returns to scale there is a general tendency for the level of productivity on the least-cost path to move above the trend level. In summary, since the level of productivity on the least-cost productivity path is higher than on the actual path during the heavy business cycle period between 1956 and 1961, the least-squares growth rate of productivity is less on the long-run path during the mid-fifties to mid-sixties interval.

Of course, the reason that the levels of least-cost productivity exceed the corresponding actual levels during periods of heavy business cycle activity is that the least-cost path reflects the instantaneous-adjustment property of the long-run model (14). Thus, when the relative prices of production worker services and/or output change there is an immediate response in the labor input to the new least-cost position. Conversely, actual or observed productivity reflects the lags in adjusting labor input to the new equilibrium. The extent to which the business cycle affects the convergence of the short-run adjustment path to the long-run equilibrium path is clearly highlighted by the average cycle effects in production worker hours in tables 2.6A–2.15A. For example, except for

SIC 20, 22, and 330, the average percentage amount by which the actual level of production worker hours exceeds the desired levels is higher in all sectors in the interval between the mid-sixties and 1972 output peaks.

In summary, the input demand patterns generated by our long-term model, which filters out the effects of the lagged adjustment process to business cycle conditions, results in a dramatically different description of the underlying long-term productivity growth rate than the description obtained by fitting a least-squares trend line to the measured productivity data. For example, the averages of the least-squares growth rates from the actual data on nondurable and durable goods manufacturing in the two peak-to-peak subintervals are 4.26 and 3.23% for nondurables and 3.05 and 1.87 for durables. In strong contrast, the corresponding least-squares growth rates from the data simulated by our long-term model give 2.28 and 3.97% for nondurables, and 1.75 and 2.33% for durables. We conclude that, net of business cycle conditions after 1966, the rate of productivity growth in manufacturing would not have slowed.

2.5 Summary and Conclusions

2.5.1 Structure of Production

In this study we have attempted to model simultaneously the long-term structure and the lagged adjustment or short-term structure of production of ten manufacturing sectors to gauge the effect of cyclical fluctuations on factor demand and factor productivity, particularly production worker productivity. The models specified and tested in each industry were based on a gross output concept of production and assume that firms in these industries attempt to minimize costs in the long run.

The F test (F_3) results shown in section 2.4 strongly indicate that the short-term or interrelated partial-adjustment structure of the model significantly contributes to the explanation of variation in the input cost shares over time. This suggests that the adjustment factor embodied in the quarterly data is strong, and that the quarterly data are especially unsuitable for the comparative static approach implied by a direct modeling of the long-term cost share equations.

It also suggests that specification and/or aggregation bias might be the source of three characteristics found in several annual time series studies in manufacturing: (1) the complementarity found by Berndt and Christensen (1973c, 1974) between capital and white collar workers; (2) the complementarity found by Berndt and Wood (1975) and Hudson and Jorgenson (1974) between capital and energy inputs; (3) the presence of serially correlated residuals reported by Berndt and Christensen (1974) and Berndt and Wood (1975).[65] In contrast to these studies, our "best" model results for all ten industries indicate that all inputs are long-term substitutes regardless of their short-term relationships. If such a result is sustained when the materials component, X_6, is disaggregated into energy and nonenergy components, it could have profound implications for forecasting future energy needs. We also obtained substantial improvement in the Durbin-Watson statistics upon those reported in the above studies.

F test (F_2) results presented in section 2.4 also lead us to reject a Cobb-Douglas formulation of the long-term structure of production as a null hypothesis to a homothetic translog formulation. Finally, additional F tests (F_1) shown in section 4 indicated acceptance of a homothetic translog formulation of (12) and (14) as a null hypothesis to a nonhomothetic formulation in all but two sectors—SIC 330 and 371. Based on our assumption that the data in each industry are the result of long-run cost-minimization process, this purely statistical basis for choosing between the homothetic and nonhomothetic versions of (12) and (14) was conditional on the fact that the version so chosen also more closely satisfied the theoretical criteria for a well-behaved translog cost function, namely, strict positivity of the fitted share equations and concavity of the function in input prices. With these theoretical considerations forming the overriding criteria, the homothetic version of (12) and (14) was chosen as the "best" model of the structure of production in eight of the industrial sectors, with the nonhomothetic version being selected as "best" only for sectors 22 and 26.

It is disappointing that the necessary condition for the concavity of the cost function in factor prices, i.e., negatively signed own Allen partials, was not explicitly satisfied by the data in most industries. However, a detailed inspection of the significance of the β_{ij} coefficients for those inputs which have $\sigma_{ii} > 0$ in each industry suggests that the β_{ii} in these cases are not significantly different from zero, and therefore that the affected σ_{ii} are not significantly different from being less than zero. Further refinements in the data may prove fruitful in strengthening the results derived from the basic model in (14). The price deflators for new investment in plant and equipment and the quarterly earnings series for nonproduction workers deserve special consideration. New quarterly data constructed by BEA back to 1958 should significantly improve the investment and rental prices of capital series, but there was not time for these data to be incorporated in the present study.

65. Neither Berndt and Christensen (1973c) nor Hudson and Jorgenson (1974) report Durbin-Watson statistics. See note 9 concerning evidence of autocorrelation in the Berndt and Wood study.

The large mid-fifties to mid-sixties disparity between the long-run and actual input expansion paths in industries 20 and 22 suggests that the maintained hypothesis (that there exists a set of constant short-term adjustment coefficients) may be inappropriate for these two sectors in the interval 1956.2 to 1972.4. Available information indicates that industries 20 and 22 were making large-scale adjustments to changing technology and/or output demand during the mid fifties to mid sixties. Thus, it is quite likely that the ensuing mid-sixties to 1972 period was characterized by a substantially different short-term adjustment structure from that which characterized the earlier period. Future research should test for this possibility.

While the foregoing discussion indicates a number of areas for improvement, time and financial considerations precluded further refinement of the statistical conclusions presented in this paper. Considering the amount of constructed data (all variables except X_1, X_2, and P_1 were the product of extensive transformation of raw data sources), the quality of the empirical results generated by the basic model (14) suggests that it is a promising vehicle for the following types of research: (1) discriminating between long-run and short-run movements in factor demand and factor productivity; (2) measuring the impact of business cycle conditions on the efficiency of factor use; (3) estimating the future course of long-run factor demand and factor productivity.

2.5.2 Productivity

The evidence overwhelmingly indicates that the labor productivity slowdown in manufacturing after the mid sixties was the result of cyclical rather than secular forces. Further, had output demand after the mid sixties been less erratic and had firms been able to plan and adjust their input mixes for more stable output growth, the levels as well as the growth rates in costs and prices for manufactured goods would have been noticeably lower than their actual levels during the interval from the mid sixties to 1972.

Moreover, in the light of the dichotomy found in the measures of the rates of growth of technical progress and returns to scale obtained for nondurable and durable goods manufacturing, it is evident that continued productivity growth in nondurable goods sectors depends greatly on developing and implementing cost-saving innovations; otherwise, sustained output growth coupled with decreasing returns to scale will lead to reduced productivity growth. In durable goods manufacturing, on the other hand, the outlook for future improvement in the rate of labor productivity growth depends more on economies of scale than on technological progress; therefore, a prolonged period of sustained output growth should increase the rate of productivity growth.

2.5.3   Capital Shortages

The capital shortages problem was discussed only peripherally in this study. Our results, while tentative, are suggestive. The five sectors showing the strongest evidence of a capital shortage include paper, chemicals, rubber and plastics, iron and steel, and nonferrous metals—industries which process basic materials for the rest of the manufacturing. Bottlenecks in the supply of these materials are often considered contributory to the very high rates of inflation in 1973–1975 shown by the three major price indices—the wholesale price index, the consumer price index, and the GNP deflator.

In ascertaining whether a shortage of plant and/or equipment existed in an industry, it is generally necessary to compare the least-cost and actual paths of plant and equipment demand prior to 1969 when the rate of growth in GNP began to fall (in the fourth quarter of 1969, the level of GNP also fell). In particular, the contraction phase of the 1970 recession began in 1969.3, and the incomplete 1971–72 expansion began in 1970.4. An inspection of figures 2.2A–2.11A shows that during the 1969–72 period the actual levels of plant and equipment were above their least-cost levels, for the most part. However, when one compares the least-cost and actual paths prior to the second half of 1969, and in particular for the relatively stable growth period between 1961 and 1969.2, a clearer picture of developing capital shortages emerges.

Simulations which use 1973 data and use the "best" model structure in each industry should prove useful in discovering whether and where bottlenecks were occurring in the 1971–73 expansion. For a more contemporary assessment of capital needs, "best" model simulations based on alternative, assumed rates of output growth from 1968.4 through 1976.4 would be very useful in analyzing whether the currently available stock of capital is sufficient to support the present expansion in a least-cost manner and for measuring the dollar amount of any shortfall.

Data Appendix

Data Sources and Methods of Construction

One of the major tasks of this study was the collection and construction of a quarterly establishment-based data bank including gross output, production worker hours, nonproduction worker employment, plant, equipment, capacity utilization, materials including energy, and prices for the respective inputs and output for each industry.[66] All data are

66. Because of space constraints, the discussion here is of necessity brief. A more complete discussion is contained in the Data Appendix of Mohr (1978).

seasonally adjusted, benchmarked to 1967 prices, standardized to millions of units, e.g. dollars or hours, expressed in quarterly rates, and available from 1953.1 to 1972.4. The development and use of quarterly constant-dollar, establishment-based series for plant and equipment is a unique feature of this study. The data used in this study are generally consistent on both a 1957 and a 1967 standard industrial classification.

2.A.1   Gross Output (Y)

Gross output for each industry is defined here as $(A1)$ $Y_t = S_t + \Delta I_t$, where $S_t =$ the current dollar value of shipments in period t, $\Delta I_t = I_t - I_{t-1} =$ the current dollar value of the change in the ending inventory of finished product in period t.

The monthly current dollar shipments and inventory data are from the Bureau of the Census. Quarterly levels were developed for each of these components in order to derive a quarterly output measure. Published shipments data for all industries except 330 and 333 are available beginning in 1953; for the latter sectors, unpublished census data are available from 1958 forward. From 1953.1 through 1957.4[67] the current dollar value of shipments for 330 and 333[68] was constructed according to Mohr (1978).

Monthly finished goods inventories are available from published census data for the period 1953 to 1972 for industry sectors 28, 30, and 32. Unpublished monthly data obtained from the Bureau of the Census were used for sectors 20, 22, 26, and 35 for the period 1958.1 to 1972.4. These monthly data were averaged to obtain a measure of average finished goods inventory levels each quarter. A combination of monthly and annual census data sources was used to construct the 1953.1–1957.4 measures of average quarterly finished goods inventory for sectors 20, 22, 26, 35, and 36, as well as the 1953.1–1972.4 measures for sectors 330, 333, and 371. The methodology is described in Mohr (1978).

2.A.2   Labor Inputs

Production Worker Hours (X_1)

The man-hours and employment used to construct total quarterly hours for production workers come from the Bureau of Labor Statistics (BLS) 790 monthly survey and are published in various issues of *Employment and Earnings*. The average weekly hours per production worker in month i (AWH$_i$) is equal to the sum of average weekly straight-time hours (AWHRS$_i$) plus average weekly overtime hours (AWHO$_i$) in month i. The AWH$_i$ for each month were multiplied by

---

67. 1953.1 stands for the first quarter of 1953.
68. See note 5 for the definitions of sectors 330 and 333.

monthly employment (E_i) times 13 to obtain total hours paid per month at quarterly rates (TQH_i). Average employment per quarter is defined as $E_p = \Sigma\, E_i/3$. Average quarterly hours per production worker at quarterly rates is defined as $\mathrm{AQH} = (\mathrm{HRS}_p + \mathrm{HRO}_p) = \Sigma \mathrm{TQH}_i/ 3E_p$. Accordingly, the total quarterly input of production worker services is defined as $(A2)\ X_1 = E_p\,(\mathrm{HRS}_p + \mathrm{HRO}_p) = \sum_{i=1}^{3} \mathrm{TQH}_i/3$.

Nonproduction Worker Employment (X_2)

An estimate of average quarterly employment of nonproduction workers was derived from the monthly BLS 790 data.

2.A.3   Constructing Quarterly Capital Stock $(X_3$ and $X_4)$

Nature of Problem

The theoretical model described in section 2.2 calls for a measure of the individual stocks of plant and equipment for each of the ten industries in note 5. These measures must be establishment-based in order to be consistent with the other data sources. The problem is that the only establishment-based investment series available at the level of detail required is the annual Faucett (1971) data. However, there is a detailed, company-based, quarterly investment series available from the Bureau of Economic Analysis (BEA). Our objective here is to give an outline of how the BEA data were used to move the Faucett data so as to construct constant (1958) dollar investment series for plant and for equipment, and finally to construct the constant (1958) dollar stocks of both.[69]

The Basic Steps

1. Aggregate the three-digit, historical dollar Faucett investment series for plant and for equipment to the desired level as per note 5.

2. Combine the plant and equipment series to form a total historical dollar investment series.

3. Using regression analysis, develop a correspondence between the series in (2) and the annual company-based investment series from BEA.

4. Use the parameter estimates from (3) and the quarterly BEA data to estimate quarterly Faucett total investment expenditures in historical dollars.

5. Use the ratio of plant expenditures to total investment expenditures from the annual Faucett data to separate the quarterly total expenditure estimates into quarterly plant and equipment expenditures.

---

69. A complete description of the methodology and its rationale along with the regression results is provided in Mohr (1978).

6. Using regression analysis, develop a correspondence between the annual Faucett plant deflator and the annual nonresidential structures deflator from BEA.

7. Use the parameter estimates from (6) and the quarterly nonresidential structures deflator to construct a quarterly Faucett deflator.

8. Construct a set of weights, appropriate to the levels of aggregation in note 5, which can be used to aggregate the Faucett deflators for equipment for the component industries within each of the ten sectors in note 5.

9. Using regression analysis, develop a correspondence between the ten equipment deflators constructed in (8) and the annual producers' durable equipment deflator from BEA.

10. Use the parameter estimates from (9) and the quarterly producers' durable equipment deflator to construct a quarterly Faucett equipment deflator.

11. For each industry, deflate the plant investment series developed in (5) by the plant deflator from (9).

12. For each industry, deflate the equipment investment series developed in (5) by the equipment deflator from (10).

13. Run the results of (11) and (12) through the Faucett STOKS[67] program to generate the quarterly stocks of plant and equipment for each industry.

Constant-Dollar Quarterly Stocks of Plant and Equipment

At this point in the discussion, we have ten quarterly constant (1958) dollar plant investment series and ten quarterly constant (1958) dollar equipment investment series. The twenty series were run through the Faucett STOKS program to develop quarterly stocks of equipment and plant for each industry. For each industry it was assumed that the limit on the service life distribution for the discard function was ±50% of the mean service life. For the decay function, beta decay[71] of .9 was assumed for plant and .5 for equipment. Thus, if a capital good has an expected life of twenty years, it will not have a 50% loss in efficiency

70. See Lineburg (1974).

71. In simple terms beta decay is a mirror image of geometric or accelerated decay patterns often assumed in the literature. (For a full discussion, see Faucett 1973, Appendix B.) It includes one-hoss shay and straight-line depreciation as limiting distributions. The capital stock estimates resulting from the β parameters assumed in the text above should conform closely to capital efficiency estimates used by Denison ("Some Major Issues in Productivity Analysis: An Examination of Estimates by Jorgenson and Griliches," *Survey of Capital Business*, pt. 2, p. 14) in which he weights gross capital stock by 3 and net capital stock based on straight-line depreciation by 1 to "obtain a series that might reasonably approximate the decline in the ability of capital goods to contribute to productivity as they grow older."

until it is between 18 and 19 years old if beta $= .9$, and between 13 and 14 years if beta $= .5$. Beta $= .9$ was chosen for plant on Coen's (1975) finding that structures suffer no efficiency loss over their service lives. A beta of .5 was chosen for equipment partly to offset the upward scaling of expected equipment lives that results when Faucett reconciles his historical dollars stock series to the book values of assets reported by the Bureau of the Census.[72]

2.A.4   Capacity Utilization (X_5)

The Wharton series was used for all sectors but 330 and 333. Since Wharton produces a capacity utilization measure only at the SIC 33 level, individual indices for sectors 330 and 333 had to be constructed using peak-to-peak interpolation.

2.A.5   Materials (X_6)

Because quarterly data were not available, it was necessary not only to treat materials and energy as a composite input but also to construct a quarterly series on this composite input. The raw data used in this construction came from the annual gross product originating (GPO) data supplied by BEA. The steps involved in constructing the quarterly series are described in Mohr (1978).

2.A.6   Gross Output Deflator

For each of the ten sectors a gross output deflator was constructed according to the methodology of Eckstein and Wyss (1972). The necessary formula to construct I-O sector level deflators and then SIC level deflators from raw WPI data were made available to the author by Charles Guy.[73]

2.A.7   Average Hourly Wage Rate (P_1)

The price per hour of production worker input comes from the BLS 790 establishment data. P_1 represents a weighted average of the straight-time hourly wage (W_s) and the overtime hourly wage rate, assumed by BLS to be $1.5\ W_s$. The weights are the proportions of overtime (HRO) and straight-time hours (HRS) in average quarterly hours paid for per production worker (AQH). Thus,

(A3) $P_1 = [(\text{HRS}/\text{AQH})W_s + (\text{HRO}/\text{AQH})1.5\ W_s]$.

---

72. See Faucett (1971), pp. 32–34, 43ff. The service lives scaled upward by Faucett fall between the Bulletin F and the 1962 IRS guidelines. Coen's results show that these prescaled lives should be close to his revealed service lives for sectors 20, 22, 26, 28, and 32, while being lower than the revealed service life in sector 30 but higher in sectors 35, 33, and 371.
73. These formulas were used by Al-Samarrie, Kraft, and Roberts (1975).

2.A.8   Average Quarterly Earnings per Nonproduction Worker (P_2)

This is another series where quarterly data are nonexistent. Annual data are available from census data. The problem we face here is the same one we faced in relation to the materials-output ration, and the procedure used to construct the quarterly earnings is similar to that detailed in points (2) and (3) under section E of the Data Appendix in Mohr (1978).

2.A.9   Capital Prices (P_3 and P_4)

The implicit rental prices of the capital stocks for each sector are computed according to a modified version of Hall and Jorgenson (1967) as follows:

$$(A4) \qquad P_{3t} = [q_{e,t-1}\, r_t - (q_{et} - q_{e,t-1}) + q_{et}\, \delta_e\, (1+Cu-\overline{Cu})^2]$$

$$\times \left[\frac{1 - u_t\, Z_{et} - k_t + v_t}{1 - u_t} \right],$$

$$(A5) \qquad P_{4t} = [q_{s,t-1}\, r_t - (q_{st} - q_{s,t-1}) + q_{st}\, \delta_s\, (1+Cu-\overline{Cu})^2]$$

$$\times \left[\frac{1 - u_t\, Z_{st}}{1 - u_t} \right],$$

where P_{3t} and P_{4t} are the implicit rental prices of equipment, e, and structures, s, respectively. Z_{et} and Z_{st} are the present values of depreciation deductions on a dollar's investment in e and s over the lifetimes, A_e and A_s, of the assets allowable for tax purposes.

Z_e and Z_s were both computed by sum-of-the-years digits. A_e was constructed as the weighted average of the ages of the sixteen equipment types purchased by each of the ten sectors. The weights used are described in Mohr (1978). The sixteen ages come from the Faucett data.

A_s was constructed directly from the two ages and two weights found in the Faucett data for each sector; u_t is the effective corporate profits tax rate; v_t is $k_t \cdot u_t \cdot Z_{et}$ for 1962–63 and zero for all other years, and is used to account for the fact that in 1962 and 1963 the investment tax credit was deducted from the value of an asset before computing depreciation; k_t is the effective rate of the investment tax credit, q_{et} and q_{st} are the constructed quarterly price deflators for new e or s (see Mohr 1978); r equals the nominal long-term market rate of interest and is assumed to be equal to Moody's AAA corporate bond rate. The terms $-(q_{et} - q_{e,t-1})$ and $-(q_{st} - q_{s,t-1})$ are measures of capital loss on the value of an asset;[70] δ_e and δ_s represent the average or expected rate

---

74. In a recent article Berndt (1976) tested several alternative forms for (A4) and (A5) in the context of estimating the elasticity of substitution from six alternative functional forms suggested by a CES production function. As a result of this, Berndt discovered that the Durbin-Watson statistic increased abruptly

of loss in efficiency units in e and s due to physical obsolescence and discards. An estimate of δ_e and δ_s was obtained from a regression suggested by the perpetual inventory formula, namely,

(A6) $$K_t - K_{t-1} = I_t - \delta K_{t-1},$$

where $K_t =$ net stock in period t and $I_t =$ gross investment in period t. For each industry and for plant and equipment separately, a regression equation corresponding to (A6) was estimated for the sample period 1950.1–1972.4. The net stock and gross investment data used were the quarterly series constructed according to the discussion in section 2.A.3. The resulting estimates for δ_e and δ_s expressed at an annual rate were used in formulas (A4) and (A5). C_u is the Wharton series for capacity utilization and $C_{\bar{u}}$ is the long-run or average postwar rate of utilization from 1947.1 to 1974.1.

The terms $q_e \cdot \delta_e \ (1 + C_u - C_{\bar{u}})^2$ and $q_s \cdot \delta_s \ (1 + C_u - C_{\bar{u}})^2$ define the replacement cost of capital and represent a significant modification of Hall and Jorgenson (1967). These formulas imply that entrepreneurs alter their rate of replacement expectations in a quadratic manner as the utilization rate varies around its long-run rate; that is, the marginal replacement cost is an increasing function of the utilization rate. When the actual and long-run rates of utilization are equal, the replacement cost simplifies to $q_e \cdot \delta_e$ and $q_s \cdot \delta_s$, that is, to a cost determined by the expected or average rate of replacement, δ_e and δ_s. Thus, there is an internal consistency between the definitions given to δ_e and δ_s and to the manner in which entrepreneurs are assumed to calculate the impact of intensifying the use of capital on replacement costs. Alternatively, using $q_e \cdot \delta_e \cdot C_u$ as a representation of a replacement cost function would imply that δ_e represents an upper limit on the rate of replacement which would be inconsistent with the way we have measured and previously defined δ_e.

Finally, while our interpolation method eliminated fourth to first quarter jumps in the levels of q_e and q_s, it did not eliminate such jumps in the movements of these series. Consequently, it was discovered that the inclusion of the terms $-(q_{et} - q_{et-1})$ and $-(q_{st} - q_{st-1})$ in the formulas for P_3 and P_4 contained a noticeable first to fourth quarter seasonal pattern. Therefore, a four-quarter moving average was used to smooth each of these price series before using them in the model.

2.A.10   Shadow Price of Capital Utilization (P_5)

In section 2.2.3 it was shown that the properly specified notion of total factor cost, RTFC, requires a measure of the shadow price of in-

---

when real rather than nominal rates of return are employed in formulas (A4) and (A5), i.e., when the terms $(q_{et} - q_{et-1})$ and $(q_{st} - q_{st-1})$ are included.

tensifying the use rate of capital. From the logic of section 2.2.3 and the definitions of the rental prices of equipment and structures it follows that the shadow price of capital utilization is defined as

$$(A7) \qquad P_5 = 2 \{ X_3 - q_{e,t} \cdot \delta_e \cdot [(1 - u_t Z_{et} - K_t + v_t)/1 - u_t]$$
$$+ X_4 \cdot q_{s,t} \cdot \delta_s \cdot [(1 - u_t Z_{st})/1 - u_t] \}$$
$$\times (1 - C_u - C_{\bar{u}}).$$

2.A.11   Price of Materials (P_6)

For each of the ten sectors a composite materials deflator was constructed according to Eckstein and Wyss (1972). The formulas used here, like the formulas used to construct the gross output deflator, were provided by Charles Guy.

Tables and Charts Appendix

Table 2.6A: SIC 20 Comparison of Actual and Long-Run Production Worker Hours, Cost Shares, Productivity, and Total Real Factor Costs

| | Production Worker | | | | | | | | |
| | Hours | | Cost Shares | | Productivity | | Real Factor Costs | | Output |
Peak to Peak	Actual	Long-Run	Actual	Long-Run	Actual	Long-Run	Actual	Long-Run	
				Annual Rate of Change					
1956.1 1972.3	−0.45	−1.76	−1.28	−2.58	3.10	4.41	4.89	4.88	2.65
1956.1 1964.2	−1.40	−1.09	−0.71	−1.22	4.31	4.00	3.04	3.86	2.91
1964.2 1972.3	0.04	−1.63	−2.00	−3.38	2.43	4.11	7.44	7.14	2.47
			Average Cycle Effect as a Percentage of Long-Run Levels						
1956.1 1972.3	− 6.13		− 6.31		7.25		0.20		0.16
1956.1 1964.2	−12.13		−11.85		14.02		− 0.29		0.16
1964.2 1972.3	− 0.20		− 0.75		0.55		0.57		0.17

Table 2.6B: SIC 20 Other Inputs: Actual and Long-Run Comparisons

| | Nonproduction Worker Employment | | Equipment | | Plant | | Capacity Utilization | | Materials | |
Peak to Peak	Actual	Long-Run	Actual	Long-Run	Actual	Long-Run	Actual	Long-Run	Actual	Long-Run
					Annual Rate of Change					
1956.1 1972.3	0.38	3.19	3.23	5.64	1.25	2.01	0.49	0.12	3.40	2.92
1956.1 1964.2	1.29	5.77	2.34	5.79	0.56	2.36	−0.19	0.72	2.87	2.99
1964.2 1972.3	−0.69	0.18	3.85	4.67	1.87	1.72	1.01	0.14	3.20	2.91
			Average Cycle Effect as a Percentage of Long-Run Levels							
1956.1 1972.3	21.13		16.64		4.96		−1.39		−3.28	
1956.1 1964.2	35.43		28.70		7.94		−3.50		−5.79	
1964.2 1972.3	6.30		4.17		1.90		0.64		−0.83	

Table 2.7A: SIC 22 Comparison of Actual and Long-Run Production Worker Hours, Cost Shares, Productivity, and Total Real Factor Costs

| | Production Worker | | | | | | | | |
| | Hours | | Cost Shares | | Productivity | | Real Factor Costs | | Output |
Peak to Peak	Actual	Long-Run	Actual	Long-Run	Actual	Long-Run	Actual	Long-Run	
				Annual Rate of Change					
1956.1 1972.3	0.23	2.77	-1.48	1.00	4.44	1.89	5.67	5.74	4.66
1956.1 1966.3	-0.36	4.48	-1.24	3.69	4.77	-0.06	3.76	3.66	4.42
1966.3 1972.3	-0.35	-0.50	-1.51	0.68	3.61	3.76	6.71	4.37	3.26
			Average Cycle Effect as a Percentage of Long-Run Levels						
1956.1 1972.3	15.69		11.61		-11.49		4.04		0.45
1956.1 1966.3	22.42		17.32		-16.12		4.96		0.50
1966.3 1972.3	3.59		1.59		-3.17		2.15		0.37

Table 2.7B: SIC 22 Other Inputs: Actual and Long-Run Comparisons

| | Nonproduction Worker Employment | | Equipment | | Plant | | Capacity Utilization | | Materials | |
Peak to Peak	Actual	Long-Run	Actual	Long-Run	Actual	Long-Run	Actual	Long-Run	Actual	Long-Run
					Annual Rate of Change					
1956.1 1972.3	2.45	2.14	2.56	3.26	1.43	3.44	1.23	1.35	5.63	4.49
1956.1 1966.3	1.46	0.63	0.91	2.03	-0.54	3.42	1.63	1.61	5.89	3.48
1966.3 1972.3	2.19	-0.37	3.96	2.29	3.23	1.77	-1.35	-3.43	5.16	1.46
			Average Cycle Effect as a Percentage of Long-Run Levels							
1956.1 1972.3	2.54		6.82		11.37		3.69		-0.20	
1956.1 1966.3	2.77		9.10		15.93		4.68		-1.53	
1966.3 1972.3	1.82		2.51		3.15		1.68		1.80	

Table 2.8A: SIC 26 Comparison of Actual and Long-Run Production Worker Hours, Cost Shares, Productivity, and Total Real Factor Costs

| | Production Worker | | | | | | | | |
| | Hours | | Cost Shares | | Productivity | | Real Factor Costs | | Output |
Peak to Peak	Actual	Long-Run	Actual	Long-Run	Actual	Long-Run	Actual	Long-Run	
				Annual Rate of Change					
1956.1 1972.4	1.17	1.13	−2.40	−2.45	3.25	3.29	7.75	7.75	4.42
1956.1 1966.3	1.19	1.40	−1.34	−1.05	3.15	2.94	6.01	5.93	4.35
1966.3 1972.4	−0.24	−1.32	−2.86	−2.55	3.17	4.25	8.78	7.40	2.93
			Average Cycle Effect as a Percentage of Long-Run Levels						
1956.1 1972.4	3.07		0.24		−2.74		2.83		0.39
1956.1 1966.3	2.85		−0.40		−2.47		3.25		0.40
1966.3 1972.4	3.09		1.26		−2.86		1.86		0.39

Table 2.8B: SIC 26 Other Inputs: Actual and Long-Run Comparisons

| | Nonproduction Worker Employment | | Equipment | | Plant | | Capacity Utilization | | Materials | |
Peak to Peak	Actual	Long-Run	Actual	Long-Run	Actual	Long-Run	Actual	Long-Run	Actual	Long-Run
				Annual Rate of Change						
1956.1 1972.4	2.98	2.57	5.50	5.05	3.72	3.45	1.37	1.54	3.31	3.59
1956.1 1966.3	3.55	2.78	5.24	4.64	3.43	3.08	1.39	1.70	3.38	3.33
1966.3 1972.4	0.91	−0.33	4.63	2.43	3.43	0.94	0.26	−0.87	1.91	1.24
		Average Cycle Effect as a Percentage of Long-Run Levels								
1956.1 1972.4	0.66		0.31		0.42		3.72		4.74	
1956.1 1966.3	0.02		−0.51		0.01		4.39		6.29	
1966.3 1972.4	1.50		1.26		0.67		2.32		2.02	

Table 2.9A: SIC 28 Comparison of Actual and Long-Run Production Worker Hours, Cost Shares, Productivity, and Total Real Factor Costs

| | Production Worker | | | | | | | | |
| | Hours | | Cost Shares | | Productivity | | Real Factor Costs | | Output |
Peak to Peak	Actual	Long-Run	Actual	Long-Run	Actual	Long-Run	Actual	Long-Run	
				Annual Rate of Change					
1956.2 1972.4	1.46	1.61	-2.44	-2.31	4.79	4.64	7.90	7.92	6.25
1956.2 1966.1	0.93	2.93	-0.11	0.92	5.42	3.41	4.48	5.45	6.34
1966.1 1972.4	-0.06	-1.15	-3.93	-3.66	5.07	6.16	9.71	8.35	5.01
			Average Cycle Effect as a Percentage of Long-Run Levels						
1956.2 1972.4	8.94		3.67		-7.71		5.01		0.37
1956.2 1966.1	7.85		3.11		-6.67		4.48		0.40
1966.1 1972.4	10.06		4.40		-8.81		5.41		0.35

Table 2.9B: SIC 28 Other Inputs: Actual and Long-Run Comparisons

| | Nonproduction Worker Employment | | Equipment | | Plant | | Utilization Capacity | | Materials | |
Peak to Peak	Actual	Long-Run	Actual	Long-Run	Actual	Long-Run	Actual	Long-Run	Actual	Long-Run
				Annual Rate of Change						
1956.2 1972.4	3.10	2.56	5.27	4.75	3.57	2.92	1.15	2.07	3.97	4.10
1956.2 1966.1	2.85	2.33	4.22	3.89	3.06	1.95	-0.67	2.98	4.17	4.77
1966.1 1972.4	1.55	0.69	5.20	3.54	3.54	1.57	0.96	-0.63	1.92	1.32
			Average Cycle Effect as a Percentage of Long-Run Levels							
1956.2 1972.4	2.57		3.11		0.50		11.41		2.83	
1956.2 1966.1	0.77		1.48		-0.85		12.83		2.95	
1966.1 1972.4	4.88		5.09		2.08		8.83		2.43	

Table 2.10A: SIC 30 Comparison of Actual and Long-Run Production Worker Hours, Cost Shares, Productivity, and Total Real Factor Costs

| | Production Worker | | | | | | | | |
| | Hours | | Cost Shares | | Productivity | | Real Factor Costs | | |
Peak to Peak	Actual	Long-Run	Actual	Long-Run	Actual	Long-Run	Actual	Long-Run	Output
				Annual Rate of Change					
1955.4 1972.4	3.89	4.12	−1.56	−1.33	2.41	2.19	8.70	8.70	6.31
1955.4 1966.1	3.00	5.54	−0.20	0.95	3.63	1.09	5.89	7.28	6.63
1966.1 1972.4	2.61	2.88	−2.40	−0.37	1.86	1.59	10.05	8.29	4.47
			Average Cycle Effect as a Percentage of Long-Run Levels						
1955.4 1972.4	3.96		1.81		−3.06		2.06		0.59
1955.4 1966.1	2.18		1.02		−1.25		1.02		0.58
1966.1 1972.4	6.44		3.13		−5.62		3.32		0.62

Table 2.10B: SIC 30 Other Inputs: Actual and Long-Run Comparisons

| | Nonproduction Worker Employment | | Equipment | | Plant | | Capacity Utilization | | Materials | |
Peak to Peak	Actual	Long-Run	Actual	Long-Run	Actual	Long-Run	Actual	Long-Run	Actual	Long-Run
				Annual Rate of Change						
1955.4 1972.4	4.03	3.82	6.64	6.46	5.25	6.35	1.15	1.46	6.57	6.51
1955.4 1966.1	3.22	4.30	5.31	6.49	3.79	7.81	−0.24	2.54	5.82	6.26
1966.1 1972.4	3.18	0.69	7.59	4.75	7.21	2.94	−0.39	−1.72	5.90	4.42
			Average Cycle Effect as a Percentage of Long-Run Levels							
1955.4 1972.4	1.08		0.75		0.92		3.26		1.97	
1955.4 1966.1	−0.41		−0.65		0.57		2.16		1.61	
1966.1 1972.4	2.93		2.45		0.96		4.55		2.35	

Table 2.11A: SIC 32 Comparison of Actual and Long-Run Production Worker Hours, Cost Shares, Productivity, and Total Real Factor Costs

Peak to Peak	Production Worker								
	Hours		Cost Shares		Productivity		Real Factor Costs		
	Actual	Long-Run	Actual	Long-Run	Actual	Long-Run	Aitual	Long-Run	Actual Long-Run
					Annual Rate of Change				
1955.4 1972.4	0.65	0.77	−1.36	−1.20	2.38	2.26	5.97	5.93	3.02
1955.4 1966.1	0.41	1.06	−1.40	−1.02	2.91	2.25	4.93	5.20	3.31
1966.1 1972.4	0.16	0.07	−1.01	−0.35	1.95	2.05	7.47	6.71	2.11
				Average Cycle Effect as a Percentage of Long-Run Levels					
1955.4 1972.4		2.25		0.74		−1.91		1.53	0.54
1955.4 1966.1		2.07		0.90		−1.76		1.21	0.58
1966.1 1972.4		2.23		0.52		−1.84		1.70	0.51

Table 2.11B: SIC 32 Other Inputs: Actual and Long-Run Comparisons

Peak to Peak	Nonproduction Worker Employment		Equipment		Plant		Capacity Utilization		Materials	
	Actual	Long-Run	Actual	Long-Run	Actual	Long-Run	Aitual	Long-Run	Actual	Long-Run
					Annual Rate of Change					
1955.4 1972.4	1.88	1.49	3.78	3.16	2.74	2.03	0.05	0.35	2.94	3.38
1955.4 1966.1	2.43	1.69	4.10	2.83	3.72	2.08	0.19	1.31	2.62	4.23
1966.1 1972.4	0.73	0.61	3.03	2.52	1.42	1.03	−0.89	−1.37	3.28	1.33
				Average Cycle Effect as a Percentage of Long-Run Levels						
1955.4 1972.4	2.15		1.75		2.51		1.76		0.97	
1955.4 1966.1	1.06		0.34		1.59		2.06		1.90	
1966.1 1972.4	3.46		3.47		3.48		1.06		−0.75	

Table 2.12A: SIC 330 Comparison of Actual and Long-Run Production Worker Hours, Cost Shares, Productivity, and Total Real Factor Costs

	Production Worker								Output
	Hours		Cost Shares		Productivity		Real Factor Costs		
Peak to Peak	Actual	Long-Run	Actual	Long-Run	Actual	Long-Run	Actual	Long-Run	
				Annual Rate of Change					
1956.2 1972.4	0.0	0.01	-1.70	-1.79	1.58	1.56	5.27	5.36	1.53
1956.2 1965.3	-0.41	-0.32	0.25	-0.02	1.47	1.38	2.44	2.78	1.06
1965.3 1972.4	-2.32	-3.43	-2.62	-2.41	0.39	1.50	6.04	4.72	-1.03
			Average Cycle Effect as a Percentage of Long-Run Levels						
1956.2 1972.4	0.34		-0.06		-0.02		0.42		1.52
1956.2 1965.3	0.83		-0.25		-0.44		1.11		1.87
1965.3 1972.4	-0.36		0.36		0.56		-0.68		1.09

Table 2.12B: SIC 330 Other Inputs: Actual and Long-Run Comparisons

	Nonproduction Worker Employment		Equipment		Plant		Capacity Utilization		Materials	
Peak to Peak	Actual	Long-Run	Actual	Long-Run	Actual	Long-Run	Actual	Long-Run	Actual	Long-Run
				Annual Rate of Change						
1956.2 1972.4	0.76	0.30	3.54	2.78	-0.93	-0.98	1.38	1.46	1.69	2.69
1956.2 1965.3	-0.20	-0.19	2.30	1.45	-1.29	-0.73	1.59	1.62	0.74	2.17
1965.3 1972.4	-0.13	-2.40	3.94	0.95	-0.52	-3.03	-1.73	-2.36	-0.22	0.44
			Average Cycle Effect as a Percentage of Long-Run Levels							
1956.2 1972.4	-0.76		-1.48		-0.11		0.64		2.44	
1956.2 1965.3	-1.92		-3.05		0.23		1.30		5.90	
1965.3 1972.4	0.41		0.18		-0.99		-0.27		-2.08	

Table 2.13A: SIC 333 Comparison of Actual and Long-Run Production Worker Hours, Cost Shares, Productivity, and Total Real Factor Costs

| | Production Worker | | | | | | | | |
| | Hours | | Cost Shares | | Productivity | | Real Factor Costs | | Output |
Peak to Peak	Actual	Long-Run	Actual	Long-Run	Actual	Long-Run	Actual	Long-Run	
					Annual Rate of Change				
1956.1 1972.4	1.49	1.77	−2.11	−1.84	2.31	2.03	7.36	7.37	3.80
1956.1 1966.3	1.30	4.10	−0.93	0.11	3.76	0.96	5.38	7.15	5.06
1966.3 1972.4	−1.62	−3.52	−3.62	−2.56	0.97	2.87	7.77	4.81	−0.65
			Average Cycle Effect as a Percentage of Long-Run Levels						
1956.1 1972.4	2.17		1.59		−1.32		0.50		0.80
1956.1 1966.3	0.71		1.40		0.28		−0.84		0.67
1966.3 1972.4	4.26		1.99		−3.67		2.34		1.08

Table 2.13B: SIC 333 Other Inputs: Actual and Long-Run Comparisons

| | Nonproduction Worker Employment | | Equipment | | Plant | | Capacity Utilization | | Materials | |
Peak to Peak	Actual	Long-Run	Actual	Long-Run	Actual	Long-Run	Actual	Long-Run	Actual	Long-Run
					Annual Rate of Change					
1956.1 1972.4	1.86	2.25	4.69	4.94	3.86	4.32	1.25	1.53	4.93	4.59
1956.1 1966.3	0.78	4.11	2.91	5.59	3.52	6.35	1.22	3.82	4.92	5.60
1966.3 1972.4	0.23	−2.84	6.50	0.89	4.39	−1.23	−0.26	−4.28	1.23	0.14
			Average Cycle Effect as a Percentage of Long-Run Levels							
1956.1 1972.4	0.71		−1.52		−2.37		0.94		1.35	
1956.1 1966.3	−0.55		−2.22		−3.37		0.17		−0.68	
1966.3 1972.4	2.17		−1.20		−1.60		1.74		4.64	

Table 2.14A: SIC 35 Comparison of Actual and Long-Run Production Worker Hours, Cost Shares, Productivity, and Total Real Factor Costs

| | Production Worker | | | | | | | | |
| | Hours | | Cost Shares | | Productivity | | Real Factor Costs | | Output |
Peak to Peak	Actual	Long-Run	Actual	Long-Run	Actual	Long-Run	Actual	Long-Run	
				Annual Rate of Change					
1956.4 1972.4	2.14	2.18	−2.35	−2.30	2.99	2.95	8.41	8.40	5.14
1956.4 1966.4	2.75	4.19	−0.67	0.22	3.07	1.62	6.62	7.17	5.81
1966.4 1972.4	−3.00	−2.78	−3.15	−2.76	3.16	2.94	5.87	5.69	0.16
			Average Cycle Effect as a Percentage of Long-Run Levels						
1956.4 1972.4	1.77		1.98		−1.45		−0.26		0.86
1956.4 1966.4	0.32		1.16		0.04		−0.91		0.84
1966.4 1972.4	4.12		3.35		−3.86		0.73		0.94

Table 2.14B: SIC 35   Other Inputs: Actual and Long-Run Comparisons

| | Nonproduction Worker Employment | | Equipment | | Plant | | Capacity Utilization | | Materials | |
Peak to Peak	Actual	Long-Run	Actual	Long-Run	Actual	Long-Run	Actual	Long-Run	Actual	Long-Run
				Annual Rate of Change						
1956.4 1972.4	3.40	3.29	6.57	6.48	4.01	3.65	1.56	1.69	5.61	5.61
1956.4 1966.4	2.75	3.58	4.57	6.09	3.31	3.30	2.17	2.80	6.26	5.88
1966.4 1972.4	1.14	3.12	7.06	9.24	3.96	5.05	−3.61	−5.37	0.13	−1.49
			Average Cycle Effect as a Percentage of Long-Run Levels							
1956.4 1972.4	0.99		1.66		−0.99		0.17		−1.78	
1956.4 1966.4	9.89		−0.87		−2.78		0.38		−1.04	
1966.4 1972.4	4.29		6.26		2.14		−0.54		−3.28	

Table 2.15A: SIC 371 Comparison of Actual and Long-Run Production Worker Hours, Cost Shares, Productivity, and Total Real Factor Costs

| | Production Worker | | | | | | | | |
| | Hours | | Cost Shares | | Productivity | | Real Factor Costs | | Output |
Peak to Peak	Actual	Long-Run	Actual	Long-Run	Actual	Long-Run	Actual	Long-Run	
				Annual Rate of Change					
1955.2 1972.4	1.25	1.46	0.14	0.48	2.96	2.74	5.52	5.39	4.21
1955.2 1965.4	0.24	1.73	−0.33	1.03	4.04	2.55	4.41	4.54	4.28
1965.4 1972.4	−0.56	0.06	0.45	1.16	2.89	2.27	5.40	5.30	2.33
			Average Cycle Effect as a Percentage of Long-Run Levels						
1955.2 1972.4	1.79		0.99		−1.30		0.79		1.27
1955.2 1965.4	0.93		0.94		−0.45		0.01		1.49
1965.4 1972.4	2.77		0.95		−2.27		1.75		1.01

Table 2.15B: SIC 371 Other Inputs: Actual and Long-Run Comparisons

| | Nonproduction Worker Employment | | Equipment | | Plant | | Capacity Utilization | | Materials | |
Peak to Peak	Actual	Long-Run	Actual	Long-Run	Actual	Long-Run	Actual	Long-Run	Actual	Long-Run
					Annual Rate of Change					
1955.2 1972.4	1.39	1.25	1.97	1.13	2.94	2.26	1.20	1.04	3.06	3.16
1955.2 1965.4	0.38	1.51	0.93	0.55	2.08	2.29	1.95	2.05	3.15	3.11
1965.4 1972.4	0.33	0.21	1.35	0.14	1.87	1.07	−1.58	−0.65	1.18	1.06
			Average Cycle Effect as a Percentage of Long-Run Levels							
1955.2 1972.4	1.09		−0.70		0.77		0.52		1.21	
1955.2 1965.4	−1.06		−4.12		−2.03		−0.80		1.81	
1965.4 1972.4	3.85		3.92		4.49		2.23		0.32	

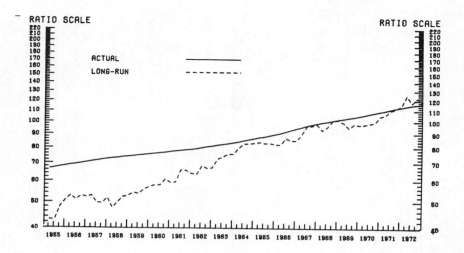

Fig. 2.2A   Equipment (hundreds of millions of dollars), Actual versus Long-Run: SIC 20

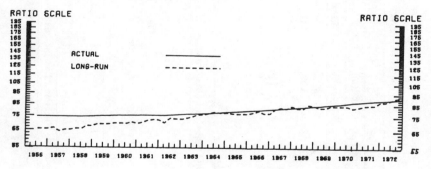

Fig. 2.2B   Plant (hundreds of millions of dollars), Actual versus Long-Run: SIC 20

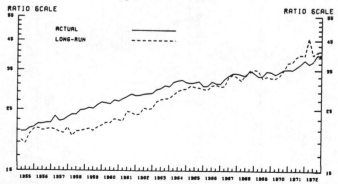

Fig. 2.2C   Average Product per Production Worker Hour, Actual versus Long-Run: SIC 20

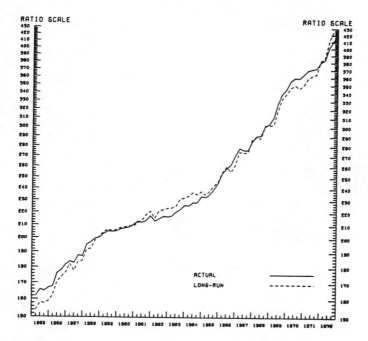

Fig. 2.2D   Real Total Factor Cost (hundreds of millions of dollars), Actual versus Long-Run: SIC 20

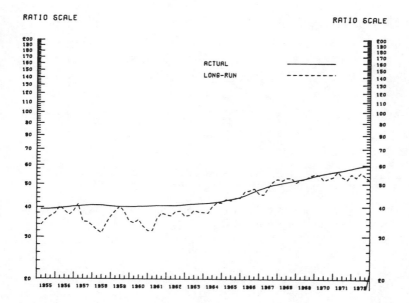

Fig. 2.3A   Equipment (hundreds of millions of dollars), Actual versus Long-Run: SIC 22

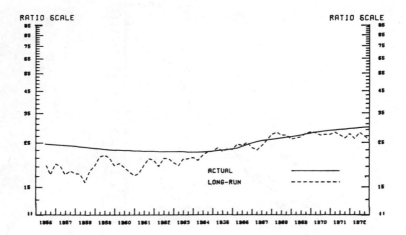

Fig. 2.3B   Plant (hundreds of millions of dollars), Actual versus
Long-Run: SIC 22

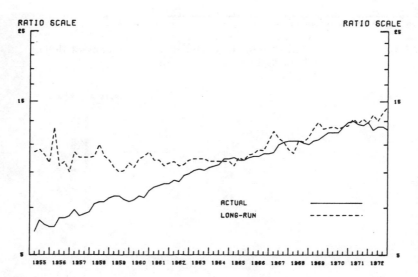

Fig. 2.3C   Average Product per Production Worker Hour, Actual
versus Long-Run: SIC 22

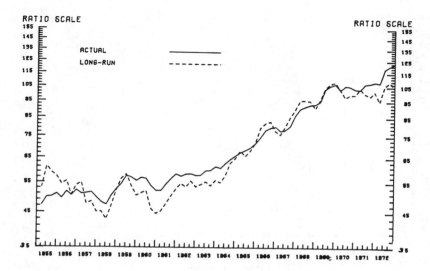

Fig. 2.3D   Real Total Factor Cost (hundreds of millions of dollars), Actual versus Long-Run: SIC 22

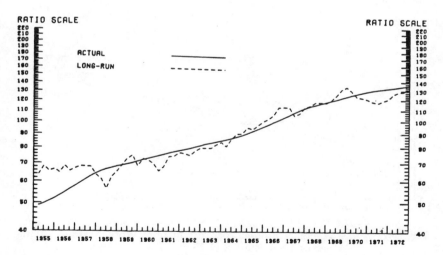

Fig. 2.4A   Equipment (hundreds of millions of dollars), Actual versus Long-Run: SIC 26

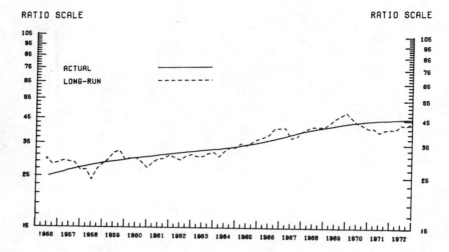

Fig. 2.4B   Plant (hundreds of millions of dollars), Actual versus Long-Run: SIC 26

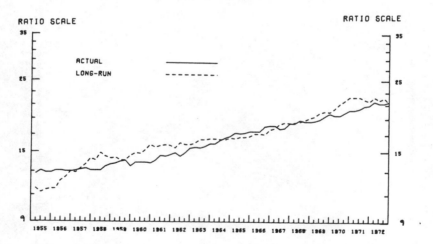

Fig. 2.4C   Average Product per Production Worker Hour, Actual versus Long-Run: SIC 26

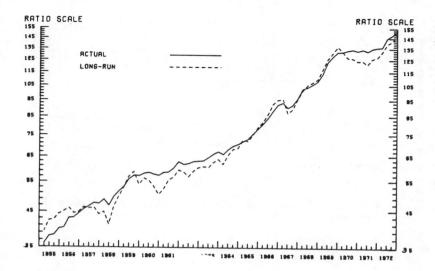

Fig. 2.4D   Real Total Factor Cost (hundreds of millions of dollars), Actual versus Long-Run: SIC 26

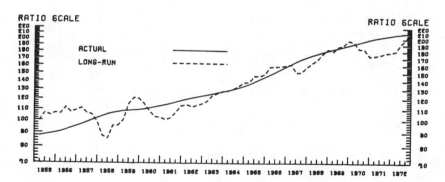

Fig. 2.5A   Equipment (hundreds of millions of dollars), Actual versus Long-Run: SIC 28

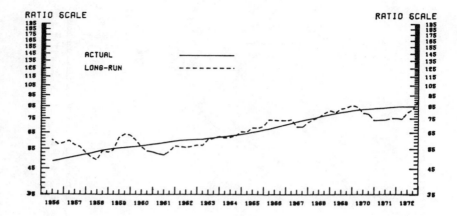

Fig. 2.5B   Plant (hundreds of millions of dollars), Actual versus Long-Run: SIC 28

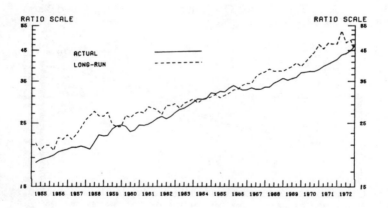

Fig. 2.5C   Average Product per Production Worker Hour, Actual versus Long-Run: SIC 28

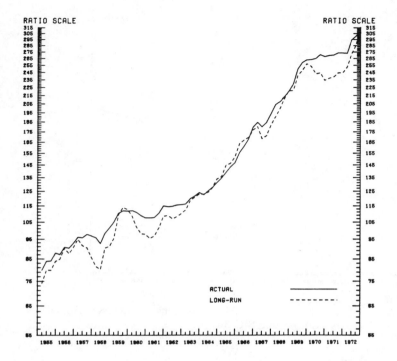

Fig. 2.5D   Real Total Factor Cost (hundreds of millions of dollars), Actual versus Long-Run: SIC 28

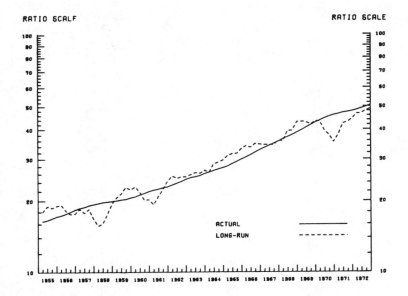

Fig. 2.6A   Equipment (hundreds of millions of dollars), Actual versus Long-Run: SIC 30

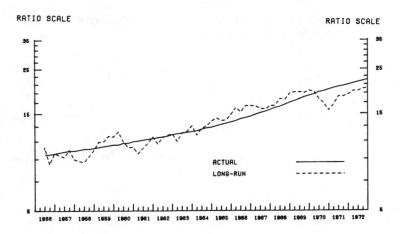

Fig. 2.6B   Plant (hundreds of millions of dollars), Actual versus Long-Run: SIC 30

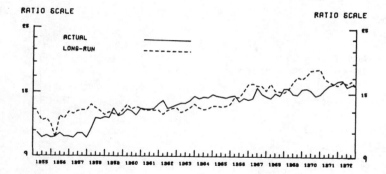

Fig. 2.6C   Average Product per Production Worker Hour, Actual versus Long-Run: SIC 30

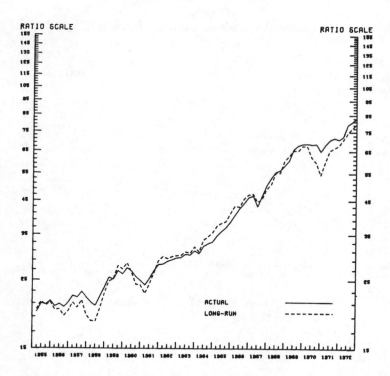

Fig. 2.6D   Real Total Factor Cost (hundreds of millions of dollars), Actual versus Long-Run: SIC 30

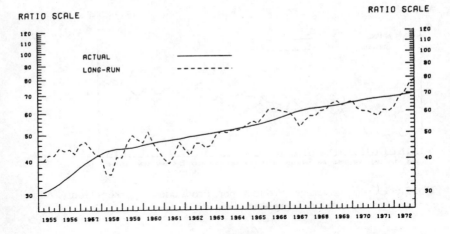

Fig. 2.7A   Equipment (hundreds of millions of dollars), Actual versus Long-Run: SIC 22

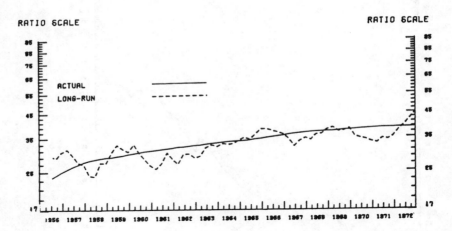

Fig. 2.7B   Plant (hundreds of millions of dollars), Actual versus Long-Run: SIC 32

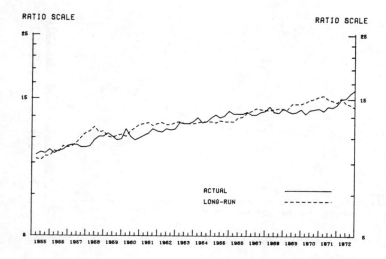

Fig. 2.7C   Average Product per Production Worker Hour, Actual versus Long-Run: SIC 32

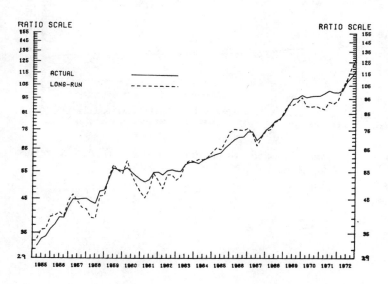

Fig. 2.7D   Real Total Factor Cost (hundreds of millions of dollars), Actual versus Long-Run: SIC 32

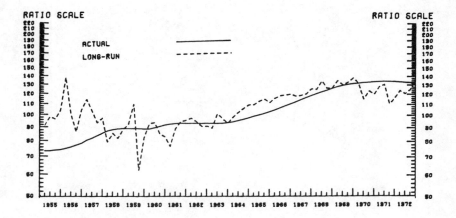

Fig. 2.8A   Equipment (hundreds of millions of dollars), Actual versus Long-Run: SIC 330

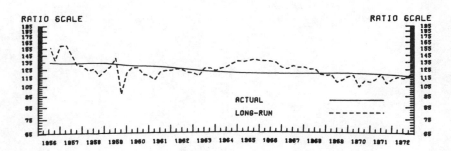

Fig. 2.8B   Plant (hundreds of millions of dollars), Actual versus Long-Run: SIC 330

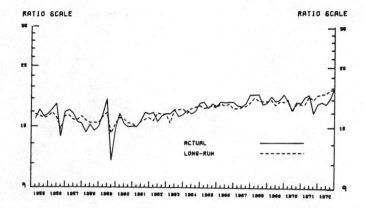

Fig. 2.8C   Average Product per Production Worker Hour, Actual versus Long-Run: SIC 330

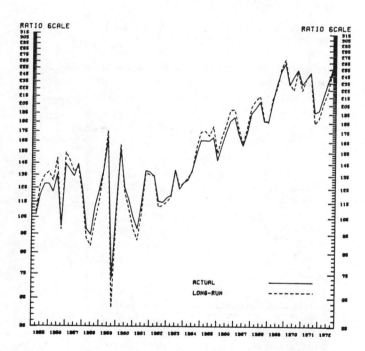

Fig. 2.8D   Real Total Factor Cost (hundreds of millions of dollars), Actual versus Long-Run: SIC 330

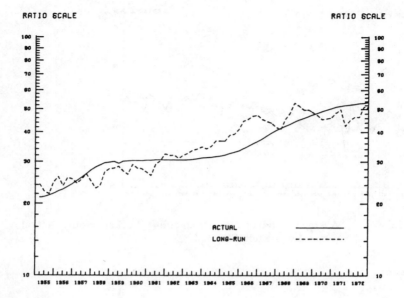

Fig. 2.9A   Equipment (hundreds of millions of dollars), Actual versus Long-Run: SIC 333

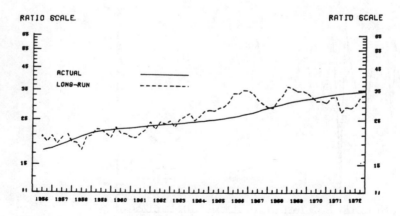

Fig. 2.9B   Plant (hundreds of millions of dollars), Actual versus Long-Run: SIC 333

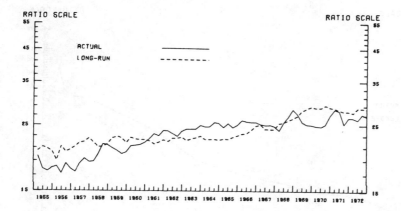

Fig. 2.9C   Average Product per Production Worker Hour, Actual versus Long-Run: SIC 333

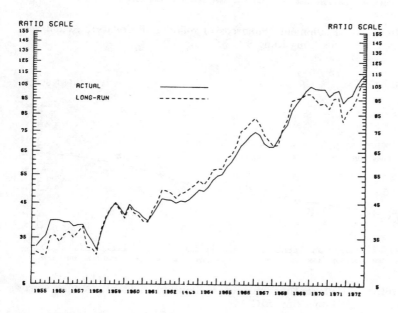

Fig. 2.9D   Real Total Factor Cost (hundreds of millions of dollars), Actual versus Long-Run: SIC 333

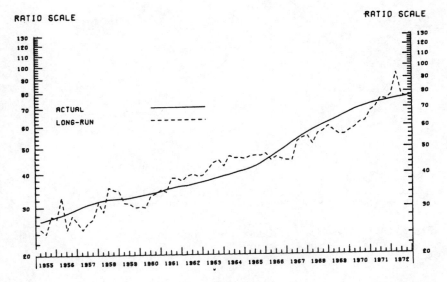

Fig. 2.10A   Equipment (hundreds of millions of dollars), Actual versus Long-Run: SIC 35

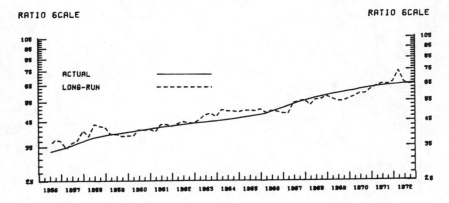

Fig. 2.10B   Plant (hundreds of millions of dollars), Actual versus Long-Run: SIC 35

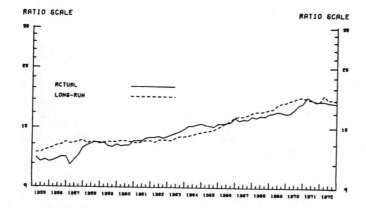

Fig. 2.10C   Average Product per Production Worker Hour, Actual versus Long-Run: SIC 35

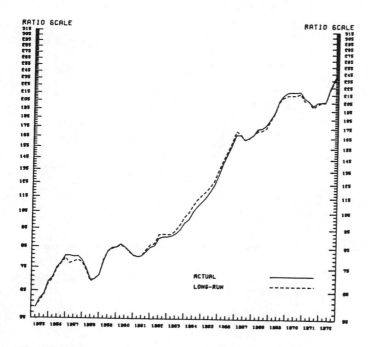

Fig. 2.10D   Real Total Factor Cost (hundreds of millions of dollars), Actual versus Long-Run: SIC 35

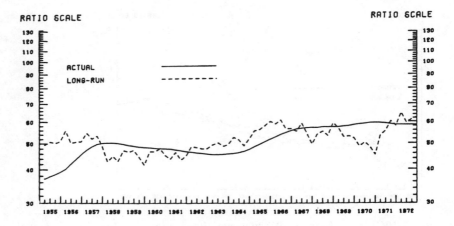

Fig. 2.11A   Equipment (hundreds of millions of dollars), Actual versus Long-Run: SIC 371

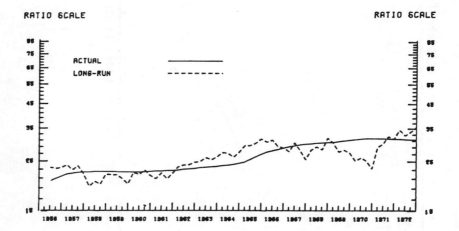

Fig. 2.11B   Plant (hundreds of millions of dollars), Actual versus Long-Run: SIC 371

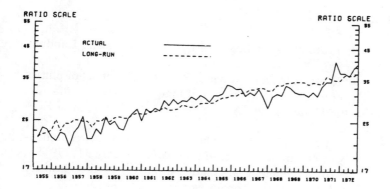

Fig. 2.11C   Average Product per Production Worker Hour, Actual versus Long-Run: SIC 371

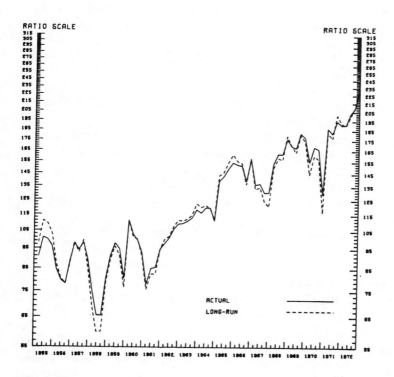

Fig. 2.11D   Real Total Factor Cost (hundreds of millions of dollars), Actual versus Long-Run: SIC 371

References

Allen, R. G. D. 1936. *Mathematical analysis for economists*. London: Macmillan.

Al-Samarrie, A.; Kraft, A. J.; and Roberts, B. 1974. The effect of phases I, II, and III on wages, prices, and profit margins in the manufacturing sector of the United States. New York: National Bureau of Economic Research.

Becker, G. S., and Lewis, H. F. 1973. On the interaction between quantity and quality of children. *Journal of Political Economy* 31:279–88.

Berndt, E. R. 1976. Reconciling alternative estimates of the elasticity of substitution. *Review of Economics and Statistics* 58:59–67.

Berndt, E. R., and Christensen, L. R. 1973*a*. The internal structure of functional relationships: separability, substitution and aggregation. *Review of Economic Studies* 40:403–10.

———. 1973*b*. The translog function and the substitution of equipment, structures, and labor in U.S. manufacturing 1929–1968. *Journal of Econometrics* 1:81–114.

———. 1973*c*. The specification of technology in U.S. manufacturing. Discussion Paper 73–117. University of British Columbia, March 1974.

———. 1974. Testing for the existence of a consistent index of labor inputs. *American Economic Review* 64:391–404.

Berndt, E. R., and Savin, N. E. 1975. Estimation and hypothesis testing in singular equation systems with autoregressive disturbances. *Econometrica* 43:937–57.

Berndt, E. R., and Wood, D. O. 1975. Technology, prices and the derived demand for energy. *Review of Economics and Statistics* 57:28–44.

Birch, E. M., and Siebert, C. D. 1976. Uncertainty, permanent demand, and investment behavior. *American Economic Review* 66:15–27.

Brainard, W. C., and Tobin, J. 1968. Pitfalls in financial model building. *American Economic Review* 58:99–122.

Christensen, L. R.; Cummings, D.; and Jorgenson, D. W. 1980. An international comparison of growth in productivity, 1947–1973. National Bureau of Economic Research. This volume.

Christensen, L. R.; Jorgenson, D. W.; and Lau, L. J. 1971. Conjugate duality and the transcendental logarithmic production function. *Econometrica* 39:255–56.

———. 1973. Transcendental logarithmic production frontiers. *Review of Economics and Statistics* 55:28–45.

Clark, C. S. 1973. Labor hoarding in durable goods industries. *American Economic Review* 63:811–24.

Clembout, S. 1968. The class of homothetic isoquant production functions. *Review of Economic Studies* 35:91–104.

Coen, R. M. 1975. Investment behavior, the measurement of depreciation, and tax policy. *American Economic Review* 65:59–74.

Denison, E. F. 1973. The shift to services and the rate of productivity change. *Survey of Current Business* 53:20–35.

―――. 1974. *Accounting for U.S. economic growth, 1929–1969.* Washington: The Brookings Institution.

Denton, F. T. 1971. Adjustment of monthly and quarterly series to annual totals: an approach based on quadratic minimization. *Journal of the American Statistical Association* 66:99–102.

Diewert, W. E. 1974. Applications of duality theory. In *Frontiers of quantitative economics*, ed. M. Intrilligator and David Kendrick, vol. 2. Amsterdam: North-Holland.

Eckstein, O., and Shields, N. S. 1974. The role of productivity in controlling inflation. Washington: Data Resources, for the National Commission on Productivity and Work Quality.

Eckstein, O., and Wyss, D. 1972. Industry price equations. *The econometrics of price determination conference*, pp. 133–65. Washington: Federal Reserve System.

Eisner, R., and Nadiri, M. I. 1968. Investment behavior and neo-classical theory. *Review of Economics and Statistics* 50:369–82.

Eisner, R., and Strotz, R. 1963. Determinants of business investment. *Impacts of monthly policy*, pp. 59–337. Englewood Cliffs, N.J.: Prentice-Hall, for Commission on Money and Credit.

Fair, R. C. 1969. *The short-run demand for workers and hours.* Amsterdam: North-Holland.

―――. 1971. *A short-run forecasting model of the United States economy.* Lexington, Mass.: Lexington Books, D. C. Heath and Co.

Faucett, Jack, Associates. 1973. *Development of capital stock series by industry sector.* Washington: Office of Emergency Preparedness.

Friedman, M. 1957. *A theory of the consumption function.* Princeton: Princeton University Press, for National Bureau of Economic Research.

Hall, R. E., and Jorgenson, D. W. 1967. Tax policy and investment behavior. *American Economic Review* 57:391–44.

Hawtrey, R. G. 1913. *Good and bad trade.* London: Constable and Co.

Hayek, Von, F. A. 1951. *Prices and production.* 2d ed. London: Routledge & Keegan Paul.

Hicks, J. R. 1950. *A contribution to the theory of the trade cycle.* London: Oxford University Press.

Hirsch, A. A. 1968. Reconciliation of the short-run employment function and the long-run production function. Mimeo. Washington: Bureau of Economic Analysis.

Hudson, E. A., and Jorgenson, D. W. 1974. U.S. energy policy and economic growth 1975–2000. *Bell J. Econ.* 5:461–514.

Johnston, J. 1972. *Econometric methods.* 2d ed. New York: McGraw-Hill.

Jorgenson, D. W., and Griliches, Z. 1967. The explanation of productivity change. *Review of Economic Studies* 34:249–84.

Jorgenson, D. W., and Stephenson, J. A. 1967a. The time structure of investment behavior in United States manufacturing, 1947–1960. *Review of Economics and Statistics* 49:16–27.

———. 1967b. Investment behavior in the U.S. *Econometrica* 35:169–220.

Kmenta, J., and Gilbert, R. F. 1968. Small sample properties of alternative estimators of seemingly unrelated regressions. *Journal of American Statistical Association* 63:1180–1200.

Lineburg, W. Z. 1974. *A user's guide for capital stock measures by industry sector.* Washington: Office of Emergency Preparedness.

Mark, J. A. 1975. *Current developments in productivity, 1973–1974.* Report 436. Washington: U.S. Department of Labor, Bureau of Labor Statistics.

Mohr, M. F. 1978. A quarterly econometric model of the long-term structure of production, factor demand, and factor productivity in ten U.S. manufacturing industries. *BLS* Staff Paper 9. Springfield, Virginia: National Technical Information Service, no. PB–282–45.

Nadiri, M. I., and Rosen, S. 1969. Interrelated factor demand functions. *American Economic Review* 59:457–71.

———. 1973. *A disequilibrium model of demand for factors of production.* New York: Columbia University Press, for National Bureau of Economic Research.

Nordhaus, W. D. 1972. The recent productivity slowdown. *Brookings Papers on Economic Activity* 3:493–545.

Parks, R. W. 1971. Price responsiveness of factor utilization in Swedish manufacturing, 1870–1950. *Review of Economics and Statistics* 53:129–39.

Perry, G. 1971. Labor structure, potential output, and productivity. *Brookings Papers on Economic Activity* 3:533–65.

Pollak, R. A., and Wales, T. J. 1969. Estimation of a linear expenditure system. *Econometrica* 37:611–28.

Roa, P., and Miller, R. L. 1971. *Applied econometrics.* Belmont, Calif.: Wadsworth Publishing Co.

Samuelson, P. A. 1963. *Foundations of economic analysis.* Cambridge: Harvard University Press.

Shepard, R. W. 1953. *Cost and production functions.* Princeton: Princeton University Press.

————. 1970. *Theory of cost and production functions.* Princeton: Princeton University Press.

Theil, H. 1971. *Principles of econometrics.* New York: Wiley.

Wales, T. J. 1977. On the flexibility of flexible functional forms: an empirical approach. *Journal of Econometrics* 5:183–93.

Wells, D. A., and Sisik, S. 1970. Steel imports: The importance of availability and cost. *MSU Business Topics* 18:57–64.

Winsatt, G. B., and Woodward, J. T. 1970. Revised estimates of new plant and equipment expenditures in the United States 1947–69. *Survey of Current Business* 50:25–40.

Wolkowitz, B. 1971. A set of explicit homothetic production functions. *American Economic Review* 61:980–83.

Zellner, A., and Revankar, N. S. 1969. Generalized production functions. *Review of Economic Studies* 36:241–50.

Comment   David Burras Humphrey

Nontechnical Summary

Observed U.S. (aggregate) private-sector labor productivity grew at an annual average rate of 3.2% over the period 1947–66 but only expanded by 2.4% from 1966 to 1973. Could this slowdown in productivity growth be attributed to cyclical differences in the rate of growth of output demand between these two periods, or are other longer run, secular causes to blame for the observed decrease in productivity growth? This question is the main focus of the Mohr paper.

Using a model of interrelated (stock-adjustment) factor demand with quarterly data on six inputs for ten two-digit SIC manufacturing industries over the period 1956–72, the author concludes that the decline in labor productivity may be attributed to increased cyclical instabilities in output demands over the 1966–72 period, compared with earlier periods when output growth was relatively more stable. When industry output growth rates exhibit greater variation, and therefore are more uncertain, Mohr contends, firms increasingly adjust to changing output demands by altering production worker labor hours and capital capacity utilization in preference to adding to stocks of plant and equipment (which are more difficult and costly to adjust in response to uncertain variations in output). Correspondingly, measured labor productivity,

David Burras Humphrey is at the Board of Governors of the Federal Reserve System.

The opinions expressed here are those of the author alone and do not reflect those of the Federal Reserve System.

output per unit of labor input, will be lower when output demands are more erratic because more of the "adjustable" short-run labor input is being utilized to produce a given output level than is utilized in periods where output growth exhibits greater stability. Since output growth rates may become more stable in the future, Mohr attributes the observed decline in measured labor productivity to potentially reversible causes and rejects the notion that labor productivity need be on a secular downward trend. Greater future stability in output growth rates should lead to a reduced reliance on labor inputs in favor of increments to stocks of capital, and output per unit of labor input should rise.

The Structural Model

Observed quarterly data on gross output (Y) and production worker man-hours (X_L) can be used to obtain a measure of labor productivity. Fluctuation in a quarterly industry labor productivity index ($PR_L = Y/X_L$) over time is due to the interaction of a number of different short-run (cyclical) and longer-run (secular) influences. These influences need to be identified and separately accounted for in order to determine the possibility that the observed decline in labor productivity over the 1966–72 period, relative to earlier periods, may be reversed in the future.

Changes in the measured U.S. aggregate private sector quarterly factor productivity index may be affected by (1) cyclical versus secular changes in the underlying composition of industry gross output (and therefore input usage); (2) changes in relative factor and intermediate input prices which affect measured input usage; (3) economies of scale which affect the efficiency of the inputs being utilized; (4) changes in relative input demands due to a differing "adjustability" among factors in response to output variation; (5) factor-biased technological change over time; and (6) shifts in the age-sex composition of the labor force. In sum, observed labor productivity measures are affected by changes in output composition or the level of industry aggregation used in the productivity index; changes in relative factor prices or operating costs; the level of output produced; the adjustment process; biased technological change; and the age-sex composition of the labor force.

To reduce the agregation or output-mix problem, the author looks at factor productivity at the two-digit SIC level of industry aggregation. The effect that changes in the adjustment process can have on input demands when output growth rates become more variable is measured by use of a model in which short-run stock-adjustment relationships are specified along with the introduction of certain short-run "inputs"— such as the degree of capital capacity utilization and production worker overtime hours—which may permit more accurate identification of the short-term adjustment aspect of factor demands between different time periods and over a business cycle. Price and output-related input substitution effects are also identified. The possible effects of factor-biased technological change or the age-sex composition of the labor force, however, are not considered in the empirical application of the model. The effect of these exclusions on the empirical results is not known.

Those familiar with the literature will find that the main specification novelty of the Mohr paper lies in the use of a so-called translog cost function in place of the Cobb-Douglas production function used in an earlier study of adjustment or disequilibrium influences on factor demand by Nadiri and Rosen (1973). Since Nadiri and Rosen's Cobb-Douglas model is unnecessarily restrictive, the specification of a translog function is reasonable, and the author is better able to measure the short-run adjustment influence on factor demands to the extent that input substitution elasticities differ from one and input demands are nonhomothetic (i.e., changes in output affect the relative composition of inputs being demanded).

The hypothesis that the translog stock-adjustment model is a significant empirical improvement over Nadiri and Rosen's use of a Cobb-Douglas stock-adjustment form was tested and accepted. As well, the (nested) hypothesis that the author's use of a translog function with a stock-adjustment sequence represents a significant improvement over a translog function without a stock-adjustment sequence (i.e., inputs "instantaneously" adjust to new equilibrium positions) was also accepted. Thus the model adopted in the paper, and applied to ten two-digit SIC U.S. manufacturing industries, is a translog cost function with a square matrix of own and cross stock-adjustment coefficients. From a statistical standpoint, this model is a close cousin to a reduced form system of derived demand equations, one for each input, with a first-order autoregressive process within and across all equations.

The model uses seasonally adjusted quarterly data over the period 1956–72 on ten industries, ranging from SIC 20 (food and kindred products) to SIC 371 (motor vehicles). Six inputs are explicitly considered: total production worker hours (including overtime hours), nonproduction worker employment, capital equipment, capital plant, a measure of capital capacity utilization (assumed to be equal for both plant and equipment), and materials inputs (including energy). The variation in total production worker hours reflects both the long-run variable of total number of workers working a "normal" workweek and the short-run adjustment input of overtime hours. Because the overtime hourly wage is almost always 1.5 times the straight-time wage, overtime and straight-time wages are highly collinear, preventing the consideration of overtime and straight-time labor hours as separate inputs. Capacity utilization is the short-run adjustment input for capital. A maintained hypothesis is that different types of intermediate inputs are functionally separable from all other inputs to the production process, thus justifying their aggregation into a composite materials input. Without estimating a model which explicitly includes these inputs as separate arguments, this aggregation assumption cannot be tested.

of labor and other factor demands which are *independent of changes in*

In essence, the approach adopted in the paper is to obtain an estimate *the adjustment sequence* brought about by changing rates of output growth over the 1956–72 period. Such a quarterly "adjustment-free" demand for production worker man-hours is denoted by X^*_L. Using actual observed quarterly data on input demands (e.g., X_L without the asterisk), input prices, and output levels, a system of translog derived demand equations with a first-order stock-adjustment sequence is estimated. The estimated parameters of these derived demand equations, *excluding* the stock-adjustment coefficients, are used along with quarterly data on prices and output to generate a predicted "equilibrium" input cost share from which the short-run adjustment process has been (in effect) removed. This "equilibrium" cost share can be expressed as $S^*_i = P_i X^*_i / C^*$ for i inputs. It is from S^*_i that the desired X^*_i estimates are obtained. The observed or constructed quarterly prices (P_i) are presumed to reflect equilibrium values so that deflating the equilibrium shares by P_i gives $S^*_i / P_i = X^*_i / C^*$. Finally, to obtain X^*_i, an estimate of the "adjustment-free" total cost C^* is required.

If Mohr had chosen to estimate the system of translog derived demand equations *jointly* with the translog total cost function where all estimated equations are subject to a first-order stock-adjustment sequence, then C^* could simply be derived by substituting the quarterly data into the estimated total cost function, again excluding the stock-adjustment coefficients. This C^* estimate would reflect the influence of all of the derived demand equation parameters (excluding the stock-adjustment coefficients) which were used to generate S^*_i and, in addition, the influence of two parameters measuring Hicks-neutral technical progress (α_t) and homothetic returns to scale (α_Y). These two additional parameters enter the total cost function but not the derived demand equations (contrast Mohr's eq. [2] with eq. [4]). As Mohr only estimates the derived demand equations, he utilizes a two-step procedure to generate an estimate of C^* (the fact that the gross output variable Y is used in eq. [2] to estimate α_Y and in [4] to estimate β_i is not a problem which prevents joint estimation of [2] with [4]).

First, using the parameters of *all* the derived demand equations (excluding all the stock-adjustment coefficients) and one year *averages* of the quarterly data, Mohr generates a predicted quarterly average total cost estimate, say, PTC. PTC is the value of predicted average quarterly total cost which is "adjustment-free" and uncorrected for neutral technical progress (α_t) or homothetic returns to scale (α_Y). To obtain an estimate of C^* from PTC, α_t and α_Y must be estimated. The second step involves this estimation.

The difference between ATC and PTC, where ATC represents the actual one-year average quarterly total cost, is regressed on time and the one-year average quarterly output value in order to estimate α_t and α_Y, respectively. Once this second step is completed, then all the parameters of the translog total cost function are known. These parameters (excluding any stock-adjustment coefficients), multiplied by the quarterly data on all inputs and output, yield an estimate of C^*.

The goal of the paper is finally reached by using S^*_i, P_i, and C^* to derive a quarterly estimate of the adjustment-free input demand: $X^*_i = (S^*_i/P_i)C^*$. Mohr then computes a quarterly "adjustment-free" input demand labor productivity index $PR^*_L = Y/X^*_L$ which measures what quarterly labor productivity would have been during 1956–72 if labor demand could have immediately adjusted to the observed current quarterly output level (Y). The important contrast of the paper is between the observed quarterly labor productivity index $PR_L = Y/X_L$, which is affected by changes in input demands due to a differing "adjustability" among factors in response to output variation (i.e., influence (4) on page 230 above), and the constructed adjustment-free index $PR^*_L = Y/X^*_L$. This contrast over 1956–72 generates the basic empirical results of the study as it relates to this Conference.

The Productivity Results

The simplest way to present Mohr's results is to take unweighted arithmetic averages of three output measures and concentrate on labor productivity (as opposed to, say, total factor productivity). In table 2.C.1 below, the unweighted average annual peak-to-peak growth rate of PR_L, PR^*_L, and Y are shown for nondurables, durables, and all industries together. As the actual peak-to-peak time periods differ slightly between most of the ten industries, the dates shown are only approximate.

Table 2.C.1   **Average Annual Peak-to-Peak Growth Rates for PR_L, PR^*_L, and Y for Durable and Nondurable Goods Sectors, 1956–72**

Sector	Peak-to-Peak	PR_L (%)	PR^*_L (%)	Y (%)
Nondurables	1956–66	4.26	2.28	4.93
(SIC 20, 22, 26, 28, 30)	1966–72	3.23	3.97	3.63
Durables	1956–66	3.05	1.75	3.90
(SIC 32, 330, 333, 35, 371)	1966–72	1.87	2.33	.40
Total	1956–66	3.66	2.02	4.42
(all 10 SIC industries)	1966–72	2.55	3.15	2.02

Source: Computed from Mohr's table 2.1 for ten SIC industries.

For the two periods shown, 1956–66 and 1966–72, a least-squares regression line is fitted to quarterly data on PR_L, PR^*_L, and Y and an implied annual growth rate is computed. The growth rate of observed production worker labor productivity PR_L for nondurables over 1956–66 is thus 4.26% per year but for the later period 1966–72 it falls to 3.23%. This observed productivity slowdown is even more marked for durables and, for all industries, the growth rate falls by 1.11 percentage points.

In contrast, the adjustment-free measure of labor productivity between these two periods rises, not falls, for durables and nondurables and increases overall by 1.13 percentage points. In effect, this contrasting result says that if output variations within both of these two periods were very similar, then the actual rate of productivity growth in manufacturing need not have fallen because the productivity growth rate computed with the adjustment process "removed" did not fall between these same two periods. As can be seen from the growth rates for gross output (Y) in table 2.C.1, average output growth was slower for the second period compared with the first; it was slower on average because during 1966–72 periods of recession were mixed in with quarters of higher growth. In sum, output demands were more erratic during 1966–72 than during 1956–66. This led firms to increasingly adjust to output variations by altering labor hours and capital capacity utilization in preference to adding to stocks of plant and equipment (which are more difficult to adjust). Mohr has demonstrated that this influence alone (given that one accepts the structural model) is sufficient to "explain" the observed decline in actual labor productivity growth.[1]

More Detailed Comments

Since the author has emphasized the more technical aspects of the topic he raises, our comments necessarily reflect a similar focus. This is somewhat unfortunate since Mohr has devoted considerable energy and time to developing new data (particularly on capital) which apparently are discussed in greater detail, and contrasted with existing series, in the referenced BLS Working Paper (Mohr 1978).

Our main comments on the Mohr paper deal with the two-step process used to generate the C^* (and thus the X^*_L) estimates, and with various "tests" or extensions of the analysis which would have usefully served to place this paper in better perspective relative to existing studies. One

---

1. Since, in the early part of the first period (1956–66), output demand was more erratic than in the latter part, the computed growth rates for PR_L can be larger than those computed for PR^*_L. This is because the *level* of PR^*_L in the late 1950s will be higher than the level of PR_L but will tend to converge to more similar values toward the mid 1960s as output growth becomes much more stable. This level difference, of course, can affect the computed growth rates.

overall comment is that the paper's technical orientation will significantly limit its audience. The model used in the paper is very complex.

The two-step process used to develop the C^* (and hence the X^*_i) estimates, summarized above, suggests a dichotomy regarding the identification of adjustment effects. Recall that the author uses the estimated parameters of each translog derived demand equation (net of the estimated stock-adjustment coefficients) in conjunction with observed quarterly data on prices and output to generate an estimate of the equilibrium quarterly adjustment-free cost share S^*_i $(= P_i X^*_i / C^*)$. Here the adjustment process is explicitly accounted for in the statistical estimation of the stock-adjustment coefficients appended to the system of translog derived demand equations. Consistency would argue that a similar method should be used to determine C^*.

Instead of *jointly* estimating the translog total cost function with the derived demand equations and explicitly identifying the stock-adjustment parameters of *both* the total cost function and the derived demand equations so that both S^*_i and C^* can be derived from the jointly estimated parameters (net of all estimated stock-adjustment coefficients), Mohr utilizes the two-step process discussed above. This process utilized the parameters of all derived demand equations (excluding the stock-adjustment coefficients) and the one-year average of quarterly values of prices and output to generate a predicted one-year average quarterly value of total cost (PTC). The actual one-year average quarterly value of total cost (ATC) was also computed. The difference ATC − PTC is then regressed on time and the average quarterly value of output in order to estimate two parameters which are in the total cost function but not in the derived demand equations—α_t and α_Y.

The reason why there is no stock-adjustment term in this second step in determining the "adjustment-free" value of C^* is that the averaged quarterly data themselves are presumed to be reflective of adjustment-free equilibrium input usage of all inputs. If this is indeed true, then the averaging process itself generates the X^*_i estimate directly, and the specification and estimation of the structural model is of course unnecessary. If the simple averaging process does not really give the author an estimate of X^*_i, then there needs to be some sort of direct, explicit stock-adjustment coefficient incorporated in the regression used to estimate α_t and α_Y; otherwise the author's estimate of C^*, used to derive X^*_i from S^*_i, will not be entirely adjustment-free as the estimates of α_t and α_Y are not entirely adjustment-free themselves.

This whole problem, and the dichotomy regarding identification of adjustment effects, could have been avoided through joint estimation of the total cost function and the system of derived demand equations where *all* equations have stock-adjustment coefficients. In all probability, the error introduced into the analysis by this two-step procedure is much more likely to affect the numbers computed from the estimated parameters than it is to reverse any conclusions already reached. Just the same, consistency would have been better served through joint estimation with stock-adjustment coefficients on all estimated equations.

Regarding estimating procedures, Mohr states that while he recognizes that iterative three-stage least squares is theoretically preferable to the iterative two-stage technique actually used, the extra effort required "seemed to be an unnecessary refinement" considering the fact that so many industries were involved and that much of the data (on capital) was constructed to begin with. This argument would have been more acceptable if for at least one industry three-stage procedures were used and, when contrasted to the two-stage results, shown to have little effect. Both estimating procedures were available on the TSP computer package which was used. In this manner, readers could indeed see if this refinement was unnecessary or not, and thus whether the possible simultaneity in the determination of input usage, input prices, and output is a problem requiring correction.

In addition, as the model represents a disequilibrium system of six interrelated factor demands by the specification of a (5×5) square matrix of own and cross stock-adjustment coefficients, it would have been of illustrative interest if these results were contrasted (again for at least one industry) with a model where the cross stock-adjustment coefficients were restricted to equal zero. In such a model only the five own adjustment coefficients are estimated. (Recall that one equation is deleted from the six-input model so that only five equations are actually estimated.) If the two sets of derived demand parameter estimates were very similar, it would be clear that specification of the cross stock-adjustment coefficients (which can easily make very large demands on the information contained in the data set) is not worth the extra effort. With fewer stock-adjustment coefficients to estimate, efficiency would increase.

Efficiency would also likely rise if the information contained in the total cost function were utilized by jointly estimating the five derived input demand equations with the total cost function. Only two extra parameters need be estimated (i.e., α_t and α_Y), but total observations would rise by 20% (instead of five equations each with n observations, we now have $6(n)$ total observations) and degrees of freedom would rise.

The author's results lead him to question whether the capital-energy and capital–nonproduction worker complementarity found by previous researchers (Berndt and Wood 1975; Berndt and Christensen 1974) could possibly be due to their use of an "instantaneous adjustment" model. Mohr, using a translog stock-adjustment model, did not find complementarity between capital and nonproduction workers (energy was included in materials inputs, so there is no direct estimate of the capital-energy relationship). Actually, this need not have been only a conjecture. Since the author estimated both a translog instantaneous adjustment model and a translog stock-adjustment model in order to apply an F-test on the significance of adding a stock-adjustment process to the translog function, estimates of substitution elasticities from both models could have been directly contrasted to see if the conjecture made is correct. The fact that the reported F-tests indicate that adding a stock-adjustment sequence to the translog model results in a significant improvement in explanatory power is not sufficient to conclude that the sign of the capital–nonproduction worker elasticity is altered in moving from one model (instantaneous adjustment) to another (stock adjustment). Unfortunately, this interesting conjecture was not "tested," although the means to do so were readily at hand.

Another candidate for reconciling the apparent difference in capital–nonproduction worker results would be the fact that Berndt and Christensen used aggregate U.S. manufacturing data while Mohr uses two-digit SIC industry data. It would have been interesting if this two-digit data were aggregated and the model rerun with and without a stock-adjustment sequence in order to assess the possible effects disaggregation can have on the identification of substitution or complementarity between inputs. In this manner the reader would be better able to see just how the present study fits in with existing studies.

On a different level, the author's use of relatively unavailable two-digit capital plant and equipment data gave him the unique opportunity to examine, through model simulation, the impact that "reasonable" changes in capital data construction can have on his results. It would be useful information indeed if Mohr were able to tell us that his results are reasonably insensitive to changes in the methodology used to construct the capital data.

It is difficult to know what to make of the empirical result that various Allen own partial substitution elasticities are positive and/or that the price concavity condition is not met. From a strict theoretical point of view, this empirical result means that the underlying data do not meet the basic duality–cost-minimization condition at all points in the data set so that use of the cost function model is, in this case, empirically unsupported. On the other hand, in some of my own work, I have found the price concavity condition to be a very sensitive restriction, a restriction in which minor changes in the data set (through use of theoretical a priori information) will generate the correct theoretical result with only small changes in coefficient estimates.

In closing, after concentrating on the apparent weaknesses of the Mohr paper, it should be emphasized that, overall, this paper represents a significant addition to our understanding of the determinants of measured labor productivity variation over time. The modeling effort described here would have been useful by itself but is further enhanced by the development and use of new data on capital by two-digit industry. These data, presented and discussed in the referenced BLS Working Paper, should provide a useful base from which other researchers will be able to further investigate the subject of this Conference.

References

Berndt, E. R., and Christensen, L. R. 1974. Testing for the existence of a consistent index of labor inputs, *American Economic Review* 64:391–404.

Berndt, E. R., and D. Wood. 1975. Technology, prices and the derived demand for energy. *Review of Economics and Statistics* 57:28–44.

Mohr, M. F. 1978. A quarterly econometric model of the long-term structure of production, factor demand, and factor productivity in ten U.S. manufacturing industries, *BLS* Staff Paper 9. Springfield, Virginia: National Technical Information Service, no. PB–282–45.

Nadiri, M. I., and Rosen, S. 1973. *A disequilibrium model of demand for factors of production.* New York: Columbia University Press.

3

A Study of High and Low "Labor Productivity" Establishments in U.S. Manufacturing

Benjamin Klotz, Rey Madoo, and Reed Hansen

3.1 Introduction

There is a consensus that policy makers concerned with both the macro problems of inflationary growth, incomes, and employment policies, and the micro problems of production and exchange at the industry level, need to know more about the productivity process at work in the economy. Productivity has often been studied by using a production function to link the growing output of an industry to increases in the quality and quantity of its labor and capital inputs. Since input-output relations are engineering concepts that apply to production processes of individual plants, the production function is most easily understood at the plant, rather than at the industry, level. However, production functions have been estimated generally from industry aggregates of plant data, despite the possibility that the estimates may not correspond to true plant production relations. This potential aggregation bias is recognized in the literature, but estimation from industry data has continued, largely due to the unavailability of plant statistics.

The causes of productivity growth in plants could be uncovered if establishment data were available to estimate production functions. These micro data would be useful because the sources of productivity

Benjamin Klotz is at Temple University. Rey Madoo is at Howard University. Reed Hansen is at The Urban Institute.

This study was supported by grants from both the National Commission on Productivity and The Urban Institute. The opinions and conclusions expressed are those of the authors and do not necessarily represent those of the Commission or the Institute.

239

advance might vary among the plants of an industry, and knowledge of any difference would help government officials assess growth policies more completely. For example, if the objective is to increase productivity growth in an industry where industry productivity is measured as a weighted average of individual establishments' productivities, the average may be elevated by shifting employment and output toward the most efficient plants, or by attempting to improve the efficiency of all plants themselves. The former effect would tend to occur naturally if efficient plants increase their share of industry sales. The latter effect, however, would require some knowledge of the technology structure in the industry. And it may be found that the productivity of some subgroup of establishments is easier to raise than that of other groups. In this instance, policymakers might find it desirable to target their efforts to the most responsive establishments.

The literature on economic growth has given much attention to the process by which new technology is carried into operation by the stream of new investment. This process supposes the existence of a spectrum of plant productivities that ranges from the best-practice establishments, using the newest techniques, to the worst-practice plants, presumably using the oldest methods. A key policy question arises in this situation: Given scarce resources for investment, should the government favor investments in "best-practice" plants or a policy that facilitates the improvement of lagging establishments? The former course has received most attention in the past, but to justify such a policy, knowledge about the sources and extent of interplant productivity variation is necessary.[1]

This study uses two complementary approaches to investigate labor productivity differences among manufacturing establishments.[2] Section 3.3 discusses the nature and significance of a plant-level data set employed in the analysis. The extent of plant productivity differences within industries is displayed and analyzed by both simple correlation and multiple regression methods. The results are examined to determine if high and low productivity can be attributed to the same factors, and if differences can be explained by postulating an underlying production function for the plants. Section 3.4 then introduces and estimates a very general production function, and we test whether the parameters of this function differ significantly between high and low productivity establishments. A corresponding cost function is also estimated. An attempt is made to incorporate such factors as monopolistic competition and plant disequilibrium into the analysis. Finally, some conclusions are

1. In the past, the USSR has also emphasized productivity advance through new construction, but it is now shifting attention toward the improvement of the plants it already has. See the *Wall Street Journal*, 12 June 1975, p. 4.

2. Throughout this paper value added per man-hour is the measurement concept of productivity that we refer to.

offered about the causes of productivity differences among plants and
how establishment data could be organized to improve the analysis of
such differences.

3.2 Census Data on Establishments

To date, little research about the nature of interplant differences in
productivity exists. Census data on a wide variety of U.S. plants have
been gathered for several years but this information has not been available for analysis because the Census Bureau has not had the resources
to do an investigation itself, and because the Census Bureau is legally
prohibited from disclosing establishment information to researchers who
are not sworn census agents. Despite these limitations, a few studies of
plant productivity differences have been done. Krishna (1967) studied
plant production relations in four four-digit manufacturing industries,
and Klotz (1970) analyzed seventeen industries using Cobb-Douglas
and constant-elasticity-of-substitution production functions. Both investigations found that various proxies for measures of the capital-labor
ratio were significant in explaining labor productivity. Furthermore,
constant returns to scale seemed to be a central tendency in these industries, so that plant size was generally not a significant cause of productivity differences.[3]

Neither of these studies, however, surveyed a wide variety of industries, and neither tried to determine if variations in the capital-labor
ratio were as successful in explaining high, as opposed to low, productivity levels in plants within industries. The high-low distinction may
reveal that low productivity plants employ different production technologies from their high productivity competitors. Recent work at the Urban
Institute investigated this question by using a special tabulation from the
1967 Census of Manufactures to inspect data for groups of high and low
productivity plants within industries.[4] Madoo and Klotz (1975) applied
simple correlation methods to 102 industries and found evidence suggestive of structural differences between the two groups of establishments. Using 40 industries, Jones (1975) found that the elasticity of
demand for production workers depended upon plant size when low

3. Griliches and Ringstad (1971) found roughly the same results in Norwegian
plant data, although some industries had increasing returns to scale. Implications
about size have been invariably drawn from estimating homogeneous production
functions and then checking the adding-up properties of proportionate changes in
all inputs. But see Hanoch (1975) for remarks on the usefulness of this approach,
and Madoo (1975) for treatment of the alternative formulation and estimation
of the elasticity of scale along the cost-minimization expansion path.
4. These data were compiled by the Census Bureau for the National Commission on Productivity.

productivity establishments were examined, but that this dependence disappeared among the high productivity groups of plants.[5]

The rest of this paper contains a report of the findings of the first study (Madoo and Klotz 1973) and subsequent work with a larger sample of industries. But first we give an account of the special characteristics of the census tabulation and an explanation of how samples of industries were selected.

3.2.1 The Special Tabulation of 1967 Data

The set of data is based on information received by the U.S. Census Bureau from each establishment in 412 four-digit manufacturing industries. The Census Bureau used this information to rank establishments in each industry by their value added per production worker man-hour in 1967. The ranking was then divided into groups with an equal number of plants in each quartile.[6] Our goal is to explain quartile differences in value added per production worker man-hour. *We here call this concept productivity.*[7]

In each quartile, data are reported for production workers, nonproduction workers, gross book value of capital, payroll, man-hours, capital expenditures, value added, value of shipment, cost of materials, and inventories. These variables are constructed by summing the corresponding statistics of all plants in the quartile. The quartile data used in this study are divided by the number of plants in the sum and are thus arithmetic averages of the plant statistics in each quartile.

Sample Size Selection

For the various stages of empirical investigation attempted we were not able to use the quartile data of all 412 four-digit industries in our analysis. Missing data, especially those pertaining to gross book value of capital, combined with obviously incorrect values for some items forced us to work with a maximum set of only 195 industries. This sample of industries is not randomly chosen, but we consider it a representative sample because the distributions of both average hourly earnings and value added per man-hour are roughly the same in the 195

---

5. Size distinctions were made by grouping plants into two classes: those with 100 or more employees and those with less.

6. Decile grouping would allow more detailed analysis, but of fewer industries. Census Bureau disclosure rules are often violated in small industries when decile data pertain to only a few plants.

7. It is neither a pure efficiency nor a total factor productivity measure. Data limitations preclude using output per unit of input, where all inputs are quality-weighted and summed.

industries and in the 217 excluded from the sample.[8] The quartile data
of the 195 industries are used in the multiple regression and production
function analysis of this study. For simple correlation our results are
based on a subset of the 195. We wanted industries whose quartile totals
contained information on current capital expenditures as well as on the
gross book value of assets. An additional criterion was to choose only
industries in which each quartile was at least 89% specialized in the
production of the industry's major commodity. Together, this screening
by product specialization and the availability of gross assets and capital
expenditures left only 102 usable industries for the simple correlation
analysis;[9] they appear similar to the set of 195.

3.3 Productivity Differences among Establishments

3.3.1 Evidence from 102 Industries

Ranking and grouping establishments reveals some dramatic productivity differences among plants within industries. Figure 3.1 shows that
value added per man-hour in the top quartile of plants is over twice as
great as the corresponding industry average in 16 of the 102 industries;
the top quartile in no industry is less than 125% of the average. Productivity in the typical top-quartile group of plants is about 65% greater
than the industry average and 200% greater than the average of low-
quartile establishments. On the other hand, productivity in the low
quartiles is less than half the industry average in almost two-thirds of
the 102 cases. This bottom quartile is always less than 70% of the
comparable industry average. Value added per man-hour in the typical
low-quartile establishment is only about 40% of the industry average.
Value-added productivity for individual industries and quartiles is listed
in the table in Appendix A for the interested reader. The table also
contains measures of productivity spread within each industry.

3.3.2 Conjectures

Great productivity differences among plants in the same industry
could be caused by a number of forces. First, establishments may not

8. In addition, average productivity in quartile 1 establishments is similar in
both data sets. However, in quartiles 1 and 4 wages are 10–15% higher in our
sample industries. In quartile 4 the excluded industries have higher average productivity but this is due to several extremely high observations caused by bad
data. Little difference remains when median productivities are compared.
9. The data are discussed extensively in Madoo and Klotz (1973). The data do
not, however, reveal the extent to which different five-digit products are produced
in seemingly homogeneous four-digit industries.

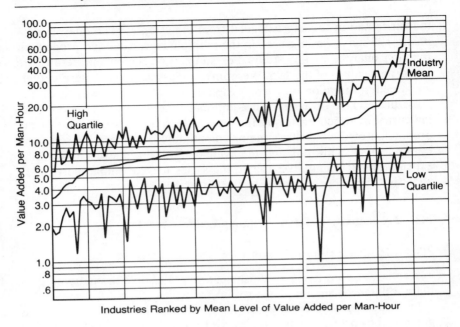

Fig. 3.1   Value added per man-hour of high and low quartiles to the
industry mean

be using the same techniques to produce industrial commodities. Economists have been giving increasing attention to the implications of the idea that a wide spectrum of technologies, corresponding to capital equipment of different ages and efficiencies, can coexist in an industry at the same time. Since new vintages of capital make use of the latest and best industrial techniques, it follows that plant productivity will depend in part on the newness of its capital equipment. The "vintage" theory assumes that new technology is carried into practice by the current stream of capital investment expenditures.[10] This reasoning leads to the first conjecture about productivity: (1) Establishments with higher (lower) productivity invest more (less) in capital assets per worker than average plants.

A second source of establishment differences in value added per production worker man-hour is the likelihood that plants are not employing the same relative quantity of other factor inputs in combination with their production workers. Most economists consider capital assets and nonproduction labor as main factors of production (in addition to

10. The idea that a spectrum of technologies can coexist in practice was first extensively explored by Salter (1962).

production workers), so it would seem likely that top-quartile plants employ relatively more of both factors than average establishments, and that low-quartile plants employ relatively less, because output per man-hour is increased if laborers are able to work with more capital assets and more skilled nonproduction technicians.[11] This argument leads to the following conjectures: (2) High (low) productivity establishments employ more (less) capital assets per production worker man-hour than average plants, (3) High (low) productivity establishments employ more (less) nonproduction workers per production worker than average plants.

A third source of productivity differences among plants could be caused by any tendency they might have to hire production laborers of various qualities. Some establishments may prefer to pay high wages and thereby accumulate a highly skilled and efficient work force; other plants may be content with lower quality production workers whose productivity and wages would therefore be lower. Higher-wage plants could therefore be expected to have higher value added per production worker man-hour. Thus the conjecture: (4) High (low) productivity plants have high (low) quality production workers and therefore pay them higher (lower) wages than average establishments.

Fourth, plants may have productivity differences simply because they are not the same size. The current body of evidence on size and productivity is mixed; there are still different methodological approaches to this issue. For example, the engineering-information questionnaire approach may be contrasted with the estimation of production functions with census data.[12]

From the data available to us, plant size is measurable by assets, shipments, or employment.[13] But use of the shipments definition of size makes it difficult to distinguish any scale economies from disequilibrium effects. Firms recently awarded large contracts will probably be expanding shipments faster than their labor force. Since value added is defined as value of shipments minus cost of materials (adjusted for inventory change), expanding plants would tend to have both supranormal shipments volume and ratios of value added per man-hour, leading to the mistaken finding that value-added productivity is associated with scale

11. For surveys of production theory and empirical findings see Brown (1967), Jorgenson (1972, 1974), Kennedy and Thirlwall (1972), and Nadiri (1970).

12. See Scherer (1970, chap. 4; 1973), and Pratten (1971) for the questionnaire approach, and Griliches and Ringstad (1971), Klotz (1970), and Krishna (1967) for production function estimation. Also, see Madoo (1975) for an adaptation of the data set of this study to measuring the optimum plant size under a cost specification for eight (SIC two-digit) industries.

13. Capacity output is ideal, but unavailable.

of plant (shipments): i.e., economies of scale would appear to exist, but this appearance could be due purely to the transitory disequilibrium experienced by the fortunate plant.[14]

Errors in the computation of value of shipments will have the same effect as short-run production oscillations in introducing a transitory component to shipments and in creating a correlation between them and value added per man-hour.[15] Since both errors and oscillations will tend to increase the correlation when plant size is defined as value of shipments, it is better practice to define size in terms of the capital assets possessed by the plant because assets are not so likely to be strongly affected by transitory movements.

These arguments lead to the final conjectures: (5) High (low) productivity plants have more (less) capital assets and more (less) output than average establishments, (6) Due to transitory output movements, value-added productivity will be more strongly linked with value of shipments than with capital assets.

A crude test of the six conjectures appears in table 3.1. The first line compares average capital expenditure per employee across the 102 industries in 1967. Their top-quartile plants spent 50% more per employee than the industry average, so this comparison is consistent with conjecture (1). But bottom-quartile plants spent only 8% less than the average, seemingly weak evidence in favor of the conjecture. This weakness may appear because capital spending for only one year, 1967, is recorded, and such investment flows may be affected by a variety of short-term events that are unrelated to the basic long-run expenditure pattern of low-quartile plants.

The second and third conjectures are clearly supported by the data. Capital assets per production worker man-hour in top-quartile establishments are almost twice the industry average, while bottom quartiles are considerably below average.[16] These differences are even more pronounced when the variable in question is the ratio of nonproduction to production workers.

Conjecture (4) also fits the data: top (bottom) quartile establishments pay higher (lower) wages than their industry average, but these wage differences are not nearly as pronounced as the value-added productivity differences between top and bottom quartiles. Variations in

14. Conversely, unluckily, plants may lose contracts and experience a temporary depression in both their shipments and value added per man-hour. This also gives the appearance of scale economies because it creates a tendency for smaller plants to register less value-added productivity.

15. In the long run, transitory effects are averaged out so plants with temporarily high (and low) productivity will tend to rebound toward the industry average in subsequent years. Evidence of this rebound effect appears in Klotz (1966).

16. Recall that the capital measure is gross book value of capital; that is, historical cost rather than constant dollar values.

Table 3.1   Average Establishment Production Statistics
             for 102 Manufacturing Industies, 1967

Statistics	Bottom Quartiles	Industry Average	Top Quartiles
Capital expenditures per employee[a]	1.03	1.11	1.62
Assets per production worker man-hour[b]	6.85	9.29	17.31
Nonproduction worker per production worker	.24	.42	1.06
Hourly wage rate of production workers[b]	2.44	2.96	3.21
Capital assets per plant[c]	1.40	2.97	3.96
Shipments per plant[c]	2.46	6.67	9.82

[a]Dollars $\times$ 1000.
[b]Dollars.
[c]Dollars $\times$ 1,000,000.

production labor quality are therefore apparently not sufficient to explain the dispersion of value-added productivity within industries.

Row 5 of the table supports the fifth conjecture: top quartile establishments tend to be almost three times as large as their bottom-quartile counterparts when plant size is defined in terms of capital assets. And, consistent with conjecture (6), the difference is even greater (four to one) when size is defined by value of shipments. Apparently there are significant transitory components in shipments, but nevertheless (due to the good performance of the asset definition of size), the evidence appears to point toward some economies of large-scale production.

The findings of table 3.1, while interesting and suggestive, do not provide clear insights into the simple correlations between value-added productivity and other variables. These correlations are reported in the next section.

3.4   Simple Correlation Results for 102 Industries

Column (1) of table 3.2 shows that the value-added productivity of bottom-quartile establishments (relative to their industry average) has only a 0.15 correlation with their capital expenditures per employee (also relative to the industry average). The top-quartile correlation is only 0.23. Therefore, for both high and low-quartile observations, *variations* in relative capital expenditures per employee are not highly correlated with variations in relative productivity—in spite of the fact that conjecture (1) is true (the average *level* of productivity and expenditures per employee is higher among top-quartile establishments). The

Table 3.2   Correlation between Value Added per Man-Hour and Selected Variables (relative to the industry mean), 1967

		Relative Variable			
Value Added per Man-Hour Relative to Industry Average	Capital Expenditures per Employee	Assets per Production Man-Hour	Nonproduction Workers per Production Worker	Average Hourly Earnings of Production Workers	Assets per Plant	Shipments Per Plant
Top quartile[a]	.23	.58	.64	.18	−.43	−.30
Bottom quartile	.15	.07	.22	−.01	.24	.49

NOTE: Correlations greater than 0.2 in absolute value are statistically significant at the 95% confidence level because 102 observations are use.

[a]Excludes book publishing (SIC 2731) because of its extremely low reported man-hours.

low correlations, if interpreted as causal relations,[17] imply that increased spending will not strongly succeed in raising either top or bottom-quartile plant productivity in relation to the industry average. More likely, however, the low correlations may be due to the fact that capital expenditures contain many transitory effects. Cumulative expenditures might have much higher correlations. This possibility appears likely because assets could be a reasonable proxy for cumulated expenditures, and variations in the degree to which top quartile productivity exceeds its industry average is strongly (0.58) correlated with the degree to which its assets per man-hour exceed the average. If high correlation is again interpreted as causation, then the value-added productivity of top-quartile establishments can be raised by increasing their assets per man-hour. Top-quartile relative productivity is also highly correlated (0.64) with a relative abundance of nonproduction workers per production worker. Therefore, the proportions with which both capital and nonproduction labor are combined with production labor seem to have a definite connection with the productivity performance of top-quartile establishments.

The other variables tend to have less association with top-quartile productivity. The quality of labor (represented by the wage rate of production workers) has an unassuming 0.18 correlation. Plant size variables (assets and shipments) are negatively correlated with variations in value-added productivity: industries where top-quartile plants are farthest above average in productivity tend to be industries where these plants are the *least* above average in size. This finding does not support a belief in economies of scale in production.

The pattern of association exhibited by bottom-quartile establishments is considerably different from the top-quartile configuration. With one exception, variations in the degree to which low-quartile productivity falls short of its industry average is *not* associated with variations in the degree to which other variables fall short of the average. Relative plant size is the exception. Both size measures exhibit positive correlation with relative value-added productivity: assets per establishment and shipments per establishment show correlations of 0.24 and 0.49, respectively. The latter correlation may be greater due to transitory components (short-run disequilibria and data errors) in value of shipments which are transmitted to value added per man-hour through their effect on value added.[18]

---

17. With 102 industry observations, correlations above 0.2 are statistically significant at the 95% confidence level. The danger of attributing causation to correlations is discussed later.

18. Remember that value added is the residual obtained by subtracting materials cost from shipments.

Surprisingly, both the relative proportions of assets and the relative proportions of nonproduction labor (per production worker), which played such a powerful role in explaining top-quartile productivity variations, have no effect on the relative performance of bottom-quartile establishments.

This diversity of results between top and bottom-quartile correlations may be due to extremely poor data submitted by bottom-quartile plants, or it may be due to something more fundamental. Errors obviously exist in the data, but Salter (1962, p. 13) indicates that moderate errors do not distort correlations unduly. Data errors therefore would have to be truly monumental to cause the vastly different correlations experienced by top and bottom-quartile plants in table 3.2.

A more promising explanation of the differences might focus on unobservable variables left out of the correlation analysis. For example, low-quartile establishments could be using completely different technologies than their top-quartile counterparts within the same industry. This technological explanation may be sufficient reason for a different correlation pattern between the two types of plants, or it may reflect some unobservable factor even more fundamental, such as management quality or five-digit product mix not captured in the four-digit statistics. For example, if there are large differences in managerial quality among low-quartile establishments, these quality differences could easily lead to large variations in plant performance. The variations would likely influence the level of technology adopted in the plant and the speed of adjustment of the plant to changing economic conditions. Data on management quality are unfortunately not directly observed.[19]

For deeper insights into plant productivity differences we must turn to a multivariate analysis. For this analysis the data set is expanded to

---

19. One good proxy for quality in the census files is the ratio of nonproduction to production workers but, as we saw, this variable was not correlated with the value-added productivity of low-quartile establishments. A better proxy might be establishment profits but this quantity is not recorded in the census data file. What is recorded is the gross margin per dollar of value added: (value added—total payroll)/value added. This is a measure of how much is left after all wages are paid. Thus the gross margin includes profits, rental payments, depreciation, and many other minor items. It is an imperfect measure of management quality, but we expect it to be correlated with value-added productivity. We find, however, that a correlation of coefficient of .01 exists between value-added productivity and gross margin (both variables expressed relative to their industry average) across industries for the top-quartile establishments, but a dramatic 0.74 results for the bottom-quartile plants. If this measure is to be taken seriously, the bottom-quartile groups could have large differences in management quality (relative to their industry average) while the top-quartile groups do not. But gross margin cannot be accepted as an unambiguous measure of productivity performance without much more analysis.

195 industries by relaxing the criterion that industries have a high product specialization ratio. This ratio is measured explicitly.

3.5 Multiple Regression Analysis Results for 195 Industries

Both economic theory and the results of our simple correlations suggest at least five variables for analysis. Two of the five (the gross book value of capital per production worker man-hour and the ratio of non-production to production workers) are chosen to represent the volume of inputs that cooperate with production labor in the production process.[20]

A third variable, the wage of production workers, is designed to capture differences in the quality of production labor between high and low-productivity plants in the same four-digit industry. The fourth variable, a measure of scale, is plant size. It is measured by the level of production worker man-hours; other measures of size (such as assets or the value of shipments) were not used because they gave unstable results when they were simply correlated with productivity. The fifth analytical variable is the plant specialization ratio, the percent of plant shipments accounted for by the primary product produced. This ratio is important because different production mixes occur among plants even though they are in the same four-digit industry, and these differences affect average plant productivity to the extent that labor productivity differs by type of product.

Since the analysis seeks to explain both high and low-productivity performance, we focus on third-quartile establishments (i.e., those just below the high-productivity quartile) as a standard of comparison. These plants tend to cluster near the productivity average for the industry, so they are a convenient proxy for the average itself. The actual industry average is not used as a standard because it is a weighted average of the productivity levels of all four quartiles, and it is therefore influenced by the productivity levels in quartiles 4 (high-productivity) and 1 (low-productivity). This influence could cause spurious correlation in the regressions when either quartile 4 or 1 is compared with the industry average.

In the multiple regression analysis the dependent variable is the percentage by which the productivity of quartile 4 establishments exceeds

20. Capital expenditures per man-hour of labor is not used as a variable because there are gaps in the data but, in any case, we observed from the sample of 102 industries that its simple correlation with productivity was small. Also, expenditures in one year do not make a sufficient contribution to the capital stock in most cases to significantly increase productivity. The effect of expenditures on productivity, however, is implicitly included in the analysis because the capital-labor ratio is used as a variable.

the productivity of plants in quartile 3. (Also, the percentage difference in productivity between establishments in quartile 3 and establishments in quartile 1 is analyzed.) This percentage difference is hypothesized to be positively related to percentage differences in (1) gross book value per production worker man-hour (K/H); (2) nonproduction workers per production worker (N/L); (3) hourly wage of production workers (W); (4) production worker man-hours (H). A fifth variable, the product specialization ratio (S), is included. It may be positively or negatively related in quartile productivity differentials because labor productivity on major products may be either higher or lower than productivity on minor products.

The five productivity hypotheses are tested by multiple regression methods and the results are displayed in table 3.3. Strikingly little of the percentage productivity differences among quartiles (of plants in the same industry) can be explained by differences in the five variables in the regression equation. The relative variables for quartile 3 versus quartile 1 yield an equation with a coefficient of determination of 0.03: only 3% of the variation in the productivity ratio (quartile 3 to quartile 1) can be explained by the five variables. In addition, none of the five variables are significantly different from zero at the 95% confidence level because no t statistic exceeds 1.7 in value (with 195 observations, if the true coefficient of regression were zero the t statistic for the coefficient would exceed 2.0 in absolute value, by chance, 5% of the time). Defining size as the level of production worker man-hours, the 0.08 regression coefficient indicates that quartile 1 plants have 0.08 lower productivity than quartile 3 establishments for every one percent that they are smaller in size than these establishments. The positive elasticity seems to indicate that plants have low productivity partly because they are undersized.

Notably, percentage differences in neither capital per production worker man-hour nor nonproduction workers per production worker play much of a role in explaining the percentage difference in productivity between quartile 3 and quartile 1 plants. Neither of the two vari-

Table 3.3   Multiple Regression Analysis of Relative Productivity Differences

Percentage Difference in Productivity: VA/H	Constant	Percentage Difference in					R^2
		K/H	N/L	W	H	S	
Quartile 4 vs. Quartile 3	.56	.16	.07	−.03	.03	−.02	.08
(t statistic)	(3.6)	(3.6)	(1.5)	(−1.0)	(1.1)	(−o.1)	
Quartile 3 vs. Quartile 1	.39	.06	.07	.13	.08	.26	.03
(t statistic)	(1.9)	(1.1)	(0.9)	(1.1)	(1.7)	(1.5)	

ables has a t value above 1.1, indicating little confidence that their impact is significantly nonzero. The capital-labor coefficient is only 0.06. If this coefficient expresses a causal relation, it suggests that a 100% increase in the capital-labor ratio of quartile 1 plants would only reduce the productivity differential between quartile 1 and 3 plants by 6%. Differences due to product mix appear also to be unimportant.

The multiple regression results for the high-productivity quartile are not much more encouraging than those for quartile 1. The regression equation in table 3.3 is able to explain only 8% of the productivity variation between quartile 4 and quartile 3 plants. In striking contrast to the low-productivity equation, differences in capital per production worker man-hour are now significantly different from zero in explaining productivity differentials. However, the regression coefficient of the capital-labor ratio is small (0.16), suggesting that a 100% increase in the ratio for quartile 3 establishments would only lower the quartile 4–quartile 3 productivity differential by 16%. Other variables in the quartile 4–quartile 3 equation have even less impact on productivity differentials, and none of their effects are significantly different from zero at the 95% level of confidence.

The results of table 3.3 indicate that interquartile productivity differences, at a point in time, cannot be well explained by variations in the five variables examined in this study. On the other hand, our results are also consistent with the theory of production which suggests that differences in output per man-hour are positively related to differences in factor proportions among establishments. The strongest variables in the multiple regression equation for the quartile 4–quartile 3 differential were capital per man-hour and nonproduction workers per production workers. We conclude, therefore, that the interquartile productivity differentials may be better explained with a framework that uses a production function as the starting point. In the next section we will try to estimate the parameters of the recently developed translog production function (Christensen, Jorgenson, and Lau 1973).

3.6 Analytical Findings

3.6.1 Models of Production

In this section we investigate the extent to which productivity differences between high and low-quartile groups are due to their being on different production functions or at different points on the same production function. In particular, we focus on differences in the partial elasticity of substitution (S) among pairs of inputs. Our assumed functional form imposes no a priori restrictions of homotheticity or additivity. Thus, partial elasticity of substitution estimates can vary with output levels, and the cross effects of various combinations of inputs on output are not assumed to be zero.

At any level of output, ease of substitution (S) will depend on the type of production technology that translates inputs into outputs. A good deal of evidence in two-input models indicates that, although S can differ considerably among some manufacturing industries at the two-digit level, it tends to be on average near 1.0 in the aggregate (Jorgenson 1974).Unfortunately, most past estimates of S have made a number of restrictive assumptions about the form of the production function. Two of them will be relaxed in this study. First, only two inputs (aggregate labor and aggregate capital) are usually introduced in the analysis for each industry; few attempts are made to disaggregate labor into two or more classes.[21] But there is accumulating evidence that the elasticity of demand for labor varies by skill class and by other divisions, such as a split between production and nonproduction workers.[22] Second, most estimates of S assume that it is a constant regardless of the relative importance of capital and labor in the production process.[23] A more flexible procedure, as in Hildebrand and Liu (1965), allows S to vary with output and input levels so that the possibility of varying rates of substitution is considered. In this study we treat S as a variable, and we also distinguish between production and nonproduction labor.

Model Specification

Because output depends on physical inputs of raw materials and other produced products, as well as on labor and capital, the theory of production suggests that the physical volume of goods produced is the appropriate concept of output. But census data on raw material inputs and other produced products used by plants are incomplete or nonexistent. Thus, in practice, we separate materials from output and work with a concept of real value added as the output of an establishment. Econometrically, this definition of output removes measurement error from the right side of the production equation (we exclude materials inputs), where it necessarily causes a bias, and puts it on the left side (in value added), where it does not necessarily distort the regression coefficients of the production equation. Furthermore, this definition is theoretically permissible if the elasticities of substitution between mate-

21. Exceptions are Berndt and Christensen (1973), Crandall, MacRae, and Yap (1975, Gramlich (1972), and Hildebrand and Liu (1965).

22. See Berndt and Christensen (1974), Diewert (1969), and Gramlich (1972).

23. This assumption is behind the popular constant-elasticity of substitution production function which is examined in Jorgenson (1974) and Brown (1967).

rials and each included (labor and capital) input are the same. Arrow (1972) discusses this separability question further.[24]

When separability holds we can write the production function as a function of primary inputs alone, so that

$$VA = f(L_1, L_2, K),$$

where VA is real value added, corresponding to the money value-added measures of our data set, and L_1, L_2, and K are the primary factors of production. Our estimation assumes that this real value-added production function is the *same* for all the plants of a given quartile across the 195 industries of our sample, but the function is allowed to vary among quartiles so that we can test for interquartile differences.

A Translog Production Function

The translog production function is given in equation (1) below. It contains three inputs and one output, and is a quadratic approximation in the logarithms of the variables for any arbitrary production function:

$$
\begin{aligned}
(1) \quad \log Q = {} & a_0 + a_1 \log L_1 + a_2 \log L_2 + a_3 \log K \\
& + a_4 (\log L_1)^2 \\
& + a_5 (\log L_2)^2 + a_6 (\log K)^2 + a_7 \log L_1 \log L_2 \\
& + a_8 \log L_1 \log K + a_9 \log L_2 \log K.
\end{aligned}
$$

The properties of this function are discussed elsewhere in great detail (Berndt and Christensen 1973, 1974; Christensen and Lau 1973). We will describe its estimation features here only to the extent necessary to furnish an understanding of how we use it to arrive at estimates of elasticity of substitution measures of L_1 with respect to the other inputs L_2 and K.

The coefficients of the translog function can be estimated directly from equation (1), but since there are nine variables (six of which are second-order terms involving squares of cross products), direct estimation risks multicollinearity. To avoid collinearity, an indirect estimation procedure can be used. If we can assume profit-maximization behavior for producers and that all markets are competitive, we can provide estimates of most of the parameters of the translog function indirectly by setting the set of three marginal productivity functions equal to their respective factor prices. Differentiating (1) with respect to $\log L_1$, log

24. For more on these issues see Hall (1973) and Diewert (1973). Apart from these theoretical considerations there is some evidence that omitting materials as an input under a value-added weight of output may not be serious because they are used in nearly fixed proportions with output (Klotz 1970).

L_2, and log K, and applying the assumption that inputs are paid the value of their marginal product, gives the marginal productivity relations:

(2)
$$d(\log Q)/d(\log L_1) = a_{10} + a_{11} \log L_1 + a_{12} \log L_2$$
$$+ a_{13} \log K,$$

(3)
$$d(\log Q)/d(\log L_2) = a_{20} + a_{21} \log L_1 + a_{22} \log L_2$$
$$+ a_{23} \log K,$$

(4)
$$d(\log Q)/d(\log K) = a_{30} + a_{31} \log L_1 + a_{32} \log L_2$$
$$+ a_{33} \log K,$$

where the a_{ij} coefficients are related to those of equation (1) in a simple manner.

Competitive profit maximization implies that $d/Q/dL_1 = P_L/P_Q$, where P_L and P_Q are the wage of labor L_1 and the price of output Q, respectively. Using the identity $d(\log Q)/d(\log L_1) = (dQ/dL_1)(L_1/Q)$, we have

(5)
$$d(\log Q)/d(\log L_1) = (P_L/P_Q)(L_1/Q) = M_1,$$

which is L_1's share in value added. Similar expressions hold for L_2 and K. Combining input (2)–(5) gives the share equations to be estimated:

(6)
$$M_1 = a_{10} + a_{11} \log L_1 + a_{12} \log L_2 + a_{13} \log K,$$
$$M_2 = a_{20} + a_{21} \log L_1 + a_{22} \log L_2 + a_{23} \log K,$$
$$M_3 = a_{30} + a_{31} \log L_1 + a_{32} \log L_2 + a_{33} \log K.$$

This set of three equations has some interesting properties that affect the way they can be estimated most efficiently. For one thing, the three cost shares in (6), M_1, M_2, and M_3, sum to unity by definition. Also, a change in log L_1 in each equation of (6) should not change the property that the cost shares sum to unity, so the sum of the three coefficients of log L_1 should be zero. The same zero-sum restriction holds if we change either log L_2 or log K. Thus there are three sets of restrictions on the a_{ij} in (6):

(7)
$$a_{11} + a_{21} + a_{31} = 0,$$
$$a_{12} + a_{22} + a_{32} = 0,$$
$$a_{13} + a_{23} + a_{33} = 0.$$

But because the three shares must add to unity, we also have the restriction that the intercepts of the equation must add to one. Thus:

(8)
$$a_{10} + a_{20} + a_{30} = 1.$$

These four restrictions are a characteristic of the translog share system. They are called the "homogeneity" restrictions because competitive cost shares sum to unity without a residual.

Estimates of the parameters of (6) help us compute the various partial elasticities of substitution among inputs. Using the notation

(9) $X_1 = L_1, X_2 = L_2$ and $X_3 = K,$

the technical definition of S is

(10) $S_{ij} = \sum_{h=1}^{3} f_h X_h |F_{ij}| / X_i X_j |F|,$

where f_h is the partial derivative of the production function with respect to input h, F is defined as the bordered matrix of derivatives of (1),

(11) $F = \begin{bmatrix} 0 & f_1 & f_2 & f_3 \\ f_1 & f_{11} & f_{12} & f_{13} \\ f_2 & f_{21} & f_{22} & f_{23} \\ f_3 & f_{31} & f_{32} & f_{33} \end{bmatrix},$

f_{ij} ($i = 1, 2, 3$ and $j = 1, 2, 3$) is the partial derivative of the production function, first with respect to input i and then with respect to input j, and F_{ij} is the cofactor of F obtained by deleting its f_{ij} row and column (see Allen 1938, pp. 503–10). $|F|$ and $|F_{ij}|$ are the determinants of F and F_{ij}. In this formulation S_{ij} is the Allen elasticity of substitution (AES). Equations (5), (6), and (10) imply that S_{ij} depends on all production function coefficients and the relative levels of all three inputs.

A Translog Cost Function

Share system (6) gives the complicated expression (10) for the S_{ij}, so confidence bounds cannot be determined to see if, for example, they differ between the plants of various quartiles. To overcome this problem we can estimate a slightly different share system whose coefficients give the S_{ij} in a very simple and direct fashion. Instead of postulating a translog production function we suppose that there is a translog average cost function derived from an underlying production function, homogeneous of degree one. Then we can write

(12) $\log C/Q = b_o + \sum_{i=1}^{3} b_i \log p_i$

     $+ \sum_{j=1}^{3} \sum_{i=1}^{3} b_{ij} \log p_i \log p_j,$

where C/Q = average cost, p_i = price of the ith input, and prices and output are exogenous. The b's are coefficients to be estimated.

Differentiating (12) gives

(13) $d\log(C/Q)/d \log p_i = b_{io}$
     $+ b_{i1} \log p_i + b_{i2} \log p_2 + b_{i3} \log p_3$

Using the results (14)–(16),

(14) $d (C/Q)/dp_i = L_i/Q,$

(15) $d\log(C/Q)/d\log p_i = [d(C/Q)/dp_i]p_i/(C/Q),$

(16) $C = VA$

(by homogeneity of Q), we have

(17) $d\log(C/Q)/d\log p_i = \dfrac{p_iL_i}{C} = \dfrac{p_iL_i}{VA} = M_i,$

(18) $M_i = b_{io} + \sum\limits_{j=1}^{3} b_{ij}\log p_j \qquad (i = 1, 2, 3).$

Since the Allen-Uzawa partial elasticities of substitution can be represented very simply by the derivatives of the cost function (Uzawa 1962), the share system (18) allows us to compute S_{ij} directly. Let the cost function be written as $C(Q_1, P_1, P_2, P_3) = Q\, g(P_1, P_2, P_3)$, then the average cost function can be written as

(19) $C/Q = g\,(p_1, p_2, p_3)$

and

(20) $S_{ij} = [g\,\partial(\partial g/\partial p_i)/\partial p_j]/(\partial g/\partial p_i)(\partial g/\partial p_j).$

For $i \neq j$ we have $S_{ij} > 0$; for $i = j$ we have $S_{ij} < 0$. Applying (20) to (13) gives

(21) $S_{ij} = b_{ij}/M_iM_j + 1 \qquad (i \neq j)$ and

             $S_{ii} = b_{ii}/M^2{}_i - M^{-1}{}_i + 1.$

Of course, since the shares add to unity, estimation of (18) is also subject to the restrictions

(22) $\sum\limits_{i} b_{io} = 1$ and $\sum\limits_{i} b_{ij} = 0 \qquad (j = 1, 2, 3).$

3.6.2   Estimating the Models

We estimate the parameters of the production function for the three different specifications just discussed. First we estimate the translog production function directly. Secondly, we estimate the share system of equation (6), and finally the share system (18) is used to provide a third set of estimates. For direct estimation of (1) we compare ordinary least-squares (OLS) and two-stage (2SLS) methods. For estimation of the translog parameters indirectly through (6) and (18), we use three-stage least-squares (3SLS). Each of the three estimation methods has its own advantages and disadvantages, depending upon whether we are estimating (1) or (6).[25]

A well known problem with OLS estimates of production function parameters is that they give inconsistent estimates of the coefficients if

---

25. A good analysis of the three methods can be found in Theil (1971).

the left-hand (dependent) and right-hand ("independent") variables are simultaneously determined. Bias arises in the structure we have imposed because the right-hand variables are not really independent of the disturbances in the regression equation, and this is the case for both the production function and the factor share system of (6). In (1), one clear chain of causation runs from the inputs on the right-side of the equation to output on the left side. In system (6), another chain runs from output back to the level of inputs through the labor demand equations represented by (6). This double chain of causation means that (1) cannot be estimated satisfactorily by OLS without bias. And in the case of (6), more efficient estimates may be obtained by estimating the system of equations jointly. The same argument for joint estimation applies to the cost system (18) as well.

Variables Used

The three inputs used in the estimation of the translog production function (1) are the man-hours of production workers (L_1), nonproduction workers (L_2), and capital (K). Data on the first two inputs are measured in physical units and the last, capital, are in dollars. For model (18), input prices are the wages of production workers (W_1), the wages of nonproduction workers (W_2), and the gross margin per unit of capital (value-added-less-payroll per dollar of gross book value of capital). In the directly estimated form (1), output is value added. Data on this variable are also given in dollar values. The problem of measurement-error bias in the direct estimates of the translog function (due to inclusion of variables measured in money units) is treated by dividing all money variables by similar money variables from neighboring quartiles. The assumption is that the output price index is the same for establishments in neighboring quartiles. All variables in the function are thus ratios of measured quantities, we hope with price effects purged.

Inputs (production workers, nonproduction workers, and gross assets, a proxy for capital) of the cost-share equation system (6) that appear on the right-hand side of the translog are left in their original measured form. The left-hand share variables represent the percentage share of total cost for each of the three inputs, with the sum of shares adding to one.

For purposes of 2SLS estimation we use nine instrumental variables: (1) the rate of growth in the price index for shipments from 1958 to 1967, (2) the rate of growth in the value of shipments from manufacturing industries from 1958 to 1967, (3) the rate of growth in the value of shipments per man-hour from 1958 to 1967, (4) the number of companies for each four-digit SIC industry, (5) the concentration ratio for each four-digit SIC industry, (6) establishments-company ratio for each four-digit SIC industry, (7) cost of materials for establishments,

(8) total beginning inventories for establishments, and (9) the specialization ratio.

In applying 3SLS to the share system, the adding-up constraints (7) and (8) imply that the disturbance terms across equations sum to zero. Any one of the three equations is a linear combination of the other two, so the covariance matrix of the disturbances has a rank of only two. Since the full 3×3 matrix is singular, one equation of (6) must be eliminated and the 3SLS procedure applied to the remaining two equations.

In principle any pair can be picked because Berndt and Christensen (1974) indicate that iterative 3SLS estimates of (6) will converge regardless of which couplet is chosen.

The 3SLS procedure can test and impose cross equation restrictions on the parameters of (6). The most important additional restrictions worth testing are the symmetry conditions. Profit-maximization in competitive markets requires that $a_{12} = a_{21}$, $a_{13} = a_{31}$, and $a_{23} = a_{32}$. Unrestricted estimates of the parameters will not in general satisfy these equalities. Symmetry simultaneously tests three important hypotheses (existence of the translog, constant returns to scale, and profit-maximizing behavior by entrepreneurs). Thus the test of $a_{ij} = a_{ji}$ is critical. 3SLS estimation of the equation system (18) derived from the cost function is also approached in a similar way.

Estimates of the Translog Production Function

Table 3.4 summarizes the first phase of our sequence of estimates. Estimates of the translog function (1) using the OLS method are reported on line 1 for quartile 1 and on line 2 for quartile 4. The first set of estimates refer to the low-productivity group of establishments (Q_1/Q_2), and the second set refer to the high-productivity group (Q_4/Q_3). The function estimated relates differences in input levels to differences in output and is written as follows:

$$(1') \qquad Y = a_o + \sum_{i=1}^{9} a_i X_i,$$

where

$$Y = \log VA_1 - \log VA_2 \text{ (subscripts refer to quartiles 1 and 2),}$$

$$X_1 = (\log L_1)_1 - (\log L_1)_2,$$

$$X_2 = (\log L_2)_1 - (\log L_2)_2,$$

$$X_3 = \log K_1 - \log K_2,$$

$$X_4 = (\log L_1)^2{}_1 - (\log L_1)^2{}_2,$$

Table 3.4   OLS and 2SLS Regression Estimates of Translog Production Function

	Constant	$\ln L1$	$\ln L2$	$\ln K$	$\ln L1^2$	$\ln L1 \times L2$	$\ln L1 \times K$	$\ln L2^2$	$\ln L2 \times K$	$\ln K^2$	Dep. Var.	R^2
$Q1/Q2$ (OLS) (t-stat.)	-370.77 (-0.896)	44.69 (0.718)	60.68 (0.995)	2.77 (0.043)	27.57 (-0.685)	-84.65 (-1.508)	96.14 (1.659)	37.67 (0.875)	-51.38 (-0.921)	-23.74 (-0.543)	lnVA	0.806
$Q4/Q3$ (OLS) (t-stat.)	-66.57 (-0.236)	-21.91 (-0.472)	24.05 (0.558)	18.23 (0.405)	30.75 (0.929)	-22.54 (-0.508)	-16.23 (-0.412)	-29.39 (-1.038)	57.33 (1.427)	-29.59 (-0.991)	lnVA	0.907
$Q1/Q2$ (2SLS) (t-stat.)	-10932.0 (-0.441)	827.62 (0.337)	800.11 (0.283)	1538.0 (0.258)	207.28 (-0.144)	481.62 (0.058)	-892.33 (-0.105)	-567.39 (-0.117)	-148.19 (-0.081)	-248.76 (-0.108)	lnVA	-0.627
$Q4/Q3$ (2SLS) (t-stat.)	-2957.4 (-0.017)	1601.0 (0.077)	287.83 (0.056)	-1032.9 (-0.031)	-2783.2 (-0.184)	2911.9 (0.114)	1058.7 (0.149)	-745.86 (-0.069)	-1705.8 (-0.198)	837.70 (0.053)	lnVA	-11.095

$$X_5 = (\log L_2)^2{}_1 - (\log L_2)^2{}_2,$$

$$X_6 = (\log K)^2{}_1 - (\log K)^2{}_2,$$

$$X_7 = (\log L_1 \log L_2)_1 - (\log L_1 \log L_2)_2,$$

$$X_8 = (\log L_1 \log K)_1 - (\log L_1 \log K)_2,$$

$$X_9 = (\log L_2 \log K)_1 - (\log L_2 \log K)_2.$$

Since we assume that the production functions for quartile 1 and quartile 2 are the same, there is no problem of identifying the various parameters of the structure. Input and value-added data for quartile 4 and 3 establishments are combined in the same manner to form ratio variables and to provide estimates of parameters for the high-productivity group. The OLS estimates for quartile 1 (line 1 of table 3.4) indicate a good fit to the data in terms of R^2 but the t statistics indicate that none of the nine input variables is significant at the 95% level ($|t| > 1.96$). This result indicates that the input variables might be highly collinear. Quartile 4 estimates have slightly higher R^2 than was the case for quartile 1 but, again, no $|t|$ value exceeds 1.96.

The 2SLS estimates (lines 3 and 4) are also insignificantly different from zero despite a great increase in their average value over the OLS case. The 2SLS fit is even worse than the OLS case, but this is a characteristic of the 2SLS approach.[26]

The Translog Production Function Share Equations

Since direct estimation of the coefficients of the production function gave poor results, we did not use them to compute estimates of the AES. Instead we turned to estimation of the share equations (6). System (6) is derived from (1) by assuming profit-maximizing behavior by establishments. Three symmetric constraints on the share equation parameters are required:

(23) $a_{12} = a_{21}, a_{13} = a_{31}$, and $a_{23} = a_{32}$.

Within the framework of 3SLS estimation, we can test (23). Because the share equations sum to unity, only two of the three share equations are independent. The capital share equation has the worst OLS fit in both quartile 1 and 4, so we chose to drop this equation.

Working with two share equations, only the symmetry restriction $a_{12} = a_{21}$ can be tested. Using 3SLS restricted estimation, we find that the hypothesis $a_{21} = a_{12}$ cannot be rejected at the 95% confidence level for either quartile 1 or 4. In addition, restrictions (7), (8), and (23)

---

26. The negative R^2s for the 2SLS cases are not reason for alarm because the formula for computed R^2 corrected for degrees of freedom can be highly negative when the true R^2 is close to zero.

imply that the sum of the three input coefficients in each share equation should sum to zero (row homogeneity): $a_{11} + a_{12} + a_{13} = 0$ and $a_{21} + a_{22} + a_{23} = 0$. Although this zero sum does not hold exactly for the unrestricted estimates, the actual coefficient sum does not depart significantly from zero at the 95% level of confidence.

Finally, imposing symmetry, we test to see if the production coefficients of quartile 1 are significantly different from those of quartile 4 at the 95% level of confidence. Estimates appear in table 3.5. The result is that we cannot reject the hypothesis that the production function coefficients are the same in both quartiles. In particular, although the fourth quartile intercepts appear different from the intercepts in the first quartile, the standard errors are so large that the hypothesis of structural equality cannot be rejected at the 95% level.

Computation of AES by Industry

We used equation (10) to compute the Allen partial elasticity of substitution S, for each of the 195 industries in quartile 1 and quartile 4. The calculation of individual elasticity estimates permits the examination of production behavior at each individual industry observation. Because industries may not have the same production structure, these calculations are a check on the appropriateness of the model.

Tables 3.6 and 3.7 present the own AES estimates for quartiles 1 and 4 based on coefficient estimates obtained using 3SLS with row homogeneity and cross equation symmetry restrictions imposed. We

Table 3.5   3SLS (with restrictions) Regression Estimates of Translog Two-Input Equation System

Equation	Constant	ln$L2$	ln$K$	ln$L1$	Dep. Var.
Quartile 1 (3 SLS with restrictions)					
Share 1	13.586	1.835	−14.675	12.841	Share L1
(*t*-stat.)	(0.902)	(0.417)	(−5.145)	(2.396)	
Share 2	43.207	−14.675	14.161	(0.515)	Share L2
(*t*-stat.)	(4.791)	(−5.145)	(4.555)	(0.209)	
Quartile 4 (3SLS with restrictions)					
Share 1	39.146	10.856	−3.700	−7.156	Share L1
(*t*-stat.)	(11.173)	(9.882)	(−4.531)	(−6.686)	
Share 2	38.198	−3.700	9.244	−5.544	Share L2
(*t*-stat.)	(15.482)	(−4.531)	(12.450)	(−7.726)	

NOTE: Each two-equation system is restricted for row homogeneity (the sum of independent variable coefficients is equal to zero) and cross equation symmetry.

Table 3.6   Frequency Distribution of Allen Elasticity of Substitution (AES) across 195 Industries (based on 3SLS estimation with restrictions)

AES Intervals		S_{11}	Quartile 1	S_{22}	Quartile 1	S_{33}	Quartile 1
	10.0+	6	(6)	52	(52)	8	(8)
5.01	10.00	4	(4)	5	(5)	1	(1)
0.01	− 5.00	42	(42)	1	(1)	3	(3)
− 0.99	− 0.0	13	(13)	0		2	(2)
− 1.99	− 1.0	47		0		28	(28)
− 2.99	− 2.0	45		3	(1)	52	(15)
− 3.99	− 3.0	14		4		39	(4)
− 4.99	− 4.0	5		7	(2)	20	(4)
− 5.99	− 5.0	4		5		9	
− 6.99	− 6.0	1		9	(1)	9	
− 7.99	− 7.0	1		6		1	
− 8.99	− 8.0	3		9		7	
− 9.99	− 9.0	1		8		3	
−19.99	−10.0	5		39	(2)	6	
	−20.0 or less	4		46		7	
Approx. Median AES		−1.68		−8.50		−3.09	

NOTE: Bracketed values represent the number of industries where calculated values for the bordered Hessians are positive and which are unacceptable for the specification of the model we have imposed. Unfortunately, we have no way of judging whether the interval around these estimates may contain negative values as well. S_{11}=production workers; S_{22}=nonproduction workers; S_{33}=capital.

note that the resulting own AES based on these coefficients vary over a wide range. The conditions of the model require that all own AES be negative but, for example, in quartile 1, 58 of the 195 own AES representing nonproduction workers, S_{22}, were positive. The same applies for quartile 4 in which there are 64 positive estimates associated with S_{22}. The remaining AES estimates also have numerous positive values. Taking these estimates on their face value, the evidence is overwhelming that the conditions for existence of the model we have imposed are not met in each industry.[27]

But the *median* values for all own AES estimates in both quartiles are negative and hence acceptable to the model specification. The bottom row of tables 3.6 and 3.7 indicates that median values for S_{11} and S_{22} are larger in quartile 4, while the S_{33} median is larger in quartile 1, suggesting greater substitution possibilities for labor in high-productivity establishments.

27. In this context we are speaking in the general sense of the suitability of our model of equilibrium behavior and the translog specification, or both.

Table 3.7   Frequency Distribution of Allen Elasticity of Substitution (AES) across 195 Industries (based on 3SLS estimation with restrictions)

AES Intervals		S_{11}	Quartile 4	S_{22}	Quartile 4	S_{33}	Quartile 4
	10.0+	20	(12)	58	(45)	1	(1)
5.01	10.00	1	(1)	5	(5)	0	
0.01	5.00	1	(1)	1	(1)	9	
— 0.99	0.0	1	(1)	0		49	(49)
— 1.99	— 1.0	2	(2)	1	(1)	115	(9)
— 2.99	— 2.0	5	(3)	0		14	(1)
— 3.99	— 3.0	7	(3)	1	(1)	5	(1)
— 4.99	— 4.0	11	(4)	3	(2)	0	
— 5.99	5.0	9	(4)	2	(1)	1	
— 6.99	6.0	20	(10)	2		0	
— 7.99	7.0	18	(2)	9		0	
— 8.99	8.0	18	(4)	7	(1)	0	
— 9.99	9.0	10	(1)	3		0	
—19.99	—10.0	46	(3)	48	(2)	1	
	—20.0 or less	27	(9)	60	(2)	0	
Approx. Median AES		—8.14		—12.19		—1.35	

NOTE: Bracketed values represent the number of industries where calculated values for the bordered Hessians are positive and which are unacceptable for the specification of the model we have imposed. Unfortunately, we have no way of judging whether the interval around these estimates may contain negative values as well. S_{11}=production workers; S_{22}=nonproduction workers; S_{33}=capital.

Cross-elasticity of substitution estimates based on the Allen formulation were also calculated, and are given in tables 3.8 and 3.9. In quartile 1 positive values occur for the median estimates of S_{12} and S_{23}, and one cross-elasticity term (S_{13}) is negative. In quartile 4, based on median cross-elasticity estimates, all pairs of inputs exhibit positive cross-elasticity effects. Positive effects imply that inputs are substitutes and negative effects imply that inputs are complements. Again, the evidence suggested by central measures is that the two quartile groups are different.

This completes the AES analysis, and we now turn to a study of the own and cross price elasticity of demand for production inputs.

Own Price Elasticities of Demand

The own AES estimates in tables 3.6 and 3.7 lead directly to the computation of own price elasticities (OPE) of demand: $\mathrm{OPE}_{ii} = M_i \mathrm{AES}_{ii}$. The distribution of OPE estimates for all inputs (not shown) is less dispersed than that of the AES estimates, the dispersion being compressed by the share weighting factor. The median OPE estimates

Table 3.8   Frequency Distribution of Allen Elasticity of Substitution (AES) across 195 Industries (based on 3SLS estimation with restrictions)

AES Intervals		S_{12}	Quartile 1	S_{13}	Quartile 1	S_{23}	Quartile 1
	10.0+	30		6	(6)	16	
5.01	10.00	40		3	(3)	19	
0.01	5.00	65	(5)	56	(56)	107	(12)
− 0.99	− 0.0	6	(6)	87		15	(15)
− 1.99	− 1.0	6	(6)	18		7	(7)
− 2.99	− 2.0	6	(6)	7		8	(8)
− 3.99	− 3.0	6	(6)	4		3	(3)
− 4.99	− 4.0	3	(3)	1		2	(2)
− 5.99	− 5.0	3	(3)	2		3	(3)
− 6.99	− 6.0	3	(3)	1		3	(3)
− 7.99	− 7.0	2	(2)	1		1	(1)
− 8.99	− 8.0	3	(3)	0		2	(2)
− 9.99	− 9.0	0		1		0	
−19.99	−10.0	12	(12)	4		4	(4)
	−20 or less	10	(10)	4		5	(5)
Approx. Median AES		2.89		−0.37		2.08	

NOTE: Bracketed values represent the number of industries where calculated values for the bordered Hessians are positive and which are unacceptable for the specification of the model we have imposed. Unfortunately, we have no way of judging whether the interval around these estimates may contain negative values as well. S_{11}=production workers; S_{22}=nonproduction workers; S_{33}=capital.

shown in table 3.10 are mostly larger in quartile 4 than in quartile 1. They differ substantially in the case of nonproduction labor and mildly in the case of capital. In the case of production labor (E_{11}) they are reasonably concentrated about the median of −0.94 for quartile 1, while they are somewhat more dispersed about the median of −1.15 for quartile 4. The median value for nonproduction labor (E_{22}) is −1.23 for quartile 1 and −2.00 for quartile 4. The median OPE for capital is −0.58 for quartile 1 and −0.63 for quartile 4.

Cross Price Elasticities of Demand

The cross price elasticity of demand estimates are computed for pairs of inputs by a generalization of the OPE formula, and are denoted by CPE:

$$(24) \qquad CPE_{ij} = M_i AES_{ij}.$$

We mention only a few of the size comparisons for median values of quartiles among factors, since OPE will take on the sign of the respective AES. Median CPE estimates for quartile 4 are all positive. All

Table 3.9   Frequency Distribution of Allen Elasticity of Substitution (AES) across 195 Industries (based on 3SLS estimation with restrictions)

AES Intervals		S_{12}	Quartile 4	S_{13}	Quartile 4	S_{23}	Quartile 4
	10.0+	42		6	(4)	9	(1)
5.01	10.0	40		9	(6)	20	(6)
0.01	5.0	52		156	(42)	129	(27)
− 0.99	0.0	1	(1)	7	(2)	19	(17)
− 1.99	− 1.0	2	(2)	6	(3)	3	(1)
− 2.99	− 2.0	2	(2)	1	(1)	1	(1)
− 3.99	− 3.0	5	(5)	4	(3)	3	(3)
− 4.99	− 4.0	1	(1)	1		1	(1)
− 5.99	− 5.0	6	(6)			0	
− 6.99	− 6.0	4	(4)			3	(1)
− 7.99	− 7.0	3	(3)			1	
− 8.99	− 8.0	5	(5)			1	
− 9.99	− 9.0	3	(3)			3	(1)
−19.99	−10.0	8	(8)	2		2	(2)
	−20.0 or less	21	(21)	3			
Approx. Median AES		+3.51		+2.35		+2.35	

NOTE: Bracketed values represent the number of industries where calculated values for the bordered Hessians are positive and which are unacceptable for the specification of the model we have imposed. Unfortunately, we have no way of judging whether the interval around these estimates may contain negative values as well. S_{11}=production workers; S_{22}=nonproduction workers; S_{33}=capital.

Table 3.10   Median Elasticity of Substitution of 195 Industries (based on 3SLS estimation with restrictions)

Elasticity Measure	Quartile 1	Quartile 4
Own price elasticity of substitution		
Production workers (E_{11})	−0.94	−1.15
Nonproduction workers (E_{22})	−1.23	−2.00
Capital (E_{33})	−0.58	−0.63
Cross price elasticity of substitution		
Production workers–nonproduction workers (E_{12})	1.87	0.98
Production workers–capital (E_{13})	−0.34	0.49
Nonproduction workers–capital (E_{23})	0.40	0.39

inputs are substitutes. In quartile 1 the median CPE for production workers and capital (E_{13}) is negative at −0.34. Thus, unlike quartile 4, capital and production workers are complements. The median CPE for production workers and nonproduction workers is positive at 1.87, indicating that they are substitutes. The median estimate of the CPE for nonproduction workers and capital is 0.40 in quartile 1.

In the next section we report the estimates from the analysis of a translog average cost function which uses price variables as inputs.

The Share Equations of a Translog Cost Function

In this part of the study we estimate the parameters of a translog cost function due to Christensen, Jorgensen, and Lau (1973), under the assumption of constant returns to scale. As demonstrated in (12)–(18), the estimating forms of the share equations also appear in the logs of the variables, but, unlike the profit-maximizing model, with the production function as the starting point, they are functions of input prices and not functions of input levels.

We separately tested for cross equation symmetry and linear homogeneity and found that the test restrictions were not rejected at the 95% level. Symmetry and homogeneity restrictions were then imposed and the system reestimated to provide estimators of Allen partial elasticities of substitution (AES). Table 3.11 summarizes the results of the regression estimation. The coefficient estimates are in general poor.

We computed the Allen partial elasticities anyway and evaluated them at the mean level of a quartile class according to formula (22):

$$S_{ij} = \frac{B_{ij}}{M_i M_j} + 1,$$

when

$$i = j, S_{ii} = \frac{B_{ii}}{M_i^2} + 1 - \frac{1}{M_i}.$$

Our results on the own and cross AES estimates are reported in table 3.12. Since all cross elasticity estimates are positive, no significant complementarity between inputs is indicated. In addition, all own-elasticity measures have the appropriate negative sign.

In table 3.12, the own AES estimates differ considerably between the two quartiles. Estimates corresponding to S_{11} and S_{22} in quartile 4 are 6 times and 2 times larger than their first-quartile counterparts. The value for S_{33} in quartile 1, however, is 6 times greater than in quartile 4. Table 3.13 gives the corresponding estimates of the OPE for the three inputs, and for comparison we repeat the results of OPE estimates obtained via the production function route in table 3.14. The estimates from both specifications are remarkably close. The clear pattern that emerges, except for E_{33}, is that quartile 4 effects are more elastic than quartile 1. This completes the analysis of translog specifications of technology differences.

Table 3.11   **3SLS (with restrictions) Regression Estimates of Translog Two–Input Price Shares Equation System**

	Constant	ln W1	ln W2	ln VK	Dep. Var.
Quartile 1 (3 SLS with restrictions)					
Share 1	48.555	−11.006	11.722	−0.716	Share L1
(*t*–stat.)	(8.863)	(−1.307)	(1.386)	(−4.117)	
Share 2	25.261	11.722	−11.608	−0.113	Share L2
(*t*–stat.)	(5.287)	(1.386)	(−1.366)	(−1.108)	
Quartile 4 (3SLS with restrictions)					
Share 1	36.823	−12.140	2.826	9.314	Share L1
(*t*–stat.)	(4.123)	(−2.525)	(0.575)	(2.115)	
Share 2	28.501	2.826	−9.255	6.429	Share L2
(*t*–stat.)	(3.540)	(0.575)	(−1.441)	(1.880)	

NOTE: Each two-equation system is restricted for row homogeneity (the sum of independent variables coefficients is equal to zero) and cross equation symmetry.

Table 3.12   **Allen Partial Elasticities of Input Substitution across 195 Industries (based on 3SLS estimation with restrictions)**

Quartile	Own		Cross	
1	$S_{11}=-0.79$		$S_{12}=$	1.82
	$S_{22}=-5.99$		$S_{13}=$	0.91
	$S_{33}=-6.31$		$S_{23}=$	0.96
4	$S_{11}=-6.214$		$S_{12}=$	1.99
	$S_{22}=-11.70$		$S_{13}=$	1.66
	$S_{33}=-0.03$		$S_{23}=$	1.74

NOTE: OPE estimates obtained from two-input price shares equation system.

Within the cost function framework, an attempt was made to see if economies of scale could be a possible explanation for differences in productivity between the two quartiles. In carrying out this test we added a proxy variable for scale, the log of man-hours of production workers, to the share equations.[28] Using 3SLS with all restrictions im-

28. This new share equation system would result if we postulated a translog average cost function with nonconstant returns to scale $[C/Q = f(p_1, p_2, p_3, Q)]$, and derived its share equations as in (12)–(18).

Table 3.13	Own Price Elasticity of Demand for Inputs across 195 Industries (based on 3SLS estimation with restrictions): Cost Function Estimates		
Quartile 1	$E_{11} = -0.51$	$E_{22} = -1.31$	$E_{33} = -0.81$
Quartile 4	$E_{11} = -1.35$	$E_{22} = -1.56$	$E_{33} = -0.02$

NOTE: OPE estimates obtained from two-input price shares equation system.

Table 3.14	Own Price Elasticity of Demand for Inputs across 195 Industries (based on 3SLS estimation with restrictions): Production Function Estimates		
Quartile 1	$E_{22} = -1.23$	$E_{11} = 0.94$	$E_{33} = -0.58$
Quartile 4	$E_{22} = -2.00$	$E_{11} = 1.15$	$E_{33} = -0.63$

NOTE: OPE estimates obtained from two-input price shares equation system.

posed, none of the coefficients of the scale variable were significant, suggesting that scale does not explain differences in labor shares and differences in labor productivity among quartiles or industries.

3.6.3 Monopoly and Growth Considerations: A Further Single-Equation Experiment

The 3SLS estimates of the three translog share equations (6) indicate that none of the corresponding coefficients differ significantly (at the 95% level) between quartiles 1 and 4. However, in general, our estimates are not very precise, and we had to appeal to average measures in many cases for the experiment to make economic sense. The theoretical specification appears to be too rich for the data we have on our hands. We speculate, therefore, that quartile 1 data, especially, may contain much "noise" and are not explainable by a static production model. The divergence of coefficients may indicate that corresponding parameters of the translog production function really differ between the quartiles, or perhaps it may indicate that the input shares of establishments in the two quartiles did not arise from long-run equilibrium conditions in 1967. This latter possibility is worth investigating because, due to the ranking of plants by their productivity, establishments may appear in the top quartile not only because they have normally high productivity but also, as mentioned previously, because they may be the beneficiary of favorable economic events which have added a positive transitory component to their value added per production worker man-hour. Similarly, bottom-quartile plants may, on the average, have some negative transitory components in their 1967 productivity. A positive component in the value-added productivity of quartile 4 plants will lift their capital share above, and reduce their labor shares below, the long-run levels. Conversely, a negative transitory element in quartile 1 establishments will depress their capital share below, and push their labor shares above, true equilibrium amounts.

The disequilibrium hypothesis cannot be checked directly because a longitudinal sample of plant data is unavailable to us. Instead, as proxies for quartile disequilibrium, we need unpublished Bureau of Labor Statistics data on the past (1958–67) trend of growth rates in industry shipments, shipments per man-hour (productivity), and shipment prices. In this instance output was defined as value of shipments deflated for price changes, and productivity was defined as deflated shipments per man-hour of production workers. In order to discover which of the three growth-rate variables was the most important indicator of disequilibrium we added all three to our previous multiple regression equation intended to explain interquartile productivity differentials. The equation is reproduced in table 3.15 along with the effects of adding the growth-rate variables. Table 3.15 indicates that the past rate of productivity increase in an industry is significantly related to its productivity differentials, not only between quartiles 4 and 3 but also between quartiles 3 and 1. This suggests that a group of leading plants experience productivity surges that tend to outstrip the industry average and to drag up the average as well. And, in addition, the accelerating average leaves the low-productivity establishments even further behind. The strong effect of past productivity advance upon productivity differentials suggests that, at some point, the plants that fall into either quartiles 1 or 4 are out of equilibrium, the former group being below their long-run level of productivity and the latter set being above it.[29]

The past rate of price increases in an industry also has a significantly positive influence on interquartile productivity differences. Perhaps this is due to unequal shifts in the demand for specific plants' products that allow these establishments to increase prices by more than their competitors. Or price increases may be due to monopoly power, in which case they would be associated with productivity differentials flowing from the same source. We will discuss this possibility shortly.

The third growth-rate variable, that of shipments, has a significantly negative effect on productivity differentials. More rapid expansion of demand for an industry's products may allow productivity laggards to catch up somewhat with their higher productivity competitors, perhaps because of a relatively faster expansion of sales which lifts their capacity utilization and their labor productivity.

All three growth-rate variables have an influence on productivity differentials between quartiles 1 and 4, and these differentials in turn

---

29. This conclusion is consistent with the erosion of plant productivity differentials through time noticed in seven of eight industries studied by Klotz (1966).

Table 3.15   Multiple Regression Analysis of Interquartile Productivity Differentials

Productivity Differential	Constant	%Δ(K/H)	%Δ(N/L)	%Δ(W)	%Δ(H)	ΔS	%ΔP	%ΔVS	%Δ(VS/H)	log(P/C)	log(Con.)	R^2
Quartile 4 to quartile 3	.559 (3.6)*	.158 (3.6)	.066 (1.5)	−.034 (−1.0)	.029 (1.1)	−.015 (−0.1)						.080
Percentage difference	.105 (0.5)	.154 (3.7)	.079 (1.8)	−.032 (−1.0)	−.007 (−0.2)	−.013 (−0.1)	.045 (3.3)	−.009 (−1.9)	.048 (4.2)	−.085 (−2.0)	.046 (1.7)	.170
Quartile 3 to quartile 1	.388 (1.9)	.061 (1.1)	.067 (0.9)	.130 (1.1)	.078 (1.7)	.261 (1.5)						.028
Percentage difference	.179 (0.6)	.042 (0.8)	.134 (1.8)	.108 (0.9)	.059 (1.3)	.157 (0.9)	.047 (1.9)	−.021 (−2.6)	.070 (3.5)	.049 (0.7)	.067 (1.4)	.107

*t values based on 195 observations: $t = 1.65$ (90% confidence); $t = 1.97$ (95% confidence)

Variables:
    K/H = capital per production worker man-hour
    N/L = nonproduction workers per production worker
    W = hourly wages of production workers
    H = production workers man-hours
    S = product specialization ratio
    P = price of shipments
    VS = value of shipments
    VS/H = shipments per production worker man-hour
    E/C = plants per company
    Con. = Concentration ratio (percent of shipments in four largest companies)

are associated with disparities in input shares between the quartiles. Thus, the growth-rate variables should be incorporated into the translog share equations in some manner. But the differential impact of the variables suggests that they may have a multiplicative, rather than an additive, effect on input shares. In this instance, each input variable in the share equations should be multiplied by some correction factor, which would be a weighted average of the past growth rates of industry output, productivity, and prices. The problem with this approach is that the weights are unknown.

In addition to disequilibrium elements, monopoly power may cause differences in the estimated coefficients of comparable share equations between quartiles 1 and 4. If quartile 4 establishments tend to have less elastic product demand than their quartile 1 competitors, then the capital share (measured as a residual in this study) will be larger in quartile 4, even if both groups of plants use the same technology and factor proportions. Conversely, because factor shares add to unity, the labor share of the quartile 4 group of plants will be less than in quartile 1.

Although monopoly affects the capital and labor share equations, we cannot incorporate it directly into the share estimates because the elasticity of product demand is unknown. However, two proxies for monopoly power were chosen for analysis: the industry concentration ratio (the fraction of industry shipments accounted for by the four largest companies) and the intensity of multiplant companies (the ratio of establishments to firms in the industry). Both should be positively related to the degree of monopoly in an industry, and the greater this degree the greater the chance that productivity differentials could occur. Table 3.15 indicates that the concentration ratio was significantly related (with 90% confidence) to the magnitude of the productivity differential between quartiles 4 and 3, but the ratio was less successful in explaining the quartile 3–quartile 1 discrepancy. This result suggests that high-productivity plants may belong to firms with market power while their low-productivity competitors have little market impact and may tend to act more like pure competitors: quartile 4 plants may belong to companies who are price makers, while quartile 1 establishments may tend to be owned by firms who are price takers. This explanation is consistent with the previous finding that, *ceteris paribus*, productivity differentials are wider in industries with larger past rates of price advance. The multiplant variable for monopoly power did not perform as well as the concentration ratio, being insignificant in the quartile 3–quartile 1 comparison and having a negative influence on the quartile 4–quartile 3 difference.

Summarizing the multiple regression results of table 3.15, we note that, although R^2s were low in all cases, the addition of both equilibrium and monopoly variables doubled the goodness of fit of the top-quartile equation and quadrupled that of the bottom quartile. These added variables did not appreciably alter the coefficients of the factor proportion variables (capital per man-hour and nonproduction workers per production worker) in the top-quartile equation, and they made these coefficients more significant statistically. On the other hand, the added variables decreased the coefficient of capital per man-hour, while increasing that of nonproduction workers per production worker, in the bottom-quartile equation; the t statistics moved accordingly. In addition, the returns to scale proxy variable (production worker man-hours) becomes insignificant in both quartile equations with the addition of monopoly and disequilibrium variables. This behavior seems to suggest that a production function explanation of the top-quartile productivity differential is more reliable than a similar explanation of the bottom-quartile difference. Our results also indicate that the incorporation of disequilibrium and monopoly elements into the translog share equations might move the estimated coefficients of comparable share equations, between high and low-productivity plants, closer together. Supposing the parameters of comparable share equations to be the same, the only technical difference among plants would then occur in the intercept terms a_o of their translog production function (1). This term, which is not estimated by the share equations, would be an index of technical ability rather than allocative wisdom. In this case the three major sources of interquartile productivity dispersion would be differences in pure technical efficiency, transitory disturbances in establishment productivity, and monopoly power.

3.7   Summary and Conclusions

Estimates from a theoretical formulation based on the translog production function and multiple regression analyses both indicate that factor proportions, represented by capital per man-hour and nonproduction workers per production worker, contribute toward an explanation of high productivity in manufacturing establishments. But these factors are less successful in explaining the level of low-productivity plants. Monopoly power also seems to be more important in explaining high, as opposed to low, productivity.

In addition to factor proportions and monopoly power effects, both high and low-productivity establishments in 1967 appear to be out of equilibrium. Their outputs, and possibly their inputs, seem to contain significant transitory elements that depend on the past growth rates of industry output, productivity, and prices. These elements appear to be strong enough to cast doubt on any static formulation of productivity differences.

In all of our regression experiments with interquartile productivity differences, unexplained factors buried in the residual were most noticeable. The combined effect of factor proportions and monopoly power explained only 17% of the quartile 4–quartile 3 productivity variation, and only 11% of the quartile 3–quartile 1 differential, across 195 industries. Differences in managerial quality and in product (at the five and seven-digit level of disaggregation) may be responsible for much of the residual variance. On the other hand, the low R^2s of the productivity equations may have been due to our poor proxies for measuring disequilibrium effects.

Klotz (1966) found that industries differ in the extent to which their high and low-productivity plants move toward the industry mean through time. This regression can be due to a competitive tendency to equalize their factor proportions, plus the attrition of their initial transitory components in output and inputs. These two effects can only be isolated and measured by tracing specific groups of high and low-productivity establishments in an industry over a period of years, while relating their differential productivity growth to their initial productivity level and the changes in their factor proportions. Ideally, for this undertaking, the analyst needs a longitudinal data set on each industry in which annual production statistics on specific groups of plants are recorded for a number of years. Such a data set would permit investigation of the dynamics of plant productivity growth, and knowledge of the dynamics of the situation would allow separation of the long-run causes of establishment productivity differentials from the transitory disturbances. The long-run causes are of most interest because the transitory forces are probably random and uncontrollable. We conclude, therefore, that due to the power of short-run disturbances in plant productivity, cross-section data for one year, such as those analyzed in this study, are of limited use for analyzing establishment differentials.

Since the preparation of data at the plant level is an expensive operation and census studies are years apart, we conclude with a few remarks as to how the usefulness of cross-section data can be improved. First, to analyze interquartile productivity differentials, the statistical theory of ranking bias (Harman and Burstein 1974) requires that plants be ranked *not by a productivity measure but by a variable that is a prime cause of productivity*. Such a ranking would reduce the difficulty of measuring transitory forces affecting particular groups. The best candidate for a causal variable may be capital per production worker man-hour. We therefore suggest that *establishments be ranked by their capital per production worker man-hour in any future tabulations designed to analyze productivity differences*. In addition, according to the ranking theory in Harman and Burstein (1974), the best ordering of plants is by a variable most strongly related to long-run productivity but not correlated with the transitory component. This variable might be a measure of plant productivity predicted from an equation estimated by regressing actual labor productivity against a number of causal variables at the individual establishment level. When this is done, the regression can be provided the analyst, along with the quartile or decile groupings of the plant data, without violating Bureau of Census rules about disclosure of individual establishment information.

Second, most empirical production-function forms suggest a double-log relation between productivity and its causal variables. This implies that *geometric as well as arithmetic averages of the data of individual plants comprising the quartile should be reported.* The arithmetic averages now derivable from census tabulations do not allow rigorous testing of production function relations which require geometric averages.

Much of the unexplained variation in quartile productivity might be due to differences in product specialization at the five-digit level, and managerial and other quality differences in inputs. Therefore, we suggest, thirdly, that *information on five-digit product specialization be included in future compilations of plant data.* Qualitative factors might be represented by the size or other attributes of the parent company as well as the work force in establishments. It is easy to provide identification codes that describe specific economic attributes of companies along with the plant information, and these might be the key to uncovering how differences arise.

Appendix A

Table 3.A.1   Value Added per Man-Hour (in dollars)

SIC	Rank	Ind. Mean ($=X$)	Quartile Means				Industry Dispersion		Coefficients of Variation	
			1	2	3	4	Range (Q4–Q1) ($=s_1$)	Range (Q3–Q1)/2 ($=s_2$)	$S1/X$	$S2/X$
2731	1	56.76	8.44	34.57	132.70	2143.00	2134.57	62.13	37.61	1.09
2087	2	54.11	7.28	14.10	22.33	109.76	102.48	7.53	1.89	0.14
2095	3	38.38	7.47	16.76	26.55	57.30	49.83	9.54	1.30	0.25
2911	4	31.31	5.18	14.01	25.16	55.12	49.94	9.99	1.59	0.32
2822	5	24.10	7.39	15.03	24.41	38.81	31.42	8.51	1.30	0.35
2085	6	23.16	5.33	13.67	23.78	43.79	38.46	9.22	1.66	0.40
2084	7	23.00	3.11	12.19	22.85	37.14	34.03	9.87	1.48	0.43
3861	8	22.26	4.82	8.19	10.39	32.97	28.15	2.79	1.26	0.13
2082	9	20.12	8.23	13.00	17.70	27.20	18.97	4.73	0.94	0.24
2026	10	18.60	5.24	11.19	18.63	36.03	30.79	6.70	1.66	0.36
3573	11	18.44	4.13	8.10	17.34	35.97	31.84	6.61	1.73	0.36
2851	12	18.06	7.88	12.86	17.20	28.42	20.54	4.66	1.14	0.26
2086	13	17.66	6.37	11.36	16.44	31.99	25.62	5.03	1.45	0.29
2042	14	16.37	2.64	7.66	13.30	32.66	30.02	5.33	1.83	0.33
3241	15	15.47	8.92	12.50	16.83	26.55	17.63	3.95	1.14	0.26
2041	16	14.97	3.56	8.18	12.23	25.87	22.31	4.33	1.49	0.29
2024	17	14.89	5.37	9.92	14.89	29.42	24.06	4.76	1.62	0.32
2647	18	14.36	3.92	8.05	12.61	21.45	17.53	4.35	1.22	0.30
2711	19	14.20	4.34	7.32	11.63	19.86	15.52	3.65	1.09	0.26
3011	20	13.36	5.82	9.66	12.57	18.51	12.70	3.38	0.95	0.25
2951	21	13.13	5.23	11.18	18.31	40.61	35.08	6.39	2.67	0.49

Table 3.A.1 (continued)

SIC	Rank	Ind. Mean ($=X$)	Quartile Means				Industry Dispersion		Coefficients of Variation	
			1	2	3	4	Range (Q4–Q1) ($=s_1$)	Range (Q3–Q1)/2 ($=s_2$)	S1/X	S2/X
3275	22	12.92	7.21	11.04	14.08	19.29	12.07	3.43	0.93	0.27
2893	23	12.33	5.03	11.11	15.09	23.74	18.71	5.03	1.52	0.41
3662	24	12.12	4.21	7.91	11.57	20.45	16.25	3.68	1.34	0.30
2831	25	11.74	3.21	7.94	13.05	24.40	21.19	4.92	1.81	0.42
3356	26	11.39	0.97	8.33	12.26	19.57	18.60	5.64	1.63	0.50
3537	27	11.20	4.27	6.75	10.16	15.28	11.01	2.94	0.98	0.26
2052	28	11.01	3.73	5.83	7.84	14.03	10.31	2.06	0.94	0.19
3351	29	10.92	5.62	9.07	11.62	18.22	12.60	3.00	1.15	0.27
2051	30	10.90	3.72	6.95	10.10	16.93	13.21	3.19	1.21	0.29
3585	31	10.49	4.65	7.42	10.29	15.83	11.18	2.82	1.06	0.27
3295	32	10.42	4.35	7.44	11.02	18.65	14.30	3.34	1.37	0.32
3519	33	10.39	4.69	7.54	9.35	14.48	9.79	2.33	0.94	0.22
2083	34	10.33	3.71	8.24	11.57	16.96	13.25	3.93	1.28	0.38
3411	35	10.13	5.01	8.61	12.13	23.62	18.61	3.56	1.84	0.35
3522	36	10.01	3.35	5.74	8.13	13.25	9.90	2.39	0.99	0.24
3612	37	9.91	3.87	6.60	9.05	13.09	9.23	2.59	0.93	0.26
2952	38	9.65	5.07	7.82	10.61	22.30	17.23	2.77	1.79	0.29
3843	39	9.62	4.33	7.20	9.94	19.13	14.79	2.80	1.54	0.29
3566	40	9.61	5.31	7.83	9.91	13.46	8.16	2.30	0.85	0.24
2094	41	9.48	2.63	6.33	9.43	20.68	18.05	3.40	1.90	0.36
2621	42	9.45	4.83	7.53	9.79	13.83	8.99	2.48	0.95	0.26
2034	43	9.33	2.03	5.57	8.97	19.31	17.28	3.47	1.85	0.37
3352	44	9.29	3.49	6.44	8.90	14.19	10.70	2.71	1.15	0.29

Table 3.A.1 (continued)

SIC	Rank	Ind. Mean ($=X$)	Quartile Means				Industry Dispersion		Coefficients of Variation	
			1	2	3	4	Range (Q4–Q1) ($=s_1$)	Range (Q3–Q1)/2 ($=s_2$)	S1/X	S2/X
3443	45	9.27	4.30	6.42	8.32	16.35	12.05	2.01	1.30	0.22
2061	46	9.23	3.66	5.75	9.03	18.16	14.50	2.69	1.57	0.29
3391	47	9.04	5.63	7.67	9.54	14.21	8.58	1.96	0.95	0.22
3452	48	9.03	4.94	7.29	9.82	14.00	9.06	2.44	1.00	0.27
3429	49	8.91	4.16	6.34	8.20	13.30	9.14	2.02	1.03	0.23
2013	50	8.82	3.75	6.67	9.14	15.74	11.99	2.70	1.36	0.31
3423	51	8.82	4.06	6.12	8.03	14.34	10.28	1.99	1.17	0.23
3292	52	8.79	4.58	6.77	9.16	14.51	9.93	2.29	1.13	0.26
2542	53	8.66	3.67	5.47	7.88	13.45	9.78	2.10	1.13	0.24
3582	54	8.58	4.00	7.31	9.29	13.26	9.26	2.65	1.08	0.31
3634	55	8.54	3.49	5.76	8.17	14.83	11.34	2.34	1.33	0.27
3691	56	8.50	4.68	6.96	8.65	13.42	8.73	1.98	1.03	0.23
2654	57	8.41	4.37	6.23	8.40	12.11	7.74	2.01	0.92	0.24
3642	58	8.39	4.34	6.28	8.22	13.55	9.21	1.94	1.10	0.23
3231	59	8.37	3.62	5.54	7.24	13.10	9.48	1.81	1.13	0.22
3621	60	8.34	3.64	5.98	8.03	12.27	8.63	2.19	1.04	0.26
3562	61	8.26	4.94	7.63	9.49	12.01	7.07	2.28	0.86	0.28
2033	62	8.14	2.78	5.19	7.83	15.21	12.42	2.52	1.53	0.31
2433	63	8.04	3.74	5.79	8.15	13.95	10.21	2.21	1.27	0.27
3461	64	7.98	4.18	6.04	7.99	11.21	7.03	1.90	0.88	0.24
2272	65	7.95	2.89	5.41	7.94	15.16	12.27	2.52	1.54	0.32
3255	66	7.91	4.31	6.46	8.23	12.27	7.96	1.96	1.01	0.25
3951	67	7.80	3.00	5.04	6.39	13.73	10.73	1.69	1.38	0.22

Table 3.A.1 (continued)

SIC	Rank	Ind. Mean ($=X$)	Quartile Means				Industry Dispersion		Coefficients of Variation	
			1	2	3	4	Range (Q4–Q1) ($=s_1$)	Range (Q3–Q1)/2 ($=s_2$)	S1/X	S2/X
3491	68	7.78	4.55	6.44	7.98	10.82	6.27	1.72	0.81	0.22
3272	69	7.73	3.49	5.59	7.96	13.89	10.40	2.24	1.35	0.29
3651	70	7.66	2.40	5.07	6.64	12.29	9.89	2.12	1.29	0.28
3544	71	7.63	4.44	6.44	8.05	11.63	7.20	1.81	0.94	0.24
3715	72	7.56	3.62	5.90	7.37	11.96	8.34	1.87	1.10	0.25
3451	73	7.24	4.33	6.21	7.92	12.16	7.83	1.79	1.08	0.25
3629	74	7.20	3.37	5.56	8.06	11.82	8.45	2.34	1.17	0.33
3742	75	7.06	2.59	6.74	9.68	13.74	11.16	3.55	1.58	0.50
3221	76	7.05	4.93	6.14	7.19	9.53	4.60	1.13	0.65	0.16
3674	77	6.94	4.00	5.73	8.53	11.47	7.47	2.27	1.08	0.33
2396	78	6.90	2.89	4.65	5.93	9.12	6.24	1.52	0.90	0.22
3481	79	6.76	3.61	5.36	7.20	11.62	8.01	1.80	1.18	0.27
2642	80	6.73	4.76	5.96	7.22	9.19	4.43	1.23	0.66	0.18
2022	81	6.67	1.53	4.15	6.37	13.66	12.14	2.42	1.82	0.36
3949	82	6.57	2.78	4.20	6.14	10.90	8.11	1.68	1.24	0.26
3479	83	6.42	3.71	5.11	6.76	12.32	8.61	1.52	1.34	0.24
3321	84	6.37	3.22	4.83	5.99	8.94	5.72	1.38	0.90	0.22
3259	85	6.27	3.42	5.11	6.73	9.77	6.35	1.66	1.01	0.26
3471	86	6.21	3.54	5.06	6.73	10.58	7.04	1.60	1.13	0.26
2121	87	6.20	1.73	4.00	5.43	7.73	5.99	1.85	0.97	0.30
3731	88	6.19	3.69	5.33	6.84	10.24	6.54	1.57	1.06	0.25
3111	89	6.01	2.88	4.87	6.55	11.76	8.88	1.83	1.48	0.31
3253	90	6.01	2.78	4.17	5.66	7.62	4.84	1.44	0.81	0.24

Table 3.A.1 (continued)

SIC	Rank	Ind. Mean ($=X$)	Quartile Means				Industry Dispersion		Coefficients of Variation	
			1	2	3	4	Range (Q4–Q1) ($=s_1$)	Range (Q3–Q1)/2 ($=s_2$)	S1/X	S2/X
3931	91	5.96	3.12	4.48	5.87	10.27	7.15	1.37	1.20	0.23
2431	92	5.95	3.20	5.01	6.81	12.09	8.89	1.81	1.49	0.30
2397	93	5.46	3.55	4.39	5.52	10.25	6.70	0.99	1.23	0.18
2512	94	5.32	3.23	4.36	5.50	8.24	5.01	1.13	0.94	0.21
2141	95	5.08	1.28	3.78	5.38	11.80	10.52	2.05	2.07	0.40
3141	96	4.57	2.67	3.75	4.64	6.81	4.13	0.98	0.90	0.21
3199	97	4.54	2.41	3.71	5.07	8.92	6.51	1.33	1.43	0.29
2852	98	4.49	2.85	3.68	4.59	7.03	4.18	0.87	0.93	0.19
2251	99	4.17	2.38	3.45	4.18	6.62	4.24	0.90	1.02	0.22
2321	100	3.72	1.81	2.62	4.28	12.03	10.22	1.23	2.75	0.33
2381	101	3.52	1.76	2.88	3.33	5.76	4.00	0.79	1.14	0.22
2426	102	3.42	2.02	2.96	3.89	5.82	3.80	0.93	1.11	0.27

Appendix B

Grouping Bias

Because the analyst is forced to work with grouped data, it is natural to wonder if the data accurately reflect relations occurring at the plant level. Under most general conditions, estimates of grouped micro data will cause biased estimates of the micro (i.e., plant) parameters to result. Theil (1971, chap. 11) has shown that the coefficients of linear regression equations using grouped data are weighted averages of the corresponding micro coefficients, but that this bias vanishes if all micro parameters are equal (i.e., all plants in the industry have the same production function parameters), or if the weights and the micro parameters are uncorrelated. Hannan and Burstein (1974), on the other hand, consider the case where the micro parameters are equal, but where the micro observations are ranked and grouped by some criterion, and a regression is performed using each group average as an observation point. In a simulation experiment, for random grouping of plants, the macro coefficient was found to be an unbiased estimate but a very inefficient estimator of the micro coefficient. An unbiased estimator of high efficiency resulted when micro observations were ranked and grouped by the values of the independent variable in the causal equation to be estimated. Conversely, grouping by values of the dependent variable lead to biased estimation.[30] The situation is worse if the micro relation to be estimated is log linear. In this case the grouped data reported should be a geometric mean of the micro data, but in practice arithmetic means are reported and this causes bias, unless the variance of the micro data is uncorrelated with the mean of the data.

Recall that for each of the 412 four-digit manufacturing industries, the census plant data used in this study have been ranked by the plant's productivity in 1967 and the ranking has been grouped into quartiles. Arithmetic sums of the quartile data are reported so that only arithmetic averages of the data pertaining to plants in the quartile could be constructed. If we were to attempt to explain productivity differences by comparing, say, capital-labor differences among the four quartiles of a given industry, then, according to Hannan and Burstein, we would

---

30. When there are several independent variables, the micro units might be ranked and grouped on the basis of a variable that is highly correlated with the combined effect of all the independent variables. The best such variable seems to be the value of the dependent variable estimated by regressing it against all independent variables, using the micro data. But this micro regression can be computed, its parameter values can be furnished to the analyst directly, obviating the need to use grouped data to estimate the micro parameters indirectly. Supposing the micro regression cannot be run (due to, say, undue cost); then the grouping might best be done on the basis of the most important explanatory variable.

obtain a biased estimate of the influence of this, presumably causal, variable. The ranking leads to an overestimate of the true differences due to the capital-labor ratio because this ratio is correlated with transitory productivity forces. The top (bottom) quartile of plants would appear to experience the greatest positive (negative) disturbance to their productivity since they tend to have the highest (lowest) capital-labor ratio.[31]

It makes sense, therefore, to carry out our investigation in relative comparisons to minimize ranking bias. If we compare productivity and capital-labor ratios in the top or bottom quartiles *across* four-digit industries, though some of this differential contains a positive transitory element, the transitory fraction of a difference can be either large or small (depending on how near the *industry* is to long-run equilibrium in input and product markets) but may be independent of the size of the differential. So, when comparing across industries, there is no special reason for industries with the highest differentials to have the largest transitory fractions.

This framework of comparing quartile productivity differentials across industries differs from a comparison of quartiles *within* industries. The latter matching is suspect because the observation with the largest differential with respect to the average is the top quartile of plants, and it also is likely to contain the greatest transitory disturbance. On the other hand, matching across industries does not force the observation with the largest differential (the industry whose top quartile of establishments is most above the average of its own industry) to have the largest transitory fraction in its differential.

When productivity differentials and transitory fractions of these differentials are uncorrelated across industries, then some theories of productivity behavior can be tested without distortion by ranking bias. For example, we hypothesized that the productivity differential between the top-quartile plants and the average establishments of an industry is positively related to their capital-labor differential. The differential measure we examined between quartile 1 and quartile 4 also contains a transitory element, but, since the fraction is not likely to be related to the differential, the element is probably not proportionately greater in industries which have the largest interquartile differential in their

---

31. Had the plants been ranked by their capital-labor ratio rather than their productivity, then the Wald-Bartlett method (Kendall and Stuart 1961, p. 404) could have been used to compute the effect of the capital-labor ratio. This method, designed to overcome the effect of measurement errors in the variables, involves ranking the data by the independent variable and joining the midpoints of the top and bottom 30% of the data points by a line whose slope is an estimate of the marginal impact of the independent variable. But this estimate is itself biased if, as is very likely, variables other than the capital-labor ratio influence productivity.

capital-labor ratios. A lack of correlation, therefore, between any transitory productivity element and the capital-labor differential means that a regression of productivity differentials on capital-labor differentials across industries will not lead to biased estimates of the latter's effect.[32]

References

Allen, R. G. D. 1938. *Mathematical analysis for economists.* London: Macmillan.

Arrow, Kenneth. 1972. *The measurement of real value added.* Technical report no. 60, Institute for Mathematical Studies in the Social Sciences, Stanford.

Berndt, Ernst, and Christensen, Laurits. 1973. The translog production function and the substitution of equipment, structures and labor in U.S. manufacturing 1929–68. *Journal of Econometrics* 1:81–114.

———. 1974. Testing for the existence of a consistent aggregate index of labor inputs. *American Economic Review* 64:391–404.

Brown, Murray, ed. 1967. *The theory and empirical analysis of production.* New York: Columbia University Press, for National Bureau of Economic Research.

Crandall, Robert; MacRae, Duncan; and Yap, Lorene. 1975. An econometric model of the low-skill labor market. *Journal of Human Resources* 10:3–24.

Christensen, Laurits; Jorgenson, Dale; and Lau, Laurence. 1973. Transcendental logarithmic production frontiers. *Review of Economics and Statistics* 55:28–45.

Diewert, W. E. 1969. *Canadian labor markets: A neoclassical econometric approach.* Project for the evaluation and optimization of economic growth. Berkeley: University of California Press.

———. 1973. Hicks' aggregation theorem and the existence of a real value added function. Technical report no. 84, Institute for Mathematical studies in the Social Sciences, Stanford.

Gramlich, Edward. 1972. *The demand for different skill classes of labor.* Washington: Office of Economic Opportunity.

Griliches, Zvi, and Ringstad, Vidar. 1971. *Economies of scale and the form of the production function.* Amsterdam: North-Holland.

Hall, Robert. 1973. The specification of technology with several kinds of output. *Journal of Political Economy* 81:750–60.

32. However, the intercept of the regression will be biased upward, because the average transitory element in top-quartiles productivity is positive, but this distortion is unimportant for explaining *variation* in the productivity differential.

Hanoch, G. 1975. The elasticity of scale and the shape of average costs. *American Economic Review* 65:492–97.

Harman, Michael, and Burstein, Leigh. 1974. Estimation from grouped observations. *American Sociological Review* 39:374–92.

Hildebrand, George, and Liu, T. C. 1965. *Manufacturing production functions in the United States.* Ithaca: Cornell University Press.

Johnston, John. 1971. *Econometric methods.* 2d ed. New York: McGraw-Hill.

Jones, Melvin. 1975. A statistical analysis of inter- and intra-industry elasticity of demand for production workers in plants with large and small employment size. WP 982–01. Washington: The Urban Institute.

Jorgenson, Dale. 1972. Investment behavior and the production function. *Bell Journal of Economics and Management Science* 3:220–51.

———. 1974. Investment and production: a review. In David Kendrick, ed., *Frontiers of quantitative economics*, vol. 2. Amsterdam: North-Holland.

Kendall, Maurice, and Stuart, Alan. 1961. *The advanced theory of statistics*, vol. 2. London: Griffin.

Kennedy, Charles, and Thirlwall, A. P. 1972. Technical progress: a survey. *Economic Journal* 82:11–72.

Klotz, Benjamin. 1966. Industry productivity projections: a methodological study. In *Technical papers*, vol. 2. Washington: National Commission on Technology, Automation and Economic Progress.

———. 1970. *Productivity analysis in manufacturing plants.* Bureau of Labor Statistics Staff Paper 3. Washington: Department of Labor.

Krishna, K. L. 1967. Production relations in manufacturing plants: an explanatory study. Ph.D. diss., University of Chicago.

Madoo, R. B. 1975. Production efficiency and scale in U.S. manufacturing: An inter-intra industry analysis. Ph.D. diss., University of California, Berkeley.

Madoo, Rey, and Klotz, Benjamin. 1973. Analysis of differences in value added per manhour among and within U.S. manufacturing industries, 1967. WP 2703–1. Washington: The Urban Institute.

Nadiri, M. I. 1970. Some approaches to the theory and measurement of total factor productivity: a survey. *Journal of Economic Literature* 8:1137–77.

Pratten, C. F. 1971. *Economies of scale in manufacturing industry.* Cambridge University Press.

Salter, W. E. G. 1962. *Productivity and technical change.* Cambridge: Cambridge University Press.

Scherer, F. M. 1970. *Industrial market structure and economic performance.* Chicago: Rand McNally.

———. 1973. The determinants of industry plant sizes in six nations. *Review of economics and statistics* 55: 135–45.
Theil, Henri. 1971. *Principles of econometrics.* New York: Wiley.
Uzawa, Hirofumi. 1962. Constant elasticity of substitution production functions. *Review of Economic Studies* 29:291–99.

Comment   Irving H. Siegel

This paper by Klotz, Madoo, and Hansen provides a wholesome reminder of the importance of the "establishment" as (1) the basic site of productive activity and (2) the source, therefore, of "atomic" information required for productivity (and other) measurement, analysis, and policy at both the micro and macro levels. Such a reminder is in order because so much of the community of quantitative economists is concerned nowadays with "the big picture," with models and aggregates pertaining to the whole economy or to components no smaller than a four-digit industry. In particular, the "postindustrial" evolution of our society has diminished the probability of early or prolonged professional exposure to the mysteries of the Census of Manufactures, which has for much more than a century been identified with the term and concept of "establishment." The census long ago also innovated the term and concept of "value added" for gauging the economic contribution of a manufacturing establishment. This census notion is the prototype of "income originating" in an industry, which is estimated by the Bureau of Economic Analysis from company, rather than establishment, data.

The authors examine closely the relationship of value added per production worker man-hour to other establishment variables for only one year, 1967, and they properly conclude from their efforts that longitudinal studies would yield more satisfying results. The tracking of value-added productivity through time would, for example, permit better assessments of transitory "noise," of the persistence of early productivity dominance, and of the relevance of market power and scale of production than the authors were able to hazard on the basis of only one year's data. At this juncture, we should recall that a promising program of direct productivity reporting by companies was inaugurated by the U.S. Bureau of Labor Statistics shortly after World War II, and that it did not long survive. Mention ought also to be made here of a current venture by the Department of Commerce to encourage companies to set up batteries of continuing productivity measurements for

Irving H. Siegel, economic adviser, Bureau of Domestic Business Development, U.S. Department of Commerce, until July 1979, is now a private consulting economist in Bethesda, Maryland.

key organizational units. This initiative, and the imitation it has inspired, should help improve the data base for longitudinal establishment studies.

Although the authors make additional recommendations concerning the design of future inquiries into value-added productivity, they omit two that merit consideration. One of these is the grouping of the establishments in each four-digit industry into a larger number of categories —into deciles, say, rather than quartiles. A finer-grain classification would permit a more sensitive analysis of interrelationships, especially at the lower end of the productivity spectrum, where heterogeneous "small businesses" tend to be concentrated.

A second needed refinement in subsequent studies is the discrimination of establishments in the same industry, insofar as possible, according to process of manufacture. Unexplained interquartile differences in productivity are surely attributable, in some degree, to differences in technology that are hardly reflected in, say, the dollar values of capital assets.[1] The authors acknowledge, in their remarks on simple correlation coefficients computed from plant data for 102 four-digit industries, "that low-productivity establishments could be using completely different technologies from their top-quartile counterparts within the same industry." Nevertheless, in their recommendations, they are silent on the need for coding of plants by process even though they would welcome information on five-digit product mix.

The patient statistical experiments and exercises of the authors, however admirable, do not encourage belief that more advanced econometric tools have much to add to the hints given by simpler ones, experience, and common sense. In particular, they offer little hope, if any, for the development from census data of reliable production functions for establishments at the various productivity levels. They show that a "causal" analysis of interplant productivity differences cannot be successfully pursued for any distance. Indeed, a summary of their attempts to wring more out of the data than is told in table 3.1—by means of simple correlation, multiple regression, the fitting of transcendental-logarithmic (translog) production functions (ordinary, two-stage, and three-stage least-squares), and the computation of Allen elasticities of substitution—would make an instructive, cautionary introductory chapter for an econometric primer. Any reader of the paper who stays the course not only feels sadder and wiser at the end but is also inclined to congratulate the data for withstanding the torments of advanced technique without confessing what they did not really know and there-

---

1. Such dollar values should, ideally, be expressed in the "same" prices for different establishments—an impossible feat. It should also be observed that, even if two establishments have the "same" technology, a difference in degree of technical integration could lead to a difference in price per "unit" of capital assets and in value added per man-hour.

fore could not tell. The following three paragraphs, which highlight the report's findings, elaborate these statements.

Pearsonian coefficients of correlation between the value-added productivity of establishments and other variables (all referred to corresponding industry means) indicate dissimilar patterns of association for top-quartile and bottom-quartile plants (table 3.2). For high-productivity plants, productivity is perceptibly correlated with both capital assets available per man-hour of production workers and with the ratio of nonproduction to production workers. For low-productivity establishments, however, the two coefficients are minuscule. The authors suggest that other variables that could not be taken into account would have substantial explanatory value—e.g., managerial quality, process technology, and product specialization. Their subsequent statistical odyssey, however, adds little new insight.

A multivariate investigation of interquartile differences in productivity in 195 industries employs five presumably "causal" variables as regressors: gross book value per production worker man-hour, nonproduction workers per production worker, hourly wages of production workers, production worker man-hours (a measure of plant size), and product specialization (the percentage of plant shipments comprised by primary products). The coefficient of determination (R^2) for the equation connecting these five variables with percentage differences in productivity between the top and third quartiles is only 0.08. The corresponding coefficient for the equation comparing the productivity rates of the third and bottom quartiles is still smaller, only 0.03 (table 3.3). The individual regression coefficients are also small.

Despite the weak apparent explanatory value of the variables, a brave try is made to learn something from translog production (and cost) functions and Allen elasticities of substitution. The nine-parameter equations (subject to subsidiary constraints) are fitted to logarithms of production worker man-hours, nonproduction workers, and gross assets. Negative R^2s are obtained for the two-stage least-square equations when degrees of freedom are taken into account; and many of the Allen elasticities have the wrong sign. The heroic undertaking seems to confirm that top-quartile and bottom-quartile plants have different dependency profiles; and it indicates that bottom-quartile data, in particular, may suffer from significant transitory distortion. Additional test computations suggest that "disequilibrium" vitiates low-quartile relationships and that "monopoly" affects top-quartile relationships. Factor inputs and monopoly, however, seem to explain only 17% of the productivity variation between the top and third quartiles, and they account for only 11% of the productivity differential between the third and bottom quartiles. Again the authors cite managerial quality and product specialization as pertinent, though omitted, explanatory variables; they do not this time mention the relevance of process of manufacture.

The gist of various marginal notes prompted by comments made by the authors may be of interest or of use to them and to other readers of their report. Accordingly, a few of these notes have been combined and restated for offering below as observations on concepts and measurement.

1. Apart from the omission of variables, it should be recorded that census information on the included variables leaves little leeway for experiment in the measurement of establishment performance. Neither production workers nor nonproduction workers are occupationally fungible; and establishment differences in compensation of production workers, which are reported, do not reflect qualitative differences with respect to such germane labor attributes as morale. Furthermore, census figures for gross assets are only crude measures of capital supply; they include a variable price element and make no allowance for age or depreciation of plant. The different plant ages, incidentally, also affect the mutual adaptation of labor and capital—a "learning-curve'" phenomenon that augments both factors in terms of "efficiency units," rather than a contribution of management.

2. The reasonableness of appealing to additional external, even nonquantitative, information for appraising the "disequilibrium" and "monopoly" distortions of census data for a particular year should not be overlooked.

3. A production function for an establishment is really an "average" of imaginable, though not necessarily computable, elemental functions relating to more detailed products. The latter functions would require the estimation of inputs that in fact are joint—such as the services of various nonproduction workers. In principle, however, the inputs of "direct" (production-worker) labor and materials can be matched readily with the quantities of detailed products.

4. The choice of value added or some other net-output concept for a production function does not require validation by a "separability" theorem. It is justified, rather, by a plausible historic interest in "economic" production functions, which are intended to "explain" output levels and income shares simultaneously by reference to inputs of remunerable factors. To imply that net output belongs to a "second-best" class of concepts is as whimsical as to say that Leontief tables of gross transactions are inherently preferable to a system of national income and product accounts.

5. An "engineering" production function is not more characteristic of measurement at a plant level than is an "economic" function. It may refer either to net or gross output, but its independent variables are not

confined to the remunerable factor inputs. Thus, it may include cost elements such as materials and energy, gifts of nature, and noneconomic variables reflecting product specifications. A hybrid engineering-economic function of special interest substitutes capital services for capital supply, and it uses energy (usually purchased) as a proxy for such services.

6. A study concerned with interquartile (or interdecile) differences in "real" value added per production worker man-hour ought ideally to (a) distinguish between quantity and price in the numerator and (b) suitably "fix" the price component. Thus, for a comparison of top and bottom quartiles (deciles), prices of one or the other or industry averages should be used in both, if feasible. Failure to make a price adjustment in the measurement process should be taken into account in interpretation.[2]

7. Since unadjusted dollar figures of value added are interpretable as both net-output and factor-input values, it matters just what "deflators" are used. For productivity measurement, of course, "real" value added should reflect output, so price should be stabilized for (a) sales adjusted for inventories and (b) subtracted energy, materials, etc.

8. Even if no price adjustment of dollar figures for value added is feasible, it would seem desirable, when interquartile (interdecile) comparisons of productivity are sought, to weight establishment ratios by production worker man-hours.[3]

9. The availability of census information for value-added productivity and other variables affords an opportunity for design, if not full construction, of systems of algebraically compatible index numbers. Establishments occupying the same ranks in different quartiles (deciles) would be treated as "identical" for the computation of comparative numbers. (As in temporal comparisons, Fisherian or Divisian principles of index-number design might be invoked, and the two approaches could even be harmonized to some degree.)

10. For the analysis of interquartile (interdecile) differences in value added and associated variables, it may be useful to start with definitional identities, then perturb all the variables, and keep the terms containing second-order (and higher) "deltas." Arc elasticities could be computed; and they could also be adjusted, if desired, to include portions of symmetrically distributed interaction terms. The perturbed equation, still an identity, is highly respectable, being an exact Taylor (difference-

2. The points made in this paragraph and the next are related to those made by another commentator (Lipsey), of which the writer has first become aware on prepublication review of edited copy.

3. This remark, referring to appropriate aggregation of establishment ratios, should not be confused with another ideal desideratum: the weighting of intra-establishment man-hours according to hourly pay.

differential) expansion without remainder. It could be modified by the introduction of behavioral statements connecting the variables (e.g., a production function) or of other simplifying relationships. (The same approach could be used, if desired, with an initial production function —say, of the Cobb-Douglas variety. The function could be perturbed without arbitrary sacrifice of discrete interaction terms, which need not be negligibly small.)

A concluding optimistic comment is warranted. Despite some introductory remarks by the authors on the utility of mathematical functions for policy, the limited success of their painstaking inquiry hardly means that programs for deliberate advancement of productivity will be frustrated. Engineering and management consultants and business and government officials can still pinpoint opportunities for the improvement of plant operations, even by the manipulation of variables that the present study may indicate to be unpromising. The Department of Commerce (or any other) program of encouraging company productivity measurement should have a salutary effect on industry averages, even if it fails to reduce the gap between low-productivity and high-productivity establishments. (Indeed, the differential ability or willingness of firms to install a measurement system could itself be an indicator of variation in management quality.) The prospect of toning up productivity at the micro level, however, does not detract from the importance of a breakthrough on the macro level. Government could still influence the acceleration of productivity most decisively if it knew how to curb inflation without inducing or prolonging economic sluggishness, and how to maintain "stable" growth of employment and production ever after—in the spirit of the Employment Act of 1946, as amended, and according to the most ambitious interpretations thereof.[4]

---

4. Achievement of substantial disinflation without recession would, for example, improve the outlook for (1) private bond and equity financing and (2) private spending on research and development, two significant sources of productivity gain.

The Full Employment and Balanced Growth (Humphrey-Hawkins) Act of 1978, which amounts to a "most ambitious interpretation" of the Employment Act of 1946, offers no encouragement of greater governmental success in achievement of price stability and productivity acceleration. See *Economic Report of the President: 1979*, pp. 106ff.

Comment   Robert E. Lipsey

The results of this study are ambiguous because there is a basic flaw in the data: the measure of "productivity" used, value added per production worker man-hour, is not really an efficiency measure but is more like a proxy for factor proportions.[1] A high value reflects high inputs of physical or financial capital, or nonproduction workers, or skilled workers per unit of unskilled labor input. There is no reason to say that high values of any such ratios imply efficient production. Since this is a type of factor proportions ratio, it is not surprising that the authors then find it correlated with other measures of or proxies for the capital-labor ratio, such as assets per production worker man-hour or nonproduction workers per production worker, or the hourly wage rate of production workers. No inferences about the effects of factor proportions on efficiency or prescriptions about methods of improving efficiency can properly be drawn. All that can be said is that value added per production worker man-hour is correlated with other measures of capital intensity.

Aside from the unsuitability of this productivity measure, cross-sectional studies of efficiency at the micro level using census data are subject to other problems that make it difficult to draw conclusions about efficiency. Value added is affected by indirect taxes and by erratic variations in profitability which can produce an impression of large differences in productivity when none exist. Furthermore, many of the individual establishments that are the units of observation are parts of larger enterprises which may, for tax or other reasons, influence the value added by manipulating such variables as the price paid by an establishment for products purchased from another unit of the same enterprise that is in another industry. Particularly in an industry in which value added is small compared with sales, such practices are another possible source of spurious variability in value added per man-hour which does not reflect differences in efficiency.

Robert E. Lipsey is with Queens College and the National Bureau of Economic Research.

1. See, for example, the use of a similar construct to measure the ratio of capital (including human capital) to labor in production in Hal B. Lary, *Imports of Manufactures from Less Developed Countries* (NBER, 1968).

II. Productivity in Selected Service Sectors

4 Measurement and Analysis of Productivity in Transportation Industries

John R. Meyer
José A. Gómez-Ibáñez

4.1 The Interest in Transportation Productivity

Recently, a great deal of interest has been expressed in measuring and improving productivity in the transportation industries. In addition to all the conventional reasons for wishing to know more about the productivity of any industry, an additional concern in the case of transportation is that several transportation modes, notably the railroads and urban mass transit, have been declining rapidly. Many analysts have argued that the decline of these modes is undesirable—because, for example, it imposes hardships on employees and certain groups of passengers and shippers who are particularly dependent on the service these modes provide; or, more recently, because these modes appear to generate less pollution and use less energy than their competitors.

It is, of course, less than fully obvious that a high rate of productivity growth will necessarily reverse the decline of these, or any other, industries. The evidence, though, suggests that productivity and growth are positively related, as shown in figure 4.1. Needless to say, one can debate cause and effect in this relationship; besides, it is not always that close: two of the more notoriously declining or stagnant industries of the U.S. postwar economy—railroads and coal mines—were also by many conventional measures good productivity performers.

John R. Meyer and José A. Gómez-Ibáñez are with Harvard University.

Research for this study was supported by the Urban Mass Transportation Administration (grant no. MA–11–0026). The views expressed do not necessarily reflect the official views or policy of the Urban Mass Transportation Administration or of the U.S. Department of Transportation.

The authors would like to thank William Vickery, the discussant for this paper, Ralph L. Nelson, and John W. Kendrick for helpful comments on earlier drafts. Of course, responsibility for all remaining errors rests with the authors.

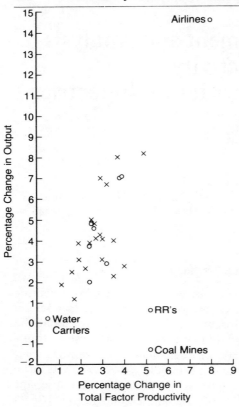

× = manufacturing groups

Source: Kendrick (1973), p. 106

Fig. 4.1   Relationship between Annual Rates of Change in Output
and in Total Factor Productivity, Thirty-Two Industry
Groups: 1948–66

Productivity improvement probably is perhaps best viewed as a helpful, perhaps sometimes necessary, but not a sufficient condition for an
industry to develop a favorable growth record. Certainly, productivity
improvement does help an industry to keep pace with other industries,
all else being equal. Moreover, few would argue with the proposition
that if productivity could be improved in some of the troubled transportation industries, the odds would at least improve, even if ever so
slightly, that these modes could be once again revived.

Interest in measuring and improving transportation productivity is
also generated by the circumstance that many of the transportation
industries are closely regulated and often subsidized by government.

The extensive public involvement in the industry has a variety of motivations, too many to list here. But whatever the motives, regulation often involves the government in decisions about the industry where information on productivity is deemed vital or at least helpful. Such decisions include the appropriate fares and rates for transportation services, valuation of transportation capital, and compensation for labor.

It is also now apparent that a common unintended consequence of public involvement may be the weakening of industry incentives to improve productivity. This possibility is perhaps most pertinent where public operating subsidies exist. Operating subsidies are common among transit firms and local service airlines, and are being implemented for northeastern railroads.

Even without direct subsidies, motivation for productivity improvement may be undermined by public regulation. One famous example is the ICC regulation on calculation of the cost of service in rate making. An unintended consequence was apparently to make it unprofitable for the railroads to use what was, under normal circumstances, the most efficient type of flat cars for piggyback service (Gellman 1971).

These concerns, new and old, have stimulated several recent analyses of productivity trends in transportation industries. Several problems in measuring productivity have been identified recurrently in these efforts. While the problems are usually not unique to transportation, they are perhaps particularly common and difficult in this sector. No insurmountable conceptual barriers may exist to finding solutions, but substantial difficulties in the accurate measurement and analysis of productivity trends are posed.

To illustrate these problems, we shall first describe some of the most difficult and common of them as encountered when measuring transportation productivity. Then we will review some recent attempts to estimate productivity trends in the trucking and railroad industries. Finally, we will present some new research on the productivity record of the urban mass transit industry from 1948 to 1970.

4.2   Problems in Measuring Transportation Productivity

In essence, measuring productivity change really involves manipulating and comparing four basic quantities: (1) rate of growth of output (Y'); rate of growth of labor inputs (L'); (3) rate of growth of capital (K'); and (4) rate of growth of intermediate goods used (I'). Using these four quantities, a standard formula for measuring change in what has come to be called total factor productivity is

$$A' = Y' - [\alpha \, (L')] - [\beta \, (K')] - [(1-\alpha-\beta) \, (I')],$$

where

$A' =$ total factor productivity change;

$\alpha =$ the "weight" attached to the labor contribution to output (e.g., the labor exponent in a Cobb-Douglas production function); and

$\beta =$ the "weight" attached to the capital contribution to output.

Obviously, the fundamental problems of productivity measurement are developing acceptable measures of the four basic rates of growth and determining the weights (e.g., α, β, and $1-\alpha-\beta$) to be attached to the different factor inputs. For a variety of reasons, these measurement and weighting problems almost always involve a certain number of assumptions and judgments. However, additional difficulties can be encountered in transportation because the sector is often of particular public interest, which commonly leads in turn to government regulation, subsidy, and other public involvement in the industry.

By way of illustration, a conventional method employed by governments for achieving social goals in transport is to keep rates low on those transport activities that are deemed most essential to promoting these objectives. Of course, if low enough, such rates may generate losses, which if not subsidized from public funds, must be made up from other activities conducted by the transport enterprise. One commonly used method of recouping is to charge high rates in so-called monopoly markets served by the carrier. Often these monopolies prove transient or nonexistent; a temptation may then emerge for the regulators to "remedy" the situation by artificially creating monopolies through various restrictions, e.g., on entry or competitor's prices.

Such policies can make it difficult to derive a meaningful measure of industry output. In most industries a single index of output is usually calculated by using relative prices to weight different types of service or outputs. In a market economy relative prices should reflect the relative value which customers place on these services and, where the industry is competitive, the relative cost of producing them. But when public policies deliberately keep some prices below and some above costs, relative prices may lose these qualities. Under these regulatory "distortions," relative price weights may mainly reflect circumstances that are largely irrelevant to normal output measurement, such as changes in the policies of regulators or in the mix of subsidized and unsubsidized outputs.

This problem is well illustrated in estimating postwar railroad productivity growth. Railroads produced both freight and passenger services, and the tariffs charged were heavily regulated and cross-subsidized. Usually passenger tariffs were far below costs and the services were continued only because the regulators so decreed, against the wishes of management and often in the absence of much market demand. At the same time, "monopoly" tariffs placed on freight to compensate for the passenger losses were in large measure forced down by truck or barge competition, so that rates charged for different types of freight services increasingly tended to reflect real demand and cost characteristics. Since passenger services declined rapidly while freight services did not, an index of railroad output constructed with passenger and freight outputs weighted by relative prices makes the postwar decline in output look less precipitous than, in some senses, it was. Productivity estimates based on such an output index would correspondingly exaggerate the growth in railroad productivity.

Even if public transport goals are advanced without distorting relative prices, say by direct government subsidy, a problem may remain of properly valuing the special "outputs" thereby achieved. For example, in recent years the transit industry has received public subsidies in order to preserve mobility and reduce air pollution, among other goals. But the worth of additional mobility in an urban area or for a small town has never been assessed very objectively. And while some attempts have been made to estimate the value of less polluted air, the estimates done to date are probably best described as rough approximations (National Academy of Sciences, Committee on the Costs and Benefits of Automobile Emission Control, 1974).

In sum, the "social" character of some transport activities may make it difficult even to define a quantitative measure of "true" output for the industry. Even if that problem can be finessed or ignored, the conventional solution of using market prices or values to construct an aggregate index of total output is not feasible or meaningful if prices are highly regulated and cross-subsidization is prevalent.

This lack of good market information permeates and complicates almost all aspects of transport productivity measurement. For example, a pervasive, special difficulty in measuring transportation output is differentiating between terminal and line-haul operations. Although both operations are essential for completing most shipments, they involve two distinct types of service, normally performed by different parts of a transportation organization or even by different organizations. To handle joint production problems of this type when measuring output and productivity, two approaches are commonly used: (1) establish that the relative proportions of the two activities are more or less constant; or (2) "unbundle" the two activities and estimate their value or costs separately.

Unfortunately, there is no reason to believe that the mix of these two functions will be the same for different transport modes or has remained constant over time within a particular mode. The extent and cost of terminal operations (which includes local pickup and delivery of freight or passengers and sorting for assignment to the appropriate vehicle) depend in the first instance on the number of shipments or passengers handled and to a lesser extent on cubage and weight; these costs are usually not overly sensitive to the distances traveled. The cost of line-haul transportation, on the other hand, is dependent on the distance moved and to a lesser extent the weight of the shipment. Obviously, shipments come in different sizes and weights; even more pronouncedly, passenger trip and shipment distances vary widely.

Most conventionally available physical measures of transportation output tend to capture changes in one of these activities and not the other. For example, if the basic measure of output is the number of shipments or passengers, it will not reflect shifts in amounts of line-haul services provided when these are caused by changes in the average distance moved or the size of shipment. On the other hand, if output is measured by the number of ton-miles transported, it will not reflect shifts in amounts of terminal services required as caused by changes in the number of shipments or of passengers carried.

In short, several measures of output may be needed to accurately reflect all the relevant dimensions of transportation output. How to combine or weight these different measures so as to create one composite index of total output is usually not obvious. Of course, if separate prices were assessed for the different services, terminal and line-haul, then fairly conventional product value weighting schemes could be followed. The difficulty is that in most, though not all, transportation operations the service charge or tariff is "bundled" and a separate market valuation for the different activities is not available. Furthermore, even if separate charges were assessed, as they are in a few instances, rate regulation would often mitigate their usefulness.

Measuring transportation output, as for most industries, can also be confounded by the problem of controlling for differences in the quality of service rendered. Important components of quality include the average speed of the journey; the frequency and convenience of scheduled services; the reliability of estimated pickup, delivery, and travel times; vibration; temperature variation and its control; noise levels; physical protection against product damage; etc.

These service qualities have been changing rapidly in recent years for many modes. The availability of new technologies, such as the jet airplane or containerized freight, is one reason. Another has been the rise in per capita income. With higher incomes, passengers have generally demanded faster, more convenient, and more comfortable transportation service. Higher incomes have also meant an increase in the share of traffic in highly manufactured goods relative to basic materials.

Because these highly manufactured goods are generally more valuable, shippers have tried to reduce inventory costs by making smaller and more frequent shipments and by using faster, more convenient, more reliable, and less damage-prone services.

The quality of service has not increased, however, on all modes. For example, the average quality of service provided by railroads has probably declined in recent years. Moreover, some service changes which at first glance may appear to be clear improvements may not be unambiguously so in all dimensions. For example, the introduction of jet airplanes improved service by making air travel faster, but it may have also degraded service at some medium and lower density airports by making operation of larger planes relatively more economical and thus decreasing flight frequency.

If transport outputs were sold in freely competitive, unregulated markets, quality differences could be measured by simply using as output weights the rates charged for services of different quality. Actually, intermodal competition, in spite of attempts to suppress it through regulation, is probably sufficient to make existing rates at least somewhat indicative of the valuations placed on some service differentials. But the corrections so derived are probably rough approximations at best.

Complications also arise in determining the factor inputs required for delivering transport services. One of the more common of these difficulties is that in many modes the firms providing the transportation services do not own outright some of the capital they use. Some important capital inputs (e.g., highways, airports, airways, ports, and waterways) conventionally are provided and owned by government. In addition, among privately owned transport firms there has been a decided move in recent years away from outright ownership and toward various kinds of leasing arrangements. The reasons for this shift are many, the most important being tax advantages and the greater availability of financing under leasing as compared with ownership (due, for example, to better subordination of existing debt, etc.).

Unfortunately, conventional measures of capital stock or capital inputs, especially at an industry level, will not always accurately capture these changes. Specifically, an implicit ownership assumption is often made in the capital goods series so that only those capital inputs actually owned by the enterprise rendering the service will be incorporated into the capital measures. Usually, these omissions can be corrected, but only at the expense of doing somewhat more in-depth analysis of the particular industry and its practices. Even then, it may be difficult to measure with any precision the changes in these practices over time.

Probably the most difficult of these problems is evaluating highway inputs with any accuracy. Complexities inherently arise when determining the amount of public investment in highways that properly should be assigned to different highway modes. Without much question, motor carrier, bus, and transit productivity have benefited from postwar highway investments. Furthermore, the total amount of capital employed in these industries may have risen more rapidly than indexes based on rolling stock alone would suggest. Thus conventional measures of the increased capital employed in an industry might understate the actual situation. The exact dimensions of this understatement, though, can be very difficult to determine.

Factor inputs, once measured, must be weighted, of course, to construct a productivity index. Factor weights attached to labor and capital in productivity measures are usually determined by the national income shares attributed to labor and property. Such weights should be reasonably satisfactory as long as wage and profit shares do indeed reflect normal market influences. Clearly, though, such an assumption is at least questionable in highly regulated industries.

Regulated transportation, for example, has generally had a relatively poor record of profitability and accordingly relatively low weights attached to capital inputs. To what extent this is due entirely to regulation is at least debatable. To some extent, though, low profitability in several transport industries almost surely reflects various attempts at cross-subsidization and particularly the failure of the transport enterprises to realize high monopoly profits needed to pay for losses on social activities. Regulation may also diminish profitability by introducing a long "regulatory lag" between an increase in costs and the realization of a compensatory tariff rate increase—a particularly troublesome problem, of course, in an inflationary economy. Finally, regulation may inhibit the ability of an enterprise to attract good managerial talent or may divert such talent away from the pursuit of operating economies and into legal and political problems.

Whatever the cause, the low rate of return to capital in many regulated transportation industries leads some productivity analysts to assign very low weights to capital inputs in these industries. Other analysts argue that the weight given to capital ought to reflect the higher rate of return in other, unregulated sectors since this higher rate represents the social opportunity cost of transportation capital. While the proper weights in these circumstances are not always readily obvious, it is clear that changes in the weights can make a great deal of difference to the calculation of total factor productivity (as shown more fully in the next section).

4.3 Recent Analyses of Trucking and Railroad Productivity

Obviously, caution would appear advisable in interpreting any single transport industry productivity measure. Indeed, there is probably no substitute for a detailed knowledge of an industry in interpreting and understanding the various productivity measures normally available. The usefulness of any particular series, moreover, is likely to depend rather crucially on the application: certain measures serve certain purposes rather better than others.

Moreover, rarely are productivity measures likely to be so precise and unambiguous as to provide clear-cut quantitative guides to many of the public and private policy decisions which productivity measures are expected to aid. In short, rough or approximate answers may be possible in some instances, but highly precise or definitive answers are not.[1] A review of work done on different modes, as discussed below, confirms this.

4.3.1 Intercity Trucking

Several estimates of postwar productivity trends in U.S. intercity trucking have been made by the Bureau of Labor Statistics and by John W. Kendrick; these are summarized in table 4.1. Both the BLS and Kendrick independently estimate that while output in intercity trucking has been growing at the rate of 6 to 8% per year in the postwar period, labor productivity (output per man-hour) has been growing at the rate of only about 3% per year. The BLS also estimates that among the general freight carriers of the intercity trucking industry, postwar output and labor productivity have been increasing by only 4.9 and 2.1% per year, respectively, rates much lower than those for the industry as a whole. Capital and total factor productivity growth was not estimated because of the lack of data on capital stocks and depreciation. Both the BLS and Kendrick use ton-miles as the basic measure of output, apparently corrected, at least in the case of the BLS estimates, for changes in the composition of commodities carried.

Daryl Wyckoff has suggested that fundamental problems may be created for these estimates because the ratio of less-than-truckload (LTL) to full-truckload shipments, the average shipment size, and the average length of haul have all been changing over time.[2] From the standpoint of productivity measurement, the importance of these shifts

---

1. As one student on the subject has summarized the situation: "At best, a productivity measure (or a group of productivity measures) may serve as guides to better understanding of the achievements and frustrations of the industry—they certainly can never be taken as final truth." D. Daryl Wyckoff, "Issues of Productivity: State of the Art and Proposed Measures of Regular Common Carrier Motor-Carrier Productivity," *Traffic World*, 18 December 1972.

2. D. Daryl Wyckoff, "Issues of Productivity," *Traffic World*, 18 September; 6 and 13 November; 18 and 25 December 1972; and 26 February 1973. D. Daryl Wyckoff, *Organizational Formality and Performance in the Motor Carrier Industry* Lexington, Mass.: D. C. Heath, 1974). Many of the same observations were also made by Darwin D. Daicofe, "Analyzing Productivity Trends in Intercity Trucking," *Monthly Labor Review* 97 (1974):41–45.

Table 4.1   **Previous Estimates of Postwar Output and Labor Productivity Trends in Intercity Trucking**

Type of Trucking	Source	Period	Estimated Average Annual Percentage Growth in	
			Output	Labor Productivity
Intercity common carriers, class I and II	Kendrick[a]	1948–66	8.4	3.1
Intercity common carriers, class I and II	Bureau of Labor Statistics[b]	1954–72	6.0	2.7
Intercity common carriers of *General Freight*, class I and II	Bureau of Labor Statistics[c]	1954–72	4.9	2.1

[a]Kendrick (1973), pp. 193, 335.
[b]Carnes (1974).
[c]Carnes (1974, p. 55).

(in LTL freight, shipment size, and distance) is to create a corresponding shift in the mix of terminal and line-haul services required by the typical common carrier. For example, if the ratio of LTL and non-truckload shipments is increasing or average shipment size and length of haul are decreasing, then an output measure based on ton-miles alone (even corrected for changes in commodity composition) will almost certainly understate output growth and therefore, all else being equal, productivity gain as well.

Such shifts may explain, in part, the disparity between the estimates of productivity growth in the trucking industry as a whole and productivity growth among general freight carriers. In the industry as a whole LTL shipment tonnage declined from about 25% of total tonnage in 1950 to 12% in 1970.[3] Over the same period the average length of haul has increased slightly from about 235 to 264 miles.[4] *Ceteris paribus*, such trends decrease the amount of terminal services required relative to line-haul services; as a result, ton-miles measures, like those used by

3. Calculated from data in Transportation Association of America, *Transportation Facts and Trends*, 11th ed. (Washington: Transportation Association of America, 1974), pp. 10, 11.
4. Data for class I carriers only from the American Trucking Association, *American Trucking Trends, 1975* (Washington: American Trucking Association, 1975), p. 32.

the BLS and Kendrick, could possibly overstate output and productivity growth in the industry as a whole.

On the other hand, general freight carriers apparently experienced trends in shipment size different from the industry as a whole. For example, Wyckoff argues that the ratio of LTL to non–LTL shipments for general freight carriers increased from 1958 to 1970.[5] To the extent this is true, a ton-mile metric would tend to underestimate postwar growth in output, and thus productivity, among general freight carriers.

Wyckoff also finds that individual elements of general motor carrier operations displayed different productivity trends over recent years. As shown in figure 4.2, line-haul operations and maintenance both improved in productivity, and handling of less-than-truckload (LTL) shipments and the administrative costs of handling individual shipments seem to have declined. To the extent that general freight carriers have become increasingly involved in these slow or negative-productivity-growth activities, their overall productivity record as measured by ton-miles would, of course, be held back.

More generally, any productivity decline in the handling of LTL shipments would only heighten skepticism about the adequacy of conventional estimates of postwar trucking productivity growth that abstract from changes in shipment size and composition. Because a ton-mile metric may exaggerate output growth when average shipment size and length of haul are increasing, intercity trucking output and labor productivity may not have increased quite as rapidly as suggested by the 8.4 to 6.0% and 3.1 to 2.7% per year estimates in table 4.1. Similarly, because ton-miles may understate output growth when shipment size is decreasing, general freight carrier output and labor productivity may have increased more rapidly than the 4.9 and 2.1% per year estimates would indicate.

4.3.2   Railroads

Railroads have always represented something of a puzzle for productivity analysts in that, to a greater extent than almost any other industry —the only possible exception being coal mining—railroading represents

---

5. Wyckoff reports data from the U.S. Interstate Commerce Commission which show that the ratio of LTL to non–LTL shipments *increased* from 1958 to 1970. However, according to Wyckoff's data LTL to non–LTL shipments *decreased* fairly steadily from 1958 to 1964 and from 1965 to 1970; the increase between 1958 and 1970 is due almost entirely to an extremely large upward shift between 1964 and 1965. The size of this shift suggests that the 1958–64 and 1965–70 data are not consistent and that better evidence of the trend in LTL general freight shipments is needed. See D. Daryl Wyckoff, "Issues of Productivity: Measures of Productivity—What Is Being Measured and For What Purpose?" *Traffic World*, 18 September 1972.

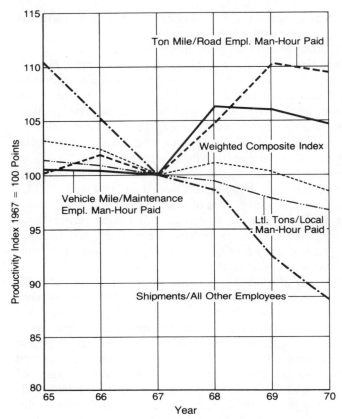

Source: D. Daryl Wyckoff, "Issues of Productivity: State
of the Art and Proposed Measures of Regular Common
Motor-Carrier Productivity," *Traffic World*, 18 December
1972.

Fig. 4.2   Comparison of Productivity of Individual Elements of
General Commodities Motor Carrier Operations

a case of an industry experiencing relatively high productivity gains
while at the same time declining, or stagnating, in terms of output
growth. This situation is aptly illustrated by referring back to figure 4.1
wherein it is shown that railroading, at least as measured by conventional productivity indices, lies well off of the relationship between
percentage change in output and percentage change in productivity
during the postwar period.

It seems highly likely that this deviation may be at least partly a
result of methods used to measure railroad productivity. Specifically,
research undertaken recently by the Task Force on Railroad Productiv-

ity suggests that postwar productivity growth in railroads may have been less than conventionally estimated earlier. Whereas previous estimates (again by the Bureau of Labor Statistics and John Kendrick) were in the range of 5%, the task force estimated rail productivity growth as probably lying somewhere between 1 and 2% (U.S. Bureau of Labor Statistics 1971; Kendrick 1973; Task Force on Railroad Productivity 1973).

Some of the differences in these estimates, as might be expected, are simply explained by the use of different concepts. The BLS focuses exclusively on estimating labor productivity and, in contrast to Kendrick, did not attempt to measure total factor productivity. Since the railroads have been substituting capital for labor rather more rapidly than industry in general, the rate of growth for total factor productivity in the industry is substantially less than that for labor productivity. However, the task force's research suggests that, even if one confines attention to labor productivity alone (which, of course, is a quite legitimate and useful measure for many purposes), simple labor productivity in the rail industry may have grown at an average rate of only 3 to 4% per year during the postwar years, substantially lower than the 5% estimated by the BLS. Nevertheless, even 3 to 4% is as great or greater than the growth of labor productivity computed for the entire private domestic economy, which is placed between 2.0 and 3.0% per year during the postwar period (Kendrick 1973, p. 41).

But the largest part of the difference between the estimates by the BLS and Kendrick and those by the task force stem from the differences in the measures of inputs and outputs. For example, unlike the task force, Kendrick does not adjust his estimates of capital inputs to count capital which is leased by the railroads. Since leasing arrangements are becoming more common, especially for railroad rolling stock, the task force estimates a higher rate of growth of capital inputs, and thus a lower rate of growth in capital and total factor productivity, than Kendrick.

More importantly, the Kendrick results are very sensitive to the weights used for combining capital and labor inputs when doing the calculations to determine total factor productivity. Kendrick follows the usual procedures for determining weights by basing these on the relative shares of labor and property in the national income originating in the industry. As noted, though, the property share of capital in national income depends upon profitability, and since the rate of profit in the highly regulated railroad industry is by most measures rather low, the relative level of capital inputs could be understated for many purposes by following this convention. Specifically, Kendrick accords to capital inputs a weighting of roughly 0.1, while labor is weighted at 0.9; any shift of ten percentile points in this weighting away from labor and to capital would reduce total productivity estimates by about three-tenths of a percentage point. For example, with a 25–75 weighting, the estimate of annual postwar total productivity growth drops by about one-half a percentage point.

As in trucking, rail productivity estimates are commonly based on ton-miles as the basic measure of output, and the mix of railroad traffic has been changing. Specifically, railroads have lost much of their short-haul, small-shipment, and high-value traffic, which generally requires more factor input per ton to carry and which incurs more terminal outlay per ton-mile. Thus, if one uses tonnage weighted by revenue (to control for changes in the commodity mix) rather than ton-miles as the major measure of output,[6] another half a percentage point or so per year of productivity growth is shaved from the standard rail estimates.

The standard productivity estimates also use relative prices, instead of relative costs, as weights in combining the rail freight and rail passenger outputs into a single index. As noted earlier, public regulators long required that passenger service be cross-subsidized by freight service, and thus the relative prices did not reflect the relative amounts of resources required to produce the services or, presumably, their relative value to society. A shift from prices to costs in weighting passenger output explains another half a percent per year difference between the standard and task force estimates of rail productivity growth.

Railroad productivity measures might also be usefully adjusted for changes in the quality of services. The prevailing view among those acquainted with the transportation industry is that the quality of railroad services, especially speed and service reliability, has been deteriorating over the postwar years, just as the conventional view is that there has been an improvement in the quality of trucking services. Accordingly, if one could develop reasonably adequate measures of service qualities for these highly regulated industries, the probability would be that the railroad productivity estimates would be scaled downward, while the trucking estimates probably would be adjusted upward.

4.3.3 Truck-Rail Comparisons

In sum, many alternatives have been suggested for measurement of productivity change in the motor-carrier and railroad industry. Each of these measures probably embodies some useful information. Clearly, though, none of the measures in and of itself is likely to be accepted as

---

6. The Task Force did not actually weight tonnage by revenue to control for the effect of systematic changes in the composition of rail freight traffic. Instead they used the analogous procedure of deflating total freight revenues by an ICC–computed index of rail rates which abstracts from changes in freight composition. See Task Force on Railroad Productivity (1973).

the definitive measure of productivity change for all purposes within the industry.

The measures are nevertheless suggestive. In particular, on the basis of the comparisons and reviews of the various measures thus far done, it would appear that the conventional measures of productivity, as reported by the BLS or Kendrick, probably tend to substantially overestimate the general rate of productivity improvement in the railroad industry, to slightly overestimate productivity improvement for the intercity trucking industry as a whole, and to underestimate productivity improvement for general freight trucking. If true, this would make it at least somewhat easier to explain why the motor-carrier industry has grown so rapidly relative to rail in the postwar years since, after revision, it may well be true that the motor-carrier industry experienced a rate of productivity improvement comparable to that of the railroad industry. In short, the seeming paradox that the growth records of these highly competitive industries being the reverse of their productivity records may be more a measurement aberration than a reflection of industry reality.

4.4   Productivity in Urban Mass Transit, 1948–70

Urban mass transit, probably to an even greater extent than railroading and trucking, has been an industry of intense public concern. The productivity record of the industry has come under particular scrutiny as the industry has drifted toward increasing governmental control and ownership. The advent of federal operating subsidies for local transit operations has heightened this interest since a major apparent worry, at least as expressed by subsidy opponents, is that the subsidies may induce "inefficiency" in the industry's use of resources. There is no reason to believe, moreover, that measures of productivity in transit will be any less ambiguous than those for the other transportation industries.

Transit includes four modes: motor bus, trolley bus, light rail transit (more commonly known as streetcars or trolleys), and heavy rail transit (such as subways). The size and character of the transit industry have been changing rapidly since World War II. According to estimates by the American Transit Association (since 1974 the American Public Transit Association), the number of revenue passengers carried dropped drastically in the postwar years. As the data in table 4.2 show, the decline in passengers was sharpest in the years immediately following the war for light rail transit and (after 1952) trolley bus modes.

The factor inputs consumed by the industry, as shown in table 4.3, have also declined. The index of capital inputs is based on estimates

Table 4.2   Millions of Transit Revenue Passengers Carried
per Year, 1948–70

Year	Heavy Rail	Light Rail	Trolley Bus	Motor Bus	All Modes
1948	2473	4740	1206	8893	17,312
1949	2203	3480	1286	8300	15,269
1950	2113	2790	1261	7681	13,845
1951	2041	2171	1231	7438	12,881
1952	1982	1714	1201	7125	12,022
1953	1903	1403	1137	6593	11,036
1954	1767	1053	993	6045	9,858
1955	1741	845	869	5734	9,184
1956	1748	625	814	5568	8,755
1957	1706	491	703	5438	8,338
1958	1635	415	593	5135	7,778
1959	1647	378	517	5108	7,650
1960	1670	335	447	5069	7,521
1961	1680	323	405	4834	7,242
1962	1704	284	361	4773	7,122
1963	1661	238	264	4752	6,915
1964	1698	213	214	4729	6,854
1965	1678	204	186	4730	6,798
1966	1584	211	174	4702	6,671
1967	1632	196	155	4633	6,616
1968	1627	187	152.2	4524.5	6,490
1969	1656.3	183.4	135.2	4335.3	6,310.3
1970	1573	172	127	4158	6,032

SOURCE: American Transit Association, *Transit Fact Book*, annual (Washington: American Transit Association, various years).

of industry capital stocks and depreciation recently developed by Jack Faucett Associates, Inc. Since buses, trolley buses, and streetcars use public highways, a portion of highway costs is included in the capital measure.[7] The labor input index is calculated from American Transit Association's (ATA) annual estimates of the industry's average employment adjusted by Bureau of Labor Statistics (BLS) figures on changes in the average number of hours worked per week by unionized local transit operating employees. The index on intermediate goods

7. Faucett Associates apportioned highway stock and depreciation costs among the various highway modes according to the formulas proposed by a 1965 government study on allocating highway costs. See Jack Faucett Associates, *Capital Stock Measures for Transportation*, report no. JACKFAU–71–04–6, prepared for the U.S. Department of Transportation, Office of the Secretary (Washington: U.S. Department of Transportation, 1974).

consumed is based on ATA annual estimates of industry expenditures for fuel and maintenance materials adjusted by BLS data on changes in the wholesale prices of fuels and transportation equipment. Finally, total factor inputs are calculated by weighting the labor, capital, and intermediate goods inputs by their relative prices in the base year, 1958.[8]

As the industry has declined, public ownership, which is usually accompanied by public subsidization, has become more important and common. Even before 1950, publicly owned firms may have carried nearly as many passengers as privately owned firms; although most firms were privately owned in 1950, the publicly owned firms included the principal properties in several large metropolitan areas where the industry's ridership is concentrated—such as New York, Chicago, Boston, and San Francisco.[9] By 1971 public ownership had become much more common, especially among large firms, and the ATA estimated that, although publicly owned firms were still only 14% of all firms, they carried 84% of all the revenue passengers (American Transit Association 1972, p. 3).

Estimates of postwar productivity in the U.S. transit industry have been previously made by Kendrick. His estimates are for privately owned firms only. Since data on transit capital stocks were not readily available at the time he did his work, Kendrick estimated labor productivity and not total factor productivity. His results, shown in table 4.4, indicate that transit productivity increased at a very slow rate in the 1940s and early 1950s and declined at an average rate of 2 to 4% per year during the late 1950s and early 1960s. Over the entire postwar period studied, from 1948 to 1966, he estimates that transit labor productivity declined at an average annual rate of 0.9%. This 0.9% annual decline in transit productivity is striking when compared to Kendrick's estimate that labor productivity in the entire private business sector increased by 3.0% per year during the postwar period (Kendrick 1973, p. 41).

Similar results were obtained by B. M. Deakin and T. Seward in a study of total factor productivity for the postwar period in the British transit and taxi industries. Their estimates, also shown in table 4.4, indicate that transit and taxi productivity declined rapidly during the mid 1950s and mid 1960s and was relatively stagnant in the intervening years. Over the entire period studied, from 1954 to 1965, they report that total factor productivity in the British taxi and transit industry declined at an average annual rate of 1.65%.

8. The opportunity cost of capital in 1958 was assumed to be 6% per year. Both the capital and total factor index were relatively insensitive to changing the cost of capital to either 4 or 10% per year.

9. These four metropolitan areas alone accounted for 50 to 55% of all transit ridership in the United States in 1970.

Table 4.3　　　**Inputs Used by the Transit Industry, 1948–70**
(1958=100.0)

Year	Labor Inputs[a]	Capital Inputs[b]	Intermediate Goods (Operating and Maintenance Materials)[c]	Total Inputs[d]
1948	171.0	153.5	146.8	160.7
1949	165.8	127.9	135.5	145.8
1950	156.9	124.9	131.1	140.0
1951	149.9	122.3	127.2	135.3
1952	143.3	119.6	122.2	130.6
1953	138.9	116.0	116.7	126.4
1954	129.8	112.6	112.7	120.4
1955	122.1	109.3	102.9	114.4
1956	114.4	106.2	101.6	109.4
1957	108.3	103.1	98.9	105.0
1958	100.0	100.0	100.0	100.0
1959	96.4	96.9	97.9	96.8
1960	94.6	93.4	98.4	94.5
1961	91.5	90.6	99.2	91.9
1962	89.9	87.7	95.6	89.5
1963	88.8	84.5	95.1	87.5
1964	86.9	81.8	95.5	85.5
1965	87.0	79.5	90.5	84.0
1966	86.4	77.9	92.8	83.3
1967	87.5	76.3	98.0	83.6
1968	86.0	75.4	101.8	82.9
1969	84.3	76.3	n.a.[f]	n.a.[f]
1970	82.6	76.0	105.6	82.1
Average annual percentage change, 1948–70[e]	−3.48	−2.97	−1.63	−3.15

[a]Calculated from American Transit Association estimates of the industry's average employment adjusted by the Bureau of Labor Statistics' estimates of changes in the average number of hours worked per week by unionized local transit operating employees. See American Transit Association, *Transit Fact Book,* annual (Washington: American Transit Association, various years); and U.S. Bureau of Labor Statistics, *Union Wages and Hours: Local-Transit Operating Employees,* annual (Washington: Government Printing Office, various years).

[b]Calculated from data in Jack Faucett Associates, Inc., *Capital Stock Measures for Transportation,* report no. JACKFAU–71–04–6, prepared for the U.S. Dept. of Transportation, Office of the Secretary (Washington: U.S. Department of Transportation, 1974).

[c]Calculated from American Transit Association estimates of industry expenditures on operating and maintenance materials adjusted by Bureau of Labor Statistics' estimates of the wholesale price indices for fuels and related products (05) and transportation equipment (14), respectively. See American Transit Association,

Table 4.4 **Previous Estimates of Postwar Productivity Trends in the U.S. Transit Industry and the British Transit and Taxi Industry**

Year	Kendrick's Estimates of Labor Productivity in Privately Owned Firms in the U.S. Transit Industry[a]	Deakin and Seward's Estimates of Total Factor Productivity in the British Taxi and Transit Industries[b]
1948	105.3	
1949	102.0	
1950	105.5	
1951	99.9	
1952	107.3	115.6
1953	106.9	114.9
1954	104.2	113.2
1955	111.6	111.8
1956	111.3	109.0
1957	112.6	103.8
1958	100.0	100.0
1959	93.8	103.2
1960	98.6	105.0
1961	99.3	104.6
1962	100.0	102.0
1963	95.0	98.3
1964	92.4	95.5
1965	88.0	88.8
1966	88.2	
Average annual percentage change[c]	−0.93	−1.65

[a]Kendrick (1973), p. 334.
[b]Deakin and Seward (1969), p. 227.
[c]Calculated from a least-squares fit of an exponential curve.

Transit Fact Book; and U.S. Bureau of Labor Statistics, *Handbook of Labor Statistics, 1972* (Washington: Government Printing Office, 1972).
[d]Weighted by 1958 relative prices for capital and labor.
[e]Calculated from a least-squares fit of an exponential curve.
[f]Not available.

While these pioneer attempts at measuring productivity in the transit industry represent a remarkable effort, given the available data, they may be misleading in some important respects, mainly because they use revenue passengers carried or revenue passenger-miles as the basic measure of transit output. Among other deficiencies, these two output measures may not adequately track basic trends in the quality of service rendered. Determining whether the quality of transit has improved or deteriorated is difficult. Many dimensions of transit service have been changing in the postwar period and, while quality has clearly improved in some respects, it has declined in others.

For example, declines have occurred on many routes because the frequency of vehicles has been reduced and service has sometimes been completely eliminated during late evening hours or on weekends. This reduction in service frequencies and service hours may force travelers to wait at stops longer or to travel at less convenient times. Quality may also be deemed to have declined because of the increases in crime on vehicles or near stops and stations—although, obviously, it is not likely that the responsibility for any such quality decline rests with the industry.

The quality of transit service has also increased in several ways during the postwar period, and these gains probably outweigh the declines. The installation of air conditioning, for example, has improved services to passengers. A more important quality improvement has been a reduction in crowding in vehicles, allowing a higher percentage of passengers to get a seat (often even in the peak hours); this reduction in crowding has mainly resulted from transit officials not reducing the frequency of service on routes as rapidly as patronage has declined.

Quality has also improved in that the average speeds at which transit vehicles travel on a given type of route appear to have increased. This seems true notwithstanding the fact that industry-wide *average* transit vehicle speeds probably declined in the postwar period, largely because transit patronage has increasingly been concentrated on those routes which generally operate at slower speeds (i.e. in the cores of the larger and more congested metropolitan areas). Conversely, ridership and service have dropped sharply during the off-peak times and on suburban routes where vehicle speeds are relatively high. On any given type of route or service, however, average vehicle speeds have probably been increasing, because of both improvements in general traffic speeds on urban arterials and the introduction of more express services by transit lines.

Service rendered per passenger has also improved because the average length of transit trips very probably increased in the postwar period. The average length of intraurban work, shopping, and recreational trips by all modes increased greatly during the postwar period as residential and employment locations dispersed. While time-series data on transit passenger trip lengths alone are not generally available in the U.S., it seems likely that transit shared in this general trend toward longer urban journeys and, if so, passengers carried (or passenger trips) as an output measure will understate the growth in output in recent years.

These various dimensions of quality changes are most inadequately or not at all reflected when revenue passengers is used as the output metric. Some are perhaps captured when revenue passenger-miles is the output measure (as in Deakin and Seward's analysis of British taxi and transit productivity). Revenue passenger miles will reflect changes in average trip length as well as in the number of transit trips taken. Unfortunately, passenger-mile data are not generally available for the U.S. industry.

Series are available, however, on the number of vehicle-miles operated, and for some purposes it may be a more appropriate measure of output than revenue passengers. Vehicle-miles would capture at least some of the reduction in crowding in transit during the postwar period as well as much or most of the increase in trip lengths. It would not reflect, on the other hand, the deterioration in schedules, the increase in crime, or improvements in amenities such as air conditioning.

As a comparison of tables 4.2 and 4.5 shows, the number of vehicle-miles operated on each transit mode declined much less rapidly than the number of revenue passengers carried. The increase in vehicle-miles operated per passenger carried may of course reflect consumer preference or demand for longer trips and less crowding, but it may represent other trends as well. In particular, maintaining the number of vehicle-miles may have been perceived as important to achieving certain public or social objectives. As widespread public regulation and subsidy of the industry suggest, other dimensions of transit output besides passengers carried may be important to society. Perhaps the most important of these other dimensions is the maintenance of some "minimum" network and schedule of transit service for the local community. A common provision of franchises granted by local governments to private transit firms almost always has been that the firms provide certain minimum levels of service, even when and where service at the normal fare was less profitable, for example during evenings and weekends or to less densely populated parts of a city. As the fortunes of the transit industry have declined, a key motivation for local public takeover and subsidy of transit in many cities was concern about preserving at least some of this service, especially services to downtown retail areas or for those residents who do not have ready access to automobiles because they are too old or too young to drive, physically disabled, or too poor to own a car.

Table 4.5   Millions of Vehicle-Miles Operated
                    by Transit Mode, 1948–70

Year	Heavy Rail	Light Rail	Trolley Bus	Motor Bus	All Modes
1948	458.1	699.3	178.0	1975.7	3311.1
1949	460.0	555.4	200.0	1968.2	3183.6
1950	443.4	463.1	205.7	1895.4	3007.6
1951	424.0	387.6	208.8	1893.0	2913.4
1952	400.4	321.2	215.2	1877.7	2814.5
1953	391.1	373.7	211.7	1819.0	2695.5
1954	375.6	215.8	196.7	1760.7	2548.8
1955	382.8	178.3	176.5	1709.9	2447.5
1956	387.1	132.9	165.7	1680.9	2366.6
1957	388.0	106.6	146.5	1648.4	2289.5
1958	386.5	89.9	131.0	1593.6	2201.0
1959	388.7	81.3	112.4	1576.5	2158.9
1960	390.9	74.8	100.7	1576.4	2142.8
1961	385.1	69.4	92.9	1529.7	2077.1
1962	386.7	61.5	84.0	1515.2	2047.4
1963	387.3	48.9	62.4	1523.1	2021.7
1964	395.8	42.9	49.2	1527.9	2015.8
1965	395.3	41.6	43.0	1528.3	2008.2
1966	378.9	42.9	40.1	1521.7	1983.6
1967	396.5	37.8	36.5	1526.0	1996.8
1968	406.8	37.5	36.2	1508.2	1988.7
1969	416.6	36.0	35.8	1478.3	1966.7
1970	407.1	33.7	33.0	1409.3	1883.1

SOURCE: American Transit Association, *Transit Fact Book*, annual (Washington: American Transit Association, various years).

If the number of vehicle-miles declined more slowly than patronage because of publicly mandated social policy (rather than passenger willingness to pay for the retained or mandated services), then a transit output index based on vehicle-miles alone could possibly exaggerate the output, and its quality, *rendered to passengers*. Such an output index should perhaps best be viewed as an upper bound for any estimate of postwar growth in services provided to passengers, just as an output index based on revenue passengers (like Kendrick's) points to a lower bound.

For these same reasons, however, vehicle-miles might be an appropriate, albeit crude, index of the social outputs which transit produces *in addition* to its services to passengers. Since the stability of vehicle-mileage is a product of both passenger demands for improved services and publicly mandated policies to maintain minimum levels of service despite declining patronage, vehicle-miles will reflect to at least some extent both the passenger and social outputs. It might even be an underestimate of the combined social and passenger services produced because it does not adjust for all of the improvements in passenger service quality.

The degree of meaning attached to any such index depends, of course, on whether maintaining transit vehicle-mileage provides significant public benefits. It should be noted that some considerable doubt exists as to whether maintaining unprofitable transit service is necessarily an effective means to advance the social objectives which proponents of transit subsidy often claim (see, for example, Meyer, Kain, and Wohl 1965, chap. 13; Gómez-Ibáñez 1975). Nevertheless, the fact that transit subsidies are enacted by legislatures does suggest that maintenance of transit services is deemed a public benefit by much of the electorate.

The choice between revenue passengers and vehicle-miles does make a significant difference when estimating transit output trends. Table 4.6 shows two indexes of transit output from 1948 to 1970, one based on passengers and the other on vehicle-miles. Output as measured by revenue passengers declines at an average annual rate of 4.94% whereas output measured in vehicle-miles declines at only 3.44% per year.

Since productivity is measured by the relation between outputs and inputs, the choice between revenue passengers and vehicle-miles will affect estimates of the postwar trends in transit productivity. The productivity estimates in table 4.7 show that if output is measured in revenue passengers carried, total factor productivity appears to have declined at an average annual rate of 1.40% per year from 1948 to 1970. This estimate is slightly more negative but otherwise quite comparable to that of Kendrick for the private sector only of the industry between 1948 to 1966. However, if output is measured in vehicle-miles operated, the average annual rate of total factor productivity decline drops by 1.29 percentage points to only 0.11%.

Moreover, if vehicle-miles are used to measure output, any productivity decline that does take place is in the years immediately after World War II and not, as Kendrick suggests, in the late 1950s and the 1960s. Indeed, with vehicle-miles as the measure, the postwar productivity record separates into two distinct periods: (1) the decade from 1948 to 1958 when total factor productivity declined at a rate of about 0.8% per year; and (2) the years from 1958 to 1968 when productivity seemingly improved at a rough rate of 0.7% annually.

When deriving these comprehensive measures of output and productivity for the entire transit industry, the outputs of the different component modes (motor and trolley buses and light and heavy rail transit) have been weighted by the relative prices of the modes. These prices may or may not well reflect differences in factor inputs required or market values placed on the services. On the whole, in a regulated and subsidized industry, relative costs are probably more appropriate weights than relative prices, especially if some modes are more heavily subsidized than others. As explained earlier, where public policy keeps the price of some outputs below costs, relative costs are at least as likely as relative prices to reflect the relative value which society places on the outputs or the relative resources which are necessary for producing them. Specifically, systematic subsidy of a service would suggest that society envisages some special social goals or outputs of value (at least equal to costs) thereby being achieved.

Table 4.6   **Effect on Output Estimates of Using Vehicle-Miles instead of Revenue Passengers as the Basic Measure of Output (1958=100.0)**

Year	Index of Output Based on Revenue Passengers	Index of Output Based on Vehicle-Miles
1948	228.6	171.8
1949	200.4	161.2
1950	181.4	150.1
1951	168.1	143.0
1952	156.5	136.1
1953	143.4	129.2
1954	127.7	120.4
1955	118.8	114.5
1956	112.9	109.1
1957	98.0	104.6
1958	100.0	100.0
1959	98.3	97.6
1960	96.5	96.5
1961	92.9	93.4
1962	91.3	91.7
1963	88.5	89.9
1964	87.7	89.2
1965	86.9	88.7
1966	85.3	87.5
1967	84.6	88.0
1968	83.0	87.7
1969	80.6	86.9
1970	77.1	83.2
Average annual percentage change, 1948–70[a]	−4.42	−3.23

NOTE: The outputs of the different modes are weighted by the modes' relative prices in 1958.
[a]Calculated from a least-squares fit of an exponential curve.

Table 4.7 Effect on Productivity Estimates of Using Vehicle-Miles instead of Revenue Passengers as the Basic Measure of Output (1958=100.0)

Year	Labor Productivity		Capital Productivity		Total Factor Productivity	
	Passengers Measure Output	Vehicle-Miles Measure Output	Passengers Measure Output	Vehicle-Miles Measure Output	Passengers Measure Output	Vehicle-Miles Measure Output
1948	133.7	100.5	148.9	111.9	142.3	106.9
1949	120.9	97.2	156.7	126.0	137.4	110.6
1950	115.6	95.2	145.2	120.2	129.6	107.2
1951	112.1	95.4	137.4	116.9	124.2	105.7
1952	109.2	95.0	130.9	113.8	119.8	104.2
1953	103.2	93.0	123.6	111.4	113.4	102.2
1954	98.4	92.8	113.4	106.9	106.1	100.0
1955	97.3	93.8	108.7	104.8	103.8	100.1
1956	98.7	95.4	106.3	102.7	103.2	99.7
1957	90.5	96.6	95.1	101.5	93.3	99.6
1958	100.0	100.0	100.0	100.0	100.0	100.0
1959	102.0	101.2	101.4	100.7	101.5	100.8
1960	102.0	102.0	103.3	103.3	102.1	102.1
1961	101.5	102.1	102.5	103.1	101.1	101.6
1962	101.6	102.0	104.1	104.6	102.0	102.6
1963	99.7	95.6	104.7	100.5	101.1	97.0
1964	100.9	102.6	107.2	109.0	102.6	104.3
1965	99.9	102.0	109.3	111.6	103.5	105.6

Table 4.7 (continued)

Year	Labor Productivity		Capital Productivity		Total Factor Productivity	
	Passengers Measure Output	Vehicle-Miles Measure Output	Passengers Measure Output	Vehicle-Miles Measure Output	Passengers Measure Output	Vehicle-Miles Measure Output
1966	98.7	101.3	109.5	112.3	102.4	105.0
1967	96.7	100.6	110.9	115.3	101.2	105.3
1968	96.5	102.0	110.1	116.3	100.1	105.8
1969	95.6	103.1	105.6	113.9	n.a.[b]	n.a.[a]
1970	93.3	100.7	101.4	109.5	93.9	101.3
Average annual percentage change, 1948–70[b]	−0.93	+0.35	−1.45	−0.14	−1.40	−0.11

NOTE: The outputs of the different modes are weighted by the modes' relative prices in 1958.
[a]Not available.
[b]Calculated from a least-squares fit of an exponential curve.

Within the transit industry, heavy and light rail transit service tends to be more heavily subsidized than trolley bus and, especially, motor bus. Although the situation varied from firm to firm, in the industry as a whole during 1958, the base year for our estimates, the revenues collected on each mode were only about sufficient to cover operating expenses. The two rail transit modes, though, have relatively high directly identifiable capital costs and thus may have been subsidized more (i.e., a bigger gap is created between fares and total factor input requirements for these modes). On the other hand, the trolley and the motor bus may have been the beneficiaries of equal but disguised capital inputs through their use of public highways. A firm determination of the extent and incidence of subsidy to various classes of highway users has been a matter of some contention in highway circles and would require an analysis well beyond the scope of the present study to settle. Jack Faucett Associates, quite heroically, attempted such an allocation when measuring highway inputs in their transit industry capital estimates. Nevertheless, the issue is probably best regarded as still open.

It would seem highly improbable, though, that any "highway subsidy" bestowed on trolleys, and especially buses, could be substantial, given that the highways are shared by so many modes and the costs are prorated or spread over a very large volume of traffic, particularly in urban areas. Furthermore, quite a bit of evidence suggests that urban arterials of the type commonly used by transit are actually sources of subsidy (via user taxation) for covering the costs of less intensively utilized roads in rural areas (Meyer, Kain, and Wohl 1965, chap. 4). On balance, therefore, it may not be too misleading to ignore the possibility of unrecouped or unrecognized highway costs for trolley and bus, but we admit this is a subjective judgment and debatable.

To better gauge the possibility of differential modal subsidies, table 4.8 shows estimates of average revenues and two estimates of average costs per revenue passenger trip and per vehicle-mile on the different modes in 1958. Two cost estimates are given because with the available data it is difficult to know exactly how to allocate industry costs, especially capital costs, among the modes. In our view, the most reasonable estimate assumes that heavy rail transit is responsible for most of the rail capital costs reported by Faucett Associates. Our "less likely estimate" assigns more of the capital costs to light rail transit and trolley buses.[10]

---

10. Unfortunately, Faucett did not make separate estimates of stocks and depreciation for the four basic modes but only for the bus mode and for the three "rail" modes (heavy and light rail and trolley bus) together. For both bus and "rail" modes Faucett made separate estimates of costs associated with equipment and with structures and way. For years before 1968 separate estimates of capital

Because the different transit modes declined at different rates during the postwar period, a shift from price to cost-based weights can make a difference in estimates of postwar trends of industry output and thus productivity. The impact, moreover, is very sensitive to the particular cost estimates used. Tables 4.9 and 4.10 show output estimates measured in revenue passengers and vehicle-miles using three different weighting schemes. The data show that a shift from weights based on relative prices to weights based on what seems to be the most likely estimate of relative costs alters the estimated postwar average annual percentage decline in revenue passengers from 4.42 to 4.24 and the annual percentage decline in vehicle-miles from 3.23 to 2.43. This occurs because the most likely estimates of relative costs strongly weight heavy rail transit output, and heavy rail transit has not declined as rapidly as other modes. However, the data in tables 4.9 and 4.10 also show that a shift from price-based weights to weights based on a less likely (but not totally indefensible) estimate of relative costs increases the estimated annual rate of decline. The "less likely" relative cost estimates weight light rail output more strongly than heavy rail transit output, and light rail transit declined relatively rapidly, especially in the years immediately after World War II.

A shift to weights based on relative costs also changes, of course, the estimates of productivity. Tables 4.11 and 4.12 show estimates of labor, capital, and total factor productivity using weights based on relative prices and on the more and less likely estimates of relative costs. The data show that a shift from weights based on relative prices to weights based on the most likely estimates of relative costs makes the trend in transit productivity look slightly more favorable. For example, if output

---

stocks for the four basic modes were made by the American Transit Association (ATA). However, the derivation of the ATA estimates was never documented, and they must be considered less reliable than those by Faucett. See Jack Faucett Associates, *Capital Stock Measures for Transportation* and American Transit Association, "Gross Investment of the Transit Industry as of December 31, 1940–1967, Segregated as to Mode of Service," unpublished, 1968.

For the "most likely" estimate of the relative costs of transit modes, Faucett's estimates of "rail" capital costs (both for structures and equipment) were allocated among the heavy rail, light rail, and trolley bus in proportion to the 1958 ATA estimates of the stocks of these three modes. For the "less likely" estimate of relative costs, Faucett's estimates of "rail" structure costs were allocated among the three modes on the basis of the number of line-miles each mode served, assuming that a light rail line-mile and a trolley bus line-mile were only one-fourth and one-tenth as expensive, respectively, as a heavy rail line-mile; Faucett's estimates of "rail" equipment costs were allocated on the basis of vehicles owned, assuming that a light rail vehicle and a trolley bus vehicle were only two-thirds and one-sixth as expensive, respectively, as heavy rail vehicle.

Table 4.8   **Indexes of Revenue and Cost per Vehicle-Mile and per Revenue Passenger for Transit Modes in 1958 (motor bus=100.0)**

Mode	Relative Revenue[a]	Relative Cost[b]	
		Using the Most Likely Allocation of Capital Costs	Using a Less Likely Allocation of Capital Costs
Per vehicle-mile operated			
Heavy rail	124.8	425.2	330.1
Light Rail	199.5	354.0	656.3
Trolley bus	142.5	159.0	232.3
Motor bus	100.0	100.0	100.0
Per revenue passenger carried			
Heavy rail	95.0	323.9	251.4
Light rail	139.2	247.1	458.1
Trolley bus	101.5	113.2	105.3
Motor bus	100.0	100.0	100.0

[a]Calculated from data in American Transit Association, *Transit Fact Book, 1959* (Washington: American Transit Association, 1959).

[b]See footnote 10 for a description of the two methods of allocating capital costs among the modes.

NOTE: These estimates of the relative costs of heavy rail, light rail, trolley bus, and motor bus trips do not necessarily indicate the relative efficiency or effectiveness of the four transit modes. One mode's average cost may be higher than another's because that mode tends to provide better quality service or operates in localities where factor prices are higher. For example, heavy rail transit costs may be higher because this mode generally serves longer passenger trips and is more heavily concentrated in the largest cities, where wages are higher.

is measured in revenue passengers, the shift from price-based weights to weights based on most likely estimates of relative costs alters the estimated average change in total factor productivity from −1.40 to −1.21% per year. Similarly, if output is measured in vehicle-miles, the shift from weights based on prices to those based on most likely costs alters the estimated average change in total factor productivity from −0.11 to +0.63% per year. However, a shift from price-based weights to weights based on the less likely estimates of relative costs makes the postwar trend in productivity look much less favorable, whether output is measured in revenue passengers or vehicle-miles.

Table 4.13 summarizes what seem to be the best estimates of the industry's productivity trends from 1948 to 1970. In broad outline, the postwar productivity record of the transit industry can be placed as lying somewhere between ±1% per year. Estimates lying outside that

Table 4.9   Revenue Passenger Output Indexes Calculated Using Relative Costs and Relative Prices as Weights (1958=100.0)

Year	Weights Based on Relative Prices	Weights Based on Most Likely Estimate of Relative Costs	Weights Based on Less Likely Estimates of Relative Costs
1948	228.6	222.6	320.1
1949	200.4	196.1	262.9
1950	181.4	178.0	229.7
1951	168.1	152.8	202.4
1952	156.5	154.6	181.0
1953	143.4	141.9	162.3
1954	127.7	126.7	139.8
1955	118.8	118.1	127.1
1956	112.9	112.6	116.9
1957	98.0	107.2	98.8
1958	100.0	100.0	100.0
1959	98.3	98.4	97.6
1960	96.5	96.7	95.2
1961	92.9	93.1	92.4
1962	91.3	91.6	90.3
1963	88.5	88.9	86.2
1964	87.7	88.1	85.2
1965	86.9	87.4	84.0
1966	85.3	85.8	82.0
1967	84.6	85.1	81.6
1968	83.0	83.4	80.2
1969	80.6	81.1	78.9
1970	77.1	77.5	75.2
Average annual percentage change, 1948–70[a]	−4.42	−4.24	−5.85

[a]Calculated using a least-squares fit of an exponential equation.

range could be justified, though, under certain circumstances, especially beyond the lower bound.

Exactly which estimate one might prefer within the range of ±1% will depend to some considerable extent upon one's purposes and assumptions. If the emphasis is upon output as reflected in market prices paid by passengers, then a relatively negative productivity record can be justified. On the other hand, if one chooses instead to stress the social goals ostensibly achieved through transit operations (which seems to be the emphasis increasingly favored by the governments which subsidize such operations), then a more favorable productivity record

Table 4.10   Vehicle-Mile Output Indexes Calculated Using Relative Costs and Relative Prices as Weights (1958=100.0)

Year	Weights Based on Relative Prices	Weights Based on Most Likely Estimate of Relative Costs	Weights Based on Less Likely Estimate of Relative Costs
1948	171.8	150.4	225.6
1949	161.2	144.6	201.8
1950	150.1	136.6	182.7
1951	143.0	132.4	167.9
1952	136.1	127.9	154.3
1953	129.2	122.4	143.4
1954	120.4	115.8	129.5
1955	114.5	111.2	121.0
1956	109.1	107.5	112.0
1957	104.6	104.0	105.5
1958	100.0	100.0	100.0
1959	97.6	98.1	97.1
1960	96.5	97.4	95.4
1961	93.4	94.3	92.2
1962	91.7	93.0	90.1
1963	89.9	91.9	86.8
1964	89.2	91.6	85.8
1965	88.7	91.2	85.2
1966	87.5	90.1	83.6
1967	88.0	90.7	84.2
1968	87.7	90.4	84.5
1969	86.9	89.4	84.3
1970	83.2	85.6	81.1
Average annual percentage change, 1948–70[a]	−3.23	−2.43	−4.37

[a]Calculated using a least-squares fit of an exponential equation.

can be demonstrated. However, even using the most favorable estimate (of +0.63% per year), transit's productivity record still has fallen far short of the average annual total factor productivity increase of 2 to 3% in the private domestic economy as a whole.

4.5   Some Implications

To recapitulate, recent research suggests some dramatic changes in the estimates of productivity trends in several transportation industries. A comparison of these old and new estimates appears in table 4.14.

Table 4.11   Productivity Estimates Using Revenue Passengers as Output Measure

Year	Labor Productivity Output Weighted by Relative Prices	Labor Output Weighted by Estimates of Relative Costs Most Likely	Labor Less Likely	Capital Productivity Output Weighted by Relative Prices	Capital Output Weighted by Estimates of Relative Costs Most Likely	Capital Less Likely	Total Factor Productivity Output Weighted by Relative Prices	TFP Output Weighted by Estimates of Relative Costs Most Likely	TFP Less Likely
1948	133.7	130.2	187.2	148.9	145.0	208.5	142.3	138.5	199.2
1949	120.9	118.3	158.6	156.7	153.3	205.6	137.4	134.5	180.3
1950	115.6	113.4	146.4	145.2	142.5	183.9	129.6	127.1	164.1
1951	112.1	101.9	135.0	137.4	124.9	165.5	124.2	112.9	149.6
1952	109.2	107.9	126.3	130.9	129.3	151.3	119.8	118.4	138.6
1953	103.2	102.2	116.8	123.6	122.3	139.9	113.4	112.3	128.4
1954	98.4	97.6	107.9	113.4	112.5	124.2	106.1	105.2	116.1
1955	97.3	96.7	104.1	108.7	108.1	116.3	103.8	103.2	111.1
1956	98.7	98.4	102.2	106.3	106.0	101.1	103.2	102.9	106.9
1957	90.5	99.0	91.2	95.1	104.0	95.8	93.3	102.1	94.1
1958	100.0	100.0	100.0	100.0	100.0	100.0	100.0	100.0	100.0
1959	102.0	102.1	101.2	101.4	101.5	100.7	101.5	101.7	100.8
1960	102.0	102.2	100.6	103.3	103.5	101.9	102.1	102.3	100.7
1961	101.5	101.7	101.0	102.5	102.8	102.0	101.1	101.3	100.5
1962	101.6	101.9	100.4	104.1	104.4	103.0	102.0	102.3	100.9
1963	99.7	100.1	97.1	104.7	105.2	102.0	101.1	101.6	98.5
1964	100.9	101.4	98.0	107.2	107.7	104.2	102.6	103.0	99.6
1965	99.9	100.5	96.6	109.3	109.9	105.7	103.5	104.0	100.0

Table 4.11 (continued)

Year	Labor Productivity			Capital Productivity			Total Factor Productivity		
	Output Weighted by Relative Prices	Output Weighted by Estimates of Relative Costs		Output Weighted by Relative Prices	Output Weighted by Estimates of Relative Costs		Output Weighted by Relative Prices	Output Weighted by Estimates of Relative Costs	
		Most Likely	Less Likely		Most Likely	Less Likely		Most Likely	Less Likely
1966	98.7	99.3	94.9	109.5	110.1	105.3	102.4	103.0	98.4
1967	96.7	97.3	93.3	110.9	111.5	106.9	101.2	101.8	97.6
1968	96.5	97.0	93.3	110.1	110.6	106.4	100.1	100.6	96.7
1969	95.6	96.2	93.6	105.6	106.3	103.4	n.a.[b]	n.a.[b]	n.a.[b]
1970	93.3	93.8	91.0	101.4	102.0	98.9	93.9	94.4	91.6
Avg. annual percentage change, 1948–70[a]	−0.93	−0.75	−2.37	−1.45	−1.27	−2.86	−1.40	−1.21	−2.92

[a]Calculated from a least-squares fit of an exponential curve.
[b]Not available.

Table 4.12 Productivity Estimates Using Vehicle-Miles as Output Measure

	Labor Productivity			Capital Productivity			Total Factor Productivity		
	Output Weighted by Relative Prices	Output Weighted by Estimates of Relative Costs		Output Weighted by Relative Prices	Output Weighted by Estimates of Relative Costs		Output Weighted by Relative Prices	Output Weighted by Estimates of Relative Costs	
Year		Most Likely	Less Likely		Most Likely	Less Likely		Most Likely	Less Likely
1948	100.5	88.0	131.9	111.9	98.0	147.0	106.9	93.6	140.4
1949	97.2	87.2	121.7	126.0	113.1	157.8	110.6	99.2	138.4
1950	95.2	87.1	116.4	120.2	109.4	146.3	107.2	97.6	130.5
1951	95.4	88.3	112.0	116.9	108.3	137.3	105.7	97.9	124.1
1952	95.0	89.3	107.7	113.8	106.9	129.0	104.2	97.9	118.1
1953	93.0	88.1	103.2	111.4	105.5	123.6	102.2	96.8	113.4
1954	92.8	89.2	99.9	106.9	102.8	115.0	100.0	96.2	107.6
1955	93.8	91.1	99.1	104.8	101.7	110.7	100.1	97.2	105.8
1956	95.4	94.0	97.9	102.7	101.2	105.5	99.7	98.3	102.4
1957	96.6	96.0	97.4	101.5	100.9	102.3	99.6	99.0	100.5
1958	100.0	100.0	100.0	100.0	100.0	100.0	100.0	100.0	100.0
1959	101.2	101.8	100.7	100.7	101.2	100.2	100.8	101.3	100.3
1960	102.0	103.0	100.8	103.3	104.3	102.1	102.1	103.1	101.0
1961	102.1	103.1	100.8	103.1	104.1	101.8	101.6	102.6	100.3
1962	102.0	103.4	100.2	104.6	106.0	102.7	102.6	103.9	100.7
1963	95.6	103.5	97.7	100.5	108.8	102.7	97.0	105.0	99.2
1964	102.6	105.4	98.7	109.0	112.0	104.9	104.3	107.1	100.4
1965	102.0	104.8	97.9	111.6	114.7	107.2	105.6	108.6	101.4

Table 4.12 (continued)

Year	Labor Productivity			Capital Productivity			Total Factor Productivity		
	Output Weighted by Relative Prices	Output Weighted by Estimates of Relative Costs		Output Weighted by Relative Prices	Output Weighted by Estimates of Relative Costs		Output Weighted by Relative Prices	Output Weighted by Estimates of Relative Costs	
		Most Likely	Less Likely		Most Likely	Less Likely		Most Likely	Less Likely
1966	101.3	104.3	96.8	112.3	115.7	107.3	105.0	108.2	100.4
1967	100.6	103.7	96.2	115.3	118.9	110.4	105.3	108.5	100.7
1968	102.0	105.1	98.3	116.3	119.9	112.1	105.8	109.0	101.9
1969	103.1	106.0	100.0	113.9	117.2	110.5	n.a.[a]	n.a.[a]	n.a.[a]
1970	100.7	103.6	98.2	109.5	112.6	106.7	101.3	104.3	98.8
Avg. annual percentage change, 1948–70[b]	+0.35	+1.05	−0.89	−0.14	+0.54	−1.40	−0.11	+0.63	−1.40

[a]Not available.
[b]Calculated from a least-squares fit of an exponential curve.

Table 4.13   **Final Transit Productivity Estimates**

	Average Annual Rate of Productivity Change, 1948–70		
Basic Measure of Output Used	Total Factor Productivity	Labor Productivity	Capital Productivity
Revenue passengers	−1.21	−0.75	−1.27
Vehicle-miles	+0.63	+1.05	+0.54

NOTE: Output weighted by the most likely estimates of the relative costs of the modes.

Given these results, it is difficult to escape the conclusion that, at least in transportation, productivity measurement is an art in which interpretation and understanding is enhanced by knowledge of the industry involved and, equally important, careful consideration of the purpose for which any estimate might be used. In transportation, moreover, it is crucial to understand the social characteristics of the output and the effect of public involvement on prices and returns to factors, especially capital. A particularly difficult "joint-production" problem also complicates output and productivity measurement in most transport undertakings, specifically the common practice of jointly providing terminal and line-haul services. Difficulties are also introduced, as in many industries, by changes in the quality of service provided and in the form of ownership or financing employed for capital inputs. The normal remedy for most of these complications involves weighting by market prices. Unfortunately, in highly regulated transport industries market data may lose much of its conventional meaning and therefore usefulness in such applications.

Some troublesome implications are also suggested for comparisons made of productivity trends among a large number of industries. In order to generate the required data series, large-scale comparative studies must rely on simple, standard conventions for estimating the output and input trends in each industry. These conventions generate data series which are, at least in some narrow sense, consistent. But given that the interpretations are so sensitive to purpose and the particular characteristics of an industry, the question arises of whether the resulting estimates can be meaningfully compared across time and industry sector.

By way of amelioration, it is tempting to argue that measuring productivity in transportation is more difficult than in other sectors. We suspect, though, that while other industries may not share the particular

Table 4.14 **"Conventional" and Adjusted Estimates of the Postwar Output and Productivity Changes in Selected Transportation Industries**

Industry	Average Annual Percentage Change[a] in Output		Average Annual Percentage Change[a] in Total Factor Productivity		Labor Productivity	
	"Conventional" Estimate	Adjusted Estimate	"Conventional" Estimate	Adjusted Estimate	"Conventional" Estimate	Adjusted Estimate
Intercity trucking						
All class I and II carriers	6.0,[b] 8.4[c]	< 6.0, 8.4[d]			2.7,[b] 3.1[c]	< 2.7, 3.1[d]
General freight carriers only	4.9[b]	> 4.9[d]			2.1[b]	> 2.1[d]
Railroad	0.4,[e] 0.3[c]	− 0.7[f]	5.0[e]	1.8 to 0.8[f]	4.9,[e] 6.0[e]	3.7[f]
Urban Mass Transit	− 4.8,[c] − 2.6[g]	− 4.2 to − 2.4[h]	− 1.6[g]	− 1.2 to + .6[h]	− 0.9[e]	− .7 to + 1.0[h]

[a]Annual changes calculated from a least-squares fit of an exponential curve.

[b]Estimates from 1954 to 1972 in Carnes (1974).

[c]Estimates for 1948 to 1966 from data in Kendrick (1973), pp. 329, 334, and 335.

[d]See the discussion of Daryl Wyckoff's work in section 4.3.

[e]Estimates for 1948 to 1970 from data at U.S. Bureau of Labor Statistics, *Indexes of Output Per Man-Hour, Selected Industries*, bulletin no. 1827 (Washington: Government Printing Office, 1974), pp. 89, 90, and 93.

[f]Estimates for 1947 to 1970 from Task Force on Railroad Productivity (1973), pp. 75 and 78.

[g]Estimates for the British taxi and transit industries between 1952 and 1965 from data in Deakin and Seward (1969), p. 227.

[h]See Section 4.4.

characteristics which complicate measurement in transportation, they may well have their own special attributes and complications that are at least equally confusing and obfuscating.

References

American Transit Association. 1972. *Transit fact book, '71–'72,* p. 3. Washington: American Transit Association.

Carnes, Richard. 1974. Productivity trends in intercity trucking. *Monthly Labor Review* 97:53–57.

Deakin, B. M., and Seward, T. 1969. Productivity in transport: A study of employment, capital, output, productivity, and technical change. Cambridge University Department of Applied Economics, Occasional Papers no. 17. Cambridge: Cambridge University Press.

Gellman, Aaron J. 1971. Surface freight industries. In *Technological change in regulated industries,* ed. William Capron, pp. 166–96. Washington: Brookings Institution.

Gómez-Ibáñez, José A. 1975. Assessing the arguments for urban mass transportation operating subsidies. Harvard University, Department of City and Regional Planning, Working Paper no. 75–1.

Jack Faucett Associates. 1974. *Capital stock measures for transportation,* report no. JACKFAU–71–04–6, prepared for the Office of the Secretary, U.S. Department of Transportation. Washington: U.S. Department of Transportation.

Kendrick, John. 1973. *Postwar productivity trends in the United States, 1948–1969,* p. 106. New York: National Bureau of Economic Research.

Meyer, John R.; Kain, John F.; and Wohl, Martin. 1965. *The urban transportation problem.* Cambridge: Harvard University Press.

National Academy of Sciences, Committee on the Costs and Benefits of Automobile Emission Control. 1974. Final Report, vol. 4.

Task Force on Railroad Productivity. 1973. *Improving railroad productivity.* Report to the National Commission on Productivity and the Council of Economic Advisors. Washington: National Council on Productivity.

U.S. Bureau of Labor Statistics. 1971. Indexes of output per man-hour, selected industries, 1939 and 1947–1970, Bulletin no. 1692. Washington: Government Printing Office.

Wyckoff, D. Daryl. 1972–73. Issues of productivity. *Traffic World,* 18 September, 6 and 13 November, 18 and 25 December 1972; 26 February 1973.

———. 1974. *Organizational formality and performance in the motor carrier industry.* Lexington, Mass.: D. C. Heath.

5   Current Efforts to Measure Productivity in the Public Sector: How Adequate for the National Accounts?

Allan D. Searle and Charles A. Waite

5.1   Introduction

The federal government is currently engaged in a broad program to measure productivity in the federal sector.

The present effort to measure federal productivity is an immediate outgrowth of work undertaken in fiscal 1972 by a joint interagency task force (composed of the Office of Management and Budget, the General Accounting Office, and the Civil Service Commission) which collected data for fiscal years 1967–71 from 114 organizational units in 17 agencies representing about 55% of the federal civilian work force. In July 1973, the Office of Management and Budget endorsed the continuation of the project, and full responsibility for collecting input, output, and related information and for developing the productivity measures shifted to the Bureau of Labor Statistics (BLS).

In fiscal years 1974 and 1975, the Bureau expanded the data base, expanded coverage to include organizational units not previously covered, improved the quality of some of the input and output data, and refined the methodological procedures used by the original task force. Currently, about 65% of the federal civilian work force is covered by the BLS survey.

The question to which this paper is directed may be summarized thusly: Does this effort to measure productivity and the more modest efforts undertaken by certain state and local governments provide a basis for adjusting existing measures of government output in the national income and product accounts?

Charles A. Waite is at the Bureau of Economic Analysis. Allan D. Searle was a consultant to the Bureau from 1973 to 1978.

The opinions and conclusions expressed are those of the authors and do not necessarily represent those of the Bureau of Economic Analysis.

333

Our answer is No if government output in the national accounts is viewed as including the ultimate public goods and services which government provides, such as national security, education, or fire protection. However, the answer is Maybe if one views government output more narrowly, namely as the flow of governmental processes, such as passports issued, vouchers examined, or audits completed.

Although we prefer the broader concept of output, we find no consensus on this matter, and there is certainly no way to measure changes in output under this concept. Nevertheless, the narrower output concept also poses serious conceptual and measurement problems.

This paper will review alternative output concepts as well as pragmatic considerations which affect both national accounts and existing productivity measures. The current federal productivity measurement program is examined as to its possible use in improving the existing national accounts measures. Problems in developing productivity measures for the state and local government sector also will be examined briefly.

5.2   Government Output in National Accounts

Value added by government to national output, like value added in all nonbusiness sectors of the economy, is measured by total factor cost incurred. In the case of government, factor cost is confined to the compensation of employees. Interest payments are not regarded as measuring value added because they are subject to fluctuations which cannot be regarded as representing corresponding changes in the value of national production. (Of course, inclusion of business interest in GNP excludes explicit consideration of its behavior because any of its fluctuations not reflecting productive activity are offset by changes in profits.) Government output also excludes the return to government-owned property because the statistical basis for making a realistic imputation is inadequate. This is largely because a realistic market value of the rental value of government property is not available, nor is an estimate for the total value of government real capital assets (BEA is currently working to develop such estimates, however).

In real terms, government output is obtained for any year as the product of full-time equivalent employment in that year and base-year compensation per full-time equivalent employee.[1] We may add that the estimates are made in eleven categories including officers and enlisted

---

1. Subsequent to the preparation of this paper, the methodology for estimating real government output was revised as part of the comprehensive revision of the national income and product accounts. See the January 1976 issue of the *Survey of Current Business* (p. 22) for a summary of the revised methodology.

men by major military service, federal civilian workers, state and local education and noneducation employees. Also, federal and state and local work relief (and recently, public service job holders) are treated separately in the period they appear. Productivity changes within each category are conventionally assumed to be zero.

It is important to realize what is *not* measured. What is not measured is the amount of education, defense, etc., which the government provides from its expenditures. The government is not transformed from a final consumer to a producer selling products to individuals at an imputed value. This is because no one knows how to obtain an output index for any important government function except by measuring inputs.

This is not to say the present method of deflating government compensation cannot be refined. One possibility, which BEA is seriously investigating, is use of specification pricing for employment inputs as outlined by Denison. In specification pricing for any group of commodities or services, one seeks to select as specifications those characteristics which (1) can be readily identified and do not change over time so that one can get continuous series; (2) are reliably associated with the biggest price differentials—either because they are characteristically important to the buyer or because they are associated with such characteristics; and (3) are possessed in varying proportions by the class of commodities under consideration. One does not examine the use of the product or service. BEA is considering a classification of government compensation based on age, occupation, and education, all of which are associated with substantial earnings differentials. Base-year pay of age/occupation/education groups would be extrapolated by hours worked in order to obtain real compensation. The proposition is that work by government employees in the same age/occupation/education group with the same amount of hours worked represents a purchase of the same quality of labor at different dates. Statistically, BEA might use data on shifts in the pattern of the federal grade structure (adjusted for "grade-creep") as a proxy for shifts in age/occupation/education. The functional distribution of labor is irrelevant.

In summary, since BEA does not have market values to place on the services produced by government, it is not possible to price these services and therefore not possible to arrive at a real value of government output. As a result, BEA has adopted the convention of valuing government output in terms of input, namely employee compensation. Changes in real compensation/output result only from changes in employment. (Output in the household sector is derived in a similar manner.) Research is under way to modify this method by taking into consideration changing characteristics of the government work force that are associated with earnings differentials.

5.3   Alternative Concepts of Government Output

Many of the problems of measuring government output are similar to problems found in measuring output in the service sector of the private economy. Estimating the quantity and quality of service output is inherently difficult since no physical unit of standard quality is available. How does one quantify an auto repair in the private sector? Or police protection in the public sector?

At least two methods are used. They are ably explained by Ross and Burkhead in their excellent book, *Productivity in the Local Government Sector*. First, the number of direct outputs, for example cars repaired or arrests made, may be used. However, this does not take account of quality change, nor does the direct output represent the desired service output. For example, the number of spark plugs replaced may be a good direct output measure, but the service output is the properly operating auto. Similarly, the number of arrests made may be a direct output, but the service output is a decreasing crime rate. To overcome these problems, a second method may be used, that of calculating the effects or consequences of the service; in our example, this would be the number of properly operating autos, or the lower crime rate. This method has been criticized because it confuses services output and consequences of output. The consequences are not necessarily a direct result of the service, but of the service and the environment. In our example, your car can be inoperative because of bad roads and not because of too few spark plugs installed, or crime may increase because of the easy availability of handguns and not because of too few arrests made.

Difficult as private-sector service output is to measure, it has one distinct advantage over public-sector output: it has a market price, and thus the total value of private-sector services can be estimated.

Not only do we lack market values to place on services produced by the government, we also lack a consensus on what is really meant by public-sector output in the national accounts. It is clear how government value added is currently measured, but it is far from clear what concept of public-sector output is being estimated. Is the concept one of direct outputs, such as arrests made, tons of garbage collected, or bombs dropped, or is it more general, such as a secure environment or international peace? Our investigation turned up enough diversity of opinion on this point to make it difficult to assess the applicability of current productivity measurement efforts to the national accounts.

The statistical method employed in the national accounts for measuring government output, namely by measuring the value of inputs, is the most common, but perhaps the least sophisticated, method of measuring government output. Two other methods, each aimed at the different output concepts discussed above, are used outside the national accounts. As we have seen, the first method estimates changes in output from changes in the quantity of direct outputs. The second method calculates output changes by estimates of changes in consequences; program-planning budgeting systems (PPBS) use this method. Bradford, Malt, and Oates (1969) have clearly drawn a distinction between the two. They separate output into what they term "D-output" (method 1) of the services directly produced, such as classroom hours taught, and "C-output" (method 2), the things of primary interest to the consumer, such as Johnny's ability to read—in other words, the consequences. As Ross and Burkhead (1971) pointed out, the C-output is functionally dependent on the D-output of that service, upon the D-output of any other public service that may influence it, and upon other environmental factors. To illustrate, let C-output be safety from crime and D-output be number of blocks patrolled by police. Although safety is related to number of blocks patrolled, many other variables also affect it. As is obvious, selecting C-output rather than D-output multiplies the problem of estimating public-sector productivity, particularly the problem of adjusting for quality change.

All studies of federal productivity, including the latest BLS effort, have focused on D-output. This is not only because it is more susceptible to measurement, but because it preserves the distinction between output and evaluation of effectiveness. Furthermore, to use consequences as estimates of government services output, as noted earlier, requires that one be able to separate those effects which directly result from the measured input from those resulting from the environment within which that service is performed. Moreover, changes in D-output measures are more nearly comparable to changes in most private-sector output measures. In the private sector, changes in output are measured in terms of physical units and not in terms of consequences, although consequences are a factor in determining relative values by buyers and sellers in the market place.

For these reasons, criticism of methods of measuring output in government productivity studies should not center on their use of direct outputs, but rather on other questions. Are the direct outputs final or intermediate? Should factor inputs in addition to labor be examined? Should the labor inputs be adjusted for characteristics associated with earnings differentials such as age, occupation, and education? Is it appropriate to derive a total government productivity index by combining the results for individual agencies? How appropriate is the sample of federal activities? Can the federal civilian results be extended to the military? To state and local governments?

5.4 Productivity Link between Input and Output

As implied earlier, if government direct output could be measured in physical terms and valued, then there would be no need to seek a suitable productivity measure with which to adjust the national accounts. Quantity, value, and price data would be available at the output end and presumably at the input end, and an index of value added at constant prices for the government sector would be attainable. The lack of comprehensive output quantity measures—under either the C-output or D-output definitions given above—precludes construction of both output-price and productivity measures for the government sector as a whole. Before casting aside all hope, however, some questions must be answered: Can deflated input values somehow be adjusted by some form of productivity measure to arrive at an *estimate* of government output? Or can the current employment series now used be similarly adjusted? If so, what is the appropriate form of productivity and output measure, and what are the assumptions involved? Are data available? What is now being done?

The link between input price and output price can be formulated in a variety of ways with output price as a function of productivity (or unit-labor requirements) and input prices. One formulation, for example, links input price, unit man-hours, unit materials requirements, unit labor requirements, wage rates, material prices, and output price.

Whatever use is made of government productivity measures requires certain compromises from an ideal concept and demands acceptance of a number of assumptions. If one accepts the national accounts assumptions that employment change is proportional to output change, then one might adopt suitable productivity measures as modifiers of the employment series.

Alternatively, one might apply a productivity index to the purchase price indexes to arrive at an estimate of output price. In this event, a productivity index using labor and materials as inputs would be required. However, on the assumption that unit material requirements tend to be stable in the short run and that unit profits data are inapplicable, one might be willing to confine attention to analyses of the type of labor productivity (output per man-hour) measure which would be an acceptable compromise.

For usefulness as adjustment factors in the national accounts, it would seem that the appropriate productivity measure would be one which consists of component unit-man-hour series weighted with labor cost—not with labor requirements (man-hours) as is usual in most of the Bureau of Labor Statistics industrial productivity series. The BLS series are conceptually suitable for technological-change analysis. The national accounts, on the other hand, require dollar weights in order to attain consistency with the value and price series of the national accounts. It follows that the total man-hours indexes used to obtain the productivity measures would be weighted by the wage or salary rate in each job category.

These formulation problems are not particularly serious, however, for data are available to provide the necessary weighting systems for the productivity measures. Of paramount importance is another question altogether: How useful are the productivity measures which can be constructed for component parts (departments, offices, activities, etc.) of the government? The question inquires not only as to their accuracy, coverage, sample, representativeness, etc., but whether a conceptually meaningful combination of the various series can be made which would be of use in the national accounts system.

To illustrate the problem raised by the last question: If an improved method of constructing walls requires fewer nails and thus less labor time, yet carpenters continue hammering at a constant rate of nails-per-hour, productivity based on nails-per-hour is constant while productivity based on walls-constructed-per-hour is higher. Similarly, if better paint allows painters to use one instead of two coats per wall, and the number of gallons of paint applied per man-hour is constant, productivity from the painter's standpoint is unchanged, but productivity from the standpoint of the seller of the painted wall is doubled. If a "total" index of productivity for wall construction were constructed from the indexes for carpenters and painters (or carpenter shops and paint shops), the combined index would be unchanged. An index based on "final" output—(walls or houses) would increase because account has been taken of the change in relationship between the outputs of intermediate processes and of the final product. In addition to the problems involved in combining measures of productivity, the example highlights the importance of obtaining an appropriate measure of output.

Output measures for final product are not simply averages of component process indexes, but consists also of an interaction or "activity-mix" factor which can even pull the total index outside the range of the highest-lowest component index. A productivity index constructed as an average for component departments of an organization or of processes is likely to miss the improvement which comes from elimination or reduction in importance of tasks or processes or from the introduction of new processes. In general, this failure would tend to result in a downward-biased productivity measure.

5.5   Early Efforts to Measure Federal Productivity Change

Before examining the current federal productivity measurement program, it may be useful to review the relatively few earlier efforts by federal agencies to measure the productivity of an entire organization or selected organizational components, following broadly the review by Ross and Burkhead (1971). In 1932, the first empirical study of productivity in the federal government was done for the Post Office by Bowden. He identified thirteen separate outputs—seven classes of mail weighted by relative average labor time required to handle units of that class and six special-service transactions weighted by average costs (since labor cost is the predominant cost element in both categories, he argued that the two types of output were additive.) Bowden's inputs were full-time equivalent postal workers based on hours actually paid.

Bowden's research was not sophisticated by present-day standards (he omitted certain types of labor, did not correct for changes in hours worked, etc.) but his basic methodology has been used by all studies of federal government productivity since then.

That methodology may be summarized in four steps: First, the organizations to be studied within the federal government are identified. The choice depends on the availability of output measures. Second, the quantity of inputs associated with each output is estimated. Capital inputs are not measured. Third, each output is weighted by the percentage of total inputs, usually man-hours used in the production of that output in the base year. Last, both outputs and inputs are expressed as indexes; dividing the output index by the input index yields an index of productivity.

Other works in federal productivity measurement were published in the late 1950s by Vogely and by Litton. Vogely's primary effort was to devise output measures for the Bureau of Land Management of the Department of Interior. He divided the Bureau into its major programs —minerals, lands, grazing, and forestry—and identified output measures for each, such as cases closed. In the process, he developed unit cost measures which suggested the direction of productivity change.

Lytton estimated productivity indexes for five separate agencies, covering 56% of total federal nondefense agency employment and included 139 indicators of the work of the federal government. His measures of output were developed, in some cases, by the agency itself (as in the case of the Social Security Administration), but his list of outputs has led some analysts to question whether his outputs were final and whether double-counting existed. It is also difficult to ascertain how he combined the five indexes into one government-wide productivity index.

The first major effort at measuring federal productivity for more than one agency began in 1962 and was published in 1964 by the Bureau of the Budget (Executive Office of the President, Bureau of the Budget 1964). The study covered 24% of total civilian federal employees in the fiscal year 1962. The period covered depended on the agency included and varied widely; as a result, no aggregate index was attempted.

The outputs selected met two criteria: (1) they were related to the mission of the agency as defined by law; (2) they were "final" in the sense that some person or unit other than the agency providing the service was the recipient. They were not adjusted for quality, although agencies submitted lists of quality improvements.

Some of the output measures used are comparable with the approach used in today's measures. For the Post Office Department, output measures were straightforward, being based on weighted series of twenty-one types of mail handled. For Treasury's Division of Disbursement, however, output was based on payments made and number of bonds issued. The output of the Department of Insurance of the Veterans Administration was based on policies in force (maintenance), number newly issued (separately by type), termination, and disability cases. For the Systems Maintenance Services of the Federal Aviation Agency, output was defined as the facility year, i.e., maintenance of an operating facility for a year; 318 such outputs were identified.

Three separate input indexes were used for each agency: (1) the unweighted man-hours; (2) dollar payroll costs; and (3) real total budget costs. For the latter, each agency developed its own price index to deflate current budget cost (how an agency could do this without making explicit productivity assumptions about its own work force is not explained).

The most important finding of the BOB study was that productivity could be measured at reasonable cost and that it could be a useful tool for government management and budgeting. The study found that the principal obstacle in the development of productivity measures was the requirement that products or service be measurable over time on a consistent basis. It is undoubtedly true that more or less satisfactory output measures were obtained for those agencies dealing with products and even well-defined services. Whether the output measures were "final" depended on the scope of the activity measured. How the BOB study might have dealt with agencies such as Defense, Labor's BLS, or Commerce's BEA, however, is not clear.

5.6 Current Productivity Measurement Efforts for the Federal Sector

In 1971, the federal government began a much more ambitious effort to measure federal productivity, initially mounted as a joint effort of the Civil Service Commission, Office of Management and Budget, and the General Accounting Office. In mid-1973, the responsibility for further improvement, maintenance, and expansion of these productivity measures was placed in the Bureau of Labor Statistics. During fiscal 1972, a task force under the Joint Federal Management Improvement Program (JFMIP) surveyed the use of quantitative measures within seventeen Federal agencies and demonstrated how they could be improved for management purposes. Data were gathered for the construction of an overall productivity index. Special studies were carried out, aimed at improving measures of unit cost and effectiveness. The latest report shows that 48 agencies reported on activities of 245 organizational elements covering over 1.8 million staff years (Joint Financial Management Improvement Program 1975). For purposes of these measures, productivity is defined as output per unit of labor, rather than per unit of a combination of inputs. These measures compare actual changes in output per unit input, without regard to the mission of the organizational units. Thus, according to Ardolini and Hohenstein,

> they must be distinguished from measures of effectiveness which provide a means of determining whether an agency is proceeding toward its objectives by establishing a relationship between organizational actions and mission accomplishment. Both types of measures are useful tools: the productivity measures indicate changes in the real cost of producing an agency's output and the effectiveness measures determine the value of the agency's output to the recipients of its goods and services [Ardolini and Hohenstein 1974].

The authors continue with the statement that "ideally a productivity measure should relate final outputs to their associated direct and indirect inputs." "Ideally"—aye, there's the rub!

5.6.1 The Output Measure

The data-reporting instructions for this project remind the various agencies that "the output series for an organizational unit should ideally reflect every final output activity of the organizational element" and go on to say, "While it may be possible to separate output activities, assigning appropriate employee-years to each may be impossible. Therefore the output detail will be constrained by the availability of actual base-year, employee-year data or estimates of base-year weights (e.g., relative weights)." Cautions are included to count joint outputs only once. Also, the instructions state that each output measure should (1) consist of units which are relatively homogeneous with respect to their labor requirements; (2) should be repetitive; (3) should directly reflect the work loads of the organizational element (and not that of contractors, for example); (4) should reflect changes in output quality (e.g., adjust for quality change); (5) should reflect the amount of work done in a fiscal year; and (6) should reflect the final products, services, and treatments of an organization. In connection with point (6), the instructions specifically call for the outputs to be final *"from the perspective of the organization providing the information."*

In fact, the output data are often "final" with respect to an organizational unit providing productivity data, but may be intermediate from an overall government point of view. For example, the productivity of payroll offices in issuing checks to employees is final from the viewpoint of the payroll office, but intermediate for the government as a whole.

At best, the total productivity measures are a weighted average of the separate productivity changes. Furthermore, not all the measures are output measures, even from this restricted view. For example, the JFMIP project identifies a number of tasks within the organizational element and defines output in terms of accomplishment of the task. Among the tasks are such activities as soil survey reports, contracts administered, patent disposals, weather observations, engine overhauls, claims adjudicated, number of applications examined, cubic feet of helium extracted, items printed. As one means of analyzing the quality of the data, the outputs were classified as (1) direct measures of work performed, e.g., engines overhauled; (2) partial measures, e.g., procurement contracts closed; (3) proxies, e.g., patients admitted; (4) population support, e.g., personnel served. According to the tabulations of the JFMIP, 85% of the outputs (weighted on a basis of man-years worked) are direct measures, with 5% more represented by partial indicators. Another classification shows that 71% of the outputs are "final," e.g., directly associated with performance of the mission, and the rest are intermediate.

Little need be said about the pitfalls attendant on the use of the proxy and population support measures. It is evident, for example, that a building maintenance measure based on square feet or floor area could result in a productivity measure which would show improvement if some of the work force were absent or if services were performed less frequently. "Population served" as measures for fire fighting and education are also unsatisfactory. But these categories of data represent only 10% of the total, and efforts are being made to upgrade the measures based on this type of data.

The 85–90% of the index which consists of direct and partial measures needs further scrutiny also. These series may very well be adequate for the specific tasks whose output they are designed to measure. The instructions do caution reporters to be alert for quality change and to adjust output measures in order to avoid measuring spurious productivity changes. Ways of measuring long-cycle production (e.g., ships) are presented and the need to match man-hours with output is stressed.

The man-hour measures include not only the direct labor but indirect labor which can be allocated to the output.

Many problems connected with measuring output trends arise because most federal activities result in production of services. The summary report for June 1973 (Joint Measurement Systems Project 1973) indicated that agencies sometimes state that an improvement in service has caused a productivity decline—that is, the measure takes no account of this type of quality change. The Bureau of Labor Statistics is attempting to correct this kind of misinterpretation of the instructions.

There are other types of quality change which affect the indexes. The BLS can solve some of these by constructing more detailed measures—for example, as BLS suggests, by means of separate indexes for high labor-intensive deliveries of mail to private residences and low labor-intensive deliveries to office buildings. Other quality changes—particularly those which cannot be solved by setting up such subproject categories—may be most difficult—for example, changes in time required from posting to delivery, or increased or decreased responsiveness of officials dealing with the public, or the efficiency of tax collection. Nevertheless, efforts need to be made. Sometimes an adjustment in quantity may be feasible on the basis of either the labor time or cost of an additional service feature instituted in connection with the basic service which is being measured.

5.6.2   Inputs

The early reports also state that two man-year indexes were prepared —one based on aggregate man-years and the other consisting of an index of current dollar compensation divided by an unpublished deflator for federal government general employee compensation covering salaries and fringe benefits. This latter index conforms more closely than the former to the concepts needed for national accounts deflators, but later JFMIP reports make no mention of it so far as we can ascertain. One hopes this index, as well as the associated productivity series, will be maintained together with subindexes as appropriate.

5.7   Productivity Measurement at the State and Local Level

As compared to the work done by the federal government, local efforts are fairly primitive. There is very little information available on the direct outputs of local governments; most do not keep data to measure outputs, and those that do have begun only recently. There is also controversy as to what is to be measured—direct outputs or consequences.

Hatry and Fisk, of the Urban Institute, in a report prepared for the National Commission on Productivity, state that "the main thing to be said about the productivity of local governments in the United States is that little is known about it" (Hatry and Fisk 1971).

The earliest studies of local government output such as those of Ridley and Simon in 1938 or Schmardt and Stephens in 1960 define output in terms of consequences rather than direct outputs.[2] This emphasis was carried over into the area of planning-programming budgeting systems (PPBS) evaluation of government programs at the national and local level. However, the relationship of inputs to outputs was not examined in the early studies.

The first empirical studies relevant to local productivity and direct local output was published in 1969 by Bradford, Malt, and Oates, who estimated the increase in cost of direct output for local education, health and hospitals, police, fire, and public welfare activities. Their output measures, such as pupil-days for education and patient-days for hospitals, are crude, however, and their means of deflating input costs are open to question.

A more ambitious effort to examine local government productivity was undertaken in 1971 by the Urban Institute. The institute's position on output measurement is quite different from Bradford, Malt, and Oates in that it argues that output should be broadly defined to include effectiveness and quality, not merely efficiency and quantity. The implication is that multiple measures of local productivity should be developed. As an example, the institute suggests a way for estimating the components of the productivity of garbage collection. The output measure suggested is tons of garbage collected adjusted for quality change where the latter is calculated by rating average street cleanliness by a local official on a scale of 1 to 4 and the percentage of population expressing satisfaction with garbage collection based on a survey. The input measure is real dollar costs. The institute also examined ways in which police crime control output may be measured, but again focused on output as measured by consequences or effects rather than from services directly produced.

Hatry and Fisk could find no local government function for which nation-wide productivity data had been or could be calculated. They found no consensus, at the local level, of what to measure, much less how to measure it.

They did identify at least three types of statistics collected by local governments which might be used in measuring productivity—cost data, work load measures, and, in a very few cases, effectiveness measures. Cost data, such as dollars expended by function or program, are most common, but they are rarely expressed in real terms. Moreover, existing measures of price change for local governments, such as BEA's implicit

2. From Ross and Burkhead (1971).

deflator for state and local government, are not available by function or level of government. (However, BEA is currently working on detailed deflators and expects to publish them in the near future.)

Work load measures, such as miles of streets swept, number of students per school, etc., are collected by many governments. Hatry and Fisk found that the most ambitious programs were in Chicago, Dayton, Fort Worth, Los Angeles, New York, Philadelphia, San Diego, and Savannah. Relating costs to work loads is also done in some cities, but rarely in real terms.

The measurement of effectiveness, or the quality of the government service as it impacts on the citizens of the community, has been tried in only a few jurisdictions, such as Chicago and Dayton.

Information collected by the federal government bearing on the effectiveness of local programs is beset with many problems. Important areas of government activity, such as garbage collection and fire protection, are largely ignored. Reports are often voluntary and response rates poor. Output data are not related to input data. Definitions are inconsistent among governments. Most important, none of the special surveys or the routinely collected data compiled by federal agencies or others have been specifically designed to provide nationwide information on state or local government productivity.

In summary, although local and state governments comprise over two-thirds of government output as now estimated in the GNP accounts, efforts to measure their productivity are still in their infancy and lag well behind federal efforts. Until new data are collected and existing data improved, it will not be possible to produce productivity measures suitable for use in the state-local sector of the GNP accounts.

5.8 Do the Federal Productivity Measures Meet the Needs of National Accounts Measurement?

5.8.1 In Concept?

If one's concept of government output includes the consequences of government activity, such as national security, the new federal productivity measures are of little use for adjusting the existing national account measures. As noted, BLS does not attempt to estimate the real market value of government services. If such data were available, they could be used with presently available input data to derive real value added for government. With such an output measure, productivity measurement would be redundant. Instead, the current federal productivity measurement effort is studying the output of processes, for example, claims processed. As illustrated earlier, the weighted average of productivity changes in the processes which go into the provision of a final product is not the same as the productivity gain in providing the final product. Eliminating, reorganizing, and replacing processes is the very essence of a most important way that productivity rises in the private economy. As noted, adjusting existing national-account government output measures by the new government productivity indexes would not give one the amount of defense, education, or other products the government provides. Neither could change in output per man-hour be used to adjust for change in labor quality.

5.8.2   As a Practical Alternative?

But this verdict cannot be the end of the matter, for we are a long way from measuring the market value of government services. A more reasonable approach must take realities into account and assess whether the use of currently available productivity measures would improve the national accounts. This paper is a modest effort to provide such an assessment.

The following section will touch on some of the more important measurement problems.

First, the new federal productivity measures combine intermediate with final outputs for individual agencies, although there is an attempt to avoid this. This duplication cannot be altogether offset in the weighting system, because of the problem of "activity-mix change" to which reference has been made earlier.

Second, the combining of agency outputs into a total ignores the interagency mix problem. The aggregate productivity measure represents a weighted average of agency measures.

These two points are related, but the current effort seems to view the *intraagency* duplication as an error to be corrected, but to view the *interagency* duplication as desirable. From the standpoint of the national accounts, both create problems, and we would suggest "netting out" of "final" *outputs* of one unit which are inputs to another, on an *intraagency* and *interagency* basis. Certainly, for use in national accounts, this netting would be essential. A year-to-year assessment would have to include an estimate of the bias caused by failure of the current indexes to measure the productivity change originating in "activity-mix" changes. It may be that in some years during which there has been little organizational change, the current measures would suffice. In other years, some estimates might be made—based perhaps on cost-effectiveness studies.

Third, many of the measures, as indicated above, are not really based on direct output or even intermediate output, but are in the nature of proxies, consisting of such measures as "personnel served" or "population support." We think these, together with indirect measures, may amount to 10–20% of the coverage, in weighted terms.

In order to ameliorate this problem, further experimentation might be conducted on measurement of final outputs of agencies where measurement problems are especially severe. For example, Marvin Mundel (1973) prepared an experimental measure for grants administration activities, in connection with the research work preceding the institution of the JFMIP project. He discussed two measures: (1) a performance (output per man-hour) measure constructed as the product of "standard time" for each current period, times quantity of work done, and divided by actual current man-hours; (2) a productivity index constructed by multiplying quantity, each year, by "standard time" of each type grant in the base period, summing, and dividing by actual man-hours. The first index could *decline* if today's actual performance compared to expected (standard time) is relatively poorer than yesterday's performance. The second index might increase if today's output per man-hour increased with respect to that of the base period. This latter concept seems more closely related to the productivity measures discussed earlier.

What makes Mundel's approach interesting, however, is not so much the choice offered between two indexes, each suitable for its own purpose, but his attempt to quantify *final* output of a service agency. In essence, he examines various kinds of grants (the end products) and then traces the associated man-hours and standard times throughout the agency.

Fourth, labor is treated as a homogeneous input. The experimental work which led to this study made mention of another labor series based on use of a deflator of current dollar compensation. This series, or some version of it, might be examined as an alternate labor measure. Also, such characteristics as wage rates, occupation, education, and experience might be considered along the general lines indicated by Denison and the BEA's experimental work along similar lines.

Fifth, capital inputs are not included. It is perhaps unfair to insist on this point in view of the dearth of work in this area, but the development of these measures would greatly enhance the results.

Sixth, it should be recognized that while the coverage of the federal civilian sector alone is relatively large, this coverage is not based on a random sample. One does not know how representative of the government's total civilian productivity experience the coverage is. This is because availability of output data happens to have been the most important criterion for inclusion. All agencies having 200 or more employees were asked to participate in the project. From this high point, fallouts occurred as organizations were unable to identify measurable outputs or matching inputs. As a result, the sample may not be as representative as one could wish, being biased, perhaps, by data from agencies with more routine or mechanized processes, more readily organized data, or even more enthusiasm for the project. While the overall coverage is good, a more nearly representative sample should be sought. Coverage of some important government departments is well below average—for example, Defense (35%), State (9%), Commerce (23%)—compared with high coverage for Veterans Administration (95%), Transportation (85%), and HEW (79%).

5.8.3   As to Comprehensiveness?

The Federal productivity measurement project covered 65% of federal civilian employment in fiscal 1974, and coverage may eventually increase to 70%. The 1974 data include 1.8 million man-years out of a total of 2.8 million. While this coverage appears impressive, it is much less so when it is adjusted by removing government enterprises such as the Postal Service whose output is excluded by definition from general government in the GNP accounts. (Postal output is included with private-sector output in the GNP.) Excluding enterprises, the coverage drops to 50%. More important, it represents only about 25% of total federal general government (civilian and military) man-years, and only 8% of total general government (federal, state, and local) man-years.

In other words, even if the GNP accounts were to incorporate the new federal civilian productivity measures, it would have only a negligible impact on the current government output measures.[3] Certainly, even the most enthusiastic backer of the current productivity effort would not suggest using the new measures to estimate productivity in the military or the state-local sector.

5.9   What of the Future?

As discussed in the previous section, current federal productivity measures are less than ideal in concept and comprehensiveness, and have several statistical shortcomings from the standpoint of the national accounts.

However, this judgment should not be interpreted too harshly. First, there appears to be little agreement on the precise concept of government output, and the broadest output concept has never been calculated for the government as a whole. Second, although the existing measures cover only a small part of total government, they may point the way to new efforts covering the rest of the federal sector and the state and local sectors. Third, we believe many of the statistical problems in the BLS project can be overcome, perhaps by the means suggested earlier.

---

3. Rough calculations by BEA indicate that total government output in 1974 would be only 1% higher than currently estimated if the new federal productivity measures—available back to 1967—were used to adjust that part of federal output covered.

Nevertheless, it would be unwise, in our judgment, to introduce the existing federal measures into the national accounts. National accountants have to do more thinking about what should be measured as government output and how to measure government input, and productivity experts need to broaden the scope and refine the methods currently employed in measuring public-sector productivity. It is encouraging to see the BLS program underway, and we hope that eventually it will help to provide some of the tools necessary to construct a much-improved measure of government output.

References

Ardolini, Charles, and Hohenstein, Jeffrey. 1974. "Measuring productivity in the federal government." *Monthly Labor Review* 97 (Nov.): 13–20.

Bradford, D. F.; Malt, R. A.; and Oates, W. E. 1969. "The rising cost of local public services: Some evidence and reflections." *National Tax Journal* 22 (June):185–202.

Hatry, H., and Fisk, D. M. 1971. *Improving productivity and productivity measurement in local governments*. The Urban Institute, Working Paper 2700–01.

Joint Financial Management Improvement Program. 1964. *Measuring productivity of federal government organizations*. Executive Office of the President, Office of Management and Budget.

———. *Productivity programs in the federal government, FY 1974*, vol. 1, *Current efforts and future prospects*.

Joint Measurement Systems Project. 1973. *Measuring and enhancing productivity in the federal government*, pt. 3, *Summary report*. Executive Office of the President, Office of Management and Budget.

Mundel, Marvin D. 1973. Measuring productivity of grants administration activities. *Special studies of measurement problems*, Special Report no. 3, section 2, Joint Measurement Systems Project, Executive Office of the President, Office of Management and Budget.

Ross, J. P., and Burkhead, J. 1974. *Productivity in the local government sector*. Lexington, Mass.: D. C. Heath.

Comment   Jerome A. Mark

The problems associated with measuring government output in the national accounts are perhaps the most frequently discussed and least resolved of all the problems with the accounts. But the need for some improvement in the existing procedures has long been recognized. In view of the recent attempts to measure productivity in the public sector, it is very appropriate that Searle and Waite examine these measurements to see how adequate they are for use in the accounts.

Their paper reviews the various conceptions of government output and the problems associated with implementing them. It describes how government output is currently being measured in the accounts and what form productivity adjustments should take to transform input to output. The paper then examines the productivity measurement work in the areas of federal, state, and local government to assess the usefulness of the results of these efforts for the accounts. Since productivity measurement at the state and local level is very limited, this assessment is almost entirely devoted to the current measurement program for the federal government.

This program to measure the productivity of federal agencies is a continuation of the work undertaken by a joint interagency task force composed of the Office of Management and Budget, the General Accounting Office, the Civil Service Commission, and the Bureau of Labor Statistics. It was established as a continuing program in July 1973, with the BLS given responsibility for collecting input, output, and related data and for improving the measures; and the Civil Service Commission, the General Services Administration, and the Joint Financial Management Improvement Program (consisting of the GAO and five executive departments) given responsibility for productivity enhancement efforts.

I mention the productivity enhancement aspect to point out that the main thrust of the program has been toward the development of productivity measures as an aid to government managers for decision-making, planning, and evaluation. Some functional groupings whose activities may be intermediate to the total government are useful for these purposes, whereas they would not be for national accounting purposes.

The federal sample includes 245 organizational elements from 48 agencies encompassing 65% of total federal civilian employment. It includes civilian components of the military, but does not include the armed forces directly. Government enterprises which, in the national accounts, are in the private sector, are also included in the sample. Their exclusion reduces the employment coverage in the federal general

Jerome A. Mark is with the Bureau of Labor Statistics.

government to about 50% and the number of organizational elements to 232. Separate labor productivity indexes were developed for each of these organizational elements and these in turn were aggregated into functional areas of government activity.

In determining the output indicators upon which the productivity indexes were based, the agencies, with some assistance from the BLS, had to identify specific units of service which were final to the organization, quantifiable, and fairly homogeneous over time. The nature of the indicators varies substantially; they include such items as currency notes delivered, trademarks disposed, passports issued, tanks repaired, weather observations, square feet of buildings cleaned, and deportable aliens located.

The question Searle and Waite initially address themselves to is, Does this effort to measure productivity provide a basis for adjusting existing measures of government accounts? Their answer is No, if government output in the national accounts is viewed as including ultimate public goods and services which the government provides, such as national security and education.

But Searle and Waite point out that, although this concept may be preferred (and there is no consensus on that), it cannot be implemented. Therefore, a narrower concept, the flow of government processes, must be considered. Under this concept, they say there may be possibilities for using the results of the efforts to measure government productivity.

In reviewing alternative concepts of government output, Searle and Waite point out that the problems are similar to measuring output in the private service sector, and thus are inherently difficult. Based on some work of Ross and Burkhead, Searle and Waite cite two methods for measuring output in service and/or government activities—either counting the number of direct outputs (such as cars repaired)or calculating the effects or consequences of the service. They feel the first method, counting direct output, does not take account of quality change, nor does it represent desired service output. The second method—calculating the consequences of services—is criticized because consequences are not necessarily a direct result of the service.

They point out that all studies of federal productivity, including the BLS one, have focused on the first method of counting direct output, which they feel is appropriate not only because it is more susceptible to measurement, but also because it preserves the distinction between output and an evaluation of effectiveness. Moreover, it is more compatible with private-service sector output measures which are in terms of physical units.

Their assessment of the methods of measuring output in government, therefore, is in terms not of the appropriateness of the concept which they accept as being direct output of specific government activities, but rather of how adequate the measures are which have been developed. On this basis, they make six observations on the problems with the currently available productivity measures: (1) The measures combine intermediate with final outputs for individual agencies—although there is an attempt to avoid this. (2) The combining of agency outputs into a total ignores the interagency mix problem. (3) Many of the measures are not based on direct output, but are proxies. (4) Labor is treated as a homogeneous input. (5) Capital inputs are not included. (6) The coverage is not based on a random sample which, although large, may not be representative.

For these reasons, they conclude it would be unwise to introduce the existing federal measures into the national accounts.

The criticisms of the current federal government productivity efforts that Searle and Waite have made are in part valid and I agree with some of them, but I am more optimistic about the potential usefulness of the measures for the national accounts. My difference with the paper largely is in the perspective or framework in which the work is being assessed.

There *are* some serious limitations with the existing measures, and I would not recommend *blanket* inclusion of the current measures into the national accounts. In my opinion, it is not a question of the measures failing to meet an "ideal" definition of direct output; rather, it is whether better estimates of productivity change for component parts of the federal government sector can be derived from the measures developed than the assumed zero productivity change currently being used for the entire government sector.

Let me be somewhat more specific with regard to the paper's criticisms of the project's measures.

On the intermediate-final output problem there are, as Searle and Waite indicate, two aspects to it. The first relates to those output indicators for activities which are intermediate to the organizational element, whether or not the functions of the organization as a whole are external to the government. The second relates to those organizations whose output indicators are final to the organization, but whose organizational output is intermediate to other government agencies.

On the first—the intraagency problem—it may not be as serious as Searle and Waite imply. First of all, over 70% of the indicators presently used are final output indicators for the organizational elements, and the employee-years associated with those indicators represent almost 90% of the sample. Second, the problem is being reduced insofar as reporting is concerned. The reporting instructions do stress the need for final output measures, and BLS has worked closely with many of the agencies in examining the indicators and eliminating the intermediate measures when possible.

With regard to the interagency duplication, for national accounts purposes, of course, it would be essential to net out these intermediate outputs. For the purposes of the current program which are directed toward using the measures as an aid in the enhancement of government productivity, the combining of measures for organizations whose final outputs are intermediate to other government organizations is useful, particularly when examining functional areas across agency lines; for example, examining the productivity changes among support service organizations within the federal government.

The interagency duplication can be reduced since separate productivity indexes for the 245 organizational elements have been developed and efforts can be made to net out organizations with activities that are intermediate to the federal government. Organizational units providing support services such as all the elements in the General Services Administration, the Civil Service Commission, and the Defense Supply Agency are cases in point. Exploration of the possibilities along these lines would have been useful in the paper.

With regard to use of proxy indicators, which represent only about 10% of the coverage, it should only present a problem if a bias exists, and this hasn't been examined in this paper, but would have to be in any assessment.

On the treatment of labor as a homogeneous input, in order to separate the quality changes in labor input from productivity changes in the output-per-employee measures, it would be desirable to adjust the present measures for changes in the composition of labor input.

But for the purposes of using the measures in the national accounts, I do not believe the criticism is relevant. The purpose for using the productivity indexes from the federal project in the existing accounts is to adjust the employment change to derive an estimate of output change. For this purpose, it would *not* be desirable to make the adjustments for quality change in labor input to the productivity measure. If that were done, the resultant output would not reflect the direct effect of changes in labor quality on output. The unadjusted measures, as developed in the project, would be the appropriate ones.

If the Bureau of Economic Analysis introduces the adjustments to labor inputs to take account of shifts in the composition of labor along the lines Searle and Waite mention, then the project productivity indexes needed to transform government input into output would have to be modified, but until then, in this connection the present ones are the appropriate ones.

On the absence of capital inputs from the measures, I also do not believe that the criticism is relevant. This is only a limitation if we are concerned with developing a total factor productivity measure for the federal government. However, again as in the case of the labor quality changes, it is not a limitation if the productivity measures of the project are used as an independent method for deriving government output. As in the previous case, if a total factor productivity measure could be developed and were used, the resultant output measure would not reflect the direct effects of capital inputs.

Finally, with regard to the absence of random sampling, I agree with Searle and Waite that there could be a problem of representativeness of a measure for the entire federal government. It would not arise, however, from an absence of random sampling since all agencies with 200 or more employees were asked to participate. If present, it would arise from the inability of some agencies to respond because of inadequate data. Of necessity, the availability of adequate output and input data had to be the principal criterion for inclusion.

In the eventuality that there might possibly be component measures useful for the accounts, they might, in addition to being included with their individual weight, also serve as a basis for imputation to uncovered parts. Imputations are used directly or indirectly in many components of the existing accounts. For example, a significant portion of the accounts rests on the use of wholesale price index information, and yet for a substantial part of the WPI imputations are used. Even in the part that is directly collected, coverage is limited and not based on a random sample.

In summary, then, in assessing the usefulness of the results of the current effort to measure productivity in the federal government, I believe they have to be examined in relation to what is currently being done—namely, assuming zero productivity change. This approach consists of addressing the following questions: Are the estimates of productivity derived based on reasonable procedures? Do they result in biased estimates? Can appropriate adjustments be made to overcome some of the problems, such as the intermediate output problem? How do the methods employed compare with some of the procedures and imputations currently used for deriving measures in the private sector of the accounts?

It is only on the basis of such considerations that the possible usefulness of the measures for the accounts can be assessed.

Searle and Waite point out that even if the accounts were to incorporate the federal general government productivity measures, it would only have a negligible impact on the total government output measures. I would agree that the potential effect is very small, and it certainly points out the need for additional, extensive efforts in the difficult area of state and local government productivity measurement. Perhaps, as Searle and Waite state, "although the existing measures cover only a small part of total government, they point the way to new efforts covering the rest of the federal sector and the state and local sector."

I share their belief that "many of the statistical problems in the BLS project can be overcome." Moreover, I agree that blanket inclusion on an overall basis of the productivity measures now available is not warranted. However, I do think that some degree of selective inclusion may be feasible and worth exploring, and with the continued development of the government productivity measurement program, more extensive inclusion might be possible.

III.   The Effects of Research and Development, Energy, and Environment on Productivity Growth

6 Direct and Indirect Effects of Industrial Research and Development on the Productivity Growth of Industries

Nestor E. Terleckyj

6.1 Introduction

In an earlier study by the author, rather high estimates were obtained of the effects of industrial R and D on the rate of productivity growth of industries (Terleckyj 1974). Two kinds of such effects were identified using the total factor productivity data compiled by John W. Kendrick (1973): direct effects in the industries in which the R and D is conducted, and indirect effects in the industries purchasing intermediate and capital inputs from the industries conducting the R and D. Indications of presence of these effects were obtained for the privately financed R and D, but not for government financed R and D, and for the manufacturing industries but not for the nonmanufacturing industries. Because human capital was not included in earlier research, the resulting estimates of productivity returns to R and D might be inflated by the possible effects of increases in the employment of human capital if such increases were correlated with increased use of R and D inputs.

In this paper these results are tested for independence from possible effects of increased use of human capital and other input characteristics, first by introduction of an explicit variable measuring increases in the use of human capital by industry and then by repeating estimation of the R and D effects using the measures of total factor productivity

Nestor E. Terleckyj is with the National Planning Association.

The author greatly appreciates the helpful suggestions and comments received from Milton Moss, Neil McMullen, and B. J. Stone, and the help in obtaining data given by Dale W. Jorgenson, John W. Kendrick, and Elizabeth Wehle. The present revised version of this paper incorporates changes made in response to the original comments by Steven Globerman, who discussed this paper at the conference. The research for this paper was supported by grant GSOC74–17574 from the National Science Foundation.

growth prepared by Gollop and Jorgenson (1979) which are already
adjusted for the use of human capital, as well as for other characteristics
of input.

6.2   The Analytical Model

The theoretical model underlying the present analysis treats the research capital as a third input in addition to the labor and capital inputs.
This model has been formulated by Griliches (1973). Its adaptation to
the present analysis has been discussed in earlier work by the author
(Terleckyj 1974, pp. 3–8, 19). Hence, only a very brief discussion of
the model will be provided here.

In this model the production function for time, t, is represented by:

$$(1) \qquad Q = Ae^{\lambda t} L^{\beta}K^{(1-\beta)}R^{\alpha},$$

where Q, L, K, and R are the output, and the inputs of labor, tangible
capital, and R and D capital, respectively; β, $(1-\beta)$, and α are the
respective elasticity parameters for the three inputs; A is a constant
specifying the level of output in the base year; and the parameter λ
represents the disembodied growth of productivity.

The productivity ratio at time t can then be expressed as a product
of a component representing cumulative effects of disembodied technical change and the stock of R and D capital raised to an exponent
representing the elasticity of output with respect to research capital:

$$(2) \qquad P_t = \frac{Q_t}{L^{\beta}_t K^{(1-\beta)}_t} = Ae^{\lambda t} R^{\alpha}_t.$$

Differentiating this equation with respect to time, one can show that the
rate of growth in productivity is the sum of the autonomous disembodied
component and a component representing the product of the relative
growth of research capital and the elasticity of output with respect to
that capital:

$$(3) \qquad p = \frac{\dot{P}}{P} = \lambda + \alpha \frac{\dot{R}}{R}.$$

Because the rate of growth of research capital usually cannot be
directly observed, an alternative formulation of equation (3) may be
used, provided one assumes that the gross investment in R and D,
i.e., the expenditure for R and D in the base year, also represents
the net R and D investment (i.e., that there is no depreciation of R
and D or that it can be ignored). One can then express the second term
on the right-hand side of equation (3) by a product of the marginal
product of capital, v, and the ratio of R and D investment to output, I:

$$(4) \qquad p = \lambda + vI,$$

(because $v = dQ/dR$, $I = \dot{R}/Q$, and $\alpha = dQ/dR \cdot R/Q$, $\alpha\dot{R}/R = vI$).

The present research results are based on the statistical estimates of an expanded version of equation (4). The equation is expanded by introducing successively different components of research investment: first, by separating R and D conducted in industry according to its source of financing—into the cost of research conducted with private funds of the industry and research conducted with the federal government funds—and then by estimating the R and D embodied in purchases from other industries separately for the privately financed and the government-financed R and D. The equation is also expanded by the introduction of variables other than R and D which have been found to be correlated with productivity growth and the omission of which might distort estimates of the net effect of R and D on productivity. The general form of the equations estimated in this study can be stated as follows:

$$(5) \qquad p = a_0 + \sum_i a_i X_i + \sum_j b_j I_j.$$

Here a_0 is the constant of regression representing (when normalized) the remaining unexplained residual growth. The a_i's are the regression coefficients of the variables X_i, which represent factors other than R and D, and the b_j's are the coefficients of the research intensity ratios, I_j's.

The coefficients b_j are the estimates of the marginal products of the respective types of R and D capital. They also represent the productivity rates of return on the different types of R and D expenditures. Because the costs of labor and of capital used in R and D are already included in the input index used to estimate productivity, the regression coefficients b_j measure the "excess" or additional rates of return to R and D, i.e., net of its cost. Thus, the statistical estimates of the productivity rates of return approximate the concept of "internal rates of return." The accuracy of this statistical approximation actually achieved depends among other things on the extent to which the cost and the effects of *same* R and D projects are included in the data for the period used. The period 1948–66 used in the present analysis covers 18 years. It should be sufficient to include a predominance of complete lifetimes of R and D projects and their productivity effects. The time series data on costs and on private and social returns to innovations developed by Mansfield and his associates in their case studies of specific innovations support this assumption (Mansfield et al. 1975).

6.3 Previous Estimates

In the following discussion, only the main results and the basic data of previous research are summarized. The methods of estimation of data, various qualifications, and details regarding specific assumptions were discussed in the publication in which these results were first given (Terleckyj 1974).

The basic data are shown in tables 6.1 and 6.2. Kendrick's (1973, pp. 78, 79) data for the rates of change in total factor productivity for the period 1948–66 which were used as the dependent variable, are shown in table 6.1 together with the author's estimates of the four R and D investment intensity ratios for the base year 1958. Estimates of R and D embodied in purchased goods were derived by summing the R and D of the conducting industries, redistributed in proportion to their sales as given in the 1958 Department of Commerce input-output matrices for intermediate and capital flows among industries. Table 6.2 contains the data for the three non–R and D variables introduced to hold productivity effects of R and D constant. One of these variables is the percent of sales to the private sector, which tends to have positive effects on productivity. Another is the unionization rate of the work force of the industry. It was found by Kendrick (1973) to have significant negative correlation with productivity growth. It is also included here for a different year (1953 rather than 1958, because nonmanufacturing data could not be obtained for 1958). The third variable is an index of cyclical instability of output of the industry which in another study by the present author was found to have a negative effect on productivity (Terleckyj 1960).

The highlights of the results obtained are shown in table 6.3, which contains a series of estimates of equation (5) for twenty manufacturing industries. The table follows the sequence of analysis of the R and D variables. First, the total ratio for all R and D conducted in the industry was introduced. Its coefficient was not statistically significant at the 5% level. After dividing the total R and D into privately financed and government-financed R and D, the estimated rate of productivity return to private R and D was highly significant and amounted to 37%, while the return estimated for the government-financed R and D was not significant (and numerically near zero). Based on this result, the ratio of government-financed R and D was omitted from further analyses, and the total R and D embodied in purchases from other industries was introduced. The coefficient for industry's own R and D continued to be significant, but its magnitude dropped from 37 to 28%. The estimate of return to total imputed R and D was 45% and significant at the 5% level. External R and D was then divided into government-financed and privately financed components. This division of the embodied R and D resulted in an overall improvement in the fit of the equation and increases in the significance of almost all coefficients but one (sales not to government). The coefficient obtained for privately financed R and D embodied in purchased inputs is equivalent to a 78% rate of productivity return, while the coefficient estimated for the government-financed purchased R and D is near zero, negative, and not significant.

Table 6.1 Rates of Growth in Total Factor Productivity, 1948–66, and the 1958 R and D Value Added Ratios for Privately Financed R and D and for Government Financed R and D Conducted in the Industry and for Privately Financed and Government Financed R and D Embodied in Purchased Goods, Thirty-three Industries in the Private Domestic Economy (R and D amounts as percent of value added)

Industry (arranged in order of descending productivity growth)	Productivity Growth Rate, Annual Average 1948–66 (percent)	R and D Intensity Ratios, 1958			
		R and D Conducted in Industry		R and D Embodied in Purchased Goods	
		Privately Financed R and D (percent)	Government Financed R and D (percent)	Privately Financed R and D (percent)	Government Financed R and D (percent)
*Air transportation	8.0	0	0	1.6	1.5
*Coal mining	5.2	0	0	.3	.1
*Railroads	5.2	0	0	.2	.1
Chemicals	4.9	6.8	1.8	1.8	.8
*Electric and gas utilities	4.9	.1	0	.3	.3
Textiles	4.0	.4	0	2.1	.1
Rubber products	3.9	1.1	.4	2.3	.3
*Communication utilities	3.8	.3	.1	.6	1.1
Electrical machinery	3.7	5.5	12.0	1.9	3.3
Lumber products	3.5	.2	0	.3	.1
*Farming	3.3	.5	0	.6	.1
*Oil and gas extraction	3.2	.2	0	.1	.1
Transportation equipment and ordnance	3.2	6.9	18.6	3.8	3.8
Foods	3.0	.5	0	.6	.1
Petroleum refining	3.0	4.3	.2	.9	.3
Furniture	2.9	.2	0	.4	.1
Instruments	2.9	4.2	3.6	2.1	2.2

Table 6.1 (cont.)

Industry (arranged in order of descending productivity growth)	Productivity Growth Rate, Annual Average 1948–66 (percent)	R and D Intensity Ratios, 1958			
		R and D Conducted in Industry		R and D Embodied in Purchased Goods	
		Privately Financed R and D (percent)	Government Financed R and D (percent)	Privately Financed R and D (percent)	Government Financed R and D (percent)
Printing and publishing	2.7	0	0	.2	.2
Machinery, excluding electrical	2.6	3.7	2.5	1.1	.9
*Nonmetal mining	2.6	0	0	.4	.1
Paper	2.5	.9	0	.5	.1
*Wholesale trade	2.5	0	0	.1	.1
*Metal mining	2.4	0	0	.4	.2
*Retail trade	2.4	0	0	.1	.1
Stone, clay, and glass products	2.4	.9	0	.5	.1
Beverages	2.2	0	0	.6	.1
Apparel	1.9	.1	0	.3	0
Fabricated metal products	1.9	.7	.5	.7	.3
Leather Products	1.7	.2	0	.2	.1
Primary metal products	1.6	.9	.1	.6	.2
*Contract construction	1.5	0	0	.6	.3
Tobacco products	1.1	0	0	.3	0
*Water transportation	0.5	0	0	.4	0

*Nonmanufacturing industries.

SOURCES: Productivity Growth Rate data reproduced by permission from the author: Kendrick (1973) table 5–1, pp. 78–79; R and D intensity ratios from Terleckyj (1974), pp. 13, 15. Note revision of data for beverages industry R & D conducted in industry ratios.

Table 6.2   **Variables Other than R and D Tested for Possible Effects on Productivity Growth, Thirty-three Industries in the Private Domestic Economy**

Industry (arranged in order of descending productivity growth)	Sales Other than to Government as Percent of Total Sales 1958 PVTS (percent)	Union Members as Percent of All Workers in Producing Establishments 1953 UN (percent)	Index of Cyclical Instability of Industry Output 1948–66 CYC (percent)
*Air transportation	95	51	0
*Coal mining	98	84	16.1
*Railroads	95	95	10.4
Chemicals	95	39	5.7
*Electric and gas utilities	96	41	0
Textiles	100	30	7.4
Rubber products	97	54	9.5
*Communication utilities	97	52	0
Electrical machinery	90	56	11.0
Lumber products	100	21	8.7
*Farming	98	1	3.2
*Oil and gas extraction	100	14	5.4
Transportation equipment and ordnance	77	65	11.0
Foods	100	45	0
Petroleum refining	94	67	2.5
Furniture	95	29	8.7
Instruments	85	50	9.2
Printing and publishing	98	38	3.2
Machinery, excluding electrical	95	45	13.1
*Nonmetal mining	99	32	4.6

Table 6.2 (cont.)

Industry (arranged in orders of descending productivity growth)	Sales Other than to Government as Percent of Total Sales 1958 PVTS (percent)	Union Members as Percent of All Workers in Producing Establishments 1953 UN (percent)	Index of Cyclical Instability of Industry Output 1948–66 CYC (percent)
Paper	99	45	6.7
*Wholesale trade	99	4	4.1
*Metal mining	92	70	10.6
*Retail trade	99	14	3.6
Stone, clay and glass products	100	45	7.4
Beverages	100	44	3.2
Apparel	99	53	4.1
Fabricated metal products	99	45	8.4
Leather products	99	39	5.0
Primary metal products	98	55	15.2
*Contract construction	71	72	4.1
*Tobacco products	100	58	2.0
*Water transportation	95	76	7.0

*Nonmanufacturing industries.

SOURCES: Data on industry sales to government is from U.S. Department of Commerce, Office of Business Economics, "The Transactions Table of the 1958 Input-Output Study and Revised Direct and Total Requirements Data," *Survey of Current Business*, 9 (1965): 34–39; percent unionization is from H.G. Lewis, *Unionization and Wages in the United States* (Chicago: University of Chicago Press, 1963), pp. 289–290; cyclical instability index of industry output is based on annual output data from Kendrick (1973) calculated in a manner described in Terleckyj (1960). See note 6, p. 16, in Terleckyj (1974).

Table 6.3   Regression Coefficients Obtained in the Analysis of the Annual Rates of Change in Total Factor Productivity for the Period 1948–66, Twenty Manufacturing Industries (*t*-ratios in parentheses)

Constant of Regression a_o	Cost of R and D/Value-added Ratios for Different R and D Components						Other Variables			R^2 Corrected
	R and D Conducted in Industry			R and D Embodied in Purchases from Other Industries			Percent of Sales Not to Government, 1958	Union Members as Percent of Workers in Producing Establishments, 1953	Annual Rate of Cyclical Change in Output, 1948–66	
	Total, 1958	Privately Financed, 1958	Government Financed, 1958	Total, 1958	Privately Financed, 1958	Government Financed, 1958				
	IRDI	IRDN	IRDG	PRDI	PRDN	PRDG	PVTS	UN	CYC	
2.29 (0.31)	0.12 (1.76)						0.02 (0.33)	−0.04 (2.38)	−0.03 (0.56)	0.39
1.62 (0.25)		0.37 (3.31)	0.01 (0.12)				0.03 (0.46)	−0.05 (2.94)	−0.03 (0.56)	0.44
−7.83 (1.36)		0.28 (2.84)		0.45 (2.49)			0.12 (2.20)	−0.05 (3.54)	−0.05 (1.25)	0.62
−3.72 (0.71)		0.29 (3.43)			0.78 (3.79)	−0.09 (0.34)	0.08 (1.54)	−0.05 (4.03)	−0.04 (1.30)	0.72

SOURCE: Terleckyj (1974), pp. 20, 22, 26, 29.

The effects estimated for the three non–R and D variables remained rather stable, in the course of these substitutions of the R and D variables.

These results for the manufacturing industries constituted the main findings of the earlier study. The results for nonmanufacturing (not reproduced here) were rather erratic. No indication of positive returns to R and D conducted in the industry was obtained. But, for this group of industries, it is not surprising. It may simply reflect the fact that most nonmanufacturing industries conduct little or no R and D. (Also, the R and D data for the nonmanufacturing industries were derived from the NSF data by a series of additional assumptions.) On the other hand, a statistically significant coefficient was obtained for indirect returns, suggesting a very high rate of productivity return of 187%. Dividing the indirect R and D by sources of financing gave large and positive coefficients for both components which, however, were not statistically significant.

The overall fit of the equation for all industries combined was consistently lower than for either manufacturing or nonmanufacturing industries alone. Among the coefficients for the R and D intensity ratios, only the one for the total R and D cost embodied in purchases was statistically significant.

6.4 Productivity Returns to R and D with Consideration of Human Capital

Human capital is not included in the measures of input used in estimating productivity growth. The underlying indexes of labor input used in constructing the indexes of total factor productivity from which the growth data are derived are based on the number of man-hours. Consequently, a part of growth in productivity may represent productivity returns to a growing stock of human capital. Moreover, if increases in the use of human capital are correlated with increased use of R and D capital, the regression coefficients intended to measure the productivity return to R and D may be biased upward to the extent that they (also) reflect returns to human capital. Use of human capital may be correlated either with own R and D, if use of human capital in production is complementary with the conduct of R and D, or with purchased R and D, if human capital is complementary with the use of R and D–intensive, "high-technology" inputs. Thus, the regression coefficients for both direct and indirect return to R and D are subject to potential bias from this source.

In testing the hypothesis that the previously obtained statistical estimates of returns to R and D do not include the returns to human capital as well, the estimating equations are revised to include human capital investment intensity as an additional variable. This variable is formulated in the same manner as the R and D investment intensity variable. After the introduction of human capital, equations (2), (3), and (4) discussed earlier become equations (6), (7), and (8):

(6) $$P_t = A e^{\lambda t} R^{a}{}_t H^{\gamma}{}_t,$$

(7) $$p = \frac{\dot{P}}{P} = \lambda + \alpha \frac{\dot{R}}{R} + \gamma \frac{\dot{H}}{H},$$

(8) $$p = \lambda + v \frac{\dot{R}}{Q} + r \frac{\dot{H}}{Q}.$$

Here γ is the elasticity parameter, analogous to α, and r in equation (8) is the productivity rate of return to human capital, analogous to v for research capital. Both parameters are estimated as regression coefficients of the respective net investment intensity ratios in the estimating equation for productivity growth. However, while the basic cost of R and D activities conducted in an industry is included in the labor and capital input indexes (except for the effect of differences in labor cost per man-hour), the cost of human capital is not included in the input data.

No direct measures of human capital stock or investment exist that could be readily applied in estimating its productivity effects. Human capital has to be measured indirectly, by schooling or by an indicator of its market value. In this paper, the indicator of human capital is investment intensity. It is based on the increases in real wages per man-hour worked.

This indicator of growth of human capital is based on its evident market value. The advantage of basing the measure of human capital on wages rather than on schooling is that such a measure includes both schooling and experience components of earning power (Mincer 1974), which presumably reflects productivity and at the same time excludes consumption components of schooling and the variability of the learning content of years of schooling over time. However, there are also disadvantages in using the relative real wage growth as a measure of human capital investment. One is that other factors unrelated to worker productivity affect this growth to an unknown extent. Such factors as wage bargaining or legislation have autonomous effects on wages.

Also, because, statistically, the growth in labor compensation is a major component of growth in output and output per man-hour is by definition a large part of the total factor productivity growth, the human capital investment rate estimated from growth in real wages is subject to some possibility of the simultaneous equation bias. However, this bias would not arise if the competitive working of the labor market equalized the earnings within occupations rapidly relative to the length of time over which the productivity growth is measured. Then the observed long-term increases in wages in the individual industries would be independent of the increases in productivity in the same industries because the period of observation would be sufficiently long for the correlation to reflect only the effects of increases in human capital on productivity.

The best approach to resolve the uncertainties resulting from the nature of the indicator used for human capital is to test the results obtained by alternative indicators. Use of alternative indicators was not possible within the scope of this paper because of the lack of the available data in comparable industry detail or for the period studied. It should be possible in future research to develop or adapt indicators of average education and of the skill mix of labor input in individual industries. Here, a more general further test of independence of the estimated effects of R and D from previously unmeasured inputs is undertaken by estimating the effects of industrial R and D on the total factor productivity growth measured after an adjustment for human capital and other inputs.

The real wage growth was calculated from unpublished NBER data used in Kendrick's study. The original data were in the form of period averages of actual hourly earnings for the period 1948–53 and again for the period 1960–66. These averages were converted to 1958 dollars by the Consumer Price Index. The difference between the two period averages was divided by 12.5, the number of years between the midpoints of the two periods. The result is shown in the first column in table 6.4. Equation (8) requires the net rate of investment in human capital in the aggregate in the industry rather than per hour. Therefore, the amount per hour in the first column is multiplied by the man-hours worked in the industry in the base year, 1958, used in this study. The result, giving the investment in human capital in millions of 1958 dollars, is shown in the second column. This result is then divided by the 1958 value added by industry in order to obtain the desired variable, $\dot{H}/Q$, i.e., the human capital investment intensity ratio which is shown in percentages in the third column.

It may be noted that, while, theoretically, human capital investment intensity ratios are commensurate with the R and D investment intensity ratios used in the regression analysis, statistically their estimates are much stronger. The human capital data are actually based on change for the entire period rather than on the experience in the base year. Also, they are based on net investment in human capital rather than on the gross investment as was the R and D ratio.

The results of introducing human capital investment into the estimating equation for productivity growth for the twenty manufacturing industries are given in table 6.5. The estimated effect of the human capital

Table 6.4 Estimates of the Net Investment Rate in Human Capital, Thirty-three Manufacturing and Nonmanufacturing Industries, 1958 (dollar amounts in 1958 dollars)

Industry (listed in order of descending rate of productivity growth)	Average Annual Increase in Real Wage per Hour Worked, 1948–66 (1)	Estimated Industry Investment[a] 1958 (millions) (2)	Industry Investment as Percent of Value Added, 1958 (3)
*Air transportation	$.1015	$ 36.5	2.4%
*Coal mining	.0711	27.6	1.6
*Railroads	.1112	216.4	2.6
Chemicals	.1080	172.7	1.9
*Electric and gas utilities	.0952	127.4	1.2
Textiles	.0340	60.9	1.5
Rubber products	.0678	46.2	1.6
*Communications	.0817	141.2	1.6
Electrical machinery	.0751	182.2	2.0
Lumber products	.0503	67.9	2.1
*Farming	.0166	208.8	1.0
*Oil and gas extraction	.0591	44.5	.5
Transportation equipment and ordnance	.1171	414.4	2.6
Foods	.0743	235.2	1.9
Petroleum refining	.1430	63.5	2.0
Furniture	.0477	36.2	1.9
Instruments	.0917	59.4	2.3
Printing and publishing	.0433	77.1	1.3
Machinery, excluding electrical	.0847	232.6	2.1
*Nonmetal mining	.0695	19.3	1.9

Table 6.4 (cont.)

Industry (arranged in order of descending productivity growth)	Average Annual Increase in Real Wage per Hour Worked, 1948–66 (1)	Estimated Industry Invesment[a] 1958 (millions) (2)	Industry Investment as Percent of Value Added, 1958 (3)
Paper	.0769	89.5	1.9
*Wholesale trade	.0706	468.7	1.6
*Metal mining	.0800	15.3	1.4
*Retail trade	.0415	892.4	2.0
Stone, clay, and glass products	.0812	93.4	2.0
Beverages	.0569	23.8	1.0
Apparel	.0284	60.0	1.3
Fabricated metal products	.0736	159.6	2.0
Leather products	.0369	24.1	1.6
Primary metal products	.1142	250.7	2.3
*Contract construction	.0858	607.6	3.0
Tobacco products	.0907	16.2	.6
*Water transportation	.0455	43.0	2.9

*Nonmanufacturing industries.

[a]Average annual increase in real wages per hour worked from column (1) multipled by the number of man-hours worked in 1958, as

Sources: John W. Kendrick and the National Bureau of Economic given in Kendrick (1973), pp. 196–97. Research, unpublished data on real wages.

Table 6.5　Regression Coefficients Obtained in the Analysis of the Annual Rates of Change in Total Factor Productivity for the Period 1948–66 with Additional Variables, Twenty Manufacturing Industries (t-ratios in parentheses)

Constant of Regression a_o	Cost of R and D/Value-added Ratios for Different R and D Components				Other Variables				R^2 Corrected
	R and D Conducted in Industry		R and D Embodied in Purchases from Other Industries		Percent of Sales Not to Government, 1958	Union Members as Percent of Workers in Producing Establishments, 1953	Annual Rate of Cyclical Change in Output, 1948–66	Human Capital Investment Intensity Ratio Based on Growth of Real Wages 1958	
	Privately Financed, 1958	Government Financed, 1958	Privately Financed, 1958	Government Financed, 1958					
	IRDN	IRDG	PRDN	PRDG	PVTS	UN	CYC	HCIW	
-6.58 (1.53)	.25 (3.00)		.82 (3.99)		.10 (2.62)	-.04 (3.38)	-.07 (1.73)	.39 (1.04)	.73
-6.17 (1.02)	.25 (2.50)	-.05 (.59)	.85 (3.78)	.17 (.37)	.10 (1.70)	-.04 (3.41)	-.07 (1.56)	.38 (.93)	.69

variable is not statistically significant, while, on the whole, the previous results remain unaffected by its introduction.

6.5   Results with Productivity Data Based on an Inclusive Concept of Input

In their paper, Gollop and Jorgenson have developed a set of estimates of output, input, and total factor productivity for individual industries (as well as economic sectors and the economy) which are based on different measurement concepts than the estimates by Kendrick, which are used to derive the estimates of the effects of R and D on productivity. Thus, while Kendrick measures the net output and the net input, Gollop and Jorgenson use gross measures of output and input, i.e., including intermediate inputs.

Also, the Gollop-Jorgenson method attempts to account for quality characteristics of inputs, and their input index accordingly includes "quality" index components for labor and for capital.

To the extent that research and development activities result in improved intermediate and capital inputs, one would expect the estimates of productivity rates of returns to R and D to be lower when productivity is derived from the input data already adjusted for the quality changes than when the calculation of productivity growth is based on the unadjusted inputs.

The two sets of productivity data also differ in the underlying theoretical formula. Kendrick implicitly used a reduced form of the Cobb-Douglas production function. The Gollop-Jorgenson data are derived from a translog production function. The two sets of productivity estimates also differ in the method of estimating the man-hours input and in the estimate of depreciation of physical capital. But in contrast to the input quality adjustments, there is no apparent reason to expect these differences in measurement to have a systematic effect on the observed correlations between productivity growth and the R and D variables.

The results of substituting Gollop-Jorgenson estimates for Kendrick estimates of productivity change[1] for the twenty manufacturing industries and with the same independent variables are shown in table 6.6. The Gollop-Jorgenson estimates are not available for the nonmanufacturing industries.

---

1. With two minor changes in the Gollop-Jorgenson data to make consistent the industry definitions: (1) Productivity growth for "food and kindred products" is used for both "food products" and "beverages," and (2) the arithmetic average of growth rates for "motor vehicles" and for "transportation equipment, other than motor vehicles, and ordnance" was used for "Transportation equipment and ordnance."

Table 6.6 Regression Coefficients Obtained with Alternative Estimates of the Annual Rates of Change in Total Factor Productivity, Twenty Manufacturing Industries, 1948–66 (t-ratios in parentheses)

	Constant of Regression	Cost of R and D/Value-added Ratios for Different R and D Components				Other Variables			R^2 Corrected
		R and D Conducted in Industry		R and D Embodied in Purchases from Other Industries		Percent of Sales Not to Government, 1958	Union Members as Percent of Workers in Producing Establishments, 1953	Annual Rate of Cyclical Change in Output, 1948–66	
		Privately Financed, 1958	Government Financed, 1958	Privately Financed, 1958	Government Financed, 1958				
	a_0	IRDN	IRDG	PRDN	PRDG	PVTS	UN	CYC	
Kendrick data	−4.01 (.73)	.27 (2.92)	−.05 (.53)	.81 (3.66)	.12 (.26)	.08 (1.52)	−.04 (3.69)	−.05 (1.37)	.69
Gollop-Jorgenson data	−32.26 (1.79)	.20 (.64)	−.18 (.63)	1.83 (2.53)	1.67 (1.10)	.33 (1.87)	−.03 (.88)	−.02 (.14)	.30

Compared to the estimates based on Kendrick's data, the estimates derived with the Gollop-Jorgenson data in table 6.6 have a much poorer statistical fit. But the two sets of estimates are qualitatively consistent. The signs of all coefficients are the same in both equations, and their general magnitudes are comparable. Among the four R and D variables, only the coefficient for privately financed purchased R and D is statistically significant at the 5% level. It is also considerably larger (1.83) than the coefficient derived with the Kendrick data (0.81), despite the much lower estimates of productivity growth by Gollop-Jorgenson (averaging 0.9% a year for the twenty manufacturing industries during the period 1948–66) than by Kendrick (averaging 2.8%).

Somewhat surprisingly, perhaps, the equation based on Gollop-Jorgenson data suggests the possibility of positive "spillover" effects of government R and D to the industries purchasing inputs from the industries conducting government-financed R and D. In this equation the respective coefficient for the government-financed R and D is larger and stronger than in all the earlier analyses, but it is still not statistically significant.

Among the non–R and D variables, the estimated coefficients are generally similar, but their statistical significance is eliminated, except perhaps for the share of sales in private markets.

6.6   Conclusions

Significant effects of the privately financed industrial R and D on the productivity growth of manufacturing industries were found in earlier research by the author. These effects were two-fold: (1) direct increases in productivity of industries conducting the privately financed R and D, and (2) indirect increases in productivity of industries purchasing capital and intermediate inputs from the industries conducting the privately financed R and D. The estimated indirect effects were considerably larger, per dollar of R and D expenditure, than the direct effects. No comparable effects were found for government-financed industrial R and D.

These findings were tested in this paper for independence of the R and D effects from the possible effects of the previously unmeasured inputs and input characteristics, in general, for human capital, intermediate goods, and composition of physical capital, and for human capital in particular.

The results continue to uphold strongly significant and large estimates of indirect effects of privately financed R and D. There was a weakening of the significance of the estimated direct effects of privately financed R and D, a continued absence of any indication of direct productivity effects of government-financed R and D, and some indication of possible indirect effects of the government-financed industrial R and D. Qualitatively, the results of the tests were consistent with the earlier findings. More detailed research is needed in the future to permit an evaluation of the possible effects of the previously unmeasured inputs, one at a time.

References

Gollop, Frank, and Jorgenson, Dale W. 1979. U.S. total factor productivity by industry, 1947–73, this volume.

Griliches, Zvi. 1973. Research expenditures and growth accounting. In *Science and technology in economic growth*, ed. B. R. Williams. New York: John Wiley & Sons, Halsted Press.

Kendrick, John W. 1973. *Postwar productivity trends in the United States, 1948–1969.* New York: National Bureau of Economic Research.

Mansfield, Edwin; Rapoport, John; Romeo, Anthony; Wagner, Samuel; and Beardsley, George. 1975. Returns from industrial innovation: Detailed description of 17 case studies. University of Pennsylvania, preliminary and unpublished.

Mincer, Jacob. 1974. *Schooling, experience, and earnings.* New York: National Bureau of Economic Research.

Terleckyj, Nestor E. 1960. Sources of productivity advance. A pilot study of manufacturing industries, 1899–1953. Ph.D. diss., Columbia University.

————. 1974. *Effects of R&D on the productivity growth of industries: an exploratory study.* Washington: National Planning Association.

Comment   Steven Globerman

Introduction

Terleckyj's paper is an extension of a rich and interesting study of a slightly earlier vintage (Terleckyj 1974). The earlier study sought to identify separately returns to the R and D conducted within industries and the R and D "purchased" from other industries in the form of embodied technology in capital and intermediate goods. A related concern was to estimate the separate returns to privately financed R and D (both

Steven Globerman is at York University.

"own" and "purchased") and government-financed R and D. The main findings of that study are as follows:

1. For manufacturing industries, direct returns to private R and D were on the order of 30%, in terms of productivity growth; indirect returns were on the order of 80%. The productivity returns, both direct and indirect, to government-financed R and D were estimated at zero.

2. For nonmanufacturing industries, no indication of positive returns to R and D conducted in the industry was obtained. Indirect returns were on the order of 187%.

This conference paper extends earlier findings by attempting to hold constant (either explicitly or implicitly) the effects of increased use of human capital, relative increases in the use of intermediate inputs, and changes in the composition of labor and capital which may have been correlated with increased direct and indirect investment in R and D by the industry.

Before summarizing Terleckyj's empirical results, the basic model underlying the estimation procedure should be briefly reviewed. The underlying model for most estimations is a Cobb-Douglas production function with labor, physical capital, research capital, and a "disembodied" rate of growth of productivity as arguments of the function. By making the usual assumption about equality of factor prices to marginal value products and taking time derivatives of the variables, a reduced-form equation is derived in which the rate of change in an industry's total factor productivity is a linear function of the rate of growth of the intangible stock of R and D capital. Since the growth rate of the R and D capital stock cannot be directly measured, the ratio of gross investment in R and D to output is substituted into the equation. For purposes of estimation, it is assumed that depreciation in R and D capital can be ignored and that the gross investment in R and D capital over the sample period can be measured by the industry's R and D intensity in 1958.

In the estimating equations, the aggregate R and D intensity variable is decomposed by source of financing (private versus public) and by location of conduct (within or without the industry). Additional non–R and D standardizing variables included in all reported estimating equations are percent of sales not made to government, union members as a percent of workers in producing establishments, and annual rate of cyclical change in output. The initial dependent variable is Kendrick's index of total factor productivity compiled for thirty-three manufacturing and nonmanufacturing industries, covering the period 1948–66.

The initial estimation results reported for the sample of twenty manufacturing industries are essentially those of Terleckyj's earlier study, and exclude the effect of changes in input quality and in the use of intermediate inputs. Results for the nonmanufacturing sample are not reproduced, but are reported as above.

In the first extension of his preceding findings, Terleckyj introduces a measure of human capital intensity, based upon the increase in real wages per man-hour worked over the period 1948–66, into earlier estimating equations. He finds that introduction of the human capital measure leaves previous results essentially unaffected, and the coefficient for the human capital variable itself is statistically insignificant.

In a second extension, Gollop-Jorgenson total factor productivity estimates for the twenty manufacturing industries are substituted for Kendrick's estimates in the initial set of estimating equations. The overall statistical results are much poorer than those obtained employing the Kendrick estimates: the adjusted R^2 coefficients decrease substantially, and the "own" privately financed R and D coefficient becomes statistically insignificant. Interestingly, the "purchased" privately financed R and D coefficient remains statistically significant using the Gollop-Jorgenson measure of total factor productivity, and, furthermore, has a greater impact upon productivity than in the earlier equations. Thus, the various specifications of the productivity/R and D relationship provide a range of estimates of the direct and indirect effects of R and D expenditures.

The following discussion will focus primarily upon issues relating to the model specifications, measurement of variables, and potential problems associated with the single-equation estimation procedure. I have no great difficulty in accepting the general nature of Terleckyj's findings. Specifically, to the extent that the performance (or purchase) of R and D is associated with improved quality of conventional factor inputs, one would expect the estimated returns to R and D to be lower when increases in the "quality" of labor and capital are otherwise accounted for. Furthermore, since the numerator of Kendrick's total factor productivity measure is gross output while the denominator excludes intermediate inputs, one would expect estimates of returns to "purchased" R and D to be biased upward if embodied R and D expenditures are positively correlated with the relative use of intermediate inputs. This is bound to be the case for Terleckyj's sample since the imputations of embodied R and D were done by redistributing the R and D expenditures of each industry in proportion to the distribution of sales of that industry to other industries and them summing the amounts attributed to each of the sample industries. The fact that the "purchased" privately financed R and D coefficient increases substantially in the equation employing the Gollop-Jorgenson data suggests the possibility that other, unspecified sources of bias may be present in the estimations.

The observation that the productivity effect of "own" privately financed R and D essentially disappears when "quality" adjustments for labor and capital and the relative use of intermediate inputs are incorporated into the dependent variable (i.e., the Gollop-Jorgenson index) is somewhat difficult to accept on intuitive grounds. If labor and capital resources employed in R and D activities have less risky employment alternatives, one would expect R and D resources to earn their users "excess" returns or be shifted into other activities over time. Part of the explanation for the different results reported in table 6.6 may, indeed, rest in the different methodologies employed to construct the dependent variables. In any case. since the attribution of the productivity effects of R and D will ultimately depend upon how the factor productivity residual is defined, we are somewhat less concerned about explanations of differences in estimated rates of return to R and D across different productivity measures than we are with the identification of returns to R and D employing any given productivity measure. It is the latter concern we will primarily address in our discussion.

Model Specification

The inclusion of input "quality" measures reflects Terleckyj's concern about possible estimation biases arising from the omission from the estimating equation of one (or more) variables whose values differed across sample industries. To the extent that differences in the values of other omitted variables are unsystematically related to the included variables over the sample period, the slope parameters would remain unaffected. However, the brace of standardizing variables employed by Terleckyj excludes certain variables that may be systematically related to the rate of growth in R and D investment.

One such variable is the rate of growth in output in the sample industries over the estimation period. There is ample evidence that industries enjoying above-average productivity growth rates (associated in part, with investments in R and D) also enjoy above-average rates of growth in output. Relative increases in output growth rates could, in turn, affect industry differences in productivity through differential scale and learning economies. Including an output growth rate variable in the estimating equation would raise an identification problem; however, one suspects that its exclusion leads to an upward bias in the estimated R and D parameters.

Another potential source of bias arises from changes in the relative degree of product specialization within industries over time. The derivation of productivity and R and D data along establishment (and product) lines reduces but does not obviate this possibility, particularly given the level of aggregation of the sample industries. One might hypothesize that over the sample period, R and D–intensive industries were becoming relatively more specialized (on an establishment basis), both because a rapidly expanding market for their output facilitated increased specialization and because specialization facilitated entry into high-technology industries.[1] The production and, perhaps more importantly, the learning economies associated with increased product specialization would support the productivity effects of both disembodied and embodied R and D, leading to upward biases in the estimated parameters.

The effect of differential rates of growth in "x-efficiency," in turn related to changes in industrial market structure, might also be embodied in the estimated R and D parameters. An upward bias could be imparted to the R and D coefficients if technological change brings about a decline in average plant size relative to market size. Such a decline could facilitate easier entry into the industry, thereby fostering greater competition and a more efficient allocation of resources, including faster interfirm rates of technological diffusion. Evidence relating changes in concentration ratios to technological change is far from conclusive but, on balance, points to the existence of a negative relationship between the two variables.[2]

The variable used by Terleckyj to standardize for changes in labor quality is the increase in real wages per man-hour worked. The original data for this variable were in the form of period averages of actual hourly earnings for the periods 1948–53 and 1960–66, deflated to 1958 dollars. The annualized percentage change between the two periods was multiplied by the man-hours worked in the industry in the base year, 1958, to obtain the rate of growth in aggregate human capital. The resulting term was then divided by the 1958 value added by the industry to obtain the desired variable.[3] The author acknowledges the possibility of a simultaneous-equation bias arising from the feedback of increased productivity to higher wages, but argues that this bias would not arise if the competitive working of the labor market equalized the earnings within occupations rapidly relative to the length of the period over which the productivity growth is measured. Even if adjustments in the relative supply of labor for different occupations proceeded rapidly (a phenomenon which is certainly at variance with recent evidence on the signifi-

---

1. The process of entry through specialization in the innovation process is illustrated in the case of the semiconductor industry. See John Tilton, *International Diffusion of Technology: The Case of Semi-Conductors* (Washington: The Brookings Institute), 1971.

2. Examining concentration ratios at the establishment level for different industries over time might provide some feel for the magnitude of this potential bias.

3. Since the numerator of the productivity measure is gross output, it is not evident why the human capital variable, as well as the other standardizing variables, are deflated by value-added in the base year rather than by gross output.

cance of information costs in factor markets), a simultaneous-equation bias might still be obtained if wages (to any significant extent) incorporate expected productivity gains. While it is likely that the Gollop-Jorgenson labor quality measure, based on the shift of workers among different categories, is subject to a smaller simultaneity bias, some bias will still be present if higher wages, in part, are realized in the form of job upgrading.

In light of the acknowledged shortcomings of the labor-quality variable employed, other measures, including the average education level of employees, might have been tested. Median years of schooling of the labor force by industry are available for censal years. While the available censal years 1959 and 1969 do not provide a perfect overlap with the estimation sample period, such exact concordance might not be necessary if relative differences in education levels across industries are reasonably stable over time. The assumption that differences in education levels at a point in time reflect differences in growth rates over the preceding period seems no more heroic than a similar assumption invoked by the author in specifying the R and D variables.

In fact, we reestimated the basic productivity equation across the twenty manufacturing industry sample using Kendrick's index of average education per employee for 1959 (Kendrick 1973) and obtained results quite similar to those obtained by Terleckyj for the growth-in-real-wages variable. The failure to identify a statistically significant positive return to human capital investment for those estimations employing Kendrick's productivity index as the dependent variable is a surprising result. A possible explanation of this result is the existence of multicollinearity between the human capital variables and other included variables. Indeed, the zero-order correlation coefficient between Terleckyj's human capital measure and "own" privately financed R and D equals .58, while the correlation coefficient between the human capital measure and the cyclical change in output is .69. Thus, the influence of human capital investment on productivity growth may be largely assigned to collinear variables in the estimation process.

Measurement of Variables

I will not comment extensively on the problems associated with measurement of variables since Terleckyj considers most of the obvious problems in some detail in his earlier study. Many of the problems are, in any case, intractable given the state of the available data.

The failure of conventional productivity measurements to adequately reflect product quality changes is well-recognized and presumably leads to an underestimation of real rates of productivity change. Insofar as the bias differs among products, the industry comparisons would be affected and, on balance, this probably imparts a downward bias to the estimated

R and D parameters. To the extent that federally financed R and D is primarily directed towards improvements in product quality as opposed to cost reduction, the methodology used in deriving industry productivity estimates could contribute to the finding that government-financed R and D is not significantly related to productivity change. Furthermore, while the period 1948–66 might be long enough compared to the time lag one would expect between privately financed R and D intensity ratios in 1958 and their productivity effects, it might be too short to fully incorporate the effects of federally financed R and D which is presumably aimed at effecting greater changes in underlying production conditions. While Terleckyj's finding of no productivity return to government-financed R and D accords with similar results obtained by Leonard (1971) in a study of interindustry output growth differences, the latter study is subject to the same sorts of criticisms.

The imputations of purchased R and D to the sample industries were done by redistributing the R and D expenditures of each industry in proportion to the distribution of sales of that industry to other industries and then summing the amounts attributed to each of the industries. While imputing embodied R and D as a strict proportion of sales might be no more arbitrary than any other procedure, I would expect that industries performing R and D intensively are more likely to purchase complex and technically advanced equipment than are those industries which perform little R and D. Another imputation procedure might therefore attribute the R and D transferred from a supplier industry to any given purchasing industry as a proportion of the percentage of total sales made to the purchasing industry weighted by the relative "own" R and D intensity of the purchasing industry. In any case, it would be enlightening to evaluate the sensitivity of the statistical results to the imputation procedure used.

A more serious concern is the use of a single year's set of observations to calculate interindustry flows of purchased inputs.[4] Albeit they are dictated by available data, it is certainly possible that observed factor ratios in the given year were not long-run equilibrium values. Indeed, a similar concern might be expressed about most of the independent variables. For example, the "own" R and D intensity variables are measured for a given base year, 1958. In his earlier study, Terleckyj argues that differences in base year R and D intensity levels are likely to reflect differences in preceding R and D growth rates. While this assumption might be quite tenable when comparing high and low R and D–intensive industries, it is somewhat more objectionable for the seven

---

4. Data for 1958 were employed in developing the "purchased" privately financed R and D intensity variable and the relative growth rate in intermediate inputs variable.

manufacturing industries with "own" privately financed R and D intensity ratios ranging between .2 and .5.

Estimation Procedure

Given the substantial differences in the parameters estimated across the separate samples of manufacturing and nonmanufacturing industries, it is inappropriate to fit common slope parameters for the R and D variables across the full sample of thirty-three industries.

Terleckyj notes that the results for nonmanufacturing industries were erratic, and they can be shown to be highly sensitive, in particular, to the inclusion or exclusion of the air transportation industry. Part of the reason for the sampling instability of the parameters for the nonmanufacturing industry sample might be the substantial collinearity that exists along the basic set of independent variables. Substantial collinearity also exists among specific independent variables for the manufacturing industry sample. Specifically, the zero-order correlation coefficients for pairs of the four R and D intensity variables provided in Terleckyj's table 6.1 (for the sample of twenty manufacturing industries) range between .73 and .95. The simple correlation coefficients between sales other than to government as a percent of total sales and the various R and D intensity variables range between —.79 and —.91. The fact that coefficients for the privately financed R and D variables tend to be unaffected by inclusion or exclusion of the government-financed R and D variables provides a reason for optimism about the reliability of the estimated returns to privately financed R and D. However, this stability might simply reflect the fact that rate-of-return estimates for government-financed R and D are confounded by collinearity with other variables, and particularly with the nongovernment sales variable, so that the private R and D variables are assigned the joint effect of the entire set.

One might also conjecture that the relationship between productivity change and returns to federally funded R and D depends upon the nature and the level of the R and D performed. Specifically, contract R and D performed in the electrical machinery and transportation equipment industries is largely defense-related. Thus, the effects of R and D performance on productivity may be atypical for those two industries. Our own estimation provides some indication that returns to government-financed R and D (both embodied and disembodied) are higher in the above-mentioned industries than in other manufacturing industries. The difference might reflect the existence of increasing returns to federally financed R and D or the possibility that government R and D support to other manufacturing industries is, in effect, a subsidy to offset low rates of productivity growth. These possibilities may be worthy of further investigation.

Concluding Comments

Terleckyj's general findings (for the specifications employing Kendrick's productivity index) are directionally in accord with existing evidence in the literature; however, differences among the various studies in the nature of the samples, the measurement of variables, and the techniques of estimation make specific comparisons rather tenuous. For example, Griliches (1973) obtained an estimated productivity return to R and D of around 40% for a sample of eighty-five two, three, and four-digit manufacturing industries. This estimate includes both direct (i.e., intraindustry) and indirect (i.e., interindustry) productivity effects. Terleckyj's estimates of total R and D returns (employing Kendrick's productivity index) range between 100 and 110% and lie substantially above Griliches's estimated total returns. In another study using a partial productivity measure, Griliches (1975) estimated the rate of return to R and D for 883 large R and D–performing U.S. manufacturing companies. The average gross excess rate of return to R and D was 27% in 1963. It should be noted that this estimate includes the productivity effects of intercompany as well as interindustry technology transfers. Mansfield (1965) found that marginal rates of return to R and D averaged about 40 to 60% for a sample of petroleum firms; for a sample of chemical firms, returns averaged about 30% if technical change was assumed to be capital-embodied but only about 7% if it was disembodied.[5]

Thus, various alternative estimates of the productivity returns to R and D tend to lie somewhat below estimates obtained by Terleckyj, although all of the estimated returns are substantial. Terleckyj's study performs the valuable service of demonstrating that these substantial returns (at least for one productivity measure) cannot be significantly reduced by statistically standardizing for human capital investments in an industry. It also provides us with dramatic evidence that estimated returns to R and D are extremely sensitive to the way in which productivity is measured. However, Terleckyj's study shares a weakness with other studies in failing to hold constant the effects of such factors as changes in average plant size, changes in plant-level specialization, and changes in organizational structure (including intrafirm and interfirm rates of technology diffusion) which may be related to the performance of R and D. An attempt to incorporate the influence of the above-mentioned factors into the basic productivity equation might make a significant contribution to our understanding of the influence of R and D on industrial performance.

---

5. Mansfield's estimated returns also include the indirect effects of the R and D conducted outside the sample firms.

Finally, Terleckyj should be complimented for the thoughtful inclusion and careful description of the data series included in his estimation work. The inclusion facilitates extension of his interesting work by other researchers.

References

Griliches, Zvi. 1973. Research expenditures and growth accounting. In *Science and technology in economic growth*, ed. B. R. Williams. New York: John Wiley and Sons.

———. 1975. Returns to research and development expenditures in the private sector. Paper presented at Conference on Research in Income and Wealth.

Kendrick, John. 1973. *Post-war productivity trends in the United States, 1948–1969*. New York: National Bureau of Economic Research.

Leonard, W. N. 1971. Research and development in industrial growth. *Journal of Political Economy* 79:232–56.

Mansfield, Edwin. 1965. Rates of return from industrial research and development. *American Economic Review* 55:310–22.

Terleckyj, Nestor E. 1974. *Effects of R & D on the productivity growth of industries: an exploratory study*. Washington: National Planning Association.

7 Research and Development Expenditures and Labor Productivity at the Firm Level: A Dynamic Model

M. Ishaq Nadiri and George C. Bitros

7.1 Introduction

The importance of innovative activities to the development and growth of the aggregate economies, various industries, and firms has been clearly established (see Kamien and Schwartz 1975). Issues such as the determinants of R and D expenditure, the rate and process of dissemination of innovative activities, the rates of return on R and D investment, the role of uncertainty in the undertaking of these efforts, and finally the industrial and organizational aspects of innovative activities have been the subject of numerous investigations.[1] Though there is considerable uncertainty about the quantitative evidence, the importance of research and development efforts in increasing productivity and developing new products has been generally accepted. However, one issue that has not received sufficient attention is the integration of the demand for research and development expenditure of the firm with its demand for conventional inputs such as labor and physical capital. The need for such undertakings is clear; R and D, like expenditure on plant and equipment and labor, is an input to the production process and therefore an integral part of the overall decision framework of the firm.

The primary purpose of this study is to investigate the determinants of research and development expenditure in the context of a general

M. Ishaq Nadiri is at New York University and the National Bureau of Economic Research. George C. Bitros is with the Bank of Greece.

The research for this paper was supported by the National Science Foundation (SOC 74–16295). We are indebted to Shoshona Livnat and Susan Chen for their diligent assistance in assembling the data and computation of the results.

1. Some examples of such studies are Baily (1972), Grabowski (1968), Kamien and Schwartz (1974, 1975), Mansfield (1968), Mansfield et al. (1971), and Scherer (1965).

dynamic model of a set of input demand functions. The consequences of research and development for other inputs and the impact of changes in demand for labor and physical capital on R and D decisions are treated together using a disequilibrium adjustment model of input demands. Within the context of this model the following issues are analyzed: (a) the short-run effects of changes in output and relative prices on demand for innovative activities, measured by stocks of R and D expenditure, employment, and capital stock; (b) the effects of the excess demand in any of these inputs on the short-run demand for the other inputs; (c) the effects of research and development and plant and equipment expenditures on labor productivity in the short, intermediate, and long runs; and (d) the responses of the inputs of firms of different asset sizes to changes in relative prices and output changes and the pattern of interactions among their inputs over time.

The main results of this study can be summarized briefly:

1. Changes in output and relative input prices significantly affect, in the short and long runs, the firm's demand for labor, research and development activity, and capital goods.

2. The transitory or distributed lag responses of the inputs to changes in output and relative prices are interdependent, i.e., a dynamic and asymmetrical feedback system is operative among the input responses which traces the adjustment of the system of input demands toward its long-run equilibrium.

3. Substantial differences exist among the cross-section of firms in their employment, research and development activity, and physical capital accumulation. Also, there is evidence of systematic overtime differences in their demand for labor, research and development activities, and capital goods.

4. Research and development investment exerts significant influence on the short and long-run behavior of labor productivity.

5. Finally, no discernible differences in input demand functions were found when firms in our sample were classified by the size of their assets.

The plan of the study is as follows: The rationale of the disequilibrium approach to the analysis of input demands is described in section 7.2. An example to illustrate the issues is provided and the outlines of the structure of the model are stated in this section. In section 7.3, the estimating equations, the characteristics of the data, and some estimation problems are described. The structural estimates of the model using data for sixty-two firms for the period 1965 to 1972 are presented and discussed in section 7.4.1. In section 7.4.2 the structural estimates of the model fitted to samples of firms classified by their asset sizes are presented. The stability of the model is also examined. In section 7.5, the cross-sectional differences among firms in their demand for inputs are noted and the overtime differences among input demands are analyzed. Furthermore, the long-run output and price elasticities of employment, research and development, and capital stock are discussed in this section. Also, the short, intermediate, and long-run effects of research and development on labor productivity are examined. The summary and conclusions are stated in section 7.6, followed by an appendix where the sources of data, construction of the regression variables, and the names and classification of the firms by the size of their assets are reported.

7.2   The Rationale for a Dynamic Disequilibrium Model

Existing cross-section and time series models of the determinants of R and D behavior assume fixed stocks of capital and labor. Also, no allowance is made in the employment and investment literature for the fact that a firm's R and D activities will affect its cost structure and thus its demand for labor and capital. That is, decisions with respect to the conventional inputs will be influenced depending on when and how vigorously the firm engages in innovative activities. In turn, a firm's demand for research and development effort will be affected by the magnitudes and characteristics of its capital and labor. In this type of interactive process, all the inputs are essentially variable and are only differentiated from each other by the *degree* of their flexibility or adjustment over time.

The dynamic model described below permits interaction among these inputs over time. The main feature of the model is that the disequilibrium in any of the inputs has a spill-over effect on demand for other inputs in the short run, while in the long run all excess demands disappear and the spill-over effects vanish.[2] However, in the very short run, as the firm attempts to adjust its stocks of inputs it will increase the utilization of its existing stocks to meet current demand. As the stock adjusts, the utilization rates return to their optimum levels.

7.2.1   An Example

To illustrate the nature of dynamic interactions among time paths of inputs, consider a simple two-factor example. Suppose the production function is $x = f(y_1, y_2)$, where x is output, y_1 and y_2 are inputs, and f has the usual continuity properties. Two isoquants are illustrated in figure 7.1. The dotted line AB is the locus of efficient expansion points

2. We recognize that the dynamic input and output paths are jointly determined, contingent on future product price expectations. But their joint estimation requires a full market theory not yet available. Therefore, we set the limited goal of estimating optimum input paths consistent with an optimum and given output path. This allows us to concentrate on interactions among changes and on factor substitution.

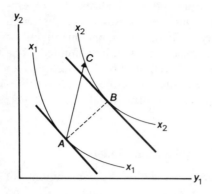

Fig. 7.1   Interactions among Time Paths of Inputs

along which total costs are minimized and is derived in the conventional way. Though this may be an adequate description of long-run behavior, there is plenty of evidence to suggest that firms do not remain along AB at every moment, and several explanations for this divergence have been offered. Most important, in addition to direct rental charges of factors, there are costs involved in changing their levels; that is, there are substantial transactions costs, and these must be viewed as additional investment costs if they are to be undertaken. There are search, hiring, training, and layoff costs and associated morale problems among workers. Similarly, there are searching, waiting, and installation costs in purchasing new capital goods, and there are adjustment costs associated with changing the level of the R and D activities such as acquisition of the appropriate facilities, search cost in hiring and training of scientists and engineers, etc. If initial input values deviate from their long-run equilibrium levels, existence of these costs implies that optimum adjustment paths to equilibrium are not instantaneous. Since exogenous variables are generally subject to change and uncertainty, these costs often make it profitable for firms to engage in hoarding of input stocks.

The conventional way of incorporating adjustment costs is the well-known partial adjustment model:

$$(1)\qquad y_{1t} - y_{1t-1} = \beta(y^*_{1t} - y_{1t-1}), \quad 0 < \beta < 1,$$

where y^*_1 is the desired level of y_1 as defined by AB and β is the adjustment coefficient. Suppose the firm wants to increase output to x_2, given initial condition A in figure 7.1. Equation (1) implies an immediate move from A to (say) C, with convergence along the new isoquant to the new equilibrium point B. The diagram indicates a corresponding and implied adjustment path for y_2.[3] In general, two independent adjustments imply additional hypotheses concerning the role of the production function during the adjustment period. There are two possibilities:

i) If the production function constraint always holds as an equality, independent adjustments imply an output decision function, which may not be optimum.

ii) If output is taken as exogenous, two independent specifications mean that firms must be off their production functions, i.e., they must be capable of producing more than they actually do during the adjustment period.[4]

An intermediate position is also possible—that is, to assume output to be exogenous, but input adjustments are specified to be interrelated. For example, a generalization of equation (1) is

$$(2) \qquad \begin{bmatrix} y_{1t} - y_{1t-1} \\ y_{2t} - y_{2t-1} \end{bmatrix} = \begin{bmatrix} \beta_{11} & \beta_{12} \\ \beta_{21} & \beta_{22} \end{bmatrix} \begin{bmatrix} y^*_{2t} - y_{2t-1} \\ y^*_{1t} - y_{1t-1} \end{bmatrix}.$$

This incorporates exogenous output and allows firms to remain on their production functions during the adjustment process, since input adjustments are not independent.[5] Refer again to figure 7.1. If the true adjustment path is described by ACB, β_{21} and β_{22} must be sufficiently positive to initially push y_2 above its ultimate value. This overshooting sets up forces that ultimately decrease y_2 to its equilibrium value at B. The net values of β_{11} and β_{12} must be positive for y_1 to increase monotonically to its equilibrium at B. Obviously, there must be restrictions on the B_{ij} to insure that the firm remains along isoquant x_2x_2.

7.2.2 The Model of the Input Demand Functions

Assume that the firm minimizes costs subject to a Cobb-Douglas production function with three inputs: labor (L), capital stock (K), and stock of research and development activities (R). The input and

---

3. Assume f is Cobb-Douglas, $x = (y_1)^a (y_2)^b$. The demand for y_2 may be derived from a logarithmic form of equation (1) and from $y_2 = (x)^{1/b}(y_1)^{-a/b}$. It is given by

$$y_{2t} = (x_t)^{1/b}(y_{it})^\beta (y_{1t-1})^{(1-\beta)-a/b}.$$

4. Nerlove (1967). Nerlove adopts the second approach. In his model, firms react not to observed values of output and relative prices, but to forecasts of unobserved (trend-cycle) components. Desired and actual output are identical, but firms may be off their production functions.

5. It is interesting to note that a similar hypothesis has been proposed by Brainard and Tobin (1968) in the related context of portfolio adjustment among assets. These authors have assumed the wealth path to be exogenous and have addressed themselves to determining optimum adjustments of various assets consistent with that path.

output prices are assumed to be exogenously given. More formally, the general problem considered is to minimize costs,

(3) $$C = wL + cK + rR$$

subject to the production function

(4) $$Q = AL\alpha_1\, K\alpha_2\, R\alpha_3\, U\alpha_4\, e^{\lambda t},$$

where w, c, and r are respectively the user costs associated with employment, stock of plant and equipment, and stock of research and development. Q is the level of output, A is a constant, α_1, α_2, and α_3 are the long-run output elasticities of the inputs, and λ is the rate of disembodied technical change. We have assumed that the input utilization rates are functions of an overall rate of utilization, U. Also note that the utilization rate U does not explicitly enter the cost function, but implicitly through the rate of depreciation, δ, of capital stock. Depreciation depends on the rate of utilization, U, as well as time, i.e., $\delta = \delta(U,t)$.

The user costs are defined to include the purchase price, the opportunity costs of funds, depreciation expenses due to utilization and passage of time, tax considerations, and capital gains. For example, the user costs of capital goods can be stated as

$$c = \frac{P_k(r + \delta)(1 - \bar{k} - v_z + v_z k')}{(1 - v)},$$

where P_k is the deflator for capital goods; r is the cost of capital, measured as $r = i - (P/P)^e$, where i is long-term interest rate and $(\dot{P}/P)^e$ is the expected change in prices; δ is the depreciation rate; P and $\dot{P}$ are the level and change in general price level; $\bar{k}$ is the Long tax credit amendment; k' is the effective rate of tax credit; z is the present value of depreciation; and v is the corporate tax rate. The user costs for labor services and for research and development efforts are in principle similar to c. The Langrangian method for minimizing costs (3) subject to the production function (4) will yield the long-run solution of the determinants of the inputs.[6] That is,

$$y^*_1 = L = g_1(x^*, \bar{P}),$$
$$y^*_2 = R = g_2(x^*, \bar{P}),$$
(5)
$$y^*_3 = K = g_3(x^*, \bar{P}),$$
$$y^*_4 = U = g_4(P),$$

where $\bar{P}$ is a vector of the relative prices of inputs and the coefficient of x^* is $1/\rho = (\alpha_1 + \alpha_2 + \alpha_3)$, the reciprocal of returns-to-scale pa-

6. See Nadiri and Rosen (1973), pp. 19–21, for derivation of these expressions.

rameter. Assuming that the adjustment cost of each input is proportional to the gap between its long-run equilibrium and actual levels and is also affected by the disequilibrium of the other inputs, it can be shown that the approach to the long-run equilibrium of the system of inputs is approximated by the following set of difference equations (Nadiri and Rosen, 1973, pp. 24–25).

$$(6) \qquad y_{it} - y_{it-1} = \sum_{j=1}^{4} \beta_{ij} \left[g_i(x_t, \bar{P}_t) - y_{jt} \right] + v_{it},$$

$$(i = 1, \ldots, 4),$$

where β_{ij} is a nondiagonal matrix of adjustment coefficients and $v_1,$ $\ldots, v_4$ are random terms with zero means and variance-covarance matrix Ω. From the generalized adjustment model (6) we can find (*a*) the short-term impact of changes in output and relative input prices, (*b*) the transition or distributed lag patterns of the inputs to a change in these variables, and (*c*) the long-run price and output elasticities of the inputs. Since the technical details of these problems are discussed elsewhere (Nadiri and Rosen 1969), we may state that the short-term transitory responses are calculated by computing $[I - (I - B) Z]^{-1}$ and the long-run elasticities by calculating $A[I - B]^{-1}$; $B = [\beta_{ij}]$ is the nondiagonal matrix of adjustment coefficients, Z is the lag operator, and A is the matrix of the coefficients of the exogenous variables.

7.3   Estimating Equations: Data and Estimation Problems

The model specified in section 7.2 has been estimated using cross-section and time series data on sixty-two firms for the period 1965–72. The main source of our firm data is the Compustat tapes. The sixty-two firms are drawn from five industries: five from Metal extraction (SIC 10), twenty-eight from Chemicals and allied products (SIC 28), twelve from Nonelectrical machinery (SIC 35), eight from Electrical equipment and supplies (SIC 36), and nine from instruments (SIC 38). Thus, our sample is dominated by firms in the Chemical and allied products categories.

The empirical specification of the model differs somewhat from (6). The user costs of labor and research and development efforts have been omitted due to lack of appropriate data. The real wage rates for the appropriate two-digit industries are used as a proxy for these two user-cost variables. The user cost of capital for each firm is approximated by a measure constructed for the total manufacturing sector.[7] The output prices are not available at the firm level; therefore, we have used appro-

---

7. See the appendix for the specific formulation and source of data to generate this variable.

priate wholesale price indices of the two-digit manufacturing industries as the deflators for output, nominal wage rate, and the user cost of capital.

The proper concept for the research and development is the services of a given stock of R and D to the production of current output. Reliable estimates of the benchmark and depreciation rates for R and D at the individual firm level are not available. We constructed the stock of R and D by assuming an arbitrary depreciation rate of 10% per annum for each firm. The 1965 R and D investment in constant dollars is used as the benchmark for those firms that did not report any figures prior to 1965, while for firms with more extended data, the first year of consistent reporting was chosen as the benchmark.[8] Capital stock series for R and D and plant and equipment for each firm were constructed by the recursive formula,

$$(7) \qquad K_{it} = I_{it} + (1 - \delta_i)K_{it-1}, \quad (i = 1, \ldots, 62),$$

where I_{it} is the deflated individual firm expenditure on R and D or new plant and equipment; the deflator used for converting nominal expenditure on R and D and plant and equipment into constant dollars is the deflator for plant and equipment $(1958 = 100)$. The δ_i are the individual firm depreciation rates calculated for plant or equipment as the ratio of depreciation expenses to the benchmark capital stock obtained from the firm's balance sheet. As noted earlier, the depreciation rates for R and D are assumed to be fixed at 10%. The employment data refer to total employment of each firm. Unfortunately, it is not possible to break this aggregate series into production and nonproduction or scientists and engineers, etc. Similarly, it is not possible to separate the research and development expenditure into privately and publicly financed categories.

The specific estimating equations used are

$$
\begin{aligned}
(8) \qquad
L_t &= \alpha_0 + \alpha_1 Q_t + \alpha_2 (w/c)_t + \alpha_3 L_{t-1} + \alpha_4 R_{t-1} \\
&\quad + \alpha_5 K_{t-1} + \alpha_6 U_{t-1} + \epsilon_1, \\
R_t &= \beta_0 + \beta_1 Q_t + \beta_2 (w/c)_t + \beta_3 L_{t-1} + \beta_4 R_{t-1} \\
&\quad + \beta_5 K_{t-1} + \beta_6 U_{t-1} + \epsilon_2, \\
K_t &= \gamma_0 + \gamma_1 Q_t + \gamma_2 (w/c)_t + \gamma_3 L_{t-1} + \gamma_4 R_{t-1} \\
&\quad + \gamma_5 K_{t-1} + \gamma_6 U_{t-1} + \epsilon_3, \\
U_t &= \delta_0 + \delta_1 Q_t + \delta_2 (w/c)_t + \delta_3 L_{t-1} + \delta_4 R_{t-1} \\
&\quad + \delta_5 K_{t-1} + \delta_6 U_{t-1} + \epsilon_4,
\end{aligned}
$$

8. The regressions were also run with the flow measure of R and D expenditure. The overall results were generally similar to those reported in table 7.1.

where all the variables are in logarithms; R_t is the measure of research and development expenditures; L_t and K_t are the levels of employment and capital stock of the firm; Q_t is the level of output; (w_t/c_t) is the ratio of nominal wage rate and the user cost of capital goods. U_t is the rate of utilization of the appropriate two-digit industries used as a proxy for firms' utilization rate, R_{t-1}, L_{t-1}, and K_{t-1} are the lagged dependent variables, and ϵ_1, ϵ_2, ϵ_3, and ϵ_4 are the error terms.[9]

The adjustment processes are embedded in the coefficients of the lagged dependent variables. The own adjustment coefficient in each equation can be obtained from the regression coefficient associated with the lagged dependent variable, while the cross-adjustment coefficients are from the regression coefficients related to the lagged values of other dependent variables. For example, in the first equation of (8), the own adjustment coefficient is $\hat{\beta}_{11} = (1 - \hat{\alpha}_3)$ and the cross-adjustment effects of disequilibria in R and D and plant and equipment on employment are measured by $-\beta_{12} = \alpha_4$ and $-\beta_{13} = \alpha_5$. The matrix

$$B = \begin{bmatrix} \alpha_3 & \alpha_4 & \alpha_5 & \alpha_6 \\ \beta_3 & \beta_4 & \beta_5 & \beta_6 \\ \gamma_3 & \gamma_4 & \gamma_5 & \gamma_6 \\ \delta_3 & \delta_4 & \delta_5 & \delta_6 \end{bmatrix}$$

constitutes the 4×4 nondiagonal adjustment matrix which traces the interdependence of the adjustment paths of the three inputs and the utilization rate over time.

Before estimating these equations, the problem of heteroscedasticity in our sample had to be considered. Except for the three aggregate industry-wide variables w_t, c_t, and U_t, the remaining variables in (8) are specific to each firm. Error variances for large firms will substantially exceed those of small firms and therefore the possibility that the cross-section within-cell regression functions will have unequal error variances will exist. As is well known, there are two ways to handle this possibility; the first is to test for the existence of heteroscedasticity among firms and eliminate the statistically significant outliers. The second approach is to transform variables so that the error variances will be homogenous (Kuh 1963). We have followed the second alternative. Two possibilities exist: (1) log transformation of the variables which equalizes the error variances on the assumption that they are strictly proportional to the size of the independent variables; (2) fitting the model in ratio form, which means dividing the firm-specific variables by an appropriate scale variable such as the total assets of the firm. Though we have used both of these procedures (using total deflated

9. See the appendix for definition, sources, and construction of the regression variables.

assets of the firms as the denominator in the ratio form of the model), we shall report only the logarithmic results.

Another important estimation problem that arises immediately is whether or not to impose the implicit constraint on the adjustment coefficients of model (8). If the adjustment coefficients are unconstrained, one of two hypotheses about the production function is implied: (1) if the production function constraint always holds as an equality, then the adjustment process implies that output is endogenous during the adjustment period; (2) on the other hand, if output is taken as exogenous, independent adjustments imply that firms may not be on their production functions. The values of the adjustment coefficients, then, will determine whether the firms are inside or outside of their production surface.

We have not imposed the necessary constraints on the adjustment coefficients, mainly because of the unreliability of the underlying data. Instead, we have assumed that output is endogeneous and have examined the unconstrained estimates of the adjustment coefficients to see whether the constraints implied by the model are met. The structural equation for each input is estimated by two-stage least-squares and the characteristic roots of matrix B are examined to check whether the implicit constraints are reasonably met.

7.4 The Structural Estimates

The model is estimated using the variance components technique for pooling cross-section and time series data developed by G. S. Maddala (1971). This method allows estimating the cross-section and time series effects separately and generates generalized least-squares estimates of the parameters of the model.[10]

The model (8) is estimated using the overall sample of sixty-two firms and three subsamples: twenty-eight firms with total assets below $300 million, twenty firms with assets greater than $300 million but smaller than one billion dollars, and fourteen firms of over one billion dollars in total assets. The estimation of the model using the stratified samples should provide a test of its stability and insight into whether firms of different sizes differ in their input decisions. We have also estimated both the ratio and logarithmic forms of (8) for all four samples. Only the generalized least-squares estimates of the model in logarithmic form are presented here.

10. The computer program based on this technique generates four regressions: the ordinary least squares (OLS), generalized least squares (GLS) without taking effect of cross-section and time effects, the least squares plus dummy variables (LSDV), which takes account of these effects, and finally the generalized least squares with dummy variables.

7.4.1   The Structural Estimates: The Overall Sample

The results in table 7.1 are the generalized least-squares estimates with cross-section and time dummies. Note that Q_t is the estimated value of the output variable Q_t.

The results indicate a consistent picture: the coefficients generally are statistically significant in both the OLS and GLS versions, the results of the ratio and logarithmic forms of the model were fairly similar, and the signs of the coefficients of all the variables except a few remained stable in the various versions of the model.

As can be seen from table 7.1, the statistical goodness of fit of the model measured by R^2 and sum of squared residuals (SSR) and estimated variance of errors (EEV) are very good. A separate test using the TSP regression program indicated that the Durbin-Watson test values were about 2.0 for each of the equations. However, this test is not only biased when a lagged dependent variable is included as an explanatory

Table 7.1   **Generalized Least-Squares Estimates of the Model in Logarithmic Form, Period 1965–72**

Independent Variables	Generalized Least-Squares Equations			
	$\text{Log } L_t$	$\text{Log } R_t$	$\text{Log } K_t$	$\text{Log } U_t$
Constant	−.3458	.6793	−.3035	−.2013
	(−.5135)	(1.889)	(−.8140)	(−2.077)
Log Q	.3355	.1970	.2279	.0290
	(5.482)	(7.614)	(5.758)	(2.933)
Log $(w/c)_t$	−.1742	−.2418	.0254	.0300
	(−1.6855)	(−1.876)	(.1773)	(.8151)
Log L_{t-1}	.5173	−.0904	−.0353	−.0253
	(8.507)	(−3.422)	(−.9482)	(−2.745)
Log R_{t-1}	.0997	.6999	−.0046	.0074
	(2.75)	(42.40)	(−.2094)	(1.34)
Log K_{t-1}	−.0544	.0804	.8175	−.0099
	(−1.62)	(5.391)	(40.33)	(−1.95)
Log U_{t-1}	−.3859	−.1772	−.4388	.6504
	(−2.220)	(−2.52)	(−3.565)	(20.42)
R^2	.9283	.9767	.9878	.8851
SSR	.3469	.3531	.3475	.3353
Degrees of freedom	365	365	365	365
EEV	.0105	.0017	.0054	.00033

NOTE: Abbreviations are explained in the text.

variable, but also may not be invariant with respect to the ordering of the firm data in our sample.

The estimates in table 7.1 indicate the immediate responses of the inputs to changes in output, relative input prices, their own lags, and cross-adjustment effects of other inputs. The coefficient of output is positive and statistically significant in each equation. The output elasticities indicate that changes in output have the strongest effect on employment (.34), followed by stocks of capital goods and research and development. The output elasticity of the utilization rate, U, which should be very high, is rather small. The explanation for this is that our measure of the utilization rate is an industry measure which may not respond greatly to movements of demand of the individual firms. The relative price variable is also statistically significant and negative in both research and development and employment equations; it has the correct positive sign but is not statistically significant in the capital stock equation or in the utilization equation.

The own lag coefficients of the three stock variables indicate that employment adjusts very rapidly $(1 - .52 = .48)$, followed by stock of research and development expenditures, $(1 - .70 = .30)$, while capital stock adjusts very slowly $(1 - .82 = .18)$. These patterns of adjustment are consistent with our a priori notion and previous results. They suggest, if we ignore the spill-over effects, an average lag of a year for employment, two and one-half years for research and development, and about four years for the capital stock.[11] The adjustment coefficient for the utilization rate is unexpectedly long. Again, part of the reason is that U is an industry measure and cannot be explained readily by movements of firm data. There are significant cross-adjustment effects in each demand equation, though of varying magnitudes. These are calculated as $-\hat{\beta}_{ij}$, $i \neq j$—that is, the negative of the cross-adjustment coefficients shown in table 7.1. For example, $-\hat{\beta}_{ij}$, $j = 2,3,4$ measures the effects of excess demand in employment on stocks of research and development and capital and the utilization rate; they are shown by the coefficients in row L_{t-1} in table 7.1. The signs and magnitudes of the cross-adjustment coefficients vary among the equations, indicating an asymmetrical and varying disequilibrium effect. As noted, the direction of these effects will be the opposite of the signs of the coefficients shown in table 7.1.

1. Employment disequilibrium has strong positive effects on the utilization rate and stock of research and development expenditure. It also affects demand for capital goods positively, but the effect is not statistically significant. Thus, excess demand for labor increases the utilization rate and demand for plant and equipment and research development.

11. These calculations are only very tentative, for the adjustment patterns are interdependent and they cannot be ignored.

2. Excess demand in stocks of research and development has a strong negative effect on demand for labor; its impact on capital stock is positive but not very significant; its effect on the utilization rate, though positive, is barely significant statistically. Thus, disequilibrium in R and D capital reduces demand for labor but increases that of physical capital, implying a complementary relation with labor and a substitutional relation with physical capital.

3. Disequilibrium in physical capital has statistically significant positive effects on demand for labor and the utilization rate while it has a strong negative and statistically significant impact on demand for research and development expenditures. These patterns of response suggest a short-run complementary relation between stocks of capital goods and research and development and a substitutional relation with employment.

4. The cross effect of the rate of utilization on the demand for employment, research and development, and capital goods is positive and statistically significant in all cases. That is, disequilibrium in the utilization rate leads to increased demand for productive inputs.

5. These disequilibrium effects suggest that a firm faces excess demand in one of its inputs by increasing its rate of utilization and adjusting its demand for other two inputs. Thus, strong feedbacks and dynamical relations exist among the inputs in the short run.

From these results we conclude that there are strong and statistically significant short-term effects of changes in output and input prices on research development, employment, and investment demand of the firm. Also, there are some lags in achieving the desired levels of these inputs. The lags arise not only because of factors generating disequilibria in the specific input's own market but also because of disequilibria in other inputs as well. Dynamic feedback or spill-over effects among the three inputs do exist, and they tend to be asymmetrical in character. The utilization rate serves as a buffer allowing the firm to change its stocks of input. That is, when current demand increases, firms utilize their existing stocks of inputs first and then, if the demand is perceived as more permanent, they will adjust their stocks of inputs.

7.4.2 Structural Estimates for the Subsamples

The results in table 7.1 are essentially repeated when the model is fitted to the three subsamples mentioned earlier. The structural estimates for the subsamples are presented in table 7.2. The striking overall conclusion that emerges from a comparison of the results in tables 7.1 and 7.2 is the stability of the model in terms of signs and significance of the coefficients, and the goodness-of-fit statistics such as R^2 and sum-of-squares errors. The magnitudes and statistical significance of the coefficients vary somewhat across different asset sizes. The output vari-

Table 7.2   Generalized Least-Squares Estimates of the Model in Logarithmic Form for Three Samples of Firms, Period 1965–72

Independent Variables	Twenty-Eight Small Firms Equations				Twenty Medium-Sized Firms Equations				Fourteen Large Firms Equations			
	$\log L_t$	$\log R_t$	$\log K_t$	$\log U_t$	$\log L_t$	$\log R_t$	$\log K_t$	$\log U_t$	$\log L_t$	$\log R_t$	$\log K_t$	$\log U_t$
Constant	−.0175 (−.0198)	.8677 (1.888)	−.4155 (−.7361)	−.1795 (−1.518)	−3.4175 (−2.031)	.1419 (.4093)	.3517 (.5351)	−.3415 (−1.432)	.6690 (.4639)	.0917 (.1921)	.7089 (1.059)	−.0591 (−.1638)
$\log Q_t$	.1828 (2.003)	.2093 (5.755)	.2459 (3.408)	.0231 (1.725)	.5640 (5.274)	.1072 (2.424)	.1977 (3.821)	.0341 (1.745)	.9619 (5.692)	.0913 (1.9345)	.2290 (3.7395)	.0428 (1.1480)
$\log (w/c)_t$	−.1410 (−.4254)	−.3216 (−1.975)	.0615 (.2779)	.0319 (.6954)	.6427 (1.187)	−.0057 (−.0396)	−.0190 (−.0821)	.0797 (.9506)	−.6367 (−1.285)	.0718 (.4457)	−.0990 (−.4410)	.0024 (.0185)
$\log L_{t-1}$	.6587 (7.309)	−.1394 (−3.7)	−.0324 (−.4831)	−.0175 (−1.3793)	.1329 (1.015)	.0038 (.0832)	−.0342 (−.5525)	−.0331 (−1.571)	.1581 (1.417)	−.0241 (−.7772)	−.0589 (−1.4703)	−.0333 (−1.3625)
$\log R_t$	.1028 (2.1625)	.6569 (32.981)	−.0164 (−.472)	.0042 (.6090)	.4347 (3.7784)	.9365 (35.532)	.0768 (1.605)	.0157 (1.1005)	−.0386 (−.4965)	.7835 (34.787)	−.0101 (−.3428)	.0141 (.7913)
$\log K_{t-1}$	−.0649 (−1.516)	.1079 (6.2154)	.7994 (24.609)	−.0114 (−1.8116)	−.2485 (−1.2013)	−.0801 (−2.831)	.6827 (15.182)	−.0185 (−1.1888)	−.3430 (−3.0043)	.0596 (1.6578)	.7417 (15.172)	−.0350 (−1.4667)
$\log U_{t-1}$	−.3049 (−1.0693)	−.1769 (−1.683)	−.5847 (−2.466)	.6607 (13.85)	−.3088 (−1.2013)	−.1775 (−1.481)	−.1429 (−1.1042)	.6272 (10.988)	−1.3089 (−3.922)	−.2421 (−2.534)	−.4469 (−3.546)	.6265 (8.3232)
R^2	.9648	.9923	.9897	.9443	.9632	.9968	.9835	.9668	.7802	.9798	.9515	.7675
SSR	.1562	.1608	.1568	.1537	.1099	.1062	.1079	.1037	.07604	.07927	.07672	.07610
Degrees of freedom	161	161	161	161	113	113	113	113	77	77	77	77
EEV	.0134	.0018	.0105	.0003	.0052	.0014	.0013	.0002	.0078	.0006	.0009	.0004

able is statistically significant in all of the regressions; the magnitudes of the coefficients are larger and similar to that of the overall sample for the firms with assets greater than one billion and those with assets less than 300 million dollars. For the "medium" size firms the short-term responses of the inputs to changes in output, except in the employment equation, is somewhat smaller. The relative price variable (w/c) has the correct sign in most cases, but in most of the regressions its magnitude and statistical significance varies. However, except in the employment equations, the coefficients of the relative price variable are statistically insignificant.

The own and cross-adjustment coefficients are quite strong in some of the regression equations in table 7.2. The asymmetrical pattern noted for the whole sample holds in the subsample regressions as well; the magnitudes of the own and cross-adjustment coefficients, however, vary among firms with different asset sizes. The weakest links in the feedback among the input disequilibria are observed in the effects of excess demand for R and D of firms with assets over one billion dollars. Disequilibrium in capital stock has strong effects on the demand for research and development of firms in all asset categories. The utilization rate positively affects the demand for all the inputs as we noted earlier for the whole sample of firms. The employment disequilibrium has a fairly weak effect on demand for R and D and capital stock in the medium-size and large firms.

Though these differences in individual coefficients may exist, still the overall significance of these differences may not be very significant. To test the stability of the model across the asset classifications, we computed the relevant F statistics for each set of input demand equations,

$$F = \frac{SSR_T - (SSR_{14} + SSR_{20} + SSR_{28})/k}{(SSR_{14} + SSR_{20} + SSR_{28})/N - 3k}$$

where SSR_T is the sum-of-squared residuals from the regression for the 62 firms and SSR_{14}, SSR_{20}, SSR_{28} are the sum-of-squared residuals from the regressions for the subsamples of firms. N is the overall number of observations and k is the number of the parameters estimated. The calculated F statistics for L, R, and K equations are 0.689, 0.9504, 0.8927 and 0.2652, respectively, and the critical value of $F(7,344)$ at the 1% level is 2.69. Therefore, the null hypothesis of an unchanging structure of demand functions for labor, research and development, and capital goods cannot be rejected.

The Cross Section and Overtime Differences among Firms

The analysis of variance employed in estimating the demand equations permits testing whether cross-section and time series differences exist among our sample of firms in their input decisions. We have calculated the F statistics based on the estimates generated by the least-squares plus dummy variables (LSDV) of the analysis of variance. The results in table 7.3 pertain to the logarithmic form of the model using the entire sample and the three subsamples of firms. They indicate an interesting pattern: substantial cross-sectional differences exist among firms with respect to *all* of the inputs and, except for the demand for research and development expenditure in the small and medium-size firms, all the input functions also vary over the span of time considered.

It is difficult to precisely state the causes of the cross-sectional and time series differences among the samples of firms in their input decisions. The cross-sectional difference may arise from the differences in the characteristics of firms such as being in different industries, producing different types of products, having different degrees of monopoly or monopsony in the markets, etc. The overtime differences may be due to differing adjustment processes, responses to external shocks, and technological changes. Though very desirable, a closer look into the

Table 7.3   **Values of F-Statistics from Analysis of Variance for the Entire Sample and Three Subsamples of Firms, Period 1965–72**

Group	Dependent Variable	Effects	
		Cross Section	Time-Series
Overall sample: sixty-two firms	L_t	63.5776	5.2096
	R_t	245.087	10.3005
	K_t	21.6712	7.6988
	U_t	19.5848	173.861
Fourteen large firms	L_t	81.5190	3.5241
	R_t	161.635	9.2359
	K_t	204.780	18.0309
	U_t	45.4924	31.5152
Twenty medium-sized firms	L_t	481.675	62.9452
	R_t	38.3298	1.1649
	K_t	267.811	9.7051
	U_t	47.5290	90.3784
Twenty-eight small firms	L_t	357.410	41.1140
	R_t	321.932	3.6381
	K_t	14.5643	2.5744
	U_t	16.1273	90.8643

NOTE: The critical values of F for the cross-section estimates at .05 are approximately as follows: $F(61,305) = 1.47$ for the entire sample, $F(13,65) = 2.42$ for the fourteen large firms, $F(19,95) = 2.09$ for the medium-sized firms, $F(27,135) = 1.85$ for the twenty-eight small firms. The critical values of F for the time series estimates at .05 are respectively $F(5,305) = 3.09$, $F(5,65) = 3.29$, $F(5,95 = 3.20$, and $F(5,135) = 3.17$.

sources of these differences in input demand functions of the firms is beyond the scope of our present research.

7.5 The Long-Run Elasticities of Inputs and Labor Productivities

From the structural estimates reported in tables 7.1 and 7.2, we can calculate the implied long-run output and price elasticities of the three inputs. Using these statistics, it is possible to obtain the long-run labor productivity estimates for the total number of firms and for the sample of firms classified by asset size. The long-run elasticities are identical to the coefficients of equation (5) (in log form) and are computed from the stationary solutions of the structural equations (8). Note that the long-run output elasticities of employment, research and development, and capital stock demand functions estimate the inverse of returns to scale, $1/\rho = 1/(\alpha_1 + \alpha_2 + \alpha_3)$.

Several features of these figures in table 7.4 should be noted:

1. The surprising similarity of the output elasticities among the inputs. Long-run elasticities of capital, however, tend to be somewhat larger in the overall sample and the sample of small firms.

Table 7.4   **Long-Run Output and Price Elasticities for the Overall Sample and Subsamples of Firms**

	Variables	
Sample Size	Output	Relative Prices
Sixty-two firms		
L	.7103	−.5954
R	.7142	−.6946
K	1.0521	.0029
U	.0172	.1143
Fourteen large firms		
L	.8495	−.7816
R	.5212	.1656
K	.6822	−.4230
U	−.0056	.1222
Twenty medium-sized firms		
L	.8365	−.6632
R	.7922	−.1836
K	.7179	−.2474
U	.0149	.1597
Twenty-eight small firms		
L	.5393	−.9202
R	.7105	.3758
K	1.0394	.3058
U	.0141	.0434

2. The output elasticities in the labor, research and development, and capital stock demand equations, except for the two cases noted, are less than unity, which implies in general a slightly increasing return to scale in the production process. The output elasticity of the utilization rate, as we expect, is approximately zero in the long run.

3. The elasticity of employment, stock of research and development, and capital stock with respect to relative input prices are generally larger for employment than for other inputs. The sign of the relative price is volatile for the stocks of research and development and capital goods. The relative price variable has a small but positive effect on the rate of utilization.

As we noted earlier, certain relationships among the adjustment coefficients, β_{ij}'s, are implied by the model. The relevant restriction we seek is for

$$\alpha(I - B) = 0,$$

where α is a vector of Cobb-Douglas exponents and B is the matrix of adjustment coefficients. Since each α_j is nonzero, then $|I - B| = 0$. In principle, this provides the test of the restrictions; otherwise the production function will be overidentified. One way to fulfill this test is to look for the characteristic roots of $|I - B|$ to have modules less than unity which would insure that $|I - B|$ will approach zero.

In table 7.5, the characteristics roots of $|I - B|$ for the entire sample of firms and its subcategories are listed. These roots are complex and less than unity in absolute values, suggesting that the response patterns of the inputs display damped oscillations and that the restriction of $|I - \hat{B}|$ $= 0$ is approximately met.

7.5.1   Research and Development and Labor Productivity

To illustrate the influence of research and development expenditures on labor productivity we can perform certain conceptual experiments using the estimates shown in tables 7.1 and 7.2. We can generate short and long-run labor productivity indices depending on what factor of production we assume to be fixed. To obtain the short-run partial pro-

Table 7.5	**Characteristic Roots of $\|I-B\|$** (calculated using estimates from tables 7.1 and 7.2)		
Entire Sample	14 Large Firms	20 Medium-Sized Firms	28 Small Firms
$.8293I \pm .3519i$	$.8023I \pm .0569i$	$.9201I \pm .1443i$	$.8242I \pm .2428i$
$.6857I \pm .1247i$	$.6728I \pm .5489i$	$.7241I \pm .1576i$	$.6838I \pm .6616i$
$.4844$	$.0325$	$.1018$	$.5839$

ductivity index, we consider the employment functions in these tables in isolation and assume that the levels of both research and development and capital stock of the firm are exogenously given and fixed in the short run. Thus, with our model (8) reduced into a single employment equation, we transform the employment functions in tables 7.1 and 7.2 into short-run productivity equations where labor productivity will be a function of output, relative input prices, previous levels of capital stock, employment, and research and development expenditures. From the magnitude of the output coefficient in the equation it is possible to infer whether employment moves proportionately with output in the short run. As indicated in table 7.6 the short-run coefficient of output in the productivity equation, $1/\alpha_q$, is positive and smaller than unity in each case except for the firms with total assets greater than one billion dollars. In other cases there is evidence of increasing return to labor in the very short run (Sims 1974). We also observe that the short-run impact of changes in research and development and capital stock varies considerably among the samples of firms. Research and development seem to exert the most significant effect on productivity in the case of large and medium-size firms, while the capital stock seems to have the largest positive effect on labor productivity in the case of the small firms followed by a fairly sizable effect on labor productivity of medium-sized firms.[12]

To determine the behavior of the labor productivity in the intermediate run, we shall assume that both employment and research and development investment are variable and only the capital stock of the firm is fixed. This reduces the estimating model to a two-equation interrelated model in employment and research and development expenditures. Solving the two-equation system, and after appropriate conver-

12. These results should be interpreted with caution since our classification of assets by size of total assets is rather arbitrary.

Table 7.6   **Short-Run Response of Labor Productivity to Changes in Output, Research and Development, and Capital Stock in the Overall Subsamples of Firms**

	62 Firms	14 Large Firms	20 Medium-Sized Firms	28 Small Firms
$(1 - 1/a_q)$	0.333	0.085	0.462	0.502
$R_t - 1$	0.256	0.162	0.165	0.398
$K_t - 1$	0.105	0.151	0.233	0.002

NOTE: These figures are based on estimates in tables 7.1 and 7.2 which are converted to elasticities.

sions, we obtain the intermediate elasticities of labor productivity with respect to output, $(w/c)_t$, R_{t-1}, and K_{t-1}. The effects of research and development on labor productivity is transmitted now through the embedded feedback process and is reflected in the coefficients of output and relative input prices. The results of this experiment indicate that the output elasticity of employment moves generally close to unity for each of the firms in the sample.

Finally, the long-run labor productivity is calculated when all the variables are changing. The magnitudes of output elasticity of labor are the same as those reported for employment in table 7.5. These figures suggest that long-run labor productivity is independent of the cyclical changes in output and the production process is probably subject to a slight degree of increasing returns to scale.

Comparison of these experiments indicates that the reason for the large returns to labor reported from the estimated short-run employment functions is the assumption of fixity of other inputs or input services. The high estimates reported in the literature should be interpreted not as a return to labor alone, but as a short-run return for all inputs. These experiments, however, are basically conjectural since our basic model stresses the dynamic interrelationships of all factors. All variables are specified as "quasi-fixed" and none of them are really entirely fixed in the short run. Yet the procedure suggests that labor productivity is affected by cyclical changes in output in the short run, while in the intermediate run this effect declines and in the long run it finally vanishes. Labor productivity is also significantly affected in the short run and also in the long run by the level of research and development activities.

7.6   Conclusions and Summary

The results presented in this paper indicate that the firm's employment, capital accumulation, and research and development decisions are closely intertwined, and a dynamic interaction process seems to underlie these decisions. The research and development activities of the firm, like its demand for labor and capital, are influenced significantly by changes in output and relative input prices. The long-run output elasticities of the inputs, especially those of labor and research and development, are quite similar and suggest a slight increasing return to scale in production. Both labor productivity and investment demand of the firms are significantly affected by their research and development expenditures. These results are in contrast to the findings of the familiar investment and employment functions which often have ignored the explicit role of research and development. We found that the demand for the three inputs are stable when firms are stratified by size of their assets; however, there is evidence of cross-sectional and overtime differences among firms in their input decisions. The causes of such differences are not explored at the present.

To improve our empirical results some of the shortcomings of our present data base have to be remedied. It would be useful to enlarge our sample of firms both in numbers and in their distribution among wider industry classifications. The wage rates and user cost of capital could be improved by obtaining more disaggregate measures of these variables; there is need for constructing the rental price of research and development activities and developing better capital stock measures for research and development at the firm level. It would be useful, if data permit, to classify the firms by industry classification and contrast the interindustry differences in employment, capital accumulation, and research and development expenditures. A test could also be developed to estimate the sensitivity of firms' demand for inputs to changes in aggregate economy variables and to examine more closely the cyclical characteristics of these input demand functions.

Improvement in these directions will be pursued in the near future. For the present, however, it is gratifying to note the methodological integration of research and development expenditure in a unified framework of input decisions of the firm, and the empirical evidence presented here to substantiate the presence of dynamic interaction of input demand functions at the micro level.

Statistical Appendix

The Data and Specification of the Variables

The sample of firms used in this study consists of sixty-two firms mainly from five industries: metal extraction, chemicals and allied products, nonelectrical machinery, electrical equipment and supplies, and instruments. The names and SIC classification of the firms are indicated in table 7.A.1; also indicated are the classifications of these firms by their 1970 asset size. The choice of the sample was somewhat arbitrary; firms with continuous data on research and development expenditures for the period 1965–72 were chosen from the Compustat tapes. Aside from individual firm data, we have compiled data on prices, wage rates, and utilization rates on a two-digit industry basis. Absence of these data at the micro level made use of the industry-level statistics imperative.

The construction of the variables used in model estimations are as follows:

Table 7.A.1   Companies Included in the Samples of Our Experiments

Standard Industrial Classification Number (1)	Names of Companies (2)	Below $300 (M) (3)	From $300 to $1000 (M) (4)	Over $1000 (M) (5)
1000	American Smelting & Refining		X	
1000	Brush Wellman Inc.	X		
1000	Cerro Corp.		X	
1000	Molybdenum of America	X		
1031	St. Joe Minerals Corp.	X		
2801	Allied Chemical			X
2801	American Cyanamid			X
2801	Celanese Corp.			X
2801	Grace (WR) & Co.			X
2801	Hercules Inc.		X	
2801	Monsanto Inc.			X
2801	Union Carbide			X
2802	Diamond Shamrock Corp.		X	
2802	Stauffer Chemical		X	
2803	Akzona		X	
2803	Cabot		X	
2835	Abbot Laboratories		X	
2835	Lilly Eil & Co.		X	
2835	Merck & Co.		X	
2835	Pfizer		X	
2835	Schering Plough		X	
2835	Smith-Kline	X		
2835	Syntex	X		
2835	Upjohn		X	
2835	Warner Lambert			X
2836	Bristol Meyers		X	
2836	Richardson-Merell Inc.		X	
2837	Baxter Laboratories	X		
2837	Becton Dickinson	X		
2844	Nestle Lemur	X		
2899	Ansul Co.	X		
2899	Diversey Corp.	X		
2899	Lubrizol Corp.	X		
3531	FMC Corp.			X
3550	Leesona	X		
3550	McNeil Corp.	X		
3570	Addressograph-Multigraph		X	
3570	Burroughs Corp.			X
3570	National Cash Register			X
3570	Pitney-Bowes Inc.		X	
3570	Xerox Corp.			X
3571	Potter Instrument Co.	X		

Table 7.A.1 (cont.)

Standard Industrial Classification Number (1)	Names of Companies (2)	Companies Classified by Asset Size (1970)		
		Below $300 (M) (3)	From $300 to $1000 (M) (4)	Over $1000 (M) (5)
3573	Memorex Corp.	X		
3573	Systems Engineering Labs	X		
3579	Nashua Corporation	X		
3600	Sperry Rand Corp.			X
3610	Thomas & Betts Corp.	X		
3611	Bourns Inc.	X		
3622	Barnes Engineering	X		
3670	Raytheon Co.		X	
3670	Collins Radio Co.		X	
3679	Mallory (Pa) & Co.	X		
3679	Sprague Electric Co.	X		
3811	Beckman Instruments	X		
3822	Robert Shaw Controls	X		
3825	Hewlett-Packard Co.	X		
3825	Varian Assoc.	X		
3831	Bausch & Lomb Inc.	X		
3831	Perkin Elmer Corp.	X		
3861	Minnesota Mining & Manufacturing			X
3861	Eastman Kodak			X
Number of Companies: 62		28	20	14

$A_t =$ total assets of the firm taken from Compustat tapes deflated by the deflator for fixed investment series in *Survey of Current Business*, various issues.

$R =$ the stock of research and development expenditures of the individual firms. This variable was generated by the recursive formula

$$R_t = RD_t + (1 - \delta')R_{t-1},$$

where RD_t is the research and development expenditure of individual firms, and R_{t-1} is the previous stock of research and development expenditures; δ' is assumed to be .10 for each firm.

$L_t =$ number of company employees in thousands from Compustat tapes.

$K_t =$ individual capital stock of the firm generated using perpetual inventory method. The recursive formula to generate capital stock series for each firm is

$$K_{it} = I_{it} + (1 - \delta_i)K_{it-1}.$$

$\delta_i =$ the depreciation rate as calculated by (depreciation expenses)/gross plant given on each firm's balance sheet in the benchmark year. The benchmark capital stock K_t is the deflated value of net plant for most firms in 1953. The deflator is the general fixed investment price deflator (P_k). For some firms where data on net plants for 1953 were not available, we used the earliest available figures. Investment series were taken from each firm's balance sheets and deflated by P_k.

$Q_t =$ the output variable defined as

$$S/P + [I/P - (I_{t-1}/P_{t-1})];$$

S is the net sales for individual firms, obtained from Compustat tapes, and P is the wholesale price index for the relevant two-digit industry reported in various issues of *SCB*. I refers to inventories of individual firms; its values were obtained from Compustat tapes.

$w_t =$ average hourly earnings of production workers of relevant two-digit industries taken from *BLS, U.S. Employment and Earnings, 1909–1971*, and *Monthly Labor Statistics, 1972 and 1973*. These figures were deflated by the corresponding wholesale price index given in various issues of *Survey of Current Business*.

$c_t =$ the user cost of capital divided by the relevant wholesale price index at the two-digit industry level. It was assumed that the nominal value of the user cost of capital is the same for each firm within and across industries. The user cost variable was generated as follows:

$$c = \frac{P_k(r + \delta)(1 - \bar{k} - zv + zk'v)}{(1 - v)},$$

where P_k is the price of investment goods, the data of which are the implicit GNP price deflator for fixed investment series in the *Survey of Current Business*; r is the *real* rate of interest, defined as $r = i - (\dot{P}/P)^e$, where i is the discount rate, the data of which are the nominal quarterly interest rates on Moody's Aaa Bonds, and $(\dot{P}/P)^e$ is the expected inflation rate calculated as the weighted average of changes in the implicit GNP price deflator for fixed investment series, with weights taken from Robert J. Gordon, "Inflation in Recession and Recovery," *Brookings Papers on Economic Activity* 1 (1971):148; $\bar{k}$ is the effective rate of quarterly investment credit, set to be .055 per quarter following Charles W. Bischoff, *Brookings Papers on Economic Activity*, 3(1971):735–753; k' is the tax credit allowance under the Long Amendment that required firms to subtract their total tax credit from the depreciation base, the value of k' being equal to that of $\bar{k}$ (.055) when the Amendment was in force and equal to zero for other time periods; v is the corporate income tax rate; and z is the present value of the depreciation deduction, the data of which have been constructed according to Nadiri, "An Alternative Model of Business Investment Spending," *Brookings Paper on Economic Activity* 3(1972):576.

$U_t =$ the Wharton index of utilization rate for the five two-digit industries.

References

Baily, M. N. 1972. Research and development costs and returns: the U.S. pharmaceutical industry. *Journal of Political Economy* 80:70–85.

Bischoff, W. 1971. *Brookings Papers on Economic Activity* 3:735–753.

Brainard, W., and Tobin, J. 1968. Pitfalls in financial model building. *American Economic Review* 58:99–122.

Branch, B. 1973. Research and development and its relation to sales growth. *Journal of Economic Business* 25:107–11.

Gordon, J. 1971. Inflation in recession and recovery. *Brookings Papers on Economic Activity* 1:148, Table A–1.

Grabowski, H. G. 1968. The determinants of industrial research and development: a study of chemical, drug, and petroleum industries. *Journal of Political Economy* 76:292–306.

Kamien, M. I., and Schwartz, N. L. 1971. Expenditure patterns for Risky R & D projects. *Journal of Applied Problems* 8:60–73.

———. 1974. Risky R & D with rivalry. *Annals of Economic and Social Measurement* 3:267–77.

————. 1975. Market structure and innovations: a survey. *Journal of Economic Literature* 13:1–37.

Kuh, E. 1963. *Capital stock growth: a micro econometric approach.* Amsterdam: North-Holland.

Maddala, G. S. 1971. The use of variance components methods in pooling, cross section, and time series data. *Econometrica* 39:341–57.

Mansfield, E. 1968. *The economics of technical change.* New York: Norton.

Mansfield, E.; Rapoport, J.; Schnee, J.; Wagner, S.; and Hamburger, M. J. 1971. *Research and innovation in the modern corporation.* New York: Norton.

Nadiri, M. I. 1972. An alternative model of business investment spending. *Brookings Papers on Economic Activity* 3:576.

Nadiri, M. I., and Rosen, S. 1969. Interrelated factor demand functions. *American Economic Review* 26:457–71.

————. 1973. *A disequilibrium model of demand for factors of production.* New York: National Bureau of Economic Research.

Nerlove, M. 1967. Notes on the production and derived demand relations included in macro-econometric models. *International Economic Review* 8:223–42.

Scherer, F. M. 1965. Firm size, market structure, opportunity, and output of patented inventions. *American Economic Review* 55:1097–1125.

Sims, C. A. 1974. Output and labor input in manufacturing. *Brookings Papers on Economic Activity* 3:695–736.

Standard & Poors Corporation. 1972. *Compustat tapes.* New York: Standard and Poors Corporation.

United States Department of Commerce. *Survey of Current Business,* various issues.

United States Department of Labor. 1965. *Earnings and employment for the U.S., 1909–65.* Washington: Government Printing Office.

————. *Monthly Labor Bulletin,* various issues.

Comment   Richard C. Levin

Nadiri and Bitros provide an interesting new approach to the analysis of research and development and productivity growth at the firm level. There exists a considerable literature on the determinants of R and D expenditures, with particular emphasis on firm size and industry characteristics such as concentration and technological opportunities. Several studies, including the Griliches and Terleckyj pieces in this volume, have

Richard C. Levin is at Yale University.

focused on measuring the long-run returns to R and D. We also have bodies of literature concerned with the diffusion of innovations, the effects of uncertainty on research strategies, and the role of public policy in the area of R and D. Nowhere to my knowledge, however, has there been an explicit focus upon the short-run disequilibrium dynamics of R and D expenditure, embedded in a general dynamic model of input and D expenditures using an arbitrarily assumed 10% annual depreciation rate.

Nadiri and Bitros put forth a model of input demand which permits them to analyze a variety of issues:

1. They examine the short-run effects of changes in output and relative factor prices on the demand for capital, labor, and R and D activities.

2. They estimate the effects of excess demand for each of the inputs on the demand for other inputs.

3. By stratifying their sample of firms by asset sizes they are able to test whether firm size affects the pattern of input demands and dynamic interactions. In this way Nadiri and Bitros touch base with the literature on the relationship between firm size and innovative activity.

4. Finally, the authors derive from the estimated parameters of their model the effects of R and D on labor productivity in the short, intermediate, and long runs.

The dynamic model introduced in this paper is an extension of Professor Nadiri's earlier work on disequilibrium models of factor demand (Nadiri and Rosen 1973). The present paper is an extension in the sense that R and D is included as a factor of production, but it is a simplification of the earlier work of Nadiri and Rosen insofar as only stocks of inputs and the utilization rate of capital are incorporated into the production function, and not the utilization rates for each factor. Essentially, the model is a generalization of the familiar partial adjustment approach to modeling disequilibrium:

$$(1) \qquad Y_{1t} - Y_{1t-1} = \beta(Y^*_1 - Y_{1t-1}),$$

where Y^*_1 is the desired level of factor Y_1 and β the adjustment coefficient.

Nadiri and Bitros generalize this model so that each period's change in the demand for a single input reflects the deviation of actual from desired stocks for all the inputs. Thus, for the two-input case,

$$(2) \qquad Y_{1t} - Y_{1t-1} = \beta_{11}(Y^*_1 - Y_{1t-1})$$
$$+ \beta_{12}(Y^*_2 - Y_{2t-1}).$$
$$Y_{2t} - Y_{2t-1} = \beta_{21}(Y^*_1 - Y_{1t-1})$$
$$+ \beta_{22}(Y^*_2 - Y_{2t-1}),$$

If the values of the adjustment coefficients are unconstrained, one of two additional hypotheses is needed to close the model: (1) firms may be assumed to remain on the production function during the adjustment period, in which case it is implied that output is endogenous; (2) alternatively, if output is assumed to be exogenous, independent input adjustments imply that firms need not be on the production function. Indeed, firms may be inside or outside of the production surface, depending on the values of the β's.

The first hypothesis seems appealing: that disequilibrium in factor markets implies that firms fail to produce along their optimal expansion paths. It seems quite reasonable to assume that output decisions are constrained by input disequilibria. Nadiri and Bitros note that there is a third alternative which permits output to remain exogenous *and* firms to be on the production function. This approach implies severe restrictions on the adjustment coefficients. To illustrate, if output is exogenous a firm will move from output X_1 to X_2 in a certain time period (see fig. 7.C.1). If the production function constraint holds as an equality, then the firm must use a combination of inputs on the isoquant X_2. If the desired input combination is at point B, excess demand in the market for one factor will necessarily imply overshooting the target level of the other factor. In a model with several factors of production, at least one must overshoot its target level to compensate for excess demand elsewhere.

This implied hypothesis of overshooting target values of one or more inputs had considerably more intuitive appeal in the earlier work of Nadiri and Rosen than it does here. In Nadiri and Rosen (1973), utilization rates of each input entered directly (if perhaps too independently) into the production function. It seems quite reasonable to assume that excess demand for capital or labor would lead to an overshooting of target values of utilization rates, but it is not quite so obvious that stocks would overshoot in the same way. In the present paper, only the utilization rate of capital enters into the production function.

Nadiri and Bitros complete the model by substituting for the Y^* terms in the adjustment equations an approximation to the factor demand functions derived from a Cobb-Douglas production function. Embedded in the coefficients of the resulting system of equations are the estimated values of the adjustment coefficients, and the elasticities of each input with respect to factor prices and output.

The model is estimated on pooled cross-section and time series data on 62 firms for the period 1965–72. The limitations of the data are, as usual, serious. Wage rates at the two-digit industry level are used to represent the user cost of both labor *and* R and D. The utilization rate is also an industry figure, rather than firm-specific. The output variable was constructed by deflating firm revenues by the wholesale price index

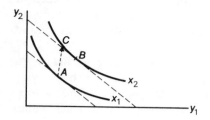

Fig. 7.C.1   Interactions among Time Paths of Inputs

of the appropriate two-digit industry. Total employment is used for the labor stock variable, which implies that R and D employees are counted twice. The R and D stock variable is constructed from cumulative R and D expenditures using an arbitrarily assumed 10% of annual depreciation rate.

Despite the limitations of the data, Nadiri and Bitros obtain a remarkably good fit of their model with generalized least-squares estimation. I shall briefly summarize the results, quibbling with a few of their interpretations along the way, before I conclude by expressing some more fundamental worries about their overall approach.

1. Nadiri and Bitros find that all inputs respond significantly to short-run changes in output—the output elasticity of labor being highest, that of R and D lowest, and that of capital in between. Employment and R and D respond significantly to short-run changes in relative factor prices, but not capital or the utilization rate. This pattern of responsiveness to factor prices in the short run is inconclusive, given the poor quality of the price data.

2. The own adjustment coefficients are all statistically significant and have the correct signs; the magnitudes suggest that employment adjusts most rapidly, followed by R and D and capital. The utilization rate adjusts more slowly than expected, but this is doubtless a consequence of using an industry-wide measure of utilization instead of a firm-specific measure.

3. When the sample is stratified by asset size into three groups, Nadiri and Bitros are able to reject the null hypothesis of an unchanging structure of input demands. Thus we have one more piece of evidence to add to the endless debate on the so-called Schumpeterian hypothesis —which we all know by now is not really a Schumpeterian hypothesis— namely, that large firms do more R and D.

4. In the final section Nadiri and Bitros calculate the long-run output elasticities of the inputs from the coefficients of their estimated equations. These results are presented in a most confusing manner, since the authors do not report the output elasticity of each input separately, but

rather they report the *sum* of the elasticities of the inputs for each of the equations. These results suggest constant or increasing returns to scale. It would be useful to have separate calculations of the output elasticity of each input.

5. Finally, the authors calculate what they interpret as the short, intermediate, and long-run responses of labor productivity by varying in turn labor alone, then labor and R and D, and finally all factors. The meaning of this conceptual experiment is not entirely clear within the context of their model, which after all requires that all inputs must vary in the short and intermediate runs. It would seem instead that if the authors were interested in the returns to R and D they would examine the long-run elasticity of output with respect to R and D, which is a way of capturing how changes in R and D affect the productivity of the conventional inputs. This elasticity can be converted, with the appropriate caveats mentioned by Professor Griliches in his paper, into a kind of crude average rate of return on R and D.

I would like to close with a more fundamental criticism of the paper. I have some difficulty in grasping the connection between the model proposed by Nadiri and Bitros and the estimation techniques they employ. In the version of the paper presented at the conference, the authors held to the pair of assumptions noted above: that firms are on the production function and that output is exogenous. They failed, however, to impose the appropriate restrictions on the β_{ij}, the own and cross-adjustment coefficients. In an effort to remedy this deficiency, the authors have chosen to leave the adjustment coefficients unconstrained and to treat output as endogenous. But merely asserting that output is endogenous and running two-stage least-squares does not get them out of the woods. Several problems remain:

1. If output is assumed to be endogenous, the behavioral assumption of cost minimization given output is no longer appropriate. Presumably, this assumption would be replaced by profit maximization subject to the production function constraint, but this will introduce product price as an exogenous variable.

2. If output is endogenous and product price enters the model, it is not obvious without further argument that the inferences made from the estimates about the parameters of the production function and the adjustment equations will hold.

3. Since the estimated equations are neither the structural nor the reduced form, it is not clear that the error terms are appropriately specified. If stochastic terms enter the structural equations in a simple linear or multiplicative fashion, they will not enter linearly and independently in the equations estimated.

4. Even if the appropriate reduced-form equations were derived, the assumption that firms are on the production function suggests that the

error terms will not be independent across equations. Joint estimation imposing the appropriate restrictions would still be warranted.

While these problems are serious, they are in principle remediable. Despite these objections, this is a very interesting paper and an important further step toward building disequilibrium dynamics into the theory of the firm. I hope the authors will further pursue this line of inquiry, with a richer data base if possible, using a more fully specified model and appropriate joint estimation techniques.

Reference

Nadiri, M. Ishaq, and Rosen, Sherwin. 1973. *A disequilibrium model of demand for factors of production.* New York: National Bureau of Economic Research.

8 Returns to Research and Development Expenditures in the Private Sector

Zvi Griliches

8.1 Introduction

In late 1965, the Bureau of the Census and the Office of Manpower Studies of the National Science Foundation asked me to consider a project to analyze the available historical data on company research and development expenditures together with other data for the same companies collected in different Census inquiries. During 1966–67, a plan of work was outlined, cut down to size, and agreed upon. The Census undertook to develop a company record, edited for consistency, to produce regressions and related outputs free of disclosures for individual companies, and to pass on the reasonableness of the various series employed. Only Census employees were to have (and have had) access to individual company data, and the treatment of outliers was in accordance with the usual criteria employed by the Census. The process of matching the same companies in different data sets and over time turned out to be quite a difficult and time-consuming task. Because the results were slow in coming, and in the context of severe budgetary cuts, the Office of Manpower Studies of the NSF bowed out as a direct partner in this study in 1968. The rest of the financing for this project

Zvi Griliches is at Harvard University.

A large number of people were essential and helpful in initiating and carrying through this work. I am grateful to, among many others, Max Conklin, Owen Gretton, L. Jack Owen, Walter Heller, Milton Eisen, and Ruth Rynyan at the Bureau of the Census; to Thomas Hogan, Pat Riley, Ken Sanow, and James Blackman at the National Science Foundation; and to Paul Ryan, Ruth Helpman, and Bronwyn Hall at Harvard University, for help, encouragement, and research assistance. I am indebted to the National Science Foundation for the financial support of this project both through the budget of the Office of Economic and Manpower Studies and through grants no. G–1812, GS–712, GS–2762X, GS–39865X, and SOC 73–05374–A01.

still came from the National Science Foundation, but in the form of a direct research grant to me rather than as a continuation of the in-house research partnership. The funding crisis and other workload pressures on the Census delayed the completion of the data match until 1970. During this long gestation period the project was greatly reduced in scope by abandoning the idea of extending the match to such additional company data sources as the IRS and Compustat tapes and by limiting the number and range of variables to be included in the final data base. First regression results for a restricted set of equations and variables became available in early 1971, and final corrected runs were delivered in 1972. This is the first report based on the results of this project. I am solely responsible for the interpretation and analysis of the results and for the delay since mid-1972.

The original universe of this study consists of large (1000-plus employees) R and D–performing U.S. manufacturing companies. There were 1,154 such companies in 1964. Our final sample is based on data for 883 such companies, accounting for about 90% of total sales and over 92% of total R and D expenditures of all firms in this universe (see table 8.1 for more detail). Since large firms account for most of the reported R and D expenditures in industry, our sample accounted for 91% of all the R and D performed in industry in 1963 including the R and D performed outside our universe of large companies. Thus, in spite of quite a few companies for which some or many of the data are missing, the coverage of our sample is rather complete, especially in comparison to other micro-data sets of this kind.

The data base consists of individual company time series on research and development expenditures (company-financed and total), on the number of research scientists and engineers, and on total company employment and sales—all based on the 1957–65 annual NSF–Census R and D surveys—and of additional company data on value added, assets, depreciation, and other economic magnitudes, based on the match with the 1958 and 1963 Census of Manufactures and Enterprise statistics. Because of problems of handling confidential data I received only matrices of correlation coefficients and standard deviations for the various variables in the data base, broken down into six rather broad industry groupings, and never had access to the actual individual observations. The restriction of this study to variables contained in the original data sets and the associated inability to add such things as prices, stock valuations, or concentration ratios, the availability of data only in the form of moment matrices, the relative shortness of the available time series, and the lack of detailed industrial breakdown, all severely limit the range of questions that can be asked and largely predetermine the feasible modes of analysis.

Table 8.1 Sample Coverage in 1963: R and D–Performing Companies with 1,000 or More Employees

SIC Industry	Number of Companies			Total Sales (billions of dollars)			Total R and D Expenditures (millions of dollars)		
	Population	Sample	Coverage Ratio	Population	Sample	Coverage Ratio	Population	Sample	Coverage Ratio
1. 28, 29, 13: Chemicals and petroleum	134	110	.82	52.6	48.4	.92	1,556	1,294	.83
2. 34, 35: Fabricated metal products and machinery	257	187	.73	32.1	23.7	.74	1,111	958	.86
3. 34, 48: Electrical and communication equipment	134	102	.76	28.2	23.2	.82	2,866	2,579	.90
4. 371, 373–9: Motor vehicles and other transport equipment	55	34	.62	32.0	29.6	.92	1,090	1,062	.97
5. 372, 19: Aircraft and missiles	53	31	.58	17.4	16.8	.97	4,712	4,619	.98
6. All others	521	419	.80	97.8	90.5	.93	1,137	922	.81
Total	1,154	883	.77	260.1	232.2	.89	12,472	11,434	.92

SOURCE: Unpublished census tabulations.

When this study was initiated in the mid 1960s, my own interests centered on sources of productivity growth and on estimating the contribution of nonmarket factors to growth using production function models and econometric estimation techniques. The study reported below bears the marks of this interest. It focuses on estimating the coefficient of cumulated R and D expenditures in company-level production functions or its equivalent in company productivity growth equations. Because the data are for individual companies, this study can explore only the magnitude of *private* returns to such expenditures. It cannot deal with the very important issue of externalities—returns that accrue to other firms and to society at large and are not captured by the original investors. In a later report I shall try to deal with this problem by comparing the estimates presented here with those derivable from aggregate industry and economy-wide time series. Here we'll limit ourselves, however, to what direct information can be gleaned from the data at hand.

The next section of this paper outlines the theoretical model used and the statistical problems associated with its estimation. The variables used in this study are described in section 8.3 and the main results are summarized in section 8.4. Section 8.5 digresses to consider the relation of R and D to firm size. Concluding remarks are contained in section 8.6, while more detail on the matching process and data construction can be found in the Appendix.

8.2 Models and Problems

Both the theoretical and empirical literature on the relationship between research and productivity have been reviewed recently by several authors (cf. Griliches 1973, 1974; Mansfield 1967, 1972; and Nordhaus 1969, among others) and we shall not go over the same ground again here except to present the simplest possible model of this process which will serve as the framework of our estimation efforts below.

This model, which is common to most analyses of the contribution of research to productivity growth, can be summarized along the following lines:

(1) $Q = TF(C,L)$,

(2) $T = G(K,O)$,

(3) $K = \Sigma w_i R_{t-i}$,

where Q is output (sales, or value added), C and L are measures of capital and labor input, respectively, T is the current level of (average) technological accomplishment (total factor productivity), K is a measure of the accumulated and still productive (social or private) research capital ("knowledge"), O represents other forces affecting productivity,

R_t measures the real gross investment in research in period t, and the w_i's connect the levels of past research to the current state of knowledge.[1]

For estimation purposes, the F and G functions are usually specialized to the Cobb-Douglas form and O is approximated by an exponential trend. The whole model then simplifies to

$$(4) \qquad Q_t = A e^{\lambda t} K^{\alpha}_t C^{\beta}_t L^{1-\beta}_t,$$

where A is constant, λ is the rate of disembodied "external" technical change, and constant returns to scale have been assumed with respect to the conventional inputs (C and L). Equations like this have been estimated by Griliches (1964) from several agricultural cross-sections, and by Evenson (1968) and Minasian (1969) from combinations of time series and cross-section data for agricultural regions and chemical firms, respectively. Alternatively, if one differentiates the above expression with respect to time and assumes that conventional inputs are paid their marginal products, one can rewrite it as

$$(5) \qquad f = q - \hat{\beta} c - (1 - \hat{\beta}) l = \lambda + \alpha k,$$

where f is the rate of growth of total factor productivity, lower-case letters represent relative rates of growth of their respective upper-case counterparts $[x = \dot{X}/X = (dX/dt)/X]$, and $\hat{\beta}$ is the estimated factor share of capital input.[2] Equation (5) is a constrained version of (4). Versions of such an equation were estimated by Evenson (1968) for agriculture and by Mansfield (1965) for manufacturing industries, among others. In either form, the estimates of α have tended to cluster around .05 for public research investments in agriculture (Evenson and Griliches) and around .1 for private research investments in selected manufacturing industries (Mansfield, Minasian, and Terleckyj).

Up to now I have been deliberately vague as to the operational construction of the various variables. The difficulties here are myriad. Perhaps the two most important problems are the measurement of output (Q) in a research-intensive industry (where quality changes may be rampant), and the construction of the unobservable research capital measure (K). Postponing the first for later consideration, we note that $K_t = \Sigma w_i R_{t-i}$ can be thought of as a measure of the distributed lag effect of past research investments on productivity. There are

1. Note that in writing equations (1) and (2) in this fashion we have implicitly assumed the separability and ultimate neutrality of the research process from the production process. Since theoretical generalization is cheap, we could have extended the model to make the coefficients of C and L also dependent on K, but our data could not sustain such complications.

2. To the extent that research inputs are included among the conventional input measures, they have already been imputed the average private rate of return.

at least three forces at work here: the lag between investment in research and the actual invention of a new technique or product, the lag between invention and the development and complete market acceptance of the new technique or product, and the disappearance of this technique or product from the currently utilized stock of knowledge due to changes in external circumstances and the development of superior techniques or products by competitors (depreciation and obsolescence). These lags have been largely ignored by most of the investigators. The most common assumption has been one of no or little lag and no depreciation. Thus, Griliches and Minasian have defined $K_t = \Sigma R_{t-i}$ with the summation running over the available range of data, while Mansfield assumed that since R has been growing at a rather rapid rate, so also has K (i.e., $\dot{K}/K \approx \dot{R}/R$). Evenson (1968) has been the only one to investigate this question econometrically, finding that in the aggregate data for U.S. agriculture, an "inverted V" distributed lag form fitted best, with the peak influence coming with a lag of five to eight years and the total effect dying out in about ten to sixteen years. There is some scattered evidence, based largely on questionnaire studies (see Wagner 1968), that such lags are much shorter in industry, where most of research expenditures are spent on development and applied topics.[3]

Because of the difficulties in constructing an unambiguous measure of K, many studies have opted for an alternative version of equation (5), utilizing the fact that

$$\alpha = \frac{dQ}{dK}\frac{K}{Q}$$

and

$$\alpha k = \frac{dQ}{dK}\frac{K}{Q}\frac{\dot{K}}{K} = \frac{dQ}{dK}\frac{K}{Q},$$

allowing one to rewrite (5) as

(5') $$f = \lambda + \alpha k = \lambda + \rho I_R/Q,$$

where ρ is the rate of return to research expenditures (the marginal product of K) while I_R/Q is the net investment in research as a ratio to total output. In practice, to make some connection between gross and net investment in research one needs information about its "depreciation" which, if available, would have allowed us to construct a measure of K in the first place.

While our models are written as if the main point of research expenditures is to increase the physical productivity of the firm's production

3. In the U.S. about three-fourths of all expenditures on R and D in industry have been spent on development and most of the rest on "applied research." Only about 5% of the total R and D expenditure has gone to "basic" research. Thus, one should not expect long lags *on the average*.

process, most of the actual research in industry is devoted to the development of new products or processes to be sold and used outside the firm in question. Assuming that, on average, the outside world pays for these products what they are worth to it, using sales or value added as our dependent variable does in fact capture the private returns to such research endeavors. However, the observed private returns may underestimate the social returns because, given the competitive structure of the particular industry, the market price of the new product or process will be significantly below what consumers might have been willing to pay for it. On the other hand, part of the increase in sales of an individual firm may come at the expense of other firms and not as the result of the expansion of the market as a whole. Also, some of the increase in prices paid for a particular new product may come from changes in the market power of a particular firm induced by the success of the research program. Moreover, some of the gains in productivity or in the sales of new products may be based on the research results of other firms in the same or some other industry. Such factors could result in the observed private returns overestimating the social returns significantly. We cannot say much about the net impact of such forces on the basis of the data at hand. It requires a detailed comparison of the individual firm results with estimates based on industry and economy-wide returns to research, a topic beyond the scope of this paper. But since expected private returns are presumably a determinant of private investment flows into this activity, the estimates presented below may be of some interest even if they cannot answer the social-returns question unequivocally.

Another important problem arises as soon as we write down a system of equations, such as (1)–(3), a problem that will stay with us throughout this paper. Ideally, we would like to distinguish between capital and labor used to produce current "output" and capital and labor used in research (the production of future knowledge and the maintenance of the current stock). In fact, we are usually unable to observe these different input components and are forced to use totals for C and L in our investigations. This leads to a misspecification of equation (4) or (5). Moreover, if components of L and C are weighted in proportion to their current returns, the resulting estimates of the contribution of K (or R) represent, errors in timing apart, excess returns above and beyond the "normal" remuneration of such factors of production.

Given the limited range of our time series, we decided early on a *two*-pronged research strategy: (*a*) Concentrate on estimating versions of equation (5) based on average *rates of growth* for the whole 1957–65 period. (*b*) Estimate equation (4) based on the 1963 cross-section levels. Equation (5) has the advantage that, dealing with rates of growth, one essentially differences out permanent efficiency differences across firms and does not allow them to influence the final results. Equation (4) has the advantage that it does *not* ignore the cross-sectional differences in levels, which are a major source of variance in the data and of intrinsic interest themselves. Given our limited data base, additional compromises had to be made in the definition and the choice of variables which are best discussed after we describe, in the next section, the available data and the variables constructed from them.

8.3   Data, Variables, and Caveats

Table 8.1 gives some detail on our sample and its coverage. We have data on 883 large R and D–performing companies, divided into six industrial groupings.[4] Unfortunately, the industrial groupings are rather coarse and the number of companies in some of them is rather small, especially in the motor vehicles and aircraft and missiles groups. Most of our attention will be devoted, therefore, to the combined total industry results, though, for comparison purposes, we will also present the individual industry group results and comment on them.

Our data base was limited to the short list of the R and D survey variables on the matched historical R and D tapes (i.e., R and D expenditures—company and total, sales, total employment, and the employment of scientists and engineers) and the limited number of variables that could be matched to them from the 1958 and 1963 Census of Manufacturers and Enterprise Statistics schedules. Moreover, since the original data could not be released except in the form of moment matrices for selected variables, an irreversible decision had to be made about the choice and functional form of the variables to be included in them. The choice was guided by the following research strategy decision: Given the fact that we have only relatively short time series at hand and assuming that much of the individual annual fluctuations in these series are of a transitory nature, our analysis will concentrate on *two* dimensions of these data—average *rates of growth* over the whole observation period (1957–65) and *levels* in 1963.

Thus, a major subset of the variables included in this study are *rates of growth* computed from regressions of the natural logarithms of the annual observations in the historical R and D tapes on a time-trend. They are the estimated slope coefficients (b's) from $\ln X = a + bt$ type equations, fitted to the whole 1957–65 period or to the sub-period of available data, provided that four or more years of data were available to compute such time-trend regressions.

4. See Appendices B and C for details on the criteria for inclusion of companies in the sample and the methods of imputation for missing data. The Standard Industrial Classification code of a company is determined by its main activity, and its entire research and development operations are classified in that industry.

Appendix table 8.A.1 lists the sixty variables for which moment matrices were released by the Census Bureau. These variables can be divided roughly into the following sets: (1) potential dependent variables; (2) various measures of R and D growth and intensity; (3) measures of physical capital and its age composition; (4) measures of total company employment; (5) quality of data measures; (6) other background variables. In what follows we shall discuss only the variables used intensively in this study.

The major dependent variable used in the growth rates section of this study is BPT (number 41 in table 8.A.1), or partial productivity growth, computed as the difference between the estimated rate of growth of total company sales in 1957–65 (31. BS) and the product of the rate of growth of total company employment (32. BE) and the average share of labor (total payroll) in sales (12. ALSS), in 1958 and 1963. That is, BPT = BS — ALSS · BE is a partial approximation to equation (5) with βc taken to the right-hand side:

$$(5'')\qquad q - (1-\beta)\, l \approx \text{BPT} \approx \lambda + \alpha k + \beta c + u,$$

where ALSS is an approximation to $(1-\beta)$, λ is the average exogenous rate of productivity growth, c is the rate of growth of physical capital, and u is a catchall mnemonic for all other systematic and random factors affecting productivity. Because we have no explicit measure of the growth of company physical capital, we could not construct an explicit total factor productivity measure (f) and use the direct version of equation (5). The procedure of using each individual firm's labor share as an approximation to its output-labor elasticity has the virtue of allowing this elasticity to differ across firms, adjusting thereby for rather wide differences in vertical integration across firms.

The missing company rate of growth of physical capital is approximated by two variables: the ratio of accumulated depreciation to the total stock of physical capital in 1963 (6. Age C = [gross fixed assets — net fixed assets]/gross fixed assets) and the depreciation rate (7. D = depreciation charged in 1963/gross fixed assets in 1963). These two proxy variables (Age C and D) taken together should approximate rather well the unobserved true rate of growth of fixed capital, assuming that it remained reasonably constant over the period in question. Moreover, it can be shown that the estimated coefficient of D should be on the order of β, the elasticity of output with respect to physical capital.[5]

---

5. Let g be the rate of growth of fixed investment and d its depreciation rate. If g has been approximately constant and d can be taken as (or approximated by) a fixed declining balance scheme, then

$$\text{Age } C = \frac{\text{Gross Stock} - \text{Net Stock}}{\text{Gross Stock}} = 1 - \frac{g}{g+d-dg} \approx \frac{d}{g+d}.$$

Our major measure of the growth in research capital (k) is the estimated rate of growth in total company expenditures on research and development during 1957–65 (34. BTRD). Note that we are approximating the rate of growth in the *stock* of research capital by the rate of growth in gross *investment* in this type of activity. For variables whose initial level is rather low while the rate of growth of investments is rather high, the assumption of proportionality in these rates of growth ($\dot{K}/K \approx \dot{R}/R$) is not a bad one (cf. Mansfield 1965).[6] Other measures of R and D growth include the rate of growth in company-financed (excluding federally supported) R and D expenditures (35. BCRD) and the rate of growth in the *number* of scientists and engineers engaged in research and development (33. BSE). In addition we also use, in various contexts, the average total R and D to sales ratio (28. AR/S, average of 1958 and 1962) as a measure of research intensity, the ratio of company funds to total cumulated R and D expenditures during

---

Fluctuations in Age C can then be approximated by a second-order Taylor expansion as

$$\text{Age } C \approx \overline{d/(g+d)} - \overline{d/(g+d)} \cdot g + \overline{g/(g+d)} \cdot d,$$

where bars indicate an evaluation at the mean levels of these variables. Now, in the function we need βg, where β is the elasticity of output with respect to fixed capital. Substituting a_1 Age $C + a_2 d$ for it, and ignoring constants, we get:

$$a_1 = -\beta \frac{(g+d)^2}{d} \text{ and } a_2 = \beta \bar{g}/\bar{d}.$$

Since $g/d \approx 1$, the estimated coefficient of d should be close to β, while the estimated coefficient of Age C (a_1) should be on the order of a quarter of β (assuming $g \approx d \approx .06$). Note that this construction made no allowance for differences in capital utilization among firms or overtime. The available data base contains no information on this topic.

6. Assume no depreciation and let research expenditures R grow at a constant rate ρ. Then the rate of growth of K, say, g, is given by

$$g_t = R_t/K_{t-1} = R_o (1+\rho)^t / \sum R_{t-1-i}$$
$$= R_o (1+\rho)^t / R_o \sum (1+\rho)^{t-1-i}$$
$$= (1+\rho) / \sum [1/(1+\rho)]^i$$
$$= (1+\rho)/1/[1 - 1/(1+\rho)] = \rho.$$

Allowing for depreciation and a variable past would make ρ an underestimate or an overestimate of g depending on whether K_o, the level of accumulated stock at the beginning of the period, was relatively small or large. For total U.S. industry during this period (1957–65), taking initial level estimates for 1948 from Kendrick (1973), extrapolating the NSF figures back from 1953 to 1948, and assuming a depreciation rate of 10% per year, gives a g of .10 instead of the observed ρ of about .07, or a 30% underestimate of g when using ρ. However, an allowance for the rising relative costs of research (deflation of these figures) would bring the two together rather closely.

1957–62 (24. FP62) as a measure of the composition of R and D funds, and the logarithm of total cumulated R and D expenditures over the 1957–62 period (54. LGK62) and the logarithm of the average number of research scientists and engineers during 1957–62 (53. LGANSE) as measures of the absolute size of the company research endeavor.

In the level regressions, the main dependent variable is the logarithm of value added in 1963 (51. LGVA63) and the main independent variables are a measure of capital services in 1963 (46. LGC2 = the logarithm of the sum of depreciation plus rentals plus 8% of net fixed assets and inventories), employment in the manufacturing establishments of the company (47. LGEM63), and the previously described cumulated R and D variable (54. LGK62). Among other variables used we should note the company's (five-digit) specialization ratio in 1963 (18. SPR 63), the fraction of the total company labor force that is employed in establishments classified as manufacturing in 1963 (11. M), and several "quality of data" variables: a dummy variable for no imputations (42. DNI), and the standard errors for the computed trend growth rates for sales (36. SBS) and for total R and D (37. SBTRD). A number of other variables are used occasionally, especially as instruments in the context of allowing for simultaneity. They will be identified as we go along. Of some intrinsic interest, however, is an estimate of the overall company profitability rate in 1963 (20. NRR), computed as value added in 1963 minus total manufacturing payroll, minus equipment rentals, and minus depreciation, all divided by net fixed assets plus inventories.

As these variables are introduced and described, several problems and difficulties immediately come to mind. First, note that in the growth-rate equations the basic data are for the company as a whole and not just for its manufacturing component, and that the dependent variable is based on the growth of sales rather than of value added. In the level equations we try to stick to the manufacturing portion of these companies, but the division of the labor force into these components is far from perfect and no separate data were available on fixed assets for the manufacturing establishments only. All of the variables except employment and the various ratio variables are in undeflated current or historical prices. Since we have no explicit information about the specific product mix of the various companies we could, at best, construct only industry-wide deflators. But then all companies within an industry would be treated alike and additively (given our largely linear-in-the-logarithms framework), affecting only the constants in the various equations. Hence, the whole deflation adjustment can be subsumed and allowed for by including separate industry dummy variables (the I's, 1–5) in the overall regressions.

Another major issue is one of lags, timing, and possible simultaneity. In the growth equations we use the growth in R and D over the whole 1957–65 period as an independent variable. On the whole, we believe that we gain more by averaging over a longer period than we lose by introducing a possible simultaneous-equation bias due to contemporaneous correlation between the disturbances in the output and R and D–determining equations. Given our data base, we did not have enough of a history to experiment with fancier lag structures. We shall attempt to check our results below for robustness with respect to the simultaneity problems by (a) using intensity rather than growth measures of R and D, and (b) estimating equation (5″) using instrumental variable methods. Similar problems of interpretation and the possibility of bias arise also in the level equations where our measure of accumulated research capital is the simple unweighted sum of total R and D expenditures for the whole 1957–62 period, allowing for little lag and no depreciation.

To recapitulate, we have to use makeshift proxies for the growth in both physical and research capital. We confound price changes with quantity changes in our productivity measures, and our treatment of lags and simultaneity is both crude and cavalier. Nevertheless, it is about the best that we could do with these data. It is our belief that in spite of their shortcomings and in spite of our many simplifications and dubious assumptions, our data are interesting and rich enough, and the underlying relationships are strong enough, to show through and yield valuable insights into the R and D process and its effects on productivity and growth.

8.4   The Main Results

The relationship between the rate of growth of partial productivity during the 1957–65 period and measures of growth in fixed capital and in R and D is investigated, for the combined sample, in table 8.2. Under the assumption of relatively constant rates of growth of fixed capital, the ratio of (gross − net)/gross stock and the depreciation rate together act as a proxy for the unobserved rate of growth of fixed capital. Each of the regressions includes five industry dummy variables, allowing for separate industry intercepts and for differential rates of price inflation in these industries. In addition to trying out various R and D variables, some of the regressions also include a set of "quality of data" variables: the estimated standard errors of the rate of growth of sales (SBS) and of R and D (SBRD), and a dummy variable signifying a record with no imputations (DNI).

For all firms combined, both the fixed capital and the R and D growth variables are "highly significant" and of the right sign. Total

Table 8.2 **All Industries Combined: Growth Rates 1957–65**
Dependent Variable BPT = BS − ALSS × BE,
Partial Productivity Growth, N = 883

Reg. No.	Age C	D	R and D Variables	LGANSE	Other Variables*	R^2	S.E.
			Coefficients of (standard errors)				
			BTRD				
1	−.069 (.011)	.334 (.077)	.076 (.013)		I's	.105	.0561
2	−.074 (.016)	.350 (.064)	.073 (.011)	−.003 (.001)	I's SBTRD−, DNI−	.113	.0559
3	−.052 (.016)	.286 (.061)	.074 (.010)		I's, SBS+, SBTRD−, DNI−	.402	.0459
			BCRD				
4	−.070 (.019)	.343 (.075)	.063 (.012)		I's	.096	.0564
5	−.054 (.016)	.301 (.061)	.063 (.010)	−.002 (.001)	I's SBS+, SBTRD−, DNI−	.399	.0460
			BSE				
6	−.072 (.019)	.345 (.076)	.087 (.014)		I's	.109	.0560
7	−.055 (.015)	.294 (.061)	.087 (.011)		I's SBS+, SBTRD−, DNI	.409	.0456

*Coefficients that are statistically significant at the conventional .05 level are identified by their respective signs.

Age C	= (gross fixed assets − net fixed assets)/gross fixed assets in 1963
D	= Depreciation rate, depreciation charged in 1963/gross fixed assets in 1963
BS	= Rate of growth of sales, 1957–65
BE	= Rate of growth of employment, 1957–65
BTRD	= Rate of growth of total R and D expenditures, 1957–65
BCRD	= Rate of growth of company R and D expenditures, 1957–65
BSE	= Rate of growth in the employment of scientists and engineers, 1957–65
LGANSE	= Logarithm of the average number of scientists and engineers, 1957–62
SBS	= Standard error of the estimated rate of growth of sales
SBTRD	= Standard error of the estimated rate of growth of total R and D expenditures
DNI	= Dummy variable = 1 when there were "no imputations" in the data
I's	= Industry dummy variables (five)

R and D growth is a somewhat better variable than company R and D growth, while the growth in the number of scientists and engineers is marginally better than either one of the dollar measures. The implied elasticity of output with respect to cumulated R and D is about .07 and there is an indication (in the more detailed results not reported here) of some diminishing returns to the absolute size of the research program (LGANSE) and of a negative impact of variability in it (SBTRD). The overall fit is low and a large fraction of the variance is accounted for by the "quality of data" variables.

Table 8.3 summarizes the results for the individual industry groups. They are roughly similar except that the .07 estimate for the combined cross-section can be seen to be an average of a somewhat higher elasticity (.1) for the research-intensive industries and a somewhat lower coefficient (.04) for the rest (the "other" half of the sample).

A complementary analysis of the problem can be had by looking at the *levels* of productivity and their relationship to the cumulated total of past R and D expenditures (K62). Table 8.4 presents estimates of such 1963 cross-sectional production relationships. They are surprisingly reasonable, and the estimated coefficient of cumulated R and D is rather close to that derived from the time series (growth rates) regressions. At the individual industry level the estimated coefficients are somewhat lower, suggesting that the time series results may be a bit biased upward due to the simultaneity between the growth in research and in sales. But the differences are not statistically significant, as we shall show below. There is no evidence in these data of increasing returns to firm size as such, while both specialization (SPR) and average *plant* (but not firm) size (LSE) are positively related to productivity.

There are interesting consistencies between the estimates given in tables 8.2 and 8.3 and those of table 8.4, though each is based on a very different cut across the data base. We noted before (in footnote 5) that the coefficients of D in table 8.2 are approximate estimates of the physical capital elasticity, and that the coefficients of Age C should be on the order of a quarter of (and of opposite sign to) the coefficients of D. Both estimates are of the right order of magnitude (about .33 and .07, respectively). Moreover, they are not too far from the directly estimated coefficients of log $C2$ in table 8.4, which hover around .4. Similarly, the R and D coefficient is about .07 in the growth equations in table 8.2, and about .06 in the level equations in table 8.4, for all industries combined. Since both the dependent and independent variables are quite different, this consistency reinforces our belief that this is the right order of magnitude for this coefficient.

We can check in greater detail whether the data are mutually consistent by estimating a combined multivariate regression, imposing the pairwise equality of the D and log $C2$ and of the BTRD and log K62 coefficients and testing whether these restrictions are rejected by the

Table 8.3   **Dependent Variable: Partial Productivity Growth BPT = BS − ALSS × BE, 1957–65, by Industry**

	Coefficients of alternative research variables, standard errors of the coefficients, R^2's and standard errors of the regressions (other variables included: Age C, D, SBS, SBTRD, DNI)		
Industry	BTRD	BCRD	BSE
1. Chemicals and petroleum $N = 110$	.093 (.038) .230(.042)	.090 (.038) .229(.042)	.089 (.042) .220(.042)
2. Metals and machinery $N = 187$	.102 (.022) .209(.043)	.087 (.023) .179(.044)	.123 (.023) .237(.042)
3. Electric Equipment $N = 101$	.106 (.030) .405(.040)	.055 (.019) .384(.040)	.093 (.029) .393(.040)
4. Motor vehicles $N = 34$	.126 (.070) .491(.036)	.143 (.055) .543(.034)	.044 (.083) .435(.038)
5. Aircraft $N = 31$	.107 (.077) .229(.042)	.034 (.050) .183(.044)	.250 (.064) .491(.034)
6. Other $N = 419$	.052 (.015) .556(.047)	.051 (.015) .555(.047)	.062 (.016) .559(.047)

See Notes to Table 8.2 for definitions of variables.

sample. Table 8.5 presents the original independent estimates, industry by industry, and the estimated constrained cross-equation coefficients. It also gives the computed chi-square values for the tests of these restrictions. It is clear, at a glance, that except for the two small sample industries (4 and 5), the different estimates are quite close. In no case do the tests reject the hypothesis that the estimates arise from a population having these parameter values in common.

A basic difficulty with the results presented in tables 8.2, 8.3 and 8.5 is the likelihood of simultaneity between the productivity and R and D *growth* measures. One way of guarding against this possibility is to treat BTRD as an endogenous variable and use instrumental variable methods to estimate its coefficient in equation (5″). The results of doing so are given in table 8.6. The instruments used are basically intensity and level variables as of 1957 and 1963, which should be less correlated with the disturbances in the 1957–65 growth equations. On the whole, the results are very encouraging. Except for industries 2 and 6, the TSLS results are similar to the original ones, indicating little simultane-

Table 8.4   **1963 Cross-sectional Production Functions by Industry**
Dependent Variable—Log VA63

Industry	Coefficients of (standard errors)			Other Variables in Regression*	R^2	S.E.
	Log C_2	Log EM	Log K62			
1. Chemicals and petroleum	.381 (.067)	.538 (.097)	.115 (.040)	Age C—, SPR+, DNI, LSE	.893	.391
2. Metals and machinery	.455 (.050)	.282 (.048)	.075 (.022)	Age C, SPR, DNI+, LSE+	.895	.305
3. Electric equipment	.534 (.065)	.439 (.071)	.029 (.020)	Age C, SPR+	.950	.272
4. Motor vehicles	−.048 (.106)	1.067 (.117)	.063 (.042)	Age C, SPR, DNI	.981	.233
5. Aircraft	.176 (.072)	.795 (.090)	.037 (.034)	Age C, SPR, DNI	.987	.173
6. Other	.414 (.028)	.542 (.035)	.045 (.012)	Age C, M—, SPR+, DNI	.920	.299
All industries combined						
a.	.422 (.018)	.435 (.022)	.069 (.009)	I's	.918	.330
b.	.376 (.021)	.527 (.026)	.061 (.008)	I's, Age C—, M—, SPR+, LSE+	.922	.322

ity bias. Only in industry 6 do the TSLS results not yield a significant R and D coefficient. If anything, the overall TSLS results give somewhat higher estimates for the R and D coefficient, indicating that our main problem may not be simultaneity but error (random noise) in the R and D data.

To the extent that the simultaneity problem is the result of too close a contemporaneity of the sales growth and R and D growth variables one could deal with it by either shortening the period over which the R and D growth is estimated or by using intensity variables such as R and D as a percentage of sales, or number of engineers and scientists as a fraction of total employment, instead of the suspect growth rates. While the results of doing so are somewhat more difficult to interpret, on the whole they do support the finding of a significant and apparently nonspurious influence of R and D on productivity growth. For example, in industry 6 (all others) where the instrumental-variables approach did not yield a significant R and D coefficient, if instead of BTRD we use LGK62/LTRD57 we get a significant coefficient on the order of .01 (.004). Assuming a constant rate of growth of R and D between 1957 and 1962, this stock over initial flow variable approximates the rate of growth of R and D times 3 (ignoring constants).[7] Thus, the implied

---

7. If we assume that $R_t = R_{57} (1+\rho)^{t-57}$, then $K62 = \sum\limits^{62} R_t = R_{57} \sum\limits^{5} (1 + \rho)^i$ $= R57 (6 + 15\rho + 20\rho^2 + \ldots)$. Ignoring terms of order ρ^3 and higher and assuming that $\rho \approx .1$ and hence $20\rho^2 \approx 2\rho$, gives

$$\log K62/R57 \approx \log 6 (1 + 17\rho/6 + \ldots)$$
$$\approx \log 6 + \log (1 + 3\rho \ldots)$$
$$\approx \log 6 + 3\rho.$$

The first term goes into the constant, implying that the estimated coefficient of $\log K62/R57$ should be multiplied by about 3 to convert it into a coefficient of ρ.

---

*Coefficients that are statistically significant at the conventional .05 level are identified by their respective signs.

VA 63   = Value added in 1963

C_2 = Capital services in 1963; depreciation plus rentals plus 8% of net fixed assets and inventories

EM   = Total employment in manufacturing establishments

SPR   = 1963 company industry (five-digit) specialization ratio

M   = Fraction of total company employment in manufacturing establishments

LSE   = Logarithm of the average size of establishment in 1963 (total employment / number of establishments)

LFP   = Logarithm of the fraction of cumulated research expenditures (by 1963) that were financed by company funds; FP = "fraction private"

See the notes to table 8.2 for the definition of the other variables. The number of observations is the same as in tables 8.2 and 8.3.

Table 8.5 Constrained Multivariate Regression Estimates

(a) Growth Rates (BPT) and (b) Levels (LVA63) Combined

	Coefficients of R and D			Coefficients of Capital			Estimated Chi-square
	Unconstrained		Constrained	Unconstrained		Constrained	
Industry	(a) BTRD	(b) LK62		(a) Deprec.	(b) LC2		
1	.122 (.030)	.186 (.041)	.140 (.023)	.303 (.241)	.360 (.047)	.355 (.045)	1.66
2	.098 (.023)	.093 (.021)	.085 (.014)	.235 (.165)	.453 (.049)	.449 (.042)	2.42
3	.077 (.033)	.031 (.020)	.041 (.016)	.320 (.111)	.507 (.064)	.456 (.054)	2.70
4	.025 (.060)	.043 (.038)	.028 (.028)	.284 (.137)	.017 (.072)	.074 (.059)	3.10
5	.114 (.063)	.032 (.031)	.048 (.024)	−.143 (.363)	.196 (.065)	.176 (.058)	1.80
6	.054 (.021)	.044 (.011)	.046 (.009)	.535 (.178)	.467 (.024)	.471 (.024)	.20
7 Total	.072 (.013)	.069 (.009)	.067 (.007)	.324 (.074)	.454 (.022)	.422 (.017)	1.60

NOTES: Estimated standard errors are given in parentheses. Other variables in equations: (a) DNI, Age C; (b) LEM63, and industry dummies in the total (industry 7) equation.

Estimated chi-square: Twice the difference in the estimated log likelihood between the unconstrained and constrained multivariate regressions. The expected value of this statistic under the null hypothesis of the validity of the two cross-equations restrictions is 2. The critical value of χ^2 with two degrees of freedom is 6 at the .05 significance level and 4.6 at the .1 level. The estimated chi-squares are thus not even close to the critical values.

Table 8.6   **Alternative Estimates of the Coefficient of R and D, by Industry**

Industry	OLS	TSLS
1	.122 (.030)	.110 (.048)
2	.098 (.023)	.232 (.069)
3	.077 (.033)	.099 (.072)
4	.096 (.067)	.117 (.094)
5	.114 (.063)	.113 (.072)
6	.054 (.021)	.011 (.035)
7 All (combined)	.072 (.013)	.139 (.049)

Dependent variable: BPT.
Included independent variables in addition to BTRD: Age C, D, DNI. Also SBTRD for industry 4. Industry dummies in the combined (all industries) equation.
Instruments (excluded independent variables): M, AV/S, AI/V; SCE 58, SPR 63, GRR, FP 62, AR/S, SE/E, SBTRD, LGW58, LGANSE, ALVA. In industry 4, SBTRD is not used as an instrument. In industry 6, the instruments were AI/V, GRR, SE/E, SBTRD, LTRD57, LGFP62, K/SC, and LGVA57. (See table 8.A.1 for definitions.)

coefficient of the rate of growth of R and D over the shorter period is about .03, not much less than the earlier estimate of .04. Alternatively, if one substitutes the ratio of research scientists and engineers to total employment (29. SE/E), one gets a coefficient of .38 with a standard error of .21. The intensity variables do a better job for all industries combined, the substitution of the average R and D to sales ratio (20. AR/S) resulting in a coefficient of .07 (.02).

Another way of asking a similar question is to relate profitability rates to past research investments. Assume profits consist of two types of returns $\Pi \approx r_1 C + r_2 K$, where r_1 is the rate of return on physical capital and r_2 is the rate of return on "knowledge" capital. Then regressing the observed profit rate $\Pi/C = r_1 + r_2 K/C$ on the ratio of cumulated R and D to fixed capital would provide an estimate r_2. Unfortunately, because we really don't have the right numbers we can only approximate such an estimate. Since the returns to R and D are distributed over time, we'd like to have a time series in profitability or some estimate of permanent or average profits. Actually, we don't have a perfect measure even for one year. What we do have is gross profits (called by Telser [1972] the "contribution to overhead") in one year (1963) as a ratio to total domestic assets. This variable (19. GRR) is computed by subtracting total payrolls and equipment rentals from value added and dividing the result by total domestic assets. It is an estimate of the gross company rate of return, before depreciation and corporate taxes. Also, bypassing the problems involved in the measurement of the stock of R and D capital (K) discussed earlier, we do not have an explicit measure of K/C. It was not one of the variables included in our matrices. But we do have log K/C and can use that to approximate it. In addition, there will be a problem in interpreting the resulting r_2 estimates, since past and current R and D expenditures are treated as current expense and subtracted from profits rather than capitalized, while the equipment used in the R and D process is already included in the total fixed capital measure (C). Thus, the resulting estimates are to some extent a measure of the *excess* rate of return, above and beyond that already imputed to the conventional factors used in the R and D process.

With these reservations out of the way, we can turn to table 8.7, which presents the results of such regressions for the six separate industrial groupings and the total sample. In addition to the log K/C measure, we include also a measure of absolute size (log $C2$)[8] and industry dummies (in the combined regression). The estimated coefficients of log K/C are always positive and significant, except in the case of industry 3. Since we used log K/C instead of K/C as our variable, we have to multiply the resulting coefficient by C/K to get at an estimate of r_2. Evaluating it at the approximate arithmetic means of C and K, i.e., at $\bar{C}/\bar{K}$, gives the numbers in column (4).[9] Dividing these numbers in turn by the ratio of average company-financed to total R and D (24. FP 62) translates them into rates of return to company-financed R and D. These are listed in the last column of table 8.7. On the whole the estimates appear to be both reasonable and high. The highest rates of return are estimated for the chemical, drugs, and petroleum industry group. Metals and machinery, motor vehicles, and all other industries show a rather high overall rate of return, in excess of 20%. Allowing for a depreciation rate of 10% still would leave an *excess* rate of return above 10%, or about double that earned by physical capital during the same period.

8. We use log $C2$ instead of log $C1$ to reduce the possible spurious relationship between the various measures. But the results of using log $C1$ are very similar to those reported here.
9. Because we were not given the actual means for our samples, but only means rounded to lower class interval boundaries, we cannot really use the supplied geometric means to evaluate anything (since being off by 1 on a natural logarithm is to be off by a factor of 2.7). But since the arithmetic means are very large, rounding introduces little error there.

Two industries, 3 (electrical equipment) and 5 (aircraft and missiles), yield the lowest estimates. These industries have the highest federal involvement in their research activity. The fraction that company-financed R and D is of the total was .65 in industry 3 and only .28 in industry 5 in 1962. The relative specificity of federally supported R and D may explain the estimated low rates of return in these industries. Since together these two industries accounted for over 60% of total R and D in 1963 (see table 8.1), they have a strong depressing effect on the estimated rate of return for the total combined sample. Still, an *excess* gross rate of return of 19% on average company R and D investment is no small matter.

Table 8.7   **Relationship between Company Profitability (GRR) and Past Research Investment (K62), by Industry**

Industry	Coefficients of (standard errors) log K62/C1 (1)	log C2 (2)	R^2 and S.E. (3)	Implied Rate of Return to R and D Investments[1] Total (4)	Company[2] (5)
1	.077 (.018)	−.039 (.018)	.344 .241	.93	1.03
2	.055 (.013)	−.041 (.014)	.112[3] .204	.25	.28
3	.015 (.010)	−.021 (.013)	.037 .148	.02	.03
4	.046 (.017)	−.014 (.015)	.191 .121	.23	.29
5	.104 (.036)	−.079 (.029)	.332 .227	.05	.17
6	.010 (.005)	−.033 (.008)	.041 .155	.23	.26
7 (combined total)	.033 (.007)	−.034 (.005)	.136 .185	.17	.19

DEFINITIONS
Log K62/C1: logarithm of cumulated total R and D as a fraction of total domestic assets in 1963; log C2: logarithm of capital services as of 1963; dependent variable: 19; GRR: approximate company gross rate of return in 1963; S.E.: estimated residual standard error.
[1]Evaluated at the ratio of arithmetic means for K62 and C2.
[2]Column (4) divided by the FP62 ratio.
[3]Also contains a significant SPR variable.

8.5   R and D and Firm Size

There are a number of important policy issues connected with the question of optimal size of an R and D program which cannot really be dealt with in this study. Nevertheless, we do have some negative results which are worth reporting.

The question of the relationship between firm size and research productivity has been recently analyzed by Fisher and Temin (1973) who show that one can tell very little, a priori, about this relationship, and that one cannot conclude much from an observed relationship between firm size and research *inputs*. Roughly speaking, it may pay a large firm to engage in more research, pushing it to a point where its marginal return is lower than that for a smaller firm. We cannot, then, conclude that just because a firm is doing relatively more research it would be a good idea to transfer additional resources to it from the smaller firms.

Actually, we can also look at the relation of R and D output to firm size, not just R and D input. The results presented earlier, however, are rather negative. There is no indication of significant increasing returns to scale in the productivity *level* results summarized in table 8.4. For most company-level production function regressions the estimated sum of coefficients *including* the coefficient of cumulated R and D is unity or less. There is some evidence that more specialized (i.e., less diversified) companies having plants of larger than average size are more efficient, but there is no evidence of increasing returns to total company size as such (except possibly in industries 1 and 4).

Nor is there any evidence of increasing returns to the relative size of the research program as such. In the productivity growth rate equations, shown in table 8.2, and in comparable estimates (not shown) for individual industry groups, an absolute measure of the level of R and D investments such as LGK62 or LGANSE always has a negative sign, and this negative relation is usually statistically significant. Similarly, the estimated functional form used in the rate-of-return regressions in table 8.7 (GRR on LGK62/LGC1) implies diminishing productivity with respect to the absolute size of the R and D programs.

There are several reasons why these findings should not be taken seriously as a positive proof of diminishing returns to R and D: some of our variables are subject to errors of measurement which could lead to downward biases in our estimates. Also, the use of rates of R and D *investment* growth as measures of R and D *stock* growth may overestimate the latter for large companies with a long R and D history, and the estimated negative coefficients for the cumulated R and D levels may be due to nothing more than an adjustment for such a specification bias. But the point to be made is that we have found no prima facie evidence that the *rate of growth* of productivity is higher in larger companies with larger R and D programs or that the *level* of productivity is proportionately higher in the largest companies.

Nor is it clear that the larger companies invest more than proportionately in R and D.[10] Ours is the first set of data which allows a look at this question at the micro level for a relatively large number of companies (almost all of the universe). In table 8.8 we present regressions which summarize, for the whole sample, the relationship between different measures of R and D and company size. The major measure of company size used is ALVA—average of the logarithm of value added in 1957 and 1963. The first measure examined is the logarithm of total cumulated R and D (LGK65) over the whole available period (1957–65).[11] The crude results, regression 1, indicate that larger companies did spend relatively more, and significantly so, on R and D than smaller companies. But once we allow for data difficulties (DNI) and differences in specialization (SPR), this relationship evaporates. What remains (in regression 3) is a strong indication that fixed capital-intensive firms tend also to be R and D–intensive. There is also some indication that larger plant firms (LSE) are more R and D–intensive, but not larger companies as such.

The other regressions reported in table 8.8 examine in turn the relationship to firm size of cumulated company (as against total, which also includes federally financed) R and D in 1962 (LGCK62), the average R and D investment to value-added ratio in 1957 and 1963 (AR/V), the average company R and D to value-added ratio (CAR/V), and the log of the fraction that cumulated company R and D was of total cumulated R and D in 1962 (LFP62). The conclusion is the same: Overall there is little evidence of anything more than just a proportional relationship between R and D and size. There is some evidence that federally financed R and D is biased towards larger, more diversified companies, and that total R and D investments are not uniformly distributed across industries and companies. Capital-intensive, large-plant companies tend to invest somewhat more in R and D, which may be related to technological differences and the differential profitability of R and D investments across industries. But holding such differences constant, none of

10. While the relationship of R and D inputs to size does not in general imply much about the relationship of R and D output to size (see Fisher and Temin 1973), for the specific model outlined in section 8.2 of this paper which is homogeneous in R and D and non–R and D input, a more than proportionate increase in input would also imply a more than proportionate increase in output.

11. Value added in 1957 was estimated from value added in 1958 using the relative change in total sales between these years.

Table 8.8   Relationship of R and D to Company Size, All Industries Combined

Dependent Variable	ALVA	LC2/ALVA	Other Variables	R^2	S.E.
LGK65					
1	1.203 (.037)		I's	.656	1.202
2	1.024 (.040)		I's, DNI+, SPR−	.692	1.138
3	1.010 (.090)	.248 (.080)	I's, DNI+, SPR−, LSE	.697	1.129
LGCK62					
1	1.149 (.036)		I's	.615	1.173
2	.967 (.088)	.202 (.077)	I's, DNI+, SPR−, LSE+	.661	1.104
AR/V					
1	.006 (.004)		I's	.198	.124
2	.004 (.010)	+.035 (.009)	I's, DNI, SPR, LSE+	.223	.123
CAR/V					
1	−.003 (.003)		I's	.05	.093
2	−.003 (.007)	+.017 (.006)	I's, LSE+	.061	.092
LFP62	LV/A63 −.062 (.035)	LC2/VA63 .077 (.031)	I's, DNI+, SPR+	.400	.446

the measures yields any evidence for the proposition that the largest firms invest more than proportionately in R and D. They do invest *more*, but not relatively to their size.

In table 8.9 we examine the relationship of the R and D to value-added ratio to company size for each of our six industry groupings separately. Again, once capital intensity is controlled for, there is no significant relationship of R and D intensity to size. The results of using only the company-financed R and D ratio as the dependent variable (not shown here) are similar. In short, in our population of already very large companies (1000-plus employees) there is no indication that either the intensity of R and D investments or their productivity is related positively to company size.

8.6   Discussion and Suggestions for Further Research

In spite of various reservations, we have found a rather consistent positive relationship between various measures of company productivity and investments in research and development. In particular, Cobb-Douglas–type production function estimates based on both levels (1963) and rates of growth (1957–65) indicate an overall elasticity of output with respect to R and D investments of about .07, which can be thought of as an average of .1 for the more R and D–intensive industries such as chemicals and .05 for the less intensive rest of the universe. These findings are consistent with the earlier findings of Mansfield and Minasian, but are based on a much larger and more recent data base.

It is rather hard to convert the estimated $\alpha = .07$ into an estimate of the rate of return to R and D investments. Accepting our estimates and the validity of our measures, and using the elasticity formula to derive the implied marginal product estimate yields .27 as the overall estimate of the average gross excess rate of return to R and D in 1963. This is an average for 1963 because it is based on a function fitted across all the firms in our sample and because it is evaluated at the average total cumulated R and D to value-added ratio in 1963 in our

DEFINITIONS

LGK65 $= \log \sum_{57}^{65}$ Total R and D; LGCK62 $= \log \sum_{57}^{62}$ Company R and D

AR/V $= \frac{1}{2}\left[\left(\frac{\text{Total R and D}}{\text{Value Added}} \right) 57 + \left(\frac{\text{Total R and D}}{\text{Value Added}} \right) 63 \right]$

ALVA $= \frac{1}{2}$ (log VA57 + log VA63), Average of log value added

CAR/V $=$ similar for company R and D

LFP62 $=$ LGCK62 − LGK62

Table 8.9   **Relationship of R and D Intensity to Company Size by Industry**
Dependent Variable—AR/V

Industry and Regression	Coefficient of (standard error)		R^2	S.E.
	ALVA	LC2/ALVA		
1 a	—.002 (.004)		.004	.043
b	—.002 (.007)	—.008 (.006)	.021	.043
2 a	.013 (.007)		.017	.091
b*	—.002 (.018)	.081 (.015)	.176	.083
3 a	.005 (.026)		.000	.311
b	.006 (.081)	.171 (.078)	.047	.305
4 a	.010 (.003)		.304	.025
b	.011 (.007)	.006 (.007)	.322	.025
5 a	.064 (.032)		.009	.239
b	.057 (.102)	.124 (.090)	.174	.236
6 a	—.000 (.001)		.000	.025
b	—.000 (.003)	—.000 (.003)	.000	.025

*Also includes DNI.

sample $(K/V = .26)$.[12] It is "gross" because neither our measures of output or of input allow for any depreciation of past R and D investments, and it is "excess" because the conventional labor and fixed capital measures already include the bulk of the current R and D expenditures once.

12. The average K suffers from conflicting biases. It contains nothing for pre-1957 R and D investments and hence it is too low, but it allows no depreciation in the past accumulation and hence is too high. The two effects are likely to cancel each other out, at least as of 1963. For total industrial R and D, taking Kendrick's (1973) estimates for 1948 cumulated R and D capital as a benchmark and assuming a 10% annual depreciation rate yields a stock estimate of K as of 1963 only about 6% higher than what we get by just summing from 1957 to 1962.

While our industry groupings differ in the estimated level of this elasticity, they also differ markedly in their R and D intensity, which actually results in much less difference in the estimated rates of return than one might have thought to start out with. Taking tables 8.5 and 8.6 together, one might conclude that α is about .1 or higher for industries 1 and 2, between .05 and .1 for industries 3, 4, and 5, and less than .05 for industry 6. Since the average K/V ratios for these industries are .23, .23, .6, .16, 1.4, and .09, respectively, the implied rates of return are approximately .43, .43, .08, .31, .04, and .44, respectively (taking α as .1 for industries 1 and 2, .05 for industries 3, 4, and 5, and .04 for industry 6). Thus, except for industries 3 and 5, the resulting estimates of the private rates of return to total R and D are on the order of 30 to 40%. These estimates are larger, but not inconsistent with those presented in table 8.7, based on an entirely different dependent variable (GRR). There, too, the two industries with the largest federal involvement in the financing of R and D (3. electrical equipment and 5. aircraft and missiles) yield the lowest rate-of-return estimates.[13]

It is interesting to note that we have stumbled on this impact of federally financed R and D in the interpretation of our results rather than in the econometric analysis itself. In our regressions we were unable to discover any direct evidence of the superiority of company-financed R and D as against federally financed R and D in affecting the growth in productivity. It may well be the case that within any company a dollar is a dollar, irrespective of the source of financing, but that in these two specific industries the externalities created by the large federally financed R and D investments and the constraints on the appropriability of the results of research that may have been associated with such investments

13. In general these estimates are of the same order of magnitude as those reported by Griliches (1973) and Terleckyj (1974) based on regressions of productivity growth on R and D investment ratios for aggregate interindustry data in the U.S. The first study, based on eighty-five manufacturing industries, yielded estimates of 32 to 40% for the rate of return to R and D. The second study, based on twenty manufacturing industries, yielded an estimated rate of return of 37% to company-financed R and D and essentially zero to federally financed R and D. Both studies were based on R and D data for 1958 only. While the results reported above are of the same order of magnitude, I have not been able to replicate this type of equation on these data and get coefficients of the same order of magnitude. The best equation for the combined sample was

$$BPT = .135\,AR/V - .042\,K/V + \text{(constant, }I\text{'s, Age }C,D); R^2 = .089$$
$$\quad (.028) \qquad (.008) \qquad\qquad\qquad\qquad \text{S.E.} = .058,$$

implying a rate of return of about a half of that discussed above and a depreciation rate of 31%, if it were to be believed. Besides pointing to the difference in time periods and the use of aggregate versus micro data, I do not have a satisfactory way of reconciling these results at the moment.

have driven down the realized private rate of return from R and D significantly below its prevailing rate in other industries.[14]

In general, this paper can be viewed as another link in a chain of a rather limited number of investigations supporting the argument that R and D investments have yielded a rather high rate of return in the recent past. In addition, we find no evidence for, and some evidence against, the notion that larger firms either have a higher propensity to invest in R and D or are more effective in deriving benefits from it.

There is little point in reiterating the various reservations outlined earlier. Some of the difficulties are inherent in the attempt to measure and discuss "research" and "productivity" as if they were clear and unequivocal concepts. But many of the problems, particularly those dealing with timing effects, spillovers, and externalities, could yield to more data and better data analysis. It would be very useful to have more detail on the firms at hand, especially information on the distribution of their research expenditures, on other measures of research output such as patents granted and papers published, on income received from royalties, and on money spent on advertising. All of this is feasible; it requires "only" the additional matching of IRS, SEC, and Patent Office and scientific abstracting services data bases. It would also help to know, for tracing out and following up potential externalities, more about the exact industrial structure of individual firms and their product mix. Finally, it should be relatively easy and quite useful to extend this study, as is, to the 1966–74 period. Such an extension would be particularly interesting since it would allow us to observe a period during which R and D growth largely came to an end for many firms (at least in real terms). Besides helping us to find out something about the structure of lags and the rate of depreciation in such data, it would also, for the first time, break sharply the confounding collinearity between growth in R and D and the growth that occurred in almost all of the other economic variables during the 1956–65 period.

Even without new data, we have not yet exhausted what can be learned from the data at hand. Additional analysis of the data on the number of scientists and engineers as against R and D dollar totals should prove illuminating. This distinction between federally and company-financed R and D has not really been explored in depth yet. Finally, a detailed comparison of the individual industry results with

14. This may explain why the aggregate studies cited in the previous footnote found much higher returns to company-financed R and D investments relative to federally financed ones than we did. Another way of looking at it is that in industries with a high rate of federally financed R and D expenditures the rate of depreciation (obsolescence) of the previously accumulated R and D capital is much higher. Again, this would be a difference which wouldn't be observed at the firm level. It is external to the firm but internal to the industry.

industry aggregates, focusing on the potential externalities (external to the firm but internal to the industry), is required before any strong conclusion could be drawn about *social* rates of return from our estimates of *private* rates of return to R and D.

Appendix A

Table 8.A.1   **Variables in the R and D Study (Total N=883)**

Variable			Overall Sample	
Number	Name	Definition	Mean (approximate)	Standard Deviation
1	ID1	Industry dummy: Chemicals and petroleum SIC 28, 29, 13	$N = 110$	
2	ID2	Metals and machinery SIC 34, 35	$N = 187$	
3	ID3	Electrical equipment and communication SIC 36, 43	$N = 102$	
4	ID4	Motor vehicles and transportation SIC 371, 373–9	$N = 34$	
5	ID5	Aircraft and missiles SIC 372, 19	$N = 31$	
6	AGE C	(gross fixed assets — net fixed assets) divided by gross fixed assets (in 1963)	.5	.105
7	D	Depreciation ratio: Depreciation charged in 1963 divided by gross fixed assets in 1963	.06	.028
8	D/V	Depreciation to value-added ratio, 1963	.06	.057
9	C3	Total domestic assets, 1963	260×10^6	766×10^6
10	S57	Sales in 1957	200×10^6	62×10^6
11	M	Ratio of employment in manufacturing establishments to total company employment	.80	.17
12	ALSS	Average share of total payroll in sales (average of the ratios for 1958 and 1963)	.30	.11
13	ALSV	Average share of labor in value added (average of payroll to value added for 1958 and 1963)	.50	.16
14	AV/S	Average ratio of value added to sales (1958 and 1963)	.50	.16

Table 8.A.1 (cont.)

Variable			Overall Sample	
Number	Name	Definition	Mean (approximate)	Standard Deviation
15	AI/V	Average ratio of investment (total capital expenditures) to value added (1958 and 1963)	.07	.07
16	VA63	Value added in 1963	120×10^6	361×10^6
17	SCE58	Average number of employees per establishment in 1958	350	751
18	SPR63	1963 company industry (five-digit) specialization ratio	60	27
19	GRR	Gross rate of return in 1963: Value added minus total manufacturing payroll minus equipment rentals divided by gross domestic assets	.26	.20
20	NRR	"Net" rate of return: Value added minus manufacturing payroll, minus equipment rentals, minus depreciation, divided by net *fixed* assets plus inventories	.50	.62
21	LGS63	Log total sales in 1963	10.00	1.20
22	LGS57	Log total sales in 1957	10.00	1.29
23	K62	Cumulated total R and D expenditures, 1957–62	50×10^6	272×10^6
24	FP62	Fraction private 62: Cumulated company R and D expenditures 1957–62 divided by K62	.90	.23
25	FP65	Fraction private 65: Cumulated company R and D expenditures 1957–65, divided by K65	.90	.23
26	AR/V	Average R and D to value-added ratio, 1957 and 1963	.05	.14
27	K/V	Cumulated R and D in 1962 to value-added in 1963 ratio	.26	.51
28	AR/S	Average (1957 and 1962) R and D to sales ratio	.03	.09
29	SE/E	Average (1957 and 1962) scientists and engineers to total employment ratio	.02	.04
30	CAR/V	Company R and D to value-added ratio 1957 and 1962 average	.03	.09

Rates of growth (b's), computed from regressions
of log $y = a + bt$, for the period 1957–65

Table 8.A.1 (cont.)

Variable Number	Variable Name	Definition	Overall Sample Mean (approximate)	Standard Deviation
31	BS	Rate of growth of sales	.06	.074
32	BE	Rate of growth of employment	.023	.065
33	BSE	Rate of growth of scientists and engineers employment	.05	.14
34	BTRD	Rate of growth of total R and D	.08	.15
35	BCRD	Rate of growth of company R and D	.08	.16
36	SBS	Standard error of estimate rate of growth of sales	.014	.015
37	SBTRD	Standard error of estimate rate of growth of total R and D	.035	.038
38	R/V57	Total R and D to value-added ratio, 1957	.05	.21
39	LTRD57	Log total R and D, 1957	6.0	2.25
40	LCRD57	Log company R and D, 1957	6.0	2.13
41	BPT	Partial productivity growth 1957–65: $BS - ALSS \times BE$	.05	.06
42	DN1	Dummy variable 1 if no imputations in the data, zero otherwise	.6	
43	LGE63	Log total employment, 1963	8.0	1.04
44	E57	Total employment, 1957	9,000	26,358
45	LGC1	Log gross fixed assets 1963	10.00	1.48
46	LGC2	Log capital services in 1963; capital services: Depreciation and rentals and 8% of net fixed assets and inventories	8.00	1.32
47	LGEM63	Log manufacturing employment, 1963	8.00	1.04
48	LGFM57	Log manufacturing employment, 1957	8.00	1.12
49	LGW58	Log average "wage" in 1958 (wage = payroll per employee)	1.6	.20
50	LGW63	Log wage rate in 1963	1.8	.20
51	LGVA63	Log value added in 1963	10.00	1.15
52	LGSCE63	Log average scale of establishments in 1963	5.00	1.0
53	LGANSE	Log average number of scientists and engineers, 1957–62	3.5	1.90
54	LGK62	Log cumulated R and D through 1962	8.0	2.1
55	LGK65	Log cumulated R and D through 1965	9.0	2.0

Table 8.A.1 (cont.)

Variable			Overall Sample	
Number	Name	Definition	Mean (approximate)	Standard Deviation
56	LGFP62	Log 1962 cumulated company R and D as a fraction of total cumulated R and D	—.18	.57
57	T63	Log absolute total factor productivity level in 1963: LGVA63 — ALSV × LGEM63 — (1 — ALSV) LGC2	2.0	.34
58	GVA	Growth in value added, 1957–63: (LGVA63 — LGVA57)/6	.06	.074
59	GPT	Growth in partial productivity 1957–63: [GVA — ALSV × (LGEM63 — LGEM57)]/6	.05	.058
60	GSCE	Growth in average scale of establishments: (LGSCE63 — LGSCE58)/5	—.02	.09

Additional variables constructed from the above set:

K/SC   = 54—53, log of cumulated R and D per scientist
LGCK   = 56+54, log of cumulated company-financed R and D, 1962
K/C   = 54—45, log of the cumulated R and D to fixed capital ratio
LGVA57 = 51—(6)×.58, log of value added, 1957
ALVA   = 51—(3)×.58, average of log value added in 1957 and 1963

Value added in 1957 estimated by extrapolating value added in 1958 using the percentage change in sales between 1957 and 1958.

NOTE: Industry group 6 is "All others," $N = 419$. All dollar figures are in thousands.

Appendix B

Criteria Used for Inclusion of a Company in the Griliches-NSF-Census Bureau Project

1. Only companies with 1,000 or more employees in one or more years and filing annual reports on Research and Development (Form RD–1 or RD–2) were included. The list was further limited to companies classified in manufacturing, Petroleum (SIC 13), and Communications (SIC 48). This is the area included under the term "manufacturing" in the Annual Survey of Research and Development in Industry conducted by the Census Bureau for the National Science Foundation.

2. Subsequently, in the final tabulations, only those companies for which we had R and D reports for four or more years during the period 1957–65 were retained.

3. All companies included were matched to the 1963 and 1958 Enterprise Statistics data. Company data in the Griliches-NSF-Census study are combined and classified according to the 1963 enterprise company composition and industry code. A few R and D companies of relatively small size, not matched to the enterprise lists, were dropped.*

4. During the search and edit routine, all cases outside four standard deviations of the various tests were rechecked by clerical and professional staff. A few small cases that could not be explained were dropped from the project.

Appendix C

Memorandum to Mr. Owen
23 November 1971
Attachment C

Imputation and Estimation Methods for Griliches-NSF-Census Project

1. Imputation of R and D data. Our primary data file contained nine years of data, 1957 through 1965, for five items reported in R and D surveys: sales, employment, employment of scientists and engineers assigned to R and D work, total R and D expenditures, and federal R and D expenditures. For each company in the survey, for each of these items, we imputed zero values as follows:

> Let X represent year with a value of 80 for 1957, 90 for 1958, etc.
>
> Let Y represent one of the R and D variables.
>
> For each nonzero Y, we cumulated N, ΣX, ΣY, ΣX^2, and ΣXY.
>
> Then, $A = \Sigma Y/N$ and $B = (N\Sigma XY - \Sigma X\Sigma Y)/(N\Sigma X^2 - (\Sigma X)^2)$.

---

*Comments on the R and D–Enterprise match: The 1958 enterprise data were placed in the 1963 format. Mergers and acquisitions during the period were reflected by the addition of two or more 1958 enterprise records to equal one 1963 enterprise record. No case came to light where a single 1958 record represented two or more 1963 records. According to the R and D survey instruction, respondents should report for the entire company. However, the results of the instructions have weaknesses that are avoided in the enterprise statistics (1958 and 1963) by a match to lists of related employer identification numbers and associated employment data. The R and D–enterprise match served to update the R and D company composition data, and to establish changes in broad industry classes,

Each zero value of Y was imputed from its matching year value by $Y = A + B(X - \bar{X})$; and each imputed value was flagged.

Negative imputed values were set to zero.

This is a straight-line imputation procedure; its effects were partially as follows:

(a) items totally not reported were left at zero and flagged as imputed; (b) items reported in only one year had that value imputed for all years.

2. Estimation of regression variables.

a) Federal R and D values were reset to zero if imputed and any federal R and D greater than total R and D was set equal to the total R and D value.

b) In the following description the numbers in parentheses refer to field positions in the primary data record, Attachment A. The variable abbreviation follows Griliches's document of 13 May 1971 as amended by notes of meetings and other conversations. Only those variables whose derivation is not direct from the Griliches definition are described below.

In all cases not explicitly covered below, the calculation of a ratio with a zero value for numerator or denominator would result in a zero value for the ratio.

   i. If $(50) = 0$, Age C $= 0$.

  ii. If R and D sales for 1957 and 1958 were not reported or 0, $S_{57} = (21)$ and $V_{57} = (39)$; i.e., no 1957 to 1958 ratio adjustment.

 iii. If R and D employment for 1957 or 1958 was not reported or 0, $EM_{57} = (29) \times M$; i.e., no 57 to 58 adjustment.

 iv. For ALSS, ALSV, AV/S, and AI/V, which require an averaging of two ratios, if either ratio was zero, the other ratio is used and not averaged. If both ratios were 0, the variable would be zero and the case listed.

  v. For AR/V, CAR/V, and R/V, which require averaging of a ratio involving a 1962 R and D item and a ratio involving a 1957 R and D item, if the 1962 data were missing, we used 1961; if that was also missing we used 1960; and, similarly, for 1957 we substituted 1958 and 1959. If all three early years were missing, the resulting zero ratio would have been averaged.

based upon Census company industry codes developed in the processing of the economic census data.

Since any four years of R and D data were sufficient to include a company, it was possible for a company with no R and D reported in 1958 or 1963 to be included in the sample. A few such cases did turn up in the development of the matched R and D–enterprise data.

vi. For AR/S and SE/E, which require an averaging of a ratio of two 1962 R and D items and a ratio of two 1957 R and D items, if either 1962 item were missing we would use 1963, if 1963 were missing we would use 1964, and if both of these were missing we would set that ratio to zero; similarly, we would substitute 1958 and 1959 for 1957. If both ratios were zero, the case would be listed.

vii. Growth rates and standard errors of the growth rates for the following R and D variables were computed: sales, employment, scientists and engineers employment, total R and D expenditures, and company R and D expenditures. For each variable, for the nine-year period, we let X represent year with a value of 1 through 9, and Y represent the log of the variable for nonzero values. For nonzero values of Y we obtained the following counts and sums: N, ΣX, ΣY, ΣX^2, ΣY^2, ΣXY. If N was less than 4 we set the growth rate and the standard error of the growth rate to zero, and set a dummy variable to one; otherwise

the dummy variable $= 0$;

the growth rate,

$$b = (N\Sigma XY - \Sigma X\Sigma Y)/[N\Sigma X^2 - (\Sigma X)^2],$$

and the standard error of the growth rate

$$= \mathrm{SQRT}\ ([N\Sigma Y^3 - (\Sigma Y)^2 - b(N\Sigma XY$$
$$- \Sigma X\Sigma Y)]/\{(N-2)[N\Sigma X^3 - (\Sigma X)^2]\}).$$

viii. If BS or BE could not be calculated, BPT $= 0$.

ix. The log of a variable with a value of zero would be set to zero.

References

Evenson, R. 1968. The contribution of agricultural research and extension to agricultural production. Ph.D. diss., University of Chicago.

Fisher, F. M., and Temin, P. 1973. Returns to scale in research and development: what does the Schumpeterian hypothesis imply? *Journal of Political Economy* 81:56–70.

Griliches, Z. 1964. Research expenditures, education, and the aggregate agricultural production function. *American Economic Review* 54: 961–74.

———. 1973a. Research expenditures and growth accounting. In B. R. Williams, ed., *Science and technology in economic growth*, pp. 59–95. London: Macmillan.

————. 1973*b*. Productivity and research. In National Commission on Productivity, *Conference on an agenda for economic research on productivity*. Washington: Government Printing Office.

Kendrick, J. W. 1976. *The formation and stocks of total capital*. National Bureau of Economic Research, General Series 100. New York: Columbia University Press.

Mansfield, E. 1965. Rates of return from industrial research and development. *American Economic Review* 55: 310–322.

————. 1967. *Econometric studies of industrial research and technological innovation*. New York: W. W. Norton.

————. 1972. The contribution of research and development to economic growth in the United States. In National Science Foundation, *R&D and economic growth productivity*, NSF 72–303. Washington: Government Printing Office.

Minasian, Jora R. 1962. The economics of research and development. In National Bureau of Economic Research, *The rate and direction of inventive activity*. Princeton: Princeton University Press.

————. 1969. Research and development, production functions, and rates of return. *American Economic Review* 59 (Proceedings issue): 80–85.

National Science Foundation. 1959. *Methodology of statistics on research and development*, NSF 59–36. Washington: Government Printing Office.

————. 1970*a*. *Research and development in industry, 1968*, NSF 70–29. Washington: Government Printing Office.

————. 1970*b*. *National Patterns of R&D Resources, 1953–71*, NSF 70–44. Washington: Government Printing Office.

Terleckyj, N. E. 1960. Sources of productivity advance. Ph.D. diss., Columbia University.

————. 1974. *Effects of R&D on the productivity growth of industries: an exploratory study*. Washington: National Planning Association.

Wagner, L. U. 1968. Problems in estimating research and development investment and stock. In ASA, *1968 Proceedings of the business and economic statistics section*, pp. 189–97. Washington: ASA.

Comment   Edwin Mansfield

Zvi Griliches comes to three principal conclusions in this interesting and useful paper. First, he estimates that the elasticity of output with respect to R and D investment is about 0.1 in the more R and D–intensive manufacturing industries, and about 0.05 for the less R and D–intensive manufacturing industries. Second, he estimates that the rate

Edwin Mansfield is at the University of Pennsylvania.

of return from R and D is on the order of 20% in all manufacturing—much lower than this in industries like aircraft and missiles and electrical equipment, where there is great federal involvement in the financing of R and D, and much higher in industries like chemicals. Third, he finds some evidence against the proposition that larger firms either have a higher propensity to invest in R and D or are more effective in deriving benefits from it.

An important advantage of Griliches's study over earlier ones is its inclusiveness. For the first time, we have, thanks to Griliches, the National Science Foundation, and the Census Bureau, results that pertain to almost 900 firms. This is a far larger sample than has been analyzed in previous studies, and Griliches's results are both interesting and welcome. For some purposes, however, it might have been preferable to use finer industrial categories. As matters stand, some results for individual industry groups are difficult to interpret. For example, the chemical industry includes petroleum, chemical, and drug firms. Thus, when R and D intensity and other variables are regressed on firm size, a considerable part of the relationship must be due to the well-known differences among the petroleum, chemical, and drug industries. Perhaps Griliches or his students may be able to extend the results in this way in the future.

The model that Griliches uses is similar to ones used by previous investigators. For example, it assumes that technological change is neutral, and that the Cobb-Douglas form is appropriate. Also, it assumes that the direction of causation runs from R and D expenditures to output, whereas to some extent there may be an identification problem. In other words, high rates of growth of output may lead to high R and D expenditures, or be associated with firm characteristics (such as the nature and quality of management) related to high R and D expenditure. Thus, there may be some bias in the estimated regression coefficients. Recognizing this fact, he computes two-stage least-squares estimates of the coefficient of R and D in table 8.6. Although he concludes that only in industry 6 do the two-stage least-squares results not yield a significant R and D coefficient, it appears that the coefficient is less than 1.6 times its standard error in industries 3, 4, and 5 as well. Thus, in two-thirds of the industries, the two-stage least-squares estimates of the R and D coefficient are not statistically significant.

Also, as Griliches emphasizes, he is forced to use proxies—"makeshift" proxies, as he characterizes them—to represent the growth in physical capital as well as the growth in R and D capital. In particular, he uses two proxies for the rate of growth of physical capital: the ratio of accumulated depreciation to the stock of physical capital in 1963, and the 1963 depreciation rate. Although these proxies may be serviceable if the growth rate (and depreciation rate) of capital is constant over time, this may not be the case. Thus, as he recognizes, these proxies may be troublesome. And the proxy for the growth rate of R and D capital is the rate of growth of R and D expenditures, which can be troublesome too. Combining the use of these proxies with the use of undeflated output data and the fact that the lag in the effects of R and D is ignored, it is clear that the results are very rough.

Yet, despite these approximations, the extent to which his findings agree with previous studies is quite striking. To begin with, recall his conclusion that the elasticity of output with respect to cumulated R and D expenditures is about 0.1 in the more research-intensive industries. This estimate is quite close to my estimate of 0.12 for chemicals and petroleum, and to Minasian's estimate of 0.11 for chemicals (Mansfield 1968; Minasian 1969). Also, consider his estimate at the end of his paper that the rate of return from R and D is perhaps 40% or more in the chemicals group. This estimate agrees quite well with previous studies (although the figure of 93% in table 8.7 is higher than obtained before).

Turning to his conclusion that the estimated rate of return from R and D is lower in industries where there is a great federal involvement in financing R and D, it is worth noting that Terleckyj, in his very interesting study (1974) of effects of R and D on productivity change, comes to a related conclusion. Terleckyj regressed the rate of growth of an industry's total factor productivity in 1948–66 on its privately financed R and D (as a percent of value added) and its government-financed R and D (as a percent of value added), as well as a number of other variables. He found that the regression coefficient of its government-financed R and D was almost precisely zero, and far from statistically significant, whereas the regression coefficient of its privately financed R and D was highly significant. Similarly, Leonard (1971) found that privately financed R and D had a much larger impact than government-financed R and D on both the growth of industry output and the growth of output per worker.

Further, Griliches's conclusion that the largest firms do not invest more, relative to their size, than somewhat smaller firms is in accord with earlier studies. In particular, I found that this was true in the petroleum, drug, steel, and glass industries; and Scherer, in his much more inclusive study, found that it was true (Scherer 1974; see also Mansfield 1968). In both Scherer and my studies, the chemical industry was an exception; and I suspect that the reason why Griliches does not obtain similar findings is that he includes chemicals, drugs, and petroleum in his chemicals group. Also, Griliches's conclusion that there is no evidence that the largest firms are more effective in deriving benefits from R and D is not at all incompatible with the limited amount of data provided by earlier studies.[1]

1. For example, Cooper (1964).

Having summarized his principal findings, discussed some of the problems he faced, and compared his results with previous studies, let me try to present some information that may help to shed light on a couple of the areas untouched by his paper. First, as Griliches points out, we know far too little concerning the lag between investment in research and the appearance of innovations stemming from the research. This lag should, of course, be incorporated into any model of this sort. Based on work carried out by George Beardsley in his doctoral thesis (1974) at the University of Pennsylvania, the estimated probability distribution of this lag in one of the nation's largest firms is as shown in table C.8.1. As you can see, the probability distribution is different for the firm's applied R and D work than for its more basic work. For the applied R and D, the median lag is about two years for work on products and about three years for work on processes; for the more basic research, it is about four years for products and about five years for processes. Also, note that the median lag for more basic work is shorter now than in the 1960s, a tendency which I believe is true of many firms besides this one.

Of course, these figures pertain to only one large firm, and cannot be regarded as typical for all manufacturing. But the results are not very different from those collected about ten years ago from a large electrical equipment firm (Mansfield 1968). Moreover, we collected data of this

Table C.8.1   Estimated Percentage of R and D Budget Devoted to Work which, if Successful, was to be Commercialized at Various Lengths of Time after the R and D Expenditure (large manufacturing firm)

Time Lag (yr.)	Applied R and D		1960s Total	Basic Research[a] 1970–72	
	Products	Processes		Products	Processes
< 1	10	15	------	3	1
1–2	45	25	------	7	4
2–3	25	20	5	15	10
3–4	15	15	10	25	10
4–5	5	10	20	25	20
5–6	------	10	20	20	10
6–7	------	5	20	5	15
> 7	------	------	25	------	5
Total	100	100	100	100	100

NOTE: All numbers exceeding 10 % are rounded to the nearest 5%.

[a]The firm's definition of "basic" research does not accord with that of the National Science Foundation. This is a segment of the firm's R and D that is relatively long-range. Its budget was about 30% of that for applied R and D in 1972.

sort from eleven major chemical firms and six major petroleum firms. These data indicated that the median length of time to completion of an R and D project and an effect on firm profits was about two years for some chemical firms and about four years for others, while it was generally about two or three years for the oil firms (Mansfield et al. 1971). Thus, the combined sample of about 19 firms indicates a median lag from R and D to innovation of about three years. And since the diffusion lag must be added to this lag, the average total lag in at least these areas of manufacturing may not be very much shorter than the figures Griliches quotes from Evenson (1968).

Second, it may be worthwhile to describe a case study of the private rate of return from investments in new technology. In his thesis, Beardsley obtained data concerning the returns from the innovative activities of one of the nation's largest firms. This firm has made estimates since 1960 of the benefits obtained from its R and D efforts, these estimates being used for internal planning purposes. This firm is among the largest members of an industry that is neither among the most research-intensive nor among the least research-intensive. In terms of the percent of sales devoted to R and D, this firm is reasonably representative of our nation's largest firms.

For each year since 1960, this firm has put together a careful inventory of the technological innovations arising from its R and D and related activities. Then it has made detailed estimates of the effect of each of these innovations on its profit stream. Specifically, in the case of product innovations, the firm has computed for each new product the expected difference in cash flows over time between the situation with the new product and without it, including the effect of the new product on its profits from displaced products. In the case of process innovations, it has computed the expected difference in cash flow between the situation with the new process and that without it, this difference reflecting, of course, the savings associated with the new process. In addition, the firm has updated these estimates each year. In other words, as time has gone on, the firm has revised its estimates of the returns from past innovations. This, of course, is of crucial importance, since it means that the firm's estimates for innovations occurring in the early and middle 1960s are based on a decade or more of actual experience, not just forecasts. The data we use are taken from the 1973 revision.

Besides these data on the private benefits from the firm's technological innovations, figures are also available concerning the firm's expenditures on R and D and related innovative activities each year. Using these cost figures, as well as the figures concerning the total cash flow of benefits stemming from the new products or new processes that came to fruition each year, we can compute the rate of return from the investment that resulted in each year's crop of innovations. It is worthwhile noting that this rate of return is based on the investment in both commercialized and uncommercialized (and successful and unsuccessful) projects.

The results, shown in table C.8.2, indicate at least two things. First, the average rate of return from this firm's total investments in innovative activities during 1960–72 was about 19%, a figure that is not too different from the average that Griliches gets. In its internal calculations, this firm regards investments with rates of return exceeding 15% as attractive. According to table C.8.2, the average rate of return from the firm's total investment in innovative activities during 1960–72 exceeded this figure. Second, innovation is a risky activity, and this is reflected in the results. Both for processes and products, the estimated private rate of return fell short of this figure of 15% in about 60% of the years. The year-to-year variation in the private rate of return seems greater for processes than for products, which may be related to the fact that the average rate of return is higher for processes than for products.

Although these figures are interesting, their limitations should be stressed. For one thing, the firm does not attempt to include in its calculations any innovation where the discounted value of its benefits

Table C.8.2   **Private Rates of Return from Total Investment in Research and Development and Related Innovative Activities, Major Industrial Firm, Process and Product Innovations, 1960–72**

Year	Both Products and Processes	Products	Processes
1960	31	21%	34
1961	9	0	15
1962	7	17	Negative*
1963	26	13	30
1964	15	9	18
1965	16	27	−1
1966	25	22	27
1967	11	11	12
1968	2	−1	5
1969	3	13	−15
1970	6	9	3
1971	12	16	10
1972	14	14	14
1960–72	19	14	22

*No major process innovations occurred in 1962.

(the discount rate being 15%) is less than $200,000. Since the firm's benefit figures omit the benefits from such minor innovations, the rates of return are almost surely underestimates. Also, the estimates for more recent years are not as reliable as those for the early and middle 1960s. Nonetheless, despite these and other defects in the data, the results seem to provide the most detailed description of a firm's returns from its investments in technological innovation that has been published to date.[2]

Third, as Griliches points out, his results pertain to private rates of return from R and D, not social rates of return. How much difference can there be between private and social rates of return? Judging from a study of seventeen industrial innovations that we have done recently (Mansfield et al. 1977), there can be very wide differences between them. As might be expected, the social rate of return tended to be higher than the private rate of return. Specifically, in our sample, the median social rate of return was about 56%, whereas the median private rate of return was about 25%. These estimates were derived from a detailed investigation of each of these seventeen innovations, the basic data being obtained to a considerable extent from the innovating firms, using firms, and relevant government agencies. The model on which these results are based is similar in spirit to the one used by Griliches in his earlier study of hybrid corn, although we have extended it in a number of major directions (Griliches 1958; Mansfield et al. 1977).

In conclusion, what sorts of implications can be derived from Griliches's study? Since his estimates relate to private, not social, rates of return, the fact that they are relatively high would seem to imply that firms should have expanded their R and D programs.[3] In fact, manufacturing firms did expand their investment in R and D during the middle and late 1960s; total annual expenditure by industry on R and D almost doubled between 1963 and 1969 (National Science Foundation 1972). Thus, this implication seems to be consistent with the facts, at least until about 1969. But from 1969 to 1972, there has been no appreciable increase in real terms in industry's annual R and D expenditures (National Science Foundation 1972). Consequently, one might guess that, if Griliches could have used more recent data, he might have found that the marginal private rate of return from R and D was considerably lower than the figures in his paper. Given the great changes that have occurred in the past 10 or 15 years in the attitude of industry toward R and D, it would be very interesting to see what more recent figures of this sort would reveal.

2. For further analysis of these data, see Beardsley and Mansfield (1978).

3. For some discussion of the limitations of estimates of this sort, see Mansfield (1972) and Mansfield et al. (1977).

References

Beardsley, G. 1974. Rates of return from investments in innovation. Ph.D. dissertation, University of Pennsylvania.

Beardsley, G., and Mansfield, E. 1978. A note on the accuracy of industrial forecasts of the profitability of new products and processes. *Journal of Business* 51:127–35.

Cooper, A. 1964. R and D is more efficient in small companies. *Harvard Business Review* 42:75–83.

Evenson, R. 1968. The contribution of agricultural research and extension to agricultural production. Ph.D. dissertation, University of Chicago.

Griliches, Z. 1958. Research costs and social returns: hybrid corn and related innovations. *Journal of Political Economy* 66:419–31.

Leonard, W. 1971. Research and development in economic growth. *Journal of Political Economy* 79:232–56.

Mansfield, E. 1968. *Industrial research and technological innovation.* New York: W. W. Norton.

————. 1972. Contribution of R and D to economic growth in the United States. *Science* 175:487–94.

Mansfield, E.; Rapoport, J.; Romeo, A.; Villani, E.; Wagner, S.; and Husic, F. 1977. *The production and application of new industrial technology.* New York: W. W. Norton.

Mansfield, E.; Rapoport, J.; Romeo, A.; Wagner, S.; and Beardsley, G. 1977. Social and private rates of return from industrial innovations. *Quarterly Journal of Economics* 91:221–40.

Mansfield, E.; Rapoport, J.; Schnee, J.; Wagner, S.; and Hamburger, M. 1971. *Research and innovation in the modern corporation.* New York: W. W. Norton.

Minasian, J. 1969. Research and development, production functions, and rates of return. *American Economic Review* 59:80–85.

National Science Foundation. 1972. *Science indicators.* Washington: National Science Foundation.

Scherer, F. M. 1970. *Industrial market structure and economic performance.* Evanston: Rand McNally.

Terleckyj, N. 1974. *Effects of R and D on the productivity growth of industries: an exploratory study.* Washington: National Planning Association.

9   Energy and Pollution Effects on Productivity: A Putty-Clay Approach

John G. Myers and Leonard Nakamura

9.1   The Problem

Among the constraints currently affecting production methods in manufacturing, three types deserve special attention: rapid increases in energy prices and interruptions in supplies of specific fuels; fixed time schedules of requirements for water, air, and land pollution abatement; and fixed time schedules of requirements under the Occupational Safety and Health Act. While constraints such as these are not entirely new, their strength, severity, and nearly simultaneous occurrence make the outcome on production patterns, and thus on productivity change, highly uncertain.[1]

One obvious way in which productivity change can be affected is by a diversion of real investment from productivity-enhancing capital additions and replacements to uses that are neutral or even negative in their productivity effects. Examples of the latter are "add-on" investments to reduce heat loss, convert to other fuels, reduce discharge of pollutants, and reduce safety and health hazards to workers. But to the extent that adjustment to the types of constraints mentioned entails the adoption of new production technology, more rapid capital turnover will result and the net effect may well be an acceleration in productivity growth.

In this paper we present the first stage of a project designed to measure the impact of these constraints on individual industries and the

John G. Myers is at Southern Illinois University; Leonard Nakamura is with Citibank.

During the preparation of this paper the authors benefited from the comments of K. S. Lee, now of the World Bank, and Norman Madrid, of The Conference Board.

1. We define productivity as gross output per man-hour. Many of the results we obtain will also apply to broader productivity concepts; we refer to some of these occasionally in the text.

derived effect on productivity change. Our aim here is to construct a mathematical model that captures the most important of these influences (which are treated as coming from outside the industry) and to examine the process of adaptation to them by the industry. The model is dynamic and is designed to represent the succession of changes that will occur over time as an industry reacts to higher energy costs and increased penalties for pollution (hereafter we will use the term "pollution" to refer to all undesirable outputs, including industrial accidents and health hazards). A logically consistent model provides the best guide to what data must be collected in order to test hypotheses and quantify the basic relationships.

The next stage will be to devise tests of the model and to estimate the principal parameters for selected industries. We have observed that, within the manufacturing sector, the impact of each constraint that interests us is highly concentrated among a few industries. For example, eight (four-digit SIC) industries accounted for more than 50% of all energy consumed by the manufacturing sector in 1967 (and these eight include three industries that are highly integrated and can be usefully treated as one industry—pulp, paper, and paperboard mills). The same eight industries accounted for nearly 70% of all water used by manufacturing in 1968, and for a similar proportion of all water pollution by the manufacturing sector. In addition, other forms of pollution and industrial accidents and health hazards appear to be similarly concentrated among the same industries. Successful measurement of the impacts of constraints on energy use and pollution in these industries will go far toward capturing the aggregate effects on the manufacturing sector. A sketch of our measurement procedure is given in section 9.9, which also contains an illustration for the petroleum refining industry.

In the third stage of the study, we will incorporate our empirical results in an existing national model in order to investigate the impact on the entire economy. Specifically, projections of input-output coefficients for individual industries, prepared in stage two, will be utilized to study interindustry reactions and aggregate effects. A working input-output model appears to be the most likely candidate for this application, and we are examining the feasibility of using the INFORUM model of the University of Maryland.

9.2 Model and Assumptions

A set of accurately measured elasticities of demand for the outputs of an industry and of the industry's demands for inputs, for relevant periods of adjustment, would provide the basis for estimating the impact we are studying. The size and speed of the changes in prices and regulations suggest that accurate estimation of such elasticities within a conventional neoclassical production function framework is unlikely to be successful.

In the course of studying energy use and water pollution abatement in manufacturing industries (Myers et al. 1974; Gelb and Myers 1976) we have seen the following mechanism at work: research and development, including pilot plant operation, creates a number of discrete bundles of production technology, each with fixed factor proportions. At any given time, the corporate decision-maker is faced with government regulations and prices, both current and prospective, and the choices of producing with present equipment, producing with new equipment, and scrapping old equipment. These choices, aggregated, determine capacity with fixed requirements of labor and raw materials. In concert with demand, productivity is then determined.

The constraints that we are investigating all affect the costs of production. The typical reaction of an industry to changes in production costs is to change its production methods in order to vary input mix or output mix. In the standard comparative statics model, this is described by a simultaneous movement along the production possibilities curve and along the isoquant.

In the real world, production shifts may take place via changes in existing plants or by new plants replacing old. The evidence is that the largest changes take place via replacement.

These changes can be made explicit in a putty-clay production function model. Entrepreneurs have a range of choices regarding input proportions and output mix until the investment is made (putty); thereafter, plant and equipment is fixed in form (clay). The approach most frequently used does not capture the effects we wish to show; in such a putty-putty model, even with embodied technical change, old equipment is just as adaptable as new.

Putty-clay models were developed from the work of Johansen (1959), Solow (1962), Phelps (1963), Pyatt (1965), Boddy and Gort (1971, 1974), Nickell (1974), Adachi (1974), and others. Our model follows those of Salter (1966) and Bliss (1968) to a considerable extent. It represents the behavior of an industry that buys and sells in competitive markets. The production function for each vintage employs investment, I, as an input, rather than capital stock. It is thus *ex ante*, describing substitution possibilities before plant and equipment have been put into place.

We make the following assumptions for each industry:

(*a*) Managerial efficiency is equal in all plants.

(*b*) Labor is homogeneous across plants and over time and is paid at the same wage rate in all plants.

(*c*) Once built, a machine embodies technology that determines the input-output coefficients of that machine throughout its life.

(*d*) Machines in production are fully utilized except in marginal plants that are near the age when they will be taken out of service.

(*e*) There are no cyclical or cobweb patterns in price or output.

(*f*) Within each vintage, constant returns to scale obtain.

(*g*) Knowledge of available techniques is general and new machines embody best-practice techniques.

(*h*) All entrepreneurs share the same expectations of future input and output prices.

(*i*) Technical advances are embodied in new plant and equipment but are neutral in their effects, saving each input in the same proportion.

(*j*) Plant and equipment are infinitely durable and are discarded only because of obsolescence.

(*k*) Investment bears fruit without a lag.

Initially, we further assume that input prices are constant.

We begin by presenting a general form of the model, with two inputs and one output. A Cobb-Douglas form follows, also for two inputs and one output; this section incorporates the uncertainty analysis. We then turn to a general form using three inputs and two outputs, which is followed by an examination of the rate of product transformation. We conclude with an examination of a Cobb-Douglas model with three inputs and two outputs.

We are aware that it is possible to present the model in a more sophisticated and compact fashion. (For excellent examples, see Nickell (1974) and Boddy and Gort (1974.) This would make it easier to present cyclic behavior, steadily rising wages, translog production functions, disembodied technical change, and other elements we omitted. At this stage, however, we are primarily concerned with presenting the model in the simplest possible form, so as to enable a step-by-step analysis of the assumptions and implications.

9.3   General Form, Two Inputs and One Output

For vintage v, the production function is of the general form

(A) $$X(v) = A(v)f[N(v),I(v)],$$

where X is output, A is technical change, N is man-hours, I is investment in constant prices, and v is measured in years. The price measure for investment is for goods of unchanged quality; that is, it measures the change in price of earlier vintage capital goods that are still produced in the given year. Quality changes in capital goods are included in the change, from vintage to vintage, in $A(v)$.

A short-run "utilization function" for vintage v, once the investment has become "clay," is of the general form

(B) $$X(v) = A(v)k(v)N(v),$$

where

$$k(v) = \frac{f[N(v),I(v)]}{N(v)}$$

is constant from vintage to vintage as long as input prices and length of life remain unchanged.

Total production from all vintages is given by

(C) $$Y(t) = \int_{v=t-n}^{v=t} A(v)k(v)N(v)dv,$$

where $(t-n)$ is the oldest vintage in production.

Labor productivity of the industry is given by

(D) $$\frac{Y(t)}{\int_{v=t-n}^{v=t} N(v)dv} = \frac{\int_{v=t-n}^{v=t} A(v)k(v)N(v)dv}{\int_{v=t-n}^{v=t} N(v)dv}.$$

Demand for the industry's (homogeneous) product is a function of current price and of the rate of growth of the economy,

(E) $$D(t) = D[p(t),\gamma],$$

where γ is the change in demand caused by the aggregate growth rate.

We assume that $A(v)$ is characterized by steady growth at a rate α, which represents the rate of technical progress in the industry. The production functions for successive vintages will therefore differ, since fixed amounts of labor and investment will produce greater and greater quantities of output. Given our assumption of constant input prices, technical change will result in lower production costs. And under competition, these will lead to lower output prices. The current price, $p(t)$, will be determined by the cost of production of the most recent vintage in use, $v=t$. And a steady rate of technical change will then lead to a steadily declining supply price at the same rate, α. The current price, $p(t)$, is related to the price that held when an older vintage, v, was introduced, by the following relation:

(F) $$p(t) = \frac{A(v)}{A(t)} p(v),$$

where

$$\frac{A(v)}{A(t)} = e^{\alpha(v-t)}.$$

The variable cost for any vintage is given by $wN(v)$, where w is the wage rate. A vintage is taken out of production when revenue no longer exceeds variable cost, or

(G) $$p(t)X(v) = w N(v).$$

Under the stated assumptions, this will occur after a fixed number of years, n (this is shown for a specific form of the production function in the Appendix). This number, n, is thus the length of life of a vintage. If we combine (F) and (G), we have the shutdown criterion

(H) $$\frac{p(v)X(v)}{e^{an}} = w N(v),$$

which indicates that when the initial total revenue of a vintage has been reduced to the wage bill by technical progress, the vintage is taken out of production. This result is shown in figure 9.1.

Here the price of the commodity, $p(t)$, declines from $p(v)$ at time v to $wN(v)/X(v)$, unit variable cost, at time $v+n$, as a result of technical progress. At time $v+n$, variable costs equal revenue and the vintage is taken out of service. The area labeled b represents the total return on the machine over its life, while the rectangle a represents total variable cost over the same period.[2]

In equilibrium, the cost of investment in a vintage will equal the present value of the quasi rents expected over the life of the vintage, n. (This analysis is similar to that of Phelps 1963.) The expected quasi rents are discounted at the going, risk-free rate (which we assume to be constant), in order to derive the present value. Now with exogenously

2. A more realistic treatment would show labor cost per unit rising over time for a given vintage, as a result of rising maintenance and repair costs (or of falling technical efficiency as machines deteriorate). This would make the mathematics more complex, but would not change the principal results of the analysis.

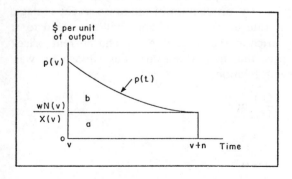

Fig. 9.1   Revenue and cost of a vintage

given wage rate, production function, and discount rate, the variable that determines the equality between investment cost and present value of quasi rents is the initial price of the (new) vintage, $p(v)$. (It is shown in the Appendix that the length of life, n, and $p(v)$ are related by α, the rate of technical progress.)

Once $p(v)$ is found, substitution into the demand equation, (E), determines aggregate production from all vintages in service, $Y(t)$. Since we know the capacity taken out of service $[v - (n+1)]$ and the sum of the capacities of the n vintages remaining in service, the volume of investment in vintage v is that which will bring the total capacity of the industry up to the quantity $Y(t)$. This mechanism is illustrated in figure 9.2 (and shown in detail in the Appendix).

In figure 9.2, $p(t)$ is the supply price of the new vintage, $v=t$. This price, together with demand, $D(t)$, determines the equilibrium quantity, $o\,e$. Gross investment in $v=t$ results in new capacity of $\overline{c\,e}$. The height of the supply curve corresponding to the distance $\overline{o\,c}$ shows the variable costs of older vintages, ranging from $v=t-1$ (with the lowest variable cost of the lot, $\overline{o\,h}$) to $v=t-n$ (the oldest in use, with variable cost at $p(t)$).

Figure 9.3 shows the change that takes place in the succeeding year. The demand curve shifts to the right, owing to growth in the economy, from $D(t)$ to $D(t+1)$. The supply price falls from $p(t)$ to $p(t+1)$, owing to technical change. The new supply price, $p(t+1)$, together with the new demand curve, $D(t+1)$, determines the new equilibrium quantity, $\overline{o\,f}$. Vintage $v=t$ is now "clay," so only its variable cost is relevant; the capacity of $v=t$ is $\overline{o\,a} = \overline{c\,e}$, and its variable cost is $\overline{o\,g}$. Gross investment in vintage $v=t+1$ results in production of $\overline{d\,f}$. Because of the decline in price, vintage $v=t-n$ is shut down and capacity $\overline{b\,c}$ is lost. The net addition to capacity is therefore $\overline{d\,f}$ minus $\overline{b\,c}$.

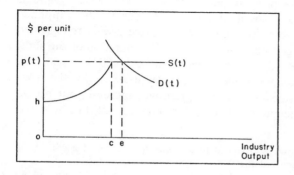

Fig. 9.2   Static equilibrium

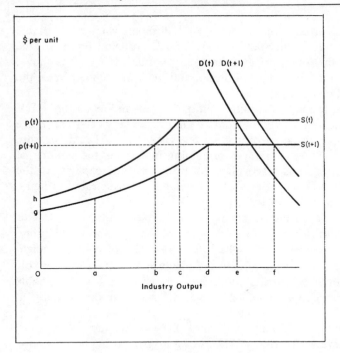

Fig. 9.3   Comparative statics

Now with steady rates of technical progress and growth in the economy and a constant price elasticity of demand for the product, it follows
that the larger (*a*) the rate of technical progress (lowering price), (*b*)
the rate of growth of the economy (shifting the demand relation to the
right), and (*c*) the price elasticity of demand, the greater will be (i)
the amount of investment in the new vintage, and (ii) the net expansion
in new capacity.

Suppose now that the price of an input rises unexpectedly and is
subsequently expected to remain at the new level.[3] In the simplified
form of the model we are now discussing, the price rise is represented
by an increase in the wage rate, from w to w^*.[4] Examination of the shutdown criterion, (*H*), reveals that the right-hand side (RHS) will now
be larger for existing vintages, since the only value affected is the wage
rate. On the left-hand side (LHS), the price will increase, but not as
much as the wage. The length of life of older vintages will thus be short-

3. The analysis that follows is designed to describe the effects of a rise in the
price of energy, such as occurred in 1973.
4. An asterisk indicates the value of a variable after a rise in the price of an
input.

ened by a rise in a variable input price; this follows from the putty-clay assumption of fixed input coefficients, which does not permit an adjustment to the new set of relative input prices.

For later vintages, such an adjustment will take place by substitution of investment for labor. A vintage constructed after the input price rise will have a higher labor productivity coefficient, k^*, and a higher initial price of output, p^*. The life of a new vintage will be longer or shorter, according to whether the numerator of the LHS of the shutdown criterion rises by a smaller or larger proportion than the RHS. In order to obtain a solution, a specific form of the production function must be chosen. This will also permit us to introduce uncertainty.

9.4   Cobb-Douglas Form, Two Inputs and One Output

By adopting a simple form of the production function, we can demonstrate that a rise in the wage rate from w to $w^* = \sigma w$ (where σ is a number greater than one), will yield the following results for new vintages: the expected length of life is the same as was expected at the time of construction of vintages built before the wage rise; the investment-labor ratio will rise by the factor σ; and the initial price will rise by a smaller proportion. These results, derived in Part B of the Appendix, are summarized in (I).

(I) $n^* = n,$

            $c^* = \sigma c,$

where c is the investment-labor ratio.

            $p^*(v) = \sigma^b p(v),$

where b is the elasticity of output with respect to labor.

In order to investigate the extent of the impact of the wage rise on old plants, which results in earlier closings owing to a sudden speeding of obsolescence, a specific form of the demand equation (E) must also be adopted:

(J) $D(t) = D(t-1)e^{\gamma}p(t)^{-\epsilon},$

where γ is the change in demand caused by the aggregate growth rate (as in (E)), and ϵ is the price elasticity of demand.

This demand function will also permit us to examine the equilibrium quantity produced by all vintages, and the portions produced by the new vintage ($v=t$) and the old vintages. The general results of this analysis, which are derived in Part C of the Appendix, are the following:

(a) Obsolescence will always increase, causing accelerated scrapping, since a new vintage will be profitable at a lower price than that which would permit the oldest equipment to remain in service. This results from the fact that the new vintage benefits from technical progress, which lowers cost, and from a lower investment-labor ratio, which also lowers cost.

(b) The more elastic the demand or the greater the wage rise, the smaller is the investment in the new vintage and the smaller the equilibrium quantity produced. The larger the increase in the wage rate, the greater the capacity of old equipment that will be shut down, and the greater the price that will be required to induce new investment. And the greater the price elasticity of demand, the smaller the equilibrium quantity demanded at the new higher price and the smaller the quantity of investment that will be profitable.

(c) If the price elasticity of demand or the increase in the wage rate is sufficiently large, no new investment will take place for a time, and the equilibrium price will be below the new vintage price, so all output will be produced from existing plants.

(d) Labor productivity will always increase, because accelerated obsolescence will lead to more rapid scrapping of old plants. The productivity increase will be enhanced by the investment, if any, in new plants, which benefit from technical progress and a lower investment-labor ratio.

(e) The steady growth of output which characterized the behavior of the model before the wage rise will now be disturbed, and oscillations in growth of labor productivity may ensue.

The impact of a sudden, unexpected rise in the price of a variable input is illustrated in figure 9.4. As a result of the input price rise, the supply curve is shifted to $S^*(t+1)$. The increase in supply price, from $p(t+1)$ to $p^*(t+1)$, is less than the price in variable cost per unit, from g to g^*, because the new vintage can partially offset the increase in the wage by varying the investment-labor ratio. Equilibrium output is smaller, at $o\,\overline{f^*}$, than would have held without the input price rise $(o\,\overline{f})$, as the higher price results in a smaller quantity demanded. Accelerated obsolescence is equal to $\overline{d^*d}$, and investment in the new vintage results in new capacity of $\overline{d^*f^*}$. Net expansion in output is $\overline{e\,f^*}$ equal to $\overline{d^*\,f^*}$ less $\overline{d^*\,e}$.

9.5   Uncertainty regarding Rise in Price of Variable Input

Instead of the sudden, unexpected rise in a variable input price discussed in the previous two sections, we now consider industry behavior during a period of uncertainty, initially of unknown duration, regarding the price increase. For simplicity, we assume that the probability of the rise in the wage rate to w^* is 0.5 during the uncertainty period, and the probability of no change is also 0.5. This is intended to parallel

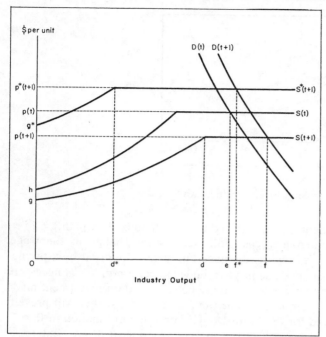

Fig. 9.4   Impact of rise in price of variable input

states of uncertainty preceding OPEC conferences, or doubts that the cartel can hold together.

Investment made during the period of uncertainty, if guided by the principle of maximizing expected profits, will have an investment-labor ratio intermediate between the two investment-labor ratios that would be appropriate for each possible future wage rate. This ratio will be inappropriate for either of the possible outcomes, yet will be cost-minimizing in view of the uncertainty surrounding either. The initial output price of a vintage constructed during the period of uncertainty must therefore be sufficiently high to recoup the loss that would otherwise ensue once the level of wages is finally determined. Vintages constructed after the period of uncertainty will embody the investment-labor ratio which is appropriate to the finally decided level of the wage, and will therefore have lower variable costs and lower initial output prices than those of the vintage built under uncertainty. So the initial price of output of the "uncertainty vintage" must be sufficiently high to equate the present value of the expected quasi rents under either outcome to the cost of investment, as illustrated in figure 9.5.

Uncertainty prevails over the period from a to b. The path $c\,d\,e\,f$ represents the price pattern with no uncertainty and no wage increase. The path $c\,d\,e\,g\,h$ represents the price pattern with no uncertainty and

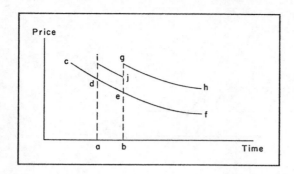

Fig. 9.5   Price path under uncertainty

a sudden, permanent increase in the wage at time b. The path $c\,d\,i\,j\,e\,f$ represents the uncertainty case followed by no change in the wage. Finally, the path $c\,d\,i\,j\,g\,h$ is the uncertainty case followed by a permanent wage increase. The rise in price under uncertainty, $d\,i$, is necessary to recoup the loss that would otherwise be sustained on investment made during the period from a to b. The minimum price rise that will prevent a net loss is derived for the Cobb-Douglas production function in Part D of the Appendix. This price rise is, in fact, a pure cost of uncertainty.

The uncertainty problem also has an effect on obsolescence. If the wage does in fact rise, vintages built before the period of uncertainty will subsequently obsolesce more rapidly than expected at the time of their construction; this is equivalent to showing that the length of life of these older vintages will be shortened, and is the same result found in the preceding sections. By a similar line of reasoning, a wage rise will result in a shorter length of life for a vintage built under uncertainty than one built thereafter; for the uncertainty vintage, a shorter span of time will ensue before variable cost per unit absorbs product price. But the acceleration of obsolescence for the uncertainty vintage will be less than for the older vintages, because the uncertainty vintage is better adjusted, though not completely so, to the new wage level.

If the wage does not rise, there will be no acceleration in the obsolescence of pre-uncertainty vintages. And the uncertainty vintage will have a longer life than those built either before or after the uncertainty period; this results from the greater investment-labor ratio of the uncertainty vintage, which delays the time when variable cost per unit will absorb the entire product price.

The uncertainty analysis does not result in a distinctive conclusion regarding labor productivity. The results depend mainly on the outcome of the uncertain input price: if the input price does rise, the conclusions of the previous section apply and labor productivity will accelerate; if the input price remains the same, the trend of labor productivity will not change by very much. During the period of uncertainty, it should be noted, the increase in the output price will tend to call back into service the vintage just shut down.

9.6   General Form, Three Inputs and Two Outputs

Three inputs are examined in order to cover explicitly the case of variations in energy prices. Study of two outputs permits us to cover the joint production of a "good" and a "bad," the latter referring to pollution, accidents, or health hazards. As before, we assume that substitution is possible among inputs before investment, but not after. Similarly, we assume that product transformation is possible before investment, but not after.[5]

The general form of the production function is given by

(K) $$X(v) = [X(1,v), X(2,v)] = A(v)f[N(v), I(v), Z(v)],$$

where boldface type indicates a vector, $X(1,v)$ the good product, $X(2,v)$ the bad product, and Z the other variable input.

A short-run utilization function may be written as

(L) $$X(v) = A(v)k[Z(v), I(v)]N(v),$$

or

(M) $$X(v) = [A(v)k(1,v)N(v), A(v)k(2,v)N(v)],$$

where

(N) $$k(i,v) = \frac{X(i,v)}{A(v)N(v)} \qquad i = 1,2.$$

The value of $k(i,v)$ will vary across vintages, but will be constant over the life of a vintage.

A utilization function can also be written for each output, because of the assumption of joint production after construction of a vintage:

(O) $$X(i,v) = A(v)k(i,v)N(v) \qquad i = 1,2.$$

As before, technical progress is assumed to occur at a constant rate, α.

The price of the first output is determined, as before, by supply and demand under competitive conditions. The second output, we assume, is subject to a legislative restriction requiring some level of treatment of

---

5. We chose to express pollution as an output rather than as a cost of production because this approach makes explicit the *ex ante* choice of the ratio of the "good" to the "bad" output; the choice is implemented by the specific product or process adopted. The quantity of the "bad" output that must subsequently be treated before discharge is, of course, dependent on (*a*) the ratio chosen and (*b*) the level of production.

wastes, in the case of pollution, or some level of worker protection, in the case of occupational safety and health. (As mentioned earlier, we are using the term "pollution" to refer to all undesirable outputs.) The cost of this treatment constitutes a negative price per unit of the second output; this price declines, in absolute value, over time as a consequence of improvements in techniques by the industries that supply pollution control equipment.[6]

When a negative price is imposed on the second output, the price of the first output must rise sufficiently to make the present value of a new vintage equal to the cost of investment. This is equivalent to the requirement that total revenue be the same for a unit of investment both before and after imposition of the penalty because input costs are unaffected. We also note that this requirement is independent of the level of $p(2,v)$, since the equal rates of decline of the two output prices will cancel regardless of the initial level of the negative price of the second output. We assume that minimization of the cost of abatement has a neutral effect on the three inputs, I, N, and Z, so that the average products of labor for both outputs can be used to express the constant revenue relationship.

(P) $$k(1,v)p(1,v) + k(2,v)p(2,v)$$

$$= \text{constant, for all } p(2,v).$$

6. We assume, for the sake of simplicity of analysis, that the rate of technical progress is the same in the industry we are studying as in the industry sector that supplies the pollution control equipment. This assumption is obviously inexact, for rates of technical progress vary among industries, so that some will have rates greater than the rate of the pollution abatement equipment sector and some will have rates that are smaller. However, incorporation into our model of a different rate for the using industry than for the equipment sector greatly complicates the analysis without a comparable gain in explanatory power. The main source of this complication is that the length of life of a vintage will vary if different rates of technical progress are assumed in the using sector and the pollution abatement sector. Variations in the length of life will, in general, be very small.

The assumption of equal rates of technical progress in the using industry and in the pollution abatement equipment sector results in both prices, the positive price of the first output and the negative price of the second output, changing at the same rate over time. Both will fall in absolute value, and the ratio of the two prices will remain constant. A vintage designed after imposition of the treatment requirement will utilize the least-cost combination of production process and purchased abatement equipment, so as to maximize profits. As technical progress occurs in our industry, new production processes will permit less production of the second output for a unit produced of the first output. And as technical progress occurs in the abatement equipment sector, the cost of a piece of equipment that will reduce the second output by one unit will also fall. So long as the ratio of prices of two outputs remains constant, the output mix will not change, from vintage to vintage, for new investment.

For vintages constructed before the imposition of $p(2,v)$, change in the production process is no longer possible, so this price will result in decreased revenue, or in plant closing.

The shutdown criterion, after the vintage has been in place for n years, is given by

(Q) $$X(1,v)p(1,v+n) + X(2,v)p(2,v+n)$$
$$- wN(v) - p(Z)Z(v) = 0.$$

This expression, which is parallel to (G), indicates that a vintage will be taken out of service when revenue no longer exceeds variable cost.

In equilibrium, the rate of product transformation (RPT) will be equal to the ratio of the prices of the two products. The RPT can be expressed by means of the output-labor ratios, so we have

(R) $$\frac{dk(1,v)}{dk(2,v)} = - \frac{p(2,v)}{p(1,v)}.$$

For new investment, the equilibrium levels of the output-labor ratios are found by equating the marginal product of labor with the ratio of the present value of the wage stream to the present value of the price stream, over the economic life, n. In a parallel fashion, the energy-output ratio is found by use of the marginal product of energy (see Part E of the Appendix).

In order to give explicit form to the rate of product transformation, we define two functions, $j(1,v)$ and $j(2,v)$. These relate the two outputs to the three inputs, removing the influences of the levels of inputs and the rate of technical change. They are therefore functionally related to one another:

(S) $$j(1,v) = f[j(2,v)].$$

As the production process is changed to reduce the output of pollution, $X(2,v)$, fewer resources are available for output of the desirable product, $X(1,v)$. This is illustrated in figure 9.6, where the terms $j(i,v)$ are used to represent the axes in order to abstract from scale effects.

The curve in figure 9.6 represents the set of possible mixes of the two outputs. We only consider points on the curve to the left of e, for this is where the quantity of the first, desirable output is at a maximum. Efforts to reduce the second output in response to penalties will lead to points on the curve that lie to the left of the vertical line above e. If the second output, pollution, is reduced to zero, the curve cuts the vertical axis—this is the other boundary of our interest.

Before the imposition of restrictions on pollution, the price of the second output is zero, and the product mix for new vintages is such as to maximize the first output. The price line is thus horizontal and tangent

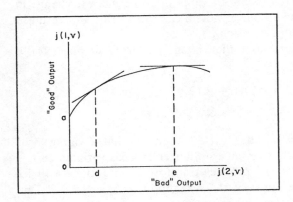

Fig. 9.6   Determination of output mix

to the RPT above *e*. A negative price of the second output will shift the product mix toward the vertical axis, and the quantities of both goods will fall for a bundle of inputs of equal cost. This is illustrated by the tangency of a price line above *d*.

By adopting particular forms of the production function and the rate of product transformation, we can derive more specific results regarding the interrelationships among an energy price increase; the imposition of restrictions on pollution; input mix; output mix; obsolescence; and product price.

9.7 Cobb-Douglas Form, Parabolic Rate of Product Transformation

A parabolic rate of product transformation conforms to our vision of a realistic representation. We define $j(1,v)$ as follows:

$$(T) \qquad j(1,v) = 1 - \frac{b^2}{4c} + b[j(2,v)] - c[j(2,v)]^2,$$

where *b* and *c* are positive and $4c > b^2$.

In terms of figure 9.6, $j(1,v) = 1$, a maximum, when $p(2,v) = 0$; this is the point above *e*. The slope of (T) is nonnegative over the range *o e*, and decreases as $j(2,v)$ increases.

When (T) is combined with a Cobb-Douglas form of the production function, the following results may be demonstrated for new vintages (see Part F of the Appendix):

(1) The energy-labor ratio, Z/N, depends only on the relative prices of these two inputs, $p(Z)$ and *w* (see eq. (F.9) in the Appendix).

(2) Similarly, the investment-labor ratio, I/N, depends only on *r* and *w* (F.10).

(3) The expected length of life of a new vintage depends only on the rate of technical progress and the discount rate (F.11). It is not affected, therefore, by variations in input or output prices.

If we now consider a sudden, unexpected rise in the price of energy, $p(Z)$, which is expected to continue, we obtain the following results for new vintages (see Part G of the Appendix):
(4) The energy-labor ratio will be reduced (G.1).
(5) The output-labor ratio will be reduced (G.5).
(6) Similarly, the output-investment ratio will be reduced (G.6), but
(7) the output-energy ratio will be increased (G.7).

Our model thus implies that a rise in the price of energy leads to substitution of labor and investment for energy, in new vintages. This result is in accordance with the findings of our case studies of manufacturing industries (Myers et al. 1974).

The increase in the price of energy will also result in a higher price of the desirable output, $p(1,v)$, for new vintages, as would be expected, but the price of pollution, $p(2,v)$, will not be affected (G.10). Therefore, the equilibrium output mix will contain more pollution and more of the desirable output, for inputs of equal cost (G.11). This can be seen by referring to figure 9.6: a rise in the relative price of the desirable output results in a movement to the right along the RPT curve, from the point above d to an intermediate point between that point and the point above e. Thus the quantity of pollution (that requires subsequent treatment) per unit of the desirable output increases as the energy price increases.

A parallel implication can be deduced for an increase in restrictions on pollution, equivalent to an increase in the absolute size of $p(2,v)$, holding the price of energy constant. This will result in a change in output mix, reducing the quantities of both outputs, for a bundle of inputs of constant cost. The output-energy ratio will therefore fall. This is in accordance with the claims of industry spokesmen that pollution abatement increases energy requirements.

The impact of an energy price rise on older vintages is to reduce their length of life below that expected at the time of construction (G.8). This is in accordance with the findings in the two-input, one-output case (section 9.3). We have thus generalized our earlier result that an increase in the price of energy will lead to accelerated obsolescence.

A similar result may be shown for the impact on old vintages of the sudden, unexpected imposition of a negative price on pollution. Total revenue of existing vintages will be reduced, thus reducing their life span below that expected at the time of construction (F.23). Obsolescence is thereby increased.

Appropriate adjustments in the three-input, two-output form of the model will yield the results found earlier with respect to (a) industry equilibrium following a rise in the price of energy (section 9.4), and (*b*) uncertainty regarding such a rise in price (section 9.5). The mathematics involved, however, are quite tedious. To avoid repetition, we will not present those derivations.

9.8   Summary of Model

The principal implications of our model are two: energy price increases and the imposition of requirements for pollution abatement lead to accelerated obsolescence of existing plant and equipment, thus tending to increase labor productivity in an industry; but the same constraints lead to higher requirements of labor and investment per unit of output for new plant and equipment, tending to reduce labor productivity. Which effect dominates over time depends on the elasticity of demand for the product and the nature of the *ex ante* production function. The empirical questions are thus clear-cut.

A reasonable deduction from our analysis is that the obsolescence effect will dominate initially and there will be an acceleration, for a time, in the rate of growth of labor productivity. Subsequent developments will depend on the vintage structure of the industry and on any possible induced acceleration in the rates of technical change in the industry under examination and in the industries supplying pollution abatement equipment.

Our model also implies that reductions in energy use and in pollution are competitive in new vintages.

9.9   Sketch of Measurement Procedure

The intent of this project is to derive and project the effects on manufacturing industries of rapid energy price increases and changes in the laws regarding pollution and occupational health and safety hazards. We have in this essay developed a model of industry behavior which leads us to focus on two effects of these changes in the economic environment: acceleration in the rate of obsolescence, and movements along the *ex ante* production function.

Were data available in sufficient detail, we should like to estimate the input and output coefficients of each unit in every plant in the industry. Such estimates, over time, would provide a robust test of the hypotheses and parameters of the model.

For our intention to be realized, however, we do not require such detail. If we can reasonably approximate the efficiency distribution of each industry, then we can derive most of the results we need.

We begin by assuming that investment is retired in order of age, the oldest investments being taken out of production first. (Of course, this assumption is not true, but it will be a good approximation if technical efficiency is a major criterion of obsolescence.)

Next we obtain estimates of the book value of the industry's gross plant and equipment for a recent period, and estimates of current dollar gross investment as far back as possible.

These investment expenditures are then cumulated back in time until their sum equals book value. These are the investments that are assumed to be still in place, and all earlier investments are assumed to have been taken out of service.

After adjusting these figures by appropriate deflators, we obtain real plant and equipment, by vintage, for the industry.

We next wish to obtain the relevant input-output coefficients for the industry, by vintage. These include the output-capital ratio, the labor-capital ratio, the energy-capital ratio, and the various pollution-capital ratios.

If the capital stock grows at a constant rate, prices remain constant, technical change is neutral, and average age is constant, then vintage-to-vintage changes in the ratios will equal year-to-year changes in the average for the entire stock. This will also hold true under the less stringent assumptions that the coefficients change steadily, the capital stock grows at a constant rate, and average age is constant.

However, even the latter assumptions are unlikely to hold over the business cycle. A correction for the cyclical effect may be made by using peak-to-peak values of the various ratios.

In a preliminary test, we applied the above procedure to the petroleum refining industry. Peak-to-peak changes in the capacity output-capital ratios (after correction for changes in the peak-to-peak rate of capacity utilization) were found to be 1.6% from 1951 to 1973.

However, we also found that the average age of capital stock in the industry had been growing for the greater part of the postwar period. The effect of this is to cause the rate of increase in the capacity output-capital ratio, from vintage to vintage, to be underestimated by the year-to-year rate of change in the average.

It also happens that from 1959 to 1966 investment was much lower than in the preceding and following periods. This causes underestimation of the change in the capacity output-capital ratio in the 1959–66 period and overestimation in the 1966–73 period.

The most accurate means for estimating the effects of these disturbances would be a simulation study. For the purposes of this illustration, we merely adjusted the series for the effects of the change in average age, which appear to be by far the most important.

With an estimate of the vintage-to-vintage rate of change in the capacity output-capital ratio, we can construct estimates of the capacity output associated with each vintage still in place.

A similar procedure can then be applied to capacity labor and capacity energy to obtain vintage estimates for these measures. Our previous studies of the petroleum refining industry indicated that a break in the trend of the ratio of energy to output occurred around 1962. At that time, expectations of falling energy prices were replaced by expectations of increasing energy prices. For this industry, therefore, the energy use series is divided into two portions (one before and one after the change in expected prices) which are adjusted separately.

The estimates thus obtained may be cross-checked with data from engineering studies and from plant operations data which are occasionally available from trade and technical journals, as well as from company sources.

Series on air, water, and land pollution for each industry do not exist for the long historical period under study, although there is a historical series on water use in the Census of Manufactures. However, considerable data are available from pollution abatement studies on the industries that interest us. Such studies often provide data on "old," "typical," and "best practice" (or "new") plants which will enable us to form very rough estimates of pollution output by vintage. This material will also be supplemented by data from individual plants, which are available in the technical literature.

We wish to measure the new level of output, the volume of new investment, and the new productivity level. Given the vintage structure outlined above, the input-output coefficients for new equipment, and the price elasticity of demand for the product, we can obtain estimates of these figures.

As a preliminary test of the magnitude of the obsolescence effects, we estimated the vintage structure for petroleum refining, including only the capacity output, energy, and labor coefficients. Since we wish to use petroleum refining as a case study for this project, we used a *ceteris paribus* analysis, in which it was assumed that all prices remained constant with the exception of the price of energy for heat and power.

From engineering studies carried out in 1973–4 (Gordian Associates 1974; Gyftopoulos et al. 1974), we estimated the new input-output coefficients caused by the rise in energy prices (which roughly doubled). This enabled us to obtain an estimate of the change in output price due to the energy price rise.

We then assumed that quasi rents for the oldest vintage in use in 1973 (the capital stock from 1949) were zero in 1973 prices. (Since we wish to estimate only the static obsolescence effect, we used the data to show effects on quasi rents without the passage of time.) Table 9.1 shows quasi rents when energy for heat and power is at 1973 prices and at 1975 prices (roughly double the 1973 level).

Table 9.1	Quasi Rents of Selected Vintages (Percent of Output Price)	
	Energy for Heat and Power	
Vintages	1973 prices	1975 prices
1973	9.2%	8.6%
1961	6.1%	4.9%
1951	1.4%	0.2%
1950	0.7%	−0.5%
1949	0.0%	−1.3%

As a result of the energy price change, the better part of two vintages go out of production that would not otherwise have done so.

To obtain the new level of output, the volume of investment, and the new productivity level, we also require estimates of the price elasticity of demand for the products of the industry. In the case of petroleum refining, the total effect of the price rises greatly exceeds the capabilities of available price elasticity studies.

At this stage, we have not established a procedure for measurement of uncertainty. There are two routes available. One would be to seek direct and indirect measures of uncertainty by obtaining estimates from decision-makers as to the degrees of uncertainty that prevailed in the past or estimates of errors in actual decisions made. The alternative route is to assume that uncertainty results in underinvestment and higher short-term profits and prices. If our model accurately measures desirable levels of investment in the absence of uncertainty, predicted and actual levels of investment and prices provide an estimate of the effect of uncertainty.

Appendix A

Two-Input, One-Output Case
General Form

The *ex ante* production function:

A.1 $(A)^7$ $X(v) = A(v) f[N(v), I(v)]$.

The *ex post* utilization function:

7. Letters in parentheses indicate equations that appear in the text.

A.2   (B) $X(v) = A(v)k(v)N(v)$

where $k(v) = f\left[1, \dfrac{I(v)}{N(v)}\right]$.

Output from all vintages:

A.3   (C) $Y(t) = \int\limits_{v=t-n}^{v=t} A(v)k(v)N(v)dv.$

Average labor productivity:

A.4   (D) $\dfrac{Y(t)}{\int\limits_{v=t-n}^{v=t} N(v)dv} = \dfrac{\int\limits_{v=t-n}^{v=t} A(v)k(v)N(v)dv}{\int\limits_{v=t-n}^{v=t} N(v)dv}.$

Demand equation:

A.5   (E) $D(t) = D[p(t),\gamma].$

Technical change:

A.6 $A(v) = A(o)e^{av},$

where the zeroth year is any convenient base year from which to count vintages.

Price:

A.7   (F) $p(t) = \dfrac{A(v)}{A(t)} p(v).$

From (A.7) and (A.6):

A.8 $p(t) = p(v)e^{a(v-t)}.$

A machine goes out of production after $t-v$ years:

A.9   (G) $p(t)X(v) = wN(v).$

The shutdown criterion:

A.10   (H) $\dfrac{p(v)X(v)}{e^{an}} = wN(v)$

from (A.8) and (A.9).

Length of life:

A.11 $n = \dfrac{1}{\alpha} \ln\left(\dfrac{p(v)X(v)}{wN(v)}\right)$

from (A.10).

A.11a
$$\frac{p(v)X(v)}{wN(v)} = \frac{p(v)A(v)k(v)}{w}$$

from (A.2).

Since $p(v)A(v)$ is constant, and $k(v)$ is constant as long as input prices are constant, it follows from (A.11) and (A.12) that length of life is constant.

Cost of investment must equal discounted quasi rents:

A.12
$$I(v) = \int_{v}^{v+n} p(t)X(t)e^{-r(t-v)}dt$$
$$- \int_{v}^{v+n} wN(v)e^{-r(t-v)}dt.$$

A.13
$$I(v) = p(v)A(v)k(v)N(v)\left[\frac{1-e^{-(a+r)n}}{\alpha+r}\right]$$
$$- wN(v)\left(\frac{1-e^{-rn}}{r}\right).$$

A.14
$$p(v) = \frac{I(v)}{N(v)} + w\left(\frac{1-e^{-rn}}{r}\right)\Big/$$
$$A(v)k(v)\left[\frac{1-e^{-(a+r)n}}{\alpha+r}\right].$$

Assuming $I(v)/N(v)$ and $k(v)$ are known from the input prices and the production function, (A.14) and (A.11) together give $p(v)$ and n. Thus, to complete the general model, we need (A.15) and (A.16).

Ex ante marginal product of labor:

A.15
$$\frac{\partial X(v)}{\partial N(v)} = A(v)\left\{\frac{\partial f[N(v),I(v)]}{\partial N(v)}\right\}.$$

Marginal product of labor is equal to the present value of the wage stream divided by present value of the price stream over the economic life, n.

A.16
$$\frac{\partial X(v)}{\partial N(v)} = \frac{\int_{v}^{v+n} we^{(t-v)r}dt}{\int_{v}^{v+n} p(v)e^{(t-v)r}dt}$$
$$= \frac{w}{p(v)}\left\{\left(\frac{1-e^{-rn}}{r}\right)\Big/\left[\frac{1-e^{-(a+r)n}}{\alpha+r}\right]\right\}.$$

Appendix B

Two-Input, One-Output Case
Cobb-Douglas Form

Ex ante production function:

B.1 $\qquad$ (A) $\quad X(v) = A(v)N(v)^b I(v)^{1-b}$.

Ex post utilization function:

B.2 $\qquad$ (B) $\quad X(v) = A(v)\, c^{1-b}\, N(v)$

$\qquad\qquad\qquad$ where $c = I(v)/N(v)$.

Output from all vintages:

B.3 $\qquad$ (C) $\quad Y(t) = c^{1-b} \displaystyle\int_{v=t-n}^{v=t} A(v)N(v)\,dv$.

Length of life:

B.4 $\qquad\qquad n = \dfrac{1}{\alpha} \ln \left[\dfrac{A(v)p(v)c^{1-b}}{w} \right].$

From (A.14):

B.5 $\qquad\qquad p(v) = c + w \left(\dfrac{1 - e^{-rn}}{r} \right)$

$\qquad\qquad\qquad\qquad \times \left[A(v)c^{1-b} \dfrac{1 - e^{-(a+r)n}}{\alpha + r} \right]^{-1}.$

From (A.15):

B.6 $\qquad\qquad \dfrac{\partial X(v)}{\partial N(v)} = bA(v)c^{1-b}.$

From (B.6) and (A.16):

B.7 $\qquad\qquad bA(v)c^{1-b} = w \left(\dfrac{1 - e^{-rn}}{r} \right)$

$\qquad\qquad\qquad\qquad \times \left[p(v) \dfrac{1 - e^{-(a+r)n}}{\alpha + r} \right]^{-1}.$

Using (B.4) and (B.7),

B.8 $\qquad\qquad rbe^{(a+r)n} - (\alpha + r)e^{rn} + (\alpha + r - rb) = 0.$

Equation (B.8) is the length-of-life formula, showing length of life determined by α, the rate of technical progress; r, the rate of discount; and b, the elasticity of output with respect to labor.

Using (B.7) and (B.5),

B.9
$$c = w \left(\frac{1-b}{b}\right)\left(\frac{1-e^{-rn}}{r}\right).$$

From (B.4),

B.10
$$p(v) = \frac{we^{an}}{A(v)c^{1-b}}.$$

The equilibrium values of the variables of interest for two different wage rates w and $w^* = \sigma w$ bear the following relationships:

B.11 $n^* = n$ (from B.8).

No change in length of life.

B.12 $c^* = \sigma c$ (from B.9).

Investment-labor ratio is proportionate to wage.

B.13 $p^*(v) = \sigma^b p(v)$ (from B.10).

Price rises but less than the wage.

Appendix C

Two-Input, One-Output Case
Cobb-Douglas with Sudden Wage Rise

Demand function:

C.1   (E) $q(v) = q(o)e^{\gamma v}p(v)^{-\epsilon} = q(o)p(o)^{-\epsilon}e^{v(\gamma + a\epsilon)}.$

Production from the new vintage:

C.2
$$X(v) = \frac{dq(v)}{dv} + X(v-n).$$

From (C.2) and assuming smooth growth in X:

C.3
$$X(v) = q(v)\frac{\gamma + \alpha\epsilon}{1 - e^{-n(\gamma + a\epsilon)}}.$$

Labor requirement per vintage:

C.4
$$N(v) = \frac{X(v)}{A(v)c^{1-b}}.$$

Total employment:

C.5
$$\int_{v-n}^{v} N(t)\,dt$$

$$= \frac{q(v)\,(\gamma+\alpha\epsilon)\,(1 - e^{-n(\gamma+a(\epsilon-1))})}{A(v)c^{1-b}[\gamma + \alpha(\epsilon - 1)][1 - e^{-n(\gamma+a\epsilon)}]},$$

unless $\gamma+\alpha(\epsilon - 1) = 0$, when

C.6
$$\int_{v-n}^{v} N(t)\,dt = nN(v).$$

Average labor productivity:

C.7
$$\frac{q(v)}{\int_{v-n}^{v} N(t)\,dt} = A(v)c^{1-b}\left[\frac{\gamma + \alpha(\epsilon - 1)}{\gamma + \alpha\epsilon}\right]$$

$$\left\{\frac{1 - e^{-n(\gamma+a\epsilon)}}{1 - e^{-n[\gamma+a(\epsilon-1)]}}\right\},$$

unless $\gamma + \alpha(\epsilon - 1) = 0$, when

C.8
$$\frac{q(v)}{\int_{v-n}^{v} N(t)\,dt} = A(v)c^{1-b}\left[\frac{1 - e^{-n(\gamma+a\epsilon)}}{n(\gamma + \alpha\epsilon)}\right].$$

(C.7) and (C.8) show that labor productivity is proportionate to technical change, $A(v)$, provided input prices are constant and $X(v)$ shows smooth growth.

Suppose now that wages rise from w to σw. The price at which new investment will be forthcoming is, from (B.13),

C.9
$$p^*(v) = \sigma^b p(v).$$

Demand corresponding to this price is

C.10
$$q^*_d(v) = q(v)\sigma^{-\epsilon b}.$$

Existing plants shut down can be found from equation (B.4):

C.11
$$n^* = n - \frac{1 - b}{\alpha}\ln\sigma.$$

Thus production from existing plants is

C.12
$$q^*_s(v) = q(v) - \int_{v-n}^{v-n^*} X(t)\,dt.$$

Solving (C.12) with (C.3):

C.13
$$q^*_s(v) = q(v)\left[\frac{1 - e^{-n^*(\gamma+a\epsilon)}}{1 - e^{-n(\gamma+a\epsilon)}}\right].$$

If $q^*_a(v) \geq q^*_s(v)$, then investment will be forthcoming and the price will in fact be $\sigma^b p(v)$. If not, price will fall until supply and demand balance.

The inequality $q^*_a(v) \geq q^*_s(v)$ holds if C.14 holds:

C.14
$$\sigma^{-\epsilon b} \geq \frac{1 - e^{-n^*(\gamma + a\epsilon)}}{1 - e^{-n(\gamma + a\epsilon)}} \qquad \text{(from C.10 and C.13)}.$$

In general, the right-hand side of (C.14) will be close to one, since $n - n^*$ will usually not be too large. Thus condition (C.14) holds only for relatively small values of ϵ, that is, for relatively inelastic demand.

We now examine the three cases; (1) $q^*_a(v) = q^*_s(v)$; (2) $q^*_a(v) > q^*_s(v)$; and (3) $q^*_a(v) < q^*_s(v)$.

If $q^*_a(v) = q^*_s(v)$, then price is $p(v)\sigma^{-\epsilon b}$.

Labor employed in the still existing plants is:

C.15
$$\int_{v-n^*}^{v} N(t)\,dt = \frac{q(v)}{A(v)c^{1-b}}\left[\frac{\gamma + \alpha\epsilon}{\gamma + \alpha(\epsilon - 1)}\right]$$
$$\times \left\{\frac{1 - e^{-n^*[\gamma + a(\epsilon - 1)]}}{1 - e^{-n(\gamma + a\epsilon)}}\right\}.$$

Average labor productivity can be shown to be

C.16
$$\frac{q^*(v)}{\int_{v-n}^{v} N(t)\,dt} = A(v)c^{1-b}\left[\frac{\gamma + \alpha(\epsilon - 1)}{\gamma + \alpha\epsilon}\right]$$
$$\times \left\{\frac{1 - e^{-n^*(\gamma + a\epsilon)}}{1 - e^{-n^*[\gamma + a(\epsilon - 1)]}}\right\}.$$

Comparing with C.7, since $n < n^*$, labor productivity has increased.

If demand is sufficiently inelastic, and so $q^*_a(v) > q^*_s(v)$, then there will be a one-time spurt in new production, equal to

C.17
$$X^*(v) = q^*_a(v) - q^*_s(v),$$

C.18
$$X^*(v) = q(v)\left[\frac{\sigma^{-\epsilon b} - 1 - e^{-n^*(\gamma + a\epsilon)}}{1 - e^{-n(\gamma + a\epsilon)}}\right].$$

Labor productivity of this new production is

C.19
$$\frac{X^*(v)}{N^*(v)} = A(v)(\sigma c)^{1-b}.$$

Since average labor productivity of existing plants is (C.16), the new average labor productivity will exceed the old even further.

If demand is sufficiently elastic that $q^*_a(v) < q^*_s(v)$, then price will fall below $\sigma^b p(v)$ to $\pi^b p(v)$, where $1 < \pi < \sigma$. At this price, plants older than n^*_π will fall out of production.

C.20
$$n^*_\pi = n + \frac{b}{\alpha} \ln \pi - \frac{1}{\alpha} \ln \sigma.$$

π can be found by solving

C.21
$$\pi^{-\epsilon b} = \frac{1 - e^{-n^*_\pi (\gamma + a\epsilon)}}{1 - e^{-n(\gamma + a_\epsilon)}}.$$

Labor productivity will be

C.22
$$\frac{q^*(v)}{\int_{v^*_\pi}^{v} N(t)\,dt} = A(v)c^{1-b} \left[\frac{\gamma + \alpha(\epsilon - 1)}{\gamma + \alpha\epsilon} \right]$$

$$\times \left\{ \frac{1 - e^{-n^*_\pi (\gamma + a\epsilon)}}{1 - e^{-n^*_\pi [\gamma + a(\epsilon - 1)]}} \right\}.$$

Once price is established at $p(v)\sigma^b$, gross new production will be

C.23
$$X^*(v) = \frac{dq^*(v)}{dv} + X(v - n^*).$$

This can be shown to be

C.24
$$X^*(v) = q(v)(\gamma + \alpha\epsilon)\sigma^{-\epsilon b}$$

$$\times \left[\frac{1 - e^{-n(\gamma + a\epsilon)}\{1 - \sigma^{[\gamma(\frac{1-b}{a}) + \epsilon]}\}}{1 - e^{-n(\gamma + a\epsilon)}} \right].$$

This is faster than the smooth growth we assumed in (C.3), and the industry will exhibit oscillations in labor productivity rather than strict proportionality with technical progress.

Appendix D

Cobb-Douglas under Uncertainty

If the rise in wage to σw is uncertain, then the investment-labor ratio under uncertainty will be

D.1
$$c < c_u < \sigma c.$$

So we may define τ as

D.2
$$\tau c = c_u,$$

where $1 < \tau < \sigma$.

Suppose, after the fact, it turns out that the wage remains unchanged. In this case, the lifetime of plant built under uncertainty will be

D.3
$$n_u = \frac{1}{\alpha} \ln \left[\frac{A(v)p(v)(\tau c)^{1-b}}{w} \right],$$

D.4
$$n_u = n + \left(\frac{1-b}{\alpha} \right) \ln \tau.$$

In this case, discounted value of the quasi rents per man-hour will be, using (D.4),

D.5
$$c'_u = A(v)(\tau c)^{1-b} p(v) \left\{ \frac{1 - \exp\left[-(\alpha + r)n_u\right]}{\alpha + r} \right.$$
$$\left. - \exp(-\alpha n_u) \left[\frac{1 - \exp(-rn_u)}{r} \right] \right\}.$$

If, on the other hand, the wage rises, then the lifetime will be

D.6
$$n^*_u = n - \left(\frac{1-b}{\alpha} \right) \ln \left(\frac{\sigma}{\tau} \right) = n_u - \left(\frac{1-b}{\alpha} \right) \ln \sigma.$$

Discounted value of the quasi rents per man-hour is

D.7
$$c^{*\prime}_u = A(v)(\tau c)^{1-b} \sigma^b p(v) \left\{ \frac{1 - \exp\left[-(\alpha + r)n^*_u\right]}{\alpha + r} \right.$$
$$\left. - \exp(-\alpha n^*_u) \left[\frac{1 - \exp(-rn^*_u)}{r} \right] \right\}.$$

If the probability of the wage rise is assumed to be .5, then the optimum value of τ will be the one which minimizes

D.8
$$\frac{2\tau c - c'_u - c^{*\prime}_u}{2}.$$

If we differentiate D.8 with respect to τ, it can be shown that

D.9
$$\tau^b = \frac{1}{2} \left\{ \frac{1}{1 - \exp\left[-(\alpha + r)n\right]} \right\}$$
$$(1 - \exp\left[-(\alpha + r)n_u\right]$$
$$+ \sigma^b \left\{1 - \exp\left[-(\alpha + r)n^*_u\right]\right\}).$$

This may be approximated, for $1 < \sigma < 2$:

D.10
$$\tau^b \doteq \frac{1 + \sigma^b}{2},$$

D.11
$$\tau \doteq \left(\frac{1 + \sigma^b}{2} \right) 1/b.$$

Inserting D.9, it can be shown that the expected loss due to uncertainty is

D.12
$$\tau c - \frac{c_u + c^*_u}{2} = \frac{1}{2}\left\{ w\frac{1 - \exp(-rn_u)}{r} + \sigma w\right.$$

$$\left.\frac{1 - [\exp(-rn^*_u)]}{r}\right\} - \tau w\left[\frac{1 - \exp(rn)}{r}\right].$$

If the uncertainty period is one year, the price rise at the start of the period necessary to call forth investment is

D.13
$$\Delta p(v) = \left\{\frac{1}{2}\left[w\frac{1 - \exp(-rn_u)}{r} + \sigma w\right.\right.$$

$$\left.\left.\frac{1 - \exp(-rn^*_u)}{r}\right] - \tau w\frac{1 - \exp(rn)}{r}\right\} /A(v)(\tau c)^{1-b}.$$

Appendix E

Three-Input, Two-Output Case
General Form

Ex ante production function:

E.1   (A) $X(v) = A(v)f[N(v),I(v),Z(v)]$.

The bold type indicates vectors:

E.2 $X(v) = [x(1,v),x(2,v)]$.

The *ex post* utilization function:

E.3   (B) $X(v) = A(v)\,k\,(v)N(v)$.

Ex post utilization function for each output:

E.4 $X(i,v) = A(v)\,k(i,v)\,N(v)$ $i = 1, 2,$

where

E.5 $k(i,v) = \dfrac{X(i,v)}{A(v)N(v)}$ $i = 1, 2.$

Technical progress:

E.6 $A(v) = A(o)e^{av}$.

Price:

E.7   (F) $p(1,v) = p(1,0)e^{-av}$.

E.8 $\qquad$ (F) $\quad p(2,v) = p(2,0)e^{-av}$.

It is assumed that:

E.9 $\qquad A(v)[k(1,v)p(1,v) + k(2,v)p(2,v)] = \text{constant}$,

for all $p(2,0)$ and all v.

Define:

E.10 $\qquad h(Z) = \dfrac{Z(v)}{N(v)}$,

E.11 $\qquad h(I) = \dfrac{I(v)}{N(v)}$.

Length of life:

E.12 $\qquad n = \dfrac{1}{\alpha} \ln \left\{ \dfrac{A(v)[k(1,v)p(1,v) + k(2,v)p(2,v)]}{w - p(Z)h(Z)} \right\}$.

Parallel to (A.14):

E.13 $\qquad k(1,v)p(1,v) + k(2,v)p(2,v)$

$$= h(I) + [w + p(Z)h(Z)]\left(\frac{1 - e^{-rn}}{r}\right) \Bigg/$$

$$\left\{ A(v)\left[\frac{1 - e^{-(a+r)n}}{\alpha + r}\right]\right\}.$$

Rate of product transformation:

E.14 $\qquad \dfrac{dk(1,v)}{dk(2,v)} = -\dfrac{p(2,v)}{p(1,v)}$.

Marginal productivity:

E.15 $\qquad \dfrac{\partial X(1,v)}{\partial N(v)} = w \left(\dfrac{1 - e^{-rn}}{r}\right) \Bigg/$

$$\left\{\left[p(1,v) + \frac{k(2,v)}{k(1,v)}p(2,v)\right]\left[\frac{1 - e^{-(a+r)n}}{\alpha + r}\right]\right\},$$

E.16 $\qquad \dfrac{\partial X(1,v)}{\partial Z(v)} = p(Z)\left(\dfrac{1 - e^{-rn}}{r}\right) \Bigg/$

$$\left\{\left[p(1,v) + \frac{k(2,v)}{k(1,v)}p(2,v)\right]\left[\frac{1 - e^{-(a+r)n}}{\alpha + r}\right]\right\}.$$

Define rates of product transformation:

E.17 $\qquad j(1,v) = \dfrac{k(1,v)}{f[h(I),h(Z)]}$,

E.18 $$j(2,v) = \frac{k(2,v)}{f[h(I),h(Z)]}.$$

We wish to make $j(1,v)$ a function of $j(2,v)$ such that conditions (E.19) to (E.21) are fulfilled:

E.19 $$\frac{dj(1,v)}{dj(2,v)} \geq 0,$$

E.20 $$\frac{d^2j(1,v)}{dj(2,v)^2} < 0,$$

E.21 $$j(1,v) = 1$$

when $p(2,v) = 0$.

These are fulfilled by:

E.22 $$j(1,v) = 1 - \frac{b^2}{4c} + b[j(2,v)] - c[j(2,v)]^2,$$

where b, c are positive and $4c > b^2$.

From (E.22):

E.23 $$\frac{dj(1,v)}{dj(2,v)} = b - 2cj(2,v).$$

From (E.14):

E.24 $$b - 2cj(2,v) = -\frac{p(2,v)}{p(1,v)}.$$

Appendix F

Three-Input, Two-Output Case
Cobb-Douglas Form

Ex ante production function:

F.1 (A) $X(v) = A(v)f[p(1,v),p(2,v)]N(v)^{1-s-s'}$
$$\times I(v)^s Z(v)^{s'}.$$

Ex post utilization functions:

F.2 (B) $X(1,v) = A(v)[1 - (b^2/4c) + bj(2,v)$
$$- cj^2(2,v)]h(I)^s h(Z)^{s'}N(v),$$

F.3 (B) $X(2,v) = A(v)j(2,v)h(I)^s h(Z)^{s'}N(v).$

If $p(2,v) = 0$, then

F.4
$$j(1,v) = 1, \qquad j(2,v) = \frac{b}{2c}.$$

So (F.2) and (F.3) become

F.5
$$X(1,v) = A(v)h(I)^s h(Z)^{s'} N(v),$$

F.6
$$X(2,v) = A(v)(b/2c)h(I)^s h(Z)^{s'} N(v).$$

Marginal product of labor, from (F.1):

F.7
$$\frac{\partial X(1,v)}{\partial N(v)} = (1 - s - s')A(v)h(I)^s h(Z)^{s'}.$$

Marginal product of Z:

F.8
$$\frac{\partial X(1.v)}{\partial Z(v)} = s'A(v)h(I)^s h(Z)^{s'-1}.$$

Using (F.7), (F.8), (E.15), and (E.16) we obtain

F.9
$$h(Z) = \frac{ws'}{p(Z)(1 - s - s')}.$$

Using (E.13), (F.9), (F.8), and (E.16) we obtain

F.10
$$h(I) = \frac{ws}{1 - s - s'} \left(\frac{1 - e^{-rn}}{r} \right).$$

Using (E.12), (F.7), (E.15), and (F.9) we obtain:

F.11
$$(r - sr)e^{(a+r)n} - (\alpha + r)e^{rn} + sr + \alpha = 0.$$

And also:

F.12
$$p(1,v) = \frac{e^{an}(1 - s)w}{h(I)^s h(Z)^{s'} A(v)(1 - s - s')}.$$

We are now ready to introduce $p(2,v) < 0$. Using (E.24) and (E.22),

F.13
$$j(2,v) = \frac{p(2,v)}{2cp(1,v)} + \frac{b}{2c},$$

F.14
$$j(1,v) = 1 - \frac{1}{4c} \frac{p(2,v)}{p(1,v)}^2.$$

Defining:

F.15
$$p_o(1,v) = p(1,v) \qquad \text{when } p(2,v) = 0.$$

Using (E.9):

F.16
$$j(1,v)p(1,v) + j(2,v)p(2,v) = p_o(1,v).$$

Using (F.13), (F.14), and (F.16),

F.17
$$p(1,v) + \frac{p^2(2,v)}{4cp(1,v)} + \frac{b}{2c}p(2,v) = p_o(1,v).$$

Using the quadratic formula to solve (F.17),

F.18
$$p(1,v) = \frac{1}{2}\left\{ p_o(1,v) - \frac{b}{2c}p(2,v) + \right.$$
$$\left. [p^2{}_o(1,v) - \frac{b}{c}p_o(1,v)p(2,v) + \frac{b^2-4c}{4c^2}p^2(2,v)]^{1/2}\right\}.$$

This formula, of course, holds only for positive values of $j(2,v)$.

Let us now consider the effect on existing plant of the imposition $p(2,v) < 0$. The price of $X(1,v)$ will rise from $p_o(1,v)$ to $p(1,v)$.

For existing equipment, revenue with $p(2,v) = 0$:

F.19
$$p_o(1,v)[A(v)h(I)^s h(Z)^{s'} N(v)].$$

The new revenue, with $p(2,v) < 0$:

F.20
$$p(1,v)X(1,v) + p(2,v)X(2,v) = [p(1,v)$$
$$+ (b/2c)p(2,v)][A(v)h(I)^s h(Z)^{s'} N(v)].$$

(F.19) is greater than (F.20) since, using (F.17),

F.21
$$p(1,v) + \frac{b}{2c}p(2,v) = p_o(1,v) - \frac{p^2(2,v)}{4cp(1,v)}.$$

Length of life of existing equipment will therefore decline to

F.22
$$n = \frac{1}{\alpha}\ln\left\{ A(v)h(I)^s h(Z)^{s'}\left[p_o(1,v) - \frac{p^2(2,v)}{4cp(1,v)}\right]\right/$$
$$[w - p(Z)h(Z)]\right\}.$$

Appendix G

Three-Input, Two-Output Case
Cobb-Douglas, Energy Price Increase

We turn to the case of an energy price rise, represented as an increase in $p(Z)$ to $\sigma p(Z)$. We consider the comparative dynamics, and begin with the case $p(2,v) = 0$.

The energy-labor ratio, from (F.9):

G.1
$$h^*(Z) = (1/\sigma)h(Z).$$

The price $p_o(1,v)$ for $p(2,v) = 0$, using (F.12):

G.2 $$p^*_{\ o}(1,v) = \sigma^{s'} p_o(1,v).$$

From (F.10),

G.3 $$h^*(I) = h(I).$$

Define

G.4 $$h(X) = \frac{X_o(1,v)}{N(v)}.$$

From (G.1), (G.3), and (F.3),

G.5 $$h^*(X) = \sigma^{-s'} h(X).$$

Using (G.3) and (G.5),

G.6 $$\frac{I^*(v)}{X^*_{\ o}(1,v)} = \sigma^{s'} \frac{I(v)}{X_o(1,v)}.$$

Using (G.5) and (G.1),

G.7 $$\frac{Z^*(v)}{X^*_{\ o}(1,v)} = \sigma^{-(1-s')} \frac{Z(v)}{X_o(1,v)}.$$

Using (F.9) in (E.12), we obtain the length of life for existing capital faced with the energy price increase:

G.8 $$n^* = n + \frac{1}{\alpha} \ln \left[\frac{\sigma^{s'}(1 - s)}{(1 - s) + (\sigma - 1)s'} \right].$$

Since the term in brackets in (G.8) is less than 1, the energy price increase lowers the length of life of existing capital.

Relaxing the assumption that $p(2,v) = 0$, we can evaluate (F.17) to show that

G.9 $$1 < \frac{p^*(1,v)}{p(1,v)} < \sigma^{s'} = \frac{p^*_{\ o}(1,v)}{p_o(1,v)}.$$

Since $p(2,v)$ does not change while $p(1,v)$ increases, we have

G.10 $$-\frac{p(2,v)}{p^*(1,v)} < -\frac{p(2,v)}{p(1,v)}.$$

By (E.14) and (G.10),

G.11 $$\frac{dj^*(1,v)}{dj^*(2,v)} < \frac{dj(1,v)}{dj(2,v)}.$$

Since $d^2j(1,v)/[dj(2,v)^2]$ is negative, (G.11) results in higher values of both $j(1,v)$ and $j(2,v)$. Whether this results in increased pollution output depends on the elasticity of demand.

References

Adachi, Hideyuki. 1974. Factor substitution and durability of capital in a two-sector putty-clay model. *Econometrica* 42:773–801.

Bliss, C. J. 1968. On putty-clay. *Review of Economic Studies* 35:105–32.

Boddy, Raford, and Gort, Michael. 1971. The substitution of capital for capital. *Review of Economics and Statistics* 53:179–88.

———. 1974. Obsolescence, embodiment, and the explanation of productivity change. *Southern Economic Journal* 40:553–62.

Gelb, Bernard A., and Myers, John G. 1976. *Measuring the cost of industrial water pollution control.* New York: The Conference Board.

Gordian Associates. 1974. *Petroleum refining.* The potential for energy conservation in nine selected industries, the data base, vol. 2. Springfield, Va.: National Technical Information Service (PB 243 615).

Gyftopoulos, Elias P., et al. 1974. *Potential fuel effectiveness in industry.* Cambridge: Ballinger.

Johansen, L. 1959. Substitution versus fixed production coefficients in the theory of economic growth: a synthesis. *Econometrica* 27:157–76.

Myers, John G., et al. 1974. *Energy consumption in manufacturing.* Cambridge: Ballinger.

Nickell, Stephen. 1974. On the role of expectations in the pure theory of investment. *Review of Economic Studies* 41:1–19.

Phelps, Edmund S. 1963. Substitution, fixed proportions, growth, and distribution. *International Economic Review* 4:265–88.

Pyatt, G. 1965. A production functional model of United Kingdom manufacturing industry. *Econometric Analysis for Economic Planning.* Bristol, England: Colston Research Society Symposium.

Salter, W. E. G. 1966. *Productivity and technical change.* Cambridge: Cambridge University Press.

Solow, Robert M. 1962. Substitution and fixed proportions in the theory of capital. *Review of Economic Studies* 29:207–18.

Comment   John E. Cremeans

Summary of the Paper

Purpose of the Paper

The purpose of the paper is to examine the effects on investment and productivity of (*a*) rapid and unexpected increases in the price of

John E. Cremeans is with the Bureau of Economic Analysis.

energy, and (*b*) fixed time schedules for meeting requirements for air and water pollution abatement and occupational safety and health.

The paper reports on the first "stage" of a project of three stages: The first stage is to construct a mathematical model that captures the most important influences and may be used as a guide to data to be collected to test hypotheses; the second stage is to devise tests of the model and estimate principal parameters for selected industries; and the third stage is to incorporate empirical results into an existing national model to determine its effect on the economy.

Description of the Model

The first section of the paper is a review of existing putty-clay literature, mostly from Salter and Bliss (see Myers's and Nakamura's references). The paper does not include an analysis of data or a discussion of relevant data, but the authors' previous research indicated to them that changes in proportion of inputs take place largely through new plants replacing old, with little chance to adjust proportions of inputs in existing plants. Once built, a plant embodies technology that determines input and output coefficients. *Ex ante*, there may be considerable choice, but *ex post*, there is little choice. Therefore, they reject the "putty-putty" approach and use the "putty-clay" approach. This is, of course, a critical choice.

Assumptions (abbreviated) are as follows: (*a*) competition is pure, returns to scale are constant, input prices are constant; (*b*) labor and managerial efficiency is equal everywhere; (*c*) technology advances at a steady, predictable pace so that a series of vintages is produced over time (each vintage is more efficient than the preceding—each vintage permits production at lower real cost than the preceding—therefore product prices steadily fall as new vintages appear); (*d*) advancing technology is neutral; and (*e*) demand increases at a constant predictable pace.

The ex ante investment decision. The *ex ante* investment decision (see fig. 9.1) is made with the expectation that the assumptions just reviewed will hold over the life of the vintage. A vintage is expected to produce at its designated level of output and will continue producing at that level until the market price [$p(t)$] is less than the variable costs per unit of production. The price line $p(t)$ is a predictable result of steadily advancing technology and pure competition. The investor estimates the life of the plant and makes his decision based on expectations for the costs and returns over the life of the investment.

Capital (fixed) costs are "sunk costs" and therefore do not affect the decision to produce or to close the plant. Once investment is made there is no turning back. Therefore, (*a*) variable costs only are entered into the decision to produce or not. The (*ex ante*) investment decision is based on return over total cost—but the decision to stop production is based on variable costs only. (*b*) The *ex ante* investor's decision involves the proportions of the inputs and designed capacity of the plant —the *ex post* operator's decision is a simple on-off. Shall I close the plant or not? The vintage is operated so long as the current price is greater than or equal to the "quit price."

The ex post market decisions. The short-term supply curve h is made up of two segments (see fig. 9.2). The segment to the left is the composite output schedule of all vintages now producing at their minimum supply prices—i.e., at their quit prices. $S(t)$, the effective supply price, is set by the unit cost (fixed and variable) of the latest vintage as shown in the segment to the right. $S(t)$, in conjunction with the demand schedule, determines the market price and quantity.

Replacement of capital over time. Moving to the next period $(t + 1)$, (see fig. 9.3) the vintage $(V = t)$ is constructed and goes into place (it now has the lowest quit price). The oldest vintage $(V = t - N)$ in the previous time period goes out of production and a new vintage $(V = t + 1)$ is being considered. Demand is expected to shift from $D(t)$ to $D(t + 1)$ and investors now consider the construction of plants with new technology $(V = t + 1)$ with price $p(t + 1)$, $[p(t + 1) < p(t)]$. Vintage(s) with quit price $\geq p(t + 1)$ drop out and the supply curve shifts to "g."

The new vintage is built to produce quantity df and the process continues. The size of vintage $V = t + 1$ is determined by the quantity demanded at $p(t + 1)$ less the quantity produced by all plants with quit price $\geq p(t + 1)$.

Myers-Nakamura Modifications

The Salter-Bliss model with two inputs and one output is modified to three inputs and two outputs. The conventional inputs are labor and capital with one output good. The Myers-Nakamura modification permits the treatment of labor, capital, and energy as inputs and one good and one bad as outputs. The model thus explicitly treats energy as an important and separate input and recognizes that pollutants and safety hazards are joint products with the production of goods. Economic models have rarely, if ever, recognized this phenomenon in the past, even though it has always been with us. This modification is important and is a part of a number of similar changes that should be made in our models and our thinking.

The modified putty-clay model is actually a putty-double-clay because, *ex post*, not only are input proportions fixed, but so are the proportions of the outputs. That is, energy requirement per unit of output are fixed as are requirements for labor; the output of bads (i.e., pollution and safety hazards) is also fixed. The input and the output coefficients are determined for the vintage once and for all and change can only be effected *ex ante* as new vintages are planned and put in place. Indeed, the only change that can be made to an existing plant is to close it. This is really putty-brick.

Regulation of pollution and OSHA hazards is treated in the model as a penalty price—that is, the effective price is a weighted average of the price of the good and the negative price of the "bad." Thus the quit price formula includes a negative price for the "bad" outputs. Production will continue as long as

$$(P_g G + P_b B) \geqslant V,$$

where P_g = price of goods; P_b = price of "bads" ($P_b < 0$); G = quantity of goods; B = quantity of bads; V = variable costs. Myers-Nakamura thus depart from the strict consequences of their model when discussing pollution abatement. Few jurisdictions handle pollution by taxing pollutants, even though this procedure is beloved of economists. Normally, pollution regulations forbid the emission of more than a stated amount. The authors handle this with an additional assumption, namely that the polluting plant can contract for treatment by others or construct a separate treatment plant at a fixed fee which equates to the negative price discussed above.

While the authors don't discuss it, it can be expected that the price (P_g) will go up immediately after the imposition of the new energy prices and regulations. The market price is established by the total costs of the last vintage put in place and, presumably, the new price (P^*_g) would be set as

$$P^*_g = P_g - (P_b B)/G,$$

where the value of $(P_b B)/G$ is determined by the costs incurred by the most recent vintage plants. That is, the higher cost of energy and of pollution abatement and safety will be passed on to the consumer.

The condition for an existing plant to remain in production can be restated as

$$P^*_g G \geqslant V^*,$$

where P^*_g = the new higher price and V^* = the new higher variable costs including the payments to contractors for the removal of pollutants.[1]

1. More accurately, the right-hand side will be ($V^* + F^*$), where F^* is the value of fixed charges for any new energy, pollution-abatement, or safety capital expenditures that might be required.

Conclusion

On the one hand, a sudden and unexpected change in the relative price of energy will accelerate the obsolescence of existing plants, and their replacement with new plants will increase productivity. The imposition of pollution abatement and OSHA requirements will also accelerate obsolescence for an analogous reason—namely that the new weighted price of outputs will be taken into account. The "bads" now get their proper negative price. On the other hand, the new vintage will have lower rates of labor productivity than it otherwise would because labor will be substituted for energy, and (in effect) more labor will be expended to produce the same goods because the new negative price on pollutants will result in a shift to a position on the product transformation curve in which less than the maximum amount of product (labor fixed) will be produced. In the authors' view, the question is whether the increased productivity brought about by the new plants, or the decreased productivity brought about by energy prices and pollution/ safety restrictions, will dominate.

Critique

The purpose of the project is certainly an important and timely one. We do need a careful examination of the impact of the new higher energy prices and the stricter pollution, safety, and health regulations. I agree wholeheartedly with the general approach of the project, namely that of modifying existing models to consider explicitly energy inputs and undesirable joint products. As much as I approve of the purpose and the general approach, I do not think the paper advances the objective very much. In my view, the authors fail to examine in detail the decision to build a new vintage, given these new considerations, and so have not designed a useful model or research plan. The model and the research plan are based on the assumption that new plants will enjoy a significant cost advantage with respect to energy, pollution, and safety, and this cost advantage will greatly accelerate the closing of existing plants. In my view, this is an unexamined assumption that must be tested systematically against empirical data.

The key question to be answered is, How much will the price of goods produced be reduced by the new vintage and, of that reduction, how much will be due to the energy, pollution, and safety considerations? Recall the condition for a plant remaining in business:

$$P^*_g G \geqslant V^* \text{ or } P^*_g \geqslant V^*/G.$$

According to the model, a condition for putting a new vintage into production is

$$(P^*_g)_t \geqslant (V/G)_{t+1} + (F/G)_{t+1}.$$

That is, the sum of the average variable and fixed costs for the new vintage must be less than or equal to the market price established by the previous vintage.

The model also tells us that with the startup of the new vintage the market price falls to

$$(P_g)_{t+1} = (V/G)_{t+1} + (F/G)_{t+1}.$$

If the new price is less than the "quit price" of the older vintages, then those older vintages will be closed. Thus, the obsolescence of existing plants is determined by

$$\Delta P_g = (P_g)_{t+1} - (P^*_g)_t.$$

It is the magnitude of ΔP_g that concerns us, since that determines whether obsolescence accelerates, decelerates, or remains unchanged. That is, we must be concerned with the differential

$$dP_g = \left[\frac{\partial V/G}{\partial T} + \frac{\partial F/G}{\partial T} \right] dT$$

$$+ \left[\frac{\partial V/G}{\partial S} + \frac{\partial F/G}{\partial S} \right] dS,$$

where dT is the change in technology and dS is the change due to energy, pollution, and safety considerations. In words, the change in price from one vintage to the next will equal the change in variable and fixed costs due to technological improvements plus the change in variable and fixed costs due to the higher energy prices, pollution regulations, and safety considerations.

It is clear that the improvement implied by the first term will (under assumptions of a constant rate of technological improvement) have occurred anyway and will not cause an acceleration of obsolescence. It is the second term that must be carefully evaluated. If it has a significant negative value, acceleration of obsolescence will occur. If it is positive and greater than the absolute value of the first term, obsolescence will decelerate. If it is insignificant (i.e., near zero), it will have a small effect on obsolescence.

The Effect of Energy, Pollution, and Safety Considerations on Variable Costs

The authors assume that

$$\frac{\partial V/G}{\partial S} dS < 0.$$

That is, variable costs will be reduced (significantly) by a shift along the production mix possibility curve. While it appears, a priori, that costs will be lower in a new vintage, in practice they are often higher.

For example, it is not uncommon for EPA and local regulatory agencies to make exceptions for existing plants—particularly if their closing would add to local unemployment—while simultaneously insisting on the most stringent standards for new plants. Also, while there are dramatic examples in which reduction in pollution or increases in safety follow process changes, there are also many cases in which the regulations are met in new plants by adding substantially the same equipment, and with the same costs, that are required to bring existing plants into compliance. Thus, it cannot be assumed that new vintages will show significant reductions in variable costs due to the energy, pollution, and safety considerations. Each industry must be carefully studied on the basis of the empirical evidence.

Although many authorities have predicted that process change will play a large role in pollution abatement, available statistics indicate that process change is neither a large nor a growing proportion of the total effort. At BEA we have conducted three surveys of pollution abatement capital spending and are now beginning a fourth (see *Survey of Current Business*, July 1976). We ask respondents to estimate their expenditures for "change in production process," i.e., changes that alter the process to reduce pollutants, in contrast to "end-of-line" equipment that treats pollutants after they are generated. Respondents reported that 24% of their pollution abatement capital spending was for change in production process in 1973, 21% in 1974, and 18% in 1975. While this is certainly not conclusive (e.g., one could argue that those who used process change got more abatement for less capital expended), it does not support the idea that process change has great competitive advantage.

The Effect of Energy, Pollution, and Safety Considerations on Fixed Charges

The authors do not explicitly discuss the effect of energy, pollution, and safety considerations on capital spending for new plants or on the cost and availability of capital. It appears that they assume

$$\frac{\partial F/G}{\partial S}\, ds \leqslant 0.$$

Many businessmen argue, however, that this term is significantly positive—that is, that more capital is required and that this increases the cost (and reduces the availability) of capital for conventional purposes.

It is clear that higher energy prices, pollution regulation, and safety requirements will tend to increase prices and that higher equipment costs will result in higher fixed charges for all investment. If interest charges also rise, then this effect will be even greater and new plants will be relatively more expensive.

Thus, it is possible that the change in fixed charges will be positive, and it is conceivable that

$$\left[\frac{\partial V/G}{\partial S} + \frac{\partial F/G}{\partial S}\right] dS \geqslant 0.$$

If there are industries in which this is the case, obsolescence will not accelerate. It may even decelerate.

The Effect of Uncertainty on Investment in New Vintages

In addition, it is my opinion that uncertainty will often decelerate obsolescence. The authors consider uncertainty in terms of two possible prices for an input and find that the solution is to design the plant for the expected price, where the expected price is the sum of the products of prices and their probability of becoming effective.

Turning again to the realm of pollution abatement, uncertainty is frequently experienced, not as an unknown future input price, but as an unknown future abatement standard. A familiar example will illustrate this point. There is a series of standards for automobile pollution emissions identified by production years, e.g., the 1977 standards specify certain maximum emissions of hydrocarbons, carbon monoxide, and oxides of nitrogen. Gasoline engines with "add-on" devices can meet the 1977 (and earlier) standards with some loss of fuel economy and performance. Conventional diesel engines meet the 1977 (and earlier) standards with excellent fuel economy. Authorities generally agree that the diesel engine is a superior way to meet the need for pollution abatement (as expressed in the 1977 standards) and the need for energy conservation. Why don't U.S. manufacturers invest massively in plants to produce diesel engines for passenger cars?

Significantly more stringent standards have been planned (and postponed) for many years and are currently scheduled for 1978.[2] These standards call for significant reduction in the emission of oxides of nitrogen. Diesel engines obtain their greater fuel economy and their reduced emissions of hydrocarbons and carbon monoxides in part because of their higher combustion temperatures which in turn generate oxides of nitrogen. Thus, the diesel engine will meet the 1977 and

2. Since this Comment was first prepared, the "1978 standard" of 0.1 gram of oxides of nitrogen per mile has been postponed again and is now included in "the 1981 standard." Only one U.S. manufacturer is offering diesel powered automobiles and four manufacturers (General Motors Corporation, Volkswagen, Inc., Daimer-Benz, and Automobiles Peugot, Incorporated) have requested a waiver from the Environmental Protection Agency, claiming that enforcement of the standard would force them to stop selling diesel-powered cars (*The Environmental Reporter*, 8 June 1979, p. 200).

earlier standards without loss in fuel efficiency, but will not meet the
1978 standards for oxides of nitrogen even with special devices. EPA
and the Congress have postponed the imposition of the more stringent
oxides of nitrogen standard in recent years, but they have not yet agreed
to eliminate it entirely. Postponement rather than elimination is justified
on the grounds that the auto manufacturers will be encouraged to keep
trying.

The auto manufacturers claim that there is no known way to reduce
emissions of oxides of nitrogen to the levels required, and so have tem-
porized with "add-on" devices for conventional gasoline engines. Had it
been certain that the "1978 standards" would not be imposed, the
manufacturers might have invested in diesel engine plants and so accelerated the obsolescence of existing gasoline engine plants. While the
manufacturers deny it, it is also possible that, had it been certain that
the "1978 standards" would be imposed, the manufacturers would have
invested in plants to build some other type of engine such as steam or
electric.

Uncertainty with respect to pollution abatement and safety regulations makes it difficult, if not impossible, to estimate the useful life of
proposed new investment. In effect, the short expected life of the plant
makes the fixed charges so high that the condition for putting a new
vintage into production is not met. In the face of this uncertainty, investment is reduced and obsolescence of existing plants is retarded.

Proposed Measurement Procedure

A proposed measurement procedure is sketched in a final section of
the paper that was prepared after the conference. In my view, the procedure leans all too heavily on assumptions of uniform growth and
smoothly changing ratios of capital to output, labor, energy, and pollution. It depends on the very assumptions that must be tested empirically.
In any event, a useful measurement procedure should include a test of
the results. I find neither a plan for testing the measures obtained nor
acknowledgment that one is needed. In fact, the last sentence of the
paper suggests that the difference between predicted and actual levels
of investment is an estimate of uncertainty.

Summary

It is my opinion that the model and the research plan should be
revised. The assumption that new vintages have significant energy, pollution, and safety cost advantages over existing vintages should be examined empirically, industry by industry. The model should be revised
to consider the cost and availability of capital explicitly. The effect of
uncertainty should be reconsidered. The problems of measurement must
be considered as an integral part of model design.

IV International Comparisons of Productivity

10 International Comparisons of Productivity in Agriculture

Saburo Yamada and Vernon W. Ruttan

10.1 Introduction

The purpose of this paper is to extend the earlier analysis of the sources and direction of agricultural productivity growth over time and of agricultural productivity differences among countries which Yujiro Hayami and Vernon W. Ruttan presented in their book on *Agricultural Development: An International Perspective*.[1] In the Hayami-Ruttan study the induced innovation hypothesis was tested against the historical experience of agricultural productivity growth in Japan and the United States for the period 1880–1960. In this paper it has been possible to include four additional countries—Denmark, France, Germany, and the United Kingdom—in the analysis and to extend the analysis for all six countries to 1970. In the Hayami-Ruttan study the analysis of the sources of productivity differences among countries was based on cross section data centered on 1960. In this paper it has also been possible to analyze the sources of productivity differences among countries using data centered on 1970, and to compare the results with the earlier analysis.

The extensions of the time series analysis to four additional countries and of the time series and cross-section analysis to 1970 adds importantly to our understanding of the interrelationships among changes in relative factor prices, technical change, productivity growth, and agricultural development. The initial test of the induced innovation hypothesis was based on the historical experience of agricultural productivity growth in two countries—the United States and Japan—with extreme differences in relative factor endowments and factor prices. The addition

1. Yujiro Hayami and Vernon W. Ruttan, *Agricultural Development: An International Perspective* (Baltimore: The Johns Hopkins University Press, 1971).

509

of the four European countries permits a test of the induced innovation hypothesis against the experience of countries characterized by less extreme differences in relative factor endowments and prices.

The addition of time series and cross section data for 1970 permits an extension of the analysis to include a period characterized by rapid productivity growth in a number of developed and developing countries. In the developed countries of western Europe and Japan completion of the process of agricultural mechanization led to rapid increases in output per worker during the 1960–70 decade. In several developing countries the new seed-fertilizer or "green revolution" technology, combined with continued decline in fertilizer prices, permitted rapid growth of land productivity during the latter half of the decade.

Both the theoretical foundations on which productivity accounting rests and the precision of productivity measurement have been subject to continuous debate. The debates have focused primarily on problems of index number construction, the proper accounting for depreciation, and the incorporation of inputs not adequately measured in conventional national accounting systems. Even while the elaboration of the theory and method of productivity and growth accounting has been going forward, the several "partial" and "total" productivity measures available have been providing new insights into the process of economic growth. They have also served as useful instruments in development planning and policy.

The comparisons presented in this paper are based primarily on partial productivity measures—output per worker and output per hectare. Our attempts to "account" for differences in productivity over time and among countries also focus on these partial productivity ratios. Total productivity estimates are available for the agricultural sector for a number of developed and developing countries.[2] However, it has been

---

2. For a survey of international productivity comparisons see Irving B. Kravis, "A Survey of International Comparisons of Productivity," *Economic Journal* 86 (March 1976):1–44. See also the literature survey by Willis Peterson and Yujiro Hayami, "Technical Change in Agriculture," in Lee R. Martin, ed., *A Survey of Agricultural Economics Literature*, vol. 1 (Minneapolis: University of Minnesota Press, 1977), pp. 498–540.

In the United States partial and total productivity indexes for the agricultural sector are published annually by the U.S. Department of Agriculture. For the most recent data see *Changes in Farm Production and Efficiency: 1974* (Washington: U.S. Department of Agriculture, Statistical Bulletin No. 233, August 1975). Data for earlier years are available in R. A. Loomis and G. T. Barton, *Productivity of Agriculture, United States, 1870–1958* (Washington: U.S. Department of Agriculture, Technical Bulletin No. 1238, 1961). We do not know of any other national or international agency which publishes annual output, input, and partial and total productivity data for the agricultural sector.

An incomplete list of published total productivity studies for developed countries includes the following: I. F. Furniss, "Agricultural Productivity in Canada:

possible to mine a richer lode of development experience by focusing our efforts on partial productivity ratios. The significance of the partial productivity measures for development theory and policy is enhanced by interpreting this experience within the framework of the induced innovation hypothesis.[3]

In agriculture it has appeared consistent with the technical conditions of production to consider growth in land area per worker and output per worker as "somewhat independent, at least over a certain range."[4,5] Increases in output per worker can be achieved through advances in technology which enable the land area cultivated per worker to rise. This is typically achieved by substitution of more efficient sources of

---

Two Decades of Gains," *Canadian Farm Economics* 5 (1970): 16–27; R. Young; "Productivity Growth in Australian Rural Industries," *Quarterly Review of Agricultural Economics* 27 (1973): 185–205; J. C. Toutain, *Le Produit de l'agriculture française, 1700 à 1958*. (Paris: L'Institut de Science Economique Appliquée, 1961); Saburo Yamada, "Changes in Conventional and Nonconventional Inputs in Japanese Agriculture since 1880," *Food Research Institute Studies*, 7 (1967): 372–413; Y. Hayami et al., *A Century of Agricultural Growth in Japan* (Minneapolis: University of Minnesota Press, 1975; Tokyo: University of Tokyo Press, 1975).

There are also several total productivity studies for less developed countries. See, for example, the studies of Taiwan (by Lee and Chen), Korea (by Ban), and the Philippines (by Chrisostomo and Barker) in Yujiro Hayami, Vernon W. Ruttan, and Herman Southworth, eds., *Agricultural Growth in Japan, Taiwan, Korea and the Philippines* (Honolulu: The University Press of Hawaii, 1979); for India by Tara Shukla, *Capital Formation in Indian Agriculture* (Bombay: Vora, 1965) and by Robert E. Evenson and Dayanatha Jha, "The Contribution of the Agricultural Research System to Agricultural Production in India," *Indian Journal of Agricultural Economics*, 27 (October–December 1973): 212–30; see also the cross section analysis for Asian countries by Saburo Yamada, *A Comparative Analysis of Asian Agricultural Productivities and Growth Patterns* (Tokyo: Asian Productivity Organization, 1975).

3. The induced innovation framework and the role of induced innovation in the process of agricultural development is elaborated in Hayami and Ruttan, *Agricultural Development*; Hans P. Binswanger and Vernon W. Ruttan, eds., *Induced Innovation: Technology, Institutions and Development* (Baltimore: The Johns Hopkins University Press, 1978). For a critical review of the theory of induced innovation see Hans P. Binswanger, "A Microeconomic Approach to Induced Innovation," *Economic Journal* 84 (December 1974): 940–58.

4. Zvi Griliches, "Agriculture: Productivity and Technology," *International Encyclopedia of the Social Sciences*, vol. 1 (New York: Macmillan and Free Press, 1968), pp. 241–45.

5. The two partial productivity measures are linked through the ratio of land area per worker. Thus:

$$\frac{Y}{L} = \frac{A}{L} \frac{Y}{A},$$

where Y = output, L = labor, A = land area, and Y/L = labor productivity, A/L = land area per worker, and Y/A = land productivity.

power (animal, mechanical, electrical) and more equipment per worker. For expositional purposes it is useful to refer to those technologies which substitute for labor as *mechanical technology*. Increases in output per worker can also be achieved through increases in land productivity, if the rate of increase in output per hectare exceeds the rate of change in the number of workers per unit of land area. It is useful to refer to those technologies which increase output per hectare as *biological technology*.

In the Hayami-Ruttan induced innovation model the process of technical change can be described in terms of a series of shifts of and along innovation possibility curves.[6] In figure 10.1 (left), for example, I^*_0 represents the land/labor isoquant of the metaproduction function (MPF) in time zero. It is the envelope of less elastic isoquants such as I_0 corresponding, for example, to different types of harvesting machinery. I^*_1 is the innovation possibility curve (IPC) of time period one. A certain technology represented by I_0—a reaper, for example—is invented when a price ratio, BB, prevails for some time. When this price ratio changes from BB to CC, another technology represented by I_1—for example the combine—is invented. Similar inducements in the livestock sector might be represented by the invention of a succession of more highly automated animal-feeding systems.

The new technology represented by I_1 which permits an expansion in land area per worker is generally associated with higher animal or mechanical power inputs per worker. This implies a complementary relationship between land and power, which may be illustrated by the line (A,M). It is hypothesized that mechanical innovation involves the substitution of land and power for labor in response to a change in the wage rate relative to land and machinery prices.

6. We no longer use the term "metaproduction function" to describe innovation possibility curves as in the empirical work of Hayami and Ruttan (*Agricultural Development*). We now define the metaproduction function (MPF) as the envelope of the production points for the most efficient countries. It describes a technological frontier which countries now lying inside it can achieve by appropriate borrowing, adaptive research activities, and investment in human capital, extension, and rural infrastructure.

The innovation possibility curve (IPC), on the other hand, can be regarded as the envelope of neoclassical production functions which might be invented. Each number of the set of innovation possibility curves corresponds to a given budget, and the larger the budget, the closer the IPC lies to the origin of the isoquant map. The IPC corresponding to an unlimited research budget is the "scientific frontier." It is unlikely that applied research will ever be carried to that frontier, however, due to diminishing returns to research. The scientific frontier shifts with advances in the basic sciences and this shift carries with it a shift in the whole set of IPCs, but not of the MPF. However, shifts in the IPCs make shifts of the MPF easier or less costly to achieve.

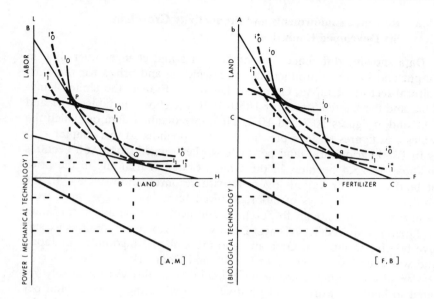

Fig. 10.1   Factor prices and induced technical change. Adopted from
Hayami and Ruttan, *Agricultural Development*, p. 126.

The process of advance in biological technology is also illustrated in
figure 1 (right panel), where i^*_0 represents the land fertilizer isoquant
of the metaproduction function. The metaproduction function is the
envelope of less elastic isoquants such as i_0 which correspond, for example, to crop varieties characterized by different levels of fertilizer
responsiveness. A decline in the price of fertilizer is regarded as inducing a response by plant breeders to develop more fertilizer-responsive
crop varieties, which might be described by the isoquant i_1 along the
IPC i^*_1, and by farmers to adopt the new varieties as they become
available.

The complementary relationship between biological technologies and
fertilizer use, represented by (F,B), also extends to the protective chemicals (insecticides, herbicides) and the institutional innovations associated with the marketing and delivery of chemical inputs and services.
Similarly, in livestock production a decline in the price of concentrated
feedstuffs (oilcake, fish meal, urea) has induced animal nutritionists
and breeders to direct their efforts to the development of feedstuffs
which incorporate a higher percentage of the lower cost proteins and to
select and breed for lines which have a more rapid rate of gain when
fed the new rations. Complementarity between breeding and nutrition
also extends to related biological and chemical technologies in the area
of animal health.

10.2   Resource Endowments and Productivity Growth in Six Developed Countries

Data showing differences among countries and changes over time in output and in factor productivity, endowments, and prices for the agricultural sectors of Japan, Germany, Denmark, France, the United Kingdom, and the United States for 1880–1970 are shown in tables 10.1 and 10.2 and in figures 10.2 and 10.3. The more detailed data on which the tables and figures rest are presented in an appendix to this chapter.

In 1880 agricultural land per male worker ranged from 0.66 hectares in Japan to 25.4 hectares in the United States. Variations in the price of land and labor varied inversely with resource endowments. In the United States 181 days of labor, at hired farm labor wage rates, were required to earn enough to purchase one hectare of arable farm land.[7] In Japan it required 1,874 days. Land was approximately half as expensive relative to labor in Germany and the United Kingdom as in Japan and was even less expensive in France and Denmark.

Variations in output per hectare among countries were inversely related to land per worker and positively related to the price of land per hectare. Output per hectare was approximately 0.5 wheat units in the United States, 1.1–1.3 wheat units in the four European countries, and 2.9 wheat units in Japan. Variations in output per hectare were sufficient to only partially offset the variations in land per worker. Output per male worker varied directly with land area per worker, ranging from 1.9 wheat units in Japan to 16.2 in the United Kingdom and 13.0 in the United States.

Limitations in resource endowments were apparently not a major constraint on growth of agricultural output over the period 1880–1970, even in countries with the most limited land resource endowments. The most rapid growth was experienced by Denmark, where output grew from an index of 100 in 1880 to 459 in 1970, and the slowest by the United Kingdom, where output rose from an index of 100 to 236 during the same period. Japan, Germany, and the United States experienced roughly comparable rates of growth in output.

7. Definitions of agricultural land are not strictly comparable among countries and over time, but generally include all land in farms, including cropland used for crops, pasture, and fallow plus permanent pasture.

Arable land generally includes only cropland used for crops, pasture, and fallow. Over time land may be added to the arable land class as a result of investment in clearing, drainage, terracing, irrigation, and fencing. In 1880 such investments in land development were much more intensive in Japan, Germany, Denmark, France and the United Kingdom than in the United States. In general it is useful to think of agricultural land as a factor created by investment rather than as an "original" factor of production. Data on agricultural land area are more generally available than for arable land area. Data on land prices are more generally available for arable land.

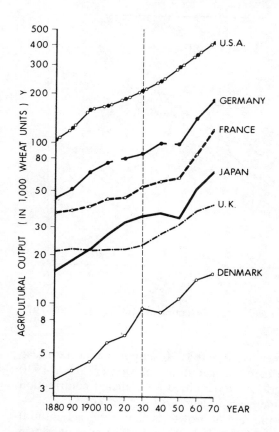

Fig. 10.2   (diagonals are land/labor ratios). Source: Appendix A.
Agricultural output in six countries (in logs), 1880–1970.

In Japan agricultural output grew at 1.6% per year during 1880–
1930 and at approximately the same rate during 1930–70. During the
earlier period growth in output per hectare accounted for approximately
70% of the growth in total output and over two-thirds of the growth
in output per worker. After 1930 growth in output per hectare rose
more rapidly than total output. Increases in land area per worker became a more important source of growth in output per worker than
output per hectare, particularly after 1960.[8]

In Germany agricultural output grew at approximately 1.3% per year
during 1880–1930 and at 1.93% per year between 1930 and 1970.
Growth in output per hectare accounted for the entire increase in output

---

8. For a detailed analysis of the sources of agricultural productivity growth in
Japan see Yujiro Hayami et al., *A Century of Agricultural Growth*.

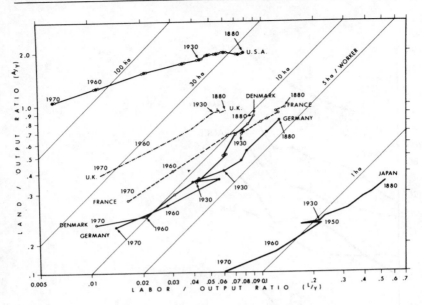

Fig. 10.3   Input-output ratios for six countries (in logs), 1880–1970

between 1880–1970. Between 1880 and 1930 output per hectare also accounted for most of the increase in output per worker. After 1930 declining employment in agriculture permitted a significant contribution to output per worker from increases in land area per worker.[9]

Among the six countries the rate of growth of both total agricultural output and output per hectare between 1880 and 1930 was highest in Denmark. It was also the only country which experienced a decline in land area per worker. Output per hectare rose more rapidly than output per worker, but slightly less rapidly than total output. Denmark was also the only country in which output per hectare rose less rapidly during 1930–70 than during 1880–1930. Output per worker continued to rise relatively rapidly, however, as a result of a reduction in the number of workers employed in agriculture.[10]

9. For an extensive review of the literature on agricultural growth in Germany see Adolf Weber, "Productivity of German Agriculture: 1850 to 1970" (Saint Paul: University of Minnesota Department of Agricultural and Applied Economics, Staff Paper 73–1, August 1973).

10. For a very useful review of Danish agricultural policies over the 1870–1970 period see Karen J. Friedman, "Danish Agricultural Policy, 1870–1970: The Flowering and Decline of a Liberal Policy," *Food Research Institute Studies* 13 (1974): 225–38. During the early part of the period, Denmark was shifting rapidly from a crop-based agriculture to a more intensive crop-livestock system.

Table 10.1 Agricultural Output, Factor Productivity, Factor Endowments, and Factor Price Ratios in Six Countries, 1880–1970

	Year	Japan	Germany	Denmark	France	United Kingdom	United States
Agricultural output index (Y)	1880	100	100	100	100	100	100
	1930	223	192	279	146	111	204
	1960	334	316	422	235	185	340
	1970	428	412	459	334	236	403
Agricultural output per male worker in wheat units (Y/L)	1880	1.89	7.9	10.6	7.4	16.2	13.0
	1930	4.60	16.0	24.1	13.2	20.1	22.5
	1960	8.41	35.4	47.5	33.4	45.3	88.8
	1970	15.77	65.4	94.4	59.9	87.6	157.4
Agricultural output per hectare of agricultural land in wheat units (Y/A)	1880	2.86	1.25	1.19	1.06	1.10	0.513
	1930	5.06	2.47	2.95	1.50	1.18	0.555
	1960	7.44	4.01	4.65	2.48	1.94	0.811
	1970	10.03	5.40	5.27	3.70	2.61	0.981
Agricultural land per male worker in hectares (A/L)	1880	0.659	6.34	8.91	6.96	14.7	25.4
	1930	0.908	6.46	8.18	8.80	17.0	40.5
	1960	1.131	8.83	10.21	13.44	23.3	109.5
	1970	1.573	12.20	17.92	16.19	33.5	160.5
Days of labor to buy one hectare of arable land (P_A/P_L)	1880	1,874	967	382	780	995	181
	1930	2,920	589	228	262	189	115
	1960	2,954	378	166	166	211	108
	1970	1,315	244	177	212	203	108

NOTES

One wheat unit is equivalent to one ton of wheat. The method of constructing output measures in terms of wheat units is described in Yujiro Hayami and Vernon W. Ruttan, *Agricultural Development: An International Perspective* (Baltimore: The Johns Hopkins University Press, 1971), pp. 308–25.

Definitions of agricultural land are not strictly comparable among countries and over time, but generally include all land in farms, including crop land used for crops, pasture, and fallow plus permanent pasture.

In Denmark the land price includes the value of agricultural land and buildings.

SOURCE: Data are from Appendix A.

Table 10.2   Annual Rates of Change in Agricultural Output, Factor Productivity, and Factor Endowments in Six Countries, 1880–1970

	Japan	Germany	Denmark	France	United Kingdom	United States
1880–1970						
Agricultural output (Y)	1.63	1.59	1.71	1.35	0.96	1.56
Output per worker (Y/L)	2.39	2.48	2.46	2.35	1.89	2.81
Output per hectare (Y/A)	1.40	1.64	1.67	1.40	0.96	0.72
Land per worker (A/L)	0.97	0.73	0.78	0.94	0.92	2.07
1880–1930						
Agricultural output (Y)	1.62	1.31	2.07	0.76	0.21	1.44
Output per worker $((Y/L)$	1.79	1.42	1.66	1.16	0.43	1.10
Output per hectare (Y/A)	1.15	1.37	1.83	0.70	0.14	0.16
Land per worker (A/L)	0.64	0.04	−0.17	0.47	0.29	0.94
1930–70						
Agricultural output (Y)	1.64	1.93	1.25	2.09	1.91	1.72
Output per worker (Y/L)	3.13	3.81	3.47	3.85	3.74	4.98
Output per hectare (Y/A)	1.73	1.97	1.44	2.28	2.00	1.43
Land per worker (A/L)	1.38	1.60	1.98	1.54	1.71	3.50
1930–60						
Agricultural output (Y)	1.36	1.67	1.39	1.60	1.72	1.72
Output per worker (Y/L)	2.03	2.68	2.29	3.14	2.75	4.68
Output per hectare (Y/A)	1.29	1.63	1.53	1.69	1.67	1.27
Land per worker (A/L)	0.73	1.05	0.74	1.42	1.06	3.37

Table 10.2 (cont.)

	Japan	Germany	Denmark	France	United Kingdom	United States
1960–70						
Agricultural output (Y)	2.51	2.69	0.84	3.58	2.45	1.71
Output per worker (Y/L)	6.49	6.35	7.11	6.02	6.82	5.89
Output per hectare (Y/A)	3.03	3.02	1.26	4.08	3.01	1.92
Land per worker (A/L)	3.35	3.29	5.79	1.88	3.69	3.90

NOTES:

One wheat unit is equivalent to one ton of wheat. The method of constructing output measures in terms of wheat units is described in Yujiro Hayami and Vernon W. Ruttan, *Agricultural Development: An International Perspective* (Baltimore: The Johns Hopkins University Press, 1971), pp. 308–25.

Definitions of agricultural land are not strictly comparable among countries and over time, but generally include all land in farms, including crop land used for crops, pasture, and fallow plus permanent pasture.

In Denmark the land price includes the value of agricultural land and buildings.

SOURCE: Data are from Appendix A.

France experienced the most dramatic transition of any of the six countries between 1880–1930 and 1930–70. During the earlier period French agriculture was essentially static. Output grew at less than 0.8% per year and output per hectare at 0.7% per year.[11] Both output and productivity growth accelerated after World War II. Between 1960 and 1970 France achieved a 3.6% annual rate of growth in agricultural output (the highest among the six countries).

The United Kingdom experienced the slowest rate of growth of agricultural output and of output per worker among the six countries during 1880–1930. The rate of growth of agricultural output rose from 0.2% per year in 1880–1930 to 1.9% per year in 1930–70. Output per worker rose from 0.4 to 3.7% per year and output per hectare from 0.1 to 2.0% per year. By the 1960s the United Kingdom was beginning to make a relatively successful transition from the earlier period of stagnation to higher modern growth rates in output and productivity. The United Kingdom has, however, been somewhat less successful than France in making the transition to modern growth rates in the agricultural sector.[12]

The United States has been on a quite different growth path than the other five countries throughout the period 1880–1970. The rate of growth in total output lagged relative to Denmark and Japan in 1880–1930 and relative to Germany and France in 1930–70. Output per worker grew less rapidly than any of the other countries except Great Britain during 1880–1930, but more rapidly than any of the other countries during 1930–70. Output per hectare lagged relative to all other countries except Great Britain in 1880–1930 and relative to all countries other than Denmark during 1930–70. The distinguishing feature of U.S. agricultural development has been the primary reliance on growth in land area per worker as a source of growth in output per worker over the entire period 1880–1970.

The periods for which data are presented in tables 10.1 and 10.2, 1880–1930 and 1930–70, are not ideal for all countries. Some of the distortions involved in selecting a common date such as 1930 for "epochal" comparisons can be visualized from figure 10.2 in which the data are plotted by decades (five-year averages centered each decade). For some countries, particularly Germany, France and Japan, growth accelerated after a long period of relative stagnation that did not end

11. This apparently represented a decline in the rate of growth of output from approximately 1.1% per year during the preceding 60 years. William H. Newell, "The Agricultural Revolution in Nineteenth Century France," *The Journal of Economic History* 33 (December 1973): 710.

12. See William W. Wade, "Institutional Determinants of Technical Change and Productivity Growth: Denmark, France and Great Britain, 1870–1965," Ph.D. diss., University of Minnesota, 1973.

until after World War II. Yet selection of 1950 as a comparison base would have also introduced significant distortions.

In figure 10.3 we have brought together the long-term trends in land per unit of output, labor per unit of output, and land area per worker. The diagonal lines represent constant land/labor ratios. Movements of land/output and labor/output ratios toward the lower left-hand corner represent improvements in the two partial productivity ratios resulting from yield-increasing (or biological) and labor-saving (or mechanical) technology (see fig. 10.1). An isoquant drawn through the 1970 input-output points describes what might be regarded as a metaproduction function (MPF). The innovation possibility curve (IPC) which describes the technology that would be feasible, given existing scientific and technical knowledge, would stand farther to the left. Investment in experiment station and industrial capacity is necessary to embody the available technical and scientific knowledge in improved crop varieties, animals, chemicals, and equipment in order to make the productivity ratios described by the 1970 metaproduction function available to farmers in countries whose productivity ratios are to the right of the 1970 metaproduction function.

Several generalizations emerge from the data presented in table 10.1 and in figures 10.2 and 10.3.

First, it is clear that there were enormous differences in factor endowment ratios among the six countries in 1880, and that these differences remain large in 1970. Yet all six countries have experienced a decline in labor intensity, whether measured in terms of labor per unit of output or in terms of land per worker. During the 1880–1970 period, Denmark was the only country that experienced a sustained decline in land per worker, comparable to the decline currently being experienced in many developing countries today.

Second, those countries in which land area per worker was relatively limited in 1880 depended primarily on increases in agricultural output per hectare as a primary source of growth in agricultural output throughout most of the period since 1880. Increases in land area per worker in these countries in recent decades have been associated primarily with declines in the number of agricultural workers rather than an increase in land area.

Third, the countries in which land area per worker has been relatively limited have been able to achieve rates of growth in total output and in output per worker that have been roughly comparable to the rates achieved by countries with more favorable resource endowments. Limitation on land per worker has apparently not represented a critical constraint on capacity for growth in agricultural output.

Fourth, the growth rates of agricultural output, and of output per hectare and output per worker, have risen sharply in most countries since 1930. In some countries these higher growth rates represent the acceleration of trends that were already apparent. In others they represent a sharp transition from earlier experiences. Modern growth rates range in the neighborhood of 2–4% per year in output, over 5% per year in output per worker, and 2–4% per year in output per hectare. This is in contrast to growth rates of output and productivity that were typically less than 2% per year before 1930.

10.3   Factor Prices and Factor Use in Six Developed Countries

In this section the relationships between factor prices and the patterns of factor use associated with growth in output per hectare and in output per worker in the six countries are explored more formally than in the previous section.

10.3.1   Biological Technology

The model of biological technology outlined earlier in this chapter (fig. 10.1) suggests that a decline in the price of fertilizer relative to the price of land can be expected to induce a rise in fertilizer use per hectare as a result of a movement to the right along the short-run production function (i_0). It can also be expected to induce advances in crop technology, such as the development and introduction of more fertilizer-responsive crop varieties, which can be characterized by a new short-run production function to the right of and below i_0, along the innovation possibility curve (IPC) i^*_1, such as i_1. A strong negative relationship is hypothesized between the price of fertilizer relative to land (P_F/P_A) and fertilizer use per hectare (F/A).

Changes in the price of labor relative to the price of land are also expected to have an impact on the level of fertilizer use per hectare. As the price of labor rises relative to the price of the land, farmers can be expected to attempt to reduce labor input per unit of land by substituting fertilizer and other chemical inputs such as herbicides and insecticides for more labor-intensive husbandry practices. A decline in the price of fertilizer can also be expected to result in the substitution of chemical fertilizers produced by the industrial sector for farm-produced fertilizers such as animal manures and green manures. Thus a positive relationship is hypothesized between the price of labor relative to land (P_F/P_A) and fertilizer use per hectare (F/A).

The strong negative relationship between the fertilizer/land price ratio and fertilizer use per hectare for all six countries is confirmed in table 10.3. Given the enormous difference in the cultural and physical environments in which farmers operate and crops are produced among the six countries, and the great differences in the level of technology and social organization over time in each country, the similarity in the response coefficients in table 10.3 is truly remarkable. The implication is not only that farmers have responded in a roughly comparable manner to similar factor/price ratios, but that farmers have been able to respond in a similar manner as a result of comparable shifts in the short-run production function. This implies a similar institutional response in making more fertilizer-responsive crop varieties available to farmers by research institutions in the several countries.

A positive relationship between the price of labor relative to land and fertilizer use per hectare hypothesized above is also confirmed in table 10.3. The relationship appears to have emerged later in France and Germany than in the other four countries.

It seems reasonable to hypothesize that the model outlined in figure 10.1 has an analogy in the livestock as well as in the crop sector. In some respects concentrate feeds, particularly the protein meals such as soybean, copra, and cottonseed meal, occupy a role in livestock production similar to fertilizer in crop production. As the price of concentrate feeds has declined over time they have been increasingly substituted for forages, hay, and other roughages. The availability of lower cost concentrates has led to the development of husbandry practices and to the selection and breeding of animals to achieve earlier maturity and more rapid rates of weight gain per day and per feed unit. In countries with limited land resources such as Western European countries and Japan concentrates are usually imported, thus reinforcing their role as land substitutes.

The relationship between the price of concentrates relative to land hypothesized above is confirmed by the data presented in table 10.4. Although the estimated relationships are not entirely comparable among countries, it is clear that the rise in the use of concentrate feeds per hectare in Germany, Denmark, and the United Kingdom has been closely associated with a continuing decline in the price of concentrates relative to land. It also seems clear that as the price of labor has risen relative to the price of land in the three Western European countries, farmers have substituted imported concentrates for labor-intensive systems of livestock feed production at home.

10.3.2 Mechanical Technology

The model of mechanical technology outlined earlier suggests that the use of land per worker rises as the price of land declines relative to the price of labor. In constructing the model it was assumed that over the long run increases in the area cultivated per worker were dependent on increased use of machinery and power per worker. Thus technical changes leading to a decline in the price of machinery relative to labor would also contribute to expansion of the area cultivated per worker. Drawing on the model, a negative relationship is hypothesized between

Table 10.3 Relationships between Fertilizer Use per Hectare and Relative Factor Prices in Six Countries

Country and Period		Coefficient of Prices of		Coefficient of Determination (R^2)	Standard Error of Estimate (S)	Degrees of Freedom
		Fertilizer Relative to Land (P_F/P_A)	Labor Relative to Land (P_L/P_A)			
Japan[a]	(1880–1960)	−1.274* (0.057)	0.729* (0.220)	0.974	0.0810	14
Germany[b]	(1880–1913)	−1.806* (0.009)	0.083 (0.515)	0.943	0.289	13
	(1950–68)	−0.377* (0.098)	0.799* (0.093)	0.954	0.100	15
Denmark[c]	(1910–65)	−1.120* (0.348)	0.958* (0.430)	0.87	0.310	9
France[d]	(1870–1965)	−0.950* (0.332)	−1.375*I (0.362)	0.56	0.776	17
	(1920–65)	−0.664* (0.259)	0.485 (0.733)	0.386	0.538	7
United Kingdom[e]	(1870–1965)	−1.130* (0.025)	1.010* (0.080)	0.92	0.218	17
United States[f]	(1880–1960)	−1.357* (0.102)	1.019* (0.168)	0.970	0.083	14

land per worker (A/L) and (a) the price of land relative to labor (P_A/P_L) and (b) the price of machinery relative to labor (P_M/P_L). Similarly, a negative relationship is hypothesized between the use of power (or machinery) per worker (M/L) and (a) the price of land relative to labor (P_A/P_L) and (b) the price of machinery relative to labor (P_M/P_L).

The results of the empirical tests of the hypotheses relating to mechanical technology are not as clear-cut as in the case of biological technology (tables 10.5 and 10.6). The hypothesis that land area per worker is negatively related to *both* the price of land relative to labor and the price of machinery relative to labor is confirmed only in the historical experience of the United States, the United Kingdom, and of Germany after 1950. In all six countries, except Germany during 1880–1913, land area per worker is, as hypothesized, negatively related to the price of machinery relative to labor. The hypothesis that power per worker is negatively related to both the price of land relative to labor and the price of machinery relative to labor is confirmed in all cases except those of Denmark, and France before 1920.

In *both* tests the price of land relative to labor performed less well than the price of machinery relative to labor. And where the test was run for both an early and a late period the results tended to be weakest for the early period.

A closer look at these equations reveals the following: In the power per worker equations only two coefficients have an inconsistent positive sign and only in one case is the coefficient significantly positive. Of the fourteen negative coefficients, on the other hand, ten are significantly so.

The land per worker equations represent the most puzzling case. Of the eighteen coefficients six are positive, although only two are significantly so (of the twelve negative coefficients, eight are significantly so).

SOURCES:

[a]Yujiro Hayami and Vernon W. Ruttan, *Agricultural Development: An International Perspective* (Baltimore: The Johns Hopkins University Press, 1971).

[b]Adolf Weber, "Productivity in German Agriculture: 1850 to 1970," University of Minnesota Department of Agricultural and Applied Economics, Staff Paper 73–1, August 1973, p. 23.

[c]William W. Wade, "Institutional Determinants of Technical Change and Agricultural Productivity Growth: Denmark, France and Great Britain, 1870–1965," Ph.D. diss., University of Minnesota, 1973, p. 128.

[d]Wade, "Institutional Determinants," pp. 134, 136.

[e]Wade, "Institutional Determinants," p. 149.

[f]Hayami and Ruttan, *Agricultural Development*, p. 132, Regression (W15).

NOTE: Equations are linear in logarithms. The numbers inside the parentheses are the standard errors of the estimated coefficients.

*Significant at 0.5 level (one-tail test); *I*: inconsistent with simple induced innovation hypothesis.

Table 10.4   **Relationship between Use of Feed Concentrates per Hectare and Factor Prices**

Country and Period	Coefficient of Prices of		Coefficient of Determination (R^2)	Standard Error of Estimate (S)	Degrees of Freedom
	Concentrates Relative to Land (P_C/P_A)	Labor Relative to Land (P_L/P_A)			
Germany[a] (1880–1913)	−3.333*	3.974*	0.712	0.337	31
(net oil cake imports)	(0.569)	(1.221)			
(1950–68)	−1.567*	2.381*	0.973	0.337	15
	(0.254)	(0.255)			
Denmark[b] (1880–1925)	−0.680*	0.494*	0.590	0.030	7
(all imported con-					
centrates per hectare)	(0.300)	(0.124)			
United Kingdom[c]	−3.642*	3.634*	0.970	0.137	17
(1870–1965) (all con-					
centrates per hectare	(0.331)	(0.331)			

NOTE: Equations are linear in logarithms. The numbers inside the parentheses are the standard errors of the estimated coefficients.

SOURCES:
[a]Adolf Weber, "Productivity Growth in German Agriculture: 1850 to 1970," University of Minnesota Department of Agricultural and Applied Economics, Staff Paper 73–1, August 1973, p. 23.
[b]William W. Wade, "Institutional Determinants of Technical Change and Agricultural Productivity Growth: Denmark, France and Great Britain, 1870–1965," Ph.D. diss., University of Minnesota, 1973, p. 128.
[c]"Institutional Determinants," p. 149.
*Significant at $P = 0.05$ (one-tail test).

Furthermore, five of the six positive coefficients are the coefficients of the land/labor price. This raises a question of whether some systematic irregularity prevents this price effect from manifesting itself in the expected manner. This behavior may be due to a fundamental or exogenous labor-saving bias in the process of technical innovation, particularly in Japan, France, and the United Kingdom. Such a bias could result from biased technology transfer opportunities by these countries from countries with higher land-labor ratios such as the United States.

The analysis presented in this section supports the hypothesis that changes in factor use in each country have been responsive to changes in relative factor prices. Fertilizer use per hectare has been responsive to the price of fertilizer and of labor relative to the price of land. And two complementary inputs—power per worker and land per worker—have been responsive to the prices of land and machinery relative to labor.

Table 10.5   **Relationship between Land per Worker and Relative Factor Prices in Six Countries**

| Country and Period | Coefficients of Prices of | | Coefficient of Determination (R^2) | Standard Error of Estimate (S) | Degrees of Freedom |
	Land Relative to Labor (P_A/P_L)	Machinery Relative to Labor (P_M/P_L)			
Japan[a]	0.159I	−0.219	0.751	0.016	14
(1880–1960)	(0.110)	(0.041)			
Germany[b]	−0.264*	0.066*I	0.393	0.012	31
(1880–1913)	(0.066)	(0.018)			
(1950–68)	−0.177	−0.476*	0.975	0.083	15
	(0.139)	(0.087)			
Denmark[c]	0.148I	−0.357*	0.910	0.030	9
(1910–65)	(0.084)	(0.072)			
France[d]	0.398*I	−0.088	0.323	0.189	17
(1870–1965)	(0.202)	(0.141)			
(1920–65)	0.050I	−0.498*	0.460	0.164	7
	(0.226)	(0.166)			
United Kingdom[e]	−0.129*	−0.139*	0.610	0.041	17
(1870–1925)	(0.033)	(0.070)			
(1925–65)	0.279I	−0.065	0.440	0.110	6
	(0.159)	(0.256)			
United States[f]	−0.451*	−0.486*	0.828	0.084	14
(1880–1960)	(0.215)	(0.120)			

NOTE: *Land* here means arable land per male worker in Japan, Denmark, France, and the United Kingdom; agricultural land per male worker in Germany and the United States.

[a]Yujiro Hayami and Vernon W. Ruttan, *Agricultural Development: An International Perspective* (Baltimore: The Johns Hopkins University Press, 1971). Land per worker (W7); power per worker (W9).

[b]Adolf Weber, "Productivity Growth in German Agriculture: 1850 to 1970," University of Minnesota Department of Agricultural and Applied Economics, Staff Paper 73–1, August 1973, p. 24. Land per worker, regressions 6 and 7; power per worker, regressions 4 and 5.

[c]William W. Wade, "Institutional Determinants of Technical Change and Agricultural Productivity Growth: Denmark, France and Great Britain, 1870–1965," Ph.D. diss., University of Minnesota, 1973, p. 128.

[d]William W. Wade, "Institutional Determinants," pp. 134, 136.

[e]Wade, "Institutional Determinants," p. 149.

[f]Hayami and Ruttan, *Agricultural Development*, p. 130. Land per worker (W1); power per worker (W5).

*Significant at $P = 0.05$ (one-tail test); I: inconsistent with simple induced innovation hypothesis.

Table 10.6   **Relationship between Power Per Worker and Relative Factor Prices in Six Countries**

| Country and Period | Coefficients of Prices of | | Coefficient of Determination (R^2) | Standard Error of Estimate (S) | Degrees of Freedom |
	Land Relative to Labor (P_A/P_L)	Machinery Relative to Labor (P_M/P_L)			
Japan[a] (1880–1960)	−0.665* (0.261)	−0.299 (0.685)	0.262	0.219	14
Germany[b] (1880–1913)	−0.238* (0.070)	−0.607* (0.020)	0.978	0.069	31
(1950–68)	−0.234 (0.329)	−1.358* (0.207)	0.979	0.213	15
Denmark[c] (1910–65)	1.494*I* (1.010)	−3.180* (0.861)	0.830	0.370	9
France[d] (1870–1965)	1.704*I* (0.880)	−0.705 (0.614)	0.160	0.810	17
(1920–65)	−0.443 (0.976)	−2.460* (0.715)	0.550	0.705	7
United Kingdom[e] (1870–1965)	−1.120* (0.295)	−1.090* (0.527)	0.810	0.075	17
United States[f] (1880–1960)	−1.279* (0.475)	−0.920* (0.266)	0.827	0.187	14

*Significant at $P = 0.05$ (one-tail test); *I*: inconsistent with simple induced innovation hypothesis.

NOTE: *Power* here means horsepower per male worker, except in Germany where machinery investment per worker was employed.

[a]Yujiro Hayami and Vernon W. Ruttan, *Agricultural Development: An International Perspective* (Baltimore: The Johns Hopkins University Press, 1971). Land per worker (W7); power per worker (W9).

[b]Adolf Weber, "Productivity Growth in German Agriculture: 1850 to 1970," University of Minnesota Department of Agricultural and Applied Economics, Staff Paper 73–1, August 1973, p. 24. Land per worker, regressions 6 and 7; power per worker, regressions 4 and 5.

[c]William W. Wade, "Institutional Determinants of Technical Change and Agricultural Productivity Growth: Denmark, France and Great Britain, 1870–1965," Ph.D. diss., University of Minnesota, 1973, p. 128.

[d]William W. Wade, "Institutional Determinants," pp. 134, 136.

[e]Wade, "Institutional Determinants," p. 149.

[f]Hayami and Ruttan, *Agricultural Development*, p. 130. Land per worker (W1); power per worker (W5).

10.4   Agricultural Productivity Differences among Countries, 1970

In this section we explore productivity differences in agriculture among developed and developing countries on different continents for 1970, and attempt to identify sources of productivity differences among countries.

First, we measure the labor and land productivities in agriculture for forty-one countries in 1970. These countries are classified into three groups on the basis of the relative dominance of biological and mechanical technology in their development experience. Second, the different technological patterns of the three country groups are analyzed in relation to the resource endowments in each country group. Third, the labor and land productivity ratios in agriculture for each country are related to the extent of industrialization or development in the nonagricultural sector of each country. Fourth, interrelationships between labor or land productivity ratios and various factor input ratios are explored on the basis of correlation analysis to illustrate the sources of productivity differences among countries. Attention has been given to the same power/labor ratios and fertilizer/land ratios that were employed in the time series analysis. Fifth, human capital variables are related to productivity differences among countries. And finally, intercountry cross section production function estimates based on the 1970 data are made. The coefficients are used to account for differences in labor and land productivities among countries that can be attributed to variations in factor inputs and shift variables.

10.4.1   Differences in Labor and Land Productivities among Countries

We have referred to agricultural technologies which increase output per worker by substitution of more efficient sources of power and equipment per worker as *mechanical technology* and to agricultural technologies which increase output per hectare of agricultural land area as *biological technology*. By comparing differences in land and labor productivities among countries we can classify the several countries by the intensity with which they employ the two types of technologies.

The land and labor productivities presented in table 10.7 were estimated as agricultural output per hectare of agricultural land area and per male worker in terms of wheat units for 1970 using the data compiled in Appendix B. The intercountry differences in these productivity ratios are large. Measured in wheat units, agricultural output per hectare ranged from 0.11 in Paraguay to 13.63 in Taiwan. Output per male worker ranged from 2.4 in India to 198.2 in New Zealand.

Figure 10.4 is an intercountry cross-section map of the labor and land productivity ratios for 1970. The wide scatter of countries on the

Table 10.7   **Factor Productivity and Input–Output Ratios in Forty-one Countries, 1970**

Country	Output per male worker in wheat units Y/L (1)	Number of male workers per wheat unit of output L/Y (2)	Output in wheat units per hectare of agricultural land Y/A (3)	Hectares of agricultural land to produce one wheat unit A/Y (4)
Argentina	51.0	0.0196	0.36	2.813
Australia	186.3	0.0054	0.12	8.607
Austria	59.0	0.0169	3.00	0.333
Bangladesh	2.9	0.3501	3.00	0.334
Belgium	116.2	0.0086	9.52	0.105
Brazil	12.0	0.0835	0.83	1.211
Canada	136.1	0.0073	0.76	1.324
Chile	18.2	0.0549	0.45	2.238
Colombia	10.3	0.0974	1.03	0.976
Denmark	86.3	0.0116	5.07	0.197
Finland	64.2	0.0156	2.63	0.381
France	65.9	0.0152	3.52	0.284
Germany, Fed.	70.1	0.0143	5.37	0.186
Greece	19.6	0.0510	1.89	0.529
India	2.4	0.4251	1.32	0.757
Ireland	34.2	0.0292	1.88	0.531
Israel	72.0	0.0139	3.66	0.273
Italy	32.0	0.0313	3.83	0.261
Japan	15.3	0.0654	10.30	0.097
Mauritius	12.1	0.0827	6.80	0.147
Mexico	8.2	0.1213	0.40	2.528
Netherlands	84.8	0.0118	10.75	0.093
New Zealand	198.2	0.0050	1.55	0.646
Norway	61.3	0.0163	3.54	0.283
Pakistan	2.6	0.3858	1.33	0.750
Paraguay	5.2	0.1928	0.11	9.221
Peru	10.6	0.0939	0.33	3.077
Philippines	4.5	0.2226	1.98	0.504
Portugal	14.1	0.0708	2.21	0.452
South Africa	16.7	0.0598	0.21	4.706
Spain	19.8	0.0506	1.46	0.687
Sri Lanka	4.2	0.2394	2.67	0.375
Surinam	27.3	0.0366	9.87	0.101
Sweden	85.5	0.0117	3.03	0.330
Switzerland	47.9	0.0209	3.52	0.284

Table 10.7 (continued)

Country	Output per male worker in wheat units Y/L (1)	Number of male workers per wheat unit of output L/Y (2)	Output in wheat units per hectare of agricultural land Y/A (3)	Hectares of agricultural land to produce one wheat unit A/Y (4)
Taiwan	10.2	0.0984	13.63	0.073
Turkey	8.3	0.1200	0.83	1.199
U.K.	90.6	0.0110	2.63	0.380
U.S.	160.2	0.0062	0.98	1.024
Venezuela	16.8	0.0596	0.45	2.222
Yugoslavia	11.5	0.0873	1.52	0.660

Source: Data from Appendix B.

map can be classified into three distinct resource endowment groupings on the basis of the relative importance of the two partial productivity ratios in each country's agriculture: (a) the countries in the new continents (and South Africa) such as New Zealand, the United States, and Australia, where labor productivity is relatively high and land productivity relatively low; (b) the countries in Asia (and a few in Africa and South America) such as Taiwan and Japan, where land productivity is relatively high and labor productivity relatively low; and (c) the countries in Europe (and a few in the Near East and South America) such as the Netherlands, Belgium, and Denmark, where labor and land productivities lie between the extremes of the other two groups.[13]

Within each group there is a scatter of countries extending out from the origin. Each scatter or path seems to reflect the long-term development process in agricultural systems characterized by alternative resource endowments. In figure 10.3 we have observed changes in labor/output ratios and land/output ratios in the course of agricultural development from 1880 to 1970 for the six developed countries. For purposes of

13. This classification is the same as based upon 1960 data in Hayami and Ruttan, *Agricultural Development*, p. 69. We have found that no fundamental changes occurred in relative international characteristics of agriculture with respect to the relative levels and combination of labor and land productivities for individual countries from 1960 to 1970. Israel and Turkey, included in the third group with European countries here, were classified into the "West Asia Mediterranean Coast Agricultural Region" in Saburo Yamada, *Comparative Analysis*. This implies that the characteristics of agriculture in the Mediterranean coast of the Near East are fundamentally the same as those of European countries.

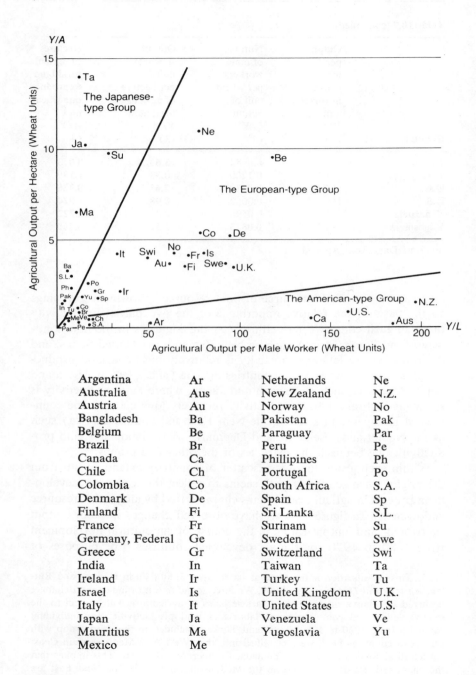

Argentina	Ar	Netherlands	Ne
Australia	Aus	New Zealand	N.Z.
Austria	Au	Norway	No
Bangladesh	Ba	Pakistan	Pak
Belgium	Be	Paraguay	Par
Brazil	Br	Peru	Pe
Canada	Ca	Phillipines	Ph
Chile	Ch	Portugal	Po
Colombia	Co	South Africa	S.A.
Denmark	De	Spain	Sp
Finland	Fi	Sri Lanka	S.L.
France	Fr	Surinam	Su
Germany, Federal	Ge	Sweden	Swe
Greece	Gr	Switzerland	Swi
India	In	Taiwan	Ta
Ireland	Ir	Turkey	Tu
Israel	Is	United Kingdom	U.K.
Italy	It	United States	U.S.
Japan	Ja	Venezuela	Ve
Mauritius	Ma	Yugoslavia	Yu
Mexico	Me		

Fig. 10.4   International comparison of labor and land productivities, 1970

comparison, figure 10.4 was converted into figure 10.5 in which productivity ratios were reversed and expressed as land per unit of output and labor per unit of output. The diagonal lines represent constant land/labor ratios. The percentage ratio of nonagricultural employment to the total economically active population is shown in parentheses. The lines make it easy to distinguish the different resource endowment ratios among countries. The nonagricultural employment percentage represents a crude indicator of the general level of development.

A comparison of figure 10.5 with figure 10.3 indicates remarkably similar patterns between the three general historical paths (of the United States, Japan, and the European countries) in figure 10.3 and the distribution of countries within each of the three groups classified in figure 10.4. In general, (*a*) the distribution of the countries in the new continents (and South Africa) falls along the historical path of the United States; (*b*) the distribution of the Asian countries (and Mauritius and Surinum) falls along the historical path of Japan; and (*c*) the distribution of the European countries (and Israel, Turkey, Brazil, and Colombia) falls along the historical paths of the four European countries. We identify the three country groups as American, Japanese, and European-type groups, respectively. These types reflect the result of different resource endowments and choice of technology paths (between mechanical and biological technology) among countries.

10.4.2   Resource Endowments and Technology Preference

We have earlier hypothesized that resource endowments as reflected by land/labor ratios are of major importance in the choice of technology, or in inducing a country to follow a particular path of technological development. In countries where land is abundant relative to labor it is efficient to emphasize mechanical technology relative to biological technology. In countries with reverse endowment conditions, biological technology would be more efficient than mechanical technology. In the former countries, the price of land is cheap relative to labor. It is expensive in the latter.

In countries of the American type, where the land/labor ratio was relatively high, ranging from 21 hectares per male worker (Mexico) to 180 (Canada) (even leaving aside the exceptional case of 1604 in Australia), the hectares used to produce one wheat unit of output (land/output ratio) ranged from 0.65 (New Zealand) to 9.22 (Paraguay), and the man years per wheat unit of output (labor/output ratio) ranged from 0.005 (New Zealand) to 0.193 (Paraguay). The land/labor ratio of the United States was 25 in 1880 and 164 in 1970, which roughly corresponds to the present range of resource endowment conditions of the group. The labor/output ratio of the United States in 1880 was 0.077, roughly comparable with 0.060 of Venezuela and 0.094 of

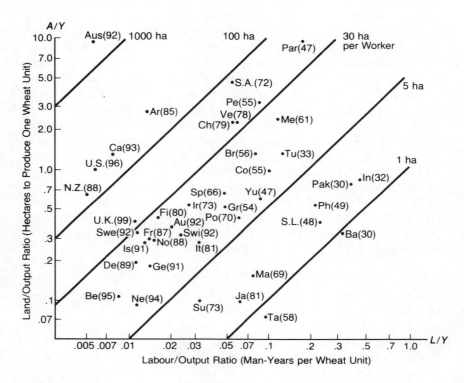

Fig. 10.5   International comparison of labor/output and land/output ratios (in logs), 1970. Source: table 10.7. Note: Diagonal lines represent land/labor ratios and numbers in parentheses are percentage ratios of nonagricultural workers to the total economically active population.

Peru in 1970. The land/output ratio of the United States in 1880 was 1.95, also roughly comparable with 2.22 of Venezuela and 2.24 of Chile in 1970.[14] In those countries of the group, such as New Zealand, the United States, and Canada, where land/labor ratios were all over 100 hectares per worker, labor/output ratios were as small as 0.005–0.117 (very high labor productivity) but land/output ratios were as high as 0.65–1.32 (low land productivity) in 1970. It is evident that mechanical technology was strongly emphasized relative to biological technology in this group.

Contrary to the above group, in the countries of the Japanese type, where the land/labor ratio was very low, ranging from only 0.8 hectares (Taiwan) to 2.8 (Surinam), the technological choice was reversed. Labor/output ratios were high, ranging from 0.037 (Surinam) to 0.425 (India), but land/output ratios ranged from 0.07 (Taiwan) to 0.76 (India). The ratios of land/labor, land/output, and labor/output in Japan in 1880 were 0.66, 0.35, and 0.53, respectively, which were roughly comparable with the present situations of India, Pakistan, Bangladesh, Philippines, and Sri Lanka. The technological leaders in this group, Taiwan and Japan, certainly chose to follow a path which gave a strong priority to biological technology relative to mechanical technology.

In the European countries, where the land/labor ratio ranged from 6.4 (Portugal) to 34.4 (The United Kingdom), intermediate between the two extreme groups, labor/output and land/output ratios were also intermediate. The ratios ranged from 0.009 and 0.11 of Belgium to 0.120 and 1.20 in Turkey. In 1880, land/labor ratios were 6.3, 7.0, 8.9, and 14.7 hectares for Germany, France, Denmark, and the United Kingdom, respectively. These are comparable with many of the present European-type countries. And labor/output and land/output ratios of the four countries in 1880 were also comparable with the ratios in countries such as Turkey, Brazil, Colombia, and Yugoslavia in 1970.

Thus resource endowments must be considered as an important factor in determining both the choice of technology and inducing an efficient path of technological development over time.

10.4.3   Industrialization and Technological Improvements

It is generally accepted that the potential for agricultural development in a country is strongly conditioned by the level of domestic industrial or nonagricultural development.[15] The close association between agri-

14. The 1880 data cited here are from tables 10.1 and 10.2. See also Appendix B.

15. See Hayami and Ruttan, *Agricultural Development*, pp. 74–81; Yujiro Hayami, "Industrialization and Agricultural Productivity: An International Comparative Study," *The Developing Economies*, 6 (September 1968): 3–21; and

cultural and industrial development holds not only for historical time sequences of individual countries but is also apparent in the intercountry cross-sectional phenomena.

Movements of land/output and labor/output ratios toward the lower left-hand corner along the same diagonal lines in figure 10.5 represent improvements in the two partial productivities under similar resource endowments of land/labor ratio conditions. And the figure reveals that the ratio of nonagricultural employment, an indicator of industrialization, for individual countries is highly correlated with movements toward the lower left-hand corner in each country group: from 47% (Paraguay) to 96% (the United States) in the American-type group; from 30% (Pakistan) to 81% (Japan) in the Japanese-type group; and from 33% (Turkey) to 95% (Belgium) in the European-type group. This association of technological improvements with industrialization in intercountry cross sections is consistent with the historical experience of the six developed countries.

Industrialization or growth of the nonagricultural sector can contribute to improvements in agricultural technology in many ways. Industrial development can (a) reduce the cost of modern agricultural inputs, such as fertilizer, chemicals, and machinery, produced by the industrial sector; (b) expand the rate of growth in the demand for farm products; and (c) increase the demand for labor. Educational development in rural areas can make farmers more productive. Advancement of knowledge in general sciences can increase the productivity of applied research in the agricultural sciences and technology. Investment in physical and institutional infrastructure develops productivity of resources devoted to agricultural production and marketing.

In the following paragraphs we will investigate interrelationships among the labor and land productivities and various factor-factor ratios to search for sources of intercountry differences in agricultural productivity. Special attention will be given to the intensity in the use of modern technical inputs as measured by power relative to labor and fertilizer relative to land.[16]

Bruce F. Johnston and Peter Kilby, *Agriculture and Structural Transformation: Economic Strategies in Late Developing Countries* (New York: Oxford University Press, 1975), for related discussions on industrialization and agricultural productivity.

16. Only physical farm inputs will be taken into account because of data availability in the study. See Hayami and Ruttan, *Agricultural Development*, pp. 90–101 for an intercountry comparative study for 1960 on sources of agricultural productivity differences including the effect of both education and modern physical inputs. See also Yujiro Hayami, et al., *Century of Agricultural Growth* for an in-depth analysis of the Japanese case.

10.4.4   Productivity Differences and Factor Proportions

Among the countries along the same land/labor ratio lines (fig. 10.5), both labor/output and land/output ratios tended to be smaller in developed countries than in less developed countries. This is because, as noted earlier, the two partial productivities are not independent but are linked through the land/labor ratio.[17] Figure 10.6 shows this relation more explicitly than figure 10.5. A higher level of labor productivity (the diagonal lines toward the upper right) can be achieved through either an increasing of the land/labor ratio, higher land productivity, or both. Developed countries in the American-type group have achieved high labor productivity principally by increasing their land/labor ratios. Those in the Japanese-type group have achieved higher labor productivity through higher land productivity. The European-type countries have experienced a more balanced pattern of productivity growth. However, the United Kingdom and Sweden are closer to the American pattern and the Netherlands and Belgium closer to the Japanese pattern.

The sources of productivity differences can be divided into two types. As noted earlier, differences in labor productivity are associated with differences in the adoption of mechanical technology. Differences in land productivity are associated with differences in the development and adoption of biological technology.

The most typical source of increase in labor productivity is more intensive use of mechanical power by farmers. The substitution of mechanical power for labor permits a rise in both the land/labor ratio and in output per worker. Figure 10.7 confirms the close association of tractor horsepower per male worker (tractor/labor ratio) and agricultural output per male worker (labor productivity) in both 1960 and 1970. In 1970 the correlation coefficient (r) was .93 for all countries —though only tractors and garden tractors (in terms of horsepower) were counted as farm machinery. The coefficient was particularly high (.96) for the American-type group. It was somewhat lower (.93) for the European-type group and even lower (.84) for the Japanese-type group.

This implies that the role of mechanical technology is critically important in achieving high levels of labor productivity. Mechanization is economically efficient, however, only in situations characterized by a high land-labor ratio and a high wage-land price ratio. The hypothesis that the use of power (or machinery) per worker is negatively related to both the price of land relative to labor and of machinery relative to labor was generally confirmed in the time series analysis. The hypothesis seems also to be plausible in international, cross-sectional perspec-

17. See footnote 5.

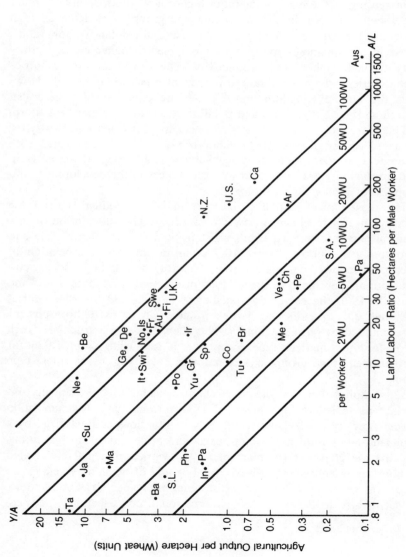

Fig. 10.6 International comparison of land/labor ratios, land productivity, and labor productivity (in logs), 1970. Source: table 10.7 and table 10.A.2. Note: Diagonal lines represent constant output/labor ratios.

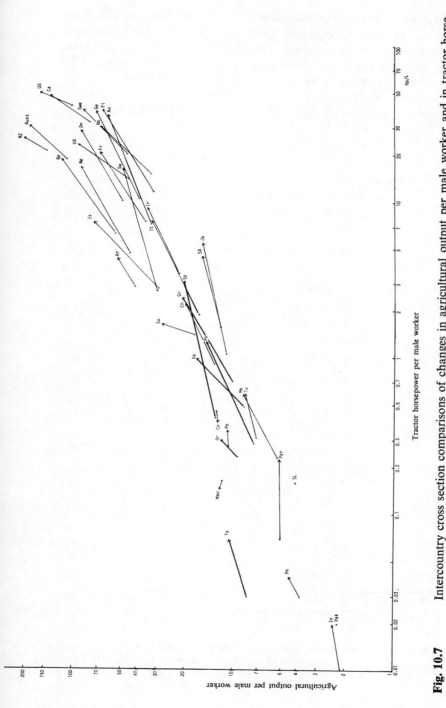

Fig. 10.7 Intercountry cross section comparisons of changes in agricultural output per male worker and in tractor horse-power per male worker, 1960–70 (in logs). Sources: table 10.7 and table 10.A.2 for 1970; and Hayami and Ruttan, *Agricultural Development,* for 1960.

tive. Because of the lack of international land price data, we could not test the relationship as rigorously in the cross section as in the time series analysis. However, a regression of tractor horsepower per male worker against the price of machinery relative to labor in figure 10.8 does confirm the plausibility of the hypothesized relationship in the cross section data. The correlation coefficient was 0.83. The elasticity coefficient was statistically significant in the following simple regression.

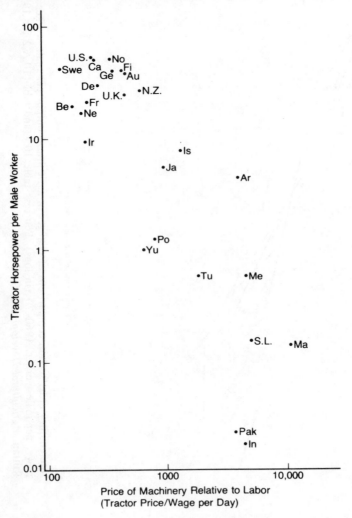

Fig. 10.8   International comparison of tractor horsepower per male worker and price of machinery relative to labor (in logs), 1970. Sources: tables 10.A.2 and 10.A.3.

$$\text{In } (M/L) = 12.230 - 1.605 \text{ In } (P_M/P_L)$$
$$(0.221)$$
$$R^2 = 0.695$$

(here 1.605 is significant at $P = 0.01$ [one-tail test]), and where M, L, P_M, and P_L represent machinery horsepower, the number of male farm workers, tractor price, and wage rate per day.

In developed countries—as New Zealand, United States, Canada, and Australia—where the ratio was more than 100 hectares per worker, the tractor/labor ratio was in the 27–53 horsepower range per worker. But in developing countries such as Mexico, Peru, and Venezuela, where the land/labor ratio was 20–40, the tractor/labor ratio was merely 0.4–1.0. The initial resource endowment conditions of the respective countries are clearly a primary source of the present differences in land/labor ratios among countries. It should be noted, however, that even in the United States it was only 25 hectares per worker in 1880. This is roughly equivalent to the level in many of the present developing countries in the American-type group. In these countries the development of mechanical technology is already a critical factor in expanding the land area that is cultivated per worker and hence in raising labor productivity (see fig. 10.7).

Unfortunately, we have not been able to explore the effect of relative factor prices on choice of biological technology in the cross section analysis. Biological technology refers not to a single technique but to an associated bundle of various technologies, particularly the use of improved varieties with more fertilizer and better irrigation. In this analysis we continue the tradition of using fertilizer as a proxy for the whole complex of biological technology. We again emphasize that this represents a gross oversimplification, though one convenient for expositional purposes.

The association between fertilizer consumption per hectare of agricultural land and land productivity levels is shown in figure 10.9. In both 1960 and 1970 there was a close association between fertilizer use per hectare and output per hectare. In 1970 the correlation coefficient was .89 for all forty-one countries. It was .81 for the American-type group, .89 for the European-type group, and .86 for the Japanese-type group. Thus it was relatively high for each resource endowment grouping. In contrast to the case of tractor use, the intensive use of fertilizer is important in raising land productivity not only in the biological-technology–oriented Japanese-type countries, but also even in the mechanical-technology–oriented countries of the American-type group. The lower level of labor productivity of developing countries such as Paraguay, Mexico, and Peru in the American-type group is not only due to their

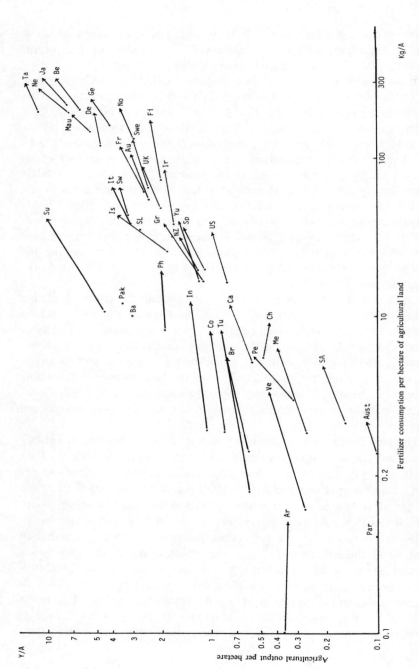

Fig. 10.9   Intercountry cross section comparison of changes in agricultural output per hectare and in fertilizer consumption per hectare of agricultural land, 1960–70 (in logs) · Source: table 10.7 and table 10.A.2, and Hayami and Ruttan, *Agricultural Development*, for 1960.

lower land/labor ratios but is also due to low land productivity. In these, as in other countries, low land productivity is associated with low levels of fertilizer use. The low level of fertilizer use typically reflects the low level of biological technology that is available to farmers and/or relatively high fertilizer prices.

Comparing each country's relative position in figure 10.7 with the same country's position in figure 10.9, we can observe the contrast among the three types of resource endowment groupings. For instance, the tractor/labor ratio was the highest but the fertilizer/land ratio was moderate for the United States. This contrast was exactly the reverse for Japan. For developed countries such as Belgium and the Netherlands in the European-type group, both ratios were relatively high.[18]

Both fertilizer and tractors are industrial products. Intensity in the use of these inputs is generally associated with the level of industrialization in individual countries. This results in a high correlation between the level of use of the two inputs in the intercountry cross section comparisons. The correlation coefficients are .84 for all countries, .93 for the American-type group, .91 for the European, and .81 for the Japanese-type group. This implies that higher labor productivity is associated not only with more tractor use per worker but also with more fertilizer use per worker ($r = .92$ between labor productivity and the fertilizer/labor ratio for all countries, .89 for the American-type group, .94 for the European-type group, and .83 for the Japanese-type group). In a technical sense, fertilizer is a substitute for land. But such a high correlation between the two variables confirms the important role of other current inputs (including agricultural chemicals, feed, and fuel) in addition to fertilizer in increasing labor productivity. This is of course consistent with the Japanese experience where yield increases have until recently represented a dominant source of labor productivity.

Factor-factor combinations among labor, land, fertilizer, and tractor horsepower have been discussed in relation to intercountry differences in labor or land productivities. In addition, farm capital stock such as livestock and perennial plants are also important agricultural resources that are used in agricultural production. Differences in the intensity of such capital inputs relative to labor or land (capital/labor or capital/land ratio) among countries must also account, in part, for the productivity differences among the several countries.

18. In Hayami and Ruttan, *Agricultural Development*, fig. 4–2, p. 72, both ratios were compared internationally for 1960. Comparing the 1960 results with the present study for 1970, relative positions of the United States and Japan were unchanged; however, relative levels of tractor/labor ratio in the developed European countries have become closer to the United States level during 1960–70 mainly due to considerable decreases in agricultural labor in those countries.

However, interrelationships between these ratios and productivity levels are not as clear-cut as in the cases of tractors and fertilizer. The correlation coefficient was .77 between the livestock/labor ratio and the labor productivity ratio and .73 between the livestock/land ratios and the land productivity ratio for all countries. It was also quite low on a regional basis (except for .86 for the first relationship in the American-type group). In the case of perennial plants, it was even lower. The ratio was .48 between perennial plants/land ratio and land productivity ratio for all countries. There was almost no correlation between perennial plants/labor ratio and labor productivity. Although such a low correlation might be due to the crudeness of our estimates for perennial plants, we conclude that productivity gaps among countries are much more closely associated with differences in the use of modern technical inputs produced in the industrial sector such as tractors and fertilizer than with differences in these forms of farm-produced capital stock.

The aggregate stock of fixed farm capital, which includes all three types of tangible fixed capital analyzed in this study (livestock, perennial plants, and tractors), is closely associated with the labor and land productivity ratios.[19] Excluding eight countries where data on perennial plants were not available, the correlation coefficient between the capital/labor ratio and the labor productivity ratio was .76 for all countries. But it was .91 for the American-type group and only .42 for the Japanese-type group (and .64 for the European-type group). This seems to imply that capital intensity is a more important factor accounting for differences in labor productivity in the American-type group, but less important in the Japanese-type group. The role of current inputs such as fertilizer would be more critical in determining agricultural productivity for the Japanese-type group. We can observe such differences among the different country groups in figure 10.10.

The correlation coefficient between the capital/land ratio and the land productivity ratio was .88 for all countries (excluding the eight countries). It was .86 in the European country group, .78 in the American-type group, and .57 in the Japanese-type group. In European countries, land productivity has been a more important concern in agricultural production than in the American-type countries. In the Japanese-type group, the contribution of capital intensity to land productivity

19. Farm capital stock estimated here includes livestock, tractors, and agricultural perennial plants only. Thus the coverage of the estimates is incomplete. Aggregation was made using Japan weights due to data availability. The estimates are therefore in terms of Japanese price relatives. See Appendix B for the estimating procedures and data. Because of the lack of data, the value of perennial plants was not included in the estimated capital stock for Bangladesh, Canada, Finland, Mauritius, Norway, Pakistan, Sweden, and the United Kingdom.

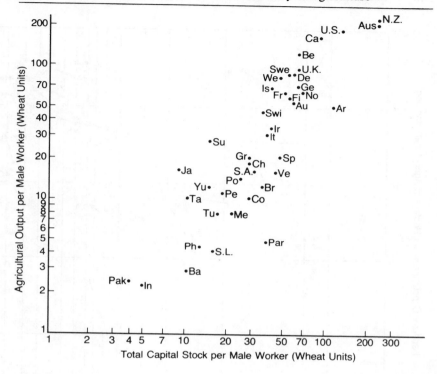

Fig. 10.10   International comparison of capital stock and agricultural output per male worker (in logs), 1970. Source: table 10.7 and table 10.A.2.

is only slightly more important than labor intensity, judging from the magnitude of the correlation coefficient.[20]

The data presented in figure 10.11 suggest that in spite of the continued differences in intensity of factor use among the three country groups there was a tendency for both the Japanese-type group and the American-type group to converge toward the European pattern of factor use between 1960 and 1970. The countries in the Japanese-type group which had achieved the highest level of fertilizer use per hectare in 1960, such as Japan, Taiwan, and Sri Lanka, experienced more rapid growth in tractor horsepower per worker than in fertilizer use per hectare between 1960 and 1970. In contrast, the countries in the American-type

20. It is not to deny the importance of capital stock in agricultural production in Asia. According to Yamada, *Comparative Analysis*, in countries where capital intensity is high, such as Japan, Taiwan, Malaysia, Hong Kong, and Sri Lanka, agricultural productivity is also relatively high.

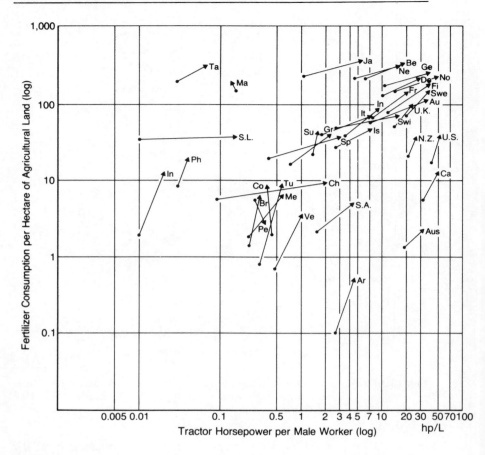

Fig. 10.11   Intercountry cross section comparison of changes in tractor
horsepower per male worker and in fertilizer consumption
per hectare of agricultural land, 1960–70 (in logs). Source:
table 10.7 and table 10.A.2 for 1970; Hayami and Ruttan,
Agricultural Development, for 1960.

group experienced more rapid increases in fertilizer use per hectare than
in tractor horsepower per worker.

The effects of these changes in factor use and factor productivity
during the 1960–70 decade were not completely consistent with our
expectations. The data presented in figure 10.7 suggest that the incremental impact of additional inputs of tractor horsepower on output per
worker between 1960 and 1970 was greater in the countries that had
already achieved high levels of mechanization than in countries characterized by a lower level of mechanization. Similarly, the data presented

in figure 10.9 suggest that the incremental impact of additional fertilizer consumption per hectare between 1960 and 1970 was greater in the countries that had already achieved high levels of fertilizer use per hectare.

This result is somewhat surprising since it was anticipated that the new "seed-fertilizer" or "green revolution" technology that was introduced in many developing countries in the mid and late 1960s would result in rapid growth in both fertilizer use and output per hectare in countries where appropriate biological technology had previously not been available. One possible explanation is that the diffusion of new biological technology had not proceeded fast enough by 1970 to exert a major impact on the patterns of productivity growth, and that the 1960–70 trends in factor use and factor productivity simply reflected the continuing momentum of historical differences in the access to mechanical and biological technology between the more advanced and the developing countries. A second alternative is that the smaller incremental contribution of increases in the use of mechanical power per worker and of fertilizer per hectare was due to lags in the introduction of complementary components in the bundle of techniques which constitutes an efficient biological or mechanical technology.

This point is illustrated with reference to the new seed-fertilizer technology in figure 10.12.

Curve A_0D_0 represents the envelope of response curves (the metaproduction function) relating fertilizer use per hectare (F/A) to yield per hectare (Y/A) for countries A, C, and D in period 0. The response curve A_0 is characteristic of a country which has access to a relatively low level of biological technology in period 0. The response curves C_0 and D_0 are characteristic of countries which have access to more advanced levels of biological technology in period 0.

The differences between the several response curves could reflect, for example, different levels of adoption of irrigation technology. The curve a_0d_0 represents the relationship between the level of biological technology and the optimum level of fertilizer use per hectare in each country. The effect of the introduction, between period 0 and period 1, of an advance in the level of biological technology, such as more fertilizer-responsive crop varieties, is to shift the individual country response curves up and to the right. If there is complementarity between irrigation technology and the new seed-fertilizer technology, the effect is a biased shift in the individual response curves. The countries characterized by low levels of biological technology in 1960 were in a weaker position to take advantage of the new seed-fertilizer technology than countries characterized by higher levels of biological technology in 1960. The new metaproduction function is shown as A_1C_1 and the new biological tech-

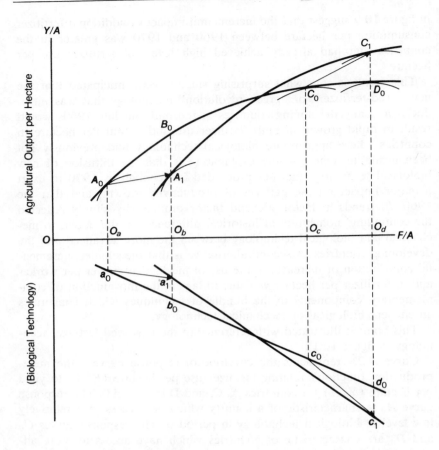

Fig. 10.12   Impact of fertilizer-using bias on fertilizer use and output per hectare

nology function is shown as a_1c_1. The changes in fertilizer use and yield per hectare presented in figure 10.9 are consistent with a shift in the metaproduction function such as that illustrated in figure 10.12.

10.4.5 Productivity Differences and Human Capital

So far, factor-factor combinations among conventional inputs have been discussed in relation to intercountry differences in labor or land productivities. In addition, the levels of nonconventional inputs such as education, research, and extension act to shift the production function and hence contribute to intercountry productivity differences in agriculture. As the proxies for these human capital inputs, two kinds of measures of education levels were related to the productivity differences:

(a) the school enrollment ratio for the primary and secondary levels, which represents the level of general education (GE), and (b) the number of graduates from agricultural colleges per 10,000 male farm workers, which stands for the level of education in the agricultural sciences and technology (TE). General education is hypothesized to influence the efficiency with which farmers make decisions with respect to the use of resources and their acquisition of skill in the use of resources. Agricultural graduates represent the major source of technological personnel for agricultural research and extension. In an attempt to convert the enrollment ratio into a measure of the stock of education, a series of averages of the data for 1960, 1965, and 1970 was used. And to check a possible lag in the effect of the general education on the adult farmers, the 1955–60–65 averages series were applied alternatively.

The association between these human capital measures and labor productivity levels in 1970 is shown in figures 10.13 and 10.14. The correlation coefficient between TE and labor productivity was relatively high —.86 as compared to .74 between $GE_{60\text{-}65\text{-}70}$ and labor productivity and .76 between $GE_{55\text{-}60\text{-}65}$ and labor productivity for all forty-one countries. It is interesting that the correlation coefficients were even higher within the different three-country groups: the correlation coefficient between TE and labor productivity was .92 for the American-type group, .85 for the European-type group, and .79 for the Japanese-type group; the correlation coefficient between $GE_{55\text{-}60\text{-}65}$ and labor productivity was .92 for the American-type group, .87 for the European-type group, and .78 for the Japanese-type group (see figs. 10.13 and 10.14).

The relationships between the human capital measures and land productivity are not as clear for the entire group of forty-one countries (fig. 10.15). The correlation coefficients between land productivity and $GE_{55\text{-}60\text{-}65}$ and $GE_{60\text{-}65\text{-}70}$ were only .22 and .17, respectively. One possible reason for such a low correlation is that the human capital measures employed here were normalized on a per capita base but not on a unit land area base. Even so, when we disaggregated by productivity groupings there was a reasonably high correlation by the three country groups: the correlation coefficient between $GE_{55\text{-}60\text{-}65}$ and land productivity was .58 for the American-type group, .77 for the European-type group, and .67 for the Japanese-type group, respectively (fig. 10.16).

The relationships between TE and land productivity are similar: the correlation coefficient was .54 for the American-type group, .72 for the European-type group, and .78 for the Japanese-type group, while it was only .21 for all forty-one countries.

These observations support the proposition that human capital as measured by general and technical education plays a significant role in increasing land productivity as well as in increasing labor productivity under conditions of similar labor/land endowments.

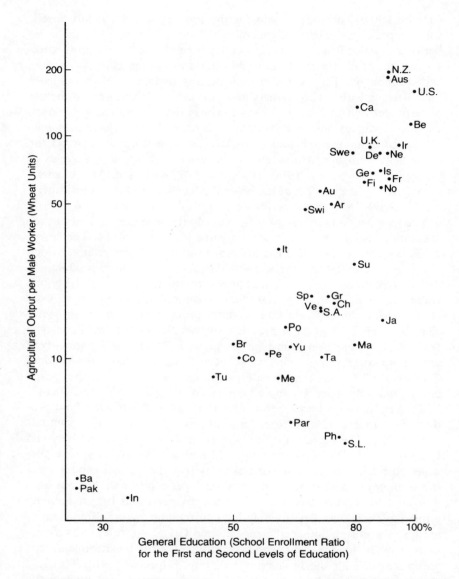

Fig. 10.13   International comparison of general education and agricultural output per male worker (in logs), 1970. Source: table 10.7 and table 10.A.3. Note: The 1955–60–65 average is used for the general education statistics.

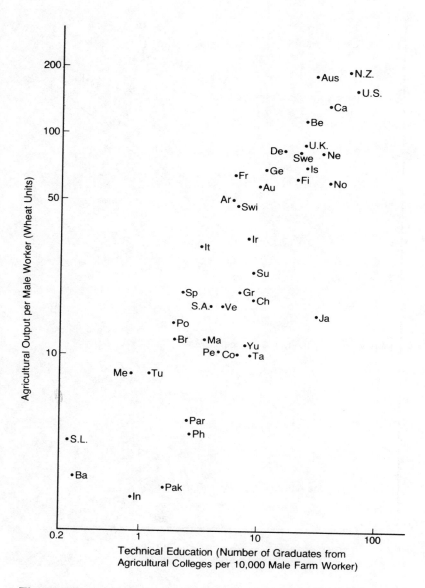

Fig. 10.14   International comparison of technical education and agricultural output per male worker (in logs), 1970. Source: table 10.7 and table 10.A.3.

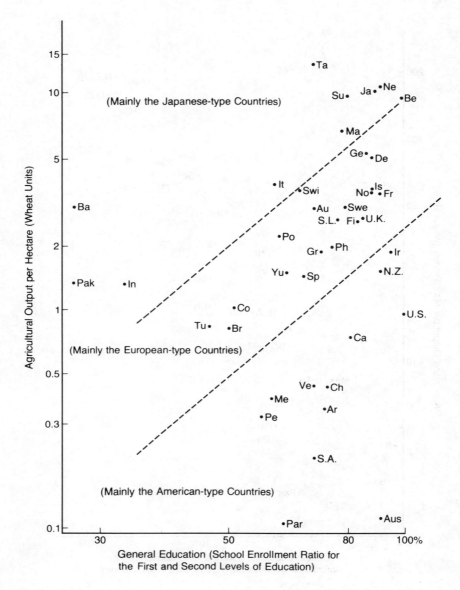

Fig. 10.15   International comparison of general education and agricultural output per hectare of agricultural land (in logs), 1970. Source: table 10.7 and table 10.A.3. Note: The 1955–60–65 average is used for the general education statistics.

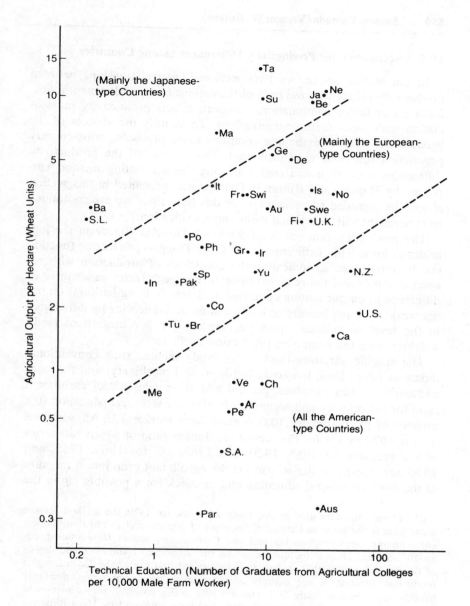

Fig. 10.16   International comparison of technical education and agricultural output per hectare of agricultural land (in logs), 1970. Sources: table 10.7 and table 10.A.3.

10.5   Accounting for Productivity Differences among Countries

In the section above, we have explored interrelationships between productivity differences and each of the various factor endowment ratios. Each factor-factor combination, however, affects productivity in association with other factor combinations. To identify the sources of the productivity differences among countries more precisely, cross-country production functions were estimated. The sources of the productivity differences were then analyzed following the accounting method employed by Hayami and Ruttan.[21] The material presented in this section should be regarded as preliminary at this time since we are continuing to experiment with functional form and specification.

The production function is of the Cobb-Douglas (linear in the logarithms) form. The coefficients of the Cobb-Douglas production function can be interpreted as indicating the elasticities of production with respect to inputs and the relative importance of each factor as a source of difference in output among countries. Differences in agricultural output per worker (or per hectare of land) can be accounted for by differences in the level of various inputs per worker (or per hectare of land) weighted with the respective production coefficients.

The specific variables used in the study include such conventional inputs as labor, land, livestock, fertilizer, and machinery, and the non-conventional shift variables, general education (the school enrollment ratio for the primary and secondary levels) and technical education (the number of graduates per 10,000 male farm workers).[22] All variables are for 1970 except for the school enrollment ratio of which two series of the averages for 1955, 1960, and 1965, and for 1960, 1965, and 1970 were used in order to convert the enrollment ratio into a measure of the stock of general education and to check for a possible lag in the

21. Though the data used in this study were new for 1970, the method for the accounting is the same as chapter 5, "Sources of Agricultural Productivity Differences among Countries," in Hayami and Ruttan, *Agricultural Development*, pp. 86–107. See the chapter for discussions on the conceptual framework and details of the method and related studies. It is recognized that use of the Cobb-Douglas production function is not entirely consistent with the factor complementarity hypothesis outlined in figure 10.1. One solution to this problem, the estimation of individual factor augmentation coefficients, has been employed by Hans Binswanger, "Measurement of Technical Change Biases with Many Factors of Production," *American Economic Review* 64 (December 1974): 964–76.

22. Perennial plants were also included in some specifications of production function estimate. Its estimated coefficient was statistically significant at $P = 0.005$ (one-tail test) but some other coefficients became negative in sign and statistically nonsignificant. Besides the variable data were lacking for the eight countries as mentioned in note 19. Hence it was excluded from the production function employed in analysis and from accounting for productivity differences.

effect of general education to the first and second levels on the farmers' decision-making and technical capacity.

Three kinds of regression models were estimated: (a) an ordinary unrestricted aggregate production function for the agricultural sector; (b) a production function on a per worker basis in which output per worker was regressed on conventional inputs per worker and on nonconventional inputs; and (c) a production function on a per hectare basis in which output per hectare was regressed on conventional inputs per hectare and on nonconventional inputs.[23] In (b) and (c) constant returns to scale were assumed and the sum of the coefficients of conventional inputs was held equal to one. The estimates were based on the data for all forty-one countries.[24] The results are summarized in table 10.8. In general the production coefficients estimated under different specifications were statistically significant except those for land and general education.[25]

The *fertilizer coefficients* were all statistically significant. They ranged from .23 to .32. This is well above the range of .09 to .16 estimated by Hayami and Ruttan for 1960.[26] The results of the regression analysis are consistent with the impression, based on figure 10.8, that between 1960 and 1970 the incremental contribution of fertilizer to output per hectare was greatest in those countries that were already using relatively high levels of fertilizer per hectare. In contrast to the fertilizer coefficient, no statistically significant *land coefficients* were estimated for 1970. This is in contrast to the 1960 results obtained by Hayami and Ruttan which typically fell in the .06–.07 range. It seems reasonable to hypothesize that at least part of this change in the fertilizer coefficient relative to the coefficient for land was due to a combination of decline

23. The production function was estimated for various groups of countries: for instance, (a) the American, Japanese, and European-style factor endowment groups, and (b) highly developed, moderately developed, and less developed country groups. Also, various regression specifications were applied in addition to those listed in table 10.8. However, most of the results were implausible because some of the coefficients were negative in sign and/or statistically nonsignificant.

24. In Hayami and Ruttan's work, the sample size of estimated regressions was 37 or 38. For comparison purposes, Bangladesh, Pakistan, Paraguay, Portugal, and Yugoslavia were also dropped from some 1970 regressions. However, there were no significant differences in the estimated coefficient in regression of the same specification between the sample sizes of forty-one and thirty-six.

25. It is possible that the low coefficient for land in 1970 may also be due in part to the high intercorrelation between land and livestock. In 1970 the correlation coefficient between land and livestock was .92. High intercorrelation was also observed between fertilizer and tractor horsepower (.84) and between labor and livestock (.76).

26. Hayami and Ruttan, *Agricultural Development*, p. 93 (Table 5–1).

Table 10.8 Estimates of the International Cross Section Production Function for Agriculture, 1970

	Regression[a]								
	Q1	Q2	Q3	Q4	Q5	Q6	Q7	Q8	Q9
Labor	.209** (.063)	.317** (.086)	.325** (.090)	.265[b]	.389[b]	.398[b]	.265** (.062)	.389** (.068)	.398** (.079)
Land	.026 (.074)	.024 (.075)	.019 (.074)	.019 (.079)	.011 (.077)	.005 (.075)	.019[b]	.011[b]	.005[b]
Livestock	.247** (.102)	.223* (.109)	.234* (.104)	.244* (.109)	.230* (.113)	.244* (.106)	.244* (.109)	.230* (.113)	.244* (.106)
Fertilizer	.312** (.082)	.247** (.088)	.243** (.089)	.323** (.087)	.237** (.090)	.226** (.090)	.323** (.087)	.237** (.090)	.226** (.090)
Machinery	.117* (.067)	.118* (.070)	.113* (.066)	.149* (.069)	.133* (.072)	.126* (.067)	.149* (.069)	.133* (.072)	.126* (.067)
General education 60–65–70 average		−.034 (.329)						.075 (.334)	
55–60–65 average			.075 (.316)		.075 (.334)	.264 (.299)			.264 (.299)
Technical education		.140* (.076)	.135* (.075)		.170* (.076)	.155* (.076)		.170* (.076)	.155* (.076)
Coef. of det.	.947	.952	.952	.923	.934	.935	.919	.930	.932
Sum of coef. for conventional inputs	.911	.929	.934	1.000	1.000	1.000	1.000	1.000	1.000

in the price of fertilizer and an induced shift in the metaproduction function associated with the introduction of the new seed-fertilizer "green revolution" technology between 1960 and 1970.

The *labor coefficients* for 1970 were almost all statistically significant. They ranged, in the several regressions, from .21 to .40. This was lower than the estimates obtained by Hayami and Ruttan for 1960, which ranged from .34 to .47. In contrast to the decline in the labor coefficients there was a tendency for the machinery coefficients to rise between 1960 and 1970. The *machinery coefficients* ranged from .11 to .15 in 1970, in contrast to .10 or below in 1960. Thus the results of the regression analysis are consistent with the impression, based on figure 10.7, that between 1960 and 1970 the incremental contribution of mechanization to output per worker was greatest in those countries that were already the most highly mechanized. The results suggest a machinery-using bias in technical change leading to increased substitution of machinery for labor between 1960 and 1970.

The *livestock coefficient* for 1970 ranged from .11 to .15. This was approximately in the same range as the Hayami-Ruttan results for 1960.

The *general education coefficient* was negative in Q2 where the averages of 1960, 1965, and 1970 were used. In the case where the averages of 1955, 1960, and 1965 were used, the general education coefficient ranged from .08 to .26, though it was still not statistically significant. The coefficient of the other nonconventional variable, technical education, however, was significant statistically, ranging from .14 to .17. This was the same level as .14–.18 for 1960 estimated by Hayami and Ruttan while the general education coefficient level estimated here was lower than the range of .29–.32 that was estimated for 1960 on a national aggregate basis as in the present study by Hayami and Ruttan. We do not know why the general education variable performed less effectively in the 1970 cross section study than in the earlier 1960 cross section study by Hayami and Ruttan.

Source: Based on the data from Appendix B.

Notes: Equations are linear in logarithms. The standard errors of the estimated coefficients are inside the parentheses.

[a]In regressions Q1, Q2, and Q3, both output and factor inputs are expressed in actual units. These three equations are estimated on an unrestricted basis.

In regressions Q4, Q5, and Q6, the output and the conventional inputs (i.e., land, livestock, fertilizer, and machinery) are expressed in per-worker terms. The sum of the conventional coefficients was restricted to equal one.

In regressions Q7, Q8, and Q9, the output and the conventional factor inputs (i.e., labor, livestock, fertilizer, and machinery) were expressed on a per-hectare basis and the sum of coefficients was restricted to equal one.

[b]Implicit coefficient.

*Significant at $P = 0.05$ (one-tail test).

**Significant at $P = 0.01$ (one-tail test).

In spite of the limitations in the 1970 cross section regression results, the following set of production elasticities was adopted for accounting purposes: .35 for labor, .02 for land, .25 for livestock, .25 for fertilizer, .13 for machinery, .25 for general education, and .15 for technical education.[27] We would feel more comfortable about the growth accounting exercise, however, if the land coefficients were higher while the fertilizer coefficients were lower and the general education coefficients were more firm.

Accounting for productivity differences was attempted between the United States and five different countries: (*a*) Argentina, a less-developed country in the American-type group; (*b*) Japan, a developed and India a less-developed country in the Japanese-type group; and (*c*) Denmark, a developed and Turkey a less-developed country in the European-type group.

The sources of differences in labor productivity between the United States and these five countries are presented in table 10.9. Each column compares the percentage differences in agricultural output per worker between each country and the United States, with the linear combinations of percentage differences in input variables weighted by the specified production elasticities. The index with the output-per-worker difference set equal to 100 is shown in parentheses.

The difference in agricultural output per worker between the United States and India was 98%; between the United States and Turkey the difference was 95%; and between the United States and Argentina the difference was 68%. The difference was 90% in the case of Japan and 46% in the case of Denmark. The four conventional variables included

27. The adopted set of coefficients for accounting in the Hayami and Ruttan work were .40 for labor, .10 for land, .25 for livestock, .15 for fertilizer, and .10 for machinery, .40 for education, and .15 for research and extension.

In a recent study Robert E. Evenson and Yoav Kislev, *Agricultural Research and Productivity* (New Haven: Yale University Press, 1975), have used a Cobb-Douglas type production function and data for 1960 and for 1955–60–65–68 to estimate international cross section production functions. The data base utilized is similar to that used by Hayami and Ruttan in *Agricultural Development*, but they added 1968 data and a new variable based on publication in agricultural sciences from 1948 to 1960 to represent research or the stock of knowledge. A comparison of the production function coefficients obtained by Evenson-Kislev and Hayami-Ruttan with the estimates obtained in this study is presented in table 10.11.

Thus the estimated coefficients of the variables were not always stable nor statistically significant in different specifications of the production function in their studies, and differed in many cases from those estimated by Hayami and Ruttan and from those in the present study. The results of these several research efforts indicate a need for further studies of the functional form and specification of the production function and of the methods used in accounting for productivity differences among countries.

Table 10.9   Accounting for Differences in Labor Productivity in Agriculture between the United States and Selected Countries, 1970

Country	American-type group — Less-developed Argentina	Japanese-type group — Developed Japan	Japanese-type group — Less-developed India	European-type group — Developed Denmark	European-type group — Less-developed Turkey
Difference in output per male worker, percent	68.2(100)[a]	90.4(100)	98.5(100)	46.1(100)	94.8(100)
Land	0.3(0)	2.0(2)	2.0(2)	1.8(4)	1.9(2)
Livestock	1.6(2)	24.2(27)	23.8(24)	11.3(25)	22.8(24)
Fertilizer	24.7(36)	22.8(25)	24.9(25)	10.1(22)	24.6(26)
Machinery	11.9(17)	11.6(13)	13.0(13)	5.6(12)	12.9(14)
Percent of difference explained by the four variables	38.5(56)	60.6(67)	63.7(65)	28.8(62)	62.2(66)
General education	6.8(10)	2.8(3)	16.8(17)	3.0(7)	13.5(14)
Technical education	13.6(20)	7.9(9)	14.8(15)	11.3(25)	14.7(16)
Percent of difference explained by human capital	20.4(30)	10.7(12)	31.6(32)	14.3(31)	28.2(30)
Percent of difference explained: total	58.9(86)	71.3(79)	95.3(97)	43.1(93)	90.4(95)

[a]Numbers inside parentheses are percentages with output per worker set equal to 100.
Accounting formula:

$$\frac{y_o - y_a}{y_a} = .02\frac{a_o - a_a}{a_a} + .25\frac{s_o - s_a}{s_a} + .25\frac{f_o - f_a}{f_a} + .13\frac{m_o - m_a}{m_a} + .25\frac{E_o - E_a}{E_a} + .15\frac{U_o - U_a}{U_a},$$

where y, a, s, f, and m are respectively output, land, livestock, fertilizer, and machinery per male worker; E and U are respectively the general education (school enrollment ratio) and the technical education variable; lower-case letter o denotes other country and a denotes United States.

in the production function accounted for 56–67% of the differences in agricultural output per worker between the United States and these countries.

Fertilizer and machinery were important sources of productivity differences between the United States and all the other countries. Livestock was also important except for Argentina, where livestock intensity per worker is similar to the United States. Land was not a significant source of difference in labor productivity between the United States and other countries in the present study. The coefficient of land in the estimated production function that was used as the accounting weight was very low (table 10.8).

The nonconventional human capital variables accounted for 30–32% of the difference in output per worker between the United States and Argentina, India, Denmark, and Turkey but only 12% of the difference between the United States and Japan. Technical education alone accounted for 15–25% of the difference between the United States and Argentina, India, Denmark, and Turkey, and 9% of the difference between the United States and Japan. Thus, even if the general education variable were to be dropped, because of its weak coefficient in the 1970 estimates, human capital would remain an important factor in accounting for intercountry productivity differences.

The case of Argentina is particularly interesting because land and labor endowments are essentially similar to the United States. The differences in output per worker due to technology embodied in fertilizer and machinery, together with the lower level of investment in technical and general education, account for most of the differences in output per worker between the United States and Argentina. The case of Japan is interesting because traditional resource endowments and embodied technology account for such a large share of the difference and human capital investment for such a small share. The case of Denmark is of interest because such a small share of the difference is explained by the variables captured by the cross-country metaproduction functions. Differences in human capital investment are highly important in all countries except Japan (table 10.9).

The sources of differences in agricultural output per hectare of agricultural land between Japan and the other countries are also presented in table 10.10. The difference in the output/land ratio between Japan and each country was 97% for Argentina, 87–92% for India, the United States, and Turkey, and 51% for Denmark. The percentage of the productivity differences accounted for by the four conventional variables ranged from 45% for India to 97% for the United States.

Technical inputs accounted for 35% of the differences in land productivity between Japan and India. Since the labor/land ratio in India does not differ very much from Japan, it accounted for only 7% of the

Table 10.10   Accounting for Differences in Land Productivity in Agriculture between Japan and Selected Countries, 1970

Country	Japanese-type group	American-type group		European-type group	
	Less-developed India	Developed U.S.	Less-developed Argentina	Developed Denmark	Less-developed Turkey
Difference in output per hectare, percent	87.2(100)[a]	90.5(100)	96.5(100)	50.8(100)	91.9(100)
Labor	5.9(7)	34.7(38)	34.6(36)	31.9(63)	29.8(32)
Livestock	−3.6(−4)	18.4(20)	18.2(19)	−9.2(−18)	15.5(17)
Fertilizer	24.1(28)	22.4(25)	25.0(26)	9.9(19)	24.4(27)
Machinery	13.0(15)	11.9(13)	12.9(13)	6.9(14)	12.8(14)
Percent of difference explained by the four variables	39.4(45)	87.4(97)	90.7(94)	39.5(78)	82.5(90)
General education	15.7(18)	−3.1(−3)	4.5(5)	0.3(1)	12.1(13)
Technical education	14.6(17)	−16.5(−18)	12.1(13)	7.3(14)	14.4(16)
Percent of difference explained by human capital	30.3(35)	−19.6(−22)	16.6(17)	7.6(15)	26.5(29)
Percent of difference explained: total	69.7(80)	67.8(75)	107.3(111)	47.1(93)	109.0(119)

NOTE: The accounting formula is the same as table 10.9, except that the variables are normalized on a per-hectare rather than a per-worker basis.

[a]Numbers inside parentheses are percentages with output per worker set equal to 100.

productivity difference. This was almost balanced by the negative contribution of the livestock/land ratio. In comparisons between Japan
and the United States, 25 and 13% of the productivity differences were
accounted for by fertilizer and by tractor use per hectare, respectively.
In addition, 27 and 20% of the productivity gap was accounted for by
labor and livestock. The sources of the differences in land productivity
between Japan, Argentina, and Turkey are very similar to the differences between Japan and the United States. Between 32 and 38% of
the difference was accounted for by labor, 17–20% by livestock, 25–
27% by fertilizer, and 13–14% by machinery. More than half the difference in land productivity between Denmark and Japan was accounted
for by differences in labor intensity. One-third of the productivity difference was accounted for by fertilizer and machinery. Since the livestock/
land ratio in Denmark is much larger than Japan, livestock carries a
negative weight of 18%. The four conventional variables account for
78% of the land productivity difference between these two countries.
Human capital is also an important source of differences in land productivity among countries as well as in labor productivity. It is particularly important in accounting for the differences between Japan and
India and Turkey.

The differences between the weights used in accounting for cross-
section productivity differences among countries in this study and those
used in the earlier Hayami-Ruttan study have been mentioned several
times. These differences appear to be due in part to nonneutral shifts in
the coefficients for fertilizer relative to land and of machinery relative
to labor. It is also possible that the indexes of mechanical technology,
biological technology, and human capital are biased or that the functional form used in the estimation is not entirely satisfactory. An attempt
was made to test the sensitivity of the particular results shown in tables
10.9 and 10.10 by using the 1960 Hayami-Ruttan weights in accounting
for the 1970 productivity differences among the six countries. In general
the percent of the total variation in land and labor productivity explained by using the 1960 weights did not differ greatly from the variation explained using 1970 weights. There was, however, a tendency for
less of the total differences in labor and in land productivity to be
explained by the four conventional variables and more by the human
capital variables when the 1960 weights were used than when the 1970
weights were used.

The analysis of the shifts in productivity coefficients and the sources
of productivity differences presented above suggests that technical inputs
such as fertilizer and machinery have become even more important
relative to raw land and labor in accounting for productivity differences
in 1970 than in 1960. However, it should be kept in mind, in interpreting these results, that both the index of biological technology (fertilizer/

hectare) and the index of mechanical technology (horsepower/worker) are clearly incomplete and may often be biased measures. In the case of biological technology, for example, it would be desirable, as implied earlier, to include other measures of biological technology such as the level of irrigation and the adoption of new crop varieties (see fig. 10.12). The effect of omission of other components of biological technology may be an upward bias in the coefficient of biological technology in 1970 relative to 1960 as a result of differences in the availability of complementary biological technology between the low-fertilizer-input and the high-fertilizer-input countries. Similarly the coefficient for mechanical technology may be biased upward in 1970 relative to 1960 due to differences in the availability of complementary components of mechanical technology.

10.6   Perspective

It is useful at this point to restate the problem that must be solved in any test of induced innovation. In figure 10.1 assume that the labor/land factor ratio in Japan can be represented by a line from the origin through P and that the labor/land factor ratio in the United States can be represented by a line from the origin through Q. Assume also that the slope of the line BB represents the factor price ratio in Japan, where land is expensive relative to labor, while the slope of CC represents the factor price ratio in the United States, where labor is expensive relative to land. If the substitution possibilities of the available agricultural technology can be represented by an isoquant map with little curvature such as $I^*_0 I^*_0$, the differences in factor ratios between Japan and the United States could be explained by simple substitution due to factor price change along a common production function. If, however, the possibilities of substitution between labor and land are represented by I_0 in Japan and I_1 in the United States, the points P and Q would not represent alternative factor combinations along production functions with equal factor intensity characteristics.

The results of both the time series and the cross section analysis are consistent with the induced innovation hypothesis. Yet they do not represent an adequate test of the hypothesis.[28] The analysis presented does not allow us to determine whether the changes in factor use describe (a) the effect of agricultural producers responding to the economic value of land relative to fertilizer or of labor relative to machinery along

28. For a rigorous test of the induced innovation hypothesis in U.S. agriculture see Hans P. Binswanger, "The Measurement of Technical Change Biases." Binswanger concludes that in the U.S. long-term decline in fertilizer prices did induce a fertilizer-using bias in technical change. In the case of mechanical technology both price-induced and autonomous effects were important.

an unchanging neoclassical macro production function, or (*b*) whether the production function available to farmers has itself shifted to the left over time and among countries as a result of the response of the technical efforts of scientists, engineers, and inventors to changing factor price relationships. The magnitude of the shifts in relative factor prices and factor use presented in the time series analysis and of the differences in factor use among countries does, however, create a presumption that the induced innovation process was involved.

The results of this analysis are consistent with the conclusion that Hayami and Ruttan drew in their earlier work—that failure to take full advantage of the potential growth from human capital and technical inputs represents a significant constraint on agricultural development. The results of the 1970 cross section analysis of the contribution of general education to agricultural productivity are somewhat less clear-cut than the results of the 1960 cross section analysis. Nevertheless, the body of evidence examined in this and in the earlier study tends to reinforce the conclusion that variations in technical inputs and human capital are typically more important than limitations in resource endowments in accounting for differences in output per worker. In the developed countries human capital and technical inputs have become the dominant sources of output growth. Differences in the natural resource base have accounted for an increasingly less significant share of the widening productivity gap among nations. Productivity differences in agriculture are increasingly a function of investments in the education of rural people and in scientific and industrial capacity rather than natural resource endowments. The decline in the coefficients for labor and land relative to the other coefficients in the relatively short period since the Hayami-Ruttan study provides additional support, over and above the relationships reported in this paper, of the declining importance of "raw" land and labor in accounting for productivity differences.

The embodiment of advances in science and technology in the inputs available to farmers clearly represents a necessary condition for releasing the constraints on agriculture imposed by inelastic supplies of traditional factors. Yet for a country in the early stages of economic development technical innovations are among the more difficult products to produce. Indeed, it seems useful to raise the question of whether, under modern conditions, the forces associated with the international transfer of agricultural technology are so dominant as to vitiate the process of induced technical change.

It might be argued, for example, that the dominance of the developed countries in science and technology raises the cost, or even precludes the possibility, of the invention of location-specific biological and mechanical technologies adapted to the resource endowments of a particular country or region. This argument has been made primarily with

Table 10.11 Various Estimates of Agricultural Production Function Coefficients from Intercountry Data

	Evenson-Kislev		Hayami-Ruttan			Present study
	1960	1955–60–65–68	1960	1965	1955–60–65	1970
Labor	.274–.438**	–.012–.259*	.335–.474**	(.390)	(.405)	.209–.398**
Land	–.002–.038	–.010–.190*	.056–.097	.043	.066**	.005–.024
Livestock	.285–.311**	.296–.450**	.191–.263**	.273**	.286**	.223–.244**
Fertilizer	.018–.173**	.048–.222**	.090–.161*	.142**	.137**	.226–.323**
Machinery	.140–.197**	.018–.138**	.040–.192*	.152**	.106**	.113–.149**
General education	.130–.168	.075–.128*	.290–.324	.356	.243**	–.034–.264
Technical education	.168–.175*	–.009–.087*	.139–.195**	.099**	.122**	.135–.170**
Research	.088–.091***	.046–.148**				

**Statistically significant at $P = 0.05$ (one-tail test).
*Statistically significant in some cases.
NOTE: Parentheses denote an implicit coefficient.

reference to the diffusion of mechanical technology from the developed to the developing countries. It has been argued that the pattern of organization of agricultural production adopted by the more developed countries—dominated by the large-scale mechanized systems of production employed in both the socialist and nonsocialist economies—precludes an effective role for an agricultural system based on small-scale commercial or semicommercial farm production units.

The potential for the development of technologies that are specific to national or regional factor endowments is, however, enhanced by the fact that in agriculture technology is highly location-specific, and even mechanical technology is relatively location-specific. It is apparently the location-specific character of agricultural technology that is responsible for the relationships between changes in factor use and productivity between 1960 and 1970 (figs. 10.7 and 10.9).

The transfer of agricultural technology occurs more through a process of adaptation to local environmental conditions than as a result of the direct transfer of materials and designs. The ability to borrow technology is dependent on the institutionalization of indigenous research and development capacity in agricultural science and technology. Thus, in order for a country or a region to acquire the capacity to borrow or transfer technology, it also needs to develop the capacity to adapt and invent technologies which are specific to its own factor endowments.[29]

In our judgment, failure to effectively institutionalize public sector agricultural research can result in serious distortion of the pattern of technical change and resource use. The homogeneity of most agricultural products and the relatively small size of the farm firm make it impossible for the individual agricultural firm to either bear the research costs or capture a significant share of the gains from scientific and technical innovation. Innovation in mechanical technology, however, has been much more responsive than biological technology to the inducement mechanism as it functions in the private sector. It has typically been more difficult for the innovating firm to capture more than a small share of the increased income stream resulting from innovation in biological than in mechanical technology.

Failure to balance the effectiveness of the private sector in responding to inducements to advances in mechanical technology (and in those areas of biological and chemical technology in which advances in knowledge can be embodied in proprietary products) with institutional innovations capable of an equally effective response to inducements to advances in biological technology leads to a bias in the productivity

29. See Robert E. Evenson and Hans P. Binswanger, "Technology Transfer and Research Resource Allocation," in Hans P. Binswanger and Vernon W. Ruttan, eds., *Induced Innovation: Technology Institutions and Development* (Baltimore: The Johns Hopkins University Press, 1978).

path that is inconsistent with factor endowments—particularly with the factor endowments of the more labor-intensive LDCs. The labor force explosion anticipated in rural areas of the LDCs in the 1970s implies that failure to design agricultural technologies consistent with higher population densities in rural areas will be extremely costly. It is possible to provide at least a partial response to this concern.

The test of the next decade for many of the developing countries will be whether they are prepared to seize the relatively inexpensive sources of growth opened up by investment in human capital and in the new potentials that can be made available through advances in biological technology.

Appendix A

Output, Factor Productivity, and Factor Price Data for Japan, Germany, Denmark, France, United Kingdom, and the United States, 1880–1970

Appendix A first appeared in Hans P. Binswanger and Vernon W. Ruttan, eds., *Induced Innovation: Technology Institutions and Development* (Baltimore: The Johns Hopkins University Press, 1978). © 1978 by The National Bureau of Economic Research.

Table 10.A.1   **Japan: Output, Factor Productivity, and Factor Price Data, 1880–1970**

Year	Output (Y) Wheat Units (000) (1)	Output (Y) Index (1880 = 100) (2)	Male Labor (L) Number (000) (3)	Male Labor (L) Index (1880 = 100) (4)	Agricultural Land (A) Hectares (000) (5)	Agricultural Land (A) Index (1880 = 100) (6)	Wheat Units per Man Year (Y/L) (7)
1880	15,706	100.0	8,332	100.0	5,493	100.0	1.89
1890	18,795	119.7	8,354	100.3	5,712	104.0	2.25
1900	21,755	138.5	8,475	101.6	6,024	109.7	2.57
1910	26,755	170.3	8,527	102.3	6,466	117.7	3.14
1920	32,249	205.3	7,626	91.5	6,940	126.3	4.23
1925	32,674	208.0	7,386	88.6	6,875	125.2	4.42
1930	35,079	223.3	7,631	91.6	6,931	126.2	4.60
1940	37,060	236.0	6,263	75.2	7,088	129.0	5.92
1950	34,608	220.3	7,692	92.4	6,792	123.6	4.50
1960	52,436	333.9	6,232	74.8	7,048	128.3	8.41
1970	67,305	428.5	4,267	51.2	6,713	122.4	15.77

NOTE: Data are five-year averages centered on year shown.
SOURCE: Yujiro Hayami, *A Century of Agricultural Growth in Japan*, (Minneapolis and Tokyo: University of Minnesota Press and University of Tokyo Press, 1975).
Output: table A-1 (col. 8), spliced with 1958–62 value of output in wheat units from Yujiro Hayami and Vernon Ruttan, *Agricultural Development, An International Perspective*, table A-5.
Land: table A-4, (col. 3), multiplied by 1.14, the ratio of agricultural land to arable land

Table 10.A.2   **Germany: Output, Factor Productivity, and Factor Price Data, 1880–1970**

Year	Output (Y)[a] Wheat units (000) (1)	Output (Y)[a] Index (1880 = 100) (2)	Male Labor (L) Number (000) (3)	Male Labor (L) Index (1880 = 100) (4)	Agricultural Land (A) Hectares (000) (5)	Agricultural Land (A) Index (1880 = 100) (6)	Wheat Units per Man year (Y/L) (7)
1880	45,137	100.0	5,684	100.0	36,040[b]	100.0	7.94
1890	52,061	115.3	5,520	97.1	35,320	98.0	9.43
1900	65,927	146.1	5,452	95.9	35,094	97.4	12.09
1910	75,367	167.0	5,746	101.1	34,878	96.8	13.12
1920	—	—	—	—	—	—	—
1925[c]	60,458 (72,103)	— (159.7)	4,808	84.6	29,249	81.2	12.57
1930	72,688 (86,644)	— (192.0)	4,547	80.0	29,375	81.5	15.99
1938[d]	83,556 (99,599)	— (220.7)	3,285	57.8	28,537	79.2	25.44
1950[e]	39,248 (97,947)	— (217.0)	2,258	39.7	14,033	38.9	17.38
1960	57,023 (142,550)	— (315.8)	1,613	28.4	14,239	39.5	35.35
1968[f]	72,073 (180,183)	— (399.2)	1,214	21.4	13,871	38.5	59.37
1970[g]	74,073 (185,964)	— (412.0)	1,142	20.1	13,578	37.7	71.40[h]

NOTE: Data are five-year averages, centered on data shown except as follows: (a) 1880–82; (b) 1925 only; (c) 1938 only; (d) 1950 only. Wheat units and indexes shown in parentheses have been adjusted for changes in land area in order to provide a long-term output series for an "undivided Germany."

Man Years per Wheat Unit (L/Y) (8)	Wheat Units per Hectare (Y/A) (9)	Hectares to Produce One Wheat Unit (A/Y) (10)	Land (Hectares) per Worker (A/L)a (11)	Wage Rate (M/day) (P_L) (12)	Land Price (M/ha) (P_A) (13)	Days Labor to Buy One Hectare (P_A/P_L) (14)
.530	2.86	.350	.659	(.183)	(343)	(1,874)
.444	3.29	.304	.684	·.183	343	1,874
.390	3.61	.277	.711	.371	968	2,609
.319	4.14	.242	.758	.469	1,613	3,439
.236	4.65	.215	.910	1.472	3,882	2,637
.226	4.75	.210	.931	1.424	3,822	2,683
.218	5.06	.198	.908	1.098	3,206	2,920
.169	5.23	.191	1.132	—	—	—
.222	5.10	.196	.883	—	—	—
.119	7.44	.134	1.131	484.	1,429,528	2,954
.0634	10.03	.0997	1.573	1,794.	2,358,431	1,315

in the 1960 Census of Agriculture.
Labor: table A-3, (col. 1).
Price of labor: table A-8, (col. 2); 1890 value used for 1880.
Price of land: table A-2, (col. 4); 1890 value used for 1880.
aThis diverges from revisions sent us by Hayami in May 1974, because Hayami did not use his latest data, as we did here, but instead calculated from Hayami and Ruttan, *Agricultural Development*, table S-2.

Man Years per Wheat Unit (L/Y) (8)	Wheat Units per Hectare (Y/A) (9)	Hectares to Produce One Wheat Unit (A/Y) (10)	Land (Hectares) per Worker (A/L) (11)	Wage Rate (M/day) (P_L) (12)	Land Price (M/ha) (P_A) (13)	Days Labor to Buy One Hectare (P_A/P_L) (14)
.1259	1.25	.798	6.34	1.36	1,315	967
.1060	1.47	.678	6.40	1.38	1,315	953
.0827	1.88	.532	6.44	1.68	1,368	814
.0762	2.16	.463	6.07	2.07	1,869	903
—	—	—	—	—	—	—
.0795	2.07	.484	6.08	3.07	2,730	889
.0626	2.47	.404	6.46	3.98	2,345	589
.0393	2.93	.342	8.69	3.50	2,188	625
.0575	2.80	.358	6.22	7.56	4,359	577
.0283	4.01	.250	8.83	18.00	6,812	378
.0168	5.20	.193	11.43	34.56	10,348	299
.0140	5.40	.185	12.20	42.12	11,448	244

SOURCE: 1880–1968 data from Adolf Weber, "Productivity Growth in German Agriculture, 1950 to 1970," University of Minnesota Department of Agricultural and Applied Economics, Staff Paper P73-1, August 1973; 1970: data provided by Adolf Weber, private communication, March 1974, from the same sources as for 1880–1968.

Table 10.A.3   Denmark: Output, Factor Productivity, and Factor Price Data, 1880–1970

Year	Output (Y) Wheat Units (000) (1)	Output (Y) Index (1880 = 100) (2)	Male Labor (L) Number (000) (3)	Male Labor (L) Index (1880 = 100) (4)	Agricultural Land (A) Hectares (000) (5)	Agricultural Land (A) Index (1880 = 100) (6)	Wheat Units per Man Year (Y/L) (7)
1880	3,408	100.0	321	100.0	2,859	100.0	10.62
1890	3,882	113.9	326	101.6	2,913	101.9	11.91
1900	4,428	129.9	312	97.2	2,912	101.9	14.19
1910	5,837	171.3	346	107.8	2,883	100.8	16.87
1920	6,341	186.1	395	123.1	3,172	110.9	16.05
1925	6,830	200.4	404	125.9	3,217	112.5	16.91
1930	9,518	279.3	395	123.1	3,229	112.9	24.10
1940	9,015	264.5	391	121.8	3,218	112.6	23.06
1950	10,956	321.5	342	106.5	3,141	109.9	32.04
1960	14,378	421.9	303	94.4	3,094	108.2	47.45
1970	15,665	459.7	166	51.7	2,975a	104.1	94.37

NOTE: Data are five-year averages centered on the year shown except for (a) 1970 only.
SOURCE: 1880–1960 data from William W. Wade, "Institutional Determinants of Technical Change and Agricultural Productivity Growth" (tables D-1 and D-4), Ph.D. diss.,

Table 10.A.4   France: Output, Factor Productivity, and Factor Price Data, 1800–1970

Year	Output (Y) Wheat Units (000) (1)	Output (Y) Index (1880 = 100) (2)	Male Labor (L) Number (000) (3)	Male Labor (L) Index (1880 = 100) (4)	Agricultural Land (A) Hectares (000) (5)	Agricultural Land (A) Index (1880 = 100) (6)	Wheat Units per Man Year (Y/L) (7)
1880	36,589	100.0	4,970	100.0	34,594	100.0	7.36
1890	38,139	104.2	4,580	92.2	34,429	99.5	8.33
1900	40,636	111.1	5,020	101.0	35,200	101.8	8.09
1910	45,457	124.2	4,910	98.8	36,799	106.4	9.26
1920	46,146	126.1	4,540	91.3	36,219	104.7	10.16
1925	49,848	136.2	4,290	86.3	36,294	104.9	11.62
1930	53,464	146.1	4,040	81.3	35,566	102.8	13.23
1940	48,657	133.0	3,860	77.7	33,488	96.8	12.61
1950	51,311	140.2	3,300	66.4	33,562	97.0	15.55
1960	86,093	235.3	2,580	51.9	34,681	100.3	33.37
1970	122,346	334.4	2,041b	41.1	33,035b	95.5	59.94

NOTE: Data are five-year averages centered on the year shown except for (a) 1968 only and (b) 1970 only.
SOURCE: 1880–1960 data from William W. Wade, "Institutional Determinants of Technical Change and Agricultural Productivity Growth" (tables F-1, F-4) Ph.D. diss., Uni-

Man Years per Wheat Unit (L/Y) (8)	Wheat Units per Hectare (Y/A) (9)	Hectares to Produce One Wheat Unit (A/Y) (10)	Land (Hectares) per Worker (A/L) (11)	Wage Rate (M/day) (P_L) (12)	Land Price (M/ha) (P_A) (13)	Days Labor to Buy One Hectare (P_A/P_L) (14)
.0942	1.192	.839	8.91	1.6	611	382
.0840	1.333	.750	8.94	1.7	536	315
.0705	1.521	.658	9.33	2.1	536	255
.0592	2.025	.494	8.33	2.8	701	250
.0623	1.999	.500	8.03	5.9	1,413	240
.0592	2.123	.471	7.96	6.2	—	—
.0415	2.948	.339	8.18	5.2	1,186	228
.0434	2.801	.357	8.23	7.8	1,233	158
.0312	3.488	.287	9.18	21.5	2,459	114
.0211	4.647	.215	10.21	35.6	5,908	166
.0106	5.266	.190	17.92	71.9	12,743	177

University of Minnesota, 1973. 1970 data provided by William Wade, private communication, from the same sources as 1880–1960.

Man Years per Wheat Unit (L/Y) (8)	Wheat Units per Hectare (Y/A) (9)	Hectares to Produce One Wheat Unit (A/Y) (10)	Land (Hectares) per Worker (A/L) (11)	Wage Rate (M/day)[a] (P_L) (12)	Land Price (M/ha) (P_A) (13)	Days Labor to Buy One Hectare (P_A/P_L) (14)
.1358	1.06	.946	6.96	2.28	1,778	780
.1201	1.11	.903	7.52	2.43	1,674	689
.1235	1.15	.866	7.01	2.69	1,584	589
.1080	1.24	.810	7.49	3.00	1,583	528
.0984	1.27	.785	7.98	11.5	2,831	246
.0861	1.37	.723	8.45	14.9	4,055	272
.0756	1.50	.665	8.80	20.6	5,405	262
.0793	1.45	.688	8.68	33.1	5,200	157
.0643	1.53	.654	10.17	479.4	125,000	261
.0300	2.48	.403	13.44	1,508.0	250,000	166
.0167	3.70	.270	16.19	37.5†	7,960†	212

versity of Minnesota, 1973. 1970 data provided by William W. Wade, private communication, from the same sources as 1880–1960.
†In new francs. One new franc is equal to 100 old francs.

Table 10.A.5   **United Kingdom: Output, Factor Productivity, and Factor Price Data, 1880–1970**

Year	Output (Y) Wheat Units (000) (1)	Output (Y) Index (1880 = 100) (2)	Male Labor (L) Number (000) (3)	Male Labor (L) Index (1880 = 100) (4)	Agricultural Land (A) Hectares (000) (5)	Agricultural Land (A) Index (1880 = 100) (6)	Wheat Units per Man Year (Y/L) (7)
1880	20,847	100.0	1,288	100.0	18,949	100.0	16.19
1890	21,696	104.1	1,235	95.9	19,331	102.0	17.57
1900	21,040	100.9	1,178	91.5	19,602	103.4	17.86
1910	21,696	104.1	1,221	94.8	19,484	102.8	17.77
1920	21,696	104.1	1,154	89.4	19,121	100.9	18.80
1925	21,889	105.0	1,199	93.1	19,798	104.5	18.26
1930	23,163	111.1	1,151	89.4	19,611	103.5	20.12
1940	27,332	131.1	1,079	83.8	19,453	102.7	25.33
1950	31,502	151.1	985	76.5	19,518	103.0	31.98
1960	38,605	185.2	853	66.2	19,894	105.0	45.26
1970	49,203	236.0	562	43.6	18,831a	99.4	87.55

NOTE: Data are five-year averages centered on the year shown, except for (a) 1970 only.
SOURCES: 1880–1960 data from William W. Wade, "Institutional Determinants of Technical Change and Agricultural Productivity Growth" (tables G-1 and G-4), Ph.D. diss.,

Table 10.A.6   **United States: Output, Factor Productivity, and Factor Prices Data, 1880–1970**

Year	Output (Y) Wheat Units (000) (1)	Output (Y) Index (1880 = 100) (2)	Male Labor (L) Number (000) (3)	Male Labor (L) Index (1880 = 100) (4)	Agricultural Land (A) Hectares (000) (5)	Agricultural Land (A) Index (1880 = 100) (6)	Wheat Units per Man Year (Y/L) (7)
1880	103,711	100.0	7,959	100.0	202,000	100.0	13.0
1890	123,416	119.0	9,142	115.0	235,000	116.4	13.5
1900	160,753	155.0	9,880	124.1	318,000	157.4	16.3
1910	170,087	164.0	10,359	130.2	333,000	164.9	16.4
1920	186,681	180.0	10,221	128.4	363,000	179.7	18.3
1925	199,126	192.0	9,818	123.4	350,000	173.3	20.3
1930	211,571	204.0	9,414	118.3	381,000	188.6	22.5
1940	240,611	232.0	8,487	106.6	411,000	203.5	28.4
1950	295,578	285.0	6,352	79.8	451,000	223.3	46.5
1960	352,619	340.0	3,973	49.9	435,000	215.3	88.8a
1970	417,957	403.0	2,655	33.4	426,000	210.9	157.4

NOTE: Data are five-year averages centered on year shown.
SOURCE: 1880–1960 data from Yujiro Hayami and Vernon W. Ruttan, *Agricultural Development, An International Perspective* (Baltimore: The Johns Hopkins University Press, 1971), table C-2 and table A-2. 1970 value: USDA; Agricultural Statistics, 1973, Index of average value per acre, March value, table 619; Changes in Production and Efficiency,

Man Years per Wheat Unit (L/Y) (8)	Wheat Units per Hectare (Y/A) (9)	Hectares to Produce One Wheat Unit (A/Y) (10)	Land (Hectares) per Worker (A/L) (11)	Wage Rate (M/day) (P_L) (12)	Land Price (M/ha) (P_A) (13)	Days Labor to Buy One Hectare (P_A/P_L) (14)
.0618	1.10	.909	14.71	2.6	2,588	995
.0569	1.12	.891	15.65	2.5	2,174	870
.0559	1.07	.932	16.64	2.6	2,065	794
.0563	1.11	.898	15.96	2.8	2,065	738
.0532	1.13	.881	16.57	7.9	1,720	218
.0548	1.11	.904	16.51	5.5	1,512	275
.0497	1.18	.847	17.04	5.8	1,096	189
.0395	1.41	.712	18.03	7.2	1,730	240
.0313	1.61	.620	19.82	17.1	4,051	237
.0221	1.94	.515	23.32	28.8	6,076	211
.0114	2.61	.383	33.51	55.5a	11,260	203

University of Minnesota, 1973. 1970 data provided by William Wade, private communication from the same sources as 1880–1960.

Man Years per Wheat Unit (L/Y) (8)	Wheat Units per Hectare (Y/A) (9)	Hectares to Produce One Wheat Unit (A/Y) (10)	Land (Hectares) per Worker (A/L) (11)	Wage Rate (M/day) (P_L) (12)	Land Price (M/ha) (P_A) (13)	Days Labor to Buy One Hectare (P_A/P_L) (14)
.07670	.513	1.95	25.4	.90	163	181
.07410	.526	1.90	25.7	.95	132	139
.06150	.506	1.98	32.2	1.00	129	129
.06090	.511	1.96	32.1	1.35	213	158
.05480	.514	1.94	35.5	3.30	352	107
.04930	.569	1.76	35.6	2.35	269	114
.04450	.555	1.80	40.5	2.15	247	115
.03530	.585	1.71	48.4	1.60	180	113
.02150	.655	1.53	71.0	4.50	389	86
.01130	.811	1.23	109.5	6.60	711	108
.00635	.981	1.02	160.5	11.58	1,247	108

1973, table 21, Index of total hours used for farmwork; Changes in Production and Efficiency, 1973, table 25, Index of farm real estate; Changes in Production and Efficiency, 1973, table 2, Index of output.

aDiffers from Hayami and Ruttan, table 8-1, col. (6). 1960 value in 8-1 is incorrect. 1960 wheat units = 352619. Table A-2; 1960. Workers = 3973. Table C-2, col. 4–9.

Appendix B

Intercountry Cross Section Data for 1970

In this appendix we explain the data used for the intercountry comparison of agricultural productivities.[1] Data were collected or estimated for forty-one countries for 1970.[2] However, to reduce the effects of yearly fluctuation, agricultural output and fertilizer consumption were measured as 1968–72 averages and 1969–71 averages, respectively.

Agricultural Output (A1)

The output variable estimated in this study[3] is specified as gross agricultural output, net of agricultural intermediate products such as seed and feed (including imported feed). The series of 1968–72 average outputs were extrapolated from the 1962–66 data, which were estimated in Yujiro Hayami et al. (1971) using the Food and Agricultural Organization's index numbers of total agricultural production (FAO, 1972) for the respective countries.[4]

1. The intercountry cross section data for 1970 used in this study were estimated partly on the basis of the intercountry data for 1962–66 compiled in Yujiro Hayami in association with Barbara B. Miller, William W. Wade, and Sachiko Yamashita, *An International Comparison of Agricultural Production and Productivities.* University of Minnesota Agricultural Experiment Station Technical Bulletin 277, March 1971. The data and analysis are recompiled in Yujiro Hayami and Vernon W. Ruttan, *Agricultural Development: An International Perspective* (Baltimore: The Johns Hopkins University Press, 1971). To maintain comparability, the concepts and methods of estimating inputs and output variables for 1970 are the same, although input categories of agricultural perennial plants stock and an aggregate of various fixed capital stock, which were not counted in the above studies at all, are estimated also in addition to them in this study. More detailed explanations on the concepts and methods are available in the above sources.

2. The number of the countries of which data were compiled in the Hayami-Ruttan studies was forty-three. However, due to the lack of data for 1970, Libya, Syria, and the United Arab Republic were excluded in this study. Instead, the old Pakistan was divided into the independent Bangladesh and the new Pakistan, resulting in the number of the countries analyzed in this study being forty-one.

3. Recently we estimated a series of aggregated agricultural production for Asian countries by using wheat-based price relatives for the 1961–65 period which were originally utilized in the FAO index numbers of agricultural production in Saburo Yamada, *A Comparative Analysis of Asian Agricultural Productivities and Growth Patterns* (Tokyo: Asian Productivity Organization, 1975). We could use the same weighting method in estimating agricultural production for this study. However, it would involve a major effort and would involve more time than the schedule for the present conference would permit.

4. The ratio of the 1968–72 average to the 1962–66 average of the index numbers (1961–65 = 100) was multiplied by the 1962–66 average of agricultural output in terms of wheat units estimated in Hayami et al., *International Comparison,* for each country. For Taiwan, the 1969–71 average was used instead of the 1968–72 average because of the lack of data.

The 1962–66 data were extended from the 1957–62 output data by using the old series of the FAO production index as well.

The series of 1957–62 average outputs were estimated as follows: (a) deduct the seed, feed (including imported feed), eggs for hatching, and milk for calf rearing from the quantities of individual agricultural commodities produced, (b) aggregate the quantities by the three sets of wheat relative prices derived from the farm-gate prices (or the imported prices of commodities not produced domestically) for the U.S.A., Japan and India, to produce three aggregate output series, and (c) combine these three series into a single composite series by taking their geometrical means.[5]

Data on the quantities produced were taken from *Production Yearbook* of FAO and data for the deduction of seed and feed from FAO's *Food Balance Sheets.*

However, there were no estimates of 1965 (1962–66 average) agricultural output for Mauritius, Paraguay, and Surinam in Hayami et al. (1971). For these countries, 1968–72 output was extrapolated from 1960 (1957–62 average) data in the book using the growth rate between 1962–66 and 1968–72 in the FAO indices of the respective countries. Since data for Pakistan in the book were those before the independence of Bangladesh, 1965 output of the old Pakistan was divided into the present two countries by using the relative ratios of agricultural production between the two for 1961–65 estimated in Yamada (1975).

Number of Male Workers in Agriculture (A2)

The number of male workers in agriculture (farm workers) was estimated from the data of the economically active male population in agricultural occupations (agriculture, forestry, hunting, and fishing), published in the *Yearbook of Labor Statistics*, various issues, by the International Labor Organization (ILO).

Due to the lack of adequate conversion factors, the number of male workers in agriculture for 1970 was transformed from the population in agricultural occupations for 1970 using 1960 conversion factors, i.e., the ratios of agricultural output to the output of agriculture, forestry, and fishing combined, assuming that labor productivities are equal between these agricultural occupations. The conversion factors were derived from Hayami and Ruttan (1971), table A–2.

For countries where 1970 data for the economically active male population in the agricultural occupations are not available in the ILO yearbooks, several methods were used for estimating 1970 data: (a) extrapolations or interpolations were conducted by using the growth rates between the nearby years data that are available in the ILO year-

5. Ibid., p. 5.

books of Hayami et al. (1971), for Australia, Austria, Greece, India, Ireland, New Zealand, Taiwan, and Turkey; (*b*) the ratios of male workers to the total workers in agriculture for a nearby year when the data were available in the ILO yearbooks were multiplied by the numbers of the total agricultural workers for 1970 which appeared in FAO (1972), table 5, for Bangladesh, Colombia, France, Mauritius, Netherlands, Pakistan, Paraguay, Spain, Sri Lanka, Surinam, and United Kingdom; (*c*) 1971 data in the ILO yearbook were used for 1970 for Yugoslavia.

In the case of Japan, the number of agricultural (farm) male workers was inferred from Bureau of Statistics (1971), pp. 73–74, instead of the ILO data, because the equal productivity assumption between agriculture and the other agricultural occupations is not plausible in Japan.[7]

Agricultural Land Area (A3)

The agricultural land area is the sum of the areas of arable land, land under permanent crops, and permanent meadows and pastures, available in FAO, *Production Yearbook*, various issues. Since we could not find appropriate weights for aggegation, the summation was made without weighting.

In countries where 1970 data for agricultural land area are not available, extrapolations or interpolations were made by using the growth rates between the nearby years data that are available in the FAO data. These countries are Argentina, Austria, Canada, Chile, Greece, India, Paraguay, Peru, Portugal, South Africa, Surinam, Switzerland, Taiwan, United Kingdom, United States, and Venezuela. Data for Bangladesh and Pakistan are referred from Yamada (1975), table 4.

Farm Capital Stock (A4–A7 and A9–A11)

Farm capital stock specified in this study is the aggregate value of livestock, agricultural machinery, and agricultural perennial plants. Values of agricultural buildings and structures, including irrigation facilities, were excluded due to lack of data. The estimation of each category of capital stock and aggregation method used in the study is as follows:

Livestock (A9)

The total value of livestock aggregates the various kinds of animals in terms of livestock units for each country. Data for the numbers of livestock animals existing on farms are taken from FAO (1972). The

6. Ibid., p. 6.
7. If we apply the same method for Japan as for other countries, the number of male workers in agriculture is 3,419 thousand in 1970, which is too small compared with the data in Japan's *Labor Force Survey*.

kind of animals and the livestock units as the aggregation weights are camels 1.1; horses, mules, and buffalo, 1.0; cattle and asses, 0.8; pigs, 0.2; sheep and goats, 0.1; and poultry, 0.01. These units appear in FAO (1971), p. 716.

Machinery (A10)

Only agricultural tractors and garden tractors are counted as agricultural machinery in the study. These numbers were aggregated in terms of horsepower by assuming that the average horsepower of farm tractors and garden tractors was 30 and 5, respectively. Data for the number of tractors in 1970 were taken from FAO (1972).

Perennial Plants (A11)

For available data, different kinds of perennial plants should preferably be weighted by their respective prices for weights and added to get an aggregate value of capital stock. But due to the lack of data on tree population or area planted to various perennial plants and unit values of perennial plants, the total area of land under permanent crops was used as a crude approximate indicator for the total amount of perennial plants as capital stock. Data for 1970 are taken from FAO, *Production Yearbook*, various issues. For countries where 1970 data were not available, extrapolations or interpolations were conducted by using the growth rates for a nearby period (Austria, India, Peru, and Switzerland), or data for a nearby year (Argentina, Chile, Greece, Paraguay, Portugal, South Africa, Surinam, United States, and Venezuela). For countries where no information is available at all for land under permanent crops, perennial plants as capital stock were not estimated.

Aggregated Value of Livestock, Perennial Plants, and Machinery (A4–A7)

The weights for aggregating the volumes of livestock, perennial plants, and machinery into an aggregated value of farm fixed capital stock should preferably be their average or representative relative prices of all countries. However, the average prices of all countries were not used due to lack of data; instead the relative prices in terms of wheat units for Japan in 1961–65 were used as the aggregating weights.

The estimated average prices assumed in this analysis are as follows: 60 thousand yen per one livestock unit, 25 thousand yen per one tractor horsepower, and 680 thousand yen per one hectare of land under permanent crops. These were estimated on the basis of various issues of *Noson Bukka Chingin Chosa Hokokusho (Survey Reports on Prices and Wages in Rural Areas), Nogyo oyobi Nokano Shakai Kanjo (Social Accounts of Agriculture and Farm Households)* and *Norinsho Tokei*

Hyo (Statistical Yearbook), all of Japan's Ministry of Agriculture and Forestry.[8]

In calculating the wheat units for each category of the capital, each of these prices was divided by 1961–65 price per ton of wheat taken from the *Price Survey* mentioned above. The weights in terms of wheat units are 1.74 per livestock unit, 0.72 per tractor horsepower unit, and 19.79 per hectare of land under permanent crops, respectively.[9]

Fertilizer Consumption (A8)

The data on fertilizer input in terms of total physical weights of N, P_2O_5, and K_2O contained in commercial fertilizers consumed in 1969–71 are taken from FAO (1972).

Ratio of Nonagricultural Labor (A12)

As an indicator of industrialization, the ratios of workers in nonagricultural occupations (other than agriculture, forestry, hunting, and fishing) to the total number of the economically active population were calculated for respective countries from the data published in ILO, *Yearbook of Labor Statistics*, various issues, and FAO (1972).

General Education–School Enrollment Ratio (A13)

The school enrollment ratio is the ratio of the number enrolled in the first and second levels of education to the population of potential enrollment. It represents the increase in the level of education. In order to convert the enrollment ratio into a measure of the stock of education, the averages of the data for 1960, 1965, and 1970, and alternatively those for 1955, 1960, and 1965, were used. The data were taken from UNESCO, *Statistical Yearbook*, 1972, and Hayami and Ruttan (1971) table A–5.

Technical Education–Number of Graduates from Agricultural Colleges per 10,000 Male Farm Workers (A14)

The number of graduates from agricultural colleges per 10,000 male farm workers was considered as a proxy variable for the level of technical education in agriculture. The data source is UNESCO, *Statistical Yearbook*, 1972 and 1973.

8. More detailed explanations on the estimating procedures are available in Yamada, *Comparative Analysis*.

9. It should be mentioned that the capital stock estimates are not nearly precise, particularly those of machinery items, as only the tractors were taken into account. In addition, aggregating weights were based on Japan data, and hence the estimates are Japan-biased.

Farm Wage Rate (A15)

The farm wage rate is defined as the wage received by a male farm worker per day. Hourly, weekly, and monthly wages presented in FAO, *Production Yearbook* (1973) are converted into daily wages by assuming eight work hours in a day, six work days in a week, and twenty-four work days in a month.

Tractor Price (A16)

Tractors and farm machinery prices paid by farmers are only available for Australia, Germany, Japan, and the United States in FAO, *Production Yearbook*. For other countries in this study the average import price of tractors for 1970 derived from FAO, *Trade Yearbook* (1972) were used as a proxy indicator of the tractor price.

Table 10.B.1 Major Intercountry Cross Section Statistical Series, 1970

Country	Agricultural output (A1) 1,000 wheat units	Number of male workers in agriculture (A2) 1,000's	Agricultural land area (A3) 1,000 hectares	Farm capital stock (WU) 1,000 wheat units — Livestock (A4)	Machinery (A5)	Perennial plants (A6)	Total (A7)	Fertilizer consumption (A8) 1,000 metric tons	Livestock (A9) 1,000 livestock units	Tractor horsepower (A10) 1,000 horsepower	Land area under permanent crops (A11) 1,000 hectares	Ratio of nonagricultural workers (A12) Percent
Argentina	60,950	1,196	171,460	84,954	3,888	42,865	131,707	87	48,824	5,400	2,177	85.2
Australia	57,759	310	497,108	64,262	7,236	3,465	74,963	1,023	36,932	10,050	176	91.6
Austria	11,685	198	3,896	4,808	5,466	1,871	12,145	418	2,763	7,592	95	83.9
Bangladesh	29,727	10,406	9,917	41,210	28	—	41,238	100	23,684	39	39	29.5
Belgium	15,218	131	1,599	6,201	1,878	669	8,748	496	3,564	2,608	34	95.4
Brazil	116,731	9,752	141,356	195,788	2,147	158,209	356,144	879	112,522	2,982	8,035	55.8
Canada	51,178	376	67,780	21,191	13,642	—	34,833	799	12,179	18,947	86	92.5
Chile	7,804	429	17,466	7,012	659	3,899	11,570	158	4,030	915	198	78.8
Colombia	22,693	2,211	22,138	32,192	602	28,708	61,502	184	18,501	836	1,458	54.8
Denmark	15,098	175	2,975	7,287	3,794	295	11,376	603	4,188	5,269	15	88.9
Finland	7,382	115	2,810	3,296	3,398	—	6,694	482	1,894	4,720	—	79.7
France	116,148	1,763	33,035	40,231	27,864	33,158	101,253	4,605	23,121	38,700	1,684	86.6
Germany, Fed.	72,852	1,039	13,575	28,922	29,971	10,593	69,486	3,197	16,622	41,626	538	91.1
Greece	16,337	834	8,633	5,277	1,440	16,756	23,473	336	3,033	2,000	851	53.5
India	235,869	100,263	178,617	368,205	1,361	83,643	453,209	2,265	211,612	1,890	4,248	32.3
Ireland	9,029	264	4,794	9,946	1,814	59	11,819	404	5,716	2,520	3	73.1
Israel	4,539	63	1,241	654	360	1,693	2,707	57	376	500	86	91.4
Italy	77,241	2,415	20,180	21,402	13,937	58,007	93,346	1,339	12,300	19,357	2,946	81.0
Japan	66,519	4,350	6,458	11,536	17,514	11,814	40,864	2,174	6,630	24,325	600	80.9
Mauritius	762	63	112	87	6	—	93	21	50	9		68.5
Mexico	38,470	4,668	97,258	63,717	1,987	33,335	99,039	606	36,619	2,760	1,693	60.5
Netherlands	23,574	278	2,193	9,246	3,378	847	13,471	623	5,314	4,692	43	93.6

Table 10.B.1 (continued)

| Country | Agricultural output (A1) 1,000 wheat units | Number of male workers in agriculture (A2) 1,000's | Agricultural land area (A3) 1,000 hectares | Farm capital stock (WU) 1,000 wheat units | | | | Fertilizer consumption (A8) 1,000 metric tons | Livestock (A9) 1,000 livestock units | Tractor horsepower (A10) 1,000 horsepower | Land area under permanent crops (A11) 1,000 hectares | Ratio of nonagricultural workers (A12) Percent |
				Livestock (A4)	Machinery (A5)	Perennial plants (A6)	Total (A7)					
New Zealand	21,014	106	13,584	23,152	2,063	276	25,491	455	13,306	2,865	14	88.3
Norway	3,374	55	954	2,020	2,015	—	4,035	201	1,161	2,798	—	88.4
Pakistan	32,583	12,571	24,447	55,289	216	—	55,505	297	31,775	300	—	29.5
Paraguay	1,499	289	13,823	9,347	48	2,402	11,797	5	5,372	66	122	46.7
Peru	9,878	928	30,393	12,156	237	4,765	17,158	89	6,986	329	242	54.9
Philippines	20,617	4,590	10,400	13,979	117	47,315	61,411	205	8,034	162	2,403	48.6
Portugal	9,338	661	4,221	3,706	608	11,735	16,049	155	2,130	845	596	70.4
South Africa	24,113	1,443	113,482	25,686	4,752	9,451	39,892	554	14,762	6,600	480	72.0
Spain	50,329	2,546	34,560	14,907	5,872	96,264	117,043	1,274	8,567	8,156	4,889	66.3
Sri Lanka	6,444	1,543	2,418	3,760	173	21,344	25,277	86	2,161	240	1,084	47.7
Surinam	464	17	47	77	20	158	255	2	44	28	8	73.2
Sweden	10,426	122	3,443	3,604	3,672	—	7,276	501	2,071	5,100	—	91.9
Switzerland	7,669	160	2,176	3,525	1,966	354	5,845	148	2,026	2,730	18	92.4
Taiwan	11,735	1,155	861	1,977	62	10,731	12,770	268	1,136	82	545	58.0
Turkey	44,630	5,357	53,513	36,074	2,257	50,899	89,230	450	20,732	3,135	2,585	33.1
U.K.	50,260	555	19,099	27,619	9,838	—	37,457	1,743	15,873	13,664	—	97.2
U.S.	424,115	2,648	434,220	201,066	101,491	34,851	337,408	15,259	115,555	140,960	1,770	95.7
Venezuela	9,507	567	21,122	13,692	415	12,838	26,945	72	7,869	576	652	78.2
Yugoslavia	22,162	1,934	14,626	13,353	1,444	13,944	28,738	628	7,674	2,006	708	46.6

Table 10.B.2 Various Factor Inputs per Male Worker and per Hectare of Agricultural Land, 1970

Country	Factor inputs per male worker						Factor inputs per hectare of agricultural land					
	Agricultural land area (F1) hectares	Fertilizer consumption (F2) kilograms	Livestock (F3) livestock units	Tractor horsepower (F4) horsepower	Area under permanent crops (F5) hectares	Total capital stock (F6) wheat units	Number of male workers (F7) number	Fertilizer consumption (F8) kilograms	Livestock (F9) livestock units	Tractor horsepower (F10) horsepower	Area under permanent crops (F11) hectares	Total capital stock (F12) wheat units
Argentina	143.4	73	40.8	4.52	1.82	110	0.007	0.5	0.28	0.031	0.013	0.77
Australia	1,603.6	3,300	119.1	32.42	0.57	242	0.001	2.1	0.07	0.020	0.001	0.15
Austria	19.7	2,111	14.0	38.34	0.48	61	0.051	107.3	0.71	1.949	0.024	3.12
Bangladesh	1.0	10	2.3	0.01	—	10	1.049	10.1	2.39	0.004	—	4.16
Belgium	12.2	3,786	27.2	19.91	0.26	67	0.082	310.2	2.23	1.631	0.021	5.47
Brazil	14.5	90	11.5	0.31	0.82	37	0.069	6.2	0.80	0.021	0.057	2.52
Canada	180.3	2,125	32.4	50.39	—	93	0.006	11.8	0.18	0.280	—	0.51
Chile	40.7	368	9.4	2.13	0.46	27	0.025	9.0	0.23	0.052	0.011	0.66
Colombia	10.0	83	8.4	0.38	0.66	28	0.100	8.3	0.84	0.038	0.066	2.78
Denmark	17.0	3,446	23.9	30.11	0.09	65	0.059	202.7	1.41	1.771	0.005	3.82
Finland	24.4	4,191	16.5	41.04	—	58	0.041	171.5	0.67	1.680	—	2.38
France	18.7	2,612	13.1	21.95	0.96	57	0.053	139.4	0.70	1.171	0.051	3.07
Germany, Fed.	13.1	3,077	16.0	40.06	0.52	67	0.077	235.5	1.22	3.066	0.040	5.12
Greece	10.4	403	3.6	2.40	1.02	28	0.097	38.9	0.35	0.232	0.099	2.72
India	1.8	23	2.1	0.02	0.04	5	0.561	12.7	1.18	0.011	0.024	2.54
Ireland	18.2	1,530	21.7	9.55	0.01	45	0.055	84.3	1.19	0.526	0.001	2.47
Israel	19.7	905	6.0	7.94	1.37	43	0.051	45.9	0.30	0.403	0.069	2.18
Italy	8.4	554	5.1	8.02	1.22	39	0.120	66.4	0.61	0.959	0.146	4.63
Japan	1.5	500	1.5	5.59	0.14	9	0.674	336.6	1.03	3.767	0.093	6.33
Mauritius	1.8	333	0.8	0.14	—	1	0.563	187.5	0.45	0.080	—	0.83
Mexico	20.8	130	7.8	0.59	0.36	21	0.048	6.2	0.38	0.028	0.017	1.02
Netherland	7.9	2,241	19.1	16.88	0.15	48	0.127	284.1	2.42	2.140	0.020	6.14

Table 10.B.2 (continued)

Country	Factor inputs per male worker						Factor inputs per hectare of agricultural land					
	Agricultural land area (F1) hectares	Fertilizer consumption (F2) kilograms	Livestock (F3) livestock units	Tractor horse-power (F4) horse-power	Area under permanent crops (F5) hectares	Total capital stock (F6) wheat units	Number of male workers (F7) number	Fertilizer consumption (F8) kilograms	Livestock (F9) livestock units	Tractor horse-power (F10) horse-power	Area under permanent crops (F11) hectares	Total capital stock (F12) wheat units
New Zealand	128.2	4,292	125.5	27.03	0.13	240	0.008	33.5	0.98	0.211	0.001	1.88
Norway	17.4	3,655	21.1	50.87	—	73	0.058	210.7	1.22	2.933	—	4.23
Pakistan	1.9	24	2.5	0.02	—	4	0.514	12.1	1.30	0.012	—	2.27
Paraguay	47.8	17	18.6	0.23	0.42	41	0.021	0.4	0.39	0.005	0.009	0.85
Peru	32.8	96	7.5	0.35	0.26	18	0.031	2.9	0.23	0.011	0.008	0.56
Philippines	2.3	45	1.8	0.04	0.52	13	0.441	19.7	0.77	0.016	0.231	5.90
Portugal	6.4	234	3.2	1.28	0.90	24	0.157	36.7	0.50	0.200	0.141	3.80
South Africa	78.6	384	10.2	4.57	0.33	28	0.013	4.9	0.13	0.058	0.004	0.35
Spain	13.6	500	3.4	3.20	1.92	46	0.074	36.9	0.25	0.236	0.141	3.39
Sri Lanka	1.6	56	1.4	0.16	0.70	16	0.638	35.6	0.89	0.099	0.448	10.45
Surinam	2.8	118	2.6	1.65	0.47	15	0.362	42.6	0.94	0.596	0.170	5.43
Sweden	28.2	4,107	17.0	41.80	—	60	0.035	145.5	0.60	1.481	—	2.11
Switzerland	13.6	925	12.7	17.06	0.11	37	0.074	68.0	0.93	1.255	0.008	2.69
Taiwan	0.8	232	1.0	0.07	0.47	11	1.341	311.3	1.32	0.095	0.633	14.83
Turkey	10.0	84	3.9	0.59	0.48	17	0.100	8.4	0.39	0.059	0.048	1.67
U.K.	34.4	3,141	28.6	24.62	—	67	0.029	91.3	0.83	0.715	—	1.96
U.S.	164.0	5,762	43.6	53.23	0.67	127	0.006	35.1	0.27	0.325	0.004	0.78
Venezuela	37.3	127	13.9	1.02	1.15	48	0.027	3.4	0.37	0.027	0.031	1.28
Yugoslavia	7.6	325	4.0	1.04	0.37	15	0.132	42.9	0.52	0.137	0.048	1.96

SOURCE: Table 10.A.1.

Table 10.B.3   **Intercountry Cross Section Data for Human Capital and Prices, 1970**

Country	School enrollment ratio 1955–60–65 average (A13-1) Percent	1960–65–70 average (A13-2)	Number of graduates from agricultural colleges per 10,000 farm workers, 1970 (A14) Persons	Farm wage rate per day, 1970 (A15) U.S. dollars	Tractor price 1970 (A16) U.S. dollars
Argentina	73	76	6.04	2.41	9,743
Australia	91	91	28.68		3,147
Austria	70	89	10.05	4.78	2,047
Bangladesh	n.a.	26	0.26		4,979
Belgium	99	93	25.11	7.04	1,154
Brazil	50	57	1.97		17,990
Canada	81	91	38.78	11.95	2,985
Chile	74	78	9.16		2,273
Colombia	51	54	2.97		3,626
Denmark	88	86	16.23	6.59	1,768
Finland	83	80	20.26	5.52	2,348
France	91	90	6.13	3.78	822
Germany, Fed.	86	88	11.06	5.63	2,029
Greece	72	83	6.73		2,182
India	33	41	0.84	0.38	1,661
Ireland	95	89	8.11	5.83	1,241
Israel	88	80	24.92	4.46	5,921
Italy	60	72	3.25		2,511
Japan	89	93	31.41	4.19	4,008
Mauritius	78	66	3.49	1.06	11,103
Mexico	59	57	0.83	1.70	7,849
Netherlands	91	86	33.31	8.96	1,717
New Zealand	91	90	57.36	4.85	3,000
Norway	88	92	38.73	9.83	3,294
Pakistan	27	26	1.60	1.43	5,241
Paraguay	62	64	2.46		4,072
Peru	57	72	4.57		8,723
Philippines	75	84	2.71		5,777
Portugal	61	74	1.91	2.54	2,046
South Africa	70	68	4.00		2,948
Spain	67	78	2.30		3,138
Sri Lanka	77	75	0.24	0.57	2,905
Surinam	80	80	9.00		5,517
Sweden	79	92	22.21	13.56	1,768
Switzerland	66	70	6.63		1,719
Taiwan	70	70	8.50		
Turkey	46	59	1.27	3.32	6,114
U.K.	85	89	24.27	7.67	3,460
U.S.	100	100	65.96	11.70	2,819
Venezuela	70	70	5.04		4,930
Yugoslavia	n.a.	78	7.91	3.21	2,131

References

Bureau of Statistics. 1971. *Rodoryoku chosa hokoki* (annual report on the labor force survey). Tokyo: Bureau of Statistics.

Food and Agricultural Organization. 1972. *Production yearbook*. Rome: Food and Agricultural Organization.

Hayami, Yujiro; Miller, Barbara B.; Wade, William W.; and Yamashita, Sachiko. 1971. *An international comparison of agricultural production and productivities*. University of Minnesota Agricultural Experiment Station technical bulletin 277.

Hayami, Yujiro, and Ruttan, Vernon W. 1971. *Agricultural development: an international perspective*. Baltimore: The Johns Hopkins University Press.

Yamada, Saburo. 1975. *A comparative analysis of Asian agricultural productivities and growth patterns*. Tokyo: Asian Productivity Organization.

Comment   G. Edward Schuh

The Yamada-Ruttan paper represents an attempt to interpret several bodies of data on partial productivity within the framework of the induced innovation hypothesis. This approach provides a richer interpretation of data on partial productivity than is usually obtained, and enables us to move beyond the mere reporting of productivity measures —important as that is to furthering our knowledge. The use of the induced innovation hypothesis provides a means of understanding development processes and development experience in a way that enables us to extend development theory while at the same time confronting that theory with a reasonably rich body of data.

The Yamada-Ruttan paper is a continuation of the work reported in Hayami and Ruttan's book, *Agricultural Development: An International Perspective*. Hayami and Ruttan reactivated Hicks's micro theory of induced innovations and applied it at the macro level in agriculture—a sector where an important share of the research has to be socialized— or in the public sector. Their particular interpretation of the theory provides insight with which to understand agricultural development processes, especially in the instrumental role they give to innovation activities. Their basic model rests on a distinction between the primary inputs of land and labor; secondary inputs of conventional capital, represented by mechanization, fertilizers, livestock, and permanent crops;

G. Edward Schuh is at the University of Minnesota.

and human capital variables, represented by general education and technical education. Innovations are specified as of two basic kinds. Biological innovations such as improved plants are viewed as a means of facilitating the substitution of fertilizer for land, while mechanical innovations are viewed as a means of facilitating the substitution of land and capital for labor.

Analytical interest focuses on the sources of productivity of land and labor, and separability of the production function is assumed so that within a range the forces determining the productivity of land can be viewed as relatively independent of the forces determining the productivity of labor. The two partial productivity measures are linked through the ratio of land area per worker. Thus $Y/L = (A/L) (Y/A)$, where $Y =$ output, $L =$ labor, and $A =$ land area. Growth in land area per worker (A/L) is also assumed to be relatively independent of output per worker.

These ideas gave rise to the concept of a metaproduction function, which the authors define in this paper as the envelope of the production points for the most efficient countries. (In previous work the metaproduction function has been equated with Ahmad's [1966] innovation possibility curve [IPC], which can be regarded as the envelope of neoclassical production functions which might be invented.) The metaproduction function describes a technological frontier which countries now lying inside it can achieve by appropriate borrowing and adaptive research activities and by investment in human capital, extension, and rural infrastructure.

Viewed in this framework, technological innovation is given the very instrumental role of opening up new areas along an innovation possibility curve, and facilitating the substitution of inputs produced in the industrial sector for primary inputs in agriculture. In the hands of Hayami and Ruttan, this factor substitution led to a theory of output growth, for it was postulated that inelasticity in factor supply of primary inputs such as land and labor imposed constraints on output growth. Biological and mechanical innovations which facilitate factor substitution permit these constraints to be eased, and a more rapid rate of output growth is the result.

The contribution of the present paper is to analyze two additional sets of data not available for the Hayami-Ruttan study. The first is a set of time series data on Germany, Denmark, France, and the United Kingdom—four developed countries which supplement the previous detailed record of the development of agriculture in Japan and the United States. The second is a set of cross-sectional data on forty-one countries for 1970, which supplements the 1960 data used in the previous study. These latter data are used to reestimate the parameters of the aggregate production function, and the new parameter estimates are then used to account for differences in productivity among countries.

There is a wealth of material presented for such a short paper. The highlights of the results obtained are as follows:

1. The first part of the paper reviews the evidence on long-term output and productivity growth in the six developed countries. The analysis shows that there were enormous differences in factor endowment among the six countries in 1880, and that these differences remained large in 1970 despite the enormous adjustments in factor use that had taken place. Those countries in which land area per worker was relatively limited in 1880 depended primarily on increases in output per hectare as a primary source of growth, and have been able to achieve rates of growth in total output and in output per worker that have been roughly comparable to the rates achieved by countries with more favorable resource endowments. Growth rates in output and in land and labor productivity have risen sharply in most countries since 1930. In contrast to growth rates of less than 2% in these variables prior to 1930, modern growth rates range in the neighborhood of 2–4% in output, over 5% in output per worker, and 2–4% in output per hectare.

2. In the second part of the paper an analysis is made of the relationship between factor prices and the pattern of factor use associated with growth in output and factor productivity in the six developed countries. The statistical results, using time series data for each of the countries, support the hypothesis that changes in factor use have been responsive to changes in relative factor prices. Fertilizer use per hectare has been responsive to the prices of fertilizer and of labor relative to the price of land. And the two complementary inputs—power per worker and land per worker—have been responsive to the prices of land and machinery relative to labor, although the statistical results are less strong in this case.

3. The third section of the paper is devoted to an examination of contemporary productivity differences among countries. Data are synthesized on land and labor productivities for forty-one countries in 1970. These countries are classified into three types of country groups on the basis of the relative dominance of biological and mechanical technology in their development experience, and differences in the technological patterns are analyzed in relation to the resource endowments for the respective country groups. The level of technological improvement is then related to the extent of industrialization or development in the nonagricultural sector of each country, and interrelationships between the land and labor productivity ratios and various input ratios are explored on the basis of correlation analysis to illustrate the sources of productivity differences among countries.

The intercountry differences in productivity ratios are quite large. The grouping of the countries is according to whether they are similar to the U.S., Japan, or the European countries. The authors note that in terms of their level of development the countries tend to align themselves in such a way as to be consistent with the historical paths followed by each of these three countries or groups of countries. Simple correlation analysis suggests again that resource endowments are an important factor both in determining the choice of technology and in inducing an efficient path of technological development over time. A strong association between industrialization and technological improvements is found. Relationships between human capital variables and labor productivity are found to be strong, but the association of these variables with land productivity is somewhat weaker.

4. In the fourth section of the paper the cross-sectional data on the forty-one countries are used to fit the parameters of a Hayami-Ruttan metaproduction function. These parameters are in turn used to account for the differences in productivity among selected countries. The production function is the Cobb-Douglas type and the specified inputs include conventional inputs as well as nonconventional inputs such as general and technical education.

The statistical results of estimating the production function were not as good as Hayami and Ruttan obtained with the 1960 data. Neither land nor general education had statistically significant coefficients, and the coefficient for fertilizer almost doubled compared to the estimate obtained with 1960 data.

Using somewhat arbitrary production elasticities, an analysis is made of the differences in labor productivity between the U.S. and five other countries (including Japan), and of the differences in land productivity between Japan and the other five countries (including the U.S.). The four conventional inputs account for 56–67% of the differences in output per worker between the U.S. and the other four countries. Differences in human capital account for around 30% of the difference in output per worker between the U.S. and four of the countries, but in the case of Japan, it accounts for only 12% of the difference.

In the case of land productivity, the four conventional inputs account for between 45 and 97% of the observed differences among the selected countries. The human capital variables also account for an important share of the differences in land productivity, and are particularly important in accounting for the differences between Japan and India and Turkey.

In a final section Yamada and Ruttan remind us that, although consistent with the induced innovation hypothesis, their results do not provide a rigorous test of that hypothesis. They believe that the evidence they produce is so strong, however, that there is a presumption that the induced innovation hypothesis was involved. In their view the results of their analysis support a conclusion that failure to take advantage of the potential growth from human capital and technical inputs represents a significant constraint on agricultural development around the world, and that differences in the natural resource base account for an increasingly less significant share of the widening productivity gap among countries.

In viewing the less developed countries, with their expected labor force explosion in the years ahead, Yamada and Ruttan believe that failure to effectively institutionalize public-sector agricultural research can seriously distort the pattern of technical change and resource use. The point is that the private sector will have ample incentive to produce mechanical innovations and those biological innovations that can be embodied in proprietary products. The private sector will *not* have adequate incentives to produce other biological innovations, however, with the result that the productivity path will not be consistent with factor endowments, especially in the more labor-intensive less developed countries.

As this brief overview should have made clear, the Yamada-Ruttan paper is a particularly rich bag, and it is difficult, in a brief synthesis, to do justice to the richness and diversity of the material presented. The authors have done yeomanly duty in bringing data together, in presenting them in imaginative and enlightening ways, and in attempting to interpret them with a larger body of development theory.

Similarly, the importance of the subject—productivity in agriculture—can hardly be denied. The problem of world hunger has dominated newspaper headlines over the last three years. It is generally recognized that the world's burgeoning population growth will be fed only with a sizable and sustained increase in productivity. Equally as important, the bulk of the world's poor are concentrated in agriculture. Their lot can be improved only through growth in productivity.

In many respects, however, the present paper is disappointing. It fails to capitalize fully on the new sets of data it uses, and treats some rather serious statistical problems in a rather cavalier fashion. When statistical results do not support preconceived notions of how the world is, the authors have somewhat of a tendency to stay with their preconceived notions. And some rather serious measurement problems or problems of correspondence are quietly swept under the rug.

In commenting on the Yamada-Ruttan paper I would like to focus on five main issues.

1. The maintained hypothesis. Considerable effort by the authors has gone into synthesizing time series data on four additional developed countries for comparison with the experience of Japan and the United States, and into generating a new set of cross-sectional data on forty-one

countries. The analysis of these data would have been considerably enriched if some a priori hypotheses about development experience had been specified and tested. The original Hayami-Ruttan analysis was rich in ideas about the role of institutional arrangements and how they might influence the technological path chosen. The theory was also capable of generating hypotheses about particular paths of development that might have been expected to be taken over the last decade, given knowledge about changes in factor price ratios. Yet the reader finds only tangential reference to such a priori thought which might have enriched the analysis of these important sets of data. We are left almost totally in the dark about why these particular four developed countries were chosen; we see no discussion of how different institutional arrangements might have influenced the particular development paths chosen; and we see little a priori discussion of how production elasticities of the aggregate production function might have been expected to change over time, if at all, or of how the development experience in 1970 might be expected to differ from the experience observed in 1960. Instead, the new data are analyzed rather mechanically, in much the same way as in the previous study, with little attention given to a priori hypotheses or to how they might be tested with the data.

As a result, there is a general tendency to fail to answer some important "why" questions. For example, why did output per hectare rise less rapidly in Denmark during 1930–70 than during 1880–1930? Why did France experience the most dramatic transition of any of the six countries between 1880–1930 and 1930–70? Why was the U.S. persistently on a quite different growth path than the other five countries? Why was Denmark the only country that experienced a sustained decline in land per worker?

2. The specification of the production function. The Cobb-Douglas production function is at best a crude approximation to the metaproduction function, or to the underlying theoretical model that the authors lay out. It was useful as the basis for a first test of the Hayami-Ruttan model. But if the authors want to advance our knowledge beyond that first approximation, they need to probe more deeply. Just a couple of points are worth noting. First, discussion early in the paper focuses on complementarity between some inputs and strong substitutability among others. Yet the Cobb-Douglas does not permit us to accomodate these differences. Similarly, the Cobb-Douglas assumes an elasticity of substitution of one. Yet their own statistical results suggest that the elasticity of substitution beween machinery horsepower and labor is greater than one.

These problems are troublesome. At the least the problems should be addressed. More importantly, if the authors are to capitalize on the insights offered by the Hayami-Ruttan model, they need to specify a production function that can accommodate the implications of that model.

3. Statistical problems. There are a number of statistical problems in the paper, some of which are rather obvious, others of which are more subtle. In the first place, the land and labor productivity equations consistent with the Cobb-Douglas production function contain for estimational purposes exactly the same variables on the right-hand side as the original production function. The only difference is that the coefficient of the input whose productivity is being considered is now equal to the production elasticity of the production function minus one, which means that the estimated coefficient will typically be negative. The coefficients of all other variables will be exactly the same as in the original production function. Put differently, there is little to be gained from estimating the parameters of both the production function and the productivity equations. In a Cobb-Douglas world they are virtually the same.

This problem would not be so serious if it were not that Yamada and Ruttan use a production elasticity of .25 for education in accounting for differences in productivity among countries, apparently on the basis that its coefficient was a statistically insignificant .26 in one version of each of the two productivity equations. These results must be taken with a grain of salt, for the productivity equations are improperly specified and hence add little to our knowledge. In point of fact, the authors have *no* statistical support for the role of general education in the production function from this particular set of data, or at least from this set of regressions.

A second statistical problem has to do with the problem of intercorrelation. This problem comes up in the lack of statistical significance for the coefficient of land and the small size of this coefficient. I agree with the authors that the importance of land is often exaggerated in the discussion of agricultural development. But to accept the notion that land has virtually no importance in the production function is to ask a bit much, especially with the particular set of countries included in their sample. What has likely happened is that the fertilizer variable has picked up the effect of the land input. These two variables would be expected to be highly interdependent, and it is worth noting that the increase in the fertilizer coefficient, compared to the 1960 data, is approximately equal to the decline in the coefficient of land. These shifts in coefficient values are very likely statistical artifacts, and of no economic significance—despite the authors' inclinations to give them an economic interpretation.

More generally, the authors are rather cavalier about statistical problems in general. Little attention is given to evaluating the statistical results obtained, or to the use of alternative procedures whereby the statistical results might have been improved.[1] Such procedures might have been especially useful in the case of the lack of statistical significance for the coefficients of both land and general education. A more careful statistical evaluation of the production function was an imperative in light of the desire to use the production elasticities in accounting for the sources of differences in productivity among countries.

4. Problems of measurement. The disappointing statistical results with the aggregate production function may also be due to measurement problems. Education is a good example. Its quality varies widely from one country to another, as does the nature of training and the goals of education. The surprise is probably that such a crude measure of education worked in the previous study, not that it performed so badly in the present case.

The problem with land is even more severe. This variable is measured as the simple sum of the areas in arable land, land under permanent crops, and permanent meadows and pastures. In other words, a hectare of pasture land on the frontier of Brazil is given the same weight as a hectare of prime Iowa farmland, or as a hectare of land on the Indo-Gangetic plain that can grow two and in some cases three crops per year.

Land is really a proxy for a very complex set of variables in these models, ranging from inherent soil quality in terms of nutrients and soil characteristics, to rainfall, temperature, and distribution of rainfall. Moreover, the degree of multiple cropping and interplanting varies widely from one place to another within a country, and from one country to another. The implication, of course, is that it makes little sense to just add up such widely differing units of an input. And if one does, he should not be very surprised that the result does not perform very well in a regression analysis.

One can sympathize with the difficulty of attempting to come to grips with this problem. But the warning flag has to be raised when the estimated coefficients do not meet the usual statistical tests. This reviewer admits to having little confidence in the results presented in the section which attempts to account for differences in productivity among the selected countries. A coefficient of .25 was used for education, when there was absolutely no statistical support for this variable in the estimation of the production function. A coefficient of .02 was used for land, yet this also was derived from a coefficient that was not statistically significant, and all the a priori information that one has suggests that land has a greater role in the production process than a coefficient of .02 implies.

1. The problem of simultaneity rears its ugly head on a number of occasions, especially when land values are used as explanatory variables. Little appreciation for that problem is found in the paper.

These difficulties are brought to the fore by the tendency of the authors to come down so heavily on the side of the human capital variables. Clearly, if one puts so little weight on land and such a large weight on general education, the results are almost foreordained.

5. Additional variables or alternative interpretations. Hayami and Ruttan and their immediate intellectual forebears in the field of agricultural development have substantially broadened our perspectives on the development process by incorporating social or infrastructure variables such as research and education into the aggregate production function. Clearly, that is to focus attention on two important variables, and the theoretical and empirical evidence for these previously omitted variables is relatively strong. But an objective observer can still be concerned about misspecification, especially in the context of drawing on international data.

Perhaps the two variables of most importance are economies of scale and specialization in production. The evidence on the first is rather mixed, but at the same time it is fair to say that few of the tests that have been made have been very rigorous or robust. On the gains from specialization in production, we know even less. But as agricultural sectors develop there is a tendency for geographic specialization in production as well as for firm specialization in production to take place. For example, farms in the American Midwest have evolved from general farms with a wide range of production activities to specialized farms with only one or two products. Moreover, there have been large shifts in the location of production within the U.S.

The problem with both of these factors, especially in the present context, is that both tend to be correlated with the level of development. Farm enlargement occurs as labor is drained out of agriculture, and specialization in production also tends to occur as development proceeds. Like it or not, general education is a good proxy for the level of development in an economy. What we do not know is whether the coefficient for education is picking up the effect of these other variables, or whether it is reflecting the effect of education as a quality adjustment for labor. That is, the problem of specification bias is still with us.

It should also be noted that general education plays a dual role in agricultural development. Although it makes labor more productive within agriculture, it at the same time increases the employability of the labor in the nonfarm labor market, thereby accelerating the rate of out-migration from agriculture, other things being equal. If this input "supply" effect should outweigh the input "demand" effect, the relationship between education and land productivity would be expected to be weak, especially in simple correlations.

To conclude on a somewhat more positive note, we are still in Yamada and Ruttan's debt, despite these statistical problems and the associated problems of interpretation. Future students of agricultural development will be indebted to them for the additional data they have synthesized. And the attempt to link the level of urban industrialization to the Hayami-Ruttan model, even if only informally, is promising.

But perhaps the most important strength of the paper is the attempt to interpret the productivity data with a theory of agricultural development. This enriches the interpretation of the data and provides insights into a more general economic problem. The Hayami-Ruttan model is a particularly insightful way of viewing the agricultural development process. It is simple but powerful in what it enables us to dig out of the data.

References

Ahmad, S. On the theory of induced innovation. *Economic Journal* 76 (1966): 344–57.

11   Economic Growth, 1947–73; An International Comparison

Laurits R. Christensen, Dianne Cummings,
and Dale W. Jorgenson

11.1   Introduction

11.1.1   Introduction

The purpose of this paper is to provide an international comparison of postwar patterns of aggregate economic growth for the United States and eight of its major trading partners—Canada, France, Germany, Italy, Japan, Korea, the Netherlands, and the United Kingdom. Our study covers the period 1947–73 for the United States and as much of this period as is feasible for each of the eight remaining countries. We compare growth in real product, real factor input, and total factor productivity for all nine countries for the period 1960–73. For all countries except Korea we compare growth during this period with growth beginning at earlier times and extending through 1960.

A complete analysis of aggregate economic growth involves the growth of real product and its sources—growth in real factor input and growth in total factor productivity. Growth in real factor input can be further divided between growth in real capital input and in real labor input. Growth in capital input involves growth in capital stock as a component of wealth through saving and capital formation. Analysis of growth in capital requires a complete accounting system, consisting of a production account, an income and expenditure account, an accumulation account, and a wealth account—all in current and constant prices.

Christensen and Jorgenson (1969, 1970, 1973a, 1973b) have developed a complete accounting system that is well adapted to the analysis of aggregate economic growth and have implemented this system for the United States for the period 1929–69. In this paper we limit considera-

Laurits R. Christensen and Dianne Cummings are at the University of Wisconsin; Dale W. Jorgenson is at Harvard University.

tion to the production account, containing data on output and input in current and constant prices. We have extended the production account for the United States through 1973 and have implemented this account for each of the eight remaining countries. Our data on output and input are compiled in a form suitable for integration into a complete system of accounts for each country.

We first provide a brief review of previous international comparisons of patterns of aggregate economic growth that are similar in scope to this study. We discuss the selection of countries to be included and the selection of an appropriate time period for our international comparisons. In section 11.2 we present our methodology for measuring real product, real factor input, and total factor productivity. This methodology is based on the economic theory of production, beginning with a production function giving output as a function of capital input, labor input, and time. We derive index numbers of real product, real capital input, real labor input, and total factor productivity from this theory.

In section 11.3 we outline the empirical implementation of our index numbers of real product, real factor input, and total factor productivity for the nine countries included in our study. In section 11.4 we present an international comparison of patterns of economic growth for all nine countries. Our principal finding is that differences in growth rates of real product for the period 1960–73 are associated with differences in growth rates of real factor input. An intertemporal comparison of growth rates during this period with growth rates during earlier periods ending in 1960 strongly reinforces this conclusion. Increases and decreases in growth rates of real product are associated with increases and decreases in growth rates of real factor input. We present a more detailed summary of our conclusions in section 11.5.

11.1.2 Alternative Methodologies

International comparisons of patterns of economic growth are no longer uncommon, but the number of studies providing real product and real factor input in both current and constant prices on an economy-wide basis is not large. We can set the stage for our detailed discussion of methodology by briefly summarizing the approaches that have been used in previous studies. In table 11.1 we present a tabular comparison among the most important of these studies for developed countries.[1]

1. Detailed surveys of the literature on total factor productivity have been given by Nadiri (1970) and by Kennedy and Thirlwall (1972). Nadiri (1972) has presented an international survey of estimates of growth of total factor productivity. Balassa and Bertrand (1970) have compared sources of economic growth in Eastern and Western Europe. Correa (1970) has compared sources of economic growth for Latin American countries. Patterns of economic growth have been studied from a more comprehensive perspective by Kuznets (1971) and by Chenery and Syrquin (1975).

Table 11.1   **International Comparisons of Growth in Total Factor Productivity**

	Authors					
	Tinbergen (1942)	Domar (1964)	Denison (1967)	Barger (1969)	Kuznets (1971)	Bergson (1974)
			Belgium			
		Canada			Canada	
	France		Denmark	Denmark		France
	Germany	Germany	France	France	France	Germany
			Germany	Germany		Italy
			Italy	Italy		Japan
		Japan				
			Netherlands	Netherlands		
			Norway	Norway	Norway	
				Sweden		
						U.S.S.R.
	U.K.	U.K.	U.K.	U.K.	U.K.	U.K.
	U.S.A.	U.S.A.	U.S.A.	U.S.A.	U.S.A.	U.S.A.
Time period	1870–1914	1948–60	1950–62	1950–64	1855–1966	1955–70

The concept of total factor productivity, defined as the ratio between real product and real factor input, was introduced in a notable but neglected article by Tinbergen (1942).[2] Among the many remarkable features of Tinbergen's study is an international comparison of growth in real product, real factor input, and total factor productivity for France, Germany, the U.K., and the U.S.A. for the period 1870–1914.

The concept of total factor productivity was developed independent of Tinbergen's work by Stigler (1947). The point of departure for this development was the measurement of real factor input by weighting real capital input and real labor input by their marginal products. Important contributions to the measurement of total factor productivity were made during the 1950s by Mills (1952), Schmookler (1952), Knowles (1954, 1960), Valavanis-Vail (1955), Abramovitz (1956), Kendrick (1956), Solow (1957), and Fabricant (1959). The initial approach to total factor productivity measurement was brought to fruition by the epochal work of Kendrick (1961). The first international comparison of growth in total factor productivity, subsequent to Tinbergen's pioneering effort, was published by Domar (1964) and five collaborators, employing the methodology of Kendrick's study for the United States. Domar's study included Canada, Germany, Japan, the U.K., and the U.S.A. and covered the period 1948–60. A notable feature of the study was the development of separate estimates for as many as eleven sectors within each of the five countries.

Griliches (1960) and Denison (1962) extended the original framework for the measurement of total factor productivity by applying the principle of weighting inputs by their marginal products to components of real labor input. Griliches and Jorgenson (1966, 1967) followed up this new departure in methodology by applying the same principle to components of real capital input. Christensen and Jorgenson (1969) developed a detailed methodology for weighting components of real capital input disaggregated by class of asset and by legal form of organization. This methodology incorporates data on the taxation of income from capital at both corporate and personal levels and data on rates of return and depreciation by asset class and legal form of organization.

Denison's study of U.S. economic growth (1962) was followed in 1967 by the appearance of his volume, *Why Growth Rates Differ*, comparing U.S. economic growth for the period 1950–62 with growth in eight European countries. Although Denison's international comparisons of growth in real product, real factor input, and total factor productivity, which he denotes output per unit of input, were limited to the nine countries listed in table 11.1, the same methodology has been

2. The first English-language reference to Tinbergen's article that has come to out attention is by Valavanis-Vail (1955).

employed by Walters (1968, 1970) in two studies for Canada and by
Denison and Chung (1976) in a study for Japan.[3] Denison (1974) has
also extended the time period of his estimates for the United States,
based on the methodology of *Why Growth Rates Differ*, to include the
years 1929–69.

Concluding our brief survey of international comparisons, we can
draw attention to Barger's (1969) comparison of growth for nine countries—Denison's list with Belgium being replaced by Sweden—for the
period 1950–64. This study incorporates embodied as well as disembodied sources of economic growth. Kuznets (1971) has provided a
comparison of Denison's results for the postwar period with his own
analysis of long-term growth trends for Canada, France, Norway, the
U.K. and the U.S.A.[4] Finally, as part of a research program on Soviet
economic growth, Bergson (1974) has compared the growth of Soviet
real product, real factor input, and total factor productivity with that
of six Western countries for the period 1955–70.

11.1.3   Selection of a Methodology

In selecting an appropriate methodology for our study, Denison's
approach in *Why Growth Rates Differ*, his subsequent studies of Japanese and U.S. economic growth, and the studies of Canada by Walters
deserve serious consideration. For present purposes Denison's approach
can be separated into three interrelated components. First, for each
country Denison has measured real product, real factor input, and total
factor productivity. Second, for each country Denison has analyzed the
growth in output per unit of input into ten separate sources, including
advances of knowledge, improved allocation of resources, balance of
the capital stock, economies of scale, and a residual factor. Third, Denison has provided a comparison of productivity levels for all nine countries for the year 1960.

Our study is limited to the development of a production account
within a complete accounting system, so that we focus attention on
Denison's measurement of real product, real factor input, and total factor productivity. Jorgenson and Griliches (1972a) have compared Denison's results for the U.S.A. with those of Christensen and Jorgenson
(1970) for the period covered by *Why Growth Rates Differ*, 1950–62.[5]

3. Denison's methodology is also employed in a study for Japan by Kanamori
(1972).
4. Hopefully this analysis will soon be complemented by a study of long-term
growth trends for France, Germany, Italy, Japan, Sweden, the U.K., and the
U.S.A. by the Social Science Research Council group under the overall direction
of Abramovitz and Kuznets.
5. Earlier, Denison (1969) had compared his results with estimates by Jorgenson and Griliches (1967). For Denison's reply to Jorgenson and Griliches
(1972a), see Denison (1972).

They conclude that the growth of real factor input accounts for a much larger proportion of growth in real product in the Christensen-Jorgenson study than in Denison's study, and that the differences in results can be traced to differences in the methodology for measuring real capital input.

Jorgenson and Griliches (1972*a*, *b*) have compared the methodology of Christensen and Jorgenson for measuring real capital input with that employed by Denison in *Why Growth Rates Differ*. They show that, by contrast with the approach of Christensen and Jorgenson, Denison's methodology fails to incorporate differences in the marginal products of capital inputs in a satisfactory way.[6] In particular, Denison fails to incorporate the effects of taxation of income from capital at both corporate and personal levels, to measure differences in rates of return and depreciation by asset class and legal form of organization, and to account properly for the impact of differences in the rate of change of the prices of different assets on rates of return. Finally, he fails to treat depreciation and replacement of capital stock in an internally consistent way.

Denison's methodology for *Why Growth Rates Differ* has been subjected to searching scrutiny from a completely different point of view by Maddison (1972). Maddison compares his own results with those of Denison as follows:

> In my accounting (like that of Jorgenson and Griliches) factor input plays a much bigger role than for Denison. It explains three-quarters of growth whereas for him it represents less than half.[7]

Maddison's critique, like that of Jorgenson and Griliches, underlines the dependence of Denison's most important substantive conclusion, the unimportance of increases in capital input per unit of labor input in explaining growth in output per unit of labor input, on his methodology for the treatment of real capital input.

From our point of view the measurement of real product, real factor input, and total factor productivity is only part of the empirical study of economic growth. In addition, it is necessary to analyze the sources of growth in real factor input, especially growth in capital stock as a component of wealth and growth in capital services as a component of factor input through saving and capital formation. As we have already emphasized, in addition to a production account in current and constant

6. Kendrick (1975), pp. 909–10, has drawn attention to the asymmetry in Denison's (1974) treatment of labor and capital input in his recent study of U.S. economic growth, which is based on the methodology of *Why Growth Rates Differ*.

7. Maddison (1972), p. 40.

prices, this necessitates accounts for income and expenditure, saving and capital formation, and wealth, also in current and constant prices. Logical inconsistencies in the treatment of real capital input would ramify into corresponding inconsistencies in the treatment of taxation and depreciation in the income and expenditure account, the treatment of revaluation and replacement in the saving and capital formation account, and the treatment of capital stock in the wealth account.

The empirical implementation of a complete accounting system necessitates an internally consistent treatment of capital in all four sets of accounts—production, income, saving, and wealth—in current and constant prices. This is a far more stringent requirement than internal consistency of the production account alone, but this requirement is met by the accounting system developed by Christensen and Jorgenson (1973a). We have adopted their methodology as the basis for our international comparisons of growth in productivity. The measurement of total factor productivity within a complete accounting system also provides a basis for overcoming a recurrent objection to conventional growth accounting. This objection is that growth of real product, real factor input, and total factor productivity are treated in isolation from other aspects of the process of economic growth, specifically from the determinants of capital formation.

11.1.4   Selection of Countries and Time Periods

Turning next to the selection of a sample of countries, our objective is to compare patterns of aggregate economic growth for the U.S.A. and its major trading partners. This leads immediately to the inclusion of Canada, Japan, and the four largest countries of Western Europe—France, Germany, Italy, and the U.K. Referring again to table 11.1, we find that all six international comparisons of productivity growth include the U.K. and the U.S.A. France and Germany are included in all but one of the studies. Italy is included in three of the six, while Canada and Japan are included in two of the six. Our selection of additional countries has been constrained by the resources available to us.

Our methods for analysis of sources of economic growth can be applied to data for industrialized countries such as Australia, Belgium, Denmark, Finland, the Netherlands, New Zealand, Norway, Sweden, and Switzerland. Among these countries Belgium, Denmark, the Netherlands, Norway, and Sweden have been included in one or more of the studies listed in table 11.1. We have selected the Netherlands for inclusion in our study as the largest of these countries. Work is currently underway on comparable studies for Belgium and Denmark. We have tested the feasibility of applying our methodology to a developing country of importance in trade with the U.S.A. by selecting Korea as a final addition to our study. Korea also provides comparative perspective for the analysis of patterns of Japanese growth that has proved to be very useful.

The selection of a time period for our study, like the selection of a sample of countries, was constrained by the objectives of our study. To provide the basis for continuing assessments of the impact of policies affecting trade and growth in each country on the pattern of world trade and growth, we require a data base that can be readily updated. These considerations made it necessary to limit our study to the postwar period and to rely as much as possible on official national accounts for the measurement of real product. The starting point for each of our country studies was determined by the first year for which a continuous time series running throughout the postwar period was available. For all nine countries we were able to develop annual time series for the period 1960–73. For all countries except Korea we have developed annual time series for the period 1955–73.

11.2   Methodology

11.2.1   Introduction

Our first objective is to separate growth in real factor input from growth in total factor productivity in accounting for growth in real product for each of the nine countries included in our study. For this purpose we require a methodology for measuring real factor input, real product, and total factor productivity. Our methodology is based on the economic theory of production and technical change. The point of departure for this theory is a production function giving output as a function of inputs and time. We consider production under constant returns to scale, so that a proportional change in all inputs results in a proportional change in output.

In analyzing changes in production patterns we combine the production function with necessary conditions for producer equilibrium. We express these conditions as equalities between shares of each input in the value of output and the elasticity of output with respect to that input. The elasticities depend on inputs and time, the variables that enter the production function. Under constant returns to scale the sum of elasticities with respect to all inputs is equal to unity, so that value shares also sum to unity.

To analyze changes in the pattern of production with time we consider the rate of technical change, defined as the rate of growth of output, holding all inputs constant. The rate of technical change, like the elasticities of output with respect to input, depends on inputs and time. Under constant returns to scale the necessary conditions for producer equilibrium can be combined with growth rates of inputs and outputs to produce an index of the rate of technical change that depends only on the prices and quantities of inputs and outputs.

11.2.2   Technical Change

Our methodology for productivity measurement is based on the *production function F*, characterized by constant returns to scale:

$$Y = F(K, L, T),$$

where Y is output, K is capital input, L is labor input, and T is time. Denoting the price of output by q_Y, the price of capital input by p_K, and the price of labor input by p_L, we can define the shares of capital and labor input in the value of output, say v_K and v_L, by

$$v_K = \frac{p_K K}{q_Y Y}, \qquad v_L = \frac{p_L L}{q_Y Y}.$$

Necessary conditions for producer equilibrium are given by equalities between each value share and the elasticity of output with respect to the corresponding input:

$$v_K = \frac{\partial \ln Y}{\partial \ln K} (K, L, T),$$

$$v_L = \frac{\partial \ln Y}{\partial \ln L} (K, L, T).$$

Under constant returns to scale the elasticities and the value shares sum to unity.

The production function is defined in terms of output, capital input, and labor input. Output and the two inputs are aggregates that depend on the quantities of individual outputs and inputs. We consider aggregates that are characterized by constant returns to scale, so that proportional changes in all components of each aggregate result in proportional changes in the aggregate:

$$Y = Y(Y_1, Y_2 \ldots Y_m),$$

$$K = K(K_1, K_2 \ldots K_n),$$

$$L = L(L_1, L_2 \ldots L_p),$$

where $\{Y_i\}$ is the set of outputs, $\{K_j\}$ the set of capital inputs, and $\{L_k\}$ the set of labor inputs.

Denoting the prices of outputs by $\{q_{Yi}\}$, the prices of capital inputs by $\{p_{Kj}\}$, and the prices of labor inputs by $\{p_{Lk}\}$, we can define the shares of individual outputs in the value of output, say $\{w_{Yi}\}$; the shares of individual capital inputs in the value of capital input, say $\{v_{Kj}\}$; and the shares of individual labor inputs in the value of labor input, say $\{v_{Lk}\}$; by

$$w_{Yi} = \frac{q_{Yi}Y_i}{q_Y Y}, \qquad (i = 1, 2, \ldots, m);$$

$$v_{Kj} = \frac{p_{Kj}K_j}{p_K K}, \qquad (j = 1, 2, \ldots, n);$$

$$v_{Lk} = \frac{p_{Lk}L_k}{p_L L}, \qquad (k = 1, 2, \ldots, p).$$

Necessary conditions for producer equilibrium are given by equalities between value shares and elasticities of the corresponding aggregate with respect to its individual components:

$$w_{Yi} = \frac{\partial \ln Y}{\partial \ln_{Yi}}, \qquad (i = 1, 2, \ldots, m);$$

$$v_{Kj} = \frac{\partial \ln K}{\partial \ln K_j}, \qquad (j = 1, 2, \ldots, n);$$

$$v_{Lk} = \frac{\partial \ln L}{\partial \ln L_k}, \qquad (k = 1, 2, \ldots, p).$$

Under constant returns to scale the elasticities and the value shares for each aggregate sum to unity.

Finally, we can define the rate of technical change, say v_T, as the growth of output with respect to time, holding capital and labor input constant:

$$v_T = \frac{\partial \ln Y}{\partial T} (K, L, T).$$

Under constant returns to scale the rate of technical change can be expressed as the rate of growth of output less a weighted average of the rates of growth of capital and labor input, where the weights are given by the corresponding value shares:

$$\frac{d \ln Y}{d T} = \frac{\partial \ln Y}{\partial \ln K} \frac{d \ln K}{d T} + \frac{\partial \ln Y}{\partial \ln L} \frac{d \ln Y}{d T} + \frac{\partial \ln Y}{\partial T}$$

$$= v_K \frac{d \ln K}{d T} + v_L \frac{d \ln L}{d T} + v_T.$$

We refer to this expression for the rate of technical change v_T as the *Divisia quantity index of technical change.*

The Divisia quantity index of technical change is defined in terms of aggregates for output, capital input, and labor input. The measurement of productivity begins with data for individual outputs and inputs. Under constant returns to scale the rate of growth of each aggregate can be expressed as a weighted average of its components, where the weights are given by the corresponding value shares:

$$\frac{d \ln Y}{d T} = \Sigma w_i \frac{d \ln Y_i}{d T},$$

$$\frac{d \ln K}{d T} = \Sigma v_j \frac{d \ln K_j}{d T},$$

$$\frac{d \ln L}{d T} = \Sigma v_k \frac{d \ln L_k}{d T}.$$

We refer to these expressions for aggregate output, capital input, and labor input as the *Divisia indexes of output, capital input, and labor input*.[8]

If the production function F gives output Y as a function of aggregate input, say X, we can write this function in the form

$$Y = G[X(K,L),T],$$

where the function G is homogeneous of degree one in aggregate input X and aggregate input is homogeneous of degree one in capital input K and labor input L, so that technical change is *Hicks-neutral*:

$$Y = A(T) X(K,L).$$

The rate of technical change depends only on time:

$$v_T = \frac{d \ln A}{d T},$$

and the rate of growth of aggregate input is a weighted average of rates of growth of capital and labor input:

$$\frac{d \ln X}{d T} = v_K \frac{d \ln K}{d T} + v_L \frac{d \ln L}{d T}.$$

We refer to this expression as the *Divisia index of input*.[9]

Under constant returns to scale a necessary condition for producer equilibrium is that the price of output and the prices of capital and labor

---

8. These quantity indexes and the analogous price indexes discussed below were introduced by Divisia (1925, 1926). The Divisia index of technical change was introduced by Solow (1957) and discussed by Richter (1966) and by Jorgenson and Griliches (1967).

9. The definition of technical change that is neutral in the sense that it leaves the ratio of marginal products of capital and labor input unchanged is due to Hicks (1963). Hulten (1973) demonstrated that the line integral defining the Divisia index of an aggregate such as input is path independent if and only if the production function is homothetically separable in the components of the aggregate.

inputs are consistent with equality between the value of output and the sum of the values of capital and labor input:

$$q_Y Y = p_K K + p_L L.$$

Given this equality, we can express the price of output as a function, say P, of the prices of capital, labor input, and time:

$$q_Y = P(p_K, p_L, T).$$

We refer to this function as the *price function*.[10] Similarly, we can express the price of each aggregate as a function of the prices of its components.

We can define the rate of technical change as the negative of the growth of the price of output with respect to time, holding the prices of capital and labor input constant:

$$v_T = - \frac{\partial \ln P}{\partial T} (p_K, p_L, T).$$

We can express the rate of technical change as the rate of growth of a weighted average of input prices less the rate of growth of the price of output, where the weights are given by the corresponding value shares:

$$\frac{d \ln q_Y}{d T} = v_K \frac{d \ln p_K}{d T} + v_L \frac{d \ln p_L}{d T} - v_T.$$

We refer to this expression for the rate of technical change as the *Divisia price index of technical change*.

We can express each aggregate price index as a weighted average of its components:

$$\frac{d \ln q_Y}{d T} = \Sigma w_i \frac{d \ln q_{Yi}}{d T},$$

$$\frac{d \ln p_K}{d T} = \Sigma v_j \frac{d \ln p_{Kj}}{d T},$$

$$\frac{d \ln p_L}{d T} = \Sigma v_k \frac{d \ln p_{Lj}}{d T}.$$

We refer to these expressions as *Divisia price indexes of output, capital input, and labor input*. If output is a function of aggregate input, the price of output can be expressed as a function of aggregate input, say p_X, so that

$$q_Y = \frac{p_X(p_K, p_L)}{A(T)},$$

10. The price function was introduced by Samuelson (1953); he refers to this function as the factor-price frontier.

and the rate of growth of the price of aggregate input is a weighted average of rates of growth of the prices of capital and labor input:

$$\frac{d \ln p_X}{d T} = v_K \frac{d \ln p_K}{d T} + v_L \frac{d \ln p_L}{d T}.$$

We refer to this expression as the *Divisia price index of input.*

Divisia indexes have the property that the product of price and quantity indexes for an aggregate is equal to the sum of the values of the components of the aggregate. For example, the product of the price and quantity of aggregate output is equal to the sum of the values of the individual outputs that make up the aggregate. Divisia indexes have the reproductive property that assures consistency among subaggregates, namely, that a Divisia index of Divisia indexes is also a Divisia index. For example, if aggregate output is composed of two subaggregates such as consumption goods and investment goods, the Divisia index of output can be defined, equivalently, as a Divisia index of the components of the two subaggregates or as a Divisia index of Divisia indexes of consumption and investment goods. By duality the reproductive property holds for Divisia price indexes.

11.2.3   Index Numbers

Although Divisia index numbers are useful in relating data on prices and quantities to aggregate output, capital input, and labor input, and to the rate of technical change, our methodology must be extended to include data at discrete points of time. For this purpose we consider a specific form of the production function F:

$$Y = \exp\,[\alpha_o + \alpha_L \ln L + \alpha_K \ln K + \alpha_T T$$
$$+ \tfrac{1}{2}\beta_{KK}\,(\ln K)^2 + \beta_{KL} \ln K \ln L + \beta_{KT}\, T \cdot \ln K$$
$$+ \tfrac{1}{2}\beta_{LL}\,(\ln L)^2 + \beta_{LT} \ln L \cdot T + \tfrac{1}{2}\beta_{TT}T^2].$$

For this production function output is a transcendental or, more specifically, and exponential function of the logarithms of inputs. We refer to this form as the *transcendental logarithmic production function* or, more simply, the translog production function.[11]

The translog production function is characterized by constant returns to scale if and only if the parameters satisfy the conditions

$$\alpha_K + \alpha_L = 1,$$
$$\beta_{KK} + \beta_{KL} = 0,$$
$$\beta_{KL} + \beta_{LL} = 0.$$

11. The translog production function was introduced by Christensen, Jorgenson, and Lau (1971, 1973). The treatment of technical change outlined below is due to Jorgenson and Lau (1977).

The value shares of capital and labor input can be expressed as

$$v_K = \alpha_K + \beta_{KK} \ln K + \beta_{KL} \ln L + \beta_{KT} T,$$

$$v_L = \alpha_L + \beta_{KL} \ln K + \beta_{LL} \ln L + \beta_{LT} T.$$

Finally, the rate of technical change can be expressed as

$$v_T = \alpha_T + \beta_{KT} \ln K + \beta_{LT} \ln L + \beta_{TT} T.$$

If we consider data at any two discrete points of time, say T and $T - 1$, the average rate of technical change can be expressed as the difference between successive logarithms of output less a weighted average of the differences between successive logarithms of capital and labor input with weights given by average value shares:

$$\ln Y(T) - \ln Y(T - 1) = \bar{v}_K[\ln K(T)$$
$$- \ln K(T - 1)]$$
$$+ \bar{v}_L[\ln L(T) - \ln L(T - 1)] + \bar{v}_T,$$

where

$$\bar{v}_K = \tfrac{1}{2}[v_K(T) + v_K(T - 1)],$$

$$\bar{v}_L = \tfrac{1}{2}[v_L(T) + v_L(T - 1)],$$

$$\bar{v}_T = \tfrac{1}{2}[v_T(T) + v_T(T - 1)].$$

We refer to this expression for the average rate of technical change v_T as the *translog index of technical change.*

We can also consider specific forms for the functions defining aggregate output Y, capital input K, and labor input L. For example, the translog form for aggregate output as a function of its components is

$$Y = \exp\,[\alpha_1 \ln Y_1 + \alpha_2 \ln Y_2 + \ldots + \alpha_m \ln Y_m$$
$$+ \tfrac{1}{2}\beta_{11}(\ln Y_1)^2 + \beta_{12} \ln Y_1 \ln Y_2 + \ldots$$
$$+ \tfrac{1}{2}\beta_{mm}(\ln Y_m)^2].$$

The translog output aggregate is characterized by constant returns to scale if and only if

$$\alpha_1 + \alpha_2 + \ldots + \alpha_m = 1,$$
$$\beta_{11} + \beta_{12} + \ldots + \beta_{1m} = 0,$$
$$\cdots \cdots \cdots \cdots \cdots$$
$$\beta_{1m} + \beta_{2m} + \ldots + \beta_{mm} = 0.$$

The value shares of individual outputs $\{w_{Yi}\}$ can be expressed as

$$w_{Yi} = \alpha_i + \beta_{1i} \ln Y_1 + \dots$$

$$+ \beta_{im} \ln Y_i, \qquad (i = 1, 2, \dots, m).$$

Considering data at discrete points of time, the difference between successive logarithms of aggregate output can be expressed as a weighted average of differences between successive logarithms of individual outputs with weights given by average value shares:

$$\ln Y(T) - \ln Y(T-1) = \Sigma \bar{w}_{Yi} [\ln Y_i(T)$$

$$- \ln Y_i(T-1)],$$

where

$$\bar{w}_{Yi} = \tfrac{1}{2}[w_{Yi}(T) + w_{Yi}(T-1)],$$

$$(i = 1, 2, \dots, m).$$

Similarly, if aggregate capital and labor input are translog functions of their components, we can express the difference between successive logarithms in the form

$$\ln K(T) - \ln K(T-1) = \Sigma \bar{v}_{Kj}[\ln K_j(T)$$

$$- \ln K_j(T-1)],$$

$$\ln L(T) - \ln L(T-1) = \Sigma \bar{v}_{Lk}[\ln L_k(T)$$

$$- \ln L_k(T-1)],$$

where

$$\bar{v}_{Kj} = \tfrac{1}{2}[v_{Kj}(T) + v_{Kj}(T-1)], \qquad (j = 1, 2, \dots, n);$$

$$\bar{v}_{Lk} = \tfrac{1}{2}[v_{Lk}(T) + v_{Lk}(T-1)], \qquad (k = 1, 2, \dots, p).$$

We refer to these expressions for aggregate output, capital input, and labor input as *translog indexes of output, capital input, and labor input.*[12]

To define price indexes corresponding to translog indexes of aggregate output, capital input, and labor input, we employ the fact that the

---

12. The quantity indexes were introduced by Fisher (1922) and discussed by Tornquist (1937), Theil (1965), and Kloek (1966). These indexes of output and input were first derived from the translog production function by Diewert (1976). The corresponding index of technical change was introduced by Christensen and Jorgenson (1970). The translog index of technical change was first derived from the form of the translog production function given above by Jorgenson and Lau (1977). The approach developed by Jorgenson and Lau does not require the assumption of Hicks neutrality. Diewert had interpreted the ratio of translog indexes of output and input as an index of technical change under the assumption of Hicks neutrality.

product of price and quantity indexes for each aggregate must be equal to the sum of the values of the components of the aggregate. For example, the price index for aggregate output is defined as the ratio of the sum of the values of the individual outputs to the translog output index. Price indexes for capital and labor input can be defined in a strictly analogous way. Although the resulting aggregate price indexes do not have the form of translog index numbers, these price indexes are nonetheless well defined. Each aggregate price index can be determined solely from data on prices and quantities of the components of the aggregate. By definition, the product of price and quantity indexes for an aggregate is equal to the sum of the values of its components. However, these indexes do not have the reproductive property that a translog index of translog indexes remains a translog index. The translog index for an aggregate depends on the structure of the subaggregates on which it is defined.[13]

11.2.4   Productivity Change

Our methodology for separating growth in real factor input from growth in total factor productivity is based on translog index numbers of aggregate output, capital input, labor input, and technical change. These index numbers provide a direct connection between the economic theory of production and technical change and data on prices and quantities of output and input at discrete points of time. We find it useful to develop further implications of our methodology for data on capital and labor input. The measurement of capital input begins with data on the stock of capital for each component of capital input. Similarly, the measurement of labor input begins with data on hours worked for each component of labor input. It is important to be explicit about the relationship between these data and the aggregates for capital and labor input defined by translog index numbers.

For a single type of capital input we first characterize the relative efficiency of capital goods of different ages by means of a sequence of nonnegative numbers—$d(0)$, $d(1)$, ... We normalize the efficiency of a new capital good at unity,

$$d(0) = 1,$$

so that the remaining elements in the sequence represent the efficiency of capital goods of every age relative to the efficiency of a new capital good. We assume that relative efficiency is nonincreasing with age, say τ, so that

$$d(\tau) - d(\tau - 1) \leqslant 0, \qquad (\tau = 1, 2, \ldots),$$

---

13. This corrects an error in Christensen and Jorgenson (1973a), p. 261.

and that every capital good is eventually retired or scrapped, so that relative efficiency eventually drops to zero:

$$\lim_{\tau \to \infty} d(\tau) = 0.$$

The stock of capital, say $A(T)$, is the sum of past investments, say $I(T - \tau)$, each weighted by relative efficiency:

$$A(T) = \sum_{\tau=0}^{\infty} d_\tau I(T - \tau).$$

Similarly, the price of acquisition of new capital goods, say $p_I(T)$, is the discounted value of the future prices of capital input, say $p_K(T + \tau)$, weighted by relative efficiency:

$$p_I(T) = \sum_{\tau=0}^{\infty} d_\tau \prod_{S=1}^{\tau} \frac{1}{1 + r(T + S)} p_K(T + \tau + 1),$$

where $r(T)$ is the *rate of return on capital* in period T and $\prod_{S=1}^{\tau} [1/1 + r(T + S)]$ is the discount factor in period T for future prices in period $T + S$.

Using data on decline in efficiency, estimates of capital stock can be compiled from data on prices and quantities of investment in new capital goods at every point of time by means of the perpetual inventory method.[14] We assume that relative efficiency of capital goods declines geometrically with age:

$$d_\tau = (1 - \delta)^\tau, \qquad (\tau = 0, 1, \ldots).$$

Under this assumption capital stock is a weighted sum of past investments with geometrically declining weights:

$$A(T) = \sum_{\tau=0}^{\infty} (1 - \delta)^\tau I(T - \tau).$$

Similarly, the price of investment goods is a weighted sum of future prices of capital input with the same weights:

$$p_I(T) = \sum_{\tau=0}^{\infty} (1 - \delta)^\tau$$

$$\prod_{S=1}^{\tau} \frac{1}{1 + r(T + S)} p_K(T + \tau + 1).$$

14. The perpetual inventory method has been employed by Goldsmith (1955) and in the BEA Capital Stock Study (1976). The dual to the perpetual inventory method, involving investment goods prices and capital input prices, was introduced by Christensen and Jorgenson (1969, 1973a). For further discussion of the underlying model of durable capital goods, see Jorgenson (1973).

Capital stock at the end of each period is equal to investment during the period less a constant proportion δ of capital stock at the beginning of the period:

$$A(T) = I(T) - \delta A(T-1).$$

Similarly, the price of capital input is equal to the sum of the nominal return to capital $p_I(T-1)$ $r(T)$ and depreciation $\delta p_I(T)$, less revaluation $p_I(T) - p_I(T-1)$:

$$p_K(T) = p_I(T-1)r(T) + \delta p_I(T)$$
$$- [p_I(T) - p_I(T-1)].$$

We can also express the price of capital input as the sum of the price of investment $p_I(T-1)$ multiplied by the *own rate of return on capital*

$$r(T) - \frac{p_I(T) - p_I(T-1)}{p_I(T-1)}$$

and depreciation:

$$p_K(T) = p_I(T-1)\left[r(T) - \frac{p_I(T) - p_I(T-1)}{p_I(T-1)}\right]$$
$$+ \delta\, p_I(T).$$

Second, for each of the components of capital input $\{K_j(T)\}$ the flow of capital services is proportional to the stock of capital at the end of the preceding period, say $\{A_j(T-1)\}$:

$$K_j(T) = Q_{Kj}A_j(T-1), \qquad (j = 1, 2, \ldots, n),$$

where the constants of proportionality $\{Q_{Kj}\}$ transform capital stock into a flow of capital services per period of time. For example, the flow of capital services from a group of machines is measured as the services of the machines per period of time while the stock of capital is measured as the number of machines. The flow of capital services reflects the own rate of return to capital and the rate of depreciation, both expressed per period of time, as well as the quantity of capital stock. The flow of services per unit of stock varies from one type of capital to another, so that the constants $\{Q_{Kj}\}$ can be taken as measures of the quality of capital stock in producing capital services.

The translog index of aggregate capital input can be expressed in terms of its components or in terms of capital stocks:

$$\ln K(T) - \ln K(T-1)$$
$$= \Sigma \bar{v}_j[\ln K_j(T) - \ln K_j(T-1)],$$
$$= \Sigma \bar{v}_j[\ln A_j(T-1) - \ln A_j(T-2)].$$

If we define the stock of capital at the beginning of the preceding time period, say $A(T-1)$, as a translog index of its components,

$$\ln A(T-1) - \ln A(T-2)$$
$$= \Sigma \bar{v}_{Aj}[\ln A_j(T-1) - \ln A_j(T-2)],$$

with weights given by the value shares of the individual capital stocks $\{v_{Aj}\}$ and

$$\bar{v}_{Aj} = \tfrac{1}{2}[v_{Aj}(T-1) + v_{Aj}(T-2)],$$
$$(j = 1, 2, \ldots, n).$$

We define an *index of the quality of capital stock*, say $Q_K(T)$, that transforms the translog index of capital stock into the translog index of capital input:

$$K(T) = Q_K(T)\, A(T-1).$$

Our index of the quality of capital stock can be expressed in the form

$$\ln Q_K(T) - \ln Q_K(T-1)$$
$$= \Sigma \bar{v}_j[\ln A_j(T-1) - A_j(T-2)]$$
$$- [\ln A(T-1) - \ln A(T-2)],$$

so that this index reflects changes in the composition of capital. If all components of capital stock are growing at the same rate, quality remains unchanged. If components with higher flows of capital input per unit of stock are growing more rapidly, quality will increase. If components with lower flows per unit of stock are growing more rapidly, quality will decline.

Second, for each of the components of labor input $\{L_k(T)\}$ the flow of labor services is proportional to hours worked, say $\{H_k(T)\}$:

$$L_k(T) = Q_{Lk}H_k(T), \qquad (k = 1, 2, \ldots, p),$$

where the constants of proportionality $\{Q_{Lk}\}$ transform hours worked into a flow of labor services per period of time. The flow of services varies from one type of labor to another, so that the constants $\{Q_{Lk}\}$ can be taken as measures of the quality of hours worked in producing labor services.

The translog index of aggregate labor input can be expressed in terms of its components or in terms of hours worked:

$$\ln L(T) - \ln L(T-1)$$
$$= \Sigma \bar{v}_k[\ln L_k(T) - \ln L_k(T-1)],$$
$$= \Sigma \bar{v}_k[\ln H_k(T) - \ln H_k(T-1)].$$

If we define hours worked, say $H(T)$, as the unweighted sum of its components,

$$H(T) = \Sigma H_k(T),$$

we can define an *index of the quality of hours worked*, say $Q_L(T)$, that transforms hours worked into the translog index of labor input:

$$L(T) = Q_L(T) \, H(T).$$

Our index of the quality of hours worked can be expressed in the form

$$\ln Q_L(T) - \ln Q_L(T-1)$$
$$= \Sigma \bar{v}_k[\ln H_k(T) - \ln H_k(T-1)]$$
$$- [\ln H(T) - \ln H(T-1)],$$

so that this index reflects changes in the composition of hours worked. Quality remains unchanged if all components of hours worked are growing at the same rate. Quality rises if components with higher flows of labor input per hour worked are growing more rapidly and falls if components with lower flows of input per hour are growing more rapidly.

We have decomposed the rate of growth of the translog index of aggregate output into the sum of a weighted average of the rates of growth of translog indexes of aggregate capital and labor input and the rate of technical change. Using the indexes of capital and labor quality, we can decompose the rate of growth of output as follows:

$$\ln Y(T) - \ln Y(T-1)$$
$$= \bar{v}_k[\ln K(T) - \ln K(T-1)] + \bar{v}_L[\ln L(T)$$
$$- \ln L(T-1)] + \bar{v}_T$$
$$= \bar{v}_K[\ln Q_K(T) - \ln Q_K(T-1)] + \bar{v}_K[\ln A(T-1)$$
$$- \ln A(T-2)] + \bar{v}_L[\ln Q_L(T) - \ln Q_L(T-1)]$$
$$+ \bar{v}_L[\ln H(T) - \ln H(T-1)] + \bar{v}_T.$$

The rate of growth of output is the sum of a weighted average of the rates of growth of capital stock and hours worked, a weighted average of the rates of growth of quality of capital stock and hours worked, and the rate of technical change.

11.3 Production Account

11.3.1 Introduction

Our next objective is to identify output, capital input, labor input, and technical change with accounts for real product, real capital input, real labor input, and total factor productivity for each of the nine countries included in our study. It is important to emphasize that only the translog indexes of output, capital input, labor input, and technical change can be derived from the theoretical model of production we have presented in section 11.2. The stock of capital, the number of hours worked, and the indexes of quality of capital stock and hours worked are purely descriptive measures. Similarly, the index of total input is a descriptive measure unless we assume that technical change is Hicks-neutral. This assumption is not required in constructing production accounts for each country in this section or in the international and intertemporal comparisons given in section 11.4 below. Wherever we provide comparisons in terms of real factor input, corresponding comparisons can be provided in terms of real product and total factor productivity without using an index of total input.

In this section we outline the principles we have followed in constructing production accounts for the nine countries in our study. A description of the complete accounting system and details of its empirical implementation for the U.S.A. can be found in Christensen and Jorgenson (1973a). A brief description of the sources and methods used to construct the production account for each country is contained in the Appendix. Our summary of sources and methods is based on detailed reports on the data construction for each country. These reports are listed among our references and are available from the authors. The Appendix also includes annual time series of real product, real capital input, real labor input, and total factor productivity for each country.

11.3.2 Product and Factor Outlay

The starting point for the construction of translog indexes of output and technical change is the measurement of the value of total product and the value of total factor outlay in current prices. The fundamental accounting identity for the production account is that the value of total product equals the value of total factor outlay. We exclude indirect business taxes unrelated to factor outlay, such as retail sales taxes and excise taxes, from the value of total product; however, indirect business taxes which are part of the outlay on factor services, such as property taxes, are retained in the value of total factor outlay and total product. Our concept of output is intermediate between output at market prices and output at factor cost.

The production account in a complete system of national economic accounts includes the activities of the private sector, the government sector, and the rest of the world. In analyzing productive activity and its distribution between consumption and investment on the output side and between capital and labor on the input side we have limited the scope of our production account to the private domestic sector of each country. Rest of the world production is excluded on the grounds that it can reflect a different physical and social environment for productive activity than the environment provided for the domestic sector.

The boundary between private and government activity varies from country to country within our study, because of variations in the role of government enterprises. While government administration must be excluded from our private domestic production account, essentially similar economic activities—telecommunications, transportation, and public utilities—are conducted by government enterprises and by private enterprises. For some of the countries included in our study it is impossible to obtain separate accounts for government and private enterprises. For the United States, on the other hand, the government enterprises are treated in a manner that is more closely analogous to the treatment of government administration than to the treatment of private enterprises. No capital accounts are maintained for government enterprises and government administration separately. Of course, government enterprises produce an almost negligible proportion of the gross national product of the U.S.A. To provide international comparability in the scope of our product measure we have included government enterprise product for all countries.

The inclusion of government enterprises in gross private domestic product should not result in confusion since "private" gross national product includes government enterprises in the official national income and product accounts of all nine countries. One unconventional aspect of our measure of total output is an imputation for the services of consumer durables. Our objective is to attain consistency in the treatment of owner-occupied residential structures and owner-utilized consumer durable equipment. It is standard procedure for national income accounts to include an imputation for owner-occupied housing in national product but not to include an analogous imputation for consumer durables. Our measure of total input is gross private domestic factor outlay, which is equal to gross private domestic product. Table 11.A.1 gives (for each country) a complete reconciliation of gross private domestic product and factor outlay with gross national product and national income.[15]

15. There are four appendix tables for each country, numbered 11.A.1 through 11.A.4. Table 11.A.1C is table 11.A.1 for Canada, and so on.

The product and factor outlay accounts are linked through capital formation and the compensation of property. To make this link explicit we divide total output between consumption and investment goods and total factor outlay between labor and property compensation. We include all services and nondurable goods in consumption goods; we include all structures and producer and consumer durable equipment in investment goods. Data for the U.S.A. are available for a complete separation of gross private domestic product between consumption goods and investment goods. For all nine countries it has been possible to separate gross private domestic product between consumption goods and investment goods, except for inventory investment and net exports. In table 11.A.2 we present time series for gross private domestic product. We also present time series for consumption goods product and investment goods product. Inventory investment and net exports are presented separately for countries where they could not be allocated between consumption goods and investment goods. The value shares of investment goods product for each country are presented in table 11.2.

To divide total factor outlay between labor and property compensation, it is necessary to allocate the factor outlay for self-employed persons between labor and property compensation. We have used the method of Christensen (1971) to impute labor compensation to self-employed workers. This involves assigning the estimated wage rate for employees to the self-employed. Christensen has shown that for the U.S.A. this method results in an allocation which is consistent with the assumption that after-tax rates of return are equal in the corporate and noncorporate sectors. The resulting division of gross private domestic factor outlay into labor and property compensation is presented in table 11.A.2 for all nine countries. The value shares of property compensation for each country are presented in table 11.3.

11.3.3   Real Capital Input

The starting point for the computation of a translog quantity index of capital input is a perpetual inventory estimate of the stock of each type of capital, based on past investments in constant prices. At each point of time the stock of each type of capital is the sum of past investments weighted by relative efficiency. Under the assumption that the efficiency of capital goods declines geometrically, the rate of replacement for the jth capital good, say δ_j, is a constant. Capital stock at the end of each period can be estimated from investment during the period and capital stock at the beginning of the period:

$$A_j(T) = I_j(T) + (1 - \delta_j)A_j(T - 1),$$

$$(i = 1, 2, \ldots, n).$$

Table 11.2 Value Share of Investment Goods Product, 1947–73

Year	Canada	France	Germany	Italy	Japan	Korea	Netherlands	United Kingdom	United States
1947	.275								.281
1948	.294								.308
1949	.300								.290
1950	.307	.243	.304						.340
1951	.294	.255	.324				.251		.340
1952	.297	.249	.336	.247	.298		.243		.321
1953	.299	.242	.321	.252	.271		.272		.317
1954	.296	.249	.339	.258	.274		.279		.306
1955	.302	.262	.368	.266	.295		.297	.213	.337
1956	.327	.264	.362	.267	.334		.310	.216	.334
1957	.332	.272	.365	.277	.372		.322	.223	.327
1958	.313	.274	.359	.272	.322		.300	.227	.298
1959	.306	.272	.363	.278	.351		.316	.235	.318
1960	.297	.276	.386	.289	.389	.126	.325	.238	.301
1961	.292	.287	.391	.300	.450	.133	.326	.238	.295
1962	.300	.292	.396	.305	.414	.152	.326	.233	.306
1963	.309	.294	.390	.309	.421	.161	.319	.234	.310
1964	.313	.309	.414	.290	.429	.139	.342	.253	.311
1965	.326	.311	.422	.269	.408	.169	.341	.251	.318
1966	.336	.317	.398	.263	.414	.227	.340	.246	.318
1967	.329	.317	.358	.269	.443	.232	.343	.253	.305
1968	.330	.319	.389	.276	.458	.270	.348	.257	.308
1969	.324	.326	.412	.281	.463	.282	.334	.250	.304
1970	.324	.327	.424	.284	.482	.264	.349	.254	.293
1971	.321	.331	.420	.284	.469	.250	.347	.258	.298
1972	.323	.333	.409	.280	.460	.224	.333	.255	.305
1973	.323	.333	.405	.281	.486	.265	.329	.264	.308

We have compiled time series of capital stock estimates for seven asset classes: consumer durables, nonresidential structures, producer durable equipment, residential structures, nonfarm inventories, farm inventories, and land. For each of the seven asset classes we derive perpetual inventory estimates of the stock as follows: First, we obtain a benchmark estimate of capital stock from data on national wealth in constant prices. Second, we deflate the investment series from the national income and product accounts to obtain investment in constant prices. Third, we choose an estimate of the rate of replacement from data on lifetimes of capital goods. Finally, we estimate capital stock in every period by applying the perpetual inventory method as outlined in section 11.2 above.

Each type of capital stock can be valued in current prices by using an index of the acquisition prices for new capital goods. We employ the investment goods price indexes to convert stocks of assets in constant prices to stocks of assets in current prices. These values can be employed in estimating value shares by class of assets. The value shares and stocks can be combined to obtain a translog quantity index of aggregate capital stock. The price index of capital stock is obtained by dividing the value of all assets by the translog quantity index. The price and quantity indexes of private domestic capital stock are presented in table 11.A.3. Value shares of the seven assets in each country are presented for 1970 in table 11.4.

To construct translog price and quantity indexes of capital input we require value shares of individual capital inputs in total property compensation and stocks of individual assets. In the absence of taxation the value of the jth capital input is the sum of depreciation and the own return to capital, defined as the nominal return less revaluation:

$$p_{Kj}(T)K_j(T) = \{p_{Ij}(T-1)r(T) + p_{Ij}(T)\delta_j$$
$$- [p_{Ij}(T) - p_{Ij}(T-1)]\}A_j(T-1)$$
$$(j = 1, 2, \ldots, n).$$

Given property compensation, the stock of assets, the price of acquisition of capital stock, and the rate of depreciation, we can determine the nominal rate of return. The nominal rate of return is equal to the ratio of property compensation less depreciation plus revaluation of assets to the value of capital stock at the beginning of the period.

In measuring the rate of return, differences in tax treatment of property compensation must be taken into account. For tax purposes the private domestic sector can be divided into corporate business, noncorporate business, and households and nonprofit institutions. Households and institutions are not subject to direct taxes on the flow of capital services which they utilize. Noncorporate business is subject to personal

Table 11.3   Value Share of Capital Input, 1947–73

Year	Canada	France	Germany	Italy	Japan	Korea	Netherlands	United Kingdom	United States
1947	.346								.368
1948	.376								.378
1949	.397								.381
1950	.413	.439	.340						.389
1951	.406	.387	.348	.419	.382		.474		.403
1952	.430	.376	.368	.420	.334		.480		.402
1953	.426	.396	.361	.394	.335		.467		.389
1954	.418	.386	.358	.403	.336		.469		.390
1955	.449	.381	.371				.483	.385	.401
1956	.443	.372	.369	.399	.351		.482	.370	.395
1957	.423	.377	.373	.400	.362		.468	.379	.386
1958	.441	.360	.369	.402	.346		.454	.381	.394
1959	.444	.366	.386	.407	.362		.459	.386	.401
1960	.444	.389	.396	.409	.391	.326	.465	.385	.400
1961	.447	.385	.389	.418	.433	.393	.448	.381	.404
1962	.448	.384	.379	.415	.401	.385	.443	.378	.408
1963	.460	.387	.385	.389	.398	.401	.437	.389	.412
1964	.470	.394	.395	.379	.422	.422	.432	.387	.415
1965	.467	.398	.400	.385	.402	.395	.432	.384	.421
1966	.462	.431	.400	.396	.415	.383	.416	.383	.428
1967	.440	.436	.405	.390	.431	.323	.424	.389	.425
1968	.442	.432	.423	.391	.442	.340	.433	.394	.418
1969	.436	.441	.421	.404	.441	.333	.422	.386	.414
1970	.434	.443	.413	.374	.436	.355	.413	.371	.404
1971	.441	.435	.405	.332	.409	.341	.415	.387	.401
1972	.430	.439	.409	.331	.405	.354	.421	.405	.410
1973	.470	.439	.404	.329	.396	.378	.410	.404	.418

Table 11.4   Value Shares of Capital Stock by Asset Class, 1970

	Canada	France	Germany	Italy	Japan	Korea	Nether-lands	United Kingdom	United States
Consumer Durables	.106	.067	.076	.081	.055	.024	.094	.086	.137
Nonresidential Structures	.233	.150	.193	.180	.376	.140	.192	.205	.157
Producer Durables	.156	.198	.222	.173		.114	.206	.316	.136
Residential Structures	.200	.276	.294	.371	.188	.146	.253	.168	.216
Nonfarm Inventories	.067	.111	.078	.077	.139	.058	.091	.105	.077
Farm Inventories	.017					.032		.019	.012
Land	.222	.198	.136	.117	.243	.485	.163	.101	.263

income taxes on income generated from capital services, while corporate business is subject to both corporate and personal income taxes. Households and corporate and noncorporate business are subject to indirect taxes on property income through taxes levied on the value of property. In order to take these differences into account we allocate each class of assets among the four sectors. For all countries, households and institutions have been treated separately from the business sector; for some of the countries it was not possible to separate the corporate and noncorporate sectors.

Property compensation associated with assets in the household sector is not taxed directly; however, part of the income is taxed indirectly through property taxes. To incorporate property taxes into our indexes of the price and quantity of capital services we add property taxes to the return to capital and depreciation in the definition of the value of the jth capital input:

$$p_{Kj}(T)K_j(T) = \{p_{Ij}(T-1)r(T) + p_{Ij}(T)\delta_j$$
$$- [p_{Ij}(T) - p_{Ij}(T-1)] + p_{Ij}(T)t_j(T)\}A_j(T-1)$$
$$(j = 1, 2, \ldots, n),$$

where t_j is the rate of property taxation. The nominal rate of return is the ratio of property compensation less depreciation plus revaluation of capital assets less property taxes to the value of capital stock at the beginning of the period.

Given the nominal rate of return for households and institutions, we can construct estimates of capital input prices for each class of assets held by households and institutions—land held by households and institutions, residential structures, nonresidential structures, producer durables, and consumer durables. These estimates require acquisition prices for each capital good, rates of replacement, rates of property taxation for assets held by households, and the nominal rate of return for the sector as a whole. We employ separate effective tax rates for owner-occupied residential property, both land and structures, and for consumer durables. Finally, we combine the price and quantity of capital input for each class of asset into a translog index of capital input for households and institutions.

To obtain an estimate of the noncorporate rate of return we deduct property taxes from noncorporate property compensation, add revaluation of assets, subtract depreciation, and divide the result by the value of noncorporate assets at the beginning of the period. The noncorporate rate of return is gross of personal income taxes on noncorporate property compensation. Property compensation of households and institutions is not subject to the personal income tax. The value of property compensation in the noncorporate sector is equal to the value of the flow of capital services from residential and nonresidential structures, producer durable equipment, farm and nonfarm inventories, and land held by the sector. All farm inventories are assigned to the noncorporate sector. Given the noncorporate rate of return, estimated from noncorporate property compensation by the method outlined above, and given data on prices of acquisition, stocks, tax rates, and replacement rates for each class of assets, we can estimate capital input prices for each class of assets. Price and quantity data are combined into a translog index of the quantity of capital input for the noncorporate sector.

We next consider the measurement of prices and quantities of capital input for corporate business. To obtain an estimate of the corporate rate of return we must take into account the corporate income tax. For the U.S.A. the value of capital input for the corporate sector, modified to incorporate the corporate income tax and indirect business taxes, becomes

$$p_{Kj}(T)K_j(T) = \left(\left[\frac{1 - u(T)z_j(T) - k_j(T) + y_j(T)}{1 - u(T)}\right]\right.$$
$$\times \{p_{Ij}(T-1)r(T) + p_{Ij}(T)\delta_j$$
$$- [p_{Ij}(T) - p_{Ij}(T-1)]\} + p_{Ij}(T)t_j(T)\Big)$$
$$\times A_j(T-1) \qquad\qquad (j = 1, 2, \ldots, n),$$

where $u(T)$ is the corporate tax rate, $z_j(T)$ is the present value of depreciation allowances on one dollar's investment, $k_j(T)$ is the investment tax credit, and $y_j(T) = k_j(T)u(T)z_j(T)$ for 1962 and 1963 and zero for all other years. The tax credit is different from zero only for producers' durables. Depreciation allowances are different from zero only for producers' durables and structures. For other countries this formula has been adopted in order to reflect the corporate tax structure in each country.

Our method for estimating the corporate nominal rate of return is the same as for the noncorporate nominal rate of return. Property compensation in the corporate sector is the sum of the value of services from residential and nonresidential structures, producer durable equipment, nonfarm inventories, and land held by that sector. To estimate the nominal rate of return in the corporate sector we require estimates of the variables that describe the corporate tax structure—the effective corporate tax rate, the present value of depreciation allowances, and the investment tax credit. We obtain estimates of all the variables—acquisition prices and stocks of assets, rates of replacement, and variables describing the tax structure—that enter the value of capital input except, of course, for the nominal rate of return. We then determine the nominal rate of return from these variables and total corporate property compensation.

To estimate the nominal rate of return in the corporate sector our first step is to subtract property taxes from total property compensation before taxes. The second step is to subtract corporate profits tax liability. We then add revaluation of assets, subtract depreciation, and divide the result by the value of corporate assets at the beginning of the period. The corporate rate of return is gross of personal income taxes, but net of the corporate income tax. We estimate the price of capital input for each asset employed in the corporate sector by substituting the corporate rate of return into the corresponding formula for the price of capital input. These formulas also depend on acquisition prices of capital assets, rates of replacement, and variables describing the tax structure. Data on the stock of each class of assets are constructed by the perpetual inventory method. Price and quantity data of capital input by class of asset are combined into a translog index of the quantity of capital input for the corporate sector.

It is interesting to compare the rate of return on capital over time and across countries. In table 11.5 we present own rates of return for the business sector. These rates of return are computed as a weighted average of own rates of return on corporate and noncorporate assets, using the value of assets at the beginning of the period in each sector as weights. Own rates of return are adjusted for differences in rates of inflation over time and across countries. Capital input prices depend only on own rates of return. Nominal rates of return for the business sector are presented in table 11.A.3 for each country included in our study.

The price and quantity index numbers for capital input in the various sectors can be combined into a price and quantity index for the private domestic sector. The quantity index is a translog index number, and the price index is defined as the ratio of property compensation to the quantity index. The price and quantity indexes of private domestic capital input are presented in table 11.A.3. Growth rates of real capital input computed from quantity indexes in table 11.A.3 are presented for each country in table 11.6. The quality of capital is defined as the ratio of the quantity index of capital services to the quantity index of capital stock. The quality of capital index is also presented in table 11.A.3.

11.3.4   Real Product and Factor Input

To construct a quantity index of labor input, it would be desirable to use the formula for a translog labor index for a large number of skill classifications. Classifications could be defined by level of education, sex, age, occupation, and so on. Following Jorgenson and Griliches (1967), we have limited our consideration to a single skill measure—

Table 11.5   Own Rate of Return to Capital in the Business Sector, 1947–73

Year	Canada	France	Germany	Italy	Japan	Korea	Netherlands	United Kingdom	United States
1947	.057								.078
1948	.068								.079
1949	.072								.063
1950	.070	.093	.053						.066
1951	.058	.069	.065	.049	.044		.057		.071
1952	.073	.058	.071	.057	.030		.045		.059
1953	.066	.066	.065	.050	.037		.053		.052
1954	.053	.063	.067	.063	.048		.066		.052
1955	.066	.062	.082				.072	.071	.061
1956	.075	.059	.079	.063	.057		.067	.072	.050
1957	.059	.059	.079	.063	.056		.065	.071	.048
1958	.061	.050	.073	.068	.042		.056	.067	.049
1959	.060	.049	.079	.073	.052		.061	.072	.051
1960	.055	.064	.087	.078	.072	.059	.067	.081	.046
1961	.050	.061	.079	.088	.102	.091	.057	.081	.049
1962	.055	.062	.069	.086	.079	.083	.055	.073	.059
1963	.060	.061	.067	.075	.085	.144	.050	.081	.061
1964	.064	.066	.072	.062	.108	.182	.057	.089	.063
1965	.067	.066	.074	.067	.092	.138	.054	.085	.072
1966	.066	.081	.069	.077	.107	.137	.046	.078	.077
1967	.053	.081	.061	.080	.129	.093	.051	.079	.068
1968	.054	.081	.075	.080	.144	.103	.053	.081	.062
1969	.046	.088	.075	.092	.138	.108	.053	.069	.054
1970	.049	.085	.079	.074	.137	.098	.051	.057	.046
1971	.047	.080	.070	.046	.109	.099	.046	.065	.048
1972	.045	.083	.067	.042	.105	.102	.047	.066	.055
1973	.065	.083	.064	.035	.101	.128	.044	.058	.058

Table 11.6   Annual Rates of Growth of Real Private Domestic Capital Input, 1947–73

Year	Canada	France	Germany	Italy	Japan	Korea	Nether-lands	United Kingdom	United States
1948	.092								.067
1949	.072								.063
1950	.071								.042
1951	.083	.054	.043						.067
1952	.073	.042	.052						.054
1953	.066	.039	.070	.019	.014				.037
1954	.074	.044	.068	.027	−.003				.039
1955	.049	.048	.075	.027	.016				.032
1956	.064	.051	.088	.034	.017		.055	.053	.052
1957	.080	.055	.080	.038	.078		.064	.035	.042
1958	.065	.052	.077	.040	.119		.062	.040	.034
1959	.049	.045	.073	.037	.054		.035	.044	.018
1960	.048	.042	.069	.042	.069		.041	.051	.034
1961	.043	.054	.082	.055	.109	.006	.061	.056	.031
1962	.036	.059	.079	.066	.157	.013	.071	.049	.023
1963	.041	.064	.079	.070	.113	.027	.073	.039	.034
1964	.045	.066	.067	.078	.089	.039	.063	.046	.039
1965	.054	.070	.077	.049	.117	.037	.073	.060	.043
1966	.065	.061	.084	.036	.089	.031	.074	.051	.053
1967	.068	.064	.066	.039	.083	.088	.062	.041	.057
1968	.054	.060	.041	.052	.117	.113	.057	.043	.044
1969	.049	.059	.055	.049	.140	.132	.059	.045	.046
1970	.051	.067	.071	.053	.138	.127	.060	.034	.046
1971	.037	.064	.076	.060	.148	.096	.076	.035	.031
1972	.044	.062	.073	.049	.123	.090	.067	.047	.035
1973	.052	.064	.062	.046	.116	.054	.062	.059	.045

educational attainment. This results in a quality of labor index which we apply to total man-hours in the private domestic sector. In table 11.A.4 we present the components of real labor input for the private domestic sector. The first column gives total persons engaged in production. The second column gives average hours worked per person engaged. The quality index is presented in the third column. The product of the first three columns provides the quantity index for private domestic labor input. The quantity index is scaled to equal labor compensation in the base year. The ratio of labor compensation to the quantity index gives the price index for private domestic labor input. Growth rates of real labor input computed from quantity indexes in table 11.A.4 are presented in table 11.7.

The quantity indexes of private domestic capital and labor input can be combined into a translog quantity index of private domestic factor input. The price index is then computed as the ratio of the value of private domestic input to the quantity index. The price and quantity indexes are presented for each country in table 11.A.5. Growth rates of real factor input computed from the quantity indexes in table 11.A.5 are presented in table 11.8.

Given measures of total product in current prices, the remaining task is to separate these data into price and quantity components. Total product is first divided between investment goods and consumption goods. These components of total product are separated into price and quantity components using deflators from the national income and product accounts. The quantity indexes for consumption and investment goods are then combined using translog index numbers. Price indexes are constructed so that the product of price and quantity indexes equals the current dollar magnitude. Since inventory investment and net exports can be negative, quantity indexes are added to the quantity index of consumption and investment goods to obtain the quantity index of gross private domestic product. For each country the price and quantity indexes of gross private domestic product are presented in table 11.A.5. Growth rates of real product computed from quantity indexes in table 11.A.5 are presented for each country in table 11.9. Finally, an index of total factor productivity, defined as the ratio of real product to real factor input, is presented for each country in table 11.A.5. Growth rates of total factor productivity computed from the data in table 11.A.5 are presented in table 11.10.

11.4   International Comparisons

11.4.1   Introduction

Our international comparisons are based on growth of output, input, and total factor productivity for the nine countries included in our study.

Table 11.7   Annual Rates of Growth of Real Private Domestic Labor Input, 1947–73

Year	Canada	France	Germany	Italy	Japan	Korea	Nether-lands	United Kingdom	United States
1948	.013								.016
1949	.017								-.039
1950	-.019								.038
1951	.020	.016	.030						.044
1952	.011	-.006	.022				-.006		.010
1953	.014	-.007	.029	.032	.049		.024		.017
1954	-.005	.010	.035	.038	.027		.024		-.034
1955	.017	.003	.044	-.001	.040		.023		.035
1956	.043	.005	.015	-.001	.077		.020	.005	.021
1957	.014	.010	-.014	.018	.049		.006	-.020	-.008
1958	-.015	-.007	-.009	.002	.035		-.006	-.012	-.027
1959	.031	-.006	-.006	.009	.046		.020	.024	.041
1960	.010	.015	.012	.027	.059		.025	.014	.013
1961	-.021	.004	-.000	.009	.013	.061	-.029	.022	-.005
1962	.029	.007	-.016	-.022	.022	.019	.026	.002	.028
1963	.017	.008	-.016	.009	.026	.041	.021	.014	.016
1964	.031	.013	.012	-.035	.030	-.002	.013	.018	.021
1965	.032	-.006	-.008	-.069	.043	.106	.014	-.002	.037
1966	.027	.012	-.019	.027	.027	.030	.011	-.013	.038
1967	.019	-.002	-.058	.034	.038	.057	-.018	-.015	.015
1968	.002	-.007	.018	.013	.034	.079	.014	-.000	.024
1969	.019	.017	.016	-.020	.014	.063	.016	.005	.032
1970	-.001	.008	.006	.019	.018	.002	-.004	-.027	-.011
1971	.019	-.002	-.022	-.025	.012	.066	-.001	-.053	.006
1972	.027	-.003	-.016	-.026	.014	.064	-.018	.010	.038
1973	.054	.007	-.003	-.004	.033	.066	-.004	.038	.050

Table 11.8   Annual Rates of Growth of Real Private Domestic Factor Input, 1947–73

Year	Canada	France	Germany	Italy	Japan	Korea	Netherlands	United Kingdom	United States
1948	.042								.035
1949	.038								−.000
1950	.017								.040
1951	.046	.032	.034						.054
1952	.037	.012	.033				.009		.027
1953	.036	.011	.044	.026	.036		.015		.025
1954	.028	.023	.047	.034	.017		.023		−.005
1955	.031	.020	.055	.010	.032		.037		.034
1956	.052	.022	.042	.013	.056		.037	.023	.033
1957	.043	.027	.021	.026	.059		.034	.001	.011
1958	.020	.014	.023	.017	.064		.025	.007	−.003
1959	.039	.013	.024	.020	.048		.027	.032	.032
1960	.027	.025	.034	.033	.063		.032	.028	.022
1961	.007	.023	.032	.028	.052	.041	.012	.035	.010
1962	.032	.027	.021	.015	.078	.017	.046	.020	.026
1963	.028	.029	.020	.034	.061	.035	.044	.024	.023
1964	.038	.034	.034	.008	.054	.015	.035	.029	.028
1965	.042	.024	.026	−.024	.073	.077	.039	.022	.040
1966	.044	.033	.022	.030	.052	.030	.038	.011	.045
1967	.041	.027	−.008	.036	.057	.068	.015	.007	.033
1968	.025	.022	.028	.028	.071	.090	.032	.017	.033
1969	.032	.036	.033	.007	.070	.086	.034	.020	.038
1970	.022	.034	.033	.032	.071	.045	.023	−.004	.012
1971	.028	.027	.019	.005	.069	.077	.031	−.020	.016
1972	.035	.026	.020	−.001	.059	.073	.017	.025	.037
1973	.053	.032	.024	.012	.066	.062	.024	.046	.048

Table 11.9   Annual Rates of Growth of Real Gross Private Domestic Product, 1947–73

Year	Canada	France	Germany	Italy	Japan	Korea	Nether-lands	United Kingdom	United States
1948	.035								.054
1949	.054								.007
1950	.097								.095
1951	.039	.025	.099						.066
1952	.090	.031	.082				.015		.037
1953	.059	.080	.085	.087	.095		.075		.046
1954	−.006	.050	.079	.036	.064		.069		−.010
1955	.087	.053	.121	.082	.103		.072		.072
1956	.095	.046	.081	.047	.043		.054	.023	.024
1957	.027	.058	.066	.045	.097		.036	.026	.016
1958	.025	.015	.041	.056	.069		—	.010	.000
1959	.042	.050	.076	.065	.069		.100	.046	.058
1960	.029	.084	.095	.064	.112		.080	.061	.022
1961	.015	.053	.055	.084	.178	.052	.035	.050	.023
1962	.060	.063	.040	.060	.106	.029	.045	.015	.056
1963	.055	.058	.041	.047	.109	.097	.033	.039	.039
1964	.069	.076	.072	.034	.119	.063	.096	.072	.053
1965	.071	.054	.063	.034	.095	.071	.062	.025	.060
1966	.066	.058	.035	.056	.076	.123	.035	.028	.060
1967	.029	.050	.000	.073	.114	.084	.049	.031	.027
1968	.053	.044	.078	.055	.125	.118	.071	.039	.045
1969	.043	.081	.070	.061	.113	.177	.067	.010	.031
1970	.038	.061	.071	.053	.123	.074	.067	.037	−.001
1971	.050	.047	.031	−.026	.093	.087	.052	.034	.035
1972	.050	.054	.044	.028	.084	.089	.062	.051	.063
1973	.066	.067	.060	.061	.081	.191	.050	.068	.063

Table 11.10   Annual Rate of Growth of Total Factor Productivity

Year	Canada	France	Germany	Italy	Japan	Korea	Nether-lands	United Kingdom	United States
1948	−.007								.018
1949	.016								.008
1950	.080								.055
1951	−.007	−.006	.064						.012
1952	.053	.019	.050				.005		.010
1953	.023	.069	.041	.061	.058		.061		.021
1954	−.034	.027	.032	.002	.047		.046		−.004
1955	.056	.033	.066	.072	.071		.034		.038
1956	.043	.024	.038	.034	−.014		.017	−.001	−.009
1957	−.016	.031	.045	.019	.038		.002	.025	.005
1958	.005	.001	.018	.039	.004		−.079	.002	.003
1959	.003	.037	.052	.044	.020		.073	.014	.026
1960	.003	.059	.061	.031	.049		.047	.033	.000
1961	.008	.030	.023	.056	.125	.011	.022	.015	.014
1962	.028	.036	.020	.045	.028	.012	−.002	−.005	.031
1963	.027	.029	.021	.013	.048	.062	−.011	.015	.015
1964	.032	.043	.038	.026	.065	.048	.061	.043	.025
1965	.029	.030	.037	.058	.022	−.006	.022	.003	.021
1966	.022	.025	.013	.025	.024	.093	−.003	.016	.015
1967	−.012	.023	.008	.037	.057	.016	.034	.025	−.006
1968	.029	.021	.051	.027	.054	.028	.038	.023	.013
1969	.010	.045	.038	.054	.043	.091	.033	−.010	−.007
1970	.016	.027	.038	.020	.053	.029	.044	.041	−.013
1971	.023	.019	.013	−.031	.024	.010	.021	.055	.019
1972	.016	.029	.024	.029	.025	.015	.045	.026	.026
1973	.013	.035	.037	.048	.015	.129	.027	.022	.015

In section 11.3 we have presented annual rates of growth of real gross
private domestic product, real gross private domestic factor input, and
total factor productivity for all nine countries.[16] We have also presented
rates of growth of real capital input and real labor input for these countries. In this section we first compare growth in real factor input and in
total factor productivity as sources of growth in real product. We then
compare growth in real capital input and in real labor input as sources
of growth in real factor input. Finally, we compare our analysis of
aggregate economic growth with an analysis based on measures of capital and labor input that do not incorporate changes in the quality of
capital stock and the quality of hours worked.

Annual growth rates of real product, real capital input, real labor
input, and total factor productivity are available for all nine countries
included in our study for the period 1960–73, so that we can compare
patterns of aggregate economic growth across countries for this period.
For all countries except Korea annual growth rates are available for
periods ending in 1960 and beginning at various times from 1947 to
1955, so that we can compare patterns of aggregate economic growth
between time periods for each country except for Korea. Since the earlier periods vary in length from country to country we do not attempt
to make systematic comparisons of growth patterns across countries for
periods before 1960–73.

11.4.2 Aggregate Economic Growth

We present average annual growth rates for real product, real factor
input, total factor productivity, real capital input, and real labor input
in table 11.11. This table provides average annual growth rates for all
nine countries included in our study for the period 1960–73. Our international comparisons of patterns of aggregate economic growth are
based on growth in real product, real factor input, and total factor
productivity for all nine countries for this period. Table 11.11 also
includes average annual growth rates for all countries except for Korea
for earlier periods beginning between 1947 and 1955 and ending in
1960. Our intertemporal comparisons of growth patterns are based on
data for the period 1960–73 and for the earlier periods.

During the 1960–73 period, average growth rates of real product fell
within the relatively narrow range of 4.3% to 5.9% for six of the nine
countries included in our study. For the two North American countries,
Canada and the U.S.A., average growth rates of real product were 5.1%
and 4.3%, respectively. For four of the European countries—France,
Germany, Italy, and the Netherlands—average growth rates were 5.9%,

16. All annual growth rates presented in this paper are computed as first differences of natural logarithms.

Table 11.11   Average Annual Growth Rates of Real Product, Real Factor Input, Total Factor Productivity, Real Capital Input, and Real Labor Input

	Canada	France	Germany	Italy	Japan	Korea	Nether-lands	United Kingdom	United States
					1960–73				
Real Product	.051	.059	.054	.048	.109	.097	.056	.038	.043
Real Factor Input	.033	.029	.024	.016	.064	.055	.030	.018	.030
Total Factor Productivity	.018	.030	.030	.031	.045	.041	.026	.021	.013
Real Capital Input	.049	.063	.070	.054	.115	.066	.066	.046	.040
Real Labor Input	.020	.004	−.007	−.007	.027	.050	.003	.000	.022
	1947–60	1950–60	1950–60	1952–60	1952–60		1951–60	1955–60	1947–60
Real Product	.052	.049	.082	.060	.081		.050	.033	.037
Real Factor Input	.035	.020	.036	.023	.047		.027	.018	.023
Total Factor Productivity	.017	.029	.047	.038	.034		.023	.015	.014
Real Capital Input	.068	.047	.069	.033	.045		.040	.045	.045
Real Labor Input	.011	.003	.016	.016	.048		.014	.002	.010

5.4%, 4.8%, and 5.6%. Growth of real product for the U.K., the fifth European country, fell below this range with an average rate of 3.8%. For the two Asian countries, Japan and Korea, growth of real product greatly exceeded this range with average rates of 10.9% and 9.7%, respectively.

Among the six countries characterized by moderate growth of real product, the range of variation in average growth rates of real factor input is the same as for real product. For France, Germany, Italy, and the Netherlands the average growth rates of real factor input are 2.9%, 2.4%, 1.6%, and 3.0%, respectively, for the period 1960–73. For this period the average rate of growth of real factor input for Canada is 3.3% and for the U.S.A. is 3.0%. By contrast, the high-growth countries, Japan and Korea, had the highest average rates of growth of real factor input, 6.4% and 5.5%, respectively. The low-growth country, the U.K., had the lowest average rate of growth in real factor input at 1.8%.

Our first conclusion is that variations in average growth rates of real product among countries during the period 1960–73 are associated with variations in growth rates of real factor input. This conclusion is based on all possible comparisons between growth rates of real product and real factor input for pairs of countries. For twenty-eight of the thirty-six possible comparisons, the differences of growth rates of real product have the same sign as the differences of growth of real factor input. For example, a comparison of patterns of economic growth for the period 1960–73 for France and the U.K. reveals average rates of growth of real product of 5.9% and 3.8%, respectively. These growth rates are associated with average rates of growth of real factor input of 2.9% and 1.8%.

If we compare patterns of aggregate economic growth between the period 1960–73 and earlier periods for each country included in our study, except for Korea, we find that average growth rates of real product have increased for France, Japan, the Netherlands, the U.K., and the U.S.A., while average growth rates have decreased for Canada, Germany, and Italy. For every country with an increased average rate of growth of real product, the average rate of growth of real factor input has also increased or remained the same. The most dramatic increases are for Japan, where the average growth rate of real product rose from 8.1% for the period 1952–60 to 10.9% for the period 1960–73, while the average growth rate of real factor input rose from 4.7% for the earlier period to 6.4% for the later period. At the opposite end of the spectrum of growth rates in real product, the rate of growth of real product for the U.K. rose modestly from 3.3% for the period 1955–60 to 3.8% for the period 1960–73, while the rate of growth of real factor input remained virtually unchanged at 1.8% for both periods.

Among countries with decreases in the average rate of growth of real product, the greatest change was for Germany with a decline from 8.2% for the period 1950–60 to 5.4% during the period 1960–73. The average growth rate of real factor input dropped from 3.6% to 2.4% between the two periods. For Canada the growth rate of real product dropped from 5.2% for the period 1947–60 to 5.1% for 1960–73, while the growth rate of real factor input dropped from 3.5% to 3.3% between the two periods. For Italy the average rate of growth of real product declined from 6.0% for the period 1952–60 to 4.8% for 1960–73, while the growth rate of real factor input declined from 2.3% for the earlier period to 1.6% for the later period. Our second conclusion is that increases and decreases in average growth rates of real factor input between the period 1960–73 and various earlier periods beginning from 1947 to 1955 and ending in 1960 are strongly associated with increases and decreases in average growth rates of real product for all eight countries for which data are available.

The most striking illustration of the association of growth of real factor input and growth in real product is provided by a comparison of patterns of aggregate economic growth for Germany and Japan. During the period 1950–60 Germany had an average rate of growth of real product of 8.2%, while for the period 1952–60 Japan had an average rate of growth of real product of 8.1%. For the period 1960–73 the average growth rate of real product rose from the earlier period for Japan to 10.9%, while the average growth rate for Germany fell to 5.4%. For Japan the average growth rate of real factor input rose from 4.7% for the earlier period to 6.4% for the 1960–73 period, while the average growth rate for Germany fell from 3.6% to 2.4%.

11.4.3   Growth in Capital and Labor Input

In analyzing the growth of real factor input among countries or between time periods for a given country, we first recall that the rate of growth of real factor input is a weighted average of rates of growth of real capital input and real labor input, with weights given by the value shares of each input. We give value shares for capital input together with ratios of the average weighted rate of growth of capital input, the average weighted rate of growth of labor input, and the average rate of growth of total factor productivity to the average rate of growth of real product in table 11.12. The rate of growth of each input is weighted by the value share of that input. Table 11.12 provides data for all nine countries included in our study for the period 1960–73, and for all countries except Korea for earlier periods ending in 1960.

Value shares for capital input vary within a narrow range from .367 for Korea to .449 for Canada for the period 1960–73, so that variations in weights assigned to capital and labor input do not account for much

Table 11.12   Value Share of Capital Input and Contributions of Growth in Real Capital Input, Real Labor Input, and Total Factor Productivity to Growth in Real Product

	Canada	France	Germany	Italy	Japan	Korea	Netherlands	United Kingdom	United States
					1960–73				
Capital Value Share	.449	.417	.401	.383	.415	.367	.429	.387	.414
Contributions of:									
Real Capital Input	.430	.444	.520	.435	.437	.250	.509	.468	.393
Real Labor Input	.209	.043	−.074	−.090	.147	.329	.031	−.006	.306
Total Factor Productivity	.361	.513	.556	.659	.414	.429	.460	.538	.301
	1947–60	1950–60	1950–60	1952–60	1952–60		1951–60	1955–60	1947–60
Capital Value Share	.420	.382	.367	.405	.352		.470	.380	.393
Contributions of:									
Real Capital Input	.549	.365	.310	.220	.197		.381	.513	.469
Real Labor Input	.127	.039	.120	.155	.380		.155	.042	.160
Total Factor Productivity	.325	.595	.568	.627	.421		.465	.445	.375

variation in average rates of growth of real factor input across countries. However, average rates of growth of real capital and labor input do vary substantially among countries as indicated in table 11.11. For the European countries the rate of growth of labor input ranges from a negative .7% for Italy to a positive .4% for France. Average rates of growth of labor input for Canada and the United States are 2.0% and 2.2%, respectively, while average rates of growth of labor input are 2.7% for Japan and 5.0% for Korea.

Comparing average rates of growth of real capital input among countries for the period 1960–73, we find that Japan and Germany have the highest average rates of growth with 11.5% and 7.0%, respectively. Canada, the U.K., and the U.S.A. have relatively low average rates of growth—4.9%, 4.6%, and 4.0%. For the remaining countries of Europe the average growth rates of capital input are higher than for the U.K. and the two North American countries, and lower than for Japan and Germany. Average rates of growth for France, Korea, Italy, and the Netherlands are 6.3%, 6.6%, 5.4%, and 6.6%.

Our third conclusion is that for the period 1960–73 very high average growth rates in real product are associated with high average rates of growth of both capital and labor input, and that low average rates of growth in real product are associated with low average rates of growth of both inputs. Average rates of growth of real product in the moderate range from 4½ to 6%, which includes five of the nine countries in our study, can be associated either with low average growth rates for labor and high growth rates for capital, as in Germany, or with high average growth rates for labor and low growth rates for capital, as in the United States. There are substantial variations among countries in average rates of growth of both capital and labor input, so that further analysis requires a study of the sources of growth of capital input through the supply of saving and capital formation and the sources of growth of labor input through the supply of work effort.

We find it useful to illustrate our third conclusion by comparing the economic performance of the U.K. and the U.S.A. for the period 1960–73. The average rate of growth of real product is higher for the U.S.A. at 4.3% than for the U.K. at 3.8%. Average rates of growth of real factor input are 3.0% for the U.S.A. and 1.8% for the U.K. Turning to average growth rates of real capital input and real labor input, we find that the difference in rates of growth of real factor input can be accounted for by the difference in average rates of growth of real labor input, zero for the U.K. and 2.2% for the U.S.A. The average rate of growth of capital input for the U.K. of 4.6% exceeded that for the U.S.A. of 4.0%. The average rate of growth of total factor productivity for the U.K. of 2.1% also exceeded that for the U.S.A. of 1.3%. The difference in average rates of growth of real labor input in the two countries accounts almost entirely for the difference in average rates of growth of real product.

If we compare the growth of real factor input between the time period 1960–73 and earlier periods we first observe that the greatest change in value shares of capital input is to .415 for the period 1960–73 from .352 for the earlier period for Japan. Changes in value shares of capital input between time periods do not account for much variation in average rates of growth of real factor input between time periods. For five of the eight countries included in our intertemporal comparisons, the value share of capital input increases between the earlier periods and the period 1960–73. If technical change were Hicks-neutral, this would imply an average elasticity of substitution in excess of unity for these five countries, since the rate of growth of capital input exceeds the rate of growth of labor input for all countries and all periods except for Japan for the period 1952–60.

Comparing the average rates of growth of real capital input and real labor input between time periods for a given country, we find that Japan's average rate of growth of real labor input for the period 1952–60 was 4.8%, while the average rate of growth of real capital input was only 4.5% for this period. For the period 1960–73 the average rate of growth of labor input declined to 2.7%, still high by international standards, while the average rate of growth of capital input jumped to 11.5%. The improvement in Japan's economic performance was due almost entirely to the increased average rate of growth of real capital input.

For Germany the decline in the average growth rate of real labor input from 1.6% during the period 1950–60 to —.7% from 1960–73 was as large as the decline for Japan from the period 1952–60 to the later period. The average rate of growth of capital input rose from 6.9% for 1950–60 to 7.0% for 1960–73, and the average rate of growth of real product fell from 8.2% in the earlier period to 5.4% in the later period. The decline in Germany's economic performance was due primarily to the decreased average rate of growth of real labor input. The contrast with changes in Japan's economic performance between 1960–73 and the earlier period is due to differences in the increase of the average rate of growth of capital input.

Our fourth conclusion is that a rise or fall in the average rate of growth of real labor input is associated with a fall or rise in the rate of growth of real capital input. This pattern reflects the process of substitution between capital and labor input in production. Germany and Japan provide the most striking illustrations of this pattern, with substantial changes in aggregate economic growth between 1960–73 and the earlier periods. However, the same pattern can be seen for two countries with moderate changes in aggregate economic growth—Canada and the U.S.A. The average rate of growth of real capital input fell from 6.8% to 4.9% for Canada, and from 4.5% to 4.0% for the U.S.A. between the periods 1947–60 and 1960–73. Average growth rates of labor input rose from 1.1% to 2.0% for Canada, and from 1.0% to 2.2% for the U.S.A. for the same two periods. France is the only exception to the general pattern; average rates of growth of real labor input and real capital input rose from .3% to .4% and from 4.7% to 6.3% between the periods 1950–60 and 1960–73.

A second illustration of our fourth conclusion involves a comparison of Korean growth for the period 1960–73 with Japanese growth for the period 1952–60. Average growth rates of real labor input were 4.8% for Japan and 5.0% for Korea. Korea had an average rate of growth of capital input at 6.6%, while Japan's average rate of growth was only 4.5%. Korea's average rate of growth of real product for the later period was 9.7%, compared with Japan's rate of growth of 8.1% for the earlier period. Korea's average rate of growth of total factor productivity for the later period was 4.1%, while for Japan in the earlier period the average was 3.4%. The difference in average rates of growth of capital inputs accounts for the bulk of the difference in economic performance.

11.4.4   Quality Change

Up to this point we have compared patterns of economic growth in terms of growth of real product, real factor input, real capital input, and real labor input. We can provide additional perspective on these results by contrasting our analysis of growth patterns and an analysis based on measures of capital and labor input that fail to incorporate changes in capital and labor quality. In table 11.13 we present average annual rates of growth of capital quality, labor quality, capital stock, and hours worked. We recall that the rate of growth of real capital input is the sum of the rates of growth of capital quality and capital stock. Similarly, the rate of growth of real labor input is the sum of the rates of growth of labor quality and hours worked.

Quality change for both capital and labor input is positive for all countries and for all time periods included in our study, except change in capital quality for Germany for the period 1952–60. An analysis based on measures of capital and labor input that fail to incorporate changes in the quality of capital stock and hours worked would assign growth in total factor productivity a much larger role in accounting for the growth in real product. For the period 1960–73 growth in total factor productivity is more important than growth in real factor input in accounting for growth in real product for four countries—France,

Table 11.13   Average Annual Growth Rates of Quality of Capital Stock, Capital Stock, Quality of Hours Worked, and Hours Worked

	Canada	France	Germany	Italy	Japan	Korea	Nether-lands	United Kingdom	United States
					1960–73				
	1947–60	1950–60	1950–60	1952–60			1951–60	1955–60	1947–60
Quality of Capital Stock	.011	.012	.005	.004	.030	.027	.020	.004	.010
Capital Stock	.038	.051	.066	.050	.085	.039	.046	.042	.030
Quality of Hours Worked	.005	.004	.001	.013	.006	.012	.005	.006	.008
Hours Worked	.015	.000	−.010	−.020	.022	.038	−.002	−.006	.014
	1947–60	1950–60	1950–60	1952–60	1952–60		1951–60	1955–60	1947–60
Quality of Capital Stock	.017	.009	−.000	.002	.013		.009	.010	.009
Capital Stock	.051	.038	.070	.031	.033		.031	.035	.035
Quality of Hours Worked	.006	.005	.001	.002	.002		.005	.006	.007
Hours Worked	.006	−.002	.011	.013	.046		.009	−.004	.003

Germany, Italy, and the U.K. Similarly, for earlier periods growth in total factor productivity is more important for three countries—France, Germany, and Italy.

If we were to replace our translog index of real labor input by hours worked as a measure of labor input and our translog index of real capital input by capital stock as a measure of capital input, total factor productivity would be more important than growth in factor input for every country and every time period included in our study, except for Japan during the period 1952–60. Our fifth conclusion is that omission of changes in quality of capital stock and hours worked would result in a completely distorted view of the relative importance of growth in real factor input and growth in total factor productivity in accounting for the growth of real product.

If we compare the role of change in quality of capital stock and hours worked between the period 1960–73 and earlier periods, we find that the differences are relatively modest except for Japan. The growth of real factor input for Japan for the period 1960–73 is 6.4%, the highest for any country and any time period included in our study. The difference between the average rate of growth in real factor input for Japan and the average rates of growth of real factor input for the remaining countries included in our study is the most important factor in accounting for the differences in rates of growth of real product between Japan and the remaining countries. The average rate of growth of real product for Japan was 10.9%, also the highest for any country and any time period included in our study. Similarly, the difference between the average rate of growth of real factor input during the period 1952–60 of 4.7% and the higher rate for the later period is an important factor in accounting for the increase in the average rate of growth from 8.1% during the earlier period.

Finally, we can analyze the role of quality change in our measures of real capital input and real labor input. Japan and Korea have the highest rates of growth of hours worked and of real labor input for the period 1960–73. A ranking based on real labor input would coincide with a ranking based on hours worked. However, the growth of hours worked is negative or zero for all five European countries, while the growth of our translog index of real labor input is nonnegative except for Germany and Italy. Omission of change in quality of hours worked from the measurement of labor input would result in a change in sign in the average rate of growth of labor input for four of the five European countries included in our study.

Growth in the quality of capital stock for Japan during the period 1960–73 is 3.0%, the highest for any country in our study. The rise in the average rate of growth of capital quality from 1.3% during the period 1962–60 is an important factor in accounting for the rise in the average rate of growth of real capital input from 4.5% in the earlier period to 11.5% in the later period. Our final conclusion is that differences among countries are greater for change in capital quality than for change in labor quality, but that omission of either results in a distortion of the relative importance of growth of real capital input and real labor input in accounting for growth in real product.

11.5   Summary and Conclusions

In section 11.2 we have outlined a methodology for separating growth in real factor input from growth in total factor productivity, based on the transcendental logarithmic production function. Beginning with a production function that gives output as a function of capital input, labor input, and time, we have defined translog indexes of output, capital input, labor input, and technical change in terms of data on prices and quantities of output and inputs at discrete points of time. We have also introduced descriptive measures of the quality of capital stock and hours worked that transform indexes of capital stock and hours worked into translog indexes of capital and labor input. These descriptive measures are useful in comparing the results of our analysis with the results of studies that fail to incorporate quality change in measures of capital and labor input.

In section 11.3 we have identified translog indexes of output, capital input, labor input, and technical change with accounts for real product, real capital input, real labor input, and total factor productivity for each of the nine countries included in our study. For all countries we have constructed annual production accounts in current and constant prices for the period 1960–73. For all countries except Korea we have constructed annual production accounts for various earlier periods, beginning from 1947 to 1955 and ending in 1960. Our first objective has been to assess the relative importance of growth in real factor input and in total factor productivity in accounting for patterns of aggregate economic growth for all nine countries for the period 1960–73. Our second objective has been to assess the relative importance of changes in growth in real factor input and in total factor productivity in accounting for changes in growth of real product between earlier periods ending in 1960 and the period 1960–73 for each country.

Our first conclusion is that variations in aggregate economic growth for the period 1960–73 for the nine countries included in our study are associated with variations in the growth of real factor input. This conclusion is strongly reinforced by a comparison of patterns of aggregate economic growth for this period with growth during earlier periods ending in 1960 for each country except Korea. An analysis that fails to incorporate changes in the quality of capital stock and hours worked in measures of capital and labor input would assign a much larger role to variations in growth of total factor productivity in accounting for international variations in the growth of real product or for variations in growth of real product over time for a given country.

The second objective of our analysis has been to assess the role of growth in real capital input and in real labor input in accounting for aggregate economic growth. For the period 1960–73 we find that very rapid growth of real product is associated with rapid growth of both real capital input and real labor input, and that slow growth of real product is associated with slow growth of both inputs. Moderate growth of real product can be associated with rapid growth of real capital input, rapid growth of real labor input, or moderate rates of growth of both inputs. Our intertemporal comparisons show that increases and decreases in the average rate of growth of real capital input are associated with decreases and increases, respectively, in the average rate of growth of real labor input. This finding provides evidence of substitution between capital and labor inputs in production.

Omission of changes in the quality of capital stock and hours worked from our measures of capital and labor input would obscure the role of differences in the growth of capital and labor input in accounting for differences in the growth of output among countries and between time periods for a given country. Further analysis of international and intertemporal differences in the growth of capital input and the growth of labor input requires a detailed characterization of sources of growth of these inputs. A complete system of accounts, like that developed by Christensen and Jorgenson (1973a), is essential to the analysis of sources of growth of capital input through saving, capital formation, and accumulation of wealth. An analysis of the sources of growth in labor input through the supply of work effort is also required. The analysis of sources of growth in capital and labor input remains an important objective for further research on patterns of aggregate economic growth.

Appendix

Canada

This summary is taken from Christensen and Cummings (1976).

Our principal data sources for Canada are the *National Income and Expenditure Accounts, Historical Revision, 1926–1971* and the recent annual issues of the *National Income and Expenditure Accounts*, both published by Statistics Canada. Except for the imputation for services of consumer durables, gross private domestic product and factor outlay are computed directly from these sources.

The capital stock benchmarks and replacement rates for all assets except residential structures and consumer durables are taken from Statistics Canada (1974), *Flows and Stocks of Fixed Nonresidential Capital, Canada*. The residential structures and consumer durables benchmarks are from Gussman (1972). The replacement rate for residential structures is from Cummings and Meduna (1973), and the replacement rate for consumer durables is our estimate. We estimate the benchmark and price index for land using Danielson (1975) and Manvel (1968). Asset deflators are from the national accounts.

Our data on employment are from the *National Income and Expenditure Accounts, Historical Revision* and annual issues of the *Bank of Canada Review*. The Productivity Measures Project, Input Output Division, Statistics Canada provided us with data for average hours worked per person employed and labor income of self-employed persons. We have constructed an educational attainment index using the educational distributions in the 1941, 1951, 1961, and 1971 censuses of Canada, published by Statistics Canada.

France

This summary is taken from Brazell, Christensen, and Cummings (1975).

Our principal data sources for France are the *National Accounts Statistics* and *Les comptes de la nation 1949–1959*, both published by the Institut national de la statistique et des études économiques. Gross private domestic product and factor outlay are computed directly from these sources, except for our estimates of the inventory valuation adjustment, the services of consumer durables, and the services of institutional durables and real estate.

The nonresidential structures and producer durable equipment benchmarks are from Mairesse (1972), the residential structures benchmark is from Carré, Dubois, and Malinvaud (1972), and the inventory benchmark is from Goldsmith and Saunders (1959). We estimate the benchmark for land using Goldsmith and Saunders (1959). Our land price index is an average European land price index based on Christensen et al. (1975), Christensen, Cummings, and Norton (1975), Christensen, Cummings, and Schoeck (1975), and Conrad and Jorgenson (1975). The replacement rates for nonresidential structures and producers' durable equipment are from Mairesse (1972), and the consumer durables and residential structures replacement rates are our estimates. The asset deflators are from the national accounts.

The data on employment are from Carré, Dubois, and Malinvaud (1972), the Institut national de la statistique et des études économiques

(*National Accounts Statistics* and "La population active par secteur d'établissement"), and the Ministère des affaires sociales, *Revue française du travail*. Average hours worked are computed from *Annuaire statistique de la France* and various other publications of the Institut national de la statistique et des études économiques, plus information on average weeks of vacation from Carré, Dubois, and Malinvaud (1972). The educational attainment index is computed from data in the French Population Census and Carré, Dubois, and Malinvaud (1972).

Germany

This summary is taken from Conrad and Jorgenson (1975).

Our principal data source for the Federal Republic of Germany is the national income and product accounts, as published by the Statistisches Bundesamt. Except for the imputation for services of consumer durables, gross private domestic product and factor outlay are computed from these accounts.

The capital stock benchmarks are from Kirner (1968) and Stobbe (1969). The replacement rates are based on service lives estimated by Kirner (1968). The asset deflators are from the national income and product accounts.

We use estimates of man-hours compiled by the Statistisches Bundesamt. The educational attainment index is based on Denison (1967). It has been updated using information published by the Statistisches Bundesamt.

Italy

This summary is taken from Christensen, Cummings, and Norton (1979).

Our principal data source for Italy is the *Annuario di contabilita nazionale* published by the Istituto Centrale di Statistica. Except for the imputation for services of consumer durables, gross private domestic product and factor outlay are computed directly from this source.

The capital stock benchmarks for nonresidential structures, producers' durable equipment, and residential structures are from Vitali (1968); the inventory benchmark is from A. Giannone (1963); and the land benchmark is based on the work of de Meo (1973). The consumer durable benchmark and replacement rate are our estimates. The other replacement rates are from de Meo (1973). The investment deflators are from the national accounts except for land and inventories. We use a wholesale price index as the inventory deflator, and the land deflator is based on de Meo (1973).

Our data on employment are from *Annali di statistica* published by the Istituto Centrale di Statistica and *Labor Force Statistics* published by the OECD. Average hours per person employed are from *Rassegna di statistiche del lavoro* published by the Istituto Centrale di Statistica. Our educational attainment index is constructed using information from the *Ninth Census of Italy* (Istituto Centrale di Statistica, 1951), *National Policies for Education, Italy* (OECD 1960, 1963, 1966), and Denison (1967).

Japan

This summary is taken from Ezaki and Jorgenson (1973) and Ezaki (1974).

Our principal data source for Japan is *Annual Report on National Income Statistics* published by the Economic Planning Agency. Except for the imputation for consumer durables, gross private domestic product and factor outlay are computed from these accounts.

The capital stock benchmarks are taken from the 1955 and 1960 national wealth surveys. The replacement rates are based on service lives estimated by Ohkawa et al. (1966). The asset deflators are from the national income and product accounts, except for the land deflator, which is based on data from the *Japanese Statistical Yearbook*.

We use estimates of man-hours made available to us by Dr. Yoichi Okita of the Economic Planning Agency. The quality of labor index is based on the work of Watanabe (1972).

Korea

This summary is taken from Christensen and Cummings (1979).

Our principal data sources for Korea are the *Economic Statistics Yearbook* and the *National Income Statistics Yearbook* published by the Bank of Korea. In addition, the Bank of Korea provided us with the unpublished data which we required. Except for the imputation for services of consumer durables, gross private domestic product and factor outlay are computed directly from Bank of Korea data.

The capital stock benchmarks for nonresidential structures, producers' durable equipment, and residential structures are from the *Report on the National Wealth Survey* of the Economic Planning Board. The benchmark for land is from Mills and Song (1977). The benchmark for consumer durables and the replacement rates for all asset types are our estimates. The investment deflators are from the Economic Statistics Yearbook except for inventories and land. The inventory deflator is a wholesale price index, and the land deflator is based on the work of Mills and Song (1977).

The Economic Planning Board provided us with unpublished data on employment and average hours worked to supplement the published figures in the *Labor Statistics Yearbook*. The educational attainment index is based on data in the *Population and Housing Census* (1960,

1966, 1970) and the *Report on Wage Survey* (1967, 1970), both published by the Economic Planning Board.

Netherlands

This summary is taken from Christensen, Cummings, and Schoech (1975).

Our principal data source for the Netherlands is the Centraal bureau voor de statistiek (1956, 1960, 1965, 1972) and the National Accounts (1950–68, 1953–69, 1960–71, 1961–72, 1962–73) published by the OECD. Except for the imputation for services of consumer durables, gross private domestic product and factor outlay are computed directly from these sources.

The capital stock benchmarks, except that for consumer durables, are from Goldsmith and Saunders (1959). The capital stock benchmark for consumer durables is our estimate. The replacement rate for consumer durables is also our estimate. All other replacement rates are based on the replacement rates used by the Centraal bureau voor de statistiek. The asset deflators are all from the OECD National Accounts except for the inventory deflator which comes from *Maandschrift van het centraal bureau voor de statistiek* (1954, 1959, 1964, 1967, 1969, 1972, 1973) and the land deflator. We estimate our own land deflator using Statistical Yearbook of the Netherlands, Goldsmith and Saunders (1959), and Revell (1967).

We use the estimate of man-years compiled by the Centraal bureau voor de statistiek (1947–66) and the Nationale rekenigen (1972–73). The number of hours worked per week is taken from data provided by the International Labour Organization (1947 through 1973). The educational attainment index is derived from Denison (1967).

United Kingdom

This summary is taken from Christensen, Cummings, and Singleton (1975).

Our principal data sources for the United Kingdom are *National Income and Expenditure, 1963–1973* and earlier issues of *National Income and Expenditure* (annual volumes from 1954 through 1966), both published by the Central Statistical Office (CSO). Except for the imputation for services of consumer durables, gross private domestic product and factor outlay are computed directly from these sources.

The capital stock benchmarks for nonresidential structures, residential structures, plant and machinery, vehicles, ships and aircraft, and inventories are taken from the CSO, *National Income and Expenditure* volume. The consumer durable benchmark is our estimate. The replacement rate for nonresidential structures is taken from the Inland Revenue

Service. The replacement rates for plant and machinery and residential structures are from *The Stock of Fixed Capital in the United Kingdom in 1961* by Geoffrey Dean. The benchmark and price index for land are estimated using J. Revell, *The Wealth of the Nation*; *Inland Revenue Statistics*, published by the Board of Inland Revenue; and CSO, *Annual Abstract of Statistics*.

Our data on employment are from the CSO, *National Income and Expenditure* volumes, except for the number of self-employed, which is taken from OECD, *Labor Force Statistics*. Our average hours worked per person is taken from *British Labour Statistics, Year Books* and the *British Labour Statistics: Historical Abstract, 1886–1968*, both published by the Department of Employment. We use the rate of growth of educational attainment estimated by R.C.O. Matthews (1975).

United States

This summary is taken from Christensen and Jorgenson (1973*a*).

Our principal data source for the United States is U.S. Office of Business Economics (1966) and the Annual National Income issue (July) of the *Survey of Current Business* published by the U.S. Department of Commerce. Except for the imputations for services of durables held by consumers and institutions, gross private domestic product and factor outlay are computed directly from these sources.

The capital stock benchmarks are from Grose, Rottenberg, and Wasson (1969) and Goldsmith (1962). The replacement rates are based on estimated service lives underlying the work by Grose, Rottenberg, and Wasson (1969). The asset deflators are all from the Bureau of Economic Analysis, except for the land deflator, which is based on Goldsmith (1962).

We use estimates of man-hours compiled by Kendrick (1973), and the index of educational attainment computed by Jorgenson and Griliches (1967). The underlying sources are the U.S. Bureau of Labor Statistics, *Special Labor Force Reports*, and the U.S. Bureau of the Census, *Census of Population and Current Population Reports*.

Table 11.A.1C   Gross Private Domestic Product and Factor Outlay, 1970

Canada

(billions of dollars)

Product

1. Gross national product	85.69
2. − Wages and salaries in general government	11.02
3. − Capital consumption allowances in general government	1.23
4. − Net interest and miscellaneous investment income of general government (net of government enterprise remittances)	.80
5. − Net interest originating in rest of world	−1.39
6. + Services of consumer durables (our imputation)	6.39
7. − Taxes not related to factor outlay	7.55
8. + Subsidies	.76
9. + Capital assistance subsidies	.12
10. − Residual error of estimate	− .35
11. = Gross private domestic product	74.08

Factor Outlay

1. National income	64.24
2. + Capital consumption allowances	9.81
3. + Services of consumer durables (our imputation)	6.39
4. − GNP originating in general government (2 + 3 + 4 above)	13.05
5. + Capital assistance subsidies	.12
6. + Indirect taxes related to factor outlay	4.50
7. − GNP originating in rest of world	−1.39
8. − Twice the residual error of estimate	− .69
9. = Gross private domestic factor outlay	74.08

Table 11.A.2C   Private Domestic Capital Input, 1947–73
Canada

Year	Private Domestic Capital Stock		Rate of Return to Capital in the Business Sector		Services per Unit of Stock	Private Domestic Capital Input	
	Price Index (1)	Quantity Index (2)	Nominal Rate (3)	Own Rate (4)	(5)	Price Index (6)	Quantity Index (7)
1947	.550	69.86	.164	.057	.098	.641	6.42
1948	.635	73.38	.217	.068	.101	.748	7.04
1949	.663	77.25	.114	.072	.103	.805	7.56
1950	.700	82.26	.125	.070	.105	.873	8.12
1951	.800	86.93	.199	.058	.107	.908	8.82
1952	.823	91.29	.103	.073	.109	1.018	9.49
1953	.836	96.60	.082	.066	.111	1.000	10.14
1954	.836	100.31	.054	.053	.113	.907	10.92
1955	.858	105.51	.098	.066	.114	1.044	11.47
1956	.902	112.46	.136	.075	.116	1.072	12.23
1957	.934	118.30	.090	.059	.118	.981	13.26
1958	.950	123.00	.079	.061	.120	.999	14.15
1959	.969	128.08	.081	.060	.121	1.020	14.86
1960	.989	132.66	.076	.055	.122	1.021	15.59
1961	1.000	136.49	.063	.050	.123	1.000	16.27
1962	1.017	141.10	.077	.055	.124	1.023	16.87
1963	1.049	146.13	.096	.060	.125	1.092	17.57
1964	1.090	152.27	.108	.064	.126	1.173	18.38
1965	1.152	159.89	.130	.067	.127	1.214	19.39
1966	1.224	168.12	.134	.066	.129	1.250	20.69
1967	1.281	174.79	.096	.053	.132	1.168	22.15
1968	1.309	181.57	.075	.054	.134	1.194	23.36
1969	1.373	189.29	.097	.046	.135	1.235	24.53
1970	1.431	195.13	.098	.049	.136	1.246	25.81
1971	1.506	202.00	.101	.047	.137	1.351	26.78
1972	1.602	209.98	.099	.045	.139	1.366	27.99
1973	1.740	219.94	.167	.065	.140	1.700	29.47

Table 11.A.3C   **Private Domestic Labor Input, 1947–73**
Canada

Year	Private Domestic Persons Engaged (1)	Private Domestic Hours per Person (2)	Index of Educational Attainment (3)	Private Domestic Labor Input	
				Price Index (4)	Quantity Index (5)
1947	4.479	1.100	.923	.440	17.71
1948	4.519	1.100	.928	.487	17.94
1949	4.611	1.091	.932	.507	18.24
1950	4.586	1.071	.936	.564	17.89
1951	4.694	1.062	.941	.643	18.26
1952	4.742	1.057	.947	.693	18.46
1953	4.785	1.055	.952	.730	18.71
1954	4.750	1.052	.958	.741	18.62
1955	4.843	1.043	.964	.775	18.94
1956	5.036	1.040	.970	.833	19.77
1957	5.136	1.028	.976	.885	20.04
1958	5.060	1.021	.982	.909	19.74
1959	5.198	1.018	.988	.931	20.36
1960	5.251	1.012	.994	.969	20.55
1961	5.172	1.000	1.000	1.000	20.13
1962	5.297	1.000	1.005	1.026	20.71
1963	5.405	.992	1.010	1.068	21.07
1964	5.585	.986	1.015	1.119	21.74
1965	5.789	.978	1.019	1.198	22.45
1966	5.987	.967	1.024	1.305	23.06
1967	6.103	.961	1.029	1.402	23.50
1968	6.154	.950	1.034	1.495	23.54
1969	6.305	.941	1.039	1.630	24.00
1970	6.334	.932	1.044	1.749	23.97
1971	6.465	.926	1.049	1.875	24.44
1972	6.652	.921	1.054	2.016	25.12
1973	6.986	.921	1.059	2.130	26.51

Table 11.A.4C   Gross Private Domestic Product and Factor Input, 1947–73
Canada
(constant dollars of 1961)

| Year | Gross Private Domestic Product | | Relative Share of Investment Goods Product | Private Domestic Factor Input | | Relative Share of Property Compensation |
	Price Index (1)	Quantity Index (2)	(3)	Price Index (4)	Quantity Index (5)	(6)
1947	.652	18.26	.275	.519	22.92	.346
1948	.740	18.91	.294	.586	23.89	.376
1949	.768	19.97	.300	.618	24.82	.397
1950	.781	22.01	.307	.681	25.24	.413
1951	.863	22.89	.294	.748	26.43	.406
1952	.897	25.04	.297	.819	27.43	.430
1953	.897	26.55	.299	.837	28.44	.426
1954	.898	26.40	.296	.810	29.26	.418
1955	.926	28.80	.302	.883	30.18	.449
1956	.934	31.68	.327	.830	31.80	.443
1957	.945	32.54	.332	.827	33.18	.423
1958	.961	33.37	.313	.948	33.84	.441
1959	.980	34.81	.306	.970	35.18	.444
1960	1.000	35.84	.897	.992	36.13	.444
1961	1.000	36.40	.292	1.000	36.40	.447
1962	.996	38.65	.300	1.024	37.58	.448
1963	1.021	40.82	.309	1.079	38.64	.460
1964	1.049	43.76	.313	1.144	40.12	.470
1965	1.073	46.99	.326	1.205	41.86	.467
1966	1.115	50.20	.336	1.279	43.76	.462
1967	1.138	51.68	.329	1.290	45.59	.440
1968	1.157	54.51	.330	1.350	46.72	.442
1969	1.220	56.89	.324	1.439	48.25	.436
1970	1.254	59.07	.324	1.502	49.31	.434
1971	1.321	62.11	.321	1.619	50.66	.441
1972	1.361	65.32	.323	1.695	52.45	.430
1973	1.528	69.74	.323	1.927	55.29	.470

Table 11.A.1F   Gross Private Domestic Product and Factor Outlay, 1970
France
(billions of francs)

Product	
1. Gross national product	808.44
2. — Inventory valuation adjustment (our estimate)	−.29
3. — Wages and salaries in general government	72.17
4. — Capital consumption allowances in general government	1.46
5. — Income originating in rest of world	1.02
6. + Services of consumer durables (our imputation)	42.92
7. + Services of durables held by institutions (our imputation)	.26
8. + Net rent on institutional real estate (our imputation)	.47
9. — Taxes not related to factor outlay	26.25
10. + Production subsidies	16.07
11. + Equipment and war damage subsidies	8.95
12. = Gross private domestic product	706.50

Factor Outlay	
1. National income	619.30
2. — Inventory valuation adjustment (2 above)	−.29
3. + Equipment and war damage subsidies (11 above)	8.95
4. + Indirect taxes, French definition	120.51
5. — Indirect taxes, our definition	130.64
6. + Capital consumption allowances	84.69
7. + Services of consumer durables (6 above)	42.92
8. + Services of durables held by institutions (7 above)	.26
9. + Net rent on institutional real estate (8 above)	.47
10. — GNP originating in general government (3 + 4 above)	73.63
11. — GNP originating in rest of world (5 above)	1.02
12. + Indirect taxes related to factor outlay	34.39
13. = Gross private domestic factor outlay	706.50

Table 11.A.2F   Private Domestic Capital Input, 1950–73
France

Year	Private Domestic Capital Stock		Rate of Return to Capital in the Business Sector	Services per Unit of Stock	Private Domestic Capital Input	
	Price Index (1)	Quantity Index (2)	Nominal Rate (3)	(4)	Price Index (5)	Quantity Index (6)
1950	.440	674.4	.156	.112	.555	71.9
1951	.512	697.8	.228	.113	.535	75.9
1952	.598	717.9	.219	.113	.589	79.2
1953	.607	744.1	.084	.115	.648	82.3
1954	.618	774.0	.084	.116	.643	86.0
1955	.636	806.4	.094	.117	.652	90.2
1956	.669	842.3	.110	.118	.661	95.0
1957	.723	877.6	.141	.119	.705	100.3
1958	.785	909.7	.131	.120	.712	105.6
1959	.833	940.9	.107	.121	.767	110.5
1960	.859	983.9	.101	.122	.879	115.2
1961	.895	1029.3	.108	.124	.904	121.6
1962	.938	1079.6	.115	.125	.942	129.1
1963	1.000	1132.4	.126	.127	1.000	137.6
1964	1.052	1195.7	.119	.130	1.060	147.0
1965	1.094	1256.1	.107	.132	1.083	157.7
1966	1.133	1324.6	.122	.133	1.197	167.6
1967	1.176	1392.1	.125	.135	1.233	178.6
1968	1.226	1462.9	.125	.136	1.262	189.7
1969	1.313	1551.7	.160	.138	1.373	201.3
1970	1.399	1642.5	.156	.139	1.453	215.3
1971	1.480	1730.1	.139	.140	1.470	229.6
1972	1.562	1824.9	.140	.141	1.573	244.4
1973	1.674	1931.1	.156	.143	1.693	260.7

Table 11.A.3F   **Private Domestic Labor Input, 1950–73**
France

Year	Private Domestic Persons Engaged (1)	Private Domestic Hours per Person (2)	Index of Educational Attainment (3)	Private Domestic Labor Input	
				Price Index (4)	Quantity Index (5)
1950	17.613	1.010	.937	.246	207.4
1951	17.688	1.017	.942	.306	210.7
1952	17.616	1.010	.947	.370	209.6
1953	17.443	1.008	.952	.390	208.1
1954	17.458	1.011	.957	.419	210.1
1955	17.433	1.010	.962	.453	210.7
1956	17.402	1.012	.966	.500	211.7
1957	17.460	1.013	.971	.548	213.8
1958	17.395	1.004	.976	.629	212.2
1959	17.247	1.002	.982	.695	211.1
1960	17.260	1.011	.987	.742	214.2
1961	17.233	1.011	.992	.817	214.9
1962	17.301	1.010	.996	.901	216.5
1963	17.531	1.000	1.000	1.000	218.1
1964	17.779	.995	1.004	1.084	221.0
1965	17.818	.983	1.008	1.173	219.7
1966	17.888	.987	1.013	1.188	222.5
1967	17.898	.981	1.017	1.283	222.1
1968	17.820	.974	1.021	1.430	220.6
1969	18.092	.972	1.025	1.564	224.4
1970	18.318	.963	1.030	1.741	226.1
1971	18.375	.955	1.034	1.944	225.7
1972	18.449	.944	1.038	2.181	225.0
1973	18.666	.935	1.043	2.488	226.6

Table 11.A.4F   Gross Private Domestic Product and Factor Input, 1950–73
France
(constant francs of 1963)

Year	Gross Private Domestic Product		Private Domestic Factor Input	
	Price Index (1)	Quantity Index (2)	Price Index (3)	Quantity Index (4)
1950	.498	182.6	.338	269.2
1951	.561	187.2	.378	277.9
1952	.643	193.1	.441	281.4
1953	.643	209.2	.473	284.4
1954	.652	219.9	.492	291.0
1955	.666	231.8	.520	296.9
1956	.695	242.7	.555	303.6
1957	.731	257.2	.602	311.8
1958	.799	261.1	.660	316.3
1959	.843	274.6	.723	320.4
1960	.871	298.6	.792	328.5
1961	.906	315.0	.849	336.1
1962	.943	335.7	.916	345.4
1963	1.000	355.8	1.000	355.8
1964	1.030	384.1	1.075	367.9
1965	1.057	405.5	1.137	377.0
1966	1.082	429.5	1.194	389.5
1967	1.119	451.5	1.263	400.0
1968	1.176	471.7	1.356	409.0
1969	1.227	511.3	1.480	423.8
1970	1.300	543.6	1.611	438.5
1971	1.363	569.6	1.723	450.6
1972	1.455	601.4	1.894	462.2
1973	1.563	642.8	2.105	477.3

Table 11.A.1G   Gross Private Domestic Product and Factor Outlay, 1970
Germany
(billions of DM)

Product	
1. Gross national product	685.6
2. — Labor compensation, government sector	59.3
3. — Government contribution to legal accident insurance	2.0
4. — Capital consumption, government	3.7
5. = Private gross national product	622.4
6. + Services of consumers' durables (our imputation)	41.9
7. — Rest of world gross national product	—1.4
8. — Indirect taxes	89.1
9. + Subsidies	9.5
10. + Contribution to legal accident insurance, business and nonprofit institutions	4.1
11. + Business tax	12.1
12. + Real estate tax + fire protection tax (see 11)	2.8
13. + Motor vehicle tax (see 11)	3.8
14. — Motor vehicle tax, private households	2.1
15. = Gross private domestic product	606.7

Factor Outlay	
1. Capital consumption allowances, business and nonprofit institutions	71.1
2. + Services of consumer durables (our imputation)	41.9
3. + Indirect tax on property (11 above + 12 + 13 — 14)	16.6
4. + Income originating in business, households, and nonprofit institutions	473.0
5. + Contribution to legal accident insurance, business and nonprofit institutions (10 above)	4.1
6. = Gross private domestic factor outlay	606.7

Table 11.A.2G   Private Domestic Capital Input, 1950–73
Germany
(billions of DM)

Year	Private Domestic Capital Stock		Rate of Return to Capital in the Business Sector	Services per Unit of Stock	Private Domestic Capital Input	
	Price Index (1)	Quantity Index (2)	Nominal Rate (3)	(4)	Price Index (5)	Quantity Index (6)
1950	.724	402.4	.046	.132	.593	50.1
1951	.805	426.9	.111	.130	.710	52.3
1952	.839	455.9	.078	.129	.809	55.1
1953	.823	486.4	.043	.130	.796	59.1
1954	.814	522.3	.049	.130	.798	63.3
1955	.831	568.6	.076	.131	.885	68.2
1956	.843	615.4	.069	.131	.895	74.5
1957	.864	663.9	.074	.131	.920	80.7
1958	.882	712.9	.067	.131	.905	87.2
1959	.895	765.7	.070	.132	.965	93.8
1960	.923	829.6	.082	.131	1.035	100.4
1961	.958	895.8	.079	.131	1.028	109.1
1962	1.000	963.5	.075	.132	1.000	118.0
1963	1.032	1026.6	.070	.133	1.006	127.8
1964	1.051	1103.3	.066	.133	1.064	136.7
1965	1.094	1188.4	.081	.134	1.095	147.7
1966	1.120	1263.2	.067	.135	1.074	160.5
1967	1.114	1318.0	.043	.136	1.022	171.5
1968	1.120	1390.7	.061	.136	1.131	178.7
1969	1.162	1482.5	.078	.136	1.182	188.8
1970	1.278	1584.1	.119	.137	1.236	202.7
1971	1.358	1685.5	.090	.138	1.241	218.8
1972	1.418	1786.9	.080	.140	1.280	235.2
1973	1.477	1888.7	.077	.140	1.323	250.3

Table 11.A.3G   Private Domestic Labor Input, 1950–73
Germany
(billions of DM)

Year	Private Domestic Persons Engaged (1)	Private Domestic Hours per Person (2)	Index of Educational Attainment (3)	Private Domestic Labor Input	
				Price Index (4)	Quantity Index (5)
1950	19.4	1.146	.991	.344	168.4
1951	19.9	1.138	.992	.402	173.4
1952	20.3	1.136	.992	.432	177.3
1953	20.8	1.131	.993	.458	182.5
1954	21.4	1.132	.994	.480	188.9
1955	22.3	1.129	.994	.519	197.3
1956	22.9	1.112	.995	.570	200.3
1957	23.3	1.076	.996	.632	197.5
1958	23.5	1.057	.997	.688	195.8
1959	23.6	1.039	.998	.738	194.5
1960	24.0	1.030	.999	.806	196.9
1961	24.2	1.017	.999	.895	196.8
1962	24.2	1.000	1.000	1.000	193.7
1963	24.2	.981	1.001	1.078	190.6
1964	24.1	.995	1.001	1.154	193.0
1965	24.1	.979	1.002	1.270	191.3
1966	24.0	.967	1.003	1.378	187.8
1967	23.0	.950	1.004	1.455	177.2
1968	23.0	.963	1.005	1.530	180.5
1969	23.4	.958	1.007	1.671	183.5
1970	23.6	.950	1.008	1.930	184.5
1971	23.5	.929	1.009	2.204	180.6
1972	23.4	.919	1.010	2.442	177.8
1973	23.3	.915	1.012	2.760	177.2

Table 11.A.4G Gross Private Domestic Product and Factor Input, 1950–73
Germany
(constant DM of 1962)

	Gross Private Domestic Product		Private Domestic Factor Input	
Year	Price Index (1)	Quantity Index (2)	Price Index (3)	Quantity Index (4)
1950	.704	124.4	.423	207.1
1951	.779	137.3	.499	214.4
1952	.813	149.1	.547	221.5
1953	.805	162.3	.564	231.4
1954	.804	175.6	.582	242.5
1955	.821	198.2	.636	256.2
1956	.842	214.9	.677	267.2
1957	.868	229.5	.730	272.8
1958	.894	239.0	.765	279.2
1959	.908	257.8	.819	285.8
1960	.926	283.5	.888	295.7
1961	.963	299.5	.944	305.4
1962	1.000	311.8	1.000	311.8
1963	1.028	325.0	1.050	318.2
1964	1.054	349.2	1.118	329.0
1965	1.088	371.9	1.199	337.6
1966	1.119	385.3	1.249	345.1
1967	1.124	385.4	1.265	342.3
1968	1.148	416.8	1.359	352.0
1969	1.185	447.2	1.456	363.7
1970	1.264	479.9	1.614	375.9
1971	1.352	495.0	1.748	382.9
1972	1.421	517.2	1.881	390.7
1973	1.493	549.5	2.051	400.1

Table 11.A.1I   **Gross Private Domestic Product and Factor Outlay, 1970**

Italy

(trillions of lire)

Product	
1. Gross national product	58.26
2. — Wages and salaries in general government	5.26
3. — Capital consumption allowances and property income of general government	.36
4. — Rest of world gross national product	.32
5. + Services of consumer durables (our imputation)	4.00
6. — Taxes not related to factor outlay	5.94
7. + Subsidies	.90
8. = Gross private domestic product	51.29

Factor Outlay	
1. National income, gross of capital consumption allowances	52.21
2. + Services of consumer durables (our imputation)	4.00
3. — GNP originating in general government (2 + 3 above)	5.62
4. — Direct taxes per the national accounts	3.56
5. + Direct taxes (our estimate)	3.08
6. + Indirect taxes (our estimate)	7.43
7. — Taxes not related to factor outlay	5.94
8. — GNP originating in rest of world	.32
9. = Gross private domestic factor outlay	51.29

Table 11.A.2I   Private Domestic Capital Input, 1952–73
Italy

Year	Private Domestic Capital Stock		Rate of Return to Capital in the Business Sector	Services per Unit of Stock	Private Domestic Capital Input	
	Price Index (1)	Quantity Index (2)	Nominal Rate (3)	(4)	Price Index (5)	Quantity Index (6)
1952	.802	50.35	.061	.134	.629	6.66
1953	.802	51.47	.056	.135	.688	6.79
1954	.805	52.68	.045	.135	.665	6.97
1955	.815	54.51	.073	.136	.727	7.16
1956	.833	56.52	.082	.136	.755	7.41
1957	.858	58.74	.094	.136	.786	7.70
1958	.860	60.95	.068	.136	.813	8.01
1959	.857	63.54	.064	.136	.844	8.31
1960	.873	66.89	.095	.136	.888	8.67
1961	.892	71.03	.109	.137	.956	9.15
1962	.935	75.65	.126	.138	1.005	9.78
1963	1.000	80.81	.144	.139	1.000	10.49
1964	1.073	84.79	.126	.140	.993	11.33
1965	1.091	88.10	.090	.140	1.006	11.91
1966	1.108	91.60	.097	.140	1.087	12.34
1967	1.136	96.06	.103	.140	1.138	12.83
1968	1.163	100.59	.102	.141	1.171	13.51
1969	1.238	105.92	.151	.141	1.293	14.18
1970	1.383	111.82	.186	.141	1.283	14.95
1971	1.468	116.65	.113	.142	1.136	15.87
1972	1.544	121.39	.094	.143	1.182	16.67
1973	1.791	127.17	.196	.144	1.356	17.46

Table 11.A.3I   **Private Domestic Labor Input, 1952–73**

Italy

Year	Private Domestic Persons Engaged (1)	Private Domestic Hours per Person (2)	Index of Educational Attainment (3)	Private Domestic Labor Input	
				Price Index (4)	Quantity Index (5)
1952	15.343	.920	.946	.399	14.58
1953	15.661	.938	.948	.429	15.05
1954	16.044	.959	.951	.455	15.64
1955	16.096	.959	.953	.495	15.62
1956	16.241	.955	.956	.541	15.61
1957	16.410	.968	.958	.570	15.90
1958	16.565	.967	.960	.608	15.94
1959	16.497	.975	.963	.634	16.09
1960	16.677	1.004	.965	.672	16.53
1961	16.808	1.001	.977	.731	16.67
1962	16.761	.982	.988	.849	16.32
1963	16.667	1.000	1.000	1.000	16.47
1964	16.654	.958	1.013	1.157	15.91
1965	16.262	.903	1.026	1.289	14.85
1966	16.048	.934	1.040	1.340	15.26
1967	16.281	.943	1.053	1.448	15.78
1968	16.299	.947	1.067	1.543	15.99
1969	16.440	.915	1.081	1.723	15.68
1970	16.536	.921	1.095	2.009	15.98
1971	16.496	.890	1.110	2.329	15.58
1972	16.334	.870	1.124	2.621	15.18
1973	16.507	.849	1.139	3.200	15.11

Table 11.A.4I   Gross Private Domestic Product and Factor Input, 1952–73
Italy
(constant lire of 1963)

	Gross Private Domestic Product		Private Domestic Factor Input	
Year	Price Index (1)	Quantity Index (2)	Price Index (3)	Quantity Index (4)
1952	.728	13.73	.480	20.85
1953	.742	14.99	.520	21.41
1954	.756	15.54	.531	22.14
1955	.767	16.87	.578	22.36
1956	.794	17.69	.619	22.66
1957	.817	18.51	.650	23.26
1958	.827	19.58	.684	23.67
1959	.824	20.89	.713	24.16
1960	.844	22.27	.753	24.98
1961	.864	24.22	.815	25.68
1962	.921	25.72	.909	26.07
1963	1.000	26.96	1.000	26.96
1964	1.064	27.89	1.091	27.19
1965	1.079	28.85	1.172	26.55
1966	1.110	30.50	1.237	27.37
1967	1.142	32.81	1.320	28.37
1968	1.169	34.66	1.388	29.18
1969	1.231	36.83	1.543	29.40
1970	1.321	38.82	1.689	30.36
1971	1.437	37.81	1.781	30.50
1972	1.529	38.89	1.952	30.46
1973	1.743	41.32	2.336	30.84

Table 11.A.1J   Gross Private Domestic Product and Factor Outlay, 1970

Japan

(trillions of yen)

Product	
1. Gross national product	70.73
2. − Net factor income from abroad	−.16
3. + Services of consumer durables	2.41
4. − Compensation of employees by public administration (general government)	2.16
5. − Rent, interest, and dividends by general government	.60
6. + Interest and dividends by general government	.42
7. = Gross private domestic product before sales tax	70.96
8. − Indirect taxes	5.31
9. + Monopoly profit	.27
10. + Current subsidies	.77
11. + Business tax (corporate + noncorporate)	.92
12. + Real estate acquisition tax	.09
13. + Motor vehicle tax (prefectural + municipal)	.19
14. + Mine-lot tax	.00
15. + Fixed estate tax (prefectural + municipal)	.52
16. = Gross private domestic product	68.41

Factor Outlay	
1. Provisions for the consumption of fixed capital	9.49
2. + Statistical discrepancy	−.21
3. + Compensation of employees	31.02
4. − Compensation of employees by public administration	2.16
5. + Income from unincorporated enterprises	11.16
6. + Income from property, rent	2.56
7. + Income from property, interest	3.29
8. − Interest on consumers' debt	.24
9. − Interest on public debt	.42
10. + Income from property, dividends	.80
11. + Corporate transfers to households and nonprofit institutions	.10
12. + Direct taxes and charges on private corporations	3.22
13. + Saving of private corporations	4.71
14. + Profit from government enterprises	.09
15. + Monopoly profit	.27
16. − Net factor income from abroad	−.16
17. + Services from consumer durables	2.41
18. + Interest and dividends by general government	.42
19. + Certain indirect taxes (above, 11 + 12 + 13 + 14 + 15)	1.72
20. = Gross private domestic factor outlay	68.41

Table 11.A.2J   Private Domestic Capital Input, 1952–73
Japan
(trillions of yen)

Year	Private Domestic Capital Stock		Rate of Return to Capital in the Business Sector	Services per Unit of Stock	Private Domestic Capital Input	
	Price Index (1)	Quantity Index (2)	Nominal Rate (3)	(4)	Price Index (5)	Quantity Index (6)
1952	.439	45.96	.102	.145	.349	6.55
1953	.468	46.89	.091	.144	.338	6.64
1954	.483	47.67	.066	.141	.372	6.62
1955	.497	48.90	.085	.141	.400	6.73
1956	.560	51.02	.193	.140	.465	6.84
1957	.611	54.17	.150	.145	.507	7.40
1958	.624	56.13	.067	.154	.446	8.33
1959	.652	58.71	.097	.157	.496	8.79
1960	.683	62.76	.121	.160	.603	9.42
1961	.723	69.39	.152	.167	.744	10.51
1962	.736	74.64	.093	.177	.653	12.29
1963	.747	80.74	.098	.184	.667	13.76
1964	.764	88.25	.129	.186	.771	15.05
1965	.781	94.44	.115	.192	.725	16.91
1966	.815	101.37	.147	.196	.795	18.48
1967	.859	111.47	.180	.198	.902	20.08
1968	.904	123.92	.199	.203	.977	22.58
1969	.949	137.68	.190	.210	.980	25.98
1970	1.000	154.29	.190	.217	1.000	29.84
1971	1.019	169.55	-.126	.224	.905	34.58
1972	1.075	185.02	.157	.231	.909	39.10
1973	1.282	203.67	.291	.237	.980	43.86

Table 11.A.3J   Private Domestic Labor Input, 1952–73
Japan
(trillions of yen)

Year	Private Domestic Persons Engaged (1)	Private Domestic Hours per Person (2)	Index of Educational Attainment (3)	Private Domestic Labor Input	
				Price Index (4)	Quantity Index (5)
1952	22.72	1.026	.936	.183	20.23
1953	23.65	1.036	.935	.210	21.25
1954	24.20	1.031	.943	.224	21.83
1955	25.32	1.038	.932	.234	22.73
1956	26.61	1.062	.936	.240	24.54
1957	28.02	1.056	.938	.257	25.76
1958	29.08	1.055	.937	.264	26.67
1959	29.91	1.066	.944	.275	27.92
1960	31.15	1.080	.949	.298	29.61
1961	31.78	1.071	.950	.342	29.98
1962	33.02	1.054	.950	.391	30.65
1963	33.93	1.047	.955	.441	31.47
1964	34.91	1.043	.960	.490	32.43
1965	36.81	1.028	.964	.539	33.84
1966	37.68	1.029	.966	.596	34.76
1967	38.92	1.028	.973	.662	36.11
1968	40.02	1.027	.981	.745	37.38
1969	40.69	1.012	.992	.851	37.91
1970	41.59	1.000	1.000	1.000	38.58
1971	42.24	.989	1.007	1.158	39.03
1972	42.80	.984	1.014	1.316	39.59
1973	44.25	.975	1.022	1.605	40.92

Table 11.A.4J   **Gross Private Domestic Product and Factor Input, 1952–73**
Japan
(constant yen of 1970)

Year	Gross Private Domestic Product		Private Domestic Factor Input	
	Price Index (1)	Quantity Index (2)	Price Index (3)	Quantity Index (4)
1952	.533	11.21	.241	24.77
1953	.544	12.32	.261	25.69
1954	.560	13.13	.281	26.13
1955	.550	14.56	.297	26.98
1956	.597	15.19	.318	28.55
1957	.619	16.74	.342	30.28
1958	.600	17.93	.333	32.30
1959	.627	19.20	.355	33.90
1960	.676	21.48	.402	36.10
1961	.704	25.65	.475	38.04
1962	.701	28.53	.486	41.14
1963	.725	31.81	.528	43.72
1964	.768	35.83	.596	46.16
1965	.774	39.41	.614	49.66
1966	.832	42.54	.676	52.33
1967	.881	47.67	.758	55.41
1968	.924	54.01	.840	59.46
1969	.955	60.47	.905	63.75
1970	1.000	68.41	1.000	68.41
1971	1.019	75.07	1.044	73.31
1972	1.074	81.63	1.128	77.72
1973	1.228	88.49	1.309	83.01

Table 11.A.1K   Gross Private Domestic Product and Factor Outlay, 1970
Korea
(billions of won)

Product	
1. Gross national product	2,589.3
2. — Wages and salaries in general government	186.9
3. — Capital consumption allowances in general government	4.8
4. — General government income from property	58.8
5. — Rest of world gross national product	11.9
6. + Services of consumer durables	89.4
7. — Taxes not related to factor outlay	197.8
8. + Subsidies	0.7
9. — Statistical discrepancy	−32.2
10. = Gross private domestic product	2,251.5

Factor Outlay	
1. National income	2,177.7
2. + Capital consumption allowances	160.2
3. + Services of consumer durables (our imputation)	89.4
4. — GNP originating in general government (2 + 3 + 4 above)	250.4
5. — Direct taxes on corporations per the national accounts	42.7
6. + Direct taxes on corporations (our estimate)	72.5
7. — Direct taxes on households per the national accounts	98.9
8. + Direct taxes on households (our estimate)	86.0
9. + Indirect taxes	235.3
10. — Taxes not related to factor outlay	197.8
11. — GNP originating in rest of world	11.9
12. — Statistical discrepancy	−32.2
13. = Gross private domestic factor outlay	2,251.5

Table 11.A.2K   Private Domestic Capital Input, 1960–73
Korea

Year	Private Domestic Capital Stock		Rate of Return to Capital in the Business Sector	Services per Unit of Stock	Private Domestic Capital Input	
	Price Index (1)	Quantity Index (2)	Nominal Rate (3)	(4)	Price Index (5)	Quantity Index (6)
1960	.174	4971.0	.152	.087	.159	433.7
1961	.203	5010.8	.306	.088	.237	436.1
1962	.231	5057.9	.239	.088	.267	442.0
1963	.266	5260.9	.312	.090	.381	453.8
1964	.346	5409.4	.407	.090	.564	472.0
1965	.413	5548.6	.267	.091	.580	489.6
1966	.498	5848.8	.273	.091	.689	505.0
1967	.572	6183.4	.203	.094	.651	551.7
1968	.678	6591.1	.227	.100	.750	618.0
1969	.868	7069.2	.243	.107	.843	704.9
1970	1.000	7483.0	.237	.113	1.000	800.2
1971	1.173	7894.2	.222	.118	1.033	880.9
1972	1.329	8192.4	.235	.122	1.234	964.3
1973	1.541	8709.9	.269	.124	1.613	1018.3

Table 11.A.3K   Private Domestic Labor Input, 1960–73
Korea

Year	Private Domestic Persons Engaged (1)	Private Domestic Hours per Person (2)	Index of Educational Attainment (3)	Private Domestic Labor Input	
				Price Index (4)	Quantity Index (5)
1960	6.785	.982	.887	.155	920.2
1961	6.975	1.003	.898	.163	977.9
1962	7.170	.982	.909	.190	996.4
1963	7.374	.982	.920	.249	1038.0
1964	7.504	.952	.931	.352	1036.0
1965	7.891	.994	.943	.378	1151.5
1966	8.093	.987	.954	.472	1186.7
1967	8.361	1.000	.965	.598	1256.8
1968	8.772	1.019	.977	.662	1359.9
1969	9.021	1.043	.988	.822	1448.5
1970	9.317	1.000	1.000	1.000	1451.3
1971	9.604	1.024	1.012	1.135	1550.5
1972	10.081	1.029	1.024	1.312	1653.5
1973	10.644	1.029	1.036	1.530	1766.6

Table 11.A.4K   Gross Private Domestic Product and Factor Input, 1960–73
Korea
(constant won of 1970)

	Gross Private Domestic Product		Private Domestic Factor Input	
Year	Price Index (1)	Quantity Index (2)	Price Index (3)	Quantity Index (4)
1960	.228	925.8	.155	1358.0
1961	.270	975.2	.186	1414.8
1962	.306	1004.0	.213	1438.6
1963	.389	1106.5	.289	1490.2
1964	.535	1178.3	.417	1512.8
1965	.568	1265.2	.440	1634.6
1966	.635	1430.9	.539	1685.1
1967	.713	1556.1	.615	1804.4
1968	.778	1751.2	.690	1975.0
1969	.854	2090.4	.829	2152.6
1970	1.000	2251.5	1.000	2251.5
1971	1.087	2456.0	1.098	2430.6
1972	1.252	2683.6	1.284	2615.7
1973	1.346	3249.5	1.562	2782.7

Table 11.A.1N   Gross Private Domestic Product and Factor Outlay, 1970
Netherlands
(billions of guilders)

Product	
1. Gross national product	114.98
2. − Wages and salaries in general government	13.48
3. − Capital consumption allowances in general government	.80
4. − Taxes paid by government	.04
5. − GNP originating in rest of world	.41
6. + Service of consumer durables (our imputation)	13.58
7. − Taxes not related to factor outlay	11.09
8. + Subsidies	1.52
9. = Gross private domestic product	104.26

Factor Outlay	
1. National income	93.70
2. + Capital consumption allowances	9.73
3. + Services of consumer durables (our imputation)	13.58
4. − National income originating in general government (2 + 3)	14.28
5. − Indirect taxes considered direct by Netherlands national accounts	.71
6. + Indirect taxes related to factor outlay	1.94
7. − GNP originating in rest of world (5 above)	.41
8. = Gross private domestic factor outlay	104.26

Table 11.A.2N   **Private Domestic Capital Input, 1951–73**
Netherlands

Year	Private Domestic Capital Stock		Rate of Return to Capital in the Business Sector	Services per Unit of Stock	Private Domestic Capital Input	
	Price Index (1)	Quantity Index (2)	Nominal Rate (3)	(4)	Price Index (5)	Quantity Index (6)
1951	.620	124.21	.199	.098	.796	11.77
1952	.666	125.15	.121	.097	.827	12.08
1953	.656	127.22	.042	.097	.827	12.13
1954	.697	132.15	.135	.097	.910	12.39
1955	.728	137.68	.115	.099	1.011	13.05
1956	.777	144.15	.137	.100	1.047	13.79
1957	.826	150.81	.127	.102	1.034	14.71
1958	.840	154.73	.071	.104	.947	15.65
1959	.842	159.63	.067	.105	.972	16.20
1960	.862	166.86	.091	.106	1.054	16.89
1961	.881	174.39	.081	.108	1.013	17.95
1962	.935	181.49	.124	.111	1.001	19.28
1963	1.000	188.11	.127	.114	1.000	20.73
1964	1.055	198.01	.113	.117	1.079	22.09
1965	1.109	207.95	.108	.120	1.126	23.75
1966	1.164	217.72	.096	.123	1.089	25.58
1967	1.179	228.01	.064	.125	1.131	27.20
1968	1.221	239.11	.087	.126	1.218	28.80
1969	1.287	251.19	.104	.128	1.279	30.56
1970	1.361	265.83	.109	.129	1.327	32.45
1971	1.496	278.86	.143	.132	1.392	35.02
1972	1.636	290.99	.144	.134	1.493	37.45
1973	1.779	304.25	.133	.137	1.550	39.83

Table 11.A.3N   Private Domestic Labor Input, 1951–73
Netherlands

Year	Private Domestic Persons Engaged (1)	Private Domestic Hours per Person (2)	Index of Educational Attainment (3)	Private Domestic Labor Input	
				Price Index (4)	Quantity Index (5)
1951	3.411	1.041	.942	.451	23.06
1952	3.367	1.043	.946	.473	22.92
1953	3.417	1.047	.951	.489	23.48
1954	3.483	1.047	.956	.530	24.05
1955	3.547	1.047	.961	.573	24.61
1956	3.602	1.047	.966	.619	25.12
1957	3.619	1.043	.970	.683	25.26
1958	3.580	1.043	.975	.711	25.11
1959	3.620	1.047	.980	.723	25.63
1960	3.692	1.047	.985	.780	26.27
1961	3.746	.998	.990	.876	25.52
1962	3.825	.998	.995	.926	26.19
1963	3.878	1.000	1.000	1.000	26.75
1964	3.952	.989	1.005	1.157	27.10
1965	3.986	.989	1.010	1.278	27.47
1966	4.009	.989	1.015	1.408	27.77
1967	3.986	.972	1.020	1.530	27.26
1968	4.021	.972	1.025	1.659	27.64
1969	4.083	.968	1.030	1.903	28.08
1970	4.129	.948	1.036	2.188	27.97
1971	4.140	.940	1.041	2.458	27.93
1972	4.082	.931	1.046	2.807	27.43
1973	4.085	.923	1.051	3.249	27.33

Table 11.A.4N   Gross Private Domestic Product and Factor Input, 1951–73
Netherlands
(constant guilders of 1963)

Year	Gross Private Domestic Product		Private Domestic Factor Input	
	Price Index (1)	Quantity Index (2)	Price Index (3)	Quantity Index (4)
1951	.728	27.15	.586	33.76
1952	.756	27.55	.611	34.08
1953	.724	29.71	.622	34.57
1954	.755	31.83	.679	35.37
1955	.799	34.19	.744	36.71
1956	.831	36.08	.787	38.09
1957	.869	37.39	.824	39.39
1958	.922	35.45	.809	40.40
1959	.875	39.17	.826	41.50
1960	.902	42.43	.893	42.87
1961	.923	43.92	.934	43.39
1962	.948	45.93	.958	45.45
1963	1.000	47.47	1.000	47.47
1964	1.056	52.26	1.122	49.16
1965	1.112	55.58	1.210	51.12
1966	1.164	57.53	1.262	53.08
1967	1.199	60.45	1.344	53.90
1968	1.247	64.88	1.454	55.68
1969	1.333	69.40	1.606	57.63
1970	1.405	74.20	1.769	58.95
1971	1.503	78.14	1.932	60.79
1972	1.598	83.16	2.148	61.86
1973	1.721	87.46	2.377	63.33

Table 11.A.1UK Gross Private Domestic Product and Factor Outlay, 1970
United Kingdom
(billions of pounds)

Product	
1. Gross national product	51.07
2. − Wages and salaries in general government	5.88
3. − Rent from government	1.12
4. − Gross trading surplus of government	.15
5. − Net property income from abroad	.53
6. + Services of consumer durables	3.81
7. + Subsidies	.90
8. + Capital transfer payments	.80
9. − Indirect taxes (our definition)	8.11
10. + Indirect taxes related to factor outlay	2.95
11. − Selective employment tax paid by government	.32
12. = Gross private domestic product	43.43

Factor Outlay	
1. National income	39.02
2. + Capital consumption allowances	4.52
3. + Services of consumer durables	3.81
4. − GNP originating in government	7.15
5. + Taxes related to factor outlay	2.95
6. + Capital transfer payments	.80
7. − GNP originating in rest of world	.53
8. = Gross private domestic product	43.43

Table 11.A.2UK   Private Domestic Capital Input, 1955–73
United Kingdom

Year	Private Domestic Capital Stock		Rate of Return to Capital in the Business Sector	Services per Unit of Stock	Private Domestic Capital Input	
	Price Index (1)	Quantity Index (2)	Nominal Rate (3)	(4)	Price Index (5)	Quantity Index (6)
1955	.624	65.51	.071	.129	.770	8.13
1956	.659	67.55	.072	.131	.748	8.57
1957	.683	69.86	.071	.131	.788	8.88
1958	.707	72.11	.067	.132	.796	9.24
1959	.708	75.00	.072	.134	.812	9.65
1960	.716	78.87	.081	.135	.826	10.16
1961	.733	82.47	.081	.136	.845	10.74
1962	.759	85.57	.073	.137	.839	11.28
1963	.772	89.17	.081	.137	.885	11.73
1964	.797	94.13	.089	.138	.907	12.27
1965	.828	98.78	.085	.138	.908	13.03
1966	.854	102.99	.078	.139	.918	13.71
1967	.869	107.42	.079	.139	.949	14.29
1968	.903	112.14	.081	.139	.993	14.91
1969	.936	116.34	.069	.139	.991	15.59
1970	1.000	120.55	.057	.139	1.000	16.12
1971	1.098	124.77	.065	.138	1.130	16.69
1972	1.261	129.26	.066	.140	1.284	17.49
1973	1.480	133.67	.058	.144	1.381	18.56

Table 11.A.3UK   Private Domestic Labor Input, 1955–73
United Kingdom

Year	Private Domestic Persons Engaged (1)	Private Domestic Hours per Person (2)	Index of Educational Attainment (3)	Private Domestic Labor Input	
				Price Index (4)	Quantity Index (5)
1955	20.903	1.068	.914	.372	26.91
1956	21.027	1.062	.919	.404	27.06
1957	20.583	1.057	.925	.433	26.53
1958	20.382	1.048	.931	.455	26.20
1959	20.448	1.064	.936	.464	26.85
1960	20.877	1.050	.942	.492	27.22
1961	21.499	1.036	.947	.530	27.84
1962	21.596	1.027	.953	.558	27.88
1963	21.537	1.039	.959	.576	28.28
1964	21.746	1.041	.965	.613	28.79
1965	21.914	1.025	.970	.659	28.74
1966	21.939	1.005	.976	.715	28.37
1967	21.382	1.009	.982	.761	27.94
1968	21.105	1.016	.988	.815	27.93
1969	21.079	1.016	.994	.875	28.07
1970	20.711	1.000	1.000	1.000	27.31
1971	19.832	.984	1.006	1.153	25.89
1972	19.778	.991	1.012	1.260	26.15
1973	20.232	1.000	1.018	1.390	27.16

Table 11.A.4UK   Gross Private Domestic Product and Factor Input, 1955–73
United Kingdom
(constant pounds of 1958)

Year	Gross Private Domestic Product		Private Domestic Factor Input	
	Price Index (1)	Quantity Index (2)	Price Index (3)	Quantity Index (4)
1955	.624	26.07	.491	33.11
1956	.650	26.67	.512	33.90
1957	.675	27.36	.545	33.93
1958	.698	27.63	.564	34.18
1959	.702	28.93	.575	35.28
1960	.709	30.75	.601	36.29
1961	.737	32.34	.634	37.59
1962	.762	32.82	.653	38.34
1963	.781	34.13	.679	39.25
1964	.785	36.66	.712	40.39
1965	.819	37.58	.746	41.29
1966	.851	38.63	.787	41.77
1967	.874	39.85	.829	42.04
1968	.907	41.44	.879	42.74
1969	.955	41.86	.917	43.62
1970	1.000	43.43	1.000	43.43
1971	1.083	44.95	1.144	42.57
1972	1.171	47.32	1.270	43.64
1973	1.251	50.65	1.387	45.71

Table 11.A.1US   Gross Private Domestic Product and Factor Outlay, 1970
United States
(billions of dollars)

Product	
1. Private gross national product	867.7
2. − Rest of the world gross national product	4.6
3. + Services of consumer durables (our imputation)	94.9
4. + Services of durables held by institutions (our imputation)	2.3
5. + Net rent on institutional real estate (our imputation)	.9
6. − Federal indirect business tax and nontax accruals	19.3
7. + Capital stock tax	—
8. − State and local indirect business tax and nontax accruals	74.7
9. + Business motor vehicle licenses	1.4
10. + Business property taxes	36.5
11. + Business other taxes	3.4
12. + Subsidies less current surplus of federal government enterprises	6.3
13. + Subsidies less current surplus of state and local government enterprises	−3.6
14. = Gross private domestic product	911.2

Factor Outlay	
1. Capital consumption allowances	90.8
2. + Business transfer payments	4.0
3. + Statistical discrepancy	−2.1
4. + Services of consumer durables (our imputation)	94.9
5. + Services of durables held by institutions (our imputation)	2.3
6. + Net rent on institutional real estate (our imputation)	.9
7. + Certain indirect business taxes (product account above, lines 8 + 10 + 11 + 12)	41.3
8. + Income originating in business	647.4
9. + Income originating in households and institutions	31.6
10. = Gross private domestic factor outlay	911.2

Table 11.A.2US   Private Domestic Capital Input, 1947–73
United States

Year	Private Domestic Capital Stock		Rate of Return to Capital in the Business Sector	Services per Unit of Stock	Private Domestic Capital Input	
	Price Index (1)	Quantity Index (2)	Nominal Rate (3)	(4)	Price Index (5)	Quantity Index (6)
1947	.439	1408.58	.249	.115	.532	155.28
1948	.473	1481.72	.164	.118	.567	166.09
1949	.469	1528.20	.051	.119	.516	176.87
1950	.491	1615.26	.116	.121	.587	184.49
1951	.532	1689.55	.162	.122	.639	197.33
1952	.540	1741.48	.072	.123	.623	208.19
1953	.544	1795.36	.057	.124	.601	215.95
1954	.547	1842.30	.064	.125	.622	224.58
1955	.560	1921.90	.086	.126	.656	231.91
1956	.588	1988.56	.107	.127	.631	244.29
1957	.610	2041.74	.093	.128	.624	254.81
1958	.618	2073.27	.065	.129	.650	263.59
1959	.633	2132.93	.078	.129	.675	268.28
1960	.645	2185.66	.069	.130	.690	277.49
1961	.656	2227.54	.067	.131	.698	286.19
1962	.671	2288.67	.083	.131	.739	292.76
1963	.684	2357.66	.084	.132	.754	302.93
1964	.700	2434.23	.091	.134	.781	314.86
1965	.720	2531.43	.105	.135	.837	328.71
1966	.746	2637.08	.120	.137	.876	346.66
1967	.776	2722.34	.109	.139	.850	367.06
1968	.813	2815.00	.111	.141	.866	383.57
1969	.862	2909.54	.113	.143	.898	401.77
1970	.905	2976.91	.103	.145	.845	420.54
1971	.954	3059.12	.105	.146	.908	433.69
1972	1.000	3167.73	.107	.147	1.000	449.07
1973	1.069	3293.41	.128	.148	1.097	469.76

Table 11.A.3US Private Domestic Labor Input, 1947–73
United States

Year	Private Domestic Persons Engaged (1)	Private Domestic Hours per Person (2)	Index of Educational Attainment (3)	Private Domestic Labor Input	
				Price Index (4)	Quantity Index (5)
1947	52.66	1.132	.825	.316	436.21
1948	53.64	1.120	.831	.341	445.21
1949	51.92	1.106	.836	.349	428.17
1950	53.54	1.107	.842	.397	444.79
1951	55.72	1.105	.847	.396	465.02
1952	56.21	1.100	.852	.419	469.48
1953	57.21	1.093	.857	.442	477.71
1954	55.59	1.081	.862	.454	461.89
1955	57.05	1.085	.867	.471	478.44
1956	58.37	1.076	.872	.497	488.61
1957	58.37	1.061	.878	.525	484.59
1958	56.62	1.052	.888	.536	471.75
1959	57.99	1.058	.899	.557	491.40
1960	58.64	1.052	.906	.575	498.05
1961	58.32	1.044	.913	.589	495.62
1962	59.41	1.046	.920	.609	509.45
1963	59.87	1.047	.927	.626	517.51
1964	60.99	1.042	.933	.654	528.53
1965	62.80	1.043	.940	.674	548.68
1966	65.13	1.036	.948	.708	570.01
1967	66.19	1.026	.956	.740	578.73
1968	67.64	1.019	.965	.790	592.99
1969	69.53	1.015	.974	.840	612.54
1970	69.18	1.000	.982	.896	605.72
1971	69.07	.998	.991	.946	609.14
1972	71.01	1.000	1.000	1.000	633.00
1973	74.15	.998	1.009	1.066	665.43

Table 11.A.4US   Gross Private Domestic Product and Factor Input, 1947–73
United States
(constant dollars of 1958)

| | Gross Private Domestic Product | | Private Domestic Factor Input | |
| | Price Index | Quantity Index | Price Index | Quantity Index |
Year	(1)	(2)	(3)	(4)
1947	.543	407.00	.388	568.72
1948	.572	429.40	.417	589.17
1949	.557	432.53	.409	589.03
1950	.571	475.60	.443	612.88
1951	.611	507.89	.480	646.67
1952	.619	526.90	.491	664.52
1953	.618	551.54	.501	681.24
1954	.640	546.30	.516	677.68
1955	.644	586.85	.539	701.09
1956	.661	601.21	.548	724.82
1957	.676	610.95	.564	733.00
1958	.694	611.26	.581	730.85
1959	.702	647.72	.603	754.26
1960	.722	662.00	.620	770.70
1961	.726	677.43	.632	778.09
1962	.735	716.60	.660	798.22
1963	.742	744.75	.676	817.05
1964	.753	785.47	.704	840.53
1965	.773	834.43	.737	874.65
1966	.798	885.64	.773	914.52
1967	.814	909.79	.783	945.24
1968	.841	952.06	.820	976.52
1969	.891	982.31	.863	1014.54
1970	.915	981.43	.875	1026.55
1971	.955	1016.02	.930	1042.80
1972	1.000	1082.07	1.000	1082.07
1973	1.063	1152.28	1.079	1135.16

References

Abramovitz, M. 1956. Resource and output trends in the United States since 1870. *American Economic Review* 46, no. 2 (May): 5–23.

Balassa, B., and Bertrand, T. J. 1970. Growth performance of Eastern European economies and comparable Western European countries. *American Economic Review* 60, no. 2 (May): 314–20.

Bank of Canada. Various dates. *Bank of Canada Review.* Ottawa: Queen's Printer.

Bank of Korea. 1972. *National Income Statistics Yearbook, 1972.* Seoul: Bank of Korea.

———. 1973. *Economic Statistics Yearbook, 1973.* Seoul: Bank of Korea.

Barger, H. 1969. Growth in developed nations. *Review of Economics and Statistics* 51, no. 2 (May): 143–48.

Bergson, A. 1974. Soviet post-war economic development. *Wicksell Lectures 1974.* Stockholm: Almqvist and Wicksell.

Brazell, D. W.; Christensen, L. R.; and Cummings, D. 1975. *Real product, real factor input, and productivity in France, 1951–1973.* Social Systems Research Institute, University of Wisconsin, Discussion Paper no. 7527.

Bureau of the Census. Various dates. *Census of Population.* Washington: U.S. Department of Commerce.

———. Various dates. *Current Population Reports.* Washington: U.S. Department of Commerce.

Bureau of Economic Analysis. 1976. *Fixed nonresidential business and residential capital in the United States, 1925–75.* Washington: U.S. Department of Commerce.

———. Various dates. *The Survey of Current Business.* Washington: U.S. Department of Commerce.

Bureau of Labor Statistics. Various dates. *Special Labor Force Reports.* Washington: U.S. Department of Labor.

Bureau of Statistics. 1975. *Japanese Statistical Yearbook.* Tokyo: Office of the Prime Minister.

Carré, J.; Dubois, P.; and Malinvaud, E. 1972. *La croissance française.* Paris; Editions du Sevil; English tran. by John P. Hatfield, *French economic growth.* Stanford: Stanford University Press (1975).

Centraal Bureau voor de Statistiek. 1967. *Arbeidsvolume in geregistrede arbeidsreserve, 1947–1966.* The Hague: Staatsuitgeverij.

———. *Jaarcijfers voor Nederland,* 1963–64, 1967–68, 1974. The Hague: Staatsuitgeverij.

———. *Maandschrift van het Centraal Bureau voor de Statistiek,* 1954, 1959, 1964, 1967, 1969, 1972, 1973, 1974. The Hague: Staatsuitgeverij.

————. *National rekeningen,* 1956, 1960, 1965, 1972, 1973, 1974. The Hague: Staatsuitgeverij.

Central Statistical Office. 1974. *National Income and Expenditure, 1963–1973.* London: Her Majesty's Stationery Office.

————. Various dates. *Annual Abstract of Statistics.* London: Her Majesty's Stationery Office.

————. *National Income and Expenditure,* annual volumes from 1954 through 1966. London: Her Majesty's Stationary Office.

Chenery, H., and Syrquin, M. 1975. *Patterns of development 1950–1970.* New York: Oxford University Press.

Christensen, L. R. 1971. Entrepreneurial income: how does it measure up? *American Economic Review* 61: 575–85.

Christensen, L. R., and Cummings, D. 1976. *Real product, real factor input, and productivity in Canada, 1947–1973.* Social Systems Research Institute, University of Wisconsin, Discussion Paper no. 7604.

————. 1979. *Real product, real factor input, and productivity in Korea, 1960–1973.* Social Systems Research Institute, University of Wisconsin, Discussion Paper no. 7917.

Christensen, L. R.; Cummings, D.; and Norton, B. 1979. *Real product, real factor input, and productivity in Italy, 1952–1973.* Social Systems Research Institute, University of Wisconsin, Discussion Paper no. 7918.

Christensen, L. R.; Cummings, D.; and Schoeck, P. 1975. *Real product, real factor input, and productivity in the Netherlands, 1951–1973.* Social Systems Research Institute, University of Wisconsin, Discussion Paper no. 7529.

Christensen, L. R.; Cummings, D.; Doerner, D.; and Singleton, K. 1975. *Real product, real factor input, and productivity in the United Kingdom, 1955–1973.* Social Systems Research Institute, University of Wisconsin, Discussion Paper no. 7530.

Christensen, L. R., and Jorgenson, D. W. 1969. Measurement of U.S. real capital input, 1929–1967. *Review of Income and Wealth,* ser. 15, no. 4: 293–320.

————. 1970. U.S. real product and real factor input, 1929–1967. *Review of Income and Wealth,* ser. 16, no. 1: 19–50.

————. 1973*a.* Measuring the performance of the private sector of the U.S. economy, 1929–1969. In M. Moss, ed., *Measuring economic and social performance.* New York: National Bureau of Economic Research, pp. 233–338.

————. 1973*b.* U.S. income, saving and wealth, 1929–1969. *Review of Income and Wealth,* ser. 19, no. 4 (December): 329–62.

Christensen, L. R.; Jorgenson, D. W.; and Lau, L. J. 1971. Conjugate duality and the transcendental logarithmic production function. *Econometrica* 39, no. 4 (July): 255–56.

————. 1973. Transcendental logarithmic production frontiers. *Review of Economics and Statistics* 55, no. 1 (February): 28–45.

Conrad, K., and Jorgenson, D. W. 1975. *Measuring performance in the private economy of the Federal Republic of Germany, 1950–1973.* Tubingen: J. C. B. Mohr.

Correa, H. 1970. Sources of economic growth in Latin America. *Southern Economic Journal* 37, no. 1 (July): 17–31.

Cummings, D., and Meduna, L. 1973. *The Canadian consumer accounts.* Ottawa: Research Projects Group, Strategic Planning and Research, Department of Manpower and Immigration.

Danielson, R. S. 1975. *Output and input data for Canadian agriculture, 1926–1970.* Ottawa: Research Projects Group, Strategic Planning and Research, Department of Manpower and Immigration.

Dean, G. 1964. The stock of fixed capital in the United Kingdom in 1961. *Journal of the Royal Statistical Society,* ser. A [General], vol. 127, pt. 3: 327–58.

de Meo, G. 1973. Sintesi statistica du un ventennio di vita economica italiana. *Annali di statistica,* ser. 8, vol. 27.

Denison, E. F. 1962. *Sources of economic growth in the United States and the alternatives before us.* Supplementary Paper 13, Committee for Economic Development.

————. 1967. *Why growth rates differ.* Washington: The Brookings Institution.

————. 1969. Some major issues in productivity analysis: an examination of estimates by Jorgenson and Griliches. *Survey of Current Business* 49, no. 5, pt. 2 (May):1–27.

————. 1972. Final comments, *Survey of Current Business* 52, no. 5, pt. 2 (May): 95–110.

————. 1974. *Accounting for United States economic growth 1929–1969.* Washington: The Brookings Institution.

Denison, E. F., and Chung, W. 1976. *How Japan's economy grew so fast.* Washington: The Brookings Institution.

Department of Employment. 1971. *British Labour Statistics: Historical Abstract 1886–1968.* London: Her Majesty's Stationery Office.

————. *British Labour Statistics Yearbook,* annual volumes from 1969 through 1973. London: Her Majesty's Stationery Office.

Diewert, W. E. 1976. Exact and superlative index numbers. *Journal of Econometrics* 4, no. 2 (May): 115–46.

Divisia, F. 1925. L'indice monétaire et la théorie de la monnaie. *Revue d'économie politique,* 39e Année, no. 4 (July-August): 842–61; no. 5 (September-October): 980–1008; no. 6 (November-December): 1121–51.

————. 1926. L'indice monétaire et la théorie de la monnaie. *Revue d'économie politique,* 40e Année, no. 1 (January-February): 49–81.

Domar, E.; Eddie, S. M.; Herrick, B. H.; Hohenberg, P. M.; Intriligator, M. D.; and Miyamato, I. 1964. Economic growth and productivity in the United States, Canada, United Kingdom, Germany and Japan in the post-war period. *Review of Economics and Statistics* 46, no. 1 (February): 33–40.

Dominion Bureau of Statistics. 1946. *Census of Canada, 1941.* Ottawa: Queen's Printer.

————. 1953. *Census of Canada, 1951.* Ottawa: Queen's Printer.

————. 1963. *Census of Canada, 1961.* Ottawa: Queen's Printer.

Economic Planning Agency. *Annual report on national income statistics.* Tokyo: Government of Japan.

Economic Planning Board. 1963. *1960 Population and housing census of Korea, 20% sample tabulation report, 11–1 Whole Country.* Seoul: Government of Korea.

————. 1967. *Report on wage survey, 1967.* Seoul: Government of Korea.

————. 1969. *1966 Population census report of Korea, 12–1 Whole Country.* Seoul: Government of Korea.

————. 1970. *Report on wage survey, 1970.* Seoul: Government of Korea.

————. 1973. *1970 Population and housing census report,* vol. 2, *10% Sample Survey, 4–1 Economic Activity.* Seoul: Government of Korea.

————. 1973. *Report on the National Wealth Survey.* Seoul: Government of Korea.

Ezaki, M. 1974. Quantitative study of Japan's economic growth, 1952–1980: an approach from the system of national accounts. Ph.D. diss., Harvard University.

Ezaki, M., and Jorgenson, D. W. 1973. Measurement of macroeconomic performance in Japan, 1951–1968. In K. Ohkawa and Y. Hayami, eds., *Economic growth: the Japanese experience since the Meiji era,* vol. 1. Tokyo: Japan Economic Research Center.

Fabricant, S. 1959. *Basic facts on productivity change,* Occasional Paper 63. New York: National Bureau of Economic Research.

Fisher, I. 1922. *The making of index numbers.* Boston: Houghton Mifflin.

Franco, M. I., ed. 1973. *Rassegna di statistiche del lavoro,* vol. 1. Rome: Istituto centrale di statistica.

Giannone, A. 1963. Evaluations of Italian national wealth in the last fifty years. *Banca Nazionale del Lavoro Quarterly Review* 16, nos. 64–67 (March).

Goldsmith, R., and Saunders, C., eds. 1959. *The measurement of national wealth.* Chicago: Quadrangle Books.

Goldsmith, R. W. 1955. *A study of saving in the United States.* Princeton: Princeton University Press.

———. 1962. *The national wealth of the United States in the postwar period.* New York: National Bureau of Economic Research.

Griliches, Z. 1960. Measuring inputs in agriculture: a critical survey. *Journal of Farm Economics* 42, no. 4 (December): 1411–27.

Griliches, Z., and Jorgenson, D. W. 1966. Sources of measured productivity change: capital input. *American Economic Review* 56, no. 2 (May): 50–61.

Grose, L.; Rottenberg, T.; and Wasson, R. 1969. New estimates of fixed business capital in the United States. *Survey of Current Business* 49, no. 2 (February): 46–52.

Gussman, T. K. 1972. *The demand for durables, nondurables, services and the supply of labour in Canada: 1946–1969.* Ottawa: Research Projects Group, Strategic Planning and Research, Department of Manpower and Immigration.

Hicks, J. R. 1963. *The Theory of Wages.* 2d ed. London: Macmillan.

Hulten, C. R. 1973. Divisia Index Numbers. *Econometrica* 41, no. 6 (November): 1017–26.

Inland Revenue. 1969. *Report of the Commissioner of Her Majesty's Inland Revenue for the year ended 31 March 1969, the 112th Report.* London: Her Majesty's Stationery Office.

———. *Inland Revenue Statistics.* London: Her Majesty's Stationery Office.

International Labour Organization. *Yearbook of Labour Statistics*, annual volumes from 1947 to 1973. Geneva: International Labour Organization.

Institut national de la statistique et des études économiques. 1961. *Annuaire statistique de la France*, vol. 67. Paris: Institut national de la statistique et des études économique.

———. 1963. Les comptes de la nation 1949–1959. *Études et Conjoncture* 18, no. 12 (December): 1105–1257.

———. 1964. *Annuaire statistique de la France*, vol. 70. Paris: Institut national de la statistique et des études économique.

———. 1964. La population active par secteur d'établissement. *Études et conjoncture* 19, no. 3 (March): 9–22.

———. 1970. *Les comptes de la nation, base 1962: résultats d'ensemble des comptes, séries 1959–1966.* Les Collections de l'I.N.S.E.E., série C, no. 7, May.

———. 1970. *Rapport sur les comptes de la nation, 1969.* Les Collections de l'I.N.S.E.E., série C, no. 8, June.

———. 1971. *Les comptes de la nation, base 1962: les comptes de biens et services*, séries 1959–1966. Les Collections de l'I.N.S.E.E., série C, no. 10, May.

————. 1971. *Rapport sur les comptes de la nation 1970.* Les Collections de l'I.N.S.E.E., série C, no. 11, June.

————. 1972. *Les comptes de la nation, base 1962: les comptes des années 1949–1959.* Les Collections de l'I.N.S.E.E., série C, no. 13, April.

————. 1972. *Rapport sur les comptes de la nation 1971.* Les Collections de l'I.N.S.E.E., série C, no. 15, June.

————. 1973. *Rapport sur les comptes de la nation 1972.* Les Collections de l'I.N.S.E.E., série C, no. 23, June.

————. 1973. *Annuaire statistique de la France,* vol. 78. Paris: Institut national de la statistique et des études économique.

————. 1974. *Rapport sur les comptes de la nation 1973.* Les Collections de l'I.N.S.E.E., série C, no. 29–30, June.

Istituto centrale di statistica. 1958. *Ninth census of Italy,* 1951, vol. 7. Rome: Istituto centrale di statistica.

————. 1973. *Annuario di contabilita nazionale,* vol. 111, tome 1 and 2.

————. 1973. *Il valore della lire dal 1861 al 1972.* Rome: Istituto centrale di statistica.

————. *Annali di statistica,* ser. 8, vol. 15–27.

Jorgenson, D. W. 1973. The economic theory of replacement and depreciation. In W. Sellekaerts, ed., *Econometrics and economic theory.* New York: Macmillan, pp. 189–221.

Jorgenson, D. W., and Griliches, Z. 1967. The explanation of productivity change. *Review of Economic Studies* 34, no. 99: 249–83.

————. 1971. Divisia index numbers and productivity measurement. *Review of Income and Wealth,* ser. 18, no. 2 (June): 227–29.

————. 1972*a.* Issues in growth accounting: a reply to Edward F. Denison. *Survey of Current Business* 52, no. 5, pt. 2 (May): 65–94.

————. 1972*b.* Issues in growth accounting: final reply. *Survey of Current Business* 52, no. 5, pt. 2 (May): 111.

Jorgenson, D. W., and Lau, L. J. 1977. *Duality and technology.* Amsterdam: North-Holland.

Kanamori, H. 1972. What accounts for Japan's high rate of growth? *Review of Income and Wealth,* ser. 18, no. 2 (June): 155–72.

Kendrick, J. W. 1956. Productivity trends: capital and labor. *Review of Economics and Statistics* 38, no. 3 (August): 248–57.

————. 1961. *Productivity trends in the United States.* Princeton: Princeton University Press.

————. 1973. *Postwar productivity trends in the United States, 1948–1969.* New York: National Bureau of Economic Research.

————. 1975. Review of Edward F. Denison, "Accounting for United States economic growth, 1929–1969." *Journal of Economic Literature* 13, no. 3 (September): 909–10.

Kennedy, C., and Thirlwall, A. P. 1972. Technical progress: a survey. *Economic Journal* 82, no. 325 (March): 11–72.

Kirner, W. 1968. Zeitreihen für das Anlagevermögen der Wirtschafts-bereiche in der Bundesrepublik Deutschland. *DIW—Beiträge zur Strukturforschung.* Berlin: Deutsches Institut für Wirtschaftsfor-schung, vol. 5.

Kloek, T. 1966. *Indexcijfers: enige methodologisch aspecten.* The Hague: Pasmans.

Knowles, J. 1954. *Potential economic growth of the United States during the next decade.* Joint Committee on the Economic Report, 83rd Congress, Second Session. Washington: Government Printing Office.

———. 1960. *The potential economic growth in the United States.* Study Paper 20, Joint Economic Committee, 86th Congress, Second Session. Washington: Government Printing Office.

Kuznets, S. 1971. *Economic growth of nations.* Cambridge: Harvard University Press.

Maddison, A. 1972. Explaining economic growth. *Banca Nazionale del Lavoro Quarterly Review*, no. 102 (September): 3–54.

Mairesse, J. 1972. *L'evaluation du capital fixe productif: méthodes et résultats.* Collections de l'I.N.S.E.E., série C, no. 18–19, November.

Manvel, A. 1968. *Three land research studies.* Washington: Govern-ment Printing Office.

Mills, E. S., and Song, B. N. 1977. *Korea's urbanization and urban problems, 1945–1975.* Korea Development Institute, Working Paper 7701.

Mills, F. C. 1952. *Productivity and economic progress.* Occasional Pa-per 38. New York: National Bureau of Economic Research.

Ministère des Affaires Sociales. 1952. *Revue française du travail*, vol. 7, nos. 1–3, January-March.

———. 1954. *Revue française du travail*, vol. 9, no. 1.

———. 1956. *Revue française du travail*, vol. 10, no. 1.

Nadiri, M. I. 1970. Some approaches to the theory and measurement of total factor productivity: a survey. *Journal of Economic Literature* 8, no. 4 (December): 1137–77.

———. 1972. International studies of factor inputs and total factor productivity: a brief survey. *Review of Income and Wealth*, ser. 18, no. 2 (June): 129–54.

Office of Business Economics. 1966. *The national income and product accounts of the United States, 1929–1965, a supplement to the sur-vey of current business.* Washington: U.S. Department of Commerce.

Office of Labor Affairs. 1974. *Year Book of Labor Statistics.* Seoul: Office of Labor Affairs.

Ohkawa, K., et al. 1966. *Shihon Stokku (Capital Stocks).* Tokyo: Toyo-kezai.

Organization for Economic Co-operation and Development. *National accounts*, 1950–1968, 1953–1969, 1960–1971, 1961–1972, 1962–1973. Paris: O.E.C.D.

————. *Labor force statistics*, 1956–1966, 1962–1973. Paris: O.E.C.D.

————. *Reviews of national policies for education, Italy*, 1960, 1963, 1966. Paris: O.E.C.D.

Revell, J. 1967. *The wealth of the nation*. Cambridge: Cambridge University Press.

Richter, M. K. 1966. Invariance axioms and economic indexes. *Econometrica* 34, no. 4 (October): 739–55.

Samuelson, P. A. 1953. Prices of factors and goods in general equilibrium. *Review of Economic Studies* 21, no. 1: 1–20.

Schmookler, J. 1952. The changing efficiency of the American economy, 1869–1938. *Review of Economics and Statistics* 34, no. 3 (August): 214–31.

Solow, R. M. 1957. Technical change and the aggregate production function. *Review of Economics and Statistics* 39, no. 3 (August): 312–20.

Statistics Canada. 1974. *1971 Census of Canada*. Labor Force and Individual Income. Ottawa: Information Canada.

————. 1975. *1971 Census of Canada*. Income of Individuals. Ottawa: Information Canada.

————. 1974. Flows and stocks of fixed non-residential capital, Canada. Ottawa: Information Canada.

————. 1974. *National income and expenditure accounts, historical revision, 1926–1971*. Ottawa: Gross National Product Division.

————. 1976. *National income and expenditure accounts*, vol. 1, 1926–1974. Ottawa: Information Canada.

Statistisches Bundesamt. *Fachserie N, Volkswirtschaftliche Gesamtrechnungen*. Reihe 1, Konten und Standardtabellen, 1969, 1970, 1971, 1972 und Vorbericht 1973. Mainz: Verlag W. Kohlhammer.

————. *Statistisches Jahrbuch für die Bundesrepublik Deutschland*. Jahrgange 1952 bis 1973. Mainz: Verlag W. Kohlhammer.

Stigler, G. J. 1947. *Trends in output and employment*. New York: National Bureau of Economic Research.

Stobbe, A. 1969. *Volkswirtschaftliches Rechnungswegen*. Berlin: Springer-Verlag.

Theil, H. 1965. The information approach to demand analysis. *Econometrica* 33, no. 1 (January): 67–87.

Tinbergen, J. 1942. Zur Theorie der langfristigen Wirtschaftsentwicklung, *Weltwirtschaftliches Archiv*, Band 55, no. 1, pp. 511–549; English translation (1959), "On the Theory of Trend Movements," in L. H. Klassen, L. M. Koyck, and H. J. Witteveen, eds., *Jan Tinbergen, Selected Papers*. Amsterdam: North-Holland.

Tornqvist, L. 1936. The Bank of Finland's consumption price index. *Bank of Finland Monthly Bulletin*, no. 10, pp. 1–8.

Valavanis-Vail, S. 1955. An econometric model of growth, U.S.A., 1869–1953. *American Economic Review* 45, no. 2 (May): 208–21.

Vitali, O. 1968. *La formazione del capitale in Italia.* Milan: E.N.I. Pubblicazione della Scuola Enrico Mattei di Studi Superiori sugli Idrocarburi.

Walters, Dorothy. 1968. *Canadian income levels and growth: an international perspective.* Staff Study no. 23, Economic Council of Canada. Ottawa: Queen's Printer.

————. 1970. *Canadian growth revisited.* Staff Study no. 28, Economic Council of Canada. Ottawa: Queen's Printer.

Watanabe, T. 1972. Improvements of labor quality and economic growth—Japan's postwar experience. *Economic Development and Cultural Change* 21, no. 1 (October): 33–53.

Comment   D. J. Daly

Summary

The authors are reporting on an intermediate stage of a larger project on intercountry growth experience. They cover nine countries (Canada, France, Germany, Italy, Japan, Korea, the Netherlands, the United Kingdom, and the United States). All of the estimates of input, output, and output in relation to total factor input are by individual years for the period 1947 to 1973 where data are available for the total private sector. The study includes thirteen tables in the text, forty-five appendix tables, with separate, more detailed, reports for individual countries available from the authors.

In many general respects the methods are broadly similar to those that were initially developed to analyze the supply determinants of economic growth in the United States over long periods (usually between years of comparable degrees of demand in relation to supply). These methods have been applied to differences between countries in sources of growth in six previous studies to which the authors refer. There are differences in the concepts used, the countries covered, and time periods examined in the various studies, however.

Recent years have witnessed major changes in the scope of international trade in relation to GNP of all the major industrialized countries, a significant relative narrowing in the real income differences among the industrialized countries, increased trade in manufactured products, differences in the degree of price change between countries, an increased role of the multinational corporation in trade and investment along with more debate about their goals and procedures in host countries, and a series of currency revaluations between industrialized and developing countries that have been more extensive since 1971 than any changes

D. J. Daly is at York University.

since 1949. Economic nationalism has intensified in a number of forms in different countries at the same time that a greater degree of freedom for capital flows and increased international specialization in manufactured products has been occurring.

The longer-term changes in labor supply, education, capital, and the flow of technology, and differences in the speed with which new technologies (both technical and organizational) are adopted in various countries are all important issues, and I welcome more resources in this field. Both government officials and businessmen are too often preoccupied with shorter-term problems, but these longer-term questions do have short-term impacts.

The paper has been extensively revised and rewritten since it was initially presented at Williamsburg, and these comments have been revised to relate to the published version.

Key Concepts

This particular paper departs from some of the previous studies of this type for the United States, and for the growth experience of the other industrialized countries. Some key points will be mentioned, especially where they lead to substantive differences in results from previous work. The study uses factor shares to combine the individual factor inputs, rather than estimating the contribution of labor and capital by econometric methods.

1. The production account is limited to the private domestic sector of each country. This procedure excludes the government sector, which has its own problems in measuring output, and makes output more homogenous for analysis. This same coverage has been followed by Denison in his more recent studies on the United States and Japan, but this has not previously been done for the other countries covered (such as the European countries and Canada).

2. This study imputes a service to consumer durables in each country. This does not seem to change the growth rate of output, but it does add appreciably to the weights used for capital, and increases the share of output in which no productivity increase can occur. For the United States this imputation is more than 10% of private GNP in 1970 and only slightly less for Canada. Table 11.4 shows that the weights for consumer durables are between 8 and 14% of the capital stock for five of the countries covered. If the authors were interested in measuring changes in welfare over time, a procedure of deleting purchases of consumer durables and adding an imputation for services of consumer durables with a measure of net output would have some merit and logic. For their purposes, however, I have serious misgivings.

3. The concept of investment and output is gross in relation to depreciation. While it is consistent to use gross weights for combining inputs

if the analysis is aimed at gross output, and net weights if the net national output is being analyzed, when the stocks of capital per worker are increasing in almost every country according to their estimates, the use of gross weights increases the relative contribution of capital to growth compared to the use of net weights. The debate on this issue has gone on for some time, and it is mentioned to remind the reader that another view persists.

4. They use the double declining balance method of calculating replacement rates for machinery and equipment and nonresidential structures. This makes the ability of an individual capital good to contribute to current production drop implausibly fast. It can also reduce the average service life below what they say they accept, but this version does not clarify how, or whether, they have prevented this.

5. In measuring capital, the authors combine consumer durables, nonresidential structures, producer durables, residential structures, nonfarm inventories, farm inventories, and land (weights for individual categories for individual countries for 1970 are given in table 11.4). The quality adjustment for capital basically reflects the difference in weights between the flows of the services of capital as they measure them and the weights for the stock of capital.

6. On labor input, the only quality adjustment is for education. Age and sex adjustments along the lines recommended in the Gallop-Jorgenson paper given at this conference are not made, but for some countries they are important over this time period. Data are available for a number of countries to do more than they have done, and this version does not go as far in using such data for Canada as the preliminary version.

Comparison of Substantive Results

Although the authors mention six previous studies of international comparisons of growth experience in table 11.1, I will concentrate on the major contrasts with the results from Denison for the United States, the Denison-Poullier results for Northwest Europe, the Denison-Chung results for Japan, and the Walters results for Canada.

1. For seven of the nine countries studied, the results in chapter 11 suggest that the contribution of total factor productivity to the growth in total income is 40% or more. For both periods, the increases in total factor productivity are *greater* absolutely and in relation to total income for every other country than for the United States. This result is in line with most of the results for the same countries that I have seen. An important and interesting question remains as to why the increases in output per unit of total factor input for all the other countries they study, and for all time periods, are larger than for the United States (tables 11.11 and 11.12). However, the authors do not go into the reasons for their results.

2. This study gives a relatively larger contribution to capital than the studies of the Denison type. This arises from the use of weights for capital that include (rather than exclude) capital consumption or depreciation, and from the inclusion of a weight for the stock of consumer durables. This contributes to a different split of total output change between total factor input change and total factor productivity change. Thus, for example, in the case of Canada, while the results on total factor productivity are roughly comparable, the contribution of capital is much greater and the contribution of labor quality is much less (and the contribution of education is somewhat less) than in the study by Dorothy Walters. My own preference is to analyze net output (excluding the imputation for services of consumer durables) and to use *net* national income weights rather than gross. This would significantly reduce the relative contribution of capital to the growth of total inputs and reduce the rate of growth in total factor input for most countries for both periods studied.

3. The result in table 11.11, that the increase in total factor productivity for the postwar period has been greater for the United Kingdom than for the United States and Canada, is hard to accept or explain. As pointed out by Professor O. J. Firestone at the Williamsburg conference, most other studies of the same countries show the United Kingdom as the lowest, a result in line with their recurrent balance of payments problems and the assessment of most observers both inside and outside the United Kingdom.

Questionable Empirical Techniques

The authors are interested in a logically consistent set of production, wealth, saving, and capital-formation accounts in current and constant prices. In implementing this, the authors sometimes make compromises for the sake of expediency which are disturbing. Let me mention some points which warrant consideration!

1. Table 11.A.4C and the related Canadian series on labor quality show a slightly smaller increase from 1960 to1973 than from 1947 to 1960, although the differences are less in the current paper than in the one presented at the conference. During the later period, the number of young people coming of labor-force age was three times the number reaching retirement age, and the differences in education levels were dramatic. The proportion going to university was up sharply and the proportion finishing high school was also up. Moreover, the increases were particularly large in the educational categories with the highest income. In view of these facts, their results are hard to explain. It is difficult to believe that the use of income weights to combine educational attainments of the various labor-force groups could completely wipe out the effect of this more rapid rise in educational level.

2. There is no reference to the fact that the procedures used to derive construction deflators for Canada, France, and the U.S. differ from the procedures used for the other countries, with the former procedures allowing for the impact of productivity change in the construction industry and the latter not. This affects comparability of changes over time in both the output and capital input measures.

3. For some countries, the authors continue to follow the practice of using the wholesale price indexes for deflating the stocks of nonfarm and farm inventories. This procedure can introduce an inappropriate set of weights. Some types of inventories have a very fast turnover, while others have a slow turnover, and thus the use of shipment weights (as are reflected in the wholesale price index) can introduce errors. Further, during a period of rising prices the accounting conventions followed should be allowed for by using prices over *previous* months, rather than the end of the period. This discussion does not refer to, and should not be confused with, the deflation of changes in inventory investment.

4. Their estimates of labor quality change associated with education look peculiar for some other countries in addition to Canada. The contribution of education shown for Japan in table 11.13 seems low in light of detailed data for that country, even apart from the significant amount of management education and retraining done by private companies. Further, the extent of increase in the index of educational attainment for Italy after 1960 shown in tables 11.13 and 11.A.4I seems unduly large.

Alternative Research Strategy Options

Thus far my comments have dealt with how well Christensen, Cummings, and Jorgenson have done the task they have set themselves. But it is also useful to consider the options open in international growth studies, especially since they point out that six similar previous studies have been published, with four previous ones being done in 1967 or since. These comments relate to future work rather than to the present paper.

1. Decomposing output in relation to total factor inputs: It is now clear that many countries have been obtaining significant increases in total factor productivity. Could this be due to such temporary factors as variations in demand pressure and agricultural output? This is more important when data for individual years are being produced than when growth rates over a series of years were being analyzed. The extent of shifts out of agriculture and self-employment have been much more important for France, Germany, Japan, and Canada than for the United States. What about the effects of tariff reductions in Europe and Canada? These need study to assess the prospects for continued high increases

in total factor productivity and to assess policies for influencing economic growth in the countries being studied.

2. Comparisons of levels of output in relation to total factor input: It is clear from *Why Growth Rates Differ* and the comparable studies for Canada and Japan that additional perspective on growth is obtained from studies at a point in time *in addition to* changes over time, rather than doing either one in isolation. It has also been established that the methods are applicable to comparisons at a point in time. Are different countries' levels of real income per person employed converging? Most of the countries covered in the Christensen-Cummings-Jorgenson paper were also covered in the International Comparisons Project by Kravis and his associates. On the whole, the differences between North America, Europe, and Japan have narrowed since the Second World War. This paper suggests that this is also happening for Korea, but this may not be the pattern in other developing countries. The study by Kravis and his associates would facilitate further analysis of the differences in level, and I hope that further work along this line will be done. It is not possible to do this from material now in the public domain as the differences in inputs between countries at a point in time are not available (especially capital stock and the quality of capital stock).

3. Industrial disaggregation: Much more attention needs to be given to the commodity producing industries, as the results for the economy as a whole and for the private sector are so heavily influenced by services and nontraded goods that are produced and consumed on a local basis. The paper at this session by Yamada and Ruttan on agriculture shows the illumination that can be provided. The U.S. Department of Labor's study of the steel industry in various countries also shows the possibilities. Another example is the recently published volume by Scherer, et al., *The Economics of Multi-Plant Operation: An International Comparisons Study* covering twelve industries in six nations. Much more study on differences within manufacturing industries between countries at a point in time is desirable, and we are aware from the Canada–U.S. work of the data and resource problems that are involved. In my opinion, however, this would be preferable, to further studies of aggregative changes over time. More work on manufacturing, agriculture, and natural resource industries would facilitate the integration of work on growth with the related areas of international trade and balance of payments.

Professor Jorgenson recognizes the desirability of additional industrial disaggregation, as in the Gallop-Jorgenson paper earlier in the current volume, and he has underway a further project comparing output and labor and capital inputs for individual manufacturing industries in Japan and the United States. Additional work by authors in the profession would also be desirable.

Reply   L. R. Christensen, D. Cummings, and D. W. Jorgenson

Daly correctly emphasizes the central importance of our approach to the measurement of capital input in our analysis of economic growth. Our methodology has very significant implications for the allocation of growth among its sources, and our results provide a very different picture from that suggested by earlier studies, such as those by Denison and his associates cited by Daly. It should also be emphasized that we cover a much broader range of historical experience.

In view of the importance of capital measurement we have taken considerable pains to provide a detailed rationale for our approach. Growth rates of inputs are weighted by their income shares; both output and income shares include depreciation. Depreciation is part of the annualized cost of using capital input, and the marginal productivity of capital is understated if depreciation is omitted. Daly concedes that our weights are appropriate for an analysis of economic growth based on gross private domestic product, the concept of output we employ.

However, Daly goes on to state his preference for a measure of productivity based on measures of output and income shares for capital that are net of depreciation. Denison and his associates have failed to supply a convincing rationale for this approach, and Daly fails to provide one. Daly also fails to confront three additional issues in capital measurement: (1) inconsistency between capital weights and capital stock measures; (2) failure to incorporate differences among capital weights due to differences in the taxation of income from capital; (3) inconsistency between the own rates of return for individual capital goods used in capital input weights and data on revaluations of assets from national wealth accounts. We must conclude that Daly's preference for net measures is unsupported and unsupportable.

Our measures of capital stock and our weights for capital input are based on declining balance depreciation and replacement. For each country we have used the best information available to estimate the replacement rates for the various classes of capital stock. For example, for Canada we employ the replacement rates implicit in the capital stock study by Statistics Canada.[1] For the United States we employ double declining balance replacement rates, one of the alternatives provided by the Bureau of Economic Analysis (U.S. Department of Commerce) in their capital stock study. The resulting capital stocks and capital input weights appear to be very reasonable for all countries included in our study.

---

1. *Fixed Capital Flows and Stocks, 1926–1973.* Information Canada, catalog 13–211.

Daly correctly points out that the stock of consumer durables is substantial for the U.S. and for some of the other countries in our study. He suggests that this large portion of the capital stock be omitted from our study. It may be desirable to consider subsets of the total capital stock for some purposes; but we believe that the full stock should be used in the analysis of sources of economic growth.

Daly expresses concern over our index of labor quality, especially for Canada. The Canadian census figures which we used are consistent with Daly's notion of the average years of education. This measure increased approximately 6% in the forties, 8% in the fifties, and 10% in the sixties. However, a correct accounting for the growth of labor input requires that the rates of growth of the various segments of the labor force be weighted by their shares in total labor earnings. When this is done, the growth of the quality of labor is much more modest than the growth of years of education per worker. Similar observations apply to our labor input indexes for other countries. In all cases our estimates are based on official census data.

Daly suggests that we use inappropriate deflators for stocks of inventories. We employ inventory stock deflators whenever they are available. In some countries, however, such deflators are simply not available. For countries which have inventory stock deflators, they do not differ substantially from wholesale price indexes. Therefore, we felt justified in using wholesale price indexes when inventory stock deflators were not available. For inventory investment flows we employ implicit deflators from the official national accounts for each country.

In a more positive vein, Daly outlines a very useful agenda for future research involving international comparisons. Analyzing sources of changes in total factor productivity and comparing levels as well as rates of growth of productivity are worthwhile objectives. We feel that disaggregation of growth sources by industry will uncover an important component of change in productivity at the aggregate level by quantifying the effects of shifts in resources among industries.

In concluding, it is a pleasure to thank Daly for the care he has taken in preparing his comments on our paper. We have found his views, expressed orally at the conference and in subsequent correspondence, to be very valuable in revising the paper for publication.

Contributors

Ernst R. Berndt
Department of Economics
University of British Columbia
2075 Wesbrook Mall
Vancouver, British Columbia
 V6T 1W5

George C. Bitros
Athens School of Economics and
 Business
A, 76 Patission Street
Athens, Greece

Laurits R. Christensen
Department of Economics
University of Wisconsin
Madison, Wisconsin 53706

John E. Cremeans
Bureau of Economic Analysis
United States Department of
 Commerce
Washington, D.C. 20230

Dianne Cummings
Department of Economics
University of Wisconsin
Madison, Wisconsin 53706

D. J. Daly
Department of Economics
York University
4700 Keele Street
Downsview, Ontario M3J 2R6

Steven Globerman
Faculty of Administrative Studies
York University
4700 Keele Street
Downsview, Ontario M3J 2R6

Frank M. Gollop
Department of Economics
University of Wisconsin
Madison, Wisconsin 53706

José A. Gómez-Ibáñez
Department of City and Regional
 Planning
Harvard University
Cambridge, Massachusetts 02138

Zvi Griliches
Department of Economics
Harvard University
Cambridge, Massachusetts 02138

Reed Hansen
Urban Institute
Washington, D.C. 20036

David Burras Humphrey
Board of Governors of the Federal
    Reserve Board
Martin Building, Room 1304
20th and C Streets N.W.
Washington, D.C. 20551

Dale W. Jorgenson
Department of Economics
Harvard University
Cambridge, Massachusetts 02138

Benjamin Klotz
Department of Economics
Temple University
Philadelphia, Pennsylvania 19122

Richard C. Levin
Department of Economics
Yale University
28 Hillhouse Avenue
New Haven, Connecticut 06520

Robert E. Lipsey
National Bureau of Economic
    Research
15–19 West 4th Street, Washington
    Square
New York, New York 10012

Rey Madoo
Howard University
Washington, D.C. 20059

Edwin Mansfield
Department of Economics
University of Pennsylvania
3718 Locust Walk
Philadelphia, Pennsylvania 19104

Jerome A. Mark
Bureau of Labor Statistics
United States Department of Labor
Washington, D.C. 20210

John R. Meyer
Harvard Business School
Morgan Hall
322 Soldier Field
Boston, Massachusetts 02163

Michael F. Mohr
Office of Industrial Economics
United States Department of
    Commerce
Washington, D.C. 20230

John G. Myers
Department of Economics
Southern Illinois University
Carbondale, Illinois 62901

M. Ishaq Nadiri
Department of Economics
New York University
8 Washington Place
New York, New York 10003

Leonard Nakamura
Economics Department
Citibank
399 Park Avenue
New York, New York 10043

Vernon W. Ruttan
Department of Agricultural and
    Applied Economics
University of Minnesota
St. Paul, Minnesota 55108

G. Edward Schuh
Department of Agricultural and
    Applied Economics
University of Minnesota
St. Paul, Minnesota 55108

Allan D. Searle
Bureau of Economic Analysis
United States Department of
    Commerce
Washington, D.C. 20230

Irving H. Siegel
8312 Bryant Drive
Bethesda, Maryland 20034

Nestor E. Terleckyj
National Planning Association
1606 New Hampshire Avenue N.W.
Washington, D.C. 20009

Charles A. Waite
Bureau of Economic Analysis
United States Department of
    Commerce
Washington, D.C. 20230

Saburo Yamada
University of Tokyo
Institute of Oriental Culture
3–1, Hongo 7-Chome, Bunkyo-ku
Tokyo, Japan

Author Index

Abramovitz, Moses, 598, 599; *Resource and Output Trends in the United States since 1870*, 4
Adachi, Hideyuki, 465
Ahmad, S., 586
Allen, R. G. D., 257, 258
Al-Samarrie, A., 192
Ardolini, Charles, 342
Arrow, Kenneth, 255

Bacharach, Michael, 31, 33, 34–35
Baily, M. N., 387
Balassa, B., 596
Ban, 511
Bancroft, Gertrude, 47
Barger, H., 597, 599
Barger, William J., 17, 43
Barker, 511
Barton, G. T., *Productivity of Agriculture, United States, 1870–1958*, 510
Beardsley, George, 457, 458, 460
Becker, G. S., 146
Bergson, A., 597, 599
Berndt, Ernst R., 6, 18, 124–36, 139, 140, 141, 150, 151, 162, 164, 170, 171–76, 185–86, 193–94, 236, 237, 254, 255, 260
Bertrand, T. J., 596
Binswanger, Hans P.: *Induced Innovation*, 511, 566; "Measurement of Technical Biases with Many Factors

of Production," 554, 563; "Microeconomic Approach to Induced Innovation," 511; "Technology Transfer and Resource Allocation," 566
Birch, E. M., 151
Bischoff, Charles W., *Brookings Papers on Economic Activity*, 411
Bitros, George C., 10–11
Blackman, James, 419
Blackorby, C., 129
Bliss, C. J., 450, 465, 499
Boddy, Raford, 465, 466
Bowden, 340
Bradford, D. F., 337, 345
Brainard, W. C., 150, 391
Brazell, D. W., 644
Brown, J. A. C., 31
Brown, Murray, 245, 254
Burkhead, J., *Productivity in the Local Government Sector*, 336, 337, 340, 345, 352
Burmeister, Edwin, 22
Burstein, Leigh, 275–76, 282–83

Carnes, Richard, 304, 331
Carré, J., 644–45
Carvalho, David, 18
Chen, 511
Chen, Susan, 387
Chenery, H., 596
Chinloy, Peter, 17, 29

Subject Index

Accelerated Depreciation Range System (US Treasury), 81–83

Accounting for the United States Economic Growth, 1948–1969 (Denison), 4

Agricultural Development: An International Perspective (Hayami and Ruttan), 509, 511, 512–13, 517, 519, 525, 527, 528, 531, 535, 536, 539, 542–43, 546, 554–56, 558, 562, 564–65, 568, 569, 572–73, 574, 575, 578, 585–86, 588, 590, 593–94

Agricultural Growth in Japan, Taiwan, Korea, and the Philippines (Hayami, Ruttan, and Southworth), 511

"Agricultural Productivity in Canada: Two Decades of Gains" (Furniss), 510–11

"Agricultural Revolution in Nineteenth-Century France" (Newell), 520

Agriculture: in Argentina, 558, 560, 562, 576, 577; in Australia, 530–32, 541, 576, 579; in Austria, 576, 577; in Bangladesh, 530, 532, 535, 544, 555, 574, 575, 576; in Belgium, 530–32, 535, 536, 537, 543; in Brazil, 530–33, 535; in Canada, 530–33, 541, 544, 576; in Chile, 530–35, 576, 577; in Colombia, 530–33, 535, 576; in Denmark, 514–32, 535, 558, 560, 562, 567–73, 586, 590; in Finland, 544; in France, 514–32, 535, 567–73, 576, 586, 590; in Germany, 514–32, 535, 567–73, 579, 586; in Greece, 576, 577; in Hong Kong, 545; in India, 529–30, 532, 560–62, 576, 577, 588; in Ireland, 576; in Israel, 530–33; in Japan, 514–33, 536, 543, 545, 558, 560–63, 567–73, 576, 577–78, 579, 586, 588, 589; in Malaysia, 545; in Mauritius, 530–33, 544, 575–76; in Mexico, 530–33, 541–43; in Netherlands, 530–32, 537, 543, 576; in New Zealand, 529–33, 541, 576; in Norway, 544; in Pakistan, 530, 532, 535, 536, 544, 555, 574, 575, 576; in Paraguay, 529–33, 536, 541–43, 555, 575, 576, 577; in Peru, 533–35, 541–43, 576, 577; in Philippines, 530, 532, 535; in Portugal, 530, 532, 535, 555, 576, 577; in South Africa 530–33, 576, 577; in Spain, 576; in Sri Lanka, 530, 532, 535, 545, 576; in Surinam, 530–33, 575, 576, 577; in Sweden, 537, 544; in Switzerland, 576, 577; in Taiwan, 529–32, 545, 576; in Turkey, 530–33, 535, 536, 558, 560, 562, 576, 588; in United Kingdom, 514–32, 535, 537, 544, 567–73, 576, 586; in United States, 514–33, 535, 536, 541, 543, 558, 560–62, 567–73, 576, 577, 579, 586, 588, 589, 590, 593; in Venezuela, 531–35, 541, 576, 577; in Yugoslavia, 535, 555, 576

"Agriculture: Productivity and Technology" (Griliches), 511